Quantitative Analysis for Business Decisions

Quantitative Analysis for Business Decisions

Eighth Edition

Harold Bierman, Jr.
Nicholas H. Noyes Professor of Business Administration
Johnson Graduate School of Management
Cornell University

Charles P. Bonini
William R. Timken Professor of Management Science and Associate Dean
Graduate School of Business
Stanford University

Warren H. Hausman
Professor and Chairman of Industrial Engineering and Engineering
Management
Department of Industrial Engineering and Engineering Management
Stanford University

IRWIN

Homewood, IL 60430
Boston, MA 02116

Sponsoring editor: *Richard T. Hercher, Jr.*
Project editor: *Susan Trentacosti*
Production manager: *Carma W. Fazio*
Designer: *John Rokusek*
Artist: *Weimer Typesetting Co., Inc.*
Compositor: *Weimer Typesetting Co., Inc.*
Typeface: *10/12 Times Roman*
Printer: *R. R. Donnelley & Sons Company*

Library of Congress Cataloging-in-Publication Data

Bierman, Harold.
  Quantitative analysis for business decisions / Harold Bierman, Charles P. Bonini, Warren H. Hausman.—8th ed.
    p.   cm.
  Includes index.
  ISBN 0-256-08267-7
    1. Industrial management—Mathematical models. 2. Decision-making—Mathematical models. I. Bonini, Charles P. II. Hausman, Warren H. III. Title.
  HD30.25.B53   1991
  658.4'033—dc20   90–48928

Printed in the United States of America
  2 3 4 5 6 7 8 9 0 DOC 8 7 6 5 4 3 2 1

Preface

In this eighth edition of *Quantitative Analysis for Business Decisions,* we have attempted to make changes that are consistent with an objective described in the preface of the first edition—to make the material understandable to a reader who does not have an extensive mathematical background. Expanded introductory material has been provided at chapter beginnings, and summaries of major concepts have been added.

Many new problems have also been added. The problems have been grouped as follows: Problems with Answers, Problems, More Challenging Problems, and Cases. Answers to the first group of problems are printed in the back of the book; they provide an opportunity for immediate feedback to the student. We have also made numerous changes throughout the book to improve the clarity of presentation.

This edition is printed in two colors and in a large book size, to highlight key concepts and communicate more effectively. We have improved the use of the second color in figures, charts, tables, and highlighting of important equations. We appreciate the aid of Joan Hausman in redesigning many of our figures and tables to take advantage of the two-color format.

The list of persons who have offered us assistance continues to grow. We want especially to thank the many users of previous editions who bothered to point out errors that we had made and offered suggestions for improving this edition. This assistance is greatly appreciated.

For the eighth edition, we have substantially reorganized and rewritten much of the linear programming material. Following the popular chapter on formulating LP programs, we now have a new chapter on graphical solution, computer solution, interpretation of dual prices, and sensitivity analysis—all based on the graphical approach and interpretation of computer solutions. The simplex procedure is discussed in a separate chapter which can be omitted if desired with no loss in the managerial insights to be gained from linear programming.

We have also substantially revised the chapter dealing with queuing theory, adding models with general and deterministic service times and emphasizing managerial insights. We have added an appendix to the simulation chapter, which shows how to perform Monte Carlo simulation on a spreadsheet. We have deleted the chapter on classical statistics, and have added a brief discussion of influence diagrams, conjoint analysis, and the "winner's curse" elsewhere in the text. We have also combined two former chapters dealing with decision theory and revision of probabilities into a single integrated chapter.

Although Lawrence Fouraker and Robert Jaedicke are no longer considered to be authors, we acknowledge that a large percentage of the book carries forward their words and ideas.

Harold Bierman, Jr.
Charles P. Bonini
Warren H. Hausman

Acknowledgments

We would like to thank these reviewers who, for recent editions, have made many helpful suggestions. We appreciate your contributions.

Thomas Boland, *University of Illinois*
Linda Salchenberger, *Loyola University*
Mary Rolfes, *Mankato State University*
George Vlahos, *University of Dayton*
Peter Ellis, *Utah State University*
Mike Middleton, *University of San Francisco*
Steve Achtenhagen, *San Jose State University*
G. John Miltenburg, *McMaster University*
Mark Walker, *State University of New York—Stonybrook*
Tim Ireland, *Oklahoma State University*
W. E. Pinney, *University of Texas*
Prem S. Mann, *California State University—Fullerton*

Extracts from the Preface to the First Edition

The administration of a modern business enterprise has become an enormously complex undertaking. There has been an increasing tendency to turn to quantitative techniques and models as a potential means for solving many of the problems that arise in such an enterprise. The purpose of this book is to describe a representative sample of the models and their related quantitative techniques. It is hoped that this book will serve as a basis for a course . . . that acts as a connecting force between the mathematical courses on the one hand and the applied business courses on the other.

This is an introductory work in the application of mathematics to problems of business. It is not an introductory work to the mathematics which are being applied. We have summarized—in a rather rough and ready manner by a mathematician's standards—some of the mathematical tools employed. Our purpose is to get our notation and a few basic relationships before the reader rather than to teach him mathematics.

We have attempted to minimize the amount of mathematical training required to read this book . . . a reader who does not have formal training in these areas should not think that this book is beyond his ability.

The book is an attempt to consider techniques which treat quite sophisticated and difficult problems; so, even though we tried to choose the simplest means of exposition—avoiding proofs and much of the characteristic rigor of such treatments—the essential subtlety of the techniques remains. These attributes can be understood only by patient application of effort over a protracted period of time.

Harold Bierman, Jr.
Lawrence E. Fouraker
Robert K. Jaedicke

viii

Contents

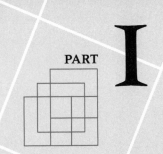

PART I

Models and Decision Making

1

Introduction to Quantitative Analysis

This book is about managerial decision making. Managerial decision making is a process whereby management, when confronted by a problem, selects a specific course of action, or "solution," from a set of possible courses of action. Since there is generally some uncertainty about the future, we cannot be sure of the consequences of the decision that is chosen, and we cannot be sure that the decision chosen will produce the best outcome. Furthermore, the problem may be quite complex because there are either a large number of alternatives to consider or many factors to take into account.

This book presents a general approach for managers to use when faced with decision problems, as well as specific quantitative tools for particular types of problems.

Business Decisions

The business manager wants to choose that course of action that will be most effective in attaining the goals of the organization. In judging the effectiveness of different possible decisions, we must use some criterion or performance measure. The most commonly used performance measure in making decisions is dollars, but we shall see in the following chapters that for some decisions, the use of dollars in judging the relative merits of different courses of action would not be adequate.

The following general process of solution is common to all types of decision situations:

1. Establish the *criterion* to be used. For example, in a simple situation the criterion may be to choose the act that maximizes profit.

2. Select a set of *alternatives* for consideration.
3. Determine the *model* to be used and the values of the parameters of the process. For example, we may decide that an adequate expression for total expenses is:

$$\text{Total expenses} = a + b(\text{units sold})$$

The parameters are a and b, and their values would have to be determined in order to use the model.

a = Fixed cost for the period or project
b = Variable (incremental) cost per unit

4. Determine which alternative *optimizes* (i.e., produces the best value for) the criterion established above in step 1.

Example   We can sell 1,000 units of product to the government at a price of $50 per unit. Should the order be accepted? The firm has excess capacity.

1. We shall use the profit maximization criterion.
2. The alternatives are to (*a*) accept the order or (*b*) reject the order. In accordance with our profit criterion, we shall accept the order if it increases profit, reject the order if it does not increase profit.
3. We need to know the incremental expenses of producing the 1,000 units. The relevant expense model is:

$$E = a + 1,000b$$

Assume that special dies costing $5,000 will have to be bought (a is equal to $5,000) and that the variable costs of producing a unit are $30 ($b$ is equal to $30). Then the total relevant expenses of filling the order are $35,000 (equal to $5,000 plus $30,000).
4. A comparison of the incremental revenues, $50,000, and incremental expenses, $35,000, indicates that we should accept the order. Profit will be greater by $15,000 if we "accept" compared with the alternative "refuse the order."

In the above example, we used basic knowledge and simple computational techniques. However, in dealing with more complex problems, we might need to use other tools of quantitative analysis, including calculus, probability, statistics, and programming (linear, integer, and dynamic).

We shall now consider some aspects of model building.

Abstraction and Simplification

Real-world problems tend to be enormously complex. There are literally an uncountable number of inherent "facts" in any empirical situation. Further, every potential course of action starts a chain of cause, effect, and interaction that logically is without end.

Consider the problem of constructing a building. An endless amount of time could be devoted to gathering factual information about this situation: for example, the precise location and physical characteristics of the building; a detailed study of the climatic conditions of the potential sites and the influence these will have on construction costs; the sources of the funds used and their cost. The decision maker might decide to consider specifically and in detail all other potential uses of the funds in this period and in future periods. If our decision maker adopts a strategy of collecting *all* the facts before acting, it follows that no action will take place. The human mind cannot consider every aspect of an empirical problem. Some attributes of the problem must be ignored if a decision is to be made. The decision maker must determine those factors most relevant to the problem. Abstraction and simplification are necessary steps in the solution of any human problem. Our objective is to improve decision making, not to provide an excuse for not making a decision.

Model Building

After the decision maker has selected the critical factors, or variables, from the empirical situation, they are combined in some logical manner so that they form a *model* of the actual problem. A *model* is a simplified representation of an empirical situation. Ideally, it strips a natural phenomenon of its bewildering complexity and duplicates the essential behavior of the natural phenomenon with a few variables that are simply related. The simpler the model, the better for the decision maker, provided the model serves as a reasonably reliable counterpart of the empirical problem. The advantages of a simple model are:

1. It is economical of time and thought.
2. It can be understood readily by the decision maker.
3. If necessary, the model can be modified quickly and effectively.

The object of the decision maker is not to construct a model that is as close as possible to reality in every respect. Such a model would require an excessive length of time to construct, and then it might be beyond human comprehension. Rather, the decision maker wants the simplest model that predicts outcomes reasonably well and is consistent with effective action.

Solutions

After the model has been constructed, conclusions may be derived about its behavior by means of logical analysis. The decision maker then bases actions or decisions on these conclusions. If the logic in deriving the conclusions from the abstracted variables is correct, and if the relevant variables have been abstracted, then the solution to the model will also serve as an effective solution for the empirical problem. For our example, the decision maker may decide that an interest rate of 15 percent measures the firm's annual opportunity cost of money. The firm can make the decision on construction of the building by computing the net present value of the cash flows, and not consider alternative investments in detail.

Errors

Two important sources of error in using models for decision making are the exclusion of important variables and mistakes in defining the relationships among the variables. For example, in the above problem involving the government contract, assume that a 40 percent loss in yield during production can be expected, due to unusually tight product specifications. If this factor were present but omitted from the analysis, the resulting model would not represent the situation adequately enough for decision purposes (the wrong decision may result).

Model-Building Techniques

Models may be represented in a variety of ways. For simple, repetitive problems, the entire decision-making process may take place in the mind of the decision maker, perhaps in a quite informal, intuitive manner. We walk, eat, and open doors every day without the aid of formal models. If the problem is somewhat more unusual or complex, we spend more time thinking about it.

The appropriate technique for describing and relating selected variables depends to a large extent on the nature of the variables. If the variables are subject to measurement of some form, and particularly if they can be given a quantitative representation, then there are strong reasons for selecting a mathematical representation of the model. First, there is a rigorous inherent discipline in mathematics that ensures an orderly procedure on the part of the investigator: you must be specific about what variables you have selected and what relationships you are assuming to exist among them. Second, mathematics is a powerful technique for relating variables and for deriving logical conclusions from given premises. Mathematics, combined with modern computers, makes it possible to handle problems that require models of great complexity, and it facilitates the decision-making process where quantitative analysis is applicable.

A large number of business problems have been given a quantitative representation successfully, leading to a general approach that has been designated as quantitative analysis, decision science, management science, or operations research. Of course, the quantitative representation and resolution of business problems is much older than these labels—witness the practice of accounting. However, quantitative analysis has been extended to many other areas of the business firm's operations and has become established as an effective way of approaching certain business decision problems. Today's managers have to be as knowledgeable about these techniques and models as they are about accounting reports.

A further word of caution is in order. The business executive should never become the captive of a quantitative model and automatically adopt its conclusions as the correct decision. The conclusion derived from the model contains some degree of error because of the abstraction process. The question of when the error becomes so large that the conclusion must be modified before it can be adopted as a solution is one of judgment. Quantification is an aid to business judgment and not a substitute for it. A certain amount of constructive skepticism is as desirable in considering quantitative analysis of business problems as it is in any other decision-making process.

Qualitative Factors. Many business decisions, particularly the most important ones, involve some variables that are qualitative rather than quantitative in nature. For example, major decisions may affect morale and leadership in the organization, or may affect employment, affirmative action, pollution, or other areas of social responsibility. Many of these factors cannot be expressed in dollar terms. How then does the decision maker deal with these qualitative variables?

First, two extreme attitudes should be avoided. One such extreme attitude would ignore qualitative factors, on the grounds that factors that cannot be measured are unimportant. An equally extreme attitude would argue that quantitative models have no value given that qualitative factors are important.

A more sensible approach is to accept the idea that the quantitative model can deal effectively with the measurable aspects of the decision problem, and that the decision maker must also be an intuitive model to deal with the qualitative variables. The manager must find some appropriate balance between the quantitative and qualitative factors.

SUMMARY

In making business decisions, one should establish the decision-making criterion, select the alternatives, determine a model, and evaluate the alternatives using the model, selecting the best alternative.

A model is an abstraction and simplification of a real problem, ideally incorporating the essential elements and relationships from the real problem. Solving a model means obtaining the logical conclusions that follow, and these conclusions should be an effective guide to decision making if the model is designed and solved properly. Decision making involves integrating the quantitative information obtained from the model with intuitive judgment about qualitative factors.

Decisions and Uncertainty

Business decisions are made in one of two essentially different contexts—under conditions approaching certainty and, more generally, under conditions of uncertainty. The quantitative analysis that supports decision making under certainty usually takes the form of maximizing some objective (for example, profit or production) subject to constraints (for example, productive capacity).

In our example at the beginning of this chapter, we compared the alternatives "accept the order" and "refuse the order" on a 1,000-unit government contract. This was a decision under conditions of certainty. We compared the two alternatives; since the profit was $15,000 greater for accepting the order, we chose that alternative.

Suppose, however, that we change the above situation slightly. We shall market our product at a price of $50 per unit. And as before, our expenses for producing X units are:

$$E = a + bX$$
$$= 5,000 + 30X$$

But now we are uncertain about the actual level of sales. Sales may be 100 units, 250 units, or 1,000 units, and we are not sure which level will actually materialize. Our two alternatives are (1) to market the product and accept whatever profit or loss materializes, or (2) to reject the whole project and obtain zero profit. Assume that the $5,000 of fixed costs must be incurred before we know the actual demand, but that the units can be produced after the demand is known (thus, there is no inventory problem).

Figure 1–1 illustrates a **decision tree** for this problem. The alternatives (market or not) are represented as branches from the square node, and the uncertain events (sales levels) as branches from the circle node. Figure 1–1 also contains the profit or loss resulting from each possible sales level, calculated as follows:

Sales	Revenue (50 per unit)	Expenses (5,000 + 30 per unit)	Profit (Revenues − Expenses)
100	5,000	8,000	−3,000
250	12,500	12,500	0
1,000	50,000	35,000	15,000

Even though we have clearly enumerated the alternatives and their consequences, the decision is not obvious. The best alternative depends on how "likely" each sales level may be. If we were certain that sales would be 1,000 units, we should market the product. If sales were to be only 100 units for sure, we should reject the whole project and avoid a loss of $3,000. If sales were 250 units, we would be indifferent as to which alternative is selected, since with both decisions the profit is $0.

When the true state of nature is unknown, the decision maker has to act with **imperfect information.** There are several possible decision-making procedures for dealing with imperfect information, and we shall investigate some of the more useful techniques later in this book. These involve the use of probabilities to represent judgment about how likely the events are to occur and procedures for determining the value of obtaining more information before acting.

Figure 1–1 ⬥ Alternatives and Consequences for Decision about Marketing a Product

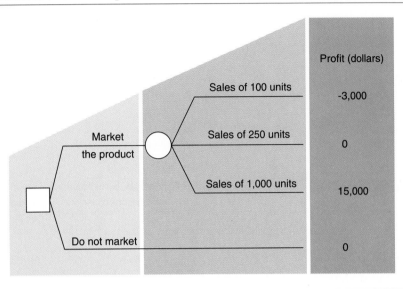

Classification of Models

There are several types of decision models that we shall discuss in this book; these are classified in Figure 1–2. Models are classified as certain if the major factors are assumed known, and uncertain if some factors are unknown.

Simple Problems

All problems must be simplified in constructing the model for any analysis. If this results in only a small number of factors or variables, and relatively few alternatives, then the model is called **simple.** Simple models may be very useful, even for very important decision problems.

A **case** or **scenario model** is a model of a decision problem that is analyzed by trying out a series of cases (possible outcomes or scenarios) using different alternatives or different assumptions. The model is not programmed to find the "best" solution directly. Rather, the manager uses the model in a trial and error process. Most of the other types of models in Figure 1–2 are **optimization** models, in which the model uses mathematical procedures to find the optimal solution. Case models are described in Chapter 2.

Decision analysis models incorporate the use of probabilities in decision making under uncertainty. They often involve the use of decision trees similar to Figure 1–1. Part II of the book presents these models.

Figure 1–2   Types of Models

Major variables in decision problems are:

	Certain	Uncertain
Decision problem is: Simple	Case models	Decision analysis (decision trees)
Complex	Case models Linear and integer programming	Simulation
Dynamic	Inventory models PERT (critical path) models Dynamic programming	Inventory models Queuing models Markov processes Dynamic programming

Complex Problems

Many decision problems involve a large number of important factors or variables, or they may have many alternatives to consider. For example, a firm may have several plants that produce goods for shipment to several hundred customers. The decision problem of scheduling the plants and determining which plants supply which customers in order to minimize cost involves hundreds of variables and constraints and may have millions of possible solutions.

Linear and integer programming models are the most widely used techniques for solving large complex business problems of this type. They use mathematical techniques to find the maximum (or minimum) value of an objective, subject to a set of constraints. These techniques are treated in Part III of the book.

Simulation is a technique for modeling large complex systems involving uncertainty. A model is designed to replicate the behavior of the system. Simulation models are usually analyzed by a case by case (versus optimization) approach. Chapter 19 introduces simulation models.

Dynamic Problems

Dynamic decision problems involve a particular type of complexity—when there is a sequence of interrelated decisions over several time periods. Part IV of the book includes several of these types of models: **inventory** models for determining when to order inventory and how much stock to hold; **PERT** or **critical path** models for scheduling projects; **queuing** models for problems involving waiting lines; and **dynamic programming** and **Markov processes** for more general dynamic problems.

Decision Support Systems

A *decision support system,* or DSS, is an integrated computer system designed to aid management decision making. A DSS generally incorporates a model that is one of the types described in this text, and the computer system performs the calculations necessary to solve the model. However, a DSS is often more than just a model. It generally involves a database that can be used to provide information directly to the manager (or to the model). A DSS sometimes involves graphics or other reports that are readily understandable by the user. Also, the DSS incorporates computer technology to make it easy to do the analysis needed for the decision problem or to query the database for needed information.

This book is not devoted to developing the computer tools necessary to build DSSs. To the extent that models are a significant part of DSSs, then understanding of the models in this book is an important step in building a DSS. Throughout the book, we shall refer to and illustrate computer software to solve particular models. This software might be a part of a DSS.

SUMMARY

Decisions may be characterized as being made under certainty or uncertainty, depending on whether or not the major factors are assumed known. Decision making under uncertainty involves the use of probabilities to express the likelihood of uncertain events.

Decision models may also be classified as simple (if there are few important variables), complex (if there are many), or dynamic (if the decisions are interrelated over time). Various types of models fitting these categories are described throughout this text.

Computer decision support systems (DSSs) often include, as a major component, a decision model of the kind studied in this book.

Bibliography

Baker, K. R., and D. H. Kropp. *Management Science: An Introduction to the Use of Decision Models.* New York: John Wiley & Sons, 1985.

Bodily, S. *Modern Decision Making: A Guide to Modeling with Decision Support Systems.* New York: McGraw-Hill, 1985.

Bonini, C. P. *Computer Models for Decision Analysis.* Palo Alto, Calif.: Scientific Press, 1980.

Buffa, E. S., and J. S. Dyer. *Management Science/Operations Research.* 2nd ed. New York: John Wiley & Sons, 1981.

Eppen, G. D.; F. J. Gould; and C. Schmidt. *Quantitative Concepts for Management.* 3rd ed. Englewood Cliffs, N.J.: Prentice Hall, 1988.

Jackson, B. B. *Computer Models in Management.* Homewood, Ill.: Richard D. Irwin, 1979.

Raiffa, H. *Decision Analysis*. Reading, Mass.: Addison-Wesley Publishing, 1968.

Schlaifer, R. *Analysis of Decisions under Uncertainty*. New York: McGraw-Hill, 1969.

Wagner, H. M. *Principles of Operations Research*. 2nd ed. Englewood Cliffs, N.J.: Prentice Hall, 1975.

Problems with Answers

1–1. Refer to the government contract example in this chapter. Suppose there was a 40 percent loss in yield due to tighter product specifications.

    a. How many units would have to enter the production process in order to obtain 1,000 "good" units?

    b. What is the total cost of obtaining 1,000 "good" units?

    c. Should the contract be accepted? Why or why not?

1–2. The XYZ Appliance Company is considering replacing a metal gear with a plastic one. The plastic gear will save $0.50 per unit but will require an expenditure of $20,000 for a special mold to produce the gear. The special mold will last for one year. Annual sales are 80,000 units.

    a. Should the company convert to the plastic gear? Why or why not?

    b. Suppose now that the plastic gear is associated with a slightly higher first-year failure rate; specifically, for every 1,000 units sold, there will be an average of two additional failures from the plastic gear as compared with the metal gear. Failures cost the company $40 (representing warranty repair costs and ill will). Now should the company convert to the plastic gear? Why or why not?

Problems

1–3. Setting the price of a product is a very important business decision. What are elements of uncertainty in the decision to change the price of a product?

1–4. In what sense are there "opponents" when a price is set for a product?

1–5. A family is planning a picnic. In what sense is nature the opponent? Is it reasonable to use probabilities to describe the likelihood of the different states of nature?

1–6. Profit maximization has sometimes been described as the prime criterion to be applied in business decision making. If you were a business manager, what additional criteria would you employ in your decision making?

1–7. The Crude Oil Company is considering drilling for oil on property it leases. Is it reasonable to specify a probability of finding oil?

1–8. Consider some business or personal decision with which you are familiar. Describe this decision in terms of:

    a. The alternatives that are available.

    b. The criterion that you would use to select among the alternatives.

    c. The important variables that should go into a model to aid in making this decision. To what extent can you quantify these variables?

    d. To what extent can you quantify the relationships among the variables suggested in (*c*)?

1–9. One management philosophy is to "fire and then aim." A second philosophy leads to "paralysis by analysis." What is your choice?

1–10. A possible model of total expenses is:

$$T = a + bX$$

where:

T = Total costs

a = Fixed costs

b = Variable costs

X = Number of units

Discuss the adequacy of this model as a predictor of the total costs associated with a given output.

More Challenging Problems

1–11. An executive is in the process of deciding on the price for a new product. The goal is to maximize profit. The alternatives are different possible prices from $2 per unit to $10 per unit. The model to be used is described below.

Let:

x = Number of units produced (and sold)
$C(x)$ = Total cost of producing x units
p = Price to be charged
NP = Total net profit (to be maximized)

Cost relationship: $C(x) = 800 + 1.25x$
Sales relationship: $x = -100 + 2,000/p$
Profit: $NP = p{\cdot}x - C(x)$

a. Comment on the model chosen by the executive in terms of the reasonableness of the relationships, the variables that were chosen (and ones left out), and the value of the model.

b. Find an approximate solution to the model by trial and error (i.e., try several values of price between $2 and $10, and try to find a price that gives a good profit).

1–12. An airport is considering installation of a sophisticated landing assistance device. The annual equivalent cost of this device (including all costs) is $800,000 a year, which will not be recoverable from the airlines. The device will reduce the expected number of crashes per year at the airport from 1.8 to 1.7.

The average flight into the airport carries 40 people (including crew), and the airplane has a resale value of $2 million.

a. If the device is rejected, what implicit value is being placed on the value of the lives of occupants of the plane?

b. How much would you be willing to pay for the device?

1–13. The product manager of Crunchy Cereal is trying to determine the advertising budget for next year. She has the following information available: selling price is $5 per case; variable cost of manufacture is $2 per case; the fixed costs for produc-

ing Crunchy Cereal totals $100,000 per year. The manager has estimated the following relationship between sales of Crunchy Cereal (called X and measured in thousands of cases) and dollars spent for advertising (called Z and measured in thousands of dollars):

$$X = 50 + 1.2Z - 0.006Z^2$$

For:

$$0 \le Z \le 100$$

a. Formulate a model for net profit for Crunchy Cereal. That is, identify all variables and relationships necessary to determine profit.

b. Find an approximate optimal solution to the model by trial and error (that is, try a few values for advertising between $0 and $100,000, and find a good profit solution).

1–14. A computer company is considering introducing a new product, model B. Some of its sales would come at the expense of model A, a best seller for the company. The economics are as follows:

	Model A	Model B
Fixed cost	$10 million	$20 million
Variable cost per unit	$500	$300
Wholesale selling price	$1,500	$1000

The fixed costs of model A have already been incurred, but not those for model B. Current sales of model A are 500,000 units annually. Introduction of model B would generate 600,000 units of B sold annually, but reduce A's sales to 300,000 units. The remaining product life for both products is one year; after that, they will be obsolete. Thus, a one-year analysis is appropriate.

a. Formulate a model to decide whether or not to introduce model B at this time. What decision would you recommend?

b. Suppose model A had not been previously introduced (and its fixed cost had not yet been incurred). Formulate a model for this situation and decide which product(s) should be introduced.

c. What other considerations would apply to the situation in (a)?

CHAPTER 2

Introduction to Model Building

Introduction

Chapter 1 introduced the basic ideas of decision making and the role that a model plays in that process. The purpose of this chapter is to go into greater depth in explaining what a model is and to show how managers can use and build a certain class of models, called case models. Other types of models—models for decision making under uncertainty, optimization models, and dynamic models—will be introduced in later sections of the book.

Basic Model Concepts

As explained in Chapter 1, a model is a simplification of a business decision problem. The simplification is accomplished by including only the important elements and omitting the nonessential considerations. A road map is a good example of a model. It excludes most of the detail of landscape, buildings, and so forth in order to show clearly the highway routes. Because it is simplified, it is highly useful. If all the detail of the real world were included, it would be much less useful, since we would be spending a large amount of time trying to sort out the highways from the other detail.

Thus, the first step in model building is to pick out the factors or variables that the decision maker considers important. These may be classified into five categories:

- Decision variables.
- Exogenous variables.
- Policies and constraints.

■ Performance measures.
■ Intermediate variables.

Decision Variables

The decision variables are those under the control of the decision maker. They represent alternative choices for the manager. Consider a marketing manager deciding on the introduction of a new product. The manager can choose to introduce the product or not; the manager may also choose the price at which to sell the product and the amount to spend on advertising. Since these are the major choices, these are the decision variables.

The manager may also have a number of minor decisions to make, such as the color of the product, the detailed content of the advertising, how the sales force is to be informed about the product, and so on. In order to simplify the analysis, the manager may choose to omit these less important factors from the model.

Exogenous Variables

Exogenous or external variables are those that are important to the decision problem but are controlled by factors outside the purview of the decision maker. Generally, economic conditions, actions of competitors, prices of raw materials, and similar factors are exogenous variables. In the case of the marketing manager considering a new product introduction, the reaction of customers (how much they will buy) is certainly an important exogenous variable. Other exogenous variables are the cost of raw materials and other elements needed to produce the product.

Policies and Constraints

A decision maker often operates within constraints imposed by company policy, legal restraints, or physical limitations. For example, there may be limited capacity available in the plant, and this may restrict the sales that can be made. A company policy may specify that materials are to be procured from certain suppliers or that certain levels of quality must be maintained.

Sometimes policies or constraints can be modified. For example, plant capacity is a constraint, but management could decide to expand the plant. This means that there may be some confusion between what is considered a decision variable and what is a constraint. It is not important to make too fine a distinction. What is important is that management recognize the presence of constraints, with the understanding that they can be modified if appropriate.

Performance Measures

In making a decision, managers have goals or objectives that they are trying to achieve. Criteria or performance measures are quantitative expressions of these objectives. For example, our marketing manager with the new product introduction decision would have profit as one performance measure. Market share and return on investment may also be performance measures.

Intermediate Variables

A number of other variables are usually needed to include all the important factors in the decision problem. Often these are accounting variables that relate to cost or revenue factors. They are used to relate the decision variables and exogenous variables to the performance measures. They are thus intermediate variables in the sense that they are between the other variables. In our example of a new product decision, total revenue (price times quantity sold) would be an intermediate variable; the components of manufacturing and sales costs would also be intermediate variables.

The Model and Relationships between Variables

Figure 2–1 shows how the various categories of variables are related. The model is in the middle. Decision variables, exogenous variables, and policies and constraints are inputs to the model, and performance measures are outputs. The model itself represents the set of all relationships among the variables. Defining these relationships is the second important step in building a model (the first step, as discussed above, is defining the important variables).

Figure 2–1   Model Inputs and Outputs

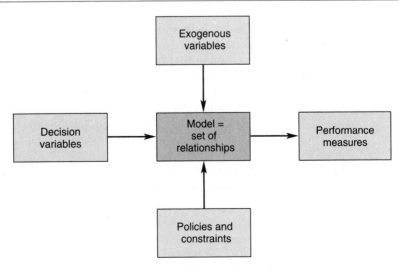

Some relationships are accounting definitions. For example, profit is revenue minus expense, a simple accounting rule. Other relationships depend on physical limits, such as determining the amount of product that can be produced from a batch of raw material. Some relationships are judgmental, representing management's understanding of how factors are related. Management's judgment about the reaction of customers to a price change is an example of such a relationship.

The model is the set of all these relationships. It is like a "black box" that transforms decision variables into performance measures for a specified set of exogenous variables and policies and constraints.

An Example: A Model of a Plywood Mill

These concepts are difficult to understand in the abstract. Hence, we introduce an example, a mill that peels logs to make plywood and sells the plywood to wholesale customers. Although the example is based on a real case,[1] it is somewhat simplified in order to show the major points. A real-world model used to make an actual business decision would usually be more complex.

Suppose the managers of a plywood mill are making their plans for next year. They face two decisions: one about plant capacity and another about labor rate. The plant capacity decision involves whether or not the firm should expand the mill, by how much, and when. Let us suppose that if they decide to expand now, additional capacity can be added in any quarter of next year.

The second decision relates to labor negotiations that are about to start with the company's labor union. The company and the union have to agree on a labor rate for the coming year. This is, of course, a joint decision, the result of the negotiation process.

The company has prepared forecasts of the prices for the plywood that it will sell next year, as well as projections for how much could be sold (i.e., an estimate of demand). The company has a policy of producing to order, so that no inventory of plywood is maintained. This means that the company can't sell more than it can produce in any period. Forecasts have also been made for the price of logs, the raw material from which plywood is made.

In order to produce plywood, the company incurs expenses for labor, supplies, and of course raw material (logs). Other expenses are related to sales. The company leases its production equipment and pays fees for these leases. There are also certain fixed (overhead) costs each period.

Table 2–1 shows a list of the important factors in this example. The abbreviation MSF stands for thousands of surface square feet and is the unit of measure for plywood. MBF stands for thousands of board feet, the unit for logs. M$ stands for thousands of dollars.

---

[1]See the Puyallup Forest Products case in Charles P. Bonini's *Computer Models for Decision Analysis* (Palo Alto, Calif.: Scientific Press, 1980), pp. 55–66.

Table 2–1 **Important Factors in Model of Plywood Mill**

Decision Variables

LABOR RATE. Average wage for mill employees (dollars per hour).
ADDITIONAL CAPACITY. Amount of capacity (MSF or thousands of surface square feet of plywood capacity) added in each quarter.

Performance Measure

PROFIT. Net profit from operating the mill each quarter, and for the year (M$ or $ thousands).

Exogenous Variables

PLYWOOD PRICE. Sales price for plywood each quarter (dollars per MSF).
DEMAND. Demand for plywood each quarter (MSF).
LOG COST. Purchase cost of logs (dollars per MBF—dollars per thousand board feet).
LABOR PRODUCTIVITY. Production output (MSF) per labor hour.

Constraints and Policies

No inventories of plywood. Production of plywood is scheduled to match sales. Analysis is to be done by quarters (i.e., three-month periods).

Intermediate Variables

REVENUE. Revenue from sale of plywood (M$ per quarter).
OPERATING EXPENSE. Expense associated directly with producing plywood (supplies expense, raw material expense, and labor expense—M$ per quarter).
SUPPLIES EXPENSE. Expense for supplies (M$ per quarter).
RAW MATERIAL EXPENSE. Cost of raw material (logs—M$ per quarter).
LABOR EXPENSE. Cost for labor (M$ per quarter).
LOGS REQUIRED. Amount of logs needed for production (MBF per quarter).
LABOR HOURS. Amount of labor hours required for production (hours per quarter).
PLYWOOD PRODUCTION. Amount of plywood produced (MSF per quarter).
CAPACITY. Actual production capacity of mill (MSF per quarter).
OTHER EXPENSE. Total of other expenses, including sales expense, fixed expense, and equipment expense (M$ per quarter).
SALES EXPENSE. Expense for marketing plywood (M$ per quarter).
FIXED EXPENSE. Fixed expense (M$ per quarter).
EQUIPMENT EXPENSE. Lease cost for equipment (M$ per quarter).

The list of variables in Table 2–1 may seem rather formidable at first, but you will see that it is really rather simple once the table is examined closely. Although the example is simplified, it is necessary to have enough complexity to illustrate how a model can be used.

Relationships: The Influence Diagram

We now turn to defining the relationships between the variables. Sometimes it is helpful to draw a diagram showing which variables relate to or influence others. For our example, Figure 2–2 is such a diagram, called an **influence diagram.**

Figure 2–2   **Plywood Mill Model—Influence Diagram**

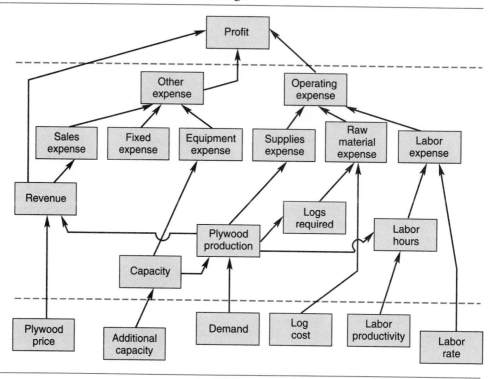

The lines with arrows indicate which variables are related to which. It isn't absolutely necessary to construct such a diagram, but it is often useful in understanding the model.

Note that there are two dashed lines across Figure 2–2. The only variable above the top line is the performance measure, PROFIT. The boxes below the bottom line contain either decision variables or exogenous variables, the inputs to the model. The variables and relationships in the middle make up the model.

We can now begin defining the relationships between the variables. We start with the physical relationships (those involving physical as opposed to dollar variables).

Physical Relationships

$$\text{CAPACITY = 9200 + ADDITIONAL CAPACITY}$$

The initial capacity of the mill is 9,200 MSF per quarter. To this is added any additional capacity that is leased.

$$\text{PLYWOOD PRODUCTION = MINIMUM (CAPACITY, DEMAND)}$$

Recall that plywood production in any quarter equals sales—the policy of no inventory requires this. If demand is higher than capacity, the firm will produce (and sell) all it can up to its capacity. That is, production is limited by capacity in this case. On the other hand, if demand is below capacity, then demand will limit production (and sales). Thus, production is limited by the smaller (i.e., minimum) of capacity or demand.

```
LOGS REQUIRED = .52 * PLYWOOD PRODUCTION
```

This relationship says that .52 MBF of logs are required for each MSF of plywood that is produced. The .52 is a constant that depends on the efficiency with which plywood can be manufactured from its raw material, logs. The asterisk * means "multiplied by." It is the standard symbol used in computer programs, and will be used as such throughout this chapter.

A short detour is needed here to explain constants. In building a model, there are numerical values, such as the .52 coefficient above, that are often estimated from cost or other data in the firm. Although these could be considered exogenous variables, they are of lesser importance, and are assumed instead to be constants. They are expected to remain fixed (i.e., constant) for the analyses performed on the model.

```
LABOR HOURS = PLYWOOD PRODUCTION/LABOR PRODUCTIVITY
```

The total hours required for labor depends on the plywood production and on how productive labor is.

Financial Relationships

The remaining relationships in the model are financial. The following are simple accounting definitions and are self-explanatory. Division by 1,000 is necessary in some equations to convert to thousands of dollars.

```
PROFIT = REVENUE - OPERATING EXPENSE - OTHER EXPENSE
REVENUE = (PLYWOOD PRODUCTION * PLYWOOD PRICE)/1000
OPERATING COST = SUPPLIES EXPENSE + RAW MATERIAL
                 EXPENSE + LABOR EXPENSE
OTHER EXPENSE = SALES EXPENSE + EQUIPMENT EXPENSE
                + FIXED EXPENSE
LABOR EXPENSE = (LABOR RATE * LABOR HOURS)/1000
RAW MATERIAL EXPENSE = (LOGS REQUIRED * LOG COST)/1000
```

A few relationships do need some explanation:

```
SUPPLIES EXPENSE = (28 * PLYWOOD PRODUCTION)/1000
```

Each MSF of plywood uses $28 in supplies in the production process. The $28 is another constant in the model.

```
SALES EXPENSE = .10 * REVENUE
```

Sales expense is 10 percent of sales revenue.

$$\mathtt{FIXED\ EXPENSE\ =\ 20}$$

Fixed expense is $20,000 per quarter.

$$\mathtt{EQUIPMENT\ EXPENSE\ =\ (11\ *\ CAPACITY)/1000}$$

Recall that the mill equipment is leased. The fees for this lease are $11 per MSF of installed capacity per quarter.

SUMMARY

Model building involves first simplifying a decision problem by selecting for study only the most important variables. These variables include decision variables (over which the decision maker has control), exogenous variables, performance measures, policies or constraints, and intermediate variables. The second step of model building is identifying the relationships among variables; that is, determining how the variables depend on one another. The model itself is the set of all these relationships.

Analysis Using the Model

The model for the plywood mill is now complete. We turn to management's use of the model. The first step is to make estimates for the exogenous variables. Let us suppose the estimates in Table 2–2 are prepared.

Note that these are predictions, based upon informed judgment of the management, but they may turn out to be incorrect. One purpose of the model is to learn how errors in these estimates may affect the mill operations.

The decision variables are ADDITIONAL CAPACITY to be added and the LABOR RATE negotiated with the union. Suppose we assume for an initial base case that no additions to capacity will be made and that the labor rate is the same as last year at $9 per hour.

This allows us to complete the calculations for the model, and these are shown in Table 2–3. Note that the base case results in profit of $387,000 for the year.

Table 2–2   **Estimates for Exogenous Variables**

Variable	Unit	First Quarter	Second Quarter	Third Quarter	Fourth Quarter
Plywood price	$/MSF	125	125	130	130
Plywood demand	MSF	10,000	10,800	8,000	10,000
Log cost	$/MBF	75	75	75	80
Labor productivity	MSF/hour	0.4	0.4	0.4	0.4

Table 2-3   Plywood Mill Model Base Case

	Units	First Quarter	Second Quarter	Third Quarter	Fourth Quarter	Year Total
Decision Variables						
Additional Capacity	MSF	0	0	0	0	
Labor Rate	$/hour	9.00	9.00	9.00	9.00	
Exogenous Variables						
Plywood Price	$/MSF	125	125	130	130	
Plywood Demand	MSF	10,000	10,800	8,000	10,000	
Log Cost	$/MBF	75	75	75	80	
Labor Productivity	MSF/hour	0.4	0.4	0.4	0.4	
Physical Factors						
Actual Capacity	MSF	9,200	9,200	9,200	9,200	36,800
Plywood Production	MSF	9,200	9,200	8,000	9,200	35,600
Logs Required	MBF	4,784	4,784	4,160	4,784	18,512
Labor Hours Required	hours	23,000	23,000	20,000	23,000	89,000
Financial Factors						
Revenue	M$	1,150	1,150	1,040	1,196	4,536
Raw Material Expense	M$	359	359	312	383	1,413
Supplies Expense	M$	258	258	224	258	997
Labor Expense	M$	207	207	180	207	801
Total Operating Expense	M$	824	824	716	847	3,211
Sales Expense	M$	115	115	104	120	454
Fixed Expense	M$	20	20	20	20	80
Equipment Expense	M$	101	101	101	101	404
Total Other Expense	M$	236	236	225	241	938
Profit	M$	90	90	99	108	387

Note: Discrepancies in totals are due to rounding.

You should pause at this point and carefully examine Table 2–3. Work through some of the numbers, using the relationships developed earlier. As an example, LOGS REQUIRED in the first quarter is 4,784, calculated as .52 * PLYWOOD PRODUCTION, one of the physical relationships described earlier. Note that plywood production is limited by capacity in the first, second, and fourth quarters, and by demand in the third.

Implementing the Model on a Computer

The calculations involved in Table 2–3 could, of course, be done by hand, and they would take perhaps 20 or 30 minutes, if you made no mistakes in arithmetic. This would be satisfactory if only one case or scenario were to be examined. However, we want to examine a whole series of cases, so a better approach would be to develop a computer version of the model. There are several ways this could be done. The model could be written in a general-purpose computer language such as BASIC, FORTRAN, or Pascal; it could be programmed in one of the financial planning languages such as IFPS or EMPIRE, designed especially for this type of problem; or it could be implemented on one of the spreadsheet programs such as Lotus 1–2–3, Excel, or Quattro that are available on personal computers. We shall illustrate this latter approach, since spreadsheet programs have become widely available, are easy to use, and are ideal for analysis of this type of problem.

A typical spreadsheet contains rows and columns, as shown in Figure 2–3. The rows are numbered starting at 1. The columns are indicated by letters,[2] starting at A. A *cell* is at the intersection of each row and column and is indicated by its column and row designation. Thus, cell B3 is the cell in column B and row 3.

A cell can contain alphanumeric information such as the label "Decision Variables"; it can contain a number such as 9.00 for the labor rate; and it can also contain a formula. Formulas include the cell designations as variables. For example, if the cell D3 contained the following formula

$$(B3 + C3)$$

this would imply that the contents of cells B3 and C3 were to be added and the total stored in the D3 cell.

Table 2–4 shows the spreadsheet formulas for the first period (quarter) of our model. The first column in Table 2–4, column A, contains only the labels for the various variables in the model. The second column contains the units of measurement, which are also alphabetic information. The first several rows in the C

---

[2]This is the way rows and columns are coded in most, but not all, spreadsheet programs.

Figure 2–3   **Layout of Spreadsheet**

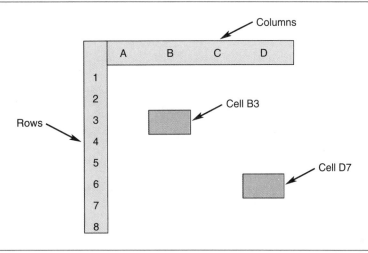

column contain numeric values for the decision variables and the exogenous variables. The formulas are in column C starting at row 14.

The first formula, in cell C14, is

$$9200 + C4$$

Since cell C4 contains ADDITIONAL CAPACITY, this formula computes the actual capacity as the initial capacity of 9200 MSF plus any additions. It is the spreadsheet equivalent of the relationship

$$\texttt{CAPACITY = 9200 + ADDITIONAL CAPACITY}$$

developed on page 20.

Similarly, the contents of cell C15 is

$$\texttt{@MIN(C9,C14)}$$

This is equivalent to the relationship

$$\texttt{PLYWOOD PRODUCTION = MINIMUM (DEMAND, CAPACITY)}$$

Note that cell C9 is Plywood Demand, and cell C14 is Actual Capacity. (The @ is a special symbol to designate functions, such as @MIN for minimum, @MAX for maximum, and @SUM for total, etc.)

You should examine the remaining formulas in Table 2–4 to be sure you understand them.

Table 2–4   **Formulas as Entered on Spreadsheet**

	A	B	C
1			First
2		Units	Quarter
3	Decision Variables		
4	Additional Capacity	MSF	0
5	Labor Rate	$/hour	9.00
6			
7	Exogenous Variables		
8	Plywood Price	$/MSF	125
9	Plywood Demand	MSF	10,000
10	Log Cost	$/MBF	75
11	Labor Productivity	MSF/hour	0.4
12			
13	Physical Factors		
14	Actual Capacity	MSF	9200+C4
15	Plywood Production	MSF	@MIN(C9,C14)
16	Logs Required	MBF	0.52*C15
17	Labor Hours Required	hours	+C15/C11
18			
19	Financial Factors		
20			
21	Revenue	M$	(C15*C8)/1000
22			
23	Raw Material Expense	M$	(C16*C10)/1000
24	Supplies Expense	M$	(28*C15)/1000
25	Labor Expense	M$	(C5*C17)/1000
26			
27	Total Operating Expense	M$	+C23+C24+C25
28			
29	Sales Expense	M$	0.1*C21
30	Fixed Expense	M$	20
31	Equipment Expense	M$	(11*C14)/1000
32			
33	Total Other Expense	M$	+C29+C30+C31
34			
35	Profit	M$	+C21−C27−C33
36			

Formulas for Other Quarters

The formulas for the other quarters of the year are similar, except they would
be in columns D, E, and F of the spreadsheet. There is a procedure within the
spreadsheet programs that allows one to copy or replicate the formulas to other
columns when they are similar, as is the case here.[3] The totals for the year are
sums of the items for the four quarters.

---

[3]Cell C14 is the one exception to the statement that the formulas can be copied to the other
columns. Cell D14 should be (C14 + D4). That is, CAPACITY (in the second period) = CAPAC-

This section is not intended to be a detailed treatment of spreadsheet packages. They have many more features than we have space to illustrate here. Our purpose, rather, is to demonstrate how a case model can be set up in the spreadsheet format.

The analysis, using the spreadsheet program, is also quite straightforward. We simply make a change in one or more of the decision or exogenous variables, and the results appear on the computer screen almost immediately. It is also possible to modify the model by changing the relationships, or by adding new variables, or by extending the model over more time periods. Some spreadsheet packages have the ability to create tables of results, and to plot the results in various types of charts.

Examples of Analysis Using the Model

In Chapter 1, and in the beginning of this chapter, we described the type of model we have built as a **case model.** This name comes from the type of analysis, which involves examining a number of cases or scenarios using the model. Each case uses different assumptions about the various variables in the model. Let us give some examples of how the managers at the plywood mill might examine a few such cases and thus use the model just developed to answer some management issues and to obtain insight into the decision problems they face.

Recall that the plywood mill management is facing negotiations with the union about the labor rate for the next year. The managers could use the model to analyze the effect of different labor rates on profitability. The current rate is $9 per hour; an increase to $10 could be entered in the model (by changing the values in the row labeled "Labor Rate" in Table 2–3). This results in a profit of $298,000 for the year, a reduction of $89,000. An even more interesting question is, "How much could the labor rate increase before the mill became unprofitable?" Eight different values for LABOR RATE are used in the model, first at $9 per hour, then $10, and so on through $16 per hour. Figure 2–4 shows a plot of the results. As can be seen, the break-even point (where profit is zero) occurs between $13 and $14 per hour, about $13.35.

Suppose that as a part of the negotiations, management is asking the union to change some work rules that would increase the productivity of the workers. Suppose that these changes would increase LABOR PRODUCTIVITY from 0.4 MSF per hour to 0.5 MSF per hour. If the union were to agree to these work rule changes in exchange for an increase in the labor rate to $11 per hour, what would be the combined effect? This is shown in Table 2–5, which is the same as Table 2–3 except for these two changes (LABOR RATE is 11 and LABOR PRO-

---

ITY (in the first period) plus second period ADDITIONAL CAPACITY. This formula should be entered in cell D14, and then it could be copied (replicated) to the third and fourth periods.

Figure 2–4   **Break-Even Analysis for Labor Rate**

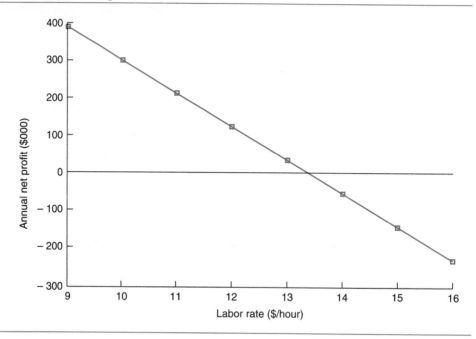

DUCTIVITY is 0.5). As you can see, there is a net increase in annual profit (from $387 thousand to $405 thousand).

Another decision is whether or not additional capacity should be added to the mill. We can start with the base case and add different amounts of capacity in the first quarter. Table 2–6 presents the results of four cases, each with a different amount of added capacity. From this, it would appear that adding about 1,000 MSF of capacity would be best, although the differences are not very large.

Management might also ask how this capacity decision would change if the forecasts for plywood demand were incorrect. In other words, how sensitive is this capacity decision to demand? To examine this, let us suppose that the pattern of demand remains the same over the four quarters (second quarter high, third low), but that we consider one case in which the actual total demand turns out to be as little as half (50 percent) of the forecast demand, another case in which it is 60 percent of forecast, and so on up to 150 percent of forecast. At 100 percent, the actual and forecast are the same. Also, we consider the installation of 1,000 MSF, or 2,000 MSF, or 3,000 MSF additional capacity. This requires entering a large number of different combinations in the model and recording the results. Actually, some spreadsheet programs have procedures to do this kind of analysis in a few simple steps. The results are plotted in Figure 2–5 (some spreadsheets can even create plots like this).

Table 2-5   Plywood Mill Model Case with Increases in Labor Productivity and Labor Rate

	Units	First Quarter	Second Quarter	Third Quarter	Fourth Quarter	Year Total
Decision Variables						
Additional Capacity	MSF	0	0	0	0	
Labor Rate	$/hour	11.00	11.00	11.00	11.00	
Exogenous Variables						
Plywood Price	$/MSF	125	125	130	130	
Plywood Demand	MSF	10,000	10,800	8,000	10,000	
Log Cost	$/MBF	75	75	75	80	
Labor Productivity	MSF/hour	0.5	0.5	0.5	0.5	
Physical Factors						
Actual Capacity	MSF	9,200	9,200	9,200	9,200	36,800
Plywood Production	MSF	9,200	9,200	8,000	9,200	35,600
Logs Required	MBF	4,784	4,784	4,160	4,784	18,512
Labor Hours Required	hours	18,400	18,400	16,000	18,400	71,200
Financial Factors						
Revenue	M$	1,150	1,150	1,040	1,196	4,536
Raw Material Expense	M$	359	359	312	383	1,412
Supplies Expense	M$	258	258	224	258	997
Labor Expense	M$	202	202	176	202	783
Total Operating Expense	M$	819	819	712	843	3,192
Sales Expense	M$	115	115	104	120	454
Fixed Expense	M$	20	20	20	20	80
Equipment Expense	M$	101	101	101	101	405
Total Other Expense	M$	236	236	225	241	938
Profit	M$	95	95	103	112	405

Note: Discrepancies in totals are due to rounding.

Table 2–6   **Results of Additional Capacity Added to Base Case in First Quarter**

Additional Capacity (MSF)	Annual Profit (M$)
0 (base case)	387
1,000	405
2,000	374
3,000	330

Figure 2–5   **Effects of Errors in Demand Estimates and Additions to Capacity**

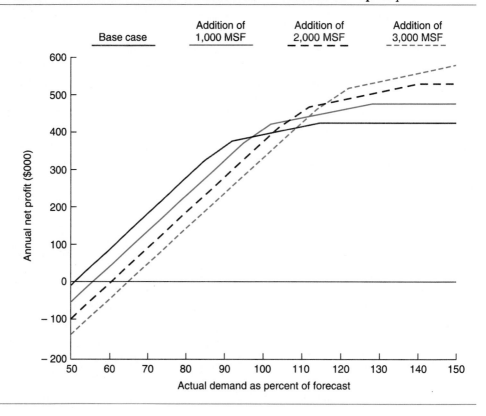

Before commenting on the results of this analysis, we should point out that investments in new capacity would generally be evaluated over a long period of time. We have restricted the model to one year to keep it simple. Thus, our conclusions below are limited.

Note in Figure 2–5 that the decision about adding capacity does not significantly affect annual profit as long as the actual demand is close to forecast or only slightly above forecast. That is, the lines in Figure 2–5 are quite close together when actual demand is between about 100 percent and 110 percent of forecast. If management is reasonably confident about the demand forecast, then the capacity decision is not a critical one—the alternatives are about equally good. The cost of adding capacity is about equal to the additional profit the capacity creates. On the other hand, if management thinks that there is a good chance that actual demand might be substantially more or substantially less than forecast, then the capacity decision is indeed critical, since there are big differences between the best and worst alternatives. The top and bottom lines in Figure 2–5 at, say, the 70 percent and 130 percent points differ by over $100,000.

This analysis does not tell management what decision to make, only whether or not a problem exists. If indeed there is a substantial uncertainty about the accuracy of the forecasts, management could use decision analysis techniques as described in Chapter 4.

One of the major benefits of spreadsheet programs is that the manager gets to see instantly how *all* the variables included in the model are affected by changes in the data. This frees the manager, to some extent, from total dependence on a single performance measure. In the discussion above, we emphasized profit. Management would also be interested in the effects of the various plans being considered on other factors: for example, how many labor hours are required (and hence how many workers need to be hired) and how much raw material is needed (MBF of logs). As can be seen in Tables 2–4 and 2–5, this information is readily available and can be taken into account by management in making its decisions.

Sensitivity Analysis

The analysis above is an example of "what if" or sensitivity analysis. This type of analysis shows what happens if this or that change is made in one of the decision or exogenous variables. The aim is to see how the performance measure (profit) is affected; that is, how sensitive profit is to the change. This approach helps managers better understand the problem they face. Rather than producing "the answer," it is an aid to insight.

We can carry this analysis further by looking at the sensitivity of profit to each of the exogenous variables. This is done by considering cases for which each of the variables is 10 percent above and 10 percent below the base case values. The variables are varied one at a time, with the others set at the base case levels. The results are shown in Figure 2–6. This is called a **spider diagram** because of its resemblance to a spider web.

The steepness of a line in the spider diagram indicates how sensitive profit is to changes in that variable. Note that the line for plywood price is very steep; even small changes in the price have a big impact on profitability. A 10 percent reduction, for example, lowers profit to zero. On the other hand, the effect of changes in demand is more modest, particularly increases in demand (production is limited by capacity in this case). Again, note that these are one-at-a-time

Figure 2–6   **Plywood Mill Model Sensitivity Analysis (Spider Diagram)**

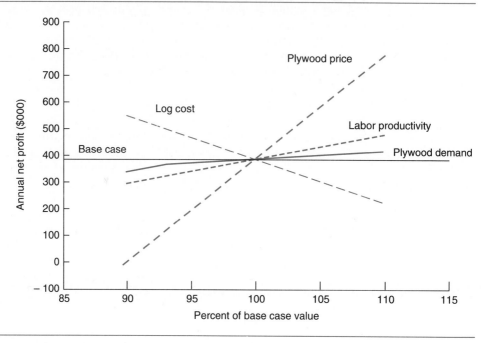

analyses, and they assume that all other factors are at base case levels. If desired, changes other than 10 percent can also be used.

An Example: *The New York Times* Model

Figure 2–7 shows the outline of a model developed for *The New York Times* newspaper.[4] Exogenous variables such as employment, prices, and gross national product are used to forecast the levels of advertising by type (e.g., auto ads, department store ads, and so forth) and the circulation for the daily and Sunday papers by geographic zones. The advertising and circulation volumes are then converted into volumes for the various operating departments of the composition room and the press room and into requirements for newsprint and ink. Also, volumes of distribution and mail are estimated. Estimates of costs, including an allowance for inflation, are combined with these volume estimates to produce variable cost estimates. Fixed costs and revenues are also included and combined into a projected income statement.

---

[4]Leonard Foreman, "*The New York Times* Newspaper Planning Model," in *Corporate Planning Models,* ed. Thomas H. Naylor (Reading, Mass.: Addison-Wesley Publishing, 1979.)

Figure 2–7   *The New York Times* Model

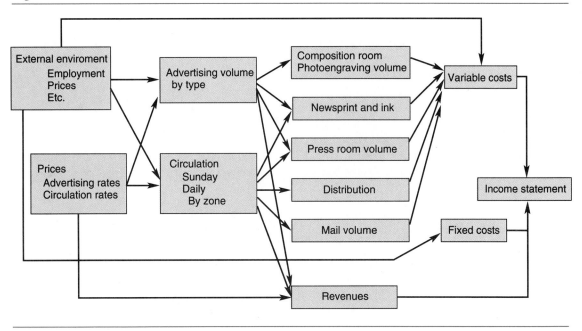

The actual model contains about 400 equations and provides detailed estimates for revenues and costs. The model has been in use for a number of years and is integrated with the budgeting and planning processes at the *Times*. The model has been used to analyze new products such as special regional editions, and to plan operations generally.

SUMMARY

A model is a set of relationships among variables. This chapter illustrated a type of model called a case model. The method of analysis is to try out many different examples or cases. In particular, sensitivity analysis examines the effect on the performance measures (e.g. profit) of changes in the decision and exogenous variables. The aim of sensitivity analysis is to increase the decision maker's understanding of the problem and the effect of different assumptions.

APPENDIX

Present Value and the Time Value of Money

Case models of the type described in this chapter often involve cash flows over several years. Most major capital investments, for example, generate cash flows that last for several years. The time period in which money is received is an important aspect of its value. You should not be indifferent to receiving $1,000 now as opposed to $1,000 in five years. Even if you had no immediate need for the $1,000 now, you could invest it and have substantially more than $1,000 in five years.

A general approach to problems involving cash flows over time is to convert all such flows to present-value equivalents using a discount or interest rate and compound interest calculations.[5] The present value of $1,000 received five years from now using a discount rate of 15 percent is:

$$\frac{1,000}{(1 + 0.15)^5} = 497.18$$

If you put $497.18 in a bank account at an interest rate of 15 percent (compounded annually), you would have $1,000 at the end of five years. In general, the present value of any amount A, with discount rate r, received in n years is:

$$\frac{A}{(1 + r)^n}$$

If there is a stream of cash flows over a number of years, then the present value of the stream is the sum of the present values of each cash flow. Thus, the present value of $10 received at the end of year 1, plus $20 received at the end of year 2, is:

$$\frac{10}{(1 + .15)^1} + \frac{20}{(1 + .15)^2} = 23.82$$

Most of the spreadsheet programs have functions available to perform these present-value calculations. For example, many programs use the function @NPV (net present value) for this purpose.

Bibliography

Bodily, S. *Modern Decision Making: A Guide to Modeling with Decision Support Systems.* New York: McGraw-Hill, 1985.

Bonini, C. *Computer Models for Decision Analysis.* Palo Alto, Calif.: Scientific Press, 1980.

Jackson, B. B. *Computer Models in Management.* Homewood, Ill.: Richard D. Irwin, 1979.

Naylor, T. H. *Corporate Planning Models.* Reading, Mass.: Addison-Wesley Publishing, 1979.

Plane, D. R. *Quantitative Tools for Decision Support Using IFPS.* Reading, Mass.: Addison-Wesley Publishing, 1986.

Problems with Answers

2–1. You have just founded MYOWN Company with the intention of manufacturing and marketing your invention—KARMA, a personal computer for turned-on people. Despite the rosy picture you paint of the company's future, the people at the bank

---

[5] For more detail on these procedures and for other techniques for evaluating cash flows over time, see H. Bierman and S. Smidt, *The Capital Budgeting Decision*, 7th ed. (New York: Macmillan, 1988).

insist on "some numbers." In particular, they want a statement showing your projected income, expenses, and profits for the first year.

The details of your planned operations are: A tentative decision has been made to set the selling price at $1,600 for each KARMA. Manufacturing costs are expected to be $300 per unit plus fixed costs of $80,000 per year. Marketing costs are projected to be 10 percent of dollar sales plus $10,000 in fixed costs. A preliminary estimate of first-year sales is 100 units.

a. Identify the decision variable(s), exogenous variable(s), performance measure, intermediate variable(s), and any policies or constraints for this problem.

b. Define the relationships between the variables identified in (a) above.

c. If you have access to a computer with a spreadsheet program, implement the model on the computer. The model format should look as shown in the adjacent column. You need to fill in the xxxxx spaces with numbers or formulas as appropriate.

d. Use the model to answer the following questions. (Note, even if you don't have access to a spreadsheet, you can answer

```
UNIT SALES                    xxxxx
PRICE                         xxxxx
VARIABLE COST/UNIT            xxxxx

       PROJECTED INCOME STATEMENT
          MYOWN COMPANY, 1992
SALES (dollars)               xxxxx
MANUFACTURING COST            xxxxx
                              -----
GROSS MARGIN                  xxxxx
MARKETING COST                xxxxx
                              -----
PROFIT BEFORE TAX             xxxxx
                              =====
```

this part using a hand calculator, since the computations are not extensive.)

(1) What is the break-even number of units sold? The break-even point is the unit sales volume at which profit is zero. Make an approximate estimate.

(2) Suppose you could lower your price to $1,400, and you believe this would increase unit sales to 130 units; or you could lower your price even further to $1,200, and unit sales would be 150 units. Which of these (the two alternatives here plus the original) would you prefer?

Problems

2–2. Refer to Problem 2–1, the MYOWN Company. Suppose that you wish to extend the model to show profit for each year for five years. The initial sales price is set at $1,600, and the sales estimate for the first year is 100 units, as above. Manufacturing cost is $300 per unit plus fixed costs of $80,000 per year for each year (again, as above). However, suppose marketing costs are 10 percent of dollar sales (as above) but fixed costs are $70,000 per year. Further, assume that unit sales increase 50 percent per year. That is, 1993 sales are 150 percent of 1992, 1994 are 150 percent of 1993, and so on.

a. Develop a model for this problem.

b. Implement the model on a spreadsheet program.

c. Use the model to answer the following questions:

(1) At the current sales estimate of 1992 sales of 100 units (growing 50 percent per year), how long will it be before your company shows a positive profit?

(2) Assuming the 50 percent growth rate continues to hold, how many units would you have to sell in the first year to just break even in the second year? How many units would you have to sell in the first year to break even in that year?

(3) Suppose that you could design KARMA to be more easily expandable as new devices come along. This would increase the unit manufactur-

ing cost to $500 per unit. However, the sales growth rate should be 100 percent per year (i.e., unit sales would double each year). Is this alternative preferable?

2–3. Refer to Problem 2–2. This problem will add some additional complications. Assume that a market study has estimated the relationship between the price for KARMA and the first-year sales as:

$$\text{Unit sales} = 300 - .125 \cdot \text{Price}$$

for prices ranging from $500 to $2,000. You can set the price, but unit sales in the first year are determined by this function. As before, unit sales will increase 50 percent per year after the first year.

Suppose, further, that when unit sales exceed 200 units, you will introduce automated equipment that will cut the unit manufacturing cost from $300 per unit to $250 per unit. However, the fixed manufacturing cost will increase from $80,000 to $90,000 per year. (You should try to build this into the model so that it happens automatically when unit sales increase above 200 units. This can be done using the spreadsheet @MIN or @IF functions.)

a. Incorporate the changes into your spreadsheet model for the MYOWN Company.

b. Use the model to find the price that produces the largest total profit (sum over the five years). (Optional: If you are familiar with the concept of net present value, you can calculate the NPV of profits for the five years [use a

15 percent discount rate], and find the price that maximizes this value.)

2–4. The city manager of Suburbia is evaluating various levels of expenditures for police protection. She has found that the average response time (in minutes) to emergency calls is inversely related to the annual budget for Suburbia's police department. The specific relationship is:

$$R = \frac{50}{C}$$

where R = Average response time in minutes and C = Annual police budget in millions of dollars.

Each citizen of Suburbia evaluates the benefit of an emergency policy response as follows:

$$B = \$100 - \$10R$$

where B = Benefit in dollars. Thus, a response time of 10 minutes produces zero benefit, and a longer time produces a negative benefit.

There are 500,000 emergency calls annually in Suburbia.

a. Develop a spreadsheet model for this problem, assuming the performance measure is total benefit minus total cost. Evaluate alternative police budgets of $5 million, $10 million, $15 million, and $20 million. Which of these is preferred?

b. Now suppose the criterion is the ratio of total benefit divided by total cost. For the same possible budgets, which is most preferred?

More Challenging Problems

2–5. You are considering the purchase of an apartment building. The building contains 25 units and is for sale for $300,000. You plan to keep the building for three years and then sell it.

You ascertain that the property taxes on the property are $6,000 per year and that it will cost about $300 per unit per

year to administer and maintain the apartments. The taxes are expected to grow at a rate of 2 percent per year, and the maintenance costs are estimated to grow at a 15 percent per year rate.

You have not decided on the rent. Currently, the rent is $300 per unit per month, but there is substantial turnover, and the occupancy rate is only 75 percent. That is, on average, 75 percent of the units are rented at any time. You estimate that if you lowered the rent to $220 per unit per month, you would have 100 percent occupancy. Intermediate rental rates would produce intermediate occupancy rates (assume a linear relationship: Occupancy rate = $168.75 - .3125 \cdot$ Rental rate). For example, a $260 rental rate would have an 87.5 percent occupancy rate. You decide to fix the rental rate for the first year and increase it 10 percent per year for years 2 and 3. Whatever occupancy rate occurs in the first year will hold for years 2 and 3 also. For example, if you decide on the $220 rate for year 1, the occupancy will be 100 percent all three years.

At the end of three years, you will sell the apartment building. The amount you expect to receive will be some multiple of the rental income (before expenses) at that time. Your estimate is that this multiple will be 5.0. That is, if the rental income in year 3 is $75,000, then the sale price will be $375,000.

Your objective is to achieve the highest total cash flow over the three-year period. Cash flow in each year is the difference between rental income and expenses. Total cash flow includes that for each year plus the cash from the sale of the property minus its purchase cost. (Optional: Use net present value as the objective, with a discount rate of 15 percent.) *Note:* For purpose of this exercise, ignore depreciation and other issues related to taxes.

a. Identify the decision variables, the exogenous variables, the performance measure, the intermediate variables, and the policies and constraints in this problem.

b. Construct the model by defining the relationships between the variables identified in (a).

c. Implement the model on a spreadsheet program. You may wish to use the suggested format given below. The x's indicate that a number or formula is in that location. The last line is appropriate only if you use present value as the objective.

```
Purchase Cost          XXXX
Initial Rental Rate    XXXX
Occupancy Rate         XXXX
Maintenance Cost/Unit  XXXX
Taxes                  XXXX
Sale Multiple          XXXX

                    Year 0   Year 1   Year 2   Year 3
Rental Rate                   XXXX     XXXX     XXXX
Rental Income                 XXXX     XXXX     XXXX
Expenses:
 Maintenance                  XXXX     XXXX     XXXX
 Taxes                        XXXX     XXXX     XXXX
  Total                       XXXX     XXXX     XXXX
Operating Cash Flow           XXXX     XXXX     XXXX

Purchase Cost        XXXX
Sale Receipt                                    XXXX

Net Cash Flow        XXXX     XXXX     XXXX     XXXX
   Total Cash Flow                              XXXX
(Present Value)                                [XXXX]
```

d. Use the model to find the initial rental rate that achieves the highest total cash flow (or highest net present value).

e. Study the sensitivity of total cash flow (or present value) to the following variables: maintenance cost per unit, annual taxes, and sale multiple. Do this by developing cases in which each of these factors is varied one at a time by 10 percent above and below the base case amounts given in the description above. Use the rental rate found in (d) for this analysis. Plot these results in a spider diagram. To which factor is total cash flow (or present value) most sensitive?

Case 2–6

Super Spuds, Inc., (SSI) purchases potatoes from growers and dehydrates them into potato flakes for sale to a large food processor. In the spring of the year, the company faces two decisions. The first involves how much of its potato requirements to purchase from the growers under a preseason contract. Such a contract in effect buys the potatoes before they are planted, and guarantees the grower a specified price—in this case, $2 per hundredweight (cwt.). The remaining potatoes are purchased in the fall on the open potato market at whatever happens to be the market price at that time.

The second decision involves what price to charge the processor to whom SSI sells its potato flakes. This decision is actually reached in negotiations with the processor and also involves the quantity of potato flakes that the processor will order for that next year. In preparing for these negotiations, SSI has estimated that if they insist on last year's price of $33 per cwt. for flakes, the processor will likely order 800 thousand cwt. It is possible to negotiate a price above or below this $33 price, but the effect will be that the processor will buy less (if higher price) or more (if lower price) than the 800 thousand cwt. Members of SSI management have expressed their judgment about the relationship between the negotiated price and the flakes ordered as:

```
FLAKES ORDERED (Thous. cwt.) = 7400 - 200 * FLAKES PRICE
```

It takes six pounds of potatoes to make one pound of potato flakes. The variable cost for dehydrating the potatoes is $13 per cwt. of potato flakes up to 750 thousand cwt., and $16 per cwt. above 750 thousand cwt. Fixed costs are $4 million per year.

The cost of raw materials (process grade potatoes) depends, of course, on the decision about how much to buy using preseason contracts. In the past, SSI has bought one half its requirements with preseason contracts. However, management at SSI is considering changing this, and could buy more or less of its requirements by preseason contract. The cost of potatoes using preseason contracts is $2 per cwt. The cost of purchasing potatoes on the open market is unknown. Management thinks that it might be anywhere from $1 per cwt. to $3 per cwt.

The profit for SSI is the revenue it gets from selling the potato flakes to the processor minus the costs of dehydrating the potatoes, the cost of purchasing the potatoes (preseason and open market), and the fixed costs.

a. Develop a model for SSI to aid in making the two decisions indicated. Identify the decision variables, exogenous variables, performance measure(s), intermediate variables, and policies and constraints. Then define the relationships between the variables.

b. Implement the model on a computer using a spreadsheet program.

c. Assume that SSI management is going to continue its policy of preseason contracting for one half its potato requirements and that the forecast for the open market price for potatoes is $2 per cwt. (the same price as for the preseason contract). Calculate the SSI profit for a series of cases in which the price of potato flakes is varied from $31 to $34 in increments of $0.50 (that is, $31, $31.50, $32, $32.50, etc.). At what price is the profit the highest? How sensitive is the profit to differences in price between $32 and $33?

d. Assume a potato flakes price of $33 per cwt. Consider the accompanying table below. Complete the table by running a series of cases and calculating the profit for the different values of open market potato price and the different policies on what fraction of the potato requirements are obtained by preseason contracting that are shown. Which of these alternatives is most "conservative"? *Note:* We shall defer until Chapter 4 a discussion of how the managers should choose which action to take in a problem such as this.

Percentage of Potatoes Obtained by Preseason Contract	*Open Market Price for Potatoes*		
	$1 per cwt.	*$2 per cwt.*	*$3 per cwt.*
25%	xxxx	xxxx	xxxx
50	xxxx	xxxx	xxxx
75	xxxx	xxxx	xxxx

CASE 2–7[6]

Chase Manufacturing is a maker of small appliances and household gadgets, with a plant in Decatur, Indiana, and sales offices in Chicago. The products are sold under a variety of brand names through manufacturers' representatives who call on retail appliance dealers, hardware stores, and housewares specialty shops.

The research department at Chase has developed a new product—a wine bottle opener with distinctive features. The product is expected to have appeal as an inexpensive gift, especially during the Christmas season.

The executive committee at Chase is meeting to consider the new product. Jane Boxer, the marketing manager, opens the discussion.

Boxer: I think this new wine bottle opener will be a winner for us. Although there are scads of openers on the market, ours is just unique enough to

[6]Source: Reprinted with permission of Stanford University Graduate School of Business, ©1985 by the Board of Trustees of the Leland Stanford Junior University.

be a hit in the Christmas market. It is an ideal gift for the person who has everything.

We plan to sell it through our normal channels and push it hard this year. By next year the novelty will have worn off, and we will probably drop it from the line.

My plan calls for pricing the opener at $8 and for spending about $50,000 on advertising and promotion to inform and sell our customers on the product. As you know, our customers are primarily buyers for chain stores, specialty shops, and hardware stores. All our sales efforts are aimed at them. We estimate a total market potential of 104,000 units at the $8 price; and with the $50,000 advertising and promotion, we should reach about 65 percent penetration [i.e., sell 65 percent of 104,000, or about 68,000 units].

I obtained estimates from accounting and manufacturing and prepared the projected income statement you have. [See Table 2–7.]

Jack Croxton, the controller, follows:

Croxton: The estimates you used seem pretty reasonable to me, except for the general and administrative costs. Where did you get that 15 percent of sales calculation? Most of our general and administrative costs are in salaries and other fixed costs, and I would think this project would add at most $40,000 to these costs.

Boxer: Our total corporate G&A expense was 15 percent of sales last year, and I simply used that same percentage. We will need to add a project man-

Table 2–7   **Chase Manufacturing Company**

New Wine Bottle Opener
Pro Forma Analysis
($000s)*

Sales	$540.8
Manufacturing costs	282.8
Marketing costs	104.1
General and administrative costs	81.1
Total costs	468.0
Profit before tax	72.8

*Assumptions:

Selling price, net of discounts—$8 per unit.
Total market potential—104,000 units.
Market penetration—65 percent.
Unit sales (65 percent of 104,000)–67,600 units.
Manufacturing costs—$80,000 plus $3 per unit.
Marketing costs—10 percent of sales (sales commissions)
  plus $50,000 for advertising and promotion.
General and administrative costs—15 percent of sales.

ager and incur some other administrative costs, which I agree probably won't add more than $40,000. But shouldn't we use the same percent as total corporate G&A?

Mr. J. L. Chase, the president, interrupts.

Chase: I agree that, on first blush, the project looks favorable. But why did you choose the $8 price and the level of $50,000 for advertising and promotion? Why not push the price down to $5? I'll guess there's a potential market of 200,000 units at that price. And perhaps we should spend more than $50,000 on advertising to ensure that we capture a good part of that potential.

Croxton: I worry, J. L., that if we cut the price, the margin will be too low to make any profit.

Manuel Olivera, the production manager, adds.

Olivera: Besides, we have limited production capacity. If we were to produce anything over 75,000 units, we would need to use overtime and do some subcontracting. This would push our variable costs up to $4 per unit for the units over 75,000. In addition, for volumes above 75,000 we would need some machinery, adding about $10,000 to the $80,000 that Jane has budgeted.

Croxton: If anything, I think we ought to consider a higher price, say $10 per unit. I realize that this would cut down on the market potential, but we would be making a healthy margin on those we sell.

Boxer: At a price of $10, I think our market potential would be only about 40,000 units.

Discussion continues for a few minutes, with no consensus about what price should be set.

Chase: Jane, I don't understand your points about market potential and how the $50,000 advertising will allow us to capture 65 percent of the market potential. Would you explain more?

Boxer: Well, J. L., you remember that research project that we have been conducting with our ad agency. This is our first chance to apply the results. Based upon interviews with a sample of customers, we have been able to assess the effectiveness of our past advertising. The result projected for this product is shown in Figure 2–8. We estimated our penetration of total market potential at three levels of advertising. Obviously, if we spend nothing at all on promotion and advertising, our customers won't even know about our product and hence can't buy it. This is the point shown at the origin in Figure 2–8. We then carefully considered how we would spend a budget of $50,000 (what ads we would use, what special deals, and so on), and estimated that we would reach about 65 percent of the market potential. That is, we would reach 65 percent of all those who would be inclined to buy. Similarly, we estimated about 88 percent

Figure 2–8   **Chase Manufacturing Market Penetration versus Advertising Expenditures**

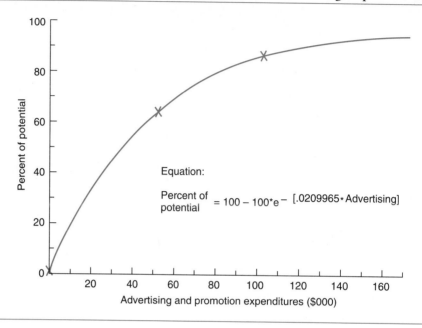

Equation:

$$\text{Percent of potential} = 100 - 100 \cdot e^{-[.0209965 \cdot \text{Advertising}]}$$

penetration of the total potential with an expenditure of $100,000. One of my assistants, who has a mathematical bent, fit the mathematical function shown to the three points. The curve makes sense to us.

Chase: But how did you settle on the $50,000 for advertising and promotion?

Boxer: Actually, it is tentative. We plan to do some more thinking about what expenditure would be optimal.

a. Build a model to aid the Chase executive committee in deciding about price and advertising for the new wine bottle opener.

As a help in this process, consider Figure 2–9. This chart shows three points relating price to total market potential. The point with a price of $8 and market potential of 104,000 units was given in the Boxer plan of Table 2–7. The point with a price of $5 and market potential of 200,000 units was suggested by Chase. The point with a price of $10 and market potential of 40,000 units was also given by Boxer.

Suppose it is reasonable to connect these points by a straight line as shown in Figure 2–9. Economists call this a demand function. The equation of a straight line is:

$$\text{Market potential} = m \cdot \text{Price} + b$$

Figure 2–9   **Chase Manufacturing Market Potential versus Price**

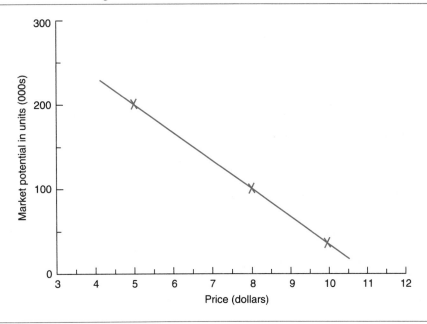

where m and b are constants to be determined. The constant m is called the slope of the line. See if you can determine the values of m and b by trial and error. If, after a while, you don't succeed, consult footnote 7.[7]

b. You should then define the other relationships in the Chase model.

c. Finally, use your model to calculate the profit for the following case:[8]

$$Price = \$7 \ per \ unit$$
$$Advertising = \$100,000$$

d. Implement your model using a spreadsheet program. Then, using trial and error, find the values for price and advertising that achieve the most profit.

e. Determine the values for profit if advertising is $70,000 and for prices from $7 to $9 (at $0.10 intervals). Plot this as a curve showing the relationship between price and profit. Repeat this for advertising of $90,000, and draw the curve on the same chart. Repeat again for advertising values of $100,000, $110,000, and $130,000. (All this can be done in a couple of steps with some spreadsheet programs.)

---

[7] The equation is: Market potential (thousand units) $= 360 - 32 \cdot Price$

[8] In case you do not have a calculator that computes powers of e, the value of $e^{-(.0209965)(100)} = .122$

Based on this curve, what can you say about the best price and advertising?

CASE 2–8[9]   The executive committee of the *Gotham City Times* newspaper is meeting to consider proposals from the promotion department and from the operations manager. You, as assistant to the publisher, have been asked to study the financial effects of these proposals.

Operations of the Times.   Most newspapers, including the *Times,* receive revenues from two sources: (1) circulation, that is, sales of newspapers to the reading public, and (2) sales of advertising space. Costs are related to (1) the distribution system (getting the newspaper to customers); (2) editorial and news coverage; (3) composition; that is, setting type, photoengraving layout, and artwork; (4) pressroom; that is, running the presses to produce the paper; and (5) newsprint (paper) and ink.

The circulation and advertising are interdependent for the *Times*. A larger circulation should lead to more advertising revenue, since the advertising would be reaching a larger audience, and advertisers would find this favorable. Similarly, readers buy a newspaper, in part, for the advertising.

The Revenues and Costs.   For purposes of planning, a month is considered as a unit, and average monthly values for circulation, advertising, and news are used. The current average daily circulation is 1 million (or 30 million total per month). The average revenue is $0.15 per paper per day.

Advertising is measured in column inches. Currently, the paper contains 225,000 column inches of advertising per month, and this generates revenue of $20 per column inch. Editorial features and news make up the rest of the newspaper and are running currently at 135,000 column inches per month. No change in the space devoted to this category is contemplated. A newspaper page at the *Times* contains 200 column inches.

The variable costs of composition are shown in Table 2–8. The variable costs for the pressroom are shown in Table 2–9. A sheet is one copy of the page of the newspaper. For example, if a given edition contains 50 pages for the 1 million

Table 2–8   **Cost of Composition**

Type of Copy	Variable Cost (per column inch)
Advertising copy	$4
News, editorial, and feature copy	$6

[9]Source: Reprinted with permission of Stanford University Graduate School of Business, © 1981 by the Board of Trustees of the Leland Stanford Junior University.

Table 2–9 **Pressroom Costs and Capacity**

	Variable Cost (per million sheets printed)	Capacity (in million sheets per month)
Regular time	$ 800	1,500
Overtime	$1,200	Unlimited

Table 2–10 **Fixed Costs**

Department	Fixed Cost ($000s per month)
Editorial, news, and features	$1,000
Composition	90
Pressroom	300
Distribution	700
	$2,090

circulation of the *Times,* this results in 50 million sheets for that day. Note that the regular-time capacity of the pressroom is 1,500 million sheets per month.

Variable distribution costs depend upon the circulation and size, and they average $40 per ton of newspaper delivered. The fixed costs for editorial, composition, pressroom, and distribution are shown in Table 2–10. The cost of newsprint is $120 per ton and is entirely variable. A ton of newsprint is sufficient for printing 90,000 sheets. Because of strikes in some pulp mills, no more than 20,000 tons of newsprint will be available to the *Times* through regular suppliers each month. Newsprint in excess of 20,000 tons can be obtained only at a cost of $160 per ton.

The Proposals. The promotion department is considering a series of alternatives to increase circulation (trial subscriptions at reduced price, for example). Two of these proposals are shown as alternatives B and C in Table 2–11, indicating both the increased circulation and the cost of obtaining this increase. The cost is incurred in the first month, and the increase in circulation generally lasts about three months.

Also shown in Table 2–11 are the advertising volumes at the current rate of $20 per column inch, and the volume if the rate were to be increased to $22. Thus, proposals for changes in this rate could be evaluated at different possible levels of circulation. Advertising also has seasonal swings, above or below the normal levels given in Table 2–11. In particular, next month should be at normal, the following month at 15 percent above normal, and the third month at 10 percent below normal.

Table 2–11   **Promotion Alternatives and Effects on Circulation at Different Advertising Rates**

Alternative	Circulation (average daily)	Cost of Obtaining Additional Circulation ($000s)	Advertising Volume (thousands of column inches) at $20 Rate	Advertising Volume (thousands of column inches) at $22 Rate
A	1,000,000*	0	225*	200
B (+10%)	1,100,000	400	235	225
C (+20%)	1,200,000	800	240	230

*Current levels.

In addition, the operations manager wants to contract out the printing of various sections of the Sunday paper, with the aim of reducing or eliminating overtime in the pressroom. (*Note:* Various sections of the Sunday paper are printed all during the week, so this outside printing would have an even effect on the pressroom schedule.) The operations manager has a quote from a local printer to do the printing *and* supply the newsprint for $2,600 per million sheets printed. The outside printer, however, insists on a three-month contract with the same amount of work each month.

a. Indicate the general objective(s) for the model and the specific performance measure(s) that you would use.

b. Indicate in general terms the decisions to be made, and then define the specific decision variables to be used.

c. Identify other important variables (exogenous and intermediate) needed in the model. Be specific, and define the variables that should be used and the units of measurement.

d. Indicate what policies limit or constrain the decisions.

e. Indicate the relationships that must be identified in building the model. Be specific; that is, show the equations.

Consider as the base case one with the following values for the decision variables:

$$\text{Initial circulation} = 1 \text{ million per day}$$
$$\text{Price of advertising} = \$20 \text{ per inch}$$
$$\text{Initial quantity of advertising} = 225{,}000 \text{ inches}$$
$$\text{Sheets printed outside} = 0$$

f. Examine the proposal to have sheets printed outside as suggested by the operations manager. Should this be done? If so, for about how many million sheets per month should the contract be made?

g. If initial circulation could be increased by 1 percent with everything else remaining the same, what would be the effect on total profit for the quarter? Does this seem strange? How would you explain it?

h. At what level of circulation would quarterly profit be at $1 million?

i. How much would the initial quantity of advertising have to drop before quarterly profit became negative?

j. Papers in some cities have recently raised the newsstand price of the paper. Suppose *Gotham City Times* were to raise its price (other things remaining the same). Would this have a major or minor effect on profitability?

k. There are six possible combinations described in Table 2–11—alternatives A, B, and C, each with an advertising rate of either $20 or $22. With each of these, there are variations depending on how many (if any) sheets are printed outside. Pick two or three plans that you think might be presented to senior management for further consideration.

l. Consider each of the five parameters in the accompanying table. Each is given a range over which it might vary. How sensitive is the total profit to these variations? To which is profit most sensitive? Draw a spider diagram.

Parameter	*Low*	*Base Case*	*High*
Newsstand price	.14	.15	.18
Pressroom capacity	1,400	1,500	1,700
Amount of editorial material	120	135	150
Initial quantity of advertising	200	225	240
Cost of purchasing newsprint (in excess of 20,000 tons)	120	160	180

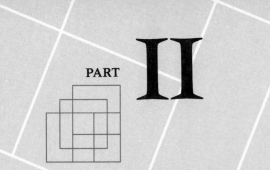

PART II

Decision Analysis

3

Basic Probability Concepts

If all business decisions could be made under conditions of certainty, the only valid justification for a poor decision would be failure to consider all the pertinent facts. With *certainty,* one can make a *perfect* forecast of the future. Unfortunately, however, the manager rarely if ever operates in a world of certainty. Usually, the manager is forced to make decisions when there is uncertainty as to what will happen after the decisions are made. In this latter situation, the mathematical theory of probability furnishes a tool that can be of great help to the decision maker.

In this chapter, we shall present some of the notation and basic relationships of probability theory the reader will apply in later chapters. Although the mathematics of probability is well defined, it will soon become obvious to the person attempting to apply the models of this book that there is a great deal of uncertainty concerning the informational inputs that are required. Also, many of the models abstract from the complexities of the real world.

Objective and Subjective Probabilities

Most of us are familiar with the laws of chance regarding coin flipping. If someone asks about the probability of a head on one toss of a coin, the answer will be one half, or 0.50. This answer is based upon common experience with coins and assumes that the coin is a *fair* coin and that it is "fairly" tossed. This is an example of **objective probability.** There are two interpretations of objective probability. The first relies on the **symmetry of outcomes** and implies that outcomes that are identical in essential aspects should have the same probability. A *fair* coin is defined to be one that is evenly balanced and has two sides that are identical (except for minor differences in the image). Hence, each side should have equal probability of one half (ignoring the possibility of the coin landing on its edge). If the coin were bent, weighted, or two-tailed, the answer would be different. As another example, suppose we have a box containing three red and seven black balls (that are the same size, have the same feel, and are otherwise identical except for color), and the balls are thoroughly mixed. The symmetry of outcome interpretation would assign a 0.10 probability to each ball, and hence a 0.30 chance of drawing a red ball.

The **relative frequency** interpretation of objective probability relies on historical experience in identical situations. Thus, if a coin has been flipped 10,000 times with 4,998 heads, we would conclude that the probability was 0.50 (i.e., 4,998/10,000 rounded) for a head the next time the coin was flipped in the same manner as before.

A **subjective interpretation** of probabilities is often useful for business decision making. In the case of objective probability, definitive historical information, common experience (objective evidence), or rigorous analysis lie behind the probability assignment. In the case of subjective interpretation, quantitative historical information may not be available; and instead of objective evidence, personal experience becomes the basis of the probability assignment. For business decision-making purposes, the subjective interpretation is frequently required, since reliable objective evidence may not be available.

In contrast to the coin flipping situation, assume a manager is trying to decide whether or not to buy a new factory, and the success of the factory depends largely on whether or not there is a recession in the next five years. A probability assigned to the occurrence of a recession would be a subjective weight. A long history and common experience that can be projected into the future with confidence are not directly available, as in the coin or ball examples. However, it may be appropriate, and indeed necessary, to consider the event "occurrence of a recession"; and after gathering evidence and using business judgment, the manager may be able to assign a probability to that event that could be used for decision-making purposes. There would certainly be less agreement on this probability than there would be on the probabilities of drawing a red ball, or a fair coin coming up heads. Since we are primarily concerned in this book with business decisions, we shall often assign subjective probabilities to events that have a critical bearing on the business decision. This device aims to assure consistency between a decision maker's judgment about the likelihood of the possible states of nature and the decision that is made.

One important objective of the suggested decision process is to allow the decision maker to think in terms of the possible events that may occur after a decision, the consequences of these events, and the probabilities of these events and consequences, rather than having the manager jump immediately to the question of whether or not the decision is desirable.

Basic Statements of Probability

Two fundamental statements about probabilities are:

1. Probabilities of all the various possible outcomes of a trial must sum to one.
2. Probabilities are always greater than or equal to zero (i.e., probabilities are never negative) and are less than or equal to one. The smaller the probability, the less likely the event.

The first statement indicates that if A and B are the only candidates for an office, the probability that A will win plus the probability that B will win must sum to one (assuming a tie is not possible).

The second statement results in the following interpretations. If an event has a positive probability, it may possibly occur; the event may be impossible, in which case it has a zero probability; or the event may be certain to occur, in which case the probability is equal to one. Regardless of whether probabilities are interpreted as objective probabilities or as subjective weights, it is useful to think in terms of a weighting scale running from zero to one. If someone tosses a coin of unknown characteristics 500 times to obtain an estimate of objective probabilities and the results are 225 heads and 275 tails, the range of possible results may be converted to a zero-to-one scale by dividing by 500. The actual results are $225/500 = 0.45$ heads and $275/500 = 0.55$ tails. Hence, if we wish to derive probabilities, we shall manipulate the data so as to adhere to the zero-to-one scale. The 0.45 and the 0.55 may be used as estimators of the true probabilities of heads and tails (the true probabilities are unknown).

Mutually Exclusive Events

Two or more events are **mutually exclusive** if only one of the events can occur on any one trial. The probabilities of mutually exclusive events can be added to obtain the probability that one of a given collection of the events will occur.

Example The probabilities shown in Table 3–1 reflect the subjective estimate of a newspaper editor regarding the relative chances of four candidates for a public office (assume a tie is not possible).

Table 3–1

Event: Elect	Probability
Democratic candidate A	0.18
Democratic candidate B	0.42
Republican candidate C	0.26
Republican candidate D	0.14
	1.00

These events are mutually exclusive, since in one election (or in one trial) only one event may occur; therefore the probabilities are additive. The probability of a Democratic victory is 0.60; of a Republican victory, 0.40; or of either B or C winning, 0.68. The probability of both B and C winning is zero, since only one of the mutually exclusive events can occur on any one trial.

Independent Events

Events may be either independent or dependent. If two events are (statistically) **independent,** the occurrence of one event will not affect the probability of the occurrence of the second event.[1]

When two (or more) events are independent, the probability of both events (or more than two events) occurring is equal to the product of the probabilities of the individual events. That is:

$$P(A \text{ and } B) = P(A) \cdot P(B) \quad \text{if } A,B \text{ independent} \tag{3-1}$$

where:

$$P(A \text{ and } B) = \text{Probability of events } A \text{ and } B \text{ both occurring}$$
$$P(A) = \text{Probability of event } A$$
$$P(B) = \text{Probability of event } B$$

Equation 3–1 indicates that the probability of A and B both occurring is equal to the probability of A times the probability of B, if A and B are independent. If A is the probability of a head on the first toss of the coin, and B is the probability of a head on the second toss of the coin, then:

$$P(A) = \tfrac{1}{2}$$
$$P(B) = \tfrac{1}{2}$$
$$P(A \text{ and } B) = \tfrac{1}{2} \cdot \tfrac{1}{2} = \tfrac{1}{4}$$

The probability of A and then B occurring (two heads) is one fourth. $P(A$ and $B)$ is the **joint probability** of events A and B. Where appropriate, the word *and* can be omitted to simplify the notation, and the joint probability can be written simply as $P(AB)$.

To define independence mathematically, we need the symbol $P(B|A)$. The symbol $P(B|A)$ is read "the probability of event B, given that event A has occurred." $P(B|A)$ is the **conditional probability** of event B, given that event A has taken place. Note that $P(B|A)$ does not mean the probability of event B divided by A—the vertical line followed by A means "given that event A has occurred."

---

[1]Statistical independence or dependence is to be distinguished from causal independence or dependence. Simply because two events are statistically dependent upon each other does not imply that one is caused by the other. Whenever we use the terms *dependence* or *independence*, we mean statistical dependence or independence.

With independent events:

$$P(B|A) = P(B) \quad \text{if } A,B \text{ independent}} \tag{3-2}$$

That is, the probability of event B, given that event A has occurred, is equal to the probability of event B if the two events are independent. With two independent events, the occurrence of the one event does not affect the probability of the occurrence of the second [in like manner, $P(A|B) = P(A)$]. Equations 3–1 and 3–2 are the basic definitions of independence between two events.

Dependent Events

Two events are **dependent** if the occurrence of one of the events affects the probability of the occurrence of the second event.

Example: Dependent Events Flip a fair coin and determine whether the result is heads or tails. If heads, flip the same coin again. If tails, flip an unfair coin that has a three-fourths probability of heads and a one-fourth probability of tails. Is the probability of heads on the second toss in any way affected by the result of the first toss? The answer here is yes, since the result of the first toss affects which coin (fair or unfair) is to be tossed the second time.

Another example of dependent events involves mutually exclusive events. If events A and B are mutually exclusive, they are dependent. Given that event A has occurred, the conditional probability of B occurring must be zero, since the two events are mutually exclusive. That is, $P(B|A) = 0$ if events A and B are mutually exclusive.

SUMMARY

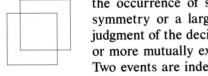

A probability is a number between zero and one representing the likelihood of the occurrence of some event. Probabilities may be objective, if based upon symmetry or a large amount of experience, or subjective, if based upon the judgment of the decision maker. The probability of the occurrence of one of two or more mutually exclusive events is the sum of the probabilities of the events. Two events are independent if the occurrence of one does not affect the probability of occurrence of the other.

Conditional, Marginal, and Joint Probabilities

We now introduce a very important probability relationship:

$$P(B|A) = \frac{P(A \text{ and } B)}{P(A)} \quad \text{if } P(A) \neq 0 \tag{3-3}$$

The conditional probability of event B, given that event A has occurred, is equal to the joint probability of A and B, divided by the probability of event A.

We can multiply both sides of the equation by $P(A)$ and rewrite Equation 3–3 as:

$$P(A \text{ and } B) = P(B|A) \cdot P(A) \tag{3–4}$$

That is, the joint probability of A and B is equal to the conditional probability of B given A times the probability of A.

Let us look at these formulas assuming independent events. By Equation 3–3:

$$P(B|A) = \frac{P(A \text{ and } B)}{P(A)}$$

But by Equation 3–1:

$$P(A \text{ and } B) = P(A) \cdot P(B)$$

for independent events. Substituting $P(A) \cdot P(B)$ for $P(A \text{ and } B)$ in Equation 3–3 gives:

$$P(B|A) = \frac{P(A) \cdot P(B)}{P(A)} = P(B) \tag{3–2}$$

This is the mathematical definition of independence given earlier in Equation 3–2.

We shall next make use of two examples to illustrate:

1. Unconditional (marginal) probabilities. The term **marginal** refers to the fact that the probabilities are found in the margins of a joint probability table (see Table 3–3, a little later in this chapter); they sum to one. A marginal probability refers to the probability of the occurrence of an event not conditional on the occurrence of another event. $P(A)$ and $P(B)$ are examples of unconditional or marginal probabilities.
2. Conditional probabilities, such as $P(A|B)$ and $P(B|A)$.
3. Joint probabilities, such as $P(A \text{ and } B)$ or $P(AB)$.

Example 1   Assume we have three boxes, which contain red and black balls as follows:

Box 1:   3 red and 7 black
Box 2:   6 red and 4 black
Box 3:   8 red and 2 black

Suppose we draw a ball from box 1; if it is red, we draw a ball from box 2. If the ball drawn from box 1 is black, we draw a ball from box 3. The diagram in Figure 3–1 illustrates the game. Consider the following probability questions about this game:

1. What is the probability of drawing a red ball from box 1? This probability is an *unconditional* or *marginal* probability; it is 0.30. (The marginal probability of getting a black is 0.70.)

Figure 3–1

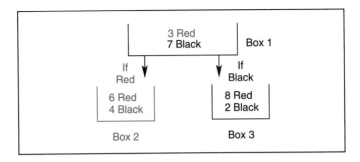

Table 3–2

Event	Marginal $P(A)$	·	Conditional $P(B\|A)$	=	Joint $P(A$ and $B)$
RR	$P(R) = 0.30$		$P(R\|R) = 0.60$		$P(RR) = 0.18$
RB	$P(R) = 0.30$		$P(B\|R) = 0.40$		$P(RB) = 0.12$
BR	$P(B) = 0.70$		$P(R\|B) = 0.80$		$P(BR) = 0.56$
BB	$P(B) = 0.70$		$P(B\|B) = 0.20$		$P(BB) = 0.14$

2. Suppose we draw a ball from box 1, and it is red; what is the probability of another red ball when we draw from box 2 on the second draw? The answer is 0.60. This is an example of a *conditional probability*. That is, the probability of a red ball on the second draw if the draw from box 1 is red is a conditional probability.

3. Suppose our first draw from box 1 was black; what is the *conditional* probability of our second draw (from box 3 this time) being red? The probability is 0.80. The draw from box 1 (the conditioning event) is very important in determining the probabilities of red (or black) on the second draw.

4. Suppose, before we draw any balls, we ask the question: What is the probability of drawing two red balls? This would be a *joint* probability; the event would be a red ball on both draws. The computation of this joint probability is a little more complicated than the above questions and some analysis will be of value. Computations are as follows:

$$P(A \text{ and } B) = P(B|A) \cdot P(A) \qquad\qquad (3\text{–}4)$$

Table 3–2 and Figure 3–2 show the joint probability of two red balls as 0.18 [i.e., $P(R$ and $R)$ or more simply $P(RR)$, the top branch of the tree]. The joint probabilities may be summarized as follows:

Two red balls	$P(RR)$ =	0.18
A red ball on first draw and a black ball on second draw	$P(RB)$ =	0.12
A black ball on first draw and a red ball on second draw	$P(BR)$ =	0.56
Two black balls	$P(BB)$ =	0.14
		1.00

Figure 3–2 is called a **tree diagram.** This is a very useful device for illustrating uncertain situations. The first fork shows that either a red or a black may be drawn, and the probabilities of these events are given. If a red is drawn, we go to box 2, where again a red or black may be drawn, but with probabilities determined by the fact that the draw will take place in box 2. For the second forks, we have conditional probabilities (the probabilities depend on whether a red or

Figure 3–2   Tree Diagram

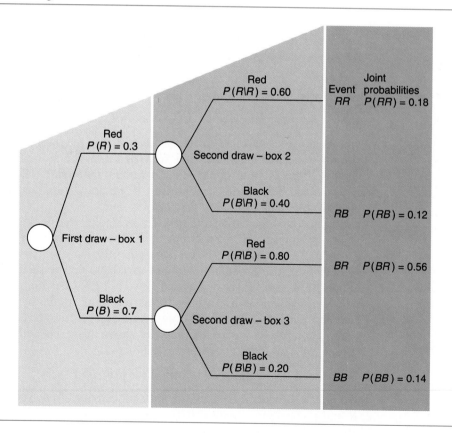

Table 3–3 **Joint Probability Table**

First Draw \ Second Draw		R	B	Marginal Probability of Outcome on First Draw
R		$P(RR)$ 0.18	$P(RB)$ 0.12	0.30
B		$P(BR)$ 0.56	$P(BB)$ 0.14	0.70
Marginal Probability of Outcome on Second Draw		0.74	0.26	1.00

a black ball was chosen on the first draw). At the end of each path are the joint probabilities of following that path. The joint probabilities are obtained by multiplying the marginal (unconditional) probabilities of the first branch by the conditional probabilities of the second branch.

Table 3–3 presents these results in a joint probability table; the intersections of the rows and columns are *joint* probabilities. The column on the right gives the unconditional probabilities (*marginals*) of the outcome of the first draw; the bottom row gives the *unconditional* or *marginal* probabilities of the outcomes of the second draw. Table 3–3 effectively summarizes the tree diagram.

Now, let us compute some additional probabilities:

1. Probability of one red and one black ball, regardless of order: $= 0.56 + 0.12 = 0.68$
2. Probability of a black ball on draw 2: $= 0.26$
   Explanatory calculation:
   Probability of red-black $= 0.12$
   Probability of black-black $= 0.14$
   Probability of black on draw 2 $= 0.26$
3. Probability of second draw being red *if* first draw is red: $= 0.60$
   If first draw is red, we are in the R row of Table 3–3, which totals 0.30. The question is, what proportion is 0.18 of 0.30? The answer is 0.60; or in terms of the appropriate formula:

$$P(R_2|R_1) = \frac{P(R_2 \text{ and } R_1)}{P(R_1)} = \frac{0.18}{0.30} = 0.60$$

Table 3–4

Event	Probability	Formula
HH	$P(HH) = \frac{1}{2} \cdot \frac{1}{2} = \frac{1}{4}$	$P(H) \cdot P(H)$
HT	$P(HT) = \frac{1}{2} \cdot \frac{1}{2} = \frac{1}{4}$	$P(H) \cdot P(T)$
TH	$P(TH) = \frac{1}{2} \cdot \frac{1}{2} = \frac{1}{4}$	$P(T) \cdot P(H)$
TT	$P(TT) = \frac{1}{2} \cdot \frac{1}{2} = \frac{1}{4}$	$P(T) \cdot P(T)$

Example 2   Suppose a fair coin is flipped twice and we ask for the following probabilities:

1. Probability of two heads.
2. Probability of one head and one tail in two flips.
3. Probability of the second toss being a head.
4. Probability of the second toss being a head, given that the first toss is a tail.

Table 3–4 gives all possible outcomes from two tosses and their probabilities. Now, using the table, we can determine the four requested probabilities:

1. $P(HH) = \frac{1}{4}$
2. $P(HT + TH) = \frac{1}{2}$
3. $P(HH + TH) = \frac{1}{2}$
4. $P(H|T) = \dfrac{P(TH)}{P(T)} = \dfrac{\frac{1}{4}}{\frac{1}{2}} = \frac{1}{2}$

One important feature of the above example is that it illustrates *independence*. Note that the last two probabilities computed are the same; the probability of a head on the second toss is one half, regardless of the outcome of the first toss. The two events are said to be *independent,* since the probability of heads on the second toss is not affected by the outcome of the first toss. That was not the case in Example 1, where the probability of a red ball on the second draw was affected by the outcome of the first draw. To summarize this result:

Dependence (Example 1)

$$\text{Conditional probability of red on second draw, given red on first draw} = \frac{\text{Joint probability of } RR \ (0.18)}{\text{Marginal probability of red on first draw } (0.30)} = 0.60$$

General formula:

$$P(B|A) = \frac{P(A \text{ and } B)}{P(A)} \qquad\qquad (3\text{–}3)$$

Independence (Example 2)

$$\frac{\text{Conditional probability of a head on second toss, given a tail on first toss}}{} = \frac{\text{Joint probability of } TH(^1/_4)}{\text{Marginal probability of tail on first toss } (^1/_2)} = \frac{0.50, \text{ marginal probability of tossing a head}}{}$$

General formula:

$$P(B|A) = P(B) \tag{3-2}$$

if B is independent of A.

Example 3 We give one further illustration of the basic probability definitions. A survey is taken of 100 families; information is obtained about family income and about whether the family purchases a specialty food product. The results are shown in Table 3–5.

Suppose a family is to be selected at random from this group.

1. What is the probability that the family selected will be a buyer? Since 38 of the 100 families overall are buyers, the probability is 0.38. Note that this is a *marginal* or *unconditional* probability.
2. What is the probability that the selected family is both a buyer and with high income? Note that this is a *joint* probability. P(Buyer and High income) = 20/100 = 0.20.
3. Suppose that a family is selected at random and you are informed that it has high income. What is the probability that this family is a buyer? Note that this asks for the *conditional* probability P(Buyer|High income). Of the 40 families with High income, 20 are Buyers. Hence, the probability is 20/40 = 0.50.
4. Are the events Buyer and High income independent for this group of families? Note from question 1 that P(Buyer) = 0.38; from question 3, P(Buyer|High income) = 0.50. These are not the same. Hence, the two events are *dependent*. Knowing that the family has high income affects the

Table 3–5   **Survey of 100 Families, Classified by Income and Buying Behavior**

	Low Income (family income below $30,000)	*High Income (family income of $30,000 or more)*	*Total Number of Families*
Family is:			
Buyer of specialty food products	18	20	38
Nonbuyer	42	20	62
Total number of families	60	40	100

probability that it is a buyer. Another way of expressing this dependence is to say that the percentage of buyers is not the same for the high- and low-income families.

Revision of Probabilities

Having discussed joint and conditional probabilities, let us investigate how probabilities are revised to take account of new information.

Suppose we do not know whether a particular coin is fair or unfair. If the coin is fair, the probability of a tail is 0.50; but if the coin is unfair, the probability of a tail is 0.10. Assume we assign a prior probability to the coin being fair of 0.80 and a probability of 0.20 to the coin being unfair. The event "fair coin" will be designated A_1, and the event "unfair coin" will be designated A_2. We toss the coin once; say a tail is the result. What is the probability that the coin is fair?

Figure 3–3 shows that the conditional probability of a tail, given that the coin is fair, is 0.50; that is, $P(\text{tail}|A_1) = 0.50$. If the coin is unfair, the probability of a tail is 0.10; $P(\text{tail}|A_2) = 0.10$.

Let us compute the joint probability $P(\text{tail and } A_1)$. There is an initial 0.80 probability that A_1 is the true state; and if A_1 is the true state, there is a 0.50 conditional probability that a tail will result. The joint probability of state A_1 being true and obtaining a tail is $(0.80 \cdot 0.50) = 0.40$. Thus:

$$P(\text{tail and } A_1) = P(A_1) \cdot P(\text{tail}|A_1) = 0.80 \cdot 0.50 = 0.40$$

Figure 3–3

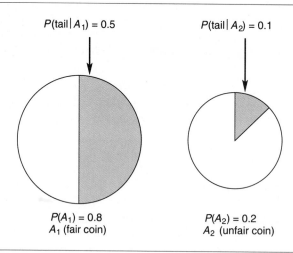

$P(\text{tail}|A_1) = 0.5$ $P(\text{tail}|A_2) = 0.1$

$P(A_1) = 0.8$
A_1 (fair coin)

$P(A_2) = 0.2$
A_2 (unfair coin)

The joint probability of a tail *and* A_2 is equal to:

$$P(\text{tail and } A_2) = P(A_2) \cdot P(\text{tail}|A_2) = 0.20 \cdot 0.10 = 0.02$$

A tail can occur in combination with the state "fair coin" or in combination with the state "unfair coin." The probability of the former combination is 0.40; of the latter, 0.02. The sum of the probabilities gives the unconditional probability of a tail on the first toss; that is, $P(\text{tail}) = 0.40 + 0.02 = 0.42$:

$$P(\text{tail and } A_2) = 0.02$$
$$P(\text{tail and } A_1) = \underline{0.40}$$
$$P(\text{tail}) = 0.42$$

If a tail occurs, and if we do not know the true state, the conditional probability of state A_1 being the true state is, using Equation 3–3:

$$P(A_1|\text{tail}) = \frac{P(\text{tail and } A_1)}{P(\text{tail})} = \frac{0.40}{0.42} = 0.95$$

Thus, 0.95 is the **revised** or **posterior probability** of A_1, given that a tail has occurred on the first toss.

Similarly:

$$P(A_2|\text{tail}) = \frac{P(\text{tail and } A_2)}{P(\text{tail})} = \frac{0.02}{0.42} = 0.05$$

In more general symbols:

$$P(A_i|B) = \frac{P(A_i \text{ and } B)}{P(B)}$$

Conditional probability expressed in this form is known as **Bayes theorem.** It has many important applications in evaluating the worth of additional information (see Chapter 4).

In this example, the *revised probabilities* for the coin are 0.95 that it is fair and 0.05 that it is unfair (the probabilities were initially 0.80 and 0.20). These revised probabilities exist after one toss when the toss results in a tail. It is reasonable that the probability that the coin is unfair has decreased, since a tail appeared on the first toss, and the unfair coin has only a 0.10 probability of a tail.

SUMMARY A joint probability is the probability of the occurrence of two or more events. A conditional probability is the probability of occurrence of some event, given that some other event is known to have occurred. A marginal probability is the unconditional probability of the occurrence of some event.

A prior probability of the occurrence of an event may be revised using Bayes theorem to produce a revised or posterior probability.

Random Variables

A **probability function** is a rule that assigns probabilities to each element of a set of events that may occur. If, in turn, we can assign a specific numerical value to each element of the set of events, a function that assigns these numerical values is termed a **random variable.** The **value** of a random variable is the general outcome of a random (or probability) experiment. It is useful to distinguish between the random variable itself and the values that it can take on. The value of a random variable is unknown until the event occurs (i.e., until the random experiment has been performed). However, the probability that the random variable will be any specific value is known in advance. The probability of each value of the random variable is equal to the sum of the probabilities of the events assigned that value of the random variable. Some examples of random variables are shown in Table 3–6.

For example, suppose we define the random variable Z to be the number of heads in two tosses of a fair coin. Then the possible values of Z, and the corresponding probabilities, are:

Possible Values of Z	Probability of Each Value
0	$^1/_4$
1	$^1/_2$
2	$^1/_4$

Random variables can be grouped into **probability distributions.** The table above is an example of a **discrete** probability distribution, in which the random variable Z can take on only specific values (0, 1, or 2 in this particular example). Note that the sum of the probabilities in a probability distribution must equal one.

Table 3–6

Random Variable (denoted by a capital letter)	Description of the Values of the Random Variable	Values of the Random Variable
U	Possible outcomes from throwing a pair of dice	2, 3, . . . , 12
X	Possible number of heads, tossing a coin five times	0, 1, 2, 3, 4, 5
Y	Possible daily sales of a newspaper, where S represents the inventory	0, 1, 2, . . . , S

The Expected Value of a Random Variable

The **expected value** or **expectation** of a random variable is the sum of the values of the random variable weighted by the probability that the random variable will take on that value. The expected value is thus the mean or weighted average value. Consider the example of Table 3–7.

In this case, 28.10 is the *expected* or *mean* demand. This is written as:

$$E(X) = 28.10$$

The expected value is calculated, as in Table 3–7, by weighting each value of the random variable by its probability, and summing. The mathematical definition of the mean, in symbols, is:

$$E(X) = \sum_{i=1}^{n} X_i P(X_i) \tag{3-5}$$

X_i is the ith value of the random variable; $P(X_i)$ is the probability of the ith value; and $\sum_{i=1}^{n}$ is the symbol meaning summation of all items for $i = 1$ to $i = n$, inclusive. The symbol Σ is read as "sigma." In our example, $n = 6$, since there are six possible values of the random variable. Hence:

$$E(X) = \sum_{i=1}^{6} X_i P(X_i) = X_1 P(X_1) + X_2 P(X_2) + \cdots + X_6 P(X_6)$$

Substituting the specific values:

$$E(X) = \sum_{i=1}^{6} X_i P(X_i) = 25(0.05) + 26(0.10) + 27(0.15) + 28(0.30)$$
$$+ 29(0.20) + 30(0.20)$$
$$= 28.10$$

Table 3–7   **Computation of the Expected Value**

Values of the Random Variable, X (tomorrow's demand)	Probability of X_i $P(X_i)$	Probability Weighted Demand, $X_i P(X_i)$
$X_1 = 25$ units	$P(X_1) = 0.05$	1.25
$X_2 = 26$ units	$P(X_2) = 0.10$	2.60
$X_3 = 27$ units	$P(X_3) = 0.15$	4.05
$X_4 = 28$ units	$P(X_4) = 0.30$	8.40
$X_5 = 29$ units	$P(X_5) = 0.20$	5.80
$X_6 = 30$ units	$P(X_6) = 0.20$	6.00
	1.00	$E(X) = 28.10$

Sums of Random Variables

The expectation of a sum of random variables is the sum of the expectations of those random variables. Thus, the mean of the random variable $(X + Y + Z)$ is:

$$E(X + Y + Z) = E(X) + E(Y) + E(Z) \qquad \textbf{(3–6)}$$

A Constant Times a Random Variable

The expectation of a constant times a random variable is the constant times the expectation of the random variable:

$$E(cX) = cE(X) \qquad \textbf{(3–7)}$$

The Variance and Standard Deviation of a Random Variable

Frequently we want to know how the values of the random variable are dispersed about the mean. The variance and the standard deviation provide measures of this dispersion.

The **variance** is defined as the sum of *squared* deviations of the values of the random variable from its mean, weighted by the probability of the deviation. The mathematical statement is as follows:

$$\mathrm{Var}(X) = \sum_{i=1}^{n} [X_i - E(X)]^2 P(X_i) \qquad \textbf{(3–8)}$$

$E(X)$ is the mean; X_i, the ith value of the random variable; and $P(X_i)$, its probability. Note that the larger the dispersion of all X_is for $i = 1$ to $i = n$, inclusive, the larger the values of $[X_i - E(X)]^2$ and the larger the variance.

The variance of a constant times a random variable is the constant squared times the variance of the random variable. That is:

$$\mathrm{Var}\,(cX) = c^2 \mathrm{Var}\,(X) \qquad \textbf{(3–9)}$$

The variance of a sum of *independent* random variables equals the sum of the variances. Thus:

$$\mathrm{Var}\,(X + Y + Z) = \mathrm{Var}\,(X) + \mathrm{Var}\,(Y) \qquad \textbf{(3–10)}$$
$$+ \mathrm{Var}\,(Z) \quad \text{if } X, Y, Z \text{ independent}$$

In Table 3–8, we calculate the variance of the random variable, demand, of our earlier example using Equation 3–8.

If the value of the random variable X is a constant, the mean is the constant value. Therefore, $[X_i - E(X)]$ would be zero for all X_i, and the variance would be zero, indicating there is no dispersion around the mean.

The **standard deviation** is the square root of the variance, and in our example, the standard deviation is $\sqrt{1.99}$, or about 1.41. The standard deviation is usually designated by σ (a small sigma), and the variance is frequently written as σ^2.

Table 3–8   Computation of the Variance

Value of the Random Variable, X_i	Probability, $P(X_i)$	Squared Deviation from the Mean of 28.1 $[X_i - E(X)]^2$	Squared Deviation Weighted by the Probability $[X_i - E(X)]^2 P(X_i)$
$X_1 = 25$	0.05	$(25 - 28.1)^2 = 9.61$	0.4805
$X_2 = 26$	0.10	$(26 - 28.1)^2 = 4.41$	0.4410
$X_3 = 27$	0.15	$(27 - 28.1)^2 = 1.21$	0.1815
$X_4 = 28$	0.30	$(28 - 28.1)^2 = 0.01$	0.0030
$X_5 = 29$	0.20	$(29 - 28.1)^2 = 0.81$	0.1620
$X_6 = 30$	0.20	$(30 - 28.1)^2 = 3.61$	0.7220
	1.00		1.9900

$$\text{Var}(X) = \left[\sum_{i=1}^{6} (X_i - 28.1)^2 P(X)_i \right] = 1.9900$$

Example This example shows how we obtain information about a random variable using the probability rules developed earlier. Suppose you have a product you are trying to sell to two customers. For Big Stores, you assess that there is a 20 percent chance that you will sell 200 cases, a 40 percent chance of a 100-case sale, and a 40 percent chance of no sale. For Little Markets, you think the chances are 40 percent for a 100-case order and 60 percent for no order. Further, you think that the sales to the two markets are dependent. If Big Stores were to buy 200 cases, the chances would be 50 percent that Little would make the 100-case order (and, of course, 50 percent chance for no order). And if Big Stores were to buy zero cases, the chances would be 50–50 that Little would also not order.

Suppose you are interested in the random variable X, the total sales to both customers. Let us develop the probability distribution for this random variable. We begin by constructing Figure 3–4, the joint probability table, and include the information we have.

Note that the overall probabilities of sales of 200, 100, and 0 cases to Big Stores are shown along the bottom margin of Figure 3–4. Similarly, the marginal probabilities of sales to Little Markets are shown in the right-hand column. We also know that $P(\text{Little sales} = 100 | \text{Big sales} = 200) = 0.5$. This conditional probability is shown in the upper corner of the upper left box. We also know $P(\text{Little sales} = 0 | \text{Big sales} = 0) = 0.5$, and this is similarly shown in the upper corner of the lower right box in Figure 3–4.

Using:

$$P(AB) = P(A|B)P(B)$$

we can calculate the joint probability:

$$P(\text{Little} = 100 \text{ and } \text{Big} = 200) = P(\text{Little} = 100|\text{Big} = 200) \cdot P(\text{Big} = 200)$$
$$= (0.5)(0.2) = 0.1$$

Similarly,

$$P(\text{Little} = 0 \text{ and } \text{Big} = 0) = P(\text{Little} = 0|\text{Big} = 0) \cdot P(\text{Big} = 0)$$
$$= (0.5)(0.4) = 0.2$$

These joint probabilities are shown in the appropriate boxes in Figure 3–4.

It is now possible to fill in the rest of Figure 3–4, using the fact that the totals of the joint probabilities in any row or column must equal the marginal probabilities. The completed table is shown as Figure 3–5.

The lower right-hand corners of the boxes in Figure 3–5 contain the values for the random variable X, the total sales, equal to the sum of the sales to Big Stores and Little Markets. The probability distribution for X is shown in columns 1 and 2 of Table 3–9.

Figure 3–4

Sales to Little Markets (cases)	Sales to Big Stores (cases)			Marginal Probability
	200	100	0	
100	0.5 / 0.1			0.4
0			0.5 / 0.2	0.6
Marginal Probability	0.2	0.4	0.4	1.0

Figure 3–5

Sales to Little Markets (cases)	Sales to Big Stores (cases)			Marginal Probability
	200	100	0	
100	0.1 / 300	0.1 / 200	0.2 / 100	0.4
0	0.1 / 200	0.3 / 100	0.2 / 0	0.6
Marginal Probability	0.2	0.4	0.4	1.0

Table 3–9   Probability Distribution for Total Sales

(1) Sales in cases X_i	(2) Probability $P(X_i)$	(3) $X_i \cdot P(X_i)$	(4) Squared Deviation from the Mean of 120 $[X_i - E(X)]^2$	(5) Squared Deviation Weighted by the Probability $[X_i - E(X)]^2 P(X_i)$
0	0.2	0	$(0 - 120)^2 = 14{,}400$	2,880
100	0.5	50	$(100 - 120)^2 = 400$	200
200	0.2	40	$(200 - 120)^2 = 6{,}400$	1,280
300	0.1	30	$(300 - 120)^2 = 32{,}400$	3,240
	1.0	$E(X) = 120$		$\text{Var}(X) = 7{,}600$

The calculation of the expected value of this distribution is shown in column 3 of Table 3–9. That is, $E(X) = 120$ cases. The expected value for total sales might also have been determined by using Equation 3–6 for sums of random variables. If random variable B is sales to Big Stores, and L is sales to Little Markets, then $E(B) = (0.2)(200) + (0.4)(100) + (0.4)(0) = 80$; and $E(L) = (0.4)(100) + (0.6)(0) = 40$. Note that $X = B + L$. And using Equation 3–6:

$$E(X) = E(B) + E(L) = 80 + 40 = 120$$

If all we were interested in was expected total sales, this could be obtained easily from the expected sales to each customer. To obtain the entire probability distribution, however, the development of Figures 3–4 and 3–5 was necessary.

The variance of total sales is also calculated in Table 3–9; see columns (4) and (5).

SUMMARY

A random variable attaches a numerical value to various outcomes of a random process. Probabilities for random variables can be displayed in a probability distribution. The expected value is the weighted average of the values of a random variable, the weights being the probabilities of occurrence. The variance and standard deviation are measures of dispersion of a random variable.

The expected value of a sum of random variables is the sum of the expected values. The variance of a sum of independent random variables is the sum of the variances.

The Bernoulli Process and the Binomial Distribution

A **Bernoulli process** may be described as follows:

1. The outcomes or results of each trial in the process are characterized as one of *two types* of possible outcomes, such as:
   a. Success, failure.

b. Yes, no.

c. Heads, tails.

d. Zero, one.

2. The probability of the outcome of any trial is "stable" and does not change throughout the process. For example, the probability of heads, given a fair coin, is 0.50 and does not change, regardless of the number of times the coin is tossed.

3. The outcome of any trial is *independent* of the outcome of any previous trial. In other words, the past history of the process would not change the probability assigned to the next trial. In our coin example, we would assign a probability of 0.50 to the next toss coming up heads, even if we had recorded heads on the last 10 trials (we assume the coin is fair).

4. The number of trials is discrete and can be represented by an integer such as 1, 2, 3, and so on.

Given a process, we may know that it is Bernoulli, but we may or may not know the stable probability characteristic of the process. With a fair coin, we may know the process is Bernoulli, with probability 0.50 of a success (say heads) and probability 0.50 of a failure (tails). However, if we are given a coin and told it is not fair, the process (flipping the coin) may still be Bernoulli, but we do not know the probability characteristic. Hence, we may have a Bernoulli process with a known or unknown probability characteristic.

Many business processes can be characterized as Bernoulli for analytical purposes, even though they are not true Bernoulli in every respect. If the "fit" is close enough, we may assume that the Bernoulli process is a reasonable characterization. Let us discuss some examples.

Example 1 Suppose we are concerned with a production process where a certain part (or product) is produced on a machine. We may be interested in classifying the parts as "good" or "defective," in which case the process may be Bernoulli. If the machine is not subject to fast wear, that is, if a setting will last for a long run of parts, the probability of good parts may be sufficiently stable for the process to qualify as Bernoulli. If, on the other hand, more defectives occur as the end of the run approaches, the process is not Bernoulli. In many such processes, the occurrence of good and defective parts is sufficiently stable (no pattern over time is observable) to call the process Bernoulli. The probability of good and defective parts may remain stable through a production run, but it may vary from run to run (because of machine setting, for example). Here, the process could still be considered Bernoulli, but the probability of a success (or failure) will change from run to run.

Example 2 A different example of a Bernoulli process is a survey to determine whether or not consumers prefer liquid to powdered soaps. The outcome of a survey interview could be characterized as "yes" (success) or "no" (failure) answers to the question. If the sample of consumers was sufficiently randomized (no pattern to the way in which the yes or no answers occur), Bernoulli (with an unknown probability) may be a useful description of the process.

Note that if the probability of a success in a Bernoulli process is 0.50, the probability of a failure is also 0.50 (since the probabilities of the event happening and the event not happening add to one). If the probability of a success is p, the probability of a failure is $(1 - p)$.

The Binomial Probability Distribution

In order to answer probability questions about a Bernoulli process, we need to know what the probability parameter of the process is, such as the 0.50 in the fair coin example. In addition, we need to know the number of trials we are going to use. Hence, to analyze a Bernoulli process, we need to know (1) the process probability characteristic, p, and (2) the number of trials, n.

The symbols and relationships given in Table 3–10 are useful.

Table 3–10

Relationship or Symbol	Interpretation
$P(R = r\|p, n)$	The probability that the unknown number of successes, R (the random variable), is *equal to* some specific number, r (say 10), given a specific number of trials, n (say 20) and some specific probability, p, of a success on each trial.
$P(R \geq r\|p, n)$	The probability that the number of successes is *greater than or equal to* a specific number, r, given values for p and n. This is called a *cumulative* probability. Table C (in the appendix at the end of the text) contains values of cumulative probabilities.
$P(R > r\|p, n)$	The probability that the number of successes is *greater than* a specific number. This inequality is exclusive; i.e., $$P(R > 10)$$ excludes 10, and includes 11 and up.
$P(R \leq r\|p, n)$	The probability that the number of successes is *less than or equal to* a specific number (say 10).
$P(R < r\|p, n)$	The probability that the number of successes is *less than* a specific number.
$P(R = 10) = P(R \geq 10) - P(R \geq 11)$	The probability of exactly 10 successes can be read from Appendix Table C by subtracting two cumulative probabilities. If $$P(R \geq 11)$$ is subtracted from $P(R \geq 10)$, the result is the probability of *exactly* 10.
$P(R < 10) = 1 - P(R \geq 10)$	Since the probabilities add to 1, if the probability of 10 or more successes is subtracted from 1, the result is the probability of less than 10 successes.

Table 3–10 (*concluded*)

Relationship or Symbol	Interpretation
$P(R \leq 10) = 1 - P(R \geq 11)$	Since *less than or equal to* 10 includes 10, subtract the probability of 11 or more successes from 1.
$P(R > 10) = P(R \geq 11)$	To read a strict inequality from Appendix Table C, add 1 to the number desired. The $$P(R > 10)$$ excludes 10, so this probability is the same as $P(R \geq 11)$, which includes 11 but excludes 10.

The Binomial Probability Function

If the assumptions of the Bernoulli process are satisfied and if the probability of a success on one trial is p, then the probability distribution of the number of successes, R, in n trials, is a **binomial distribution.** The binomial probability distribution function is:

$$P(R|n, p) = \frac{n!}{R!(n - R)!} p^R (1 - p)^{n-R} \qquad (3\text{–}11)$$

where $n!$ (called *n*-factorial) equals $n(n - 1)(n - 2) \ldots (2)(1)$ and $0!$ is defined to be equal to 1.

Performing computations using Equation 3–11 can be tedious if the number of trials is large. For this reason, tables of the cumulative binomial distribution have been provided at the end of the book in Table C. Table 3–10 illustrates a wide range of probability definitions and indicates how to use Table C in the appendix.

Example 1   Suppose we are to toss a fair coin three times and would like to compute the following probabilities:

a. The probability of three heads in three tosses.
b. The probability of two or more heads in three tosses.
c. The probability of less than two heads in three tosses.

In this example, the Bernoulli process p is 0.50, and a head constitutes a success. The number of trials (n) is three.

The first probability is the probability of three heads (successes) in three tosses (three trials), given that the probability of a head on any one toss is 0.50. This probability can be written as follows:

$$P(R = 3 | p = 0.50, n = 3) = ?$$

where P = Probability, R = Number of successes, n = Number of trials, and

p = Probability of a success on any one trial. The left side of the equation should be read "the probability of three successes, given a process probability of 0.50 and three trials."

In answering the probability questions, let us first list all the possible outcomes of the three trials and compute the probabilities (see Table 3–11).

Probabilities	Interpretation
a. $P(R = 3 \mid p = 0.50, n = 3) = \frac{1}{8}$	The probability of three heads in three trials is one eighth. This is the probability of *HHH*. See Table 3–11.
b. $P(R \geq 2 \mid p = 0.50, n = 3) = \frac{4}{8}$	The probability of two or more heads is four eighths. This is the probability of two heads plus the probability of three heads and is calculated by summing the probabilities of the following combinations: *HHH, HHT, HTH, THH*.
c. $P(R < 2 \mid p = 0.50, n = 3) = \frac{4}{8}$	The probability of less than two heads is the probability of either zero or one head and is calculated by summing the probabilities of the following combinations: *TTH, THT, HTT, TTT*.

The above probabilities can also be calculated using Equation 3–11. This is illustrated for Problem *a*.

$$P(R = 3 \mid p = 0.5, n = 3) = \frac{3!}{3!(0!)}(0.5)^3(0.5)^0 = 0.1250$$

Table 3–11

	Possible Outcomes	Probability of Each Outcome
	HHH	$\frac{1}{8}$
	HHT	$\frac{1}{8}$
	HTH	$\frac{1}{8}$
	THH	$\frac{1}{8}$
	TTH	$\frac{1}{8}$
	THT	$\frac{1}{8}$
	HTT	$\frac{1}{8}$
	TTT	$\frac{1}{8}$
		1

Finally, the probabilities can also be obtained from Appendix Table C.

Calculations	*Explanation*
a. $P(R = 3 \vert p = 0.50, n = 3) = 0.1250$	Look in Appendix Table C under $n = 3$, $p = 0.50$; read down the column to

$$P(R \geq 3) = 0.1250$$

and subtract from this:

$$P(R \geq 4) = 0$$

(four successes in three trials is impossible). The answer is 0.1250, or one eighth.

b. $P(R \geq 2 \vert p = 0.50, n = 3) = 0.5000$ — Look in Table C under $n = 3$, $p = 0.50$, and read $R \geq 2$; the answer is 0.50. If we wanted $P(R = 2)$, we would compute this as follows:

$$P(R \geq 2 \vert 0.50, 3) = 0.5000$$
$$\text{Less: } P(R \geq 3 \vert 0.50, 3) = \underline{0.1250}$$
$$P(R = 2 \vert 0.50, 3) = 0.3750$$

c. $P(R < 2 \vert p = 0.50, n = 3) = 0.5000$ — This probability is equal to

$$1 - P(R \geq 2) = 1 - 0.50 = 0.50$$

Example 2 A very large lot of manufactured goods is to be sampled as a check on its quality.[2] Suppose it is assumed that 10 percent of the items in the lot are defective and that a sample of 20 items is drawn from the lot. What are the following probabilities:

1. Probability of exactly zero defectives in the sample?
2. Probability of more than one defective in the sample?
3. Probability of less than two defectives in the sample?

We can answer as follows. Let $p = 0.10$ and $n = 20$. Then:

a. $P(R = 0 \vert p = 0.10, n = 20) = P(R \geq 0) - P(R \geq 1)$
$$= 1.0 - 0.8784 = 0.1216$$

The probability of zero or more defectives is 1.0, and $P(R \geq 1)$ is read directly from Table C.

---

[2]Strictly speaking, if the lot is of finite size, the sampled items are not independent and hence the Bernoulli assumptions are not exactly satisfied; a different distribution called the *hypergeometric distribution* should be employed. However, if the lot size is large relative to the sample, the use of the Bernoulli assumption introduces little error.

b. $P(R > 1) = P(R \geq 2) = 0.6083$ from Table C.

c. $P(R < 2) = 1.0 - P(R \geq 2) = 1.0 - 0.6083 = 0.3917$

SUMMARY

A Bernoulli process involves a specific number of trials, each with two possible outcomes; the probability of each outcome remains the same; and the trials are independent.

The binomial probability distribution gives the probabilities for each possible number of successes in a given number of trials of a Bernoulli process. Binomial probabilities can be determined using Table C in the appendix.

Bibliography

Blake, I. F. *An Introduction to Applied Probability.* New York: John Wiley & Sons, 1979.

Ewart, P. J.; J. S. Ford; and C. Y. Lin. *Probability for Statistical Decision Making.* Englewood Cliffs, N.J.: Prentice Hall, 1974.

Feller, W. *An Introduction to Probability Theory and Its Applications.* Vol 1. 3rd ed. New York: John Wiley & Sons, 1968.

Hodges, J. L., Jr., and E. L. Lehmann. *Elements of Finite Probability.* 2nd ed. San Francisco: Holden-Day, 1970.

Kemeny, J. G.; A. Schleifer, Jr.; J. L. Snell; and G. L. Thompson. *Finite Mathematics with*

Business Applications. 2nd ed. Englewood Cliffs, N.J.: Prentice Hall, 1972.

Mosteller, F.; R. E. K. Rourke; and G. B. Thomas,, Jr. *Probability with Statistical Applications.* 2nd ed. Reading, Mass.: Addison-Wesley Publishing, 1970.

Ross, S. *A First Course in Probability.* New York: Macmillan, 1976.

Samson, D. *Managerial Decision Analysis.* Homewood, Ill.: Richard D. Irwin, 1988.

Spurr, W. A., and C. P. Bonini. *Statistical Analysis for Business Decisions.* Rev. ed. Homewood, Ill.: Richard D. Irwin, 1973.

Problems with Answers

3–1. Compute the following probabilities, which pertain to flipping a fair coin three times:
  a. P (three heads).
  b. P (two or more heads in three tosses).
  c. P (one or more tails in three tosses).
  d. P (the last toss being a head).

3–2. Assume three urns:

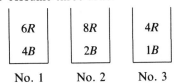

No. 1   No. 2   No. 3

  Draw a ball from no. 1: if red, go to no. 2; if black, go to no. 3.
  a. What is P (red on second draw, given red on draw 1)?
  b. What is P (black on second draw, given red on draw 1)?
  c. What is P (red on second draw, given black on draw 1)?

  d. What is P (black on second draw, given black on draw 1)?
  e. What is P (black on second draw)?
  f. Answer *(a)–(e)* if urn no. 3 was as follows:

No. 3

3–3. Assume an unfair coin has a 0.60 probability of a tail and a 0.40 probability of a head.
  Determine the following:
  a. In two tosses, the probability of:
    (1) Two heads.
    (2) Two tails.
    (3) One head.
    (4) One or more heads.

(5) One or more tails.
(6) One tail or less.
b. In three tosses, the probability of:
(1) Three heads.
(2) Two heads.
(3) One head.
(4) One or more heads.

3–4. Thirty chief executive officers in a certain industry are classified by age and by their previous functional position as shown in the table below:

Previous Functional Position	Age		
	Under 55	55 and Older	Total
Finance	4	14	18
Marketing	1	5	6
Other	4	2	6
Total	9	21	30

Suppose an executive is selected at random from this group.
a. What is the probability that the executive chosen is under 55? What type (marginal, conditional, joint) of probability is this?
b. What is the probability that an executive chosen at random is 55 or older and with Marketing as the previous functional position? What type of probability is this?
c. Suppose an executive is selected, and you are told that the previous position was in Finance. What is the probability that the executive is under 55? What kind of probability is this?
d. Are age and previous functional position independent factors for this group of executives?

3–5. The following probabilities are assigned to the possible values of the fraction defec-

tive in a manufacturing process. Compute the expected value, the variance, and the standard deviation of the random variable, fraction defective.

Event	Probability of Event
0.01 defective	0.10
0.02 defective	0.15
0.03 defective	0.20
0.04 defective	0.30
0.05 defective	0.20
0.10 defective	0.03
0.15 defective	0.02
	1.00

3–6. Using the binomial tables, look up the following probabilities:
a. $P(R = 4|0.50,10)$
b. $P(R > 4|0.50,10)$
c. $P(R \geq 4|0.40, 8)$
d. $P(R < 4|0.20,10)$
e. $P(R = 0|0.30,10)$
f. $P(R \geq 5|0.60,10)$
For (*f*), see the note at the bottom of the first page of Table C in the appendix.

3–7. Assume that the probability of a salesperson making a sale at a randomly selected house is 0.1. If a salesperson makes 20 calls a day, determine the following:
a. The probability of no sales.
b. The probability of one sale.
c. The probability of four or more sales.
d. The probability of more than four sales.
e. The probability of four sales.

3–8. Refer to the example in the chapter relating to Figure 3–3. Suppose a head occurs on the first toss. Calculate the revised (posterior) probabilities for the fair and unfair coin in this case.

Problems

3–9. Which of the following frequency distributions would be "objective" and which "subjective"?

a. Number of heads in 100,000 tosses of a fair coin.

b. Number of heads in the next 100,000 tosses of an untested coin.

c. Number of "prosperous" years in the next 10 years.

d. The earnings of the Ford Motor Company in the next five years (number of "profitable" and number of "loss" years).

e. The probability of drawing the name of a male randomly from the student directory of Cornell University.

3–10. Discuss the following statements:

a. "There is a 1.5 probability that the next president will be _____."

b. "The probability of the sun not rising tomorrow is − 1.0."

c. "There is a 0.40 probability that I'll pass and a 0.70 probability that I'll flunk the examination."

3–11. Discuss whether the following events are dependent or independent:

a. (1) The Giants winning the World Series.
   (2) The Giants winning the pennant of the National League.

b. (1) The savings from using a machine in year 2.
   (2) The savings from using the same machine in year 1.

c. (1) The successful marketing of a high-priced car following
   (2) The successful marketing of a low-priced clothing line.

3–12. Consider two urns

	Urn 1	Urn 2
Red balls	7	4
Black balls	3	6

$P(R_1) = P$ of red on first draw

$P(R_2) = P$ of red on second draw

$P(B_1) = P$ of black on first draw

$P(B_2) = P$ of black on second draw

a. Take a ball from urn 1, replace it, and take a second ball. What is the probability of:

(1) Two reds being drawn?

(2) A red on the second draw if a red is drawn on the first draw?

(3) A red on the second draw if a black is drawn on the first draw?

b. Take a ball from urn 1; replace it. Take a ball from urn 2 if the first ball was black; otherwise, draw a ball from urn 1. What is the probability of:

(1) Two reds being drawn?

(2) A red on the second draw if a red is drawn on the first draw?

(3) A red on the second draw if a black is drawn on the first draw?

3–13. Draw a tree diagram for Problem 3–12a.

3–14. Draw a tree diagram for Problem 3–12b.

3–15. Prepare a joint probability table for Problem 3–12a.

3–16. Prepare a joint probability table for Problem 3–12b.

3–17. a. What is the probability of eight heads in eight tosses of a fair coin?

b. Suppose a fair coin is flipped seven times and all the tosses are heads. What is the probability of the eighth toss being a head? Explain.

3–18. Assume that we have a box containing six red balls and four black balls. We draw two balls, one at a time, without replacing the first ball. For this experiment:

a. Draw a tree diagram showing the process.

b. Prepare a joint probability table.

c. Compute the following probabilities:

$$P(B_2|B_1)$$
$$P(R_2|B_1)$$
$$P(R_2|R_1)$$

3–19. Assume there are two urns:

6R		8R
4B		2B
No. 1		No. 2

There is equal probability of choosing each urn. You take an urn, draw one ball, and find it is red. You want to know which urn you have. You cannot look inside the urn.

a. What is the probability that you drew the ball from urn 1? From urn 2?

b. If the ball is black, what is the probability that the ball is from urn 1?

3–20. A survey was conducted among the readers of a certain magazine. The results showed that 60 percent of the readers were homeowners and had incomes in excess of $25,000 per year; 20 percent were homeowners but had incomes of less than $25,000; 10 percent had incomes in excess of $25,000 but were not homeowners; and the remaining 10 percent were neither homeowners nor had incomes in excess of $25,000.

a. Suppose a reader of this magazine is selected at random and you are told that the person is a homeowner. What is the probability that the person has income in excess of $25,000?

b. Are home ownership and income (measured only as above or below $25,000) independent factors for this group?

3–21. A survey was conducted of families in an urban and the surrounding suburban area. The families were classified according to whether or not they customarily watch two TV programs. The data are shown in the accompanying table in percentages of the total.

a. If a family is selected from this group at random, what is the probability that it views both programs?

b. If the family selected views program A, what is the probability that it also views program B?

c. Are the events (views program A) and (views program B) independent events?

d. Is the event (views program B) independent of the event (urban)?

e. Consider the event (view either program A or B or both). Is this event independent of the event (urban)?

3–22. A sales manager lists the following probabilities for various sales levels for a new product:

Probability	Sales (in units)
0.10	50
0.30	100
0.30	150
0.15	200
0.10	250
0.05	300

Calculate the mean, the variance, and the standard deviation for the random variable sales. (*Hint:* One way to make the computations easier is to treat blocks of 50 as one unit. Thus, 200 is four, 250 is five, etc.).

3–23. A manager is making a plan for her division for next year. Profit (P) is judged to be a linear function of unit sales (X) and fixed costs (Y) as follows:

$$P = \$20X - Y$$

Suppose that the manager is uncertain about the unit sales and fixed costs, but is willing to represent them as independent

	Watch Program A				
	Yes		No		
Watch Program B	Urban	Suburban	Urban	Surburban	Total
Yes	10%	14%	5%	1%	30%
No	15%	21%	20%	14%	70%
Total	25%	35%	25%	15%	100%

random variables with expected values and standard deviations as follows:

$$E(X) = 10,000 \text{ units} \quad \sigma_X = 2,000 \text{ units}$$
$$E(Y) = 150,000 \text{ dollars} \quad \sigma_Y = 50,000 \text{ dollars}$$

What is the expected value and standard deviation of the random variable P?

3–24. Refer to the example in the chapter relating to Figures 3–4 and 3–5. Assume the marginal probabilities for Big Stores and Little Markets as given in Figure 3–4, but now assume that sales to the two customers are independent. Determine the probability distribution for the random variable total sales.

3–25. Specify which of the following are Bernoulli processes:
   a. A house-to-house salesperson making sales calls.
   b. Placing coins in a slot machine that has two payoffs—zero or jackpot.
   c. Purchase of shares of common stock.
   d. Inspection of a wire coil for defects as it is being manufactured.
   e. Inspection of castings as they come off the production line.
   Give brief explanations for your answers.

3–26. Using the tables of the binomial distribution, find the following probabilities:
   a. $P(R = 6|0.28,12)$
   b. $P(R \leq 2|0.45, 8)$
   c. $P(R \geq 5|0.65,15)$
   d. $P(R < 10|0.85,20)$
   e. $P(R > 4|0.25,14)$
   f. $P(R \geq 10|0.75,18)$
   (For parts (c), (d), and (f), see the note at the bottom of first page of Appendix Table C.)

3–27. A feeder airline flies a 14-seat plane. The airline allows up to 16 confirmed reservations to be accepted for a flight. Historical experience has shown that there is a 30 percent chance that each passenger may be a "no-show." What is the probability that one or more people will be "bumped" from the flight if 16 reservations are confirmed?

3–28. Bruce Jones has applied to five schools that indicate in January to the applicant one of three classifications: "likely," "possible," or "unlikely." Bruce has received notification that he is "possible" in all five of the schools. Past results indicate the following probabilities for each school:

Likely: 0.98 probability of being accepted
Possible: 0.30 probability of being accepted
Unlikely: 0.005 probability of being accepted

   a. What is the probability of Bruce being accepted by one or more of the schools? (Assume independence.)
   b. What is the probability of Bruce being accepted by all five schools?

3–29. An accountant is about to audit 24 accounts of a firm. Sixteen of these accounts are high-volume customers. If the accountant selects four of the accounts at random, what is the probability that at least one is a high-volume account?
   Hint: First, find the probability that none of the accounts are high volume.

3–30. Two athletic teams have met 10 times, and the Big Red has won 6 of the contests. It is felt that the past experience is indicative of future outcomes. Now the two teams are going to play in an elimination tournament. Assume the outcome of each game is independent of other games.
   a. If the teams play one game, what is the probability that the Big Red will win?
   b. If the teams play a two-out-of-three series, what is the probability that the Big Red will win?
   c. If the teams play four out of seven, what is the probability that the Big Red will win?

3–31. The president of a large electric utility has to decide whether to purchase one large generator (Big Jim) or four smaller generators (Little Alices) to attain a given amount of electric generating capacity. On any given summer day, the probability of a generator being in service is 0.95 (the generators are equally reliable). Equivalently, there is a 0.05 probability of a failure.
   a. What is the probability of Big Jim being out of service on a given day?

b. What is the probability of either zero or one of the four Alices being out?

c. If five Little Alices are purchased, what is the probability of at least four operating?

d. If six Little Alices are purchased, what is the probability of at least four operating?

3–32. Suppose you flip a coin until four heads have been obtained. What is the probability that it will take exactly seven flips to obtain the four heads?

Hint: The seventh flip must be a head, and three of the first six flips must be heads to obtain the required condition.

3–33. You are in charge of the long-range planning department for a large English construction company. There is a possibility of two major construction projects during the period under consideration: a tunnel under the English Channel to France, and an expanded English missile base system for the United States Air Force. The two projects will to some extent require different engineering skills and equipment. The company that has acquired part of such specialized factors will have a decided advantage in contract negotiation. It is beyond your firm's resources to staff for both projects, and the president has instructed you to choose between them. Upon inquiry among members of Parliament, you conclude that the most critical circumstance affecting the tunnel project is the fate of England's application for trade concessions in the Common Market. If England obtains the concessions, most experts seem to think

that the probability is 0.8 that the tunnel will be built. If England is denied the concessions, the probability is reduced to 0.1 in their view. It is your estimate that the probability is about 0.3 for England to be given the concessions during the period under consideration.

You proceed to Washington to make a comparable analysis of the chances of the missile base system. To your surprise, you find that the American military planners are disturbed by the news stories regarding the tunnel. Should the tunnel be built, there is only 1 chance in 10 that the Air Force would authorize the missile system. The chances are about 50-50 if the tunnel is not constructed. If you accept the subjective probability assessments of your informants, what course of action would you suggest to your firm to maximize the probability of success?

3–34. Newspaper articles frequently cite the fact that in any one year, a small percentage (say, 10 percent) of all drivers are responsible for all automobile accidents. The conclusion is often reached that if only we could single out these accident-prone drivers and either retrain them or remove them from the roads, we could drastically reduce auto accidents. You are told that of 100,000 drivers who were involved in one or more accidents in one year, 11,000 of them were involved in one or more accidents in the next year.

a. Given the above information, complete the entries in the following joint probability table:

First Year ＼ Second Year	Accident	No Accident	Marginal Probability of Event in First Year
Accident			0.10
No Accident			0.90
Marginal Probability of Event in Second Year	0.10	0.90	1.00

b. Do you think searching for accident-prone drivers is an effective way to reduce auto accidents? Why?

More Challenging Problems

3-35. A safety commissioner for a certain city performed a study of the pedestrian fatalities at intersections. He noted that only 6 of the 19 fatalities were pedestrians who were crossing the intersection against the light (i.e., in disregard of the proper signal), whereas the remaining 13 were crossing *with* the light. He was puzzled because the figures seemed to show that it was roughly twice as safe for a pedestrian to cross against the light as with it. Can you explain this apparent contradiction to the commissioner?

3-36. Suppose a new test is available to test for drug addiction. The test is 95 percent accurate "each way"; that is, if the person *is* an addict, there is a 95 percent chance the test will indicate "yes"; if the person is *not* an addict, then 95 percent of the time the test will indicate "no." It is known that the incidence of drug addiction in urban populations is about 1 out of 10,000. Given a positive (yes) test result, what are the chances that the person being tested is addicted?

3-37. A satellite is being launched to gather data on atmospheric conditions on a distant planet. The satellite contains two power cells, and each is estimated to have a 90 percent chance of functioning correctly. The two cells are located in different parts of the satellite so that the failure of either cell is not likely to be related to the other (that is, they are independent).

There are two measuring instruments on the satellite, the primary instrument and a backup instrument. Because they are located together, the reliability of these instruments is not considered to be independent. The probabilities of failure and success are given as follows:

Primary Investment	Backup Instrument	
	Good	Fail
Good	0.6	0.2
Fail	0.1	0.1

The primary instrument requires only one power cell to function, but the backup instrument requires both power cells to operate. If either instrument works, the mission of the satellite is a success. What is the probability of a successful mission?

3-38. This is a classical probability problem. Try out your intuition before solving it systematically.

Assume there are three boxes and each box has two drawers. There is either a gold or silver coin in each drawer. One box has two gold, one box two silver, and one box one gold and one silver coin. A box is chosen at random, and one of the two drawers is opened. A gold coin is observed.

G	G	S
G	S	S

What is the probability of opening the second drawer in the same box and observing a gold coin?

3-39. Assume you can choose between two different gambles. In one gamble, you know that 50 red and 50 black balls are in a jar, and one ball is to be chosen perfectly randomly. You will receive a prize if you guess what the color of the ball drawn will be. In the second gamble, there is an undisclosed number of red and black balls in a jar, and again you are to guess the color of the draw for an identical prize.

Which gamble would you choose to participate in? Why?

3–40. A restaurant seats 100 people. The owner recently decided to provide a free birthday cake to any person having a birthday on the day he or she dined at the restaurant. Assuming $p = 1/365 = 0.003$ and $n = 100$, the owner found the following entry in an extensive binomial table:

$$P(R \geq 6|n = 100, p = 0.01) = 0.0005$$

The owner felt that, since his p was smaller than 0.01, this probability should be an upper limit on the probability of six or more birthday cakes being requested each night. He therefore ordered five cakes each night. After 10 evenings, he had "run out" of cakes three times! What do you suppose went wrong with his analysis?

3–41. The Acme Company has two warehouses located in different cities. Demand for the product is independent in each warehouse district. However, both warehouses have identical probability distributions for demand as follows:

Demand (units)	Probability
0	0.10
1	0.50
2	0.30
3	0.10
	1.00

Assume that each warehouse normally stocks two units.

a. What is the probability that one or the other of the warehouses (not both) will have more demand than stock?

b. What is the probability that both warehouses will be out of stock?

3–42. Refer to Problem 3–41. Suppose the Acme Company consolidated the two warehouses into a single one serving both cities. The consolidated warehouse would carry a stock of four units.

a. Determine the probability distribution of demand at the consolidated warehouse.

b. What is the probability that the consolidated warehouse would be out of stock by one unit? By two units? Compare these to the answers obtained in Problem 3–41.

3–43. Professor Smullyan describes an island, the inhabitants of which are either knights or knaves.[3] Knights never lie, and knaves never tell the truth. Suppose that you know that 80 percent of the inhabitants (both knights and knaves) are in favor of electing Prof. Smullyan as king of the island. The island is made up of 60 percent knights and 40 percent knaves, but you cannot tell which is which. Suppose you take a sample of 10 inhabitants at random and ask, "Do you favor Smullyan as king?" What is the probability that you will get six or more "yes" answers?

3–44. It has been found that when a malfunction occurs in an electrical system, the following parts have probabilities of causing the malfunction as indicated:

Part	Probability of Causing Malfunction
A	0.40
B	0.10
C	0.30
D	0.20
	1.00

a. Assuming it is equally fast to check each of the four parts, in what order would you suggest the parts be checked? Why?

[3]Raymond Smullyan, *What Is the Name of This Book* (Englewood Cliffs, N.J.: Prentice Hall, 1978).

b. Now suppose that the time involved in checking the parts is as follows (assume parts must be checked one at a time):

Part	Time to Check (hours)
A	2
B	1
C	¾
D	⅓

Under these conditions, in what order would you suggest the parts be checked if the malfunction is to be found in the shortest time, on average? Why?

3–45. You are interested in the price of potatoes next year. Three factors affect this price: acreage planted in winter wheat, acreage planted in potatoes, and weather conditions. A combination of large potato acreage and favorable weather conditions will result in a price of $2 per cwt. (hundred lbs). Medium potato acreage and favorable weather will result in a $4 per cwt. price. Small potato acreage and favorable weather will result in a $6 price. Unfavorable weather will increase the price in each case by $2 per cwt. You assess a 0.8 chance for favorable weather and a 0.2 chance for unfavorable weather. Weather is independent of acreage planted.

The acreage planted in potatoes depends to some extent on the acreage planted in winter wheat. Based upon past experience, you assess a 30 percent chance for heavy planting of winter wheat, and 70 percent for light planting of winter wheat. If there is heavy planting of winter wheat, the chance for large potato acreage is zero, the chance for medium potato acreage is ⅔, and the chance for small potato acreage is ⅓. If there is light planting of winter wheat, the chances for large, medium, and small potato acreage are 2/7, 3/7, and 2/7 respectively.

Consider the price of potatoes as the random variable. Determine the probability distribution for this random variable. What is the expected price?

3–46. John McEnroe has been known to exhibit anger during a tennis match. A statistician noted that John won more points than he lost immediately after he became angry. From this it was concluded that John benefited from his outbursts. Evaluate the conclusion.

3–47.[4] There are 15 blue cabs and 85 green cabs. A witness reported that a blue cab caused an accident and then drove off. However, there is evidence that witnesses are wrong 20 percent of the time (and right 80 percent of the time). What is the probability that the cab was blue?

---

[4] This question is based on S. C. Salop, "Evaluating Uncertain Evidence with Sir Thomas Bayes: A Note for Teachers," *The Journal of Economics Perspectives*, Summer 1987, pp. 155–59.

CHAPTER 4

Decision Making under Uncertainty; Revision of Probabilities

In this chapter, we consider the application of probability concepts to business decisions that must be made under conditions of uncertainty. We shall develop a means for making consistent decisions and for estimating the cost of uncertainty. We shall initially propose expected monetary value as an appropriate criterion for decision making. Later in the chapter we will describe the limitations of expected monetary value and suggest modifications in the analysis.

We will also introduce the opportunity to experiment; that is, to gather additional information and revise probabilities before making the decision.

Conditional Value

Suppose a grocer is faced with a problem of how many cases of milk to stock to meet tomorrow's demand. Assume that any milk that remains unsold at the end of the day will represent a complete loss to the grocer. Also, any unsatisfied demand bears no cost except the cost of the lost sale; the disappointed customer will come back in the future. This example is highly simplified but illustrates the basic principles of conditional and expected value.

In our analysis of the grocer's problem, it would be helpful if we knew something about past sales, on the assumption that this experience may serve as a guide to what may be expected in the future. Suppose the grocer has maintained records such as those shown in Table 4–1.

With a purchase price (variable cost) of $8 per case and a selling price of $10 per case, the table of conditional values (Table 4–2) is a description of the prob-

Table 4–1   Historical Demand

Total Demand per Day	Number of Days Each Demand Level Was Recorded	Probability of Each Event
25 cases	20	0.10
26 cases	60	0.30
27 cases	100	0.50
28 cases	20	0.10
	200	1.00

Table 4–2   Conditional Values

	Possible Actions			
Event: Demand	Stock 25	Stock 26	Stock 27	Stock 28
25 cases	$50*	$42	$34	$26
26 cases	50	52*	44	36
27 cases	50	52	54*	46
28 cases	50	52	54	56*

*Best act for the event (the largest profit in each row).

lem facing the grocer. The possible actions (number of cases to buy) facing the grocer are listed across the top of the table. It is, of course, possible to buy 24 or 29 cases, and so on; but if, in the last 200 days, sales were in the range of 25–28 cases, the grocer might view a stock of greater than 28 or less than 25 as having zero probability of occurring. We shall make this assumption. The possible (conceivable) events—in this example, the possible sales—are listed in the far left column. If the grocer is willing to assign probabilities in accordance with the historical data, then events (sales) other than those listed will carry zero probabilities; they are considered impossible events.

Table 4–2 can be thought of as a **conditional value** or conditional profit table. Corresponding to each action the grocer takes, and each event that happens, there is a given conditional profit. These profits are conditional in the sense that a certain profit results from following a specific course of action (act) and having a specific demand (event) occur. All the possible combinations are shown in Table 4–2. For example, if 26 cases were stocked and the demand turned out to be 25 cases, the grocer would have a profit of $42 (that is, $25 \cdot 10 - 26 \cdot 8$). The best act for each possible event is indicated by an asterisk.

Looking at the act column "Stock 27," let us trace through the calculations of each dollar amount. This is done in Table 4–3. Similar computations have to be made for acts "Stock 25," "Stock 26," and "Stock 28."

The calculations of Table 4–3 reflect the fact that if 27 cases are stocked, only 27 can be sold, even if the demand turns out to be 28 cases. Hence, the profit reaches a maximum of $54 for the sale of 27 units and levels off at that figure even if 28 units are demanded.

The Loss Table

In addition to making a table showing conditional profits (Table 4–2), it is possible to construct a table showing conditional *opportunity losses* (Table 4–4). Consider the act "Stock 28." If the demand turns out to be 28, the grocer will make a profit of $56. This is the best that can be achieved with a demand of 28.

Table 4–3   Conditional Profits of Act "Stock 27"

Event: Demand	Selling Price	Total Revenue	Cost of 27 Cases (27 · $8)	Conditional Profit of Act "Stock 27"
25 cases	$10	$250	$216	$34
26 cases	10	260	216	44
27 cases	10	270	216	54
28 cases	10	270	216	54

Table 4–4   Conditional Opportunity Losses

	Act			
Event: Demand	Stock 25	Stock 26	Stock 27	Stock 28
25 cases	$0	$8	$16	$24
26 cases	2	0	8	16
27 cases	4	2	0	8
28 cases	6	4	2	0

Computations of Conditional Opportunity Losses

Event: Demand	Optimum Act for Each Event	Profit of Optimum Act	Difference between Profit of Optimum Act and the Act of Stocking:			
			Stock 25	Stock 26	Stock 27	Stock 28
25	25	$50	$50 − $50 = $0	$50 − $42 = $8	$50 − $34 = $16	$50 − $26 = $24
26	26	52	52 − 50 = 2	52 − 52 = 0	52 − 44 = 8	52 − 36 = 16
27	27	54	54 − 50 = 4	54 − 52 = 2	54 − 54 = 0	54 − 46 = 8
28	28	56	56 − 50 = 6	56 − 52 = 4	56 − 54 = 2	56 − 56 = 0

With a demand of 28, if the grocer had stocked only 27, the profit would have been $54; this act would entail a $2 *opportunity loss* compared with the *best* action with a demand of 28. If the demand were 28 and the grocer stocked 26, there would be a $4 conditional opportunity loss ($56 − $52). **Opportunity loss** can be defined in general as the *amount of profit forgone by not choosing the best act for each event*. With this definition, the conditional opportunity loss table shown in Table 4–4 can be constructed.

It should be emphasized that a conditional profit (or loss) relates to a profit conditional on both:

1. An event happening.
2. A given action.

We do not know which event is going to occur; there is uncertainty. Therefore, the conditional profit for a decision is not one number but a table of profits (or losses) associated with possible events. Profit is $44 only on condition of both stocking 27 units and having an actual demand of 26 units. If the demand is different than 26 units, the actual profit will be different than $44.

Expected Monetary Value

Even though the conditional values and losses help characterize the problem facing the grocer, it is not yet possible to offer an optimum solution. The grocer could choose the best act with advance knowledge of tomorrow's demand, but this information is not available in our example. The problem facing the grocer is to assign probabilities to the possible events and then to analyze the action alternatives. If the probabilities are based on historical information (see Table 4–1), they will be as shown in Table 4–5. If the grocer believes that for some reason tomorrow's demand will vary somewhat from the observed pattern, the probability assignment should be modified.

The next step is to bring the assigned probabilities into the analysis. We accomplish this by *weighting the conditional values of each event in the conditional value table by the probability of the event occurring, and adding the products*. The resulting number is the **expected monetary value** for the act; the optimum

Table 4–5

Event: Demand	Probability of Event
25 cases	0.10
26 cases	0.30
27 cases	0.50
28 cases	0.10
	1.00

act is the one with the highest expected monetary value. The calculations are given in Table 4–6 for the acts of stocking 26 and 27 units. The calculations for 25 and 28 units would be similar.

In Table 4–6, the expected monetary value (EMV) is calculated by multiplying each conditional value by its probability and then adding the weighted conditional values. Table 4–7 shows the expected monetary values for all four acts. For the act "Stock 26," the grocer calculates an expected monetary value of $51, the highest EMV. Therefore, based on expected monetary value, 26 cases should be stocked.

Note that the EMV OF $51 will not be the profit on any one day. It is the expected or average profit. If the decision were repeated for many days (with the same probabilities), the grocer would make an average of $51 per day by stocking 26 cases of milk. Even if the decision were not repeated, the action with the highest EMV is the best alternative that the decision maker has available.

To summarize, our plan for solving the grocer's problem is as follows:

1. Construct a payoff (conditional value) table listing the acts and events that are considered to be possibilities and listing the outcomes for each act and event. In listing the events, be sure that each event is mutually exclusive (i.e., make sure that no two or more events can occur simultaneously) and that all

Table 4–6   Calculation of Expected Monetary Values

		Act: Stock 26		Act: Stock 27	
Event: Demand	*Probability of Event*	*Conditional Value (CV)*	*CV Weighted by Probability of Event*	*Conditional Value (CV)*	*CV Weighted by Probability of Event*
25 cases	0.10	$42	$ 4.20	$34	$ 3.40
26 cases	0.30	52	15.60	44	13.20
27 cases	0.50	52	26.00	54	27.00
28 cases	0.10	52	5.20	54	5.40
	1.00				
Expected monetary value			$51.00		$49.00

Table 4–7   Summary of Expected Monetary Values

Act	Expected Monetary Value
Stock 25	$50
Stock 26	51 (optimum act)
Stock 27	49
Stock 28	42

events considered together are exhaustive (i.e., that the events listed cover all the possibilities). This table includes the economics of the problem (costs, revenues, and profits) by presenting a conditional value (or loss) for each act and event combination.

2. Assign probabilities to the events.
3. Calculate an EMV for each act by weighting (multiplying) the conditional values by the assigned probabilities and adding the weighted conditional values to obtain the EMV of the act.
4. Choose the act with the largest EMV.

Expected Opportunity Loss

The grocer can also choose the best act by minimizing **expected opportunity loss (EOL).** The procedure is the same as just outlined except that instead of using the payoff table (conditional value table, Table 4–2) and conditional profits, we shall use the conditional opportunity loss table (Table 4–4) and conditional opportunity losses. The calculations for act "Stock 26" and act "Stock 27" are as given in Table 4–8.

From Table 4–9, we find that the grocer should choose act "Stock 26," which

Table 4–8   **Calculation of Expected Opportunity Losses**

		Act: Stock 26		Act: Stock 27	
Event: Demand	*Probability of Event*	*Conditional Losses (CL)*	*CL Weighted by Probability of Event*	*Conditional Losses (CL)*	*CL Weighted by Probability of Event*
25 cases	0.10	$8	$0.80	$16	$1.60
26 cases	0.30	0	0.00	8	2.40
27 cases	0.50	2	1.00	0	0.00
28 cases	0.10	4	0.40	2	0.20
	1.00				
Expected opportunity loss			$2.20		$4.20

Table 4–9   **Summary of Expected Opportunity Losses**

Act	*Expected Opportunity Losses*	*Comparison of Expected Opportunity Losses with Optimum*
Stock 25	$ 3.20	$1
Stock 26	2.20 (optimum act)	0
Stock 27	4.20	2
Stock 28	11.20	9

has an expected loss of $2.20, the lowest of the four expected opportunity losses.

SUMMARY

Let us summarize the various measures of profitability that have been introduced:

Conditional value. The actual profit that would result following a given action, conditional on a given event occurring.

Conditional opportunity loss. The relative loss (i.e., the profit not earned) following a given action, conditional on a given event occurring.

Expected monetary value. The conditional values weighted by the probability of the events occurring, and summed for each act.

Expected opportunity loss. The conditional opportunity losses weighted by the probability of the events occurring, and summed for each act.

The optimum act is the act with the greatest expected monetary value, and thus, the smallest expected opportunity loss.

Expected Utility

Although expected monetary value may be a good guide to action in many cases, it may not be in others. This does not destroy the expected value model; it means we must modify the analysis when the situation warrants it. Let us consider a major difficulty with expected monetary value.

Suppose a manager has a chance to invest $500,000 in a speculative new product. Assume that if the product is successful, there will be net profits of $1 million. However, if the product is not successful, there will be a loss of the $500,000 spent to develop, produce, and sell the new product. Our manager's conditional value table is given in Table 4–10.

If, after gathering evidence, the manager assigns a subjective probability of 0.90 of success, the EMV of the act "Invest" would be $850,000 ($1,000,000 × 0.90 − $500,000 × 0.10 = $850,000), as compared with an EMV of zero for the act "Do not invest." Suppose, however, that the firm is in a very difficult

Table 4–10   Conditional Value

	Act	
Event	*Invest*	*Do Not Invest*
Product successful	$1,000,000	0
Product not successful	− 500,000	0

financial position, and a $500,000 loss would result in certain bankruptcy. In such a case, EMV may be a poor guide to action. The manager may be unwilling to accept a 0.10 probability of losing $500,000 regardless of the size of the conditional profits or the EMV, because of the undesirable consequences of the loss. If so, the manager has a large disutility for such a loss, and this should be brought into the analysis.

If utility considerations are to be ignored, or in problems where utility for money is approximately linear (see Chapter 5), EMV is a reasonable guide to action. For example, when the potential losses are not too great and the prospective profit range is narrow, utility considerations usually are not significant. Such is the case in our grocer's problem, and EMV is adequate.

However, where actions are contemplated that involve large potential losses, it may be desirable to alter the analysis by bringing in utility considerations. This can be done by calculating the expected utility value of possible actions rather than the expected monetary value. This modification of the analysis will be discussed in Chapter 5. Here, we small assume that the situation is such that utility considerations are unimportant (i.e., the expected monetary value is a reasonable measure of the expected utility).

Expected Profit with Perfect Predictions

Returning to our example of the grocer, let us raise the following question: "What profit could the grocer *expect* to make in the future if each day's demand could be *predicted with certainty* the day before the particular demand occurred?" To answer this question, let us construct a conditional value table that will show the conditional profit for the *best* act, given each event. Table 4–11 is constructed by choosing the best act and recording the highest profit figures for each event (this information can be obtained from Table 4–2). For example, if we knew tomorrow's demand would be 27, we would stock 27 cases, for a profit of $54. If we stocked 26, we would forgo the $2 profit on one unit; and if we stocked 28, we would have to scrap one unit at a loss of $8. Table 4–11 shows the profit resulting from the best action for each possible event.

Table 4–11 **Conditional Value Table for Optimal Decisions with Perfect Prediction**

	Act			
Event: Demand	*Stock 25*	*Stock 26*	*Stock 27*	*Stock 28*
25 cases	$50			
26 cases		$52		
27 cases			$54	
28 cases				$56

Table 4–12　　　Expected Profit with Perfect Prediction

Event: Demand	Probability of Event	Conditional Profit (CP)	CP Weighted by Probability of Event
25 cases	0.10	$50	$ 5.00
26 cases	0.30	52	15.60
27 cases	0.50	54	27.00
28 cases	0.10	56	5.60
Expected profit with perfect prediction			$53.20

Let us convert these conditional optimal profit figures to an expectation. This can be done by weighting the profit for each event by the probability of the event occurring. The calculation is shown in Table 4–12, where the **expected profit with perfect prediction** ($53.20) is the profit the grocer could make on the average if each day's demand could be predicted in advance. Thus, the optimum amount would be ordered each day.

Before the perfect predictor is used, the grocer is still uncertain as to what the prediction will be, since any one of the four events may occur. Before the prediction, the profit is an *expectation,* since we do not know which event will occur. To decide whether or not to use the predictor, our grocer must assign a value to the perfect prediction and compare this value with the cost of the predictor. Remember that before buying the information, we do not know what the prediction will be.

Expected Value of Perfect Information

In many decision problems, the manager faces the question of whether to act immediately or delay action and seek more information. The important thing to the manager is to balance the *cost* of additional information against the *value* (additional profit) of the information. The cost part of this decision (cost of obtaining information) is usually easier to calculate than the value of the information. However, using the expected value model, we have a way of quantifying the value of additional information.

Referring again to our grocer example, we showed in Table 4–12 that the expected profit with perfect prediction is $53.20. Previously, in Table 4–7, we showed that the EMV of the best act under uncertainty, "Stock 26," is $51. The difference,

$$\$53.20 - \$51 = \$2.20$$

is the increase in expected profit from a free, perfect predictive device. Hence, $2.20 is the **expected value of perfect information (EVPI).** That is,

EVPI = Expected profit with perfect prediction − EMV (of optimal act)

Table 4–13

	Act			
	Stock 25	*Stock 26*	*Stock 27*	*Stock 28*
EMV (under uncertainty)	$50.00	$51.00	$49.00	$42.00
EOL	3.20	2.20	4.20	11.20
Expected profit (with perfect prediction)	$53.20	$53.20	$53.20	$53.20

Note from Table 4–9 that $2.20 is also the *expected opportunity loss* of the optimum act. We might expect this result, since the perfect predictor should reduce the opportunity loss that exists under uncertainty to zero. Hence, the expected opportunity loss of the optimum act measures the EVPI. A useful check on computations is provided by the identity:

$$\begin{array}{l} \text{EMV (of any act)} \\ + \text{ EOL (of the same act)} \end{array} = \begin{array}{l} \text{Expected profit with} \\ \text{perfect prediction} \end{array}$$

This calculation is shown in Table 4–13.

It is important to note that it is the EOL of the *optimal act* that is equal to the EVPI. If the grocer chooses the act "Stock 28," there will be an EMV of $42 and an EOL of $11.20. The EVPI is *not* $11.20, because the grocer can increase the EMV to $51 by choosing a different act ("Stock 26"), and this requires *no* additional information. The value of additional information is measured starting from the assumption that the optimal action would be chosen, given the information already available.

Sensitivity Analysis of Subjective Probabilities

Estimating probabilities is one of the most difficult steps in applying the expected monetary value decision criterion. Sometimes it is possible to avoid this step, at least partially, by leaving the estimation of probabilities to the last. For each act, a range of probabilities can be found over which the given act is optimal. The decision maker then determines in which interval the probabilities lie.

We will illustrate this using a previous example. In Table 4–10, the conditional values for a new-product decision were given ($1 million if the product is successful; −$500,000 if it fails; and zero if it is not introduced). Let p be the probability of success, and hence $(1 - p)$ is the probability of failure for the new product. Assuming the decision maker wishes to use the EMV criterion, the expected value of introducing the product is:

$$\begin{aligned} \text{EMV} &= p(1,000,000) + (1 - p)(-500,000) \\ &= -500,000 + 1,500,000p \end{aligned}$$

Table 4–14   Alternative Possible Sets of Probabilities

	Sets of Probabilities			
Event: Demand	1	2	3	4
25 cases	0.1	0.2	0.05	0.1
26 cases	0.3	0.3	0.15	0.1
27 cases	0.5	0.4	0.40	0.3
28 cases	0.1	0.1	0.40	0.5

For the product to be introduced, EMV must be greater than zero. That is:

$$-500,000 + 1,500,000p > 0$$

or

$$p > \frac{500,000}{1,500,000} = \frac{1}{3}$$

Hence, if the decision maker feels that the chances are greater than one third for success, the product should be introduced. Note that the decision maker does not have to specify an exact value for p in order to make the decision.

Example   To further clarify this concept, consider again the example of the grocer deciding how many cases of milk to stock. From Table 4–7, we determined that the optimum act was to stock 26 cases. This result was obtained using the probabilities in the first column in Table 4–14. You can check that the action "Stock 26" remains optimal for all the various sets of probabilities shown in Table 4–14.[1] Hence, the decision maker can see that the decision is not *sensitive* to the variations in the probabilities that are presented in Table 4–14. Other variations could cause a change in decision. For example, if the probability attached to the event "demand of 25 cases" is greater than 0.20, then the optimal decision changes to ordering 25 cases.

The general approach suggested by this example is *sensitivity analysis* and is similar to that introduced in Chapter 2. The decision maker makes a preliminary set of estimates (for probabilities or for payoffs). Variations in these estimates are then made. If the variations do not change the optimal decision, one need go no further. If, on the other hand, the decision is sensitive to the changes, then the manager must refine the preliminary estimates in order to arrive at a decision.

SUMMARY   The expected value of perfect information is the worth to the decision maker of a perfect forecast of an uncertain event. Sensitivity analysis examines the

---

[1]The act "Stock 26" remains optimal as long as $P(\text{demand} = 25) < 0.20$ and $P(\text{demand} \geq 27) < 0.80$. This model is developed in detail in Chapter 17.

degree to which a decision depends upon (is sensitive to) assumptions or estimates, particularly estimates of probabilities.

Decision Trees

The previous sections of this chapter developed the decision criterion of expected monetary value and analyzed simple decisions using conditional value tables. This section describes a general approach for more complex decisions that is useful both for *structuring* the decision problem and for finding a solution. The approach utilizes a **decision tree,** a graphic tool for describing the actions available to the decision maker, the events that can occur, and the relationship between these actions and events.

Decision Tree for Grocer's Problem

To illustrate the basic ideas, let us first develop the decision tree for the grocery problem of the last section. Recall that the decision involves how many cases of milk to order. The decision point is represented by a *square box* or *decision node* in Figure 4–1. The alternatives are represented as *branches* emanating from the decision node.

Suppose the grocer were to select some particular alternative, say order 28 cases. There are several possible events that can happen, each event represent-

Figure 4–1   Grocer's Alternatives

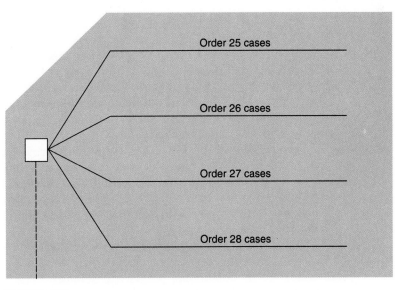

Order 25 cases

Order 26 cases

Order 27 cases

Order 28 cases

Decision node

Figure 4–2   Events for Alternative "Order 28 Cases"

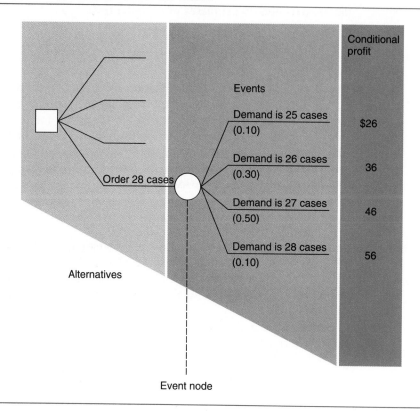

ing a number of cases of milk that customers might demand. These are shown in Figure 4–2 as branches emanating from a round node. (We are using the convention of a square box for a decision node and a circle for an event node). Note that these branches represent uncertain events over which the decision maker has no control. However, probabilities can be assigned to each event and are entered under each branch in parentheses.

At the end of each branch is the conditional profit associated with the selected action and given event (the same values as in Table 4–2). The conditional profit thus represents the profit associated with the decisions and events along the path from the first part of the tree to the end. For example, the $26 in Figure 4–2 is the profit associated with ordering 28 cases of milk, and then experiencing a demand of 25 cases.

The expected monetary value (EMV) is calculated for each event node exactly as was done in the previous section (see Table 4–6). That is, probabilities are multiplied by conditional profits and summed. The EMV is placed in the event node to indicate that it is the expected value calculated over all branches emanating from that node.

Figure 4–3   Complete Decision Tree—Grocer's Problem

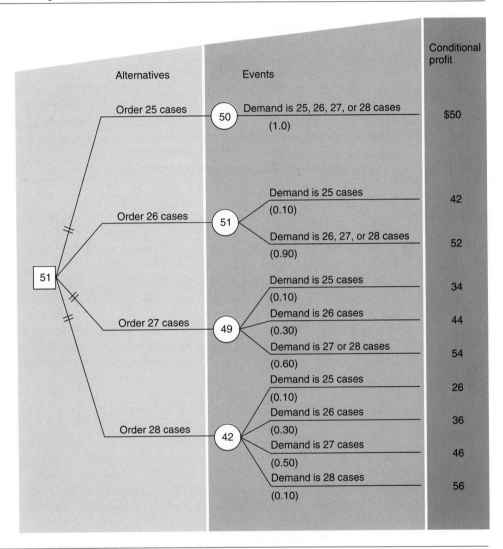

Figure 4–3 shows the complete decision tree for the grocer's problem. Note that it is not necessary to list every possible event separately for all decisions. Thus, when 26 cases are ordered, there are only two events that lead to different conditional profits: Demand is 25 cases with a profit of $42; and demand is 26 or more (that is, demand is 26, 27, or 28 cases) with a profit of $52. If the grocer orders 25 cases, there is only one outcome, namely the sale of all 25 cases with conditional profit of $50.

In Figure 4–3, the expected monetary values are shown in the event nodes. The grocer must then choose which action to take, and this choice is to select the one with the highest EMV, namely order 26 cases with EMV = $51. This is indicated in the tree by putting 51 in the decision node (square box) at the beginning of the tree. In addition, the mark ‖ is drawn across the nonoptimal decision branches, indicating that they are not to be followed.

In summary, the decision tree uses the same idea of maximizing expected monetary value developed in the previous section. For the grocery example, the use of a table, such as Table 4–2, may seem easier. However, as the decision problem becomes more complex, the decision tree becomes more valuable in organizing the information needed to make the decision. This is especially true if the manager must make a *sequence* of decisions, rather than a single decision, as the next example will illustrate.

Decision Tree
Example

Suppose the marketing manager of a firm is trying to decide whether or not to market a new product and at what price to sell it. The profit to be made depends on whether or not a competitor will introduce a similar product and on what price the competitor charges.

Note that there are two decisions: (1) introduce the product or not, and (2) the price to charge. Likewise, there are two events: (1) competition introduces a competitive product (or not), and (2) the competitor's price. The timing or sequence of these decisions and events is very important in this decision. If the marketing manager must act before knowing whether or not the competitor has a similar product, the price may be different than with such knowledge. A decision tree is useful in this type of situation, since it displays the order in which decisions are made and events occur.

Suppose in our example that the firm must introduce or decide to scrap its new product shortly. However, the price decision can be made later. If the competitor is going to act, it will introduce its product within a month. In three months, our firm will establish and announce its price. After that, the competitor will announce its price. This can be diagrammed in the decision tree in Figure 4–4. Note that this is a sequential decision problem. Our firm must make a decision *now* about introduction and *subsequently* set price, *after* learning about the competitor's action.

The decision tree shows the structure of the decision problem. To complete the analysis, conditional profits must be estimated for every combination of actions and events (that is, for every path through the tree). Suppose our marketing manager has done this, and the profits are shown in Figure 4–4 at the ends of the tree. These profit values include the costs of introducing the product and the profits made from its sale. Negative values indicate that introduction costs exceeded subsequent profit from sales.

Also, the probabilities for each event must be assessed by the decision maker; for our example they are shown under the event branches in Figure 4–4. Note that these probabilities may depend upon prior actions or events. Thus, the probabilities for the competitor's price behavior in Figure 4–4 are different when our price is high than when our price is low.

Figure 4–4   Decision Tree for Product Introduction Example

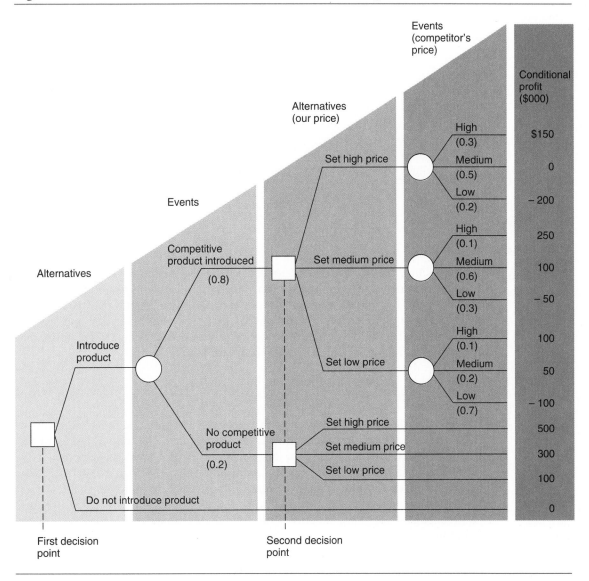

Influence Diagram

We can also represent the manager's problem using an *influence diagram,* as was done in Chapter 2. See Figure 4–5. This influence diagram is quite simple, so it may not seem particularly helpful in structuring the decision problem and the decision tree. However, for more complex situations, it may be very useful to

Figure 4–5   Influence Diagram for Product Introduction Example

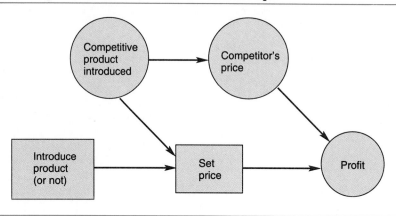

draw an influence diagram prior to developing the detailed decision tree; the influence diagram would be an excellent way to structure our assumptions about the important factors and relationships in the model. In general, we recommend using decision trees to solve problems of this type. However, for specialized cases, prototype software packages (e.g., DAVID) are emerging to solve the decision problem directly from the influence diagram.[2]

Analysis of the Decision Problem

To analyze a decision tree, we begin at the end of the tree and work backwards. For each set of event branches, the EMV is calculated as illustrated, and for each set of decision branches, the one with the highest EMV is selected. This is illustrated in Figure 4–6 for our example. First, the EMVs are calculated for the event nodes associated with competitor's price. For example, the EMV of $5,000 in the topmost right circle in Figure 4–6 represents the sum of the product of probabilities for high, medium, and low prices times the respective conditional profits:

$$EMV = (0.3)(150) + (0.5)(0) + (0.2)(-200) = 5$$

The other values are computed similarly.

Now, if we move back on the decision tree to the second decision point, we are faced with two decision situations. The first—when a competitive product

---

[2]See R. Shachter, "DAVID: Influence Diagram Processing System for the Macintosh," in *Uncertainty in Artificial Intelligence,* vol. II, ed. L. N. Kanal and J. Lemmer, North-Holland, 1988.

Figure 4–6   Completed Decision Tree for Product Introduction Example

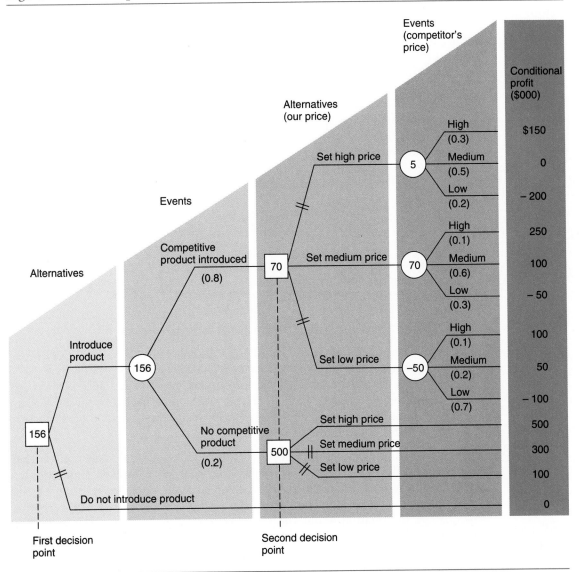

has been introduced—involves setting a high, medium, or low price with expected profits of $5,000, $70,000, and − $50,000, respectively. Assume the choice is the one with highest expected profit—the medium price. A mark ‖ is placed on the lines related to the other alternatives, indicating that they are nonoptimal, and the expected profit of $70,000 is attached to the upper box of the second decision point.

When no competitive product is introduced, the best choice is a high price, with profit of $500,000.

At the event point to the left, an expected value of $156,000 is computed by multiplying the expected profit given a competitive product ($70,000) by its probability, 0.8, and adding the profit given no competitive product ($500,000) times its probability of 0.2. The EMV in thousands is:

$$EMV = (0.8)(70) + (0.2)(500) = 156$$

Finally, the decision to market the product is made, since the expected net profit of $156,000 is greater than the zero profit from not marketing the product.

Note that the decision that results from an analysis of the decision tree is not a fixed decision, but rather a *strategy:* Introduce the product and charge a high price if there is no competitive entry; but charge a medium price if there is competition.

Developing the Decision Tree

The decision tree is a model of a decision situation, and like all models, it is an abstraction and simplification of the real problem. Only the important decisions and events are included; otherwise the tree becomes too "bushy." And judgment is required, not only about what to include, but also to assess probabilities.

In drawing a decision tree, certain rules must be observed:

1. The branches emanating from any node must be all the same logical type, either events or alternatives, and never a mix of the two.
2. The events associated with branches from any event node must be mutually exclusive and all events included, so that the sum of the probabilities is one.
3. The alternatives associated with a decision node must include all the alternatives under consideration at that point.

It is generally helpful to develop the tree in chronological sequence, so that the proper order of decisions and events is maintained. However, some aspects of drawing the tree are arbitrary. For example, in the case above, suppose the firm must announce its decision about the new product and establish the price before any information about the competitor is known. The part of the tree relating to these decisions could be drawn in either of the two equivalent ways shown in Figure 4-7. Exactly the same options would be available for diagramming the events associated with the competitor's product introduction and the competitor's price, if they occurred without any intervening decision on our firm's part.

Recall from the discussion of expected utility earlier in the chapter that expected monetary value is not an appropriate decision criterion if the conditional profits or losses are so large that the decision maker views the alternatives as having significantly different consequences. In such situations, utility values are used in the decision tree in place of conditional profits. This is considered in detail in Chapter 5.

Figure 4–7   Alternative Ways of Diagramming Decision (revised example)

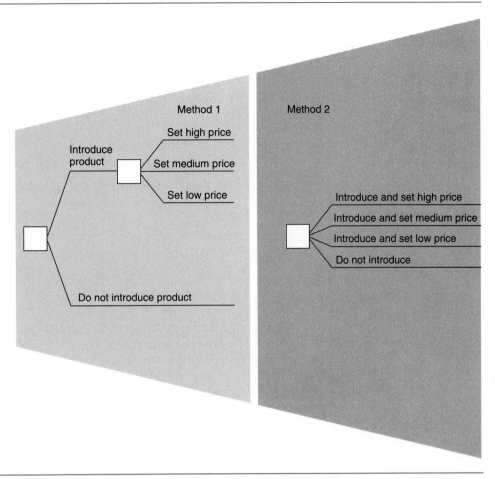

 SUMMARY A decision tree is a graphic device for showing the sequence of decision alternatives and events involved in making a decision under uncertainty. A decision tree is analyzed by calculating the expected value for each event node and choosing the alternative with the highest profit for decision nodes, starting with the end of the tree and moving backward toward the origin.

Revision of Probabilities

In this section, we introduce the opportunity to experiment; that is, to gather additional information and revise probabilities before making the decision.

We shall deal with the simplest of possible situations where there is only one unknown. For example, the decision may hinge on the demand for the product in the next year. Assume it has been decided to experiment. Demand is the only unknown. In this situation (which could be an inventory problem), the decision process is as follows:

1. Choose the decision criterion; we assume the expected value decision rule.
2. Describe the set of possible outcomes and possible decisions.
3. Assign probabilities to the possible outcomes (states of nature).
4. Determine a profit function (conditional profits).
5. Conduct an experiment.
6. Revise the assigned probabilities.
7. Compute the expected profit for each decision.
8. The optimum decision is the act with the highest expected profit.

The above process assumes that it has previously been determined that experimentation is desirable. We now investigate that question.

The Value of Imperfect Information

Here, we shall introduce a general method for evaluating the possibility of obtaining more information regarding a decision problem. Later chapters will expand this analysis.

The expected value of perfect information (EVPI) introduced earlier sets an upper limit on the value of additional information in a decision situation. Most information that we can obtain is **imperfect** in the sense that it will *not* tell us exactly which event will occur. Even so, imperfect information will still have value if it will improve the expected profit.

The term *experiment* is intended here to be very broad. An experiment may be a study by economists to predict national economic activity, a consumer survey by a market research firm, an opinion poll conducted on behalf of a political candidate, a sample of production line items taken by an engineer to check on quality, or a seismic test to give an oil well–drilling firm some indications of the presence of oil.

In general, we can evaluate the worth of a given experiment only if we can estimate the reliability of the resulting information. A market research study may be helpful in deciding whether or not to introduce a new product. However, the experiment can be given a specific economic value before the study only if the decision maker can say beforehand how closely the market research study can estimate the potential sales.

An example will make this clear. Suppose the sales of a potential new product will be either large or small (the product will be either a success or a flop). The conditional value table for this decision is shown in Table 4–15. The conditional value of $4 million is the net profit (present value) if the potential sales are large. The $-\$2$ million is the cost if the product sells poorly.

Based on expected monetary value (EMV), the indicated action is not to introduce the product. However, the decision maker, being reluctant to give up

Table 4–15   Conditional Value Table for Decision on Introduction of New Product ($ millions)

		Actions	
Outcome	Probabilities	Introduce Product	Do Not Introduce
High sales	0.3	4.0	0
Low sales	0.7	−2.0	0
Expected monetary value		−0.2	0

a probability of 0.3 of making $4 million, may consider gathering more information before action. As a first step, let us calculate the expected value of perfect information (EVPI). Recall from earlier in this chapter (page 92) that

$$\text{EVPI} = \text{Expected profit with perfect predictor} - \text{EMV (optimal act)}$$

With a perfect predictor, the company would introduce the product if sales were high, and not introduce if sales were low, resulting in an expected value of $0.3 \times 4 + 0.7 \times 0 = 1.2$. The EMV of the optimal act (do not introduce) is zero. Hence

$$\text{EVPI} = 1.2 - 0 = 1.2$$

This can also be calculated from the expected opportunity losses (EOL). Recall that:

$$\text{EVPI} = \text{EOL(optimal act)}$$

The optimal act is no introduction. If sales were low, there would be no opportunity loss. But if high sales were to occur, there would be an opportunity loss of $4 million, since the company could have made this much profit had the product been introduced. Hence, the EOL is $0.3 \times 4 + 0.7 \times 0 = 1.2$, as above.

Thus, there is an expected value of $1.2 million that can be obtained through perfect information. The value of imperfect information will be less.

The decision maker can perform an experiment in this situation. Suppose the experiment takes the form of a market survey conducted in two representative cities. The survey will cost $0.2 million.

There are three possible outcomes from the survey: (1) The survey may predict success (high sales) for the new product; (2) the survey may predict failure (low sales); or (3) the survey result may be inconclusive. In the past, surveys such as the one proposed often correctly predicted the success or failure of a new product, but sometimes success was predicted for a product that later failed, and vice versa.

If the marketing manager takes the survey before acting, the decision can be based on the survey predictions. Figure 4–8 shows the influence diagram for this problem. This problem can be expressed in terms of a decision tree, as shown in Figure 4–9. The upper part of the tree shows the decision process if no survey is taken. This is the same analysis as presented in Table 4–15, with probabilities of 0.3 and 0.7 for high and low sales, expected profit of −$0.2 million for introduction, and an indicated decision of no introduction with $0 profits.

The lower part of the tree, following the branch "Take survey," displays the possible survey results and the subsequent decision possibilities. After each of

Figure 4–8   Influence Diagram for Problem on Introduction of New Product

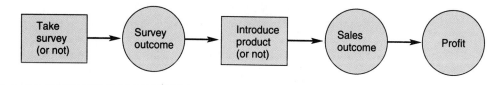

Figure 4–9   Decision Tree for Problem on Introduction of New Product

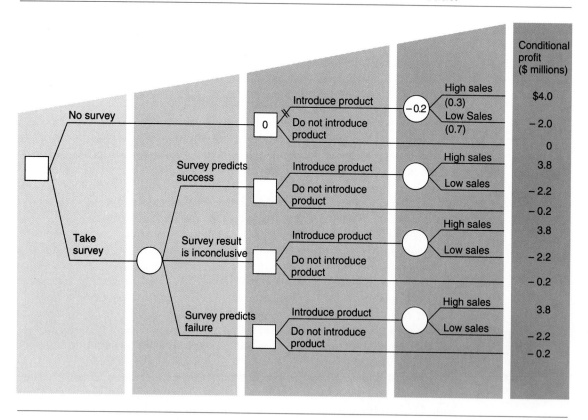

the three possible survey outcomes, a decision about whether or not to introduce the product must be made. If the product is introduced, the sales will either be high with a profit of $3.8 million, or low with a loss of $2.2 million. Note that the cost of the survey ($0.2 million) has been included in these profit and loss amounts.

Determining Probabilities

In order to complete the analysis of Figure 4–9, we need the probabilities for the various events. Let us suppose that the marketing manager estimates the probabilities shown in Table 4–16. These are the conditional probabilities for the various survey results given the potential sales level of the product. For example, when a new product has high sales potential, the survey predicts success with probability 0.4; the survey predicts failure with probability 0.2; and the survey will be inconclusive with probability 0.4. Such probabilities would reflect past experience with surveys of this type, modified perhaps by the judgment of the marketing manager.

The probabilities shown in Table 4–16 express the reliability or accuracy of the experiment. With these estimates, the marketing manager can evaluate the economic worth of the survey. Without these reliability estimates, no specific value can be attached to taking the survey.

The conditional probabilities of Table 4–16 are not directly useful in Figure 4–9. Rather, we need the *unconditional* probabilities of the various survey outcomes (all we have available are the survey probabilities conditional on sales level). We also need the conditional probabilities of a high and low sales level, given a survey prediction of success, and so on.

Table 4–17 is a joint probability table similar to those used in Chapter 3. The top part of the table shows the symbols, and the bottom displays the equivalent numerical values. In the right-hand column, we have the original probabilities assessed by the marketing manager: a 0.3 chance that the product will have high sales (H) and a 0.7 chance for low sales (L). From these, and from the conditional probabilities of Table 4–16, the joint probabilities of Table 4–17 can be calculated. Thus, the joint probability of both a prediction of "success" by the

Table 4–16 **Conditional Probabilities of Survey Predictions, Given Potential Sales**

Experimental Results (survey prediction)	Potential Level of Sales	
	High Sales (H)	Low Sales (L)
Survey predicts success (S) (i.e., high sales)	0.4	0.1
Survey inconclusive (I)	0.4	0.5
Survey predicts failure (F)(i.e., low sales)	0.2	0.4
	1.0	1.0

Table 4–17   Joint Probability Table

Potential Level of Sales	Survey Prediction			Marginal Probabilities of Sales Level
	Success (S)	Inconclusive (I)	Failure (F)	
High (H)	P(S and H)	P(I and H)	P(F and H)	P(H)
Low (L)	P(S and L)	P(I and L)	P(F and L)	P(L)
Marginal Probabilities of Survey Prediction	P(S)	P(I)	P(F)	1.00

Potential Level of Sales	Survey Prediction			Marginal Probabilities of Sales Level
	Success (S)	Inconclusive (I)	Failure (F)	
High (H)	0.12	0.12	0.06	0.30
Low (L)	0.07	0.35	0.28	0.70
Marginal Probabilities of Survey Prediction	0.19	0.47	0.34	1.00

survey (S) and high level of actual sales (H) is calculated by multiplying the conditional probability of a successful prediction, given a high sales level (which is 0.4 from Table 4–16), by the probability of a high sales level:

$$P(S \text{ and } H) = P(S|H)P(H) = (0.4)(0.3) = 0.12$$

Similarly:

$$P(S \text{ and } L) = P(S|L)P(L) = (0.1)(0.7) = 0.07$$
$$P(I \text{ and } H) = P(I|H)P(H) = (0.4)(0.3) = 0.12$$

and so on.

The marginal probabilities of sales level in Table 4–17 (the right-hand column) are equal to the sum of the joint probabilities in each row. Note that these are precisely the original probabilities for high and low sales, and they are designated **prior probabilities** because they were assessed before any information from the survey was obtained. The marginal probabilities of the survey predictions are equal to the sum of the joint probabilities in each column.

In understanding Table 4–17, it is useful to think of it as representing the results of 100 past situations identical to the one under consideration. The probabilities then represent the frequency with which the various outcomes occurred. For example, in 30 of the 100 cases, the actual sales for the product

Figure 4–10   Completed Decision Tree

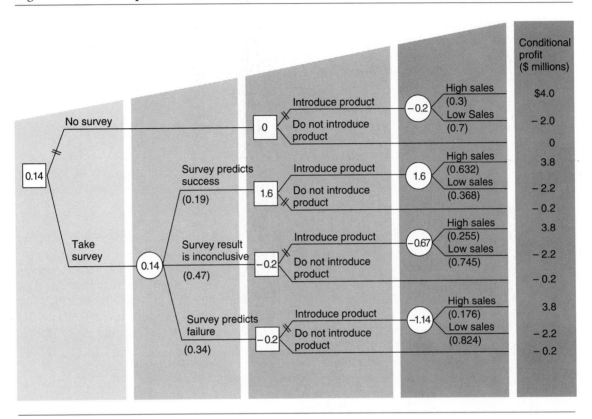

turned out to be high; and in these 30 high-sales cases, the survey predicted success in 12 instances [that is $P(H$ and $S) = 0.12$], was inconclusive in 12 instances, and predicted failure in 6 instances.

The marginal probabilities of survey prediction in the bottom row of Table 4–17 can then be interpreted as the relative frequency with which the survey predicted "success," "inconclusive," and "failure," respectively. For example, the survey predicted "success" 19 out of 100 times—12 of these times when sales actually were high and 7 times when sales were low.

These marginal probabilities of survey prediction are important to our analysis, for they give us the probabilities associated with the information received by the marketing manager before the decision to introduce the product is made. The marginal probabilities are entered beside the appropriate branches in Figure 4–10.

We still need to calculate the probabilities for the branches labeled "High sales" and "Low sales" in the lower part of Figure 4–10. We cannot use the values of 0.3 and 0.7 for these events as we did in the upper part of the tree because those probabilities were calculated independent of taking a survey. The marketing manager will have received information from a survey, and the probabilities should reflect this information. The required probabilities are the conditional probabilities for the various levels of sales given the survey result. For example, for the upper branch of the "Take survey" path, we need $P(H|S)$, the probability of high sales (H) given that the survey predicts success (S). This can be computed directly from the definition of conditional probability (see Chapter 3), using the data from Table 4–17:

$$P(H|S) = \frac{P(H \text{ and } S)}{P(S)} = \frac{0.12}{0.19} = 0.632$$

And the probability of low sales, given a survey prediction of success, is:

$$P(L|S) = \frac{P(L \text{ and } S)}{P(S)} = \frac{0.17}{0.19} = 0.368$$

These probabilities are called **posterior probabilities,** since they come after the inclusion of the information to be received from the survey. The survey has not been made yet, but the calculations are based on the possible survey results. To understand the meaning of the above calculations, think again of Table 4–17 as representing 100 past identical situations. Then, in 19 cases [since $P(S) = 0.19$], the survey predicted success. And of these 19 cases, 12 actually had high sales result. Hence, the posterior probability for high sales is, as calculated, $12/19 = 0.632$.

The posterior probabilities based on survey predictions of "inconclusive" and "failure" can be calculated similarly:

$$P(H|I) = \frac{0.12}{0.47} = 0.255$$

$$P(L|I) = \frac{0.35}{0.47} = 0.745$$

and

$$P(H|F) = \frac{0.06}{0.34} = 0.176$$

$$P(L|F) = \frac{0.28}{0.34} = 0.824$$

These values are also listed in Figure 4–10.

All the necessary information is now available, and Figure 4–10 can be analyzed—starting from the right and working backward. The expected values are shown in the circles. For example, follow out the branches "Take survey," "Survey predicts success," and "Introduce product." The expected value of 1.6 shown in the circle at the end of these branches is calculated as:

$$0.632 \times 3.8 + 0.368 \times (-2.2) = 1.6$$

Figure 4–11   Reduced Part of Decision Tree

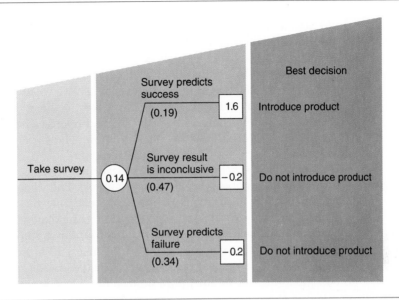

Thus, the firm can expect a profit of $1.6 million if the product is introduced after receiving a survey prediction of success. Since this is better than the $-$0.2 million associated with not introducing the product, the decision to introduce is taken, and the "Do not introduce product" branch is marked with ‖ to indicate it is not optimal.

There are expected losses of $0.67 and $1.14 (including survey costs) if the survey gives inconclusive and failure predictions, respectively. In these cases, it is better *not* to introduce the product, and the "Introduce product" branches are marked with ‖.

The part of the decision tree relating to taking the survey is now reduced to that shown in Figure 4–11. The expected value in the circle node is calculated as:

$$0.19 \times 1.6 + 0.47 \times (-0.2) + 0.34 \times (-0.2) = 0.14$$

Thus, if the survey is taken and the manager acts on the basis of the information received, the expected profit is $0.14 million. Since this is better than the zero profit that would be obtained from not taking the survey, it should be taken. Note that the decision in this case is a *strategy* involving actually two decisions: a decision now to take the survey, and the subsequent decision to introduce the product if the survey predicts success, but not to introduce it otherwise.

The Value of the Survey Information

Taking the survey in the above example is a means of obtaining additional information. The information is not perfect because the survey cannot tell exactly whether the sales will be high or low. The net expected profit from taking the survey was $0.14 million. This included the cost of the survey ($0.2 million); and if we add back this amount, the expected value from the survey will be $0.14 + $0.2 or $0.34 million. We can think of this as the expected profit from a costless survey. Hence, the **value of the imperfect information** obtained from the survey in this situation is $0.34 million. The survey would be worth taking as long as its cost did not exceed this amount.

Recall that earlier in the chapter (page 105) we calculated the expected value of perfect information (EVPI) as $1.2 million. The value of the survey (imperfect information) is substantially below this, reflecting the fact that the survey can give inconclusive or incorrect information as indicated in Table 4–16.

Taking a sample represents a means of obtaining information. This information is imperfect, since the sample is not likely to represent exactly the population from which it is taken. Chapter 8 discusses the reliability of samples and how sampling can be incorporated into the decision-making process.

SUMMARY Decision theory involves the choice of a decision criterion (i.e., a goal)—say, maximize expected profit. If possible and feasible, an experiment is conducted. The prior probabilities of the states of nature are revised, based on the experimental result. The expected profit of each possible decision is computed, and the act with the highest expected profit is chosen as the optimum act.

Before undertaking an experiment, the decision maker must determine whether the expected profit associated with acting after receiving the result of the experiment is sufficiently large to offset the cost of the experiment. The analysis involves finding the optimum rule (which tells what decision to make as a function of the experimental result) and evaluating the expected profit using that rule.

Conclusion

This chapter has been concerned with the use of probabilities in making business decisions under conditions of uncertainty. The criterion of maximization of expected monetary value was developed, and the concept of the value of information was examined. Influence diagrams and decision trees and their uses have been introduced. The value of imperfect information has also been illustrated.

Future chapters will extend many of the ideas introduced in this chapter. Chapter 5 will examine other possible decision criteria and will expand on utility analysis. Chapter 6 will treat decision problems in which uncertainty can be expressed in a continuous probability distribution.

Bibliography

Behn, R. D., and J. W. Vaupel. *Quick Analysis for Busy Decision Makers*. New York: Basic Books, 1982.

Brown, R. V.; A. S. Kahr; and C. Peterson. *Decision Analysis for the Manager*. New York: Holt, Rinehart & Winston, 1974.

Bunn, D. W. *Applied Decision Analysis*. New York: McGraw-Hill, 1984.

Holloway, C. *Decision Making under Uncertainty: Models and Choices*. Englewood Cliffs, N.J.: Prentice Hall, 1979.

McNamee, P., and J. Celona. *Decision Analysis for the Professional with Supertree*. Redwood City, Calif.: Scientific Press, 1987.

Pratt, J. W.; H. Raiffa; and R. Schlaifer. *Introduction to Statistical Decision Theory*. New York: McGraw-Hill, 1965.

Raiffa, H. *Decision Analysis*. Reading, Mass.: Addison-Wesley Publishing, 1968.

Schlaifer, R. *Analysis of Decisions under Uncertainty*. New York: McGraw-Hill, 1969.

Spetzler, C. S., and C. A. Stael von Holstein. "Probability Encoding in Decision Analysis," *Management Science,* November 1975, pp. 340–58.

Spurr, W. A., and C. P. Bonini. *Statistical Analysis for Business Decisions*. Rev. ed. Homewood, Ill.: Richard D. Irwin, 1973.

SRI Decision Analysis Group. *Readings in Decision Analysis*. Menlo Park, Calif.: Stanford Research Institute, 1976.

Vatter, P. A.; S. P. Bradley; S. C. Frey, Jr.; and B. Jackson. *Quantitative Methods in Management: Text and Cases*. Homewood, Ill.: Richard D. Irwin, 1978.

Winkler, R. L. *Introduction in Bayesian Inference and Decision*. New York: Holt, Rinehart & Winston, 1972.

Problems with Answers

4–1. Assume the following conditional value table applies to a decision:

Event	Probability of Event	Conditional Monetary Value of		
		Act 1	Act 2	Act 3
A	0.35	4	3	2
B	0.45	4	6	5
C	0.20	4	6	8

a. Present a table of expected monetary values and determine the optimum act.

b. Present a table of expected opportunity losses.

c. Compute the conditional value table, assuming a perfect predicting device.

d. Compute the expected value assuming a perfect predicting device.

e. Compute the expected value of perfect information.

4–2. A newsstand operator assigns probabilities to the demand for *Fine* magazine:

Event: Demand	Probability of Event
10 copies	0.10
11 copies	0.15
12 copies	0.20
13 copies	0.25
14 copies	0.30
	1.00

Issues sell for 50 cents and cost 30 cents.

a. If the operator *can* return any unsold copies for full credit, how many should be ordered?

b. If the operator *cannot* return unsold copies, how many copies should be ordered?

c. What is the optimum expected profit in (*b*)?

4–3. A manufacturer of hair tonic is considering production of a new hairdressing. The incremental profit is $10 per unit (on a present value basis), and the necessary investment in equipment is $500,000. The estimate of demand is as follows:

Units of Demand	Probability
30,000	0.05
40,000	0.10
50,000	0.20
60,000	0.30
70,000	0.35
	1.00

a. Should the new product be produced? What is the expected profit?

b. What is the expected value of perfect information?

c. How would the expected value of perfect information change if the probability of 30,000 units was 0.10 and the probability of 70,000 units was 0.30?

4–4. The Cooper Cola Company (CCC) must decide which of three products to introduce. Because of a shortage of working capital, only one can be introduced. The marketing manager drew up the decision tree shown in Figure 4–12. Suppose you accept this tree as a reasonable representation of CCC's decision problem, and that CCC is willing to use EMV as the decision criterion.

What is the optimal strategy for CCC, and what is the expected profit of this strategy?

4–5. A company is trying to decide about the size of a new plant currently planned for Atlanta. At present, the company has only a minimal sales effort in the southern states. However, when the Atlanta plant is completed, a major promotion effort will be undertaken. Management is somewhat uncertain about how successful this effort will be. It is estimated that there is a 0.4 chance that the company will capture a *significant* share of the market and a 0.6 chance that only a *moderate* market share will result.

A *large* plant will be needed if a significant market share is realized. A *small* plant would suffice for the moderate case. The cost of the large plant is $8 million; the cost of the small plant, $5 million.

If a significant market share materializes, the estimated present value of resulting profits (excluding cost of the plant) is $13 million; if a moderate share materializes, the present value of the resulting profits (again excluding cost of the plant) is $8 million.

Management has one other alternative. This is to build a small plant, wait to see the result of the promotion effort, and then expand the plant if the situation warrants. It would cost an additional $4.5 million to expand the small plant to the capacity of a large one.

a. Draw a decision tree for this problem.

b. What decision should the company make, and what is the expected value?

4–6. You are charged with the inventory control job in the Volant Manufacturing Company. You think there is about a 0.4 chance of a recession next year. If there is a recession next year, you should sell the AE4 model now for the last-offer price of $1 million because you could get only $800,000 for it in a recession year. These amounts would be received in one year. However, you have a promise from the purchasing agent of a leading company to buy the AE4 for $1.3 million if there is no recession (amount payable one year hence). After some preliminary calculations, you are still undecided about selling and determine to gather evidence about the chances of a recession next year. You discover that bad debts have been rising recently. A little investigation indicates that for the last 10

Figure 4–12   CCC Decision Tree (Problem 4–4)

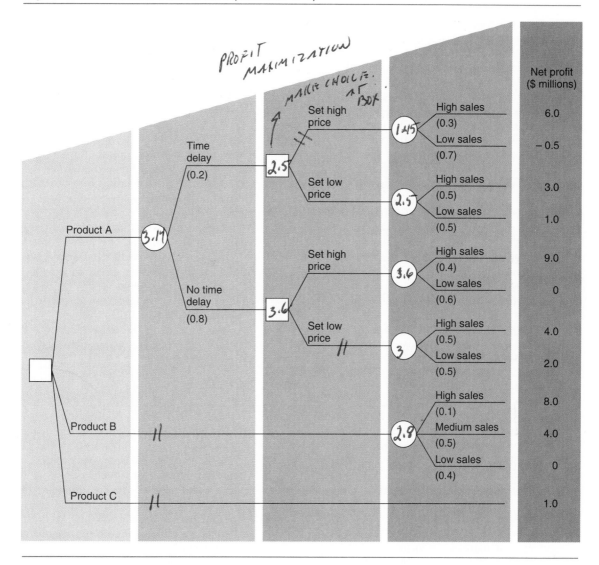

recessions, bad debts started to increase approximately a year early in eight instances. You are willing to accept 0.8 as an estimate of the probability of bad debts rising, given that a recession will occur a year later. In the same sense, you find that

for 10 randomly selected normal years, the economy experienced rising bad debts the previous year in three instances. Thus, you take 0.3 as an estimate of:

P(rising bad debts|no recession next year)

If you revise your prior probabilities as shown in the chapter, what will you do about the AE4?

4–7. The probability of two dice, if they are fair dice, giving either a 7 or an 11, is $\frac{2}{9}$. If the dice are loaded in a certain fashion, the probability of a 7 or an 11 is $\frac{4}{9}$. An acquaintance asks you to play a game with him. If he throws a 7 or an 11, he will collect $3 from you; if not, he will pay you $1. Since the game would give you an advantage if the dice were fair, you have suspicions about your acquaintance. In particular, you feel that there is a 0.7 chance that he is using loaded dice with probability $\frac{4}{9}$ for 7 or 11. To allay your fears, your opponent offers to let you roll the dice twice. You do, and you do not get a 7 or an 11 in either of the two throws.

Should you play the game with your acquaintance? Show your calculations.

4–8. Refer to the example in the chapter as shown in Figure 4–9 and Table 4–16. Suppose the reliability of the market survey was described by the following conditional probabilities:

	Actual Level of Sales	
Survey Prediction	High	Low
Success	0.3	0.2
Inconclusive	0.5	0.5
Failure	0.2	0.3
	1.0	1.0

Assuming all the other information in the example is the same, should the survey be taken?

4–9. Refer to the example in the chapter as shown in Figure 4–10. Assume that the profits are as given in Table 4–15, and the conditional probabilities as given in Table 4–16. However, now assume that management's prior probabilities are 0.5 for high sales and 0.5 for low sales.

a. What is the optimum action before consideration of a survey? What is the expected value of this action?

b. What is the expected value of the survey information?

Problems

4–10. An analysis and forecast of next month's sales results in the following probability distribution:

Event: Demand	Probability
10 units	0.10
11 units	0.70
12 units	0.20
	1.00

The profit per unit is $5. The cost of the product sold is $6. If the product is not sold during the month, it is worthless (leftover units are of no value).

a. Compute the expected (mean) sales for the month.

b. Prepare a table of conditional values for the different possible acts.

c. Prepare a table of expected monetary values, and indicate the optimum act.

4–11. (Continuation of Problem 4–10)

a. Prepare a table of conditional opportunity losses.

b. Prepare a table of expected opportunity losses.

c. Indicate the optimum act.

d. Rank the acts. Show the differences between the expected opportunity losses of each act and the EOL of the optimum act.

e. Rank the acts, using expected values. Show the differences between the

EMV of each act and the EMV of the optimum act. Compare these results with those of (d).

4–12. Refer to Problem 4–10.

a. Present the conditional value table, assuming a perfect predicting device. *3.3*

b. Compute the expected value, assuming a perfect predicting device. *2.8*

c. Compute the expected value of perfect information.

4–13. A manufacturer of sporting goods has the following demand and probability schedule for a yearly fishing guide magazine:

Event: Demand	Probability of Event
100,000	0.20
200,000	0.20
300,000	0.20
400,000	0.20
500,000	0.20
	1.00

The incremental costs of production are $4 per thousand, the selling price is $5 per thousand, and the salvage value of unsold magazines is zero.

a. The manufacturer reasons as follows: "Since there is equal chance of demand being less or greater than 300,000, I shall produce the most likely amount, 300,000." Do you agree? If not, why not?

b. What is the expected value of a perfect prediction?

c. Show that the EMV of each act plus the EOL of each act equals the expected profit with perfect prediction.

4–14. A real estate investor owns a gasoline station she has leased to a major oil company for a rental fee based on a share of profits. If the station is successful, the present value of future rentals is estimated at $1 million. If the station is not successful, the present value of the rent-

als will be $200,000. The oil company has offered the investor $600,000 to buy the property outright. On an expected monetary value basis, what probability would need to be assigned to "success" for the investor to be indifferent between selling and not selling?

4–15. A wholesaler of sporting goods has an opportunity to buy 5,000 pairs of skis that have been declared surplus by the government. The wholesaler will pay $5 a pair, and he can obtain $10 a pair by selling the skis to retailers. The price is well established, but the wholesaler is in doubt as to just how many pairs he will be able to sell. Any skis left over he can sell to discount outlets at $2 a pair. After a careful consideration of the historical data, the wholesaler assigns probabilities to demand as follows:

Retailer's Demand	Probability
1,000 pairs	0.60
3,000 pairs	0.30
5,000 pairs	0.10
	1.00

a. Compute the conditional monetary value of the different possible levels of demand.

b. Compute the expected monetary values.

c. Compute the expected profit with a perfect predicting device.

d. Compute the expected value of the perfect information.

4–16. A bookstore owner can purchase 20,000 of a publisher's leftovers for 50 cents a copy. By making use of advertising in a nationally distributed newspaper, he hopes to be able to sell the books for $2 a copy. Leftover books can be sold at 20 cents a copy to other retailers. His estimate of demand is:

Demand	Probability of Demand
5,000	0.10
10,000	0.50
20,000	0.40
	1.00

Need	Probability
Little	0.2
Medium	0.7
Much	0.1
	1.0

The cost of advertising is $12,000, and incremental costs of shipping the books that are sold are 25 cents per copy.

a. Should the bookstore owner purchase the books?

b. What is the expected profit with a perfect predicting device?

c. What is the maximum amount the owner should pay for perfect information?

4–17. When a new shopping center is built, the electric company must assign a transformer to the location. Since this is done before the occupants of the shopping center are known, there is uncertainty about the amount of electricity to be used (for example, beauty salons use much more electricity than toy stores) and hence, uncertainty about the size of the transformer needed. A too small transformer would have to be replaced, and one too large would result in more expense than necessary. A table giving these costs is shown below:

Amount of Electricity Ultimately needed	Size of Transformer Originally Installed		
	Small	Medium	Large
Little	50	100	150
Medium	140	100	150
Much	190	190	150

Suppose, for a given shopping center, the following probabilities are assigned to the amount of electricity ultimately needed:

a. Draw up an opportunity loss table.

b. What decision should be made? Why?

c. What is the expected value of perfect information?

4–18. Artex Computers has contracted to deliver two model X-60 computer systems to a Japanese university. The terms call for the payment of 150 million Japanese yen to Artex upon delivery of the computers in six months. The current exchange rate is 150 yen to the dollar. However, there is some concern in the financial markets about the future value of the yen. This is reflected in the currency future market in which yen "forward" six months can be bought or sold at the rate of 155 yen to the dollar. In particular, Artex can sell "short" the 150 million yen and receive $967,700 U.S. dollars now. The treasurer of Artex has assigned the following probabilities to the exchange rate for yen in six months:

Exchange Rate (yen per dollar)	Probability
140	0.1
150	0.6
160	0.2
170	0.1
	1.0

a. Assuming that Artex is willing to use EMV as the decision criterion, should it sell the yen short or wait until payment is received in six months?

b. Does EMV appear to be a reasonable criterion in this problem?

4-19. A company owns a lease granting it the right to explore for oil on certain property. It may sell the lease for $15,000, or it may drill for oil. The four possible drilling outcomes are listed below, together with probabilities of occurrence and dollar consequences:

Possible Outcome	Probability	Consequences
Dry well	0.16	– $100,000
Gas well only	0.40	50,000
Oil and gas combination	0.24	100,000
Oil well	0.20	200,000

Draw a decision tree for this problem, and compute the expected monetary value for the act "drill." Should the company drill or sell the lease?

4-20. The ABC Promotion Company has the opportunity to put on a "sure fire" athletic contest. However, if it rains, the game cannot be played. If the game is played, the firm stands to net $2 million. If it rains, the firm stands to lose out of pocket (not opportunity cost) $1 million. There is a 0.2 probability of rain. It wants to know whether or not to buy insurance against rain.

Draw a decision tree. How much could the firm pay for insurance to cover the $1 million loss and be no worse off on an expected value basis than if it did not buy insurance? Should it buy insurance at that price?

4-21. The Plastic Production Company needs to expand its production capacity. This can be done in one of two ways: using overtime in its current plant or leasing another plant. Overtime has a cost penalty (above regular time) of $3 per case of product produced, and can only be used for up to 15,000 cases per year. Leasing another plant would entail an annual fixed leasing cost of $25,000; however the work force of this plant would be paid on a reg-

ular-time basis and could produce any number of cases up to a maximum of 20,000 cases annually.

The company estimates that additional demand (beyond what can be produced in its current plant in regular time) may take on the following values, with corresponding probabilities:

Additional Demand (cases per year)	Probability
5,000	0.3
10,000	0.5
15,000	0.2

a. Draw a decision tree for this problem, and find the optimal decision to minimize expected costs.

b. Suppose a market research company offers to perform a survey to determine the exact quantity of additional demand that will be forthcoming. Should the company be willing to pay $1,000 for such a perfect survey? Why or why not? What is expected opportunity loss (EOL) of the best decision in (a)?

4-22. The QPC Company is deciding whether to market product A or product B. The decision depends upon the speed with which the distributors accept the product and the type of marketing strategy (promotion or advertising) employed by QPC. The company has diagrammed its decision problem as shown in Figure 4–13. The cash flows associated with the various decisions and events are shown at the end of the tree branches. Assume that QPC is willing to use EMV to make this decision.

a. What is the optimal strategy for QPC, and what is the expected cash flow for this strategy?

b. Suppose that QPC had to make a decision about the marketing strategy (promotion or advertising) *before*

Figure 4–13   QPC Decision Tree (Problem 4–22)

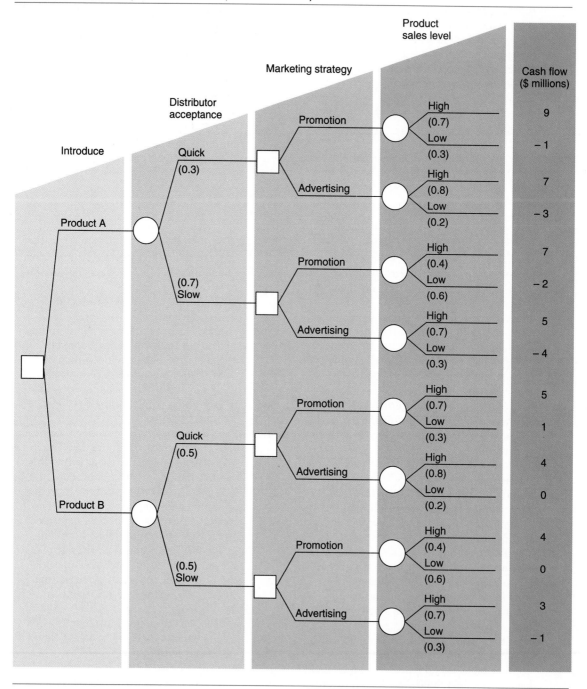

finding out about the speed of the distributors' acceptance. Would this matter, and would the optimal expected cash flow be reduced? Why? Answer without redrawing the tree.

4-23. A camera manufacturer produces two models (standard and deluxe). In preparation for the heavy Christmas selling season, production volumes must be decided upon. Variable cost of the standard camera is $10, and selling price is $20; variable cost of the deluxe model is $20, and selling price is $35. Demand is estimated as follows:

Standard Model		Deluxe Model	
Demand	*Probability*	*Demand*	*Probability*
6,000	0.30	2,000	0.20
8,000	0.70	4,000	0.80

Any cameras not sold during the Christmas season are sold at salvage price of $5 for the standard and $10 for the deluxe model. The manufacturer thinks that different segments of the market purchase the two different models; thus, the probabilities of sales given above are independent.

Suppose production capacity is unlimited. Then the two decisions can be made independently. What are the optimal quantities of each model to produce? What are the two optimal EMVs?

4-24. (Continuation of Problem 4-23) Now suppose that, due to capacity constraints, total production is limited to 10,000 cameras. Construct a decision tree for this situation, and analyze it to obtain optimal production quantities in this case. What is the EMV of the optimal action?

4-25. (Continuation of Problem 4-23) Now suppose that production is limited to a total of 10,000 cameras but that the manufacturer now thinks that the probabilities of demands are *no longer independent* for the two models. Specifically, the accompanying joint probability table describes the probabilities of demands.

Construct a decision tree for this situation, and find the optimal act and its EMV.

4-26. The Oxenol Company uses natural gas in its production-processing operations. Neighboring companies in its upstate New York area have successfully drilled for gas on their premises, and Oxenol is considering following suit. Their initial expenditure would be for drilling; this would cost $40,000. If they struck gas, they would have to spend an additional $30,000 to cap the well and provide for the necessary hardware and control equipment. At the current price of natural gas, if the well is successful it will have a value of $150,000. However, if the price of gas rises to double its current value, a

Joint Probability Table (Problem 4–25)

Standard Demand ╲ Deluxe Demand	2,000	4,000	Marginal Probability of Demand for Standard
6,000	0.20	0.10	0.30
8,000	0	0.70	0.70
Marginal Probability of Demand for Deluxe	0.20	0.80	1.00

successful well will be worth $300,000. The company thinks its chance of finding gas is 30 percent; it also believes that there is a 50 percent chance that the price of gas will double.

a. Draw a decision tree for this problem, filling in the probabilities and values.

b. Complete the tree by calculating EMVs. What should the company do?

4–27. You must bet on a toss of a coin of unknown physical characteristics. The coin is tossed by a machine. The decision you have to make is to bet heads or tails.

Assume that the payoffs are described by the table below:

	You Bet:	
Actual Result	*Heads*	*Tails*
Heads	+100	−100
Tails	−400	+100

Your prior judgment indicates that you believe that there is a one-half chance that the coin to be tossed is fair (i.e., has a 0.5 probability of heads and a 0.5 probability of tails); further, you believe that there is a one-fourth chance that the coin is two-headed (no chance of tail); and finally you believe that there is a one-fourth chance that the coin is two-tailed (no chance of head).

You are given the opportunity to experiment before you bet. The coin will be tossed twice. After observing the results, you will be required to bet either heads or tails on the next toss.

a. Suppose both experimental tosses came up heads. What decision would you make (i.e., what would you bet on the next toss)? What is the expected payoff?

b. Suppose the experimental tosses came out with one head and one tail? What would be your decision? What is the expected payoff?

c. Suppose two tails resulted? What would be your decision? What is the expected payoff?

d. Suppose you had a choice of playing or not playing in this game (before the experimental tosses are flipped). Would you play? What is the expected payoff of playing?

4–28. The UVW Music Company makes music boxes for a variety of toys and miscellaneous products. UVW has a guarantee on its music boxes against breakage for a one-year period.

The sales manager was concerned with the number of music boxes that were being returned under the guarantee. He thought an excessive number of music boxes that fail to last one year would damage the image of a quality product that UVW was trying to achieve. On checking, he found that approximately 5 percent of the music boxes were returned for repair within one year.

The production manager said that the trouble in almost every case was a break in a crucial spring mechanism within the music box. UVW was having trouble obtaining a spring that was entirely satisfactory. There was a special alloy that could be used in the spring and would guarantee virtually no breakage. A spring made of special alloy would cost $2 each as opposed to the cost of 20 cents for the spring currently used. The production manager did not feel the incidence of 1 failure out of 20 warranted using a part 10 times as expensive.

The production manager added that in the music boxes that were returned with a broken spring, the special-alloy spring was used for the repair, so that a second breakage was extremely unlikely. In addition, the cost of handling and repairing a box with a broken spring was $13 plus the $2 for the special-alloy spring.

The sales manager argued that the special-alloy spring should be used in each music box. He felt that in addition to the direct cost of repairing a broken music box, there was a goodwill cost of roughly $5 every time a customer's music box broke.

The decision was not a trivial one, since UVW had estimated sales of 20,000 music boxes over the next year.

a. Which alternative should UVW take?

b. What is the EVPI?

4-29. Refer to Problem 4-28. An alternative action is suggested by the UVW chief engineer. He has been approached by an instrument manufacturer with a test device that could measure the strength of the springs currently used and tell whether each was "strong" or "weak." An experimental program was introduced in which 100 springs were classified as either strong or weak and then put in UVW music boxes. The boxes were then put through a process designed to simulate about one year's wear. The results are shown below:

Results of Test of 100 Springs

Test Device Prediction	Actual Behavior		
	Good	Defective	Total
Strong	79	1	80
Weak	16	4	20
Total	95	5	100

The production manager did not think the test would be useful. He noted that four good springs were rejected for every bad one that was detected. Further, the test did not eliminate all defective springs.

The chief engineer thought the test would be economically feasible. He noted that the cost of the equipment and other costs associated with the test device would amount to about $4,000 for the next year.

The sales manager still preferred using all special-alloy springs but would accept

using the test since, as he noted, it would reduce the number of defectives to about 1 percent.

Should UVW obtain the test device and use it to screen springs?

Hint: Five springs need to be tested to get four that test "strong." Hence the cost of a test "strong" spring is $\frac{5}{4} \times 20¢ = 25¢$.

4-30. A publisher is evaluating a book manuscript written by a young, unknown faculty member. The publisher is considering sending the manuscript out to be reviewed by a team of well-known full professors at other universities. Historical experience comparing the reviewers' evaluations against actual success or failure is as follows:

Outcome Predicted by Reviewers	Actual Outcome	
	Success	Failure
Success	55	45
Failure	50	50

If a book is successful, the profit to the publisher is $50,000; if a failure, the loss to the publisher is $15,000. The cost of sending a manuscript out to the team of reviewers is $2,000.

a. What is the prior probability (before review) that a manuscript will be successful?

b. Draw a decision tree for this problem. Include appropriate values and probabilities. What is the optimal strategy for the publisher? *Hint:* The publisher need not send the manuscript out to review.

4-31. Refer to Problem 4-19. Suppose a test can be made at a cost of $5,000 to determine the type of underground formation (types I, II, or III). The underground formation is related to the type of well, but the relation is imperfect; of 25 wells selected at random from sites near our well, the following table illustrates historical occurrences of well type and underground formation.

Historical Occurrences (25 wells)

Type of Well \ Formation	I	II	III	Total
Dry	4	0	0	4
Gas	1	9	0	10
Gas, oil comb.	0	6	0	6
Oil	0	0	5	5
Total	5	15	5	25

If the test is made, and you subsequently decide not to drill, you can no longer sell the lease for $15,000; your prospective purchasers will conclude that since you decided not to drill, they should not also, so the lease will have zero value after a "test without drill" outcome.

Construct a decision tree for this problem. Should you sell the lease without testing, drill without testing, or test? If you decide to test, under what circumstances will you subsequently drill? What is the maximum EMV?

4–32. A large company may satisfy its fuel-oil requirements either by one annual contract or a series of separate monthly contracts throughout the winter. The cost for the annual contract is $.80 per gallon. If the year is "normal," the cost for the monthly contracts will average $.75 per gallon, while if the year is a "scarce" year with respect to fuel oil, the average cost of the monthly contracts will be $.95 per gallon. The company will use 100,000 gallons during the year, and the manager estimates a $1/10$ chance of a scarce year.

The manager may spend $500 to obtain a professional economic forecast of whether the year will be a normal or scarce one. Data on previous forecasts and actual occurrences for the past 20 years is shown:

Last 20 Years

Actual \ Forecast	Normal	Scarce	Total
Normal	15	3	18
Scarce	0	2	2
Total	15	5	20

Construct a decision tree for this problem. Should the manager purchase the forecast? What is the minimum expected monetary cost?

4–33. The credit card manager of a commercial bank must approve or reject applications for the bank's credit card. She currently uses a "scoring" procedure whereby a series of characteristics stated on an individual's credit card application are weighted by predetermined numerical weights. Based on the total weighted score, an applicant is classified either "good" or "bad" according to whether the score exceeds or falls below the predetermined cutoff score.

Recently, the manager has been considering an alternative procedure whereby an applicant would be rejected if the score fell below a new "low cutoff" score, accepted if the score fell above a new "high cutoff" score, and investigated further if it fell in between. "Further investigation" involves an extensive credit investigation at a cost of $50 each. Available data are as shown in the accompanying tables. (The "Very good" and "Very bad" groups are determined by scoring alone; the other two groups are determined after the credit bureau check.)

The bank has determined that the present value of future *profit* for an applicant who "pays" is $400, and the present value of the *losses* incurred by an applicant who "does not pay" is –$200.

a. Based on the above information, is the proposed system to be preferred to the current system? Why? For 1,000 applicants, what is the maximum EMV in present value terms?

Current System (results for 1,000 applicants) (Problem 4–33)

Current Classification by Scoring Only \ Actual Performance	Pays	Does Not Pay	Total
Good	400	100	500
Bad	*	*	500
Total	*	*	1,000

*Cannot determine payment performance of those applicants whose applications were rejected.

Proposed System (estimated results for 1,000 applicants) (Problem 4–33)

Proposed Classification by Scoring and Credit Check When Indicated \ Actual Performance	Pays	Does Not Pay	Total
Very good (scoring alone)	350	50	400
Good (scoring + check)	150	100	250
Bad (scoring + check)	*	*	50
Very bad (scoring alone)	*	*	300
Total	*	*	1,000

*Cannot determine payment performance of those applicants whose applications were rejected.

b. In order to improve on the current system above, what additional information would you like to have? How might this information be obtained in actual practice?

More Challenging Problems

4–34. The Wheeling Steel Corporation for several years had a PTO (price at the time of order) policy. A firm could order steel for future delivery and pay the price in effect at the time of order rather than at the time of delivery. Comment on this pricing policy.

4–35. Football Concessions had the franchise to sell ice cream, soft drinks, hot dogs, and so on at Wombat University home football games. This was a profitable operation, since crowds could be estimated reasonably accurately and the right amount of food purchased.

However, the November weekend Wombat was due to play its arch rival, Carbunkle U., posed a problem for the concessionnaire. Both teams were undefeated, and the winner was sure to get a Bowl bid. Advance sales of tickets indicated that if the weather was nice, a crowd of more than 80,000 people could be expected. On the other hand, it was raining on Friday, and the weather prediction called for possible showers or rain on Saturday. If the rain was heavy, it was possible that a crowd of only 20,000 would show up for the game.

The concessionnaire had to order his food on Friday. He generally ordered on the basis of $.50 per person, and this had proven reasonably accurate in the past. He had a markup of 100 percent (i.e., selling price was double cost). He could generally save about 20 percent of the value (cost) of anything that he had left over.

The concessionnaire assigned the following probabilities to the various possible crowd sizes. He generally felt that either it would clear up and a large crowd would result, or it would rain and a small crowd be present. The possibility of a medium-size crowd, he believed, was less likely.

Crowd Size	Probability
20,000	0.30
40,000	0.20
60,000	0.10
80,000	0.40
	1.00

How much food should the concessionnaire order?

4–36. Pocatello Potato Products (PPP) buys fresh Idaho potatoes and processes them into frozen french fries and other frozen potato products. PPP buys its potatoes in two ways, by preseason contract and by purchase on the open market. Under a preseason contract, entered into before the crop is planted, the processor (PPP) agrees to buy the crop of a potato grower at an agreed price per hundred-weight (cwt.) of potatoes. For the current season, the preseason contract price is $4 per cwt. Alternatively, PPP can wait until the potato crop has been harvested and buy its potato requirements on the open market at prevailing market prices. In the past few years, market prices of potatoes in Idaho have fluctuated considerably, ranging from $2 to $8 cwt. Previously, PPP has preseason contracted for about half its needs, filling the other half with open market purchases.

The president of PPP is reconsidering this decision. She thinks the preseason contract price of $4 is too high and that there are almost three chances out of four that the market price will be $4 or less. In fact, she has carefully assessed a probability distribution for possible open-market prices of potatoes:

Open Market Price ($ per cwt.)	Probability
$2.50	0.02
3.00	0.10
3.50	0.40
4.00	0.20
4.50	0.12
5.00	0.06
5.50	0.04
6.00	0.03
6.50	0.02
7.00	0.01
	1.00

Because of other requirements (storage space, etc.), PPP does not wish to have less than 30 percent of its requirements preseason contracted, nor more than 70 percent. Next year, PPP will need 2 million cwt. of potatoes for processing. Assuming that PPP wishes to minimize the expected cost of potato purchases, how much should they preseason contract? What do you recommend to the president of PPP?

4–37. A chemical company is building a plant to market Agrixon, a new chemical used primarily in agriculture. The firm is uncertain about the demand for Agrixon during the initial year of sales. However, the following probability distribution was assessed.

Demand for Agrixon for Initial Year (kilograms)	Probability
800	0.2
1,000	0.4
1,200	0.3
1,400	0.1
	1.0

Agrixon is produced on a special-purpose machine. Each such machine has a yield of 200 kilograms of Agrixon per year. The fixed cost of purchasing and operating one machine is $560,000 per year, which includes supervision, maintenance, and other fixed charges, plus annualized interest and equipment costs. Suppose the profit from one year's production of one machine (not including fixed costs) is $1.3 million, assuming demand is sufficient to run the machine for the entire year.

The problem facing the chemical company is to decide how many machines to install in the plant for the first year. The second and subsequent years pose little problem, because the firm is able to buy additional machines if needed, and any unused capacity can be absorbed in future years as sales grow.

How many machines should the firm install to maximize expected net profit in the first year?

4–38. Little Electronics Company has initiated an antitrust and unfair trade practices lawsuit against Artex Computers, asking a settlement of $10 million in damages. On November 4, Little receives an offer from Artex to settle the suit for a payment to Little of $3.5 million.

The management at Little is trying to decide whether to accept the settlement or to proceed with the suit. The lawyers agree that the chances are about 2 in 3 that Little will win. They point out, however, that even if Little wins the suit, the chances are only about 1 in 2 that the judge will award the full $10 million; he is equally likely to grant a partial settlement of $5 million. The lawyers further estimate it will cost about $200,000 in legal fees between November and June (when the case is scheduled to be heard), plus another $100,000 in legal fees to try the case (which is expected to last three months).

In making the offer for the $3.5 million settlement, Artex stressed that it was a "final offer," and that the offer would be good for only 30 days. However, Little management and lawyers agree that Artex will probably make a new offer in June, just before the trial begins. After some thought, it is decided that 0.60 is a good estimate of the probability of a new Artex offer in June. And if there is a new offer, the chances are 7 in 10 that it will be $4.5 million and 3 in 10 for a $5.5 million settlement.

If Artex makes no last minute offer in June, Little itself can initiate a settlement. In this case, Little will have to settle for $2.5 million, because Artex will interpret the action as weakness in Little's case.

Diagram the decision problem facing Little Electronics. Assuming Little is willing to use EMV in making this decision, what strategy should be used?

4-39. In early January, Etta Laboratories received an order for 10,000 ounces of its new product, Calbonite, an ingredient used to manufacture a new variety of drugs. This was by far the largest order ever received for Calbonite—total production in the previous year had been only 1,200 ounces. The order called for 5,000 ounces to be delivered in June and the remainder in November.

The process now used to synthesize Calbonite was a long one, involving processing small batches of raw material through several stages. The company would have to invest $50,000 in new equipment to bring the production capacity up to the 1,000 ounces per month level needed to meet the order. (It would take the month of January to order and set up the equipment.) The variable manufacturing cost per ounce using this process was known to be $15.

One of the research chemists at Etta had just discovered a new process for synthesizing Calbonite. If the process could be made to work on a large scale, it would greatly simplify the production process, with potentially great savings in cost. Ordinarily, a discovery of this sort would be tested thoroughly in the laboratory and in a small pilot plant to be sure it worked and to estimate production costs. This would take about a year. However, because of the potential savings, management wondered if it should shorten this test period. The engineering department suggested a crash testing program lasting five months. At the end of this period, it would be known whether or not the process would work, and estimated production costs would be determined. This test would cost $20,000 more than the more extended test.

It was estimated that there was a 0.9 chance the new process would work. Further, given that the new process worked, the chances were 4 out of 10 that the production cost would be $2 per ounce, 4 out of 10 that it would be $10 per ounce, and 2 out of 10 that it would be $18 per ounce.

If a decision was made at this stage to use the new process, the month of June would be used to set up the new manufacturing process. Thus, if this testing program were utilized, the company would have to set up and run the first 5,000 ounces using the old process.

Also, note that only the incremental testing costs associated with crashing the test program need to be charged against that alternative. Since this company would test and buy the equipment for the new process if the tests were successful independent of this decision, the costs associated with these activities need not be considered in this decision.

a. Draw a decision tree for this problem

b. What decisions should be made? What is the expected cost of filling this order?

4-40. Mary Lamb is trying to decide what to do about an apartment building she inherited from her great aunt in Walla Walla. If she were to sell it today, she could get $100,000. Since Mary doesn't need the money immediately, she is considering holding on to the property for sale later.

Suppose Mary can sell the building now, at the end of next year (year 1), or at the end of the following year (year 2). She has decided not to keep it more than two years.

For each year that Mary keeps the building, she receives $5,000 in rents (actually, rent less operating costs). Mary consults with the local Walla Walla real estate gurus and then assesses the following probabilities about increases or decreases in the value of the property: During each year (year 1 and year 2) there is a 20 percent chance that the value of the building will increase by $10,000 and an 80 percent chance that the value will decrease by $10,000 (things are a little unsettled in Walla Walla). These are the *overall* probabilities for *each* year.

However, what happens in the first

year and the second are not independent. Mary believes that if the value increases in the first year, then there is a 60 percent chance that the value will also increase in the second year. Of course, if the value decreases in the first year, there are corresponding changes in the second year probabilities, subject to the overall probabilities mentioned above.

As a first-cut analysis, Mary decides to consider only the amount received from selling the building (including the increases or decreases in value, if any) plus the amount received for rent. (Do not worry about discounting or taxes or other complications.)

a. Diagram the decision problem facing Mary. Include payoff values at the ends of the tree and probability values where appropriate.

b. What decision should Mary make?

c. (Optional.) Assume a discount rate of 15 percent. What decision should Mary make? (With a discount rate of 15 percent, cash flows received at the end of year 1 are worth $1/1.15 = 0.87$ present value dollars; cash flows received at the end of year 2 are worth 0.76 present value dollars.)

4–41. The example on pp. 101–11 used a situation that is typical of those encountered by business managers. What difficulties are encountered in applying the model described in a normal business situation?

4–42. Artex Computers is going to purchase 10,000 units of a certain part that is to be assembled into the Artex products. The order is to be placed with the lowest bidder, with the 10,000 units to be delivered at a rate of 1,000 per month over the next 10 months.

The Frank Machine Shop (FMS) is considering bidding on this order. Two factors are puzzling Mr. Frank in his attempts to fix a bid price. The first factor deals with FMS's chances of winning the bid. Mr. Frank finally decides to consider only two bids—either $12 per unit or $13 per unit. He estimates that the chances are two thirds of winning at the former

price and one third of winning at the latter price.

The second factor involved in the decision is the FMS unit manufacturing cost. Two production processes are available. The first, process A, is known to cost $10 per unit. The second, process B, is one that FMS has not used before. The chief supervisor says that there is a one-fourth chance that the per unit cost will be $9; a one-half chance that the cost will be $10; and a one-fourth chance that the cost will be $11, if process B is used.

The chief supervisor has suggested that she conduct an experiment with the new process (B). She could produce 10 or 15 units; and from the experience gained, she believes she could estimate unit cost "pretty well." The cost of this test would be $500. When asked to be more specific about how accurate the estimate of cost would be, the chief supervisor provided the table below.

Mr. Frank is not sure that this information is at all relevant to his problem. The controller has argued that the test suggested may be valuable but should be performed after the bid is awarded. Otherwise, he argues, the firm may spend $500 and then not win the contract. The supervisor believes the test should be done before the bid, since it may influence FMS's bid price.

What actions should FMS take? What is the expected profit?

Chances of Various Estimated Costs

Supervisor's Estimated Cost	Actual per Unit Cost		
	$9	$10	$11
$ 9	0.8	0.1	0.1
10	0.1	0.8	0.1
11	0.1	0.1	0.8
	1.0	1.0	1.0

4–43. The Breezy Breakfast Foods Company is considering marketing a new breakfast cereal. If the new cereal is successful, it will mean a $10 million profit (present value) over the life of the product. If unsuccessful, a $2 million loss on investment will be incurred. Management currently thinks there is a 50–50 chance that the product will be successful.

Two market research firms have approached Breezy with proposals to obtain more information. Attitude Surveys collects data on consumer attitudes with respect to specific characteristics of a product, such as sweetness, caloric content, nutritive value, and so on, and produces a forecast of "success" or "fail." Of the 50 studies this company has performed on similar products recently, their experience has been as follows:

Attitude Surveys Experience

Forecast	Actual Outcome	Success	Failure
Success		20	5
Failure		5	20

A second company, Market Competition Inc., performs analysis in an entirely different, independent manner. This company performs extensive analysis on competitive products, and produces a recommendation of "success" or "fail" based on the anticipated amount and quality of competitive products. Their experience with 50 studies has been as follows:

Market Competition Experience

Forecast	Actual Outcome	Success	Failure
Success		22	3
Failure		0	25

Attitude Surveys charges $100,000 per survey, and Market Competition charges $150,000.

a. Consider only Attitude Surveys. Use a decision tree to decide whether or not Breezy should purchase this survey.
b. Consider only Market Competition, Inc. Use a decision tree to decide whether or not Breezy should purchase this survey.

4–44. The MBA Movie Studio is trying to decide how to distribute its new movie *Claws*. The movie has the potential of being a great financial success (a "smash"), but the executives are not sure because the subject is controversial. And they have seen some films heralded as "smashes" become "flops" with disastrous financial consequences.

The decision facing MBA is whether or not to put out the movie *Claws* on a limited first run basis. This means that the movie will show only in a few select theaters during the first six months. After six months, it will be released generally. If the movie turns out to be a success, this is clearly the best approach because the studio makes considerable profit from these select theaters.

The other alternative is to release the film for wide distribution immediately.

The profits for the two alternatives are given in the table on the adjacent page, classified in terms of whether the film is a "Smash," "Medium" success, or "Flop."

There is considerable discussion in MBA about the potential of *Claws*. Management has finally agreed on the probabilities shown in the table, but which decision to make is still not clear. One possibility is to have a few sneak previews of the movie and get the audience's opinions. The cost of such a process would be about $50,000, and several executives in the company think it would be money wasted, since sneak preview audiences tend to rate a movie as good or outstanding even when it later turns out to be a flop. To support this, the following table was produced, describing the company's past experience with 40 sneak preview audience reactions.

Profits from Film *Claws*

Level of Success	Probability	Actions	
		Limited Initial Release	*Widespread Release*
Smash	0.3	$22 million	$12 million
Medium	0.4	8	8
Flop	0.3	−10	−2
	1.0		

Sneak Preview Audience Reaction

Audience Rating	Movie's Actual Success			
	Smash	*Medium*	*Flop*	*Totals*
Outstanding	9	12	3	24
Good	1	6	5	12
Poor	0	2	2	4
Totals	10	20	10	40

a. Draw the decision tree for this problem.

b. Calculate the posterior probabilities for "Smash," "Medium," and "Flop," given the various audience reactions.

c. Assume that MBA is willing to base its decision on expected monetary value. What decision should the MBA Movie Studio make about the movie *Claws?*

Case 4–45

Susan Parks, chief analyst for the state Department of Forests, is formulating a recommendation to the governor about the proposed Wabash ski area. The department had originally proposed a full-scale ski resort, but due to gasoline shortages, inflation, and other factors, the original estimates about the number of people using the resort have been questioned. Two other alternatives have also been proposed. One alternative is to build a smaller facility and expand it in two years if demand justifies it. The other alternative is to postpone the whole project for two years. Ms. Parks has collected estimates of costs, revenues, and probabilities concerning the various alternatives.

It will cost $15 million to build a full-sized facility all at one time. If a smaller facility is built and later expanded, it will cost $12 million to build the smaller initial part and $6 million to expand it later. Parks has decided to use three levels of potential demand for skiing at Wabash: high, medium, and low. The costs and revenues for these cases are shown in the table of estimates on page 132. The Department of Forests uses a measure of benefits in evaluating this type of project. The benefits measure includes revenues and costs in dollars, but also includes a value for the recreation benefits provided by the facility (at a rate of $1 per visitor day).

After consulting with her colleagues, Parks estimates that there is a 0.10 chance that demand in the *next two years* will be high, 0.60 for medium demand, and 0.30 for low demand. Demand beyond the second year depends on what occurs during the first two years. These probabilities have also been assessed and are shown in the table at the bottom of the page.

Consider a 15-year period for evaluating this project, and calculate the total 15-year net benefits. Do not include any allowance for inflation, discounting, or growth in demand other than what is indicated in the above tables. Assume that at the end of two years, the Department of Forests will be able to evaluate demand over the subsequent 13 years with certainty. Finally, assume that the department is willing to use expected net benefits as a criterion in making its recommendation to the governor.

a. Diagram this decision problem as a decision tree.
b. Fill in the probabilities and benefits in the tree.
c. What recommendation should be made to the governor?

Estimates of Visitor Days and Costs for Wabash Area

	Annual Visitor Days (000s)	Annual Revenue from Leases and Concessions ($000s)	Fixed Costs ($000s)	Net Revenue ($000s)	Weighted Net Benefits* ($000s)
Large-scale facility					
High demand	800	$2,400	$700	$1,700	$2,500
Medium demand	500	1,600	700	900	1,400
Low demand	200	600	700	−100	100
Smaller-scale facility					
High demand	500	$1,600	$400	$1,200	$1,700
Medium demand	400	1,000	400	600	1,000
Low demand	200	600	400	200	400

*Weighted net benefits includes both dollar revenue and visitor days valued at one dollar per day.

Probabilities for Demand at Wabash Facility beyond Year 2

Demand up to Year 2	Demand beyond Year 2	Probability
High	High	1.0
Medium	High	$\frac{1}{3}$
	Medium	$\frac{1}{2}$
	Low	$\frac{1}{6}$
Low	High	$\frac{1}{6}$
	Medium	$\frac{1}{3}$
	Low	$\frac{1}{2}$

Case 4–46

In June 1992, the managing director of Particular Motors, an Australian automobile manufacturer, is considering the future of the Torana model. Currently, the Torana is offered with a choice of an L4 engine (four cylinder imported from Germany), or an L6 or V8 engine, both manufactured in Australia. A major face-lift of this model is scheduled for release to the public in February 1995. A major decision involves whether or not Particular Motors should build its own L4 engine in Australia.

Australia, as elsewhere, is faced with an energy crisis. Under serious consideration by the government in Canberra is a law mandating a substantial increase in the price of gasoline. Such an increase in gasoline cost would lead to greater sales of the Torana with the smaller L4 engine, and reductions in sales of the Torana with the L6 and V8 engines. Three possible prices for gasoline may be set by the government—$1.10, $1.35, or $1.60 per gallon. The sales department estimates sales of the three models over the three-year period 1995–97 as follows (after 1997, there will be a new face-lift for the Torana):

Gasoline Price	Total Three-Years' Sales of Torana with:			
	L4 Engine	L6 Engine	V8 Engine	Total
$1.10	25,000	75,000	20,000	120,000
1.35	80,000	75,000	15,000	170,000
1.60	120,000	50,000	10,000	180,000

The contribution for each type of car is:

Model	Profit Contribution per Car
Torana with imported L4 engine	$100
Torana with Australian L4 engine	300
Torana with L6	350
Torana with V8	400

The public relations expert in Canberra is asked about the outlook for fuel prices. After serious consideration, the following probabilities are assessed:

Gasoline Price ($ per gallon)	Probability
$1.10	0.10
1.35	0.50
1.60	0.40
	1.00

A complicating factor in the decision about building the L4 engine in Australia is the possibility of passage by the government of a Local Content Bill. This bill, if passed, would force Toyota and Nissan to increase the local content of their Australian-assembled cars, and this means buying an Australian model L4 engine. There is a 60 percent chance this bill will pass, and Particular Motors would then negotiate a contract with Nissan and Toyota (assuming, of course, that it had decided to produce the L4 engine in Australia) to get the Japanese business of 100,000 L4 engines over the 1995–97 period. The contribution of each engine sold to the Japanese is expected to be $100.

In order to set up the manufacture of the Australian L4 engine, Particular Motors must commit $4 million dollars in 1992 (before the fuel price or the Local Content Bill decision is known) to build the main transfer line for the engine block. The completion of the production facility will require an additional $14 million, but this can be postponed until after the government decides about the fuel price and on whether or not to pass the Local Content Bill.

To meet the requirements for the Japanese contracts, additional investment will be required. This can be done in one of two ways. A $1 million investment now will incorporate the necessary requirements into the production system, and an additional $1 million will be required when the production system is completed later. Alternatively, the production system can be modified later (after learning about fuel prices and the Local Content Bill), but to do it at that time would require $4 million.

a. Draw up the decision tree facing Particular Motors.
b. Include only the *incremental cash flows* associated with the L4 engine decision.
c. Include the probabilities on the tree.
d. Find the optimal strategy for Particular Motors. What is the expected incremental cash flow?

Hint: To simplify the tree slightly, note that the Japanese contract will be undertaken regardless of fuel price, if the Local Content Bill passes and if, of course, Particular decides to make an Australian L4 engine.

Case 4–47

You, the manager of an automotive assembly plant, are one hour into the day shift when informed of a potential problem by your supervisor of materials control. The supervisor informs you that at hour 4, because of shipping delays, the assembly line will run out of hood-release assemblies. Two orders of hood-release assemblies are in transit, and the supervisor has traced them. The arrival of either order would solve the shortage. There is some chance (2 in 10) that the first order will arrive at hour 5; otherwise, it will arrive after the shift is over. The second order has a good chance of arriving today (6 out of 10 chances overall of arriving at hour 6); otherwise, it also arrives after the shift ends. However the chances of arrival of the two orders are not independent, since the weather is affecting both. You estimate that if the first order arrives on time (at hour 5), there is a 0.9 chance that the second order will also arrive on time (at hour 6).

You must make a decision about what to do when the shortage occurs. You have three options: (1) shut down the line and send the workers home; (2) substitute a similar part from another model; (3) assemble the cars without the hood release, and mount it tomorrow off-line. There are costs to each of these options. If you shut down the line, the production of 50 cars per hour will be lost. Your contract with the union would allow you to send home the workers without having to pay them (after they had worked four hours). However, the plant is on a tight schedule, and the lost production would have to be made up on overtime. The cost of this is $40 per car.

Substituting the hood release from a similar model also has possible limitations. The substitute release costs the same and appears to work equally well, but the substitution must be approved by the Product Engineering Committee back in Detroit. Such approval could not be obtained until tomorrow. However, you could go ahead and use the substitute hood release. If approval came through, there would be no additional cost; if approval was denied, tomorrow you would have the substitute hood release removed and the proper one installed. This would cost $120 per car. You estimate that there is a 0.6 chance that the Product Engineering Committee would approve the substitution.

The third option involves assembling the cars without any hood release and mounting it tomorrow after the parts arrive. This is done off-line, and the cost is $60 per car.

The accompanying diagram summarizes the situation. Some additional assumptions: You can shut down the plant at any time (i.e., at hour 4, or hour 5, or hour 6); however, once shut down, it stays down for the remainder of the shift. Suppose also, that once you start with either alternative, using the substitute part or not using the part, that you will continue with that alternative until either the new parts arrive or you shut down. (This would rule out, for example, using the substitute part at hour 4, and the no-part alternative at hour 5.)

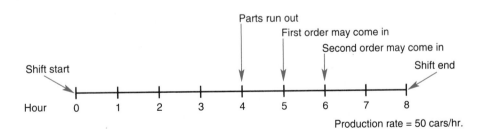

a. Diagram the decision problem described above. Include all allowable branches and decision alternatives.

b. Show the costs as end values at the *end* of the tree.

c. Show the probabilities on the tree.

d. What decisions should be made to minimize the expected cost?

Case 4–48

It is 7 P.M. on Christmas Eve at the Emergency Control Center at Telco, the San Francisco Bay Area telephone company. Larry Nettles, the manager on duty, has received several reports from Operator Services that customers are having difficulty making calls out of their local dialing areas. Checking his diagnostic printouts from key switching offices, Larry confirms what he has dreaded most—the trouble is in one of the three marine cable routes crossing San Francisco Bay.

With marine cables, it is necessary to identify as quickly as possible which one is causing the trouble and to isolate the troubled location. Only after this is done can the calls be rerouted. The only way to identify which of the three cables is at fault (and where) is to dispatch a tugboat and crew to examine each cable at selected intervals and isolate the problem. This search process has to be done on a trial and error basis, one cable at a time.

Telco has prepared for such an emergency. A detailed study has been made of the three cables, and how likely trouble might occur. The study took into account the length of the cable route, the age of the cable, and the number of shipping lanes crossed by the cable. Based upon this data, Telco assessed the probabilities of cable troubles as follows (we will assume that the probabilities for two or three cables being in trouble simultaneously are zero):

Cable	Location	Probability of Trouble
Cable 1	San Francisco/Oakland	0.3
Cable 2	Sausalito/Oakland	0.5
Cable 3	Hayward/San Francisco	0.2

The above probabilities imply, for example, that if there is a cable in trouble, it is more than twice as likely that it is in cable 2 rather than in cable 3.

Studies are also available that indicate the number of calls over each cable and the revenue generated from these calls. Christmas Eve is of course the peak time for calls, and revenue losses will be significant if Telco fails to quickly isolate a troubled cable. These are estimated to be:

Cable	Revenue Losses ($000s per hour)
Cable 1	$ 28
Cable 2	90
Cable 3	120

To locate the malfunctioning cable, the Emergency Control Center has to dispatch a tugboat and crew, at a cost of $1,000 per hour. Only one tug is available. The crew has to examine each cable in turn until the faulty one is isolated. The Emergency Center's decision problem is to tell the crew in which order to search.

Past experience indicates that if a cable were defective, it would take the crew one hour to isolate the defective location, and rerouting procedures could begin immediately thereafter. However, if a cable were not defective, it would take the crew two hours to check it out completely before moving on to the next cable. For example, if cable 3 were actually the defective one, but the crew examined cable 1 first, then cable 2 before going on to cable 3, the total search time would be five hours (two hours to check out cable 1 as OK, two hours to check out cable 2 as OK, and 1 hour to isolate the trouble in cable 3).

a. Draw a decision tree that would help the Emergency Center manager decide about the order in which the tug crew should examine the cables. Include probabilities in your tree. (In the cases where a cable has been searched and found not defective, assume that the *relative* probabilities for the other two are not changed.) Include the evaluation units (payoffs) at the end of branches of your decision tree. Assume that Telco is willing to use the total cost (revenue lost plus tug and crew cost) as the relevant payoff measure.

b. What search strategy should Telco use?

CHAPTER 5

Decision Theory

We shall define decision theory as being primarily concerned with how to assist people (or organizations) in making decisions and improving the decision process under conditions of uncertainty. Decision theory enables the decision maker to analyze a set of complex situations with many alternatives and many different possible consequences. The major objective is to identify a course of action consistent with the basic economic and psychological desires of the decision maker. Chapter 4 also dealt with decision theory but did not consider decision criteria different from the maximization of expected monetary value.

Business managers frequently deal with complicated decisions by assuming certainty. That is, the data that go into the computations are assumed to be known without question; or at most, a disclaiming statement is made, such as "Of course, the facts are not known with certainty." This approach is reasonable for many decisions. Decision making, even under certainty, can be complex. It may be desirable to start with the situation where the facts are assumed to be known. Many conventional solutions offered to such problems as inventory control, "make or buy," capital budgeting, and pricing assume certainty.

In this chapter we shall continue to discuss the art of decision making under uncertainty. The major focus will be on what **decision criterion** should be used: that is, how the decision maker should select the right course of action. In Chapter 4, we assumed that the expected value criterion was the appropriate one. In this and the following chapter, we consider alternative criteria. It will become obvious that absolutely correct answers are difficult to find when the future is uncertain, but that there are some reasonable approaches to this class of decision problems that should be understood by the manager.

The Decision Problem

We shall consider in this chapter a relatively common type of decision. There will be several possible acts and several possible states of nature. For example, the possible acts may be:

138

1. To decide the number of units of inventory to order.
2. To buy or not to buy fire insurance.
3. To make or to buy a product.
4. To invest or not to invest in a piece of equipment.
5. To add or not to add to a new product line.
6. To change the price or not to change the price of a product (and if so, the amount of the change).

By states of nature, we mean the actual possible events that may occur. One of the possible states of nature is the true state, but we do not know which one. Possible states of nature or events for each of the above acts are:

1. Demand for the product may be 0, 1, 2, 3, . . . , 50.
2. A fire may occur, or a fire may not occur.
3. If we make the product, the cost of making it may be 10 cents, 11 cents, . . . , 50 cents.
4. If we invest in the equipment, its cost saving per hour may be $1.00, $1.01, $1.02, . . . , $2.50.
5. If we add a new product line, the sales may be 1 million, 2 million, and so on.
6. If we change the price, the unit sales may be 0, 1, 2, 3, . . . , 10,000.

Not knowing which of the states of nature is the true state, we place a *probability distribution* on the possible occurrence of each event (we can have as fine a breakdown as we wish of the possible states). The probability distribution could be based on objective evidence of the past if the decision maker feels the same forces will continue to operate in the future. However, we are not restricted to objective probabilities. It may be reasonable to assign the probabilities that the decision maker thinks appropriate to the possible states of nature, so that the act chosen may be consistent with the beliefs held about the possible events and the economic consequences of those events. To the extent possible, objective evidence should be supplied to help the decision maker improve the assignment of probabilities.

An Example To illustrate the discussion, we shall develop an example. This is a basic inventory decision problem, similar to the type already introduced in Chapter 4. The problem is to determine how many units to order. The price of the product is $5, the cost is $3, and profit per unit is $2. Unsold units have no salvage value. The possible states of nature (possible demands) and their probabilities are as shown in Table 5–1.

The possible acts are to buy zero, one, or two units (it would be unreasonable to buy three, because the probability of selling three or more units is zero). The possible states of nature are that the amount demanded will be zero, one, or two units. The first step in obtaining a solution is to prepare a table (see Table 5–2) showing the profits that will result from each combination of act and state of nature. We have called this a *conditional profit or payoff* table. The profits are conditional on choosing a specific act and having a given state of nature come

Table 5-1

Demand	Probability
$q_1 = 0$	0.05
$q_2 = 1$	0.60
$q_3 = 2$	0.35
	1.00

Table 5-2 **Conditional Profit Table**

	Act		
State of Nature— Demand Is:	d_1 Buy 0	d_2 Buy 1	d_3 Buy 2
$q_1 = 0$	0	-3	-6
$q_2 = 1$	0	2	-1
$q_3 = 2$	0	2	4

true; the symbolic representation of an entry is $R(q_i, d_j)$. Thus, $R(q_2, d_3)$ would be the profit of decision d_3 if the state of nature is q_2. In this case, $R(q_2, d_3) = -1$.

The decision to be made is whether zero, one, or two units should be ordered. It is not obvious how many units should be ordered. The solution to even this relatively simple problem is complex; in fact, it is not clear what the answer "should" be. We shall now introduce several possible decision criteria.

Decision Criteria

Listed below are some possible decision criteria:

1. Assuming **equally likely** events. Choose the d_j that maximizes:

$$\frac{1}{n} [R(q_1, d_j) + R(q_2, d_j) + R(q_3, d_j)]$$

where n is the number of possible events (state of nature); here, $n = 3$.
2. Selecting the act that maximizes the maximum possible profit, the **maximax** procedure.
3. Maximizing the minimum possible profit, the **maximin** procedure (or minimizing the maximum possible cost, the **minimax** procedure).
4. Basing the decision on the profits of the event with the **maximum likelihood** of occurring.

5. Using the **expected value decision rule:** Multiply the consequences of each act by the probabilities of the several occurrences, and sum the products. The act with the largest expected value is the most desirable decision.
6. Selecting an act that **dominates** other possible acts.
7. Selecting an act that has the **highest expected utility.**

The first four criteria listed are less desirable, and we shall shortly discuss the reasons for this. The last three criteria are reasonable; the choice of which to use depends on the circumstances. We shall discuss the first six criteria in this chapter; the expected utility criterion is the subject of Chapter 6.

The type of decision being studied here may be described as a game against nature. It should be remembered that nature does not think and plot against its opponent. Criteria that may be completely reasonable in competitive situations (such as minimax) are less reasonable in a game against nature. This distinction is important, since the criticism that follows applies only in decisions involving nature, not in decisions involving a thinking opponent.

We shall assume in all of the discussion that the decision maker is willing to use money to measure the outcomes. This, of course, is not true in many decision situations. In deciding what job to take, for example, you probably would consider how challenging the job is, as well as the salary offered. This is an example of a multiattribute decision problem, and problems such as these are considered in Chapter 6.

Equally Likely

This procedure suggests that we add the possible consequences of each act and divide by the number of possible events. The act with the highest value under the equally likely assumption would be the most desirable act under this criterion. If we know little about the probability of the possible events, some would argue that we should then assume that each event is equally likely. However, it is rare that we do not have *some* idea about the probability of possible events. These probabilities, which may or may not be based on objective evidence, should be used in the analysis if our action is to be consistent with our judgment. Automatically assuming the events are equally likely will not ensure such consistency if we feel one event is more likely to occur than another. For example, in the present problem, a specific probability distribution is given (see Table 5-1). There is no reason to assume that there is equal probability that each event will occur.

As long as it is thought appropriate to use probabilities, and where there is no reason to assume the probabilities of the states of nature are equally likely, then the best estimate of the probabilities should be used, rather than the "equally likely" assumption.

Maximax

Maximax suggests that the decision maker should look for the largest possible profit for each act and choose the act that has the highest profit. This is a go-for-it strategy; it looks only at the highest possible gain and ignores the chances and consequences for other events that might occur. In our example (Table 5–2), the maximax criterion would select "Buy 2," since it offers a possible profit of $4. It ignores the possibility that this might lead to a loss of $6.

The maximax criterion is not a prudent decision rule. There are some circumstances when we may wish to take prudent risks—but we should do so fully aware of the chances and consequences of what might happen. The expected utility approach of the next chapter does include these factors in making a decision.

Minimax

Minimax suggests that we choose the act with the smallest maximum possible loss or, alternatively, with the largest minimum possible profit. That is, we should make sure that we can earn at least R dollars, and search for the act that gives the largest R (or the smallest loss, if we are discussing losses).

In the example, the minimax act would be to order zero units. The maximum possible loss with zero units is zero dollars; with the other two acts, the maximum losses are $3 and $6.

Unless there is zero probability of loss, minimax tends to lead to a decision to do nothing. It is a very conservative decision criterion. Ultimately, a minimaxer would be faced with the threat of starving to death (by doing nothing) and would be forced into action. In terms of business activity, the corporation would become stagnant and would be overcome by competition willing to innovate and to take reasonable chances of suffering losses.

In some situations, minimax may lead to a totally unreasonable decision. For example, assume Table 5–3 shows the conditional costs associated with the only two possible acts. "Buy insurance" is the best act according to minimax, since the maximum cost is $100 (the maximum cost of "Do not buy" insurance is $101). However, if the two given states of nature are equally likely, or if state q_2 is more likely than state q_1, then most individuals would label "Do not buy" as being the most desirable act. Minimax is not a desirable strategy in games against nature, but is useful against thinking opponents.

Table 5–3   Conditional Cost Table

State of Nature	Act	
	Buy Insurance	Do Not Buy
q_1	$100	$101
q_2	100	1

Maximum Likelihood

Using the **maximum-likelihood** decision criterion procedure, we consider only the consequences of the state of nature *most likely* to occur, and choose the best act for that state of nature. In the example being considered, this is state "demand is one," leading to a decision to order one unit. This is a reasonable decision in the present context, but it might not always be so. For example, assume the probability of demand being one is 0.51 and demand being two is 0.49. Now it is not clear that to order one is the best decision. To add further evidence that the maximum-likelihood decision may be faulty, reduce the loss on a leftover unit (increase the salvage value) so that there is no penalty connected with leftovers. With the 0.49 probability of selling the second unit, ordering two is a better decision.

Since the maximum-likelihood criterion ignores the consequences of all states except the state with the highest probability, it fails to make use of much of the information available to the decision maker. By failing to make use of this information, it can arrive at decisions that may not be reasonable.

Expected Value Decision Rule

With the **expected value decision rule,** already introduced in Chapter 4, we compute the expected value of each act (multiply the conditional profit by the probability of the state of nature, and sum the products for each state) and take the act with the largest expected monetary value; i.e., maximize EMV.

The expected values of the three acts from Table 5–2 are computed as shown in Table 5–4. The act with the highest expected value is "Buy 1"; thus, we should buy one unit. If the probabilities were changed, or if the conditional profits were different because of changes in price, costs, or salvage value, the expected value would be recomputed, with a possible change in decision.

In practice, the inventory problem is not solved using the payoff table and computing the expected value of each possible act. However, the procedures used are based on the above analysis. That is, conventional inventory procedure assumes it is appropriate to use the expected value decision rule. (See Chapter 17.)

Table 5–4   Computation of Expected Values

d_1 Buy 0	d_2 Buy 1	d_3 Buy 2
$0 \times 0.05 = 0$	$-3 \times 0.05 = -0.15$	$-6 \times 0.05 = -0.30$
$0 \times 0.60 = 0$	$2 \times 0.60 = 1.20$	$-1 \times 0.60 = -0.60$
$0 \times 0.35 = \underline{0}$	$2 \times 0.35 = \underline{0.70}$	$4 \times 0.35 = \underline{1.40}$
$EMV = 0$	$EMV = 1.75$	$EMV = 0.50$

The expected value criterion is sometimes called **EMV** or **expected monetary value** to distinguish it from the expected utility criterion.

The expected value decision criterion is the most sensible of those considered thus far, since it takes into account the consequences of each possible event and how likely each is to occur. But consider the following situation: An associate has offered you a gamble that involves flipping a fair coin. If a head occurs, you win $3,100; but if a tail occurs, you must pay $1,000. Note that the expected value of this gamble is $1,050 ($0.5 \times 3,100 + 0.5 \times -1,000$). As an alternative to the gamble, the associate offers you $1,000 for sure. Most people would select the sure $1,000, despite the fact that the expected value for the gamble is greater. The gamble is much riskier, and most people wish to avoid risk.

The expected value criterion does not take into account the decision maker's attitude toward risk, and this is an important limitation. If the amounts of money involved in the decision problem are small, or if the decision is a repetitive one (such as a daily decision on how much inventory to stock), risk is usually not important, and expected value is a reasonable criterion to use. On the other hand, when the amounts of money involved in the decision are large and especially if it is a one-of-a-kind decision, the expected value criterion is not adequate.

The dominance criterion (considered shortly) and the expected utility criterion (Chapter 6) do take the decision maker's risk attitude into account. But these approaches also have limitations.

The expected monetary value criterion remains as the most useful of all the decision criteria for decision making under uncertainty. It is preferred when risk is not a factor in the decision. And even for risky decisions, a sensible approach is first to calculate the expected monetary value, and then to make a subjective adjustment for the risk in making the choice.

Dominance

There are several methods by which a choice based on dominance can be made. The simplest case is called **outcome dominance,** in which the worst profit outcome from one act is at least as good as the best of some second act. As an example, consider acts d_1 and d_2 in Table 5–5.

Table 5–5   **Conditional Profit Table**

		Act			
State of Nature	*Probability*	d_1	d_2	d_3	d_4
q_1	0.3	2	-1	1	1
q_2	0.2	1	0	0	0
q_3	0.5	0	-1	-1	2

The worst profit outcome for act d_1 is 0 (when q_3 occurs); the best profit for act d_2 is also 0 (when q_2 occurs). Hence, act d_1 dominates act d_2. One is assured of doing as well or better with d_1, regardless of what happens.

A second form of dominance is called **event dominance,** and occurs if one act has a profit equal to or better than that of a second act for each event. Consider acts d_1 and d_3 in Table 5–5. For each event (that is, each state of nature), the conditional profit for act d_1 is greater than that for act d_3. Hence, d_1 dominates d_3 by event dominance. Regardless of what event occurs, d_1 is better than d_3. Note that d_1 also dominates d_2 by event dominance.

A third form of dominance is called **probabilistic dominance.**[1] To demonstrate this, we need to reorganize the information in Table 5–5 into the form shown in Table 5–6. Here, the events are defined in terms of the conditional profit and are ordered from lowest (-1) to highest (2). The probabilities for each profit are shown in the $P(X)$ columns. The columns labeled $P(X$ or more) show the probability of obtaining a profit of X or more dollars. Consider act d_1: We are sure (probability is 1.0) of obtaining a profit of -1 or more and also 0 or more. The probability is 0.5 of obtaining 1 or more; and 0.3 of obtaining 2 or more. Such probabilities as $P(X$ or more) are called *cumulative probabilities* and are discussed in more detail in Chapter 7.

One act **probabilistically dominates** a second if $P(X$ or more) for the first is at least as large as $P(X$ or more) for the second for all values of X. Compare acts d_1 and d_4 in Table 5–6. Note that for each value of X, the $P(X$ or more) probability for act d_4 is always at least as large (and is greater for X of 1 and 2) than that for act d_1. Hence, d_4 dominates d_1 by probabilistic dominance.

Consider a fixed amount of money. Obviously you prefer an alternative that has a greater chance of obtaining that amount or more. If, for any amount of

Table 5–6   Cumulative Probability Table

		Act		
		d_1		d_4
Conditional Profit X	$P(X)$	$P(X$ or more)	$P(X)$	$P(X$ or more)
-1	0.0	1.0	0.0	1.0
0	0.5	1.0	0.2	1.0
1	0.2	0.5	0.3	0.8
2	0.3	0.3	0.5	0.5

---

[1]This is also called stochastic dominance. Only first-order stochastic dominance is considered here. There are more complex forms (second and third order) that depend on characteristics of the decision maker's utility function. See Derek W. Bunn, *Applied Decision Analysis* (New York: McGraw-Hill, 1984), Chapter 4.

money, one alternative has uniformly equal or better chance of obtaining that amount or more, then that alternative dominates by probabilistic dominance.

Of the three forms of dominance, outcome dominance is the strongest, event dominance next, and probabilistic dominance the weakest. If act A dominates by outcome dominance, it will also dominate by event dominance and probabilistic dominance; but the reverse is not true. For example, act d_4 dominates d_1 by probabilistic dominance, as we have shown above, but does not dominate by either event dominance or outcome dominance.[2]

Using the dominance criterion to choose among decision alternatives is indeed a sensible procedure. The difficulty is that there may be no single alternative that dominates all the others. In fact, such is usually the case. Consider our original example in Table 5–2. None of the acts dominate any of the others by any of the three forms of dominance proposed. Hence, the dominance criterion would fail to select an action to take. This is the major limitation of dominance. However, it can be useful in eliminating some alternatives and thus narrowing down the decision process.

The dominance criterion is related to expected value in that, if one act dominates a second, this implies that the expected value of the first act is greater than the expected value of the second. The reverse, however, is not true.

Dominance in Decision Trees

It is also possible to check for dominance when a decision problem is structured as a decision tree. First we must introduce the idea of a **strategy.** A strategy is a set of decisions that completely determines a course of action. Consider the example shown in Figure 5–1. A decision maker has a choice of introducing a product or abandoning it. If introduced, the dealer acceptance can be either quick or slow. In either case, the manager can go with the product or stop. If the decision is to go, sales can be either high, medium, or low. The payoffs and probabilities are shown in Figure 5–1.

Consider the strategies available to the decision maker in this example. One easy-to-identify strategy is "Abandon the product." A second strategy is "Introduce the product: if quick acceptance, then Go; if slow acceptance, then also Go." We'll call this the Go/Go strategy. Note that both these strategy statements completely describe the decisions that must be made under all circumstances. If the product is to be abandoned, then there are no more decisions, but if the product is introduced, then a Go or Stop decision must be specified, depending upon quick or slow acceptance. In determining if a strategy statement is complete, ask yourself if it would contain sufficient instructions to enable an

---

[2]There are special cases for all three forms of dominance where both acts are tied. For outcome dominance, all profits for both acts may have exactly the same value. For event dominance, all profits for each event are exactly the same. And for probabilistic dominance, the $P(X$ or more) probabilities are the same for all X. In each of these cases, there is no dominance and the acts are considered equivalent.

Figure 5–1   Decision Tree for New Product Introduction

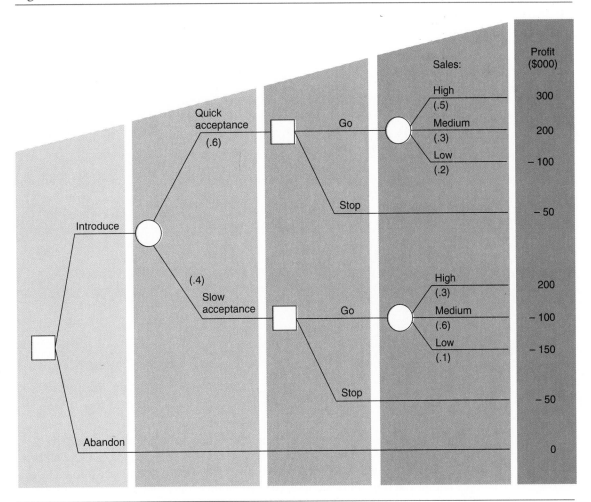

assistant to make all the decisions in your absence. If not, the statement does not specify a complete strategy.

In addition to the Abandon strategy and the Go/Go strategy, there are three other possible strategies:

- The Go/Stop strategy—"Introduce the product; if quick acceptance, then Go; if slow acceptance, then Stop."
- The Stop/Go strategy—"Introduce the product; if quick acceptance, then Stop; if slow acceptance, then Go."
- The Stop/Stop strategy—"Introduce the product; if quick acceptance then Stop; if slow acceptance, then Stop."

Figure 5–2   Abbreviated Tree for Go/Go Strategy

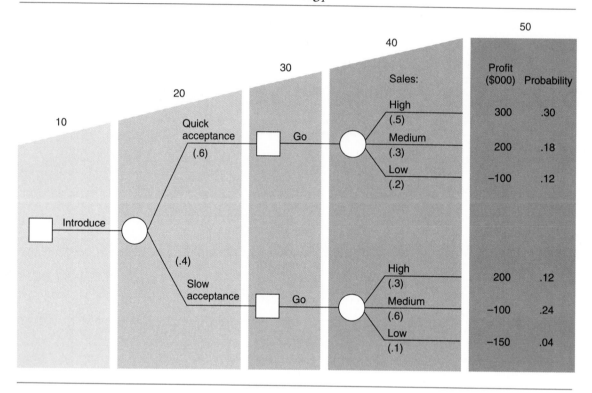

Since a strategy completely determines all the decisions, only events are left. We can redraw the decision tree for each strategy. The tree for the Go/Go strategy is shown in Figure 5–2. The probabilities for each outcome are shown at the very end of the tree. For example, the probability for a $300,000 profit (the result of quick acceptance and high sales) is $0.6 \times 0.5 = 0.30$. The other probabilities are calculated similarly. The probability distributions for profit for this strategy (Go/Go) and for the Go/Stop and Stop/Go strategies are shown in Table 5–7.

The probability distributions for profit, such as those shown in Table 5–7, are sometimes called **profit lotteries** or **risk profiles,** since they describe compactly the risks that the decision maker faces.

The strategies "Abandon product" and Stop/Stop are not included in Table 5–7. The abandon strategy has a sure profit of zero. The Stop/Stop strategy has a sure profit of − $50,000. Thus, the Abandon strategy dominates the Stop/Stop strategy by outcome dominance.

Note in Table 5–7 that strategy Go/Stop dominates strategy Stop/Go by probabilistic dominance, since the cumulative probability $P(X$ or more) is the same or greater in each case. No other dominance exists.

Table 5–7 **Probability Distributions and Cumulative Distributions for Selected Strategies**

	Go/Go Strategy		Go/Stop Strategy		Stop/Go Strategy	
Profit X	P(X)	P(X or more)	P(X)	P(X or more)	P(X)	P(X or more)
− 150	.04	1.00	0	1.00	.04	1.00
− 100	.36	.96	.12	1.00	.24	.96
− 50	0	.60	.40	.88	.60	.72
200	.30	.60	.18	.48	.12	.12
300	.30	.30	.30	.30	0	0

Figure 5–3 **Cumulative Profit Distributions**

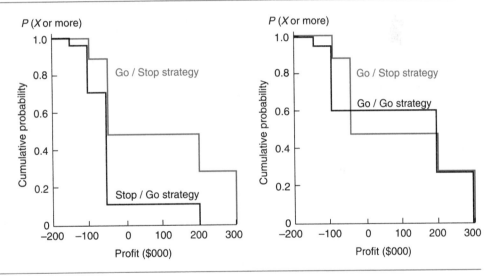

It is sometimes easier to see probabilistic dominance by looking at a graph of the cumulative distributions; that is, a plot of *P(X* or more). *One strategy dominates another if its cumulative curve is everywhere the same or above the cumulative curve of the other.* Figure 5–3 shows the case of a dominated strategy in the left half. The Go/Stop strategy dominates the Stop/Go strategy, since its curve is everywhere the same or above that for the Stop/Go strategy. On the other hand, when the curves cross, as in the right-hand part of Figure 5–3, there is no dominance. Neither distribution is always above (or the same) as the other.

When there are many outcomes in the decision tree, it is usually easier to check for dominance using cumulative curves than to use tables such as Table 5–7. When the trees become very complicated, the risk analysis procedure using

Monte Carlo simulation is used to develop the risk profiles. This method is discussed in Chapter 19.

Note in this example that we were able to eliminate only two dominated strategies (the Stop/Go and the Stop/Stop strategies). The dominance criterion does not provide a way to choose among the remaining three strategies. Hence, dominance is only a partial decision criterion.

SUMMARY

If a decision maker's attitude toward risk is not an important consideration in a decision problem, the expected value decision rule is generally preferred to other decision criteria. It is the only one that makes use of all the information available and that assures a definite choice among the alternatives.

Even when risk is present, expected monetary value is a useful first step.

The use of dominance criteria can sometimes eliminate some inferior alternatives in a decision problem.

Linear Functions

In Chapter 3 we introduced the notion of a random variable. Recall that if a random variable X is multiplied by a constant c, the expected value of the product cX can be expressed as the constant times the expected value of X (see Equation 3–7). That is:

$$E(cX) = cE(X) \qquad (5\text{–}1)$$

In this section, we will generalize this result and apply it specifically to problems involving the expected value of profit or cost.

In many business situations, an unknown or random variable is related to profit or cost by a **linear function,** such as:

$$P = a + bX$$

where P is the profit (or cost), a and b are constants, and X is the random variable. Then the **expected value** of profit (or cost) can be expressed as:

$$E(P) = a + bE(X) \qquad (5\text{–}2)$$

Note that this somewhat simplifies the computations. Instead of having to compute the conditional profit for each state of nature (i.e., for each value of X) and then calculating the expected profit, the expected value of X (i.e., the average state of nature) can be inserted in the profit equation.

As an example, suppose that the monthly costs in a given department are $10,000 plus $5 for each unit produced. That is:

$$C = 10,000 + 5X$$

where X is the random variable, number of units produced. Suppose that the expected value $E(X)$ is 1,500 units. Then the expected cost $E(C)$ is:

$$E(C) = 10,000 + 5E(X)$$
$$= 10,000 + 5(1,500) = 17,500$$

The Product of Independent Random Variables

Suppose we have two random variables, X and Y, and these variables are independent. The expected value of the product XY can be expressed as the product of the expected values. That is:

$$E(XY) = E(X) \cdot E(Y) \qquad \text{if } X, Y \text{ independent} \qquad \textbf{(5–3)}$$

Example Assume profit P is equal to unit profit times the number of units sold. We shall consider three cases. The letter b will stand for unit profit, and the letter q for units sold. When the capital letters B and Q are used, the variables will be considered random variables. When small b and q are used, the values are assumed constants and known for certain.

In the first case, the unit profit is assumed known at $1.50 each, and the number of units sold is uncertain with the probability distribution shown in Table 5–8.

The basic profit equation is:

$$P = bQ$$

(Note that since the value of B is known, it is a constant and shown in the equation with a small b). The average or expected profit is:

$$E(P) = E(bQ) = bE(Q)$$

The value of $E(Q)$ is:

$$E(Q) = 9(0.4) + 10(0.5) + 11(0.1) = 9.7$$

Thus, the expected profit is:

$$E(P) = 1.50 \cdot 9.7 = \$14.55$$

Now consider a second case, and suppose that the number of units to be sold the next period is known to be 10. We're not sure of the value of B, the unit profit. However, we do have the information shown in Table 5–9.

We now write the profit equation as:

$$P = qB$$

using a small letter q for the units sold since this is now a constant. The average or expected profit is:

$$E(P) = qE(B)$$

Table 5–8

Values of Q	Probability
9	0.4
10	0.5
11	0.1

Table 5–9

Values of B	Probability
$1.50	0.20
1.60	0.70
1.70	0.10

and $E(B)$ is calculated as:

$$E(B) = 1.50(0.20) + 1.60(0.70) + 1.70(0.10) = 1.59$$

The expected profit is:

$$E(P) = 10 \cdot 1.59 = \$15.90$$

As a third case, let us assume that neither B nor Q is known with certainty (both are random variables with probability distributions given above). We shall make the assumption that B and Q are independent. Now we write the profit equation as:

$$P = BQ$$

and the expected profit is:

$$E(P) = E(B) \cdot E(Q)$$

Substituting the values for the expectations of B and Q:

$$E(P) = 1.59 \cdot 9.7 = \$15.42$$

Thus, if we assume uncertainty for both B and Q, we have an expected profit of $15.42 and can make our plans accordingly. However, it should be noted that $15.42 is an expectation. The profit may be as low as $13.50 (if $Q = 9$ and $B = \$1.50$) or as high as $18.70 (if $Q = 11$ and $B = \$1.70$).

SUMMARY

When profit can be expressed as a linear function of the unknown variables, the calculation of the expected value can be simplified by use of Equations 5–2 and 5–3, with no loss of information (if we accept the expected value decision criterion).

Conclusion

Decision theory concerns itself with choosing the best act from a set of possible acts, given uncertainty as to the state of nature that exists. By the use of the expected value decision rule, this can be accomplished in a manner consistent with the decision maker's beliefs, even if there are no objective probabilities that can be applied to the states of nature.

A prime contribution of this procedure is that it focuses attention on all possible events and requires a calculation of the consequences of each act and each possible state of nature. Even if the analysis stopped with the conditional value table or decision tree, this would be a contribution to the art of decision making. But by the use of the expected value decision rule, it is possible to go further. For a decision maker to stop with the one computation using the most likely event is not justified in view of the techniques available for incorporating uncertainty into the analysis.

The advocacy of the expected value decision rule implies measurable utility relationships. In the real world, the input data for decisions is generally in the form of dollars, not measures of utility, and it will not always be appropriate to base a decision on expected monetary value. Other measures, such as the variance of possible outcomes, may be relevant also.

Bibliography

Bell, D.; H. Raiffa; and A. Tversky, eds. *Decision Making; Descriptive, Normative, and Prescriptive Interaction.* Cambridge: Cambridge University Press, 1988.

Bunn, D. W. *Applied Decision Analysis.* New York: McGraw-Hill, 1984.

Chernoff, H., and L. E. Moses. *Elementary Decision Theory.* New York: John Wiley & Sons, 1959.

Samson, D. *Managerial Decision Analysis.* Homewood, Ill.: Richard D. Irwin, 1988.

Weiss, L. *Statistical Decision Theory.* New York: McGraw-Hill, 1961.

Winkler, R. L. *Introduction to Bayesian Inference and Decision.* New York: Holt, Rinehart & Winston, 1972.

Problems with Answers

5–1. Consider the acts, the profits for which are shown in the accompanying table. Indicate which act or acts is best under the following criteria:
  a. Equally likely events.
  b. Minimax.
  c. Maximum likelihood.
  d. Expected value.

5–2. Refer to Problem 5–1.
  a. Which acts are involved in outcome dominance?
  b. Which acts are involved in event dominance?
  c. Which acts are involved in probabilistic dominance?
  d. Which acts are undominated by any form of dominance?

Conditional Profit Table (Problem 5–1)

		Act					
State of Nature	*Probability*	d_1	d_2	d_3	d_4	d_5	d_6
q_1	0.2	0	0	-4	5	-1	5
q_2	0.2	0	5	-4	0	2	5
q_3	0.4	0	2	3	3	5	0
q_4	0.2	0	-3	6	6	3	5

5–3. Total cost of a product is equal to:

$$T = 10,000 + BQ$$

The total revenue is $R = 20Q$. The variable cost per unit for the next period is a random variable with the following probability distribution:

Values of B	Probability
$5	0.10
6	0.50
7	0.40

a. Compute the expected profit for the coming period, assuming that 1,000 units will be sold.

b. Compute the expected profit for the coming period, assuming that there is a 0.5 probability of selling 1,000 units and a 0.5 probability of zero units (assume Q and B are independent.)

5–4. A sales manager lists the following probabilities for various demand levels for a new product.

Probability	Demand (units)
0.10	50
0.30	100
0.30	150
0.15	200
0.10	250
0.05	300

Suppose the cost of introducing the product is $500, and profit per unit sold is $5. What is the expected profit from the new product?

5–5. Refer to Figure 4–4 in Chapter 4. Assume that if no competitive product is introduced, you will set a high price. Given this assumption:

a. Make a list of all the complete strategies in the decision tree in Figure 4–4.

b. Calculate the profit lottery or risk profile for each strategy identified in (a).

c. Determine which, if any, strategies dominate others.

d. Plot the cumulative distributions for profit for all strategies.

Problems

5–6. Consider some business decision with which you are familiar. Define the acts and the states of the world, and make rough estimates of the conditional profits. What criteria do you think should be used to make the decision? Consider the relative merits of assuming equally likely events, minimax, maximum likelihood, dominance, and the expected value decision rule.

5–7. It has been stated in the text that decisions cannot always be based on computations involving only the monetary expressions of the consequences. Describe some business situations where factors other than money are important.

5–8. In the presence of decision making under uncertainty, can the expert evolve a procedure that will guarantee the correct decision? Explain.

5–9. Of the six criteria discussed in this chapter, which one(s) is consistent with individuals purchasing lottery tickets?

5–10. A decision maker has three possible investments with payoffs and probabilities as shown on the adjacent page.

a. Using the criterion of dominance, compare the alternatives. Can you find a preferred alternative? What form of dominance did you use to select your choice?

b. Using the expected value criterion, what choice would you make?

	Probabilities for Investment Payoffs		
Payoff ($000)	*Investment A*	*Investment B*	*Investment C*
−50	0.4	0.2	0.2
0	0.0	0.0	0.1
50	0.4	0.2	0.1
100	0.2	0.4	0.6
150	0.0	0.2	0.0

5–11. A manager needs a piece of equipment. She can buy either a new or used piece of equipment; the new piece costs more than the used piece, but it is much more likely to provide trouble-free service, which is of crucial importance. Of the six decision criteria discussed in this chapter, which one(s) would seem most suitable here? Why?

5–12. The following probabilities are assigned to the possible values of fraction defective in a manufacturing process:

Event	Probability of Event
0.01 defective	0.10
0.02 defective	0.15
0.03 defective	0.20
0.04 defective	0.30
0.05 defective	0.20
0.10 defective	0.03
0.15 defective	0.02
	1.00

Suppose we have a lot of 50,000 parts, and each defective costs 25 cents in rework costs. What is the expected rework cost? Would it be cheaper to inspect 100 percent of the lot if it costs 3 cents per item to inspect (assuming that all defectives are removed by inspection)?

5–13. You are president of an American corporation that manufactures aircraft. There has been some talk in Washington about

(a) going to Mars, (b) not going to Mars, and (c) going to Mars with the Russians. In your judgment, the probability of these states is 0.5, 0.4, and 0.1, respectively. You must make plans in the light of these possible states. Your alternatives are these: (a) You may continue to make airplanes only, which would provide you with an expected $10 million profit, regardless of the Mars decision. (b) You may design a payload system for the Mars shot (if the program falls through, you will lose $30 million; if it does not fall through, you will make a profit of $40 million, regardless of whether or not the Russians participate). (c) You may design a payload booster system. If the program falls through, you will lose $100 million. If we go, but with Russian participation, it is likely that we shall use Russia's booster system, and your profits will be $20 million. If we go alone, your profits will be $80 million. Base your decision on dollar profits.

a. What is the best act on the assumption of equally likely states?
b. What is the minimax act?
c. What is the maximum-likelihood act?
d. Are any of the acts dominated?
e. What is the act that maximizes expected value?
f. What decision do you prefer?

5–14. A company is considering an advertising campaign to increase the sales of the Gadgeto, the company's major product. An advertising budget of $300,000 has been proposed for the next year.

The sales manager and president agree on the probability distribution (shown in the table on the next page) for the effect of the advertising campaign on Gadgeto sales.

The company makes a profit of $1.20 on each Gadgeto sold. What is the expected incremental profit if the advertising campaign is adopted?

Sales Increase (units)	Probability
150,000	0.05
200,000	0.25
250,000	0.30
300,000	0.20
350,000	0.10
400,000	0.05
450,000	0.05
	1.00

5–15. Two students are trying to use the equally likely criterion in connection with the possible outcomes of two tosses of a coin. Student A says that each of the three following possible outcomes is considered equally likely to him:

Zero heads in two tosses.
One head in two tosses.
Two heads in two tosses.

Student B argues that each of the following possible outcomes is considered equally likely to him: HH, HT, TH, TT.

If the coin were a fair coin, which assessment would you prefer? Why?

5–16. Refer to Problem 4–19.
  a. Prepare a conditional value table for the two acts (sell lease or drill) and the four possible outcomes.
  b. What is the best act under the equally likely criterion?
  c. What is the best minimax act?
  d. What is the best maximum likelihood act?
  e. What is the best act to maximize expected value?

5–17. A manager must carry $500 worth of sample merchandise with him on an overseas trip. He estimates the probability of loss of the merchandise at 0.05. He is offered a full-risk insurance policy covering this loss for $35, and he decides to buy the insurance.
  a. Develop the conditional cost table.
  b. Which of the decision criteria pre-

sented in the chapter are consistent with his decision?

5–18. A suburban community voted on a $10,000 bond issue to finance a second fire truck. Proponents of the bond issue stated that in the past 10 years (the expected life of a truck) there were 20 fires (out of 1,000 fire calls) in which the presence of a second truck would have enabled firefighters to provide better service. The bond issue was defeated at the polls.
  a. Under the expected value criterion, what is the maximum dollar benefit per fire (out of 20 cases) resulting from having a second truck, if that criterion were followed by the voters?
  b. Now assume the voters are told that the value of having the second truck is $750 for each fire in which it is (or would have been) used. The voters still reject the bond issue. What decision criteria are consistent with their choice? Develop the conditional cost table.

5–19. An automobile manufacturer has found that a redesigned gas tank will lessen the likelihood of fire in a rear-end collision. The company estimates the total benefit to society to be $25 million. The additional cost of the redesign would be $40 million. The likelihood of a car being involved in a rear-end collision over its life is 1 percent.
  a. Under the EMV criterion, should the manufacturer implement the redesign or not?
  b. From a driver's viewpoint, if EMV is used, should the driver prefer the redesigned car (at additional cost) or not?
  c. What criteria would lead a driver to prefer the redesigned tank, among those discussed in the chapter?

5–20. Refer to Figure 4–10 on page 109.
  a. List the strategies available in this decision tree. Include all the strategies, even ones that you might consider silly.

b. Find at least two strategies that are dominated by other strategies. Show the profit lotteries (risk profiles) for these dominated strategies and for the strategies that dominate them.

c. Some of the strategies in (*a*) may have seemed silly or unreasonable. What can you now say about why they seemed unreasonable?

More Challenging Problems

5–21. The following is a letter to the editor in *The New York Times*[3] of February 28, 1971.

Yalta: Lack of Communication on Bomb
To the Editor:

Under the title "The Truth About Yalta," C. L. Sulzberger (column Feb. 14) discussed the assessment by Ambassador Charles Bohlen of the chief problems which faced President Roosevelt and the U.S. delegation at the time of the Yalta Conference, February 1945. The third point of this assessment reads in part as follows:

"While Roosevelt and a handful of advisers knew about the Manhattan Project, no one would be certain the atomic bomb would in fact explode or how effective a weapon it would be."

This problem looked different as seen from the Los Alamos Scientific Laboratory charged with the development of the bomb. By February 1945 it appeared to me and to other fully informed scientists that there was a better than 90 percent probability that the atomic bomb would in fact explode; that it would be an extremely effective weapon, and that there would be enough material to build several bombs in the course of a few months.

Thus even if the first bomb should have failed, the project was bound to succeed in a relatively short time. Few things in war and even fewer in politics have as good a chance as 90 percent.

That the full flavor of this conviction of the scientists was not transmitted to the decision makers was a failure of communication—excessive secrecy and the absence of direct channels between scientists and high Government officials were responsible. Because of this failure of direct communication, the U.S. at Yalta urged Russia to participate in the assault on Japan, with grave consequences for the future of the political situation in the Far East. Suppose there had been good communication. Should the U.S. Government have acted on a 90 percent probability of technical success? In my opinion, definitely yes.

Again, in 1958 we had a chance to arrange a ban on the testing of nuclear weapons at a time when the U.S. had a clear advantage over the Soviet Union in weapon design. However, we were afraid of the possibility of clandestine underground Russian tests of small nuclear weapons and insisted therefore on ironclad safeguards. These were unacceptable to the U.S.S.R., and no agreement was reached by 1961.

In 1961 the Russians conducted a series of nuclear weapons tests in which they managed to equal, in most of the important aspects, the

[3]© 1972 by The New York Times Company. Reprinted by permission.

performance of U.S. thermonuclear weapons. Thus here again, by insisting on certainty, the U.S. lost a clear advantage.

This letter is not meant to imply that our foreign policy should center on advantage over the U.S.S.R. I merely wish to argue that if and when the seeking of such an advantage is part of our policy, we should act on high technical probability rather than requiring certainty and should have easy communication between the knowledgeable persons and decision makers.

Hans Bethe
Ithaca, N.Y., Feb. 16, 1971

The writer, 1967 Nobel laureate in physics, headed the theoretical divisions of the Los Alamos Scientific Laboratory from April 1943 to January 1946.

Comment on this letter, noting particularly the following:

a. The decision criterion that appears to have been used at the top levels of government.

b. The decision criterion that is suggested by the author of the letter.

5–22. It has been argued that the U.S. government should strongly encourage alternative sources of energy (by subsidies, guarantees, and direct loans) even though the alternative sources may cost more than oil. Attempt to evaluate this problem using the decision theory approach. That is, define alternatives, events, payoffs, and probabilities, and recommend an alternative.

Utility as a Basis for Decision Making

In previous chapters, the maximization of expected monetary value has been emphasized. There are business situations in which maximizing expected monetary value does not lead to the course of action many experienced people would select. A framework to deal with such situations is provided by utility theory. The difference between expected monetary value and expected utility will be illustrated with an example.

Example   Assume that you are given a choice in each of the following paired alternatives. You may select one of the A choices, one of the B choices, and one of the C choices. Make a note of the set of alternatives you choose.

A_1 = The certainty of *or* A_2 = On the flip of a fair coin, nothing if it comes
a \$100,000 gift, up heads, or a tax-exempt gift of \$250,000 if
tax-free. the coin turns up tails.

B_1 = No gain or loss. *or* B_2 = One chance out of 100 of incurring a \$9,000
debt, and a 99/100 chance of winning \$100.

C_1 = A gift of *or* C_2 = A payment of 2^N cents, where N is the num-
\$10,000, tax- ber of times a fair coin is flipped until tails
free. comes up. If tails appears on the first toss,
you receive 2 cents; if the coin shows heads
on the first toss and tails on the second, you
receive 4 cents; two heads in a row followed
by tails yields 8 cents; and so forth. However, you are allowed to participate only
once; the sequence stops with the first
showing of tails.

Most people would choose the set A_1, B_1, and C_1. However, the mathematical expectation (or expected monetary value) favors the alternatives A_2, B_2, and C_2. The expected value of alternative A_2 is one half (the probability of the fair coin showing heads) times zero (the monetary value associated with heads) plus one half (the probability of tails) times $250,000, or $125,000. Since this expected value is $25,000 more than the expected value of choice A_1, you should have selected A_2 *if you wanted to maximize expected monetary value.*

Similarly, with B_2 the expected net gain is 99/100 (the appropriate probability) times $100 (the amount of gain) less 1/100 times $9,000. This amount is $9, which is larger than the zero-dollar gain associated with B_1. If you made decisions so as to maximize expected monetary gain, you would accept the very small chance of a large loss; but most of us would choose B_1.

The expected monetary value of the game described in C is infinite. The chance of the first tail appearing on the first toss is ½; on the second toss, ¼; on the third, ⅛; on the fourth, ¹⁄₁₆; and so on. The related rewards would be 2 cents, 4 cents, 8 cents, 16 cents, and so on. The expected monetary value, by definition, is the sum of the monetary outcomes, weighted by the associated probabilities. In this case:

$$\text{EMV} = \tfrac{1}{2}(2\cancel{c}) + \tfrac{1}{4}(4\cancel{c}) + \tfrac{1}{8}(8\cancel{c}) + \tfrac{1}{16}(16\cancel{c}) + \cdots$$
$$= 1\cancel{c} + 1\cancel{c} + 1\cancel{c} + 1\cancel{c} + \cdots = \infty\cancel{c}$$

The fact that no prudent person would choose this game in preference to the certainty of a modest amount provides the essentials of the famous St. Petersburg paradox. This paradox led Daniel Bernoulli to the first investigations of utility rather than the expectation of monetary value as a basis of decision making.

Utility

Since most people would choose A_1, B_1, and C_1 rather than the three alternatives with greater monetary expectation, it seems reasonable to conclude that people do not always make decisions so as to maximize expected monetary value. What, then, is an alternative criterion for decision making? Von Neumann and Morgenstern constructed a framework consistent with choices such as A_1, B_1, and C_1.[1] They argued that decisions were made so as to maximize **expected utility** rather than expected monetary value. If you selected A_1 over A_2, we would conclude that alternative A_1 had more utility for you than alternative A_2. If you were indifferent between two alternatives—say B_1 and B_2—we would conclude that each alternative offered the same expected utility to you. Indifference might be defined as your willingness to take either result at random, or have

---

[1] J. von Neumann and O. Morgenstern, *Theory of Games and Economic Behavior* (Princeton: Princeton University Press, 1944).

some stranger make the choice for you. It is possible to derive generalizations about a person's utility function for some commodity (most often money) that are consistent with logic and observation of repeated decisions. It follows that it is reasonable to assume that people make decisions so as to maximize expected utility rather than expected value. The use of expected utility is not a costless choice, for expected monetary value is an unambiguous concept and is relatively easy to calculate. It would be quite convenient if we were able to associate different monetary outcomes with indices of the decision maker's preferences. A complex set of alternatives then might be transformed into utility measures for purposes of decision making. It is our purpose in this chapter to relate money and a utility index and to derive generalizations about this relationship in situations involving risk.

Measuring Utility

Is it possible to measure the utility of money? In an attempt to answer this question, we shall consider three different types of measurement scales:

1. Nominal or classification scale.
2. Ordinal or ranking scale.
3. Cardinal or interval scale.

A **nominal scale** assigns a description to a set of elements. The elements may be a physical unit or a condition. The description may be a number, as in a numbering system for baseball players; or it may be an adjective, as when children say they are hungry or not hungry. A nominal scale can sometimes be useful for decision analysis. For example, a set of possible returns might be divided into subsets or classifications of satisfactory and unsatisfactory returns. Investments may be divided into two classes, acceptable and unacceptable, on a nominal scale. A form of grading procedure could assign two grades, passing or failing. It is not difficult to conceive of nominal measures of utility. For example, acts could be classified as having negative utility (disutility) or positive utility. However, a nominal scale that contains no ordering or ranking may not be useful in decision making.

An **ordinal measure** adds the concept of relative ordering or ranking. Objects become "more" or "less" than other objects. A person can declare a sound is louder than another sound. Different light sources may be ranked by brightness without a number measure being placed on the amount of light. We can choose the winner of a race without the use of a stopwatch. An attempt may be made to rank all investments according to their relative desirability (though this process may be easier to describe than to accomplish).

Ordinal measures of utility are used in analyzing situations with riskless choices. Indifference curve analysis collects alternatives with equal utility (i.e., a person is indifferent to these choices), and we compare any of these choices with the choices on another indifference curve that is higher (and more desirable) or lower (and less desirable). If we could rank investments, this would imply that we have an ordinal measure of desirability.

With a **cardinal measure,** a number is assigned that is an interval measure of a characteristic. Thus, a piece of wood may be a number of inches long, a number of pounds in weight, and a number of cubic inches in volume. We can measure in a cardinal sense such things as distance, weight, light, sound, time, and heat. We can do some mathematical manipulations with a cardinal measure. For example, all 5-pound bags of sugar weigh the same; and if we have two 5-pound bags, we then have 10 pounds of sugar.

The von Neumann–Morgenstern measure of utility is a special type of cardinal measure (some would say it is a special type of ordinal measure). It measures utility in situations involving risk for the individual decision maker. The use of this utility measure allows us to predict which of several lotteries an investor will prefer, and thus enables a manager to make the decision for the investor. Sometimes an investor will make decisions inconsistent with his or her utility function, but this type of inconsistency can generally be straightened out if the investor reconsiders the decisions.

Any utility function is the result of a person's attitudes toward risk. There are no right or wrong answers (though inconsistencies may arise because of misunderstandings). Thus, if you are asked what amount you will accept for certain instead of engaging in a lottery involving a 0.5 probability of losing $500 and 0.5 probability of winning $1,000, the answer is a personal preference rather than a mathematical calculation. (In a group of 50 individuals, it is likely that nearly 50 different answers will be obtained.)

The Psychological Assumptions

The use of utility for purposes of making decisions involves assumptions about how an individual reacts to outcomes. Since we are attempting to measure attitudes toward uncertain situations, it is important that the model used in making the decisions be consistent with the psychological makeup of people.

The following seven assumptions will be made:

1. With any two alternatives, we can decide whether we are indifferent to them or which one we prefer. This seems to be a trivial requirement, but it is necessary. In fact, we may find that it is difficult to determine a specific unequivocal reaction to pairs of alternatives. For example, would you prefer $200 for certain or a lottery involving a 50–50 chance of getting zero dollars or $1,000? Change the certain outcome until your preference is different. Finding the exact point of indifference between the two lotteries is very difficult, and the answer is frequently indecisive.

2. Alternatives are transitive; that is, if A is preferred to B, and B is preferred to C, then A is preferred to C. Also, if A equals B, and B equals C, then A is equal to C. It is possible, where the degree of preference is slight and the alternatives are many, for a person to give rankings of pairs that are intransitive. This means that on close decisions a person may be inconsistent. For example, a person might prefer a trip to Nassau to a trip to Bermuda, and a trip to Bermuda to a trip to Hawaii, but then prefer a trip to Hawaii to a trip to Nassau. This is intransitive, but it may result from the fact that all three trips sound fine; and although the person is trying to give preferences, there is close to indifference among the three choices. A decision maker should be able to eliminate this type of intransitivity by reexamining the choices.

3. If a person is indifferent to two lotteries, then they may be substituted for each other for purposes of analysis. For example, we previously compared a 50–50 chance of zero dollars and $1,000 with $200 for certain. If you are indifferent between these two lotteries, then we can use the second lottery ($200 for certain) as a substitute for the first. Further, we can say the utilities of the two lotteries are equal.

4. If two lotteries have the same two possible outcomes, but the outcomes have different probabilities, then the lottery with the more favorable outcome having the higher probability is the preferred lottery.[2]

Example Consider the two lotteries shown in Table 6–1. Lottery A must be preferred over lottery B.

5. If A is preferred to B, and B is preferred to C, then there is some lottery involving A and C that is indifferent to B for certain.

Example Let:

$$A = \$1,000$$
$$B = \$400$$
$$C = \$0$$

Table 6–1

Possible Outcomes	*Probability of Outcomes for Lottery*	
	A	*B*
$1,000	0.80	0.50
0	0.20	0.50

---

[2]This is a form of probabilistic dominance discussed in Chapter 5.

We shall make up a lottery involving A with probability p and C with probability $(1 - p)$. The expected *monetary* value of the lottery will be:

$$A(p) + C(1 - p) = 1{,}000p + 0(1 - p)$$

What is the value of p that will make you indifferent to the above lottery and B for certain? If there is some value, then assumption 5 is satisfied; B would be called the *certainty equivalent* of the lottery.

6. If A is preferred to B, and there is some third alternative, C, then any lottery involving A and C is preferred to a corresponding lottery of B and C, provided the probability of assignments are the same in both lotteries. It is required that the probability attached to C be less than one.

Example   Let:

$$A = \$1{,}000$$
$$B = \$400$$
$$C = \$0$$

$A(p) + C(1 - p)$ is preferred over $B(p) + C(1 - p)$. If p equals 0.6, then $\$1{,}000 \cdot 0.6 + \$200 \cdot 0.4$ is preferred over $\$400 \cdot 0.6 + \$200 \cdot 0.4$.

Assumption 6 can also be expressed as follows: If a lottery of A and C is preferred over a lottery of B and C, with C having the same probability (less than one) in both lotteries, then A is preferred to B.

7. The utility of a lottery is defined to be equal to the expectation of the utilities of its components.

The assumption that the utility of a lottery is the sum of the expectations of the component utilities is a convenient assumption for mathematical manipulation.[3] Let us assume a lottery, L_1, has the outcomes shown in Table 6–2, with

Table 6–2

Outcomes	Utility of Outcomes	Probability
A_1	$U(A_1)$	p_1
A_2	$U(A_2)$	p_2
. . .	. . .	. . .
. . .	. . .	. . .
A_n	$U(A_n)$	p_n

[3] See R. Dorfman, P. A. Samuelson, and R. M. Solow, *Linear Programming and Economic Analysis* (New York: McGraw-Hill, 1958), pp. 465–69, for a proof.

Table 6–3

Lottery	Outcomes	Utility of Outcomes	Probability
L_1 $\begin{cases} \\ \end{cases}$	$1,000 0	50 0	0.6 0.4
L_2	400	40	1.0

each outcome assigned a utility measure and a probability of occurrence. The utility of the lottery is defined as:

$$U(L_1) = p_1 U(A_1) + p_2 U(A_2) + \cdots + p_n U(A_n)$$

The lottery L_1 may itself have a probability of occurrence. Assume lottery L_1 has a probability of r, and lottery L_2 has a probability of $(1 - r)$. The utility of the two lotteries is $U(L)$:

$$U(L) = rU(L_1) + (1 - r)U(L_2)$$

Example   Assume two lotteries (see Table 6–3):

$$U(L_1) = 0.6 \cdot 50 + 0.4 \cdot 0 = 30$$
$$U(L_2) = 1.0 \cdot 40 = 40$$

Assume L_1 has a probability of 0.8, and L_2 has a probability of 0.2. The expected utility of the gamble (i.e., the two lotteries) is:

$$U(L) = 0.8 \cdot 30 + 0.2 \cdot 40 = 32$$

Rescaling

Since the scale of utility is arbitrary, we can change the scale and origin without contradicting our assumptions. In particular, if a and b are any two constants, with $b > 0$ and if $U(L)$ is a utility function, then $V(L)$ is an equivalent utility function where:

$$V(L) = a + bU(L) \quad \text{for } b > 0$$

Decisions made using the utility function $V(L)$ would be identical to those made using $U(L)$. That is to say, we can add a constant to a utility function, or we can change the unit (or the slope). It is said that a utility function is unique up to an order-preserving linear transformation.[4]

---

[4]The sense in which von Neumann and Morgenstern use the term *utility* differs somewhat from the traditional use in economics. Utility in the von Neumann sense is associated with choices involving uncertainty; in the older economic version, utility represented the intrinsic satisfaction possessed by a commodity. The distinction will be sharpened in the following discussion. The word *preference* has been used instead of *utility* in some recent books to avoid this confusion.

Derivation of a Utility Function for Money

To be of use in decision making, utility values must be assigned to all outcomes. In many circumstances, such outcomes are nonmonetary in nature. For example, in making a medical diagnosis, a physician has to weigh such factors as pain and suffering, loss of work from hospitalization, psychological effects, costs, and even death. It is possible using the von Neumann–Morgenstern approach to assign utility values to such outcomes. However, in most business decision problems, the monetary consequence is of major importance. Hence, in this book we shall be concerned primarily with evaluating the utility function for money.

The Shape of Utility Functions

Some generalizations about the usual shape of a utility function are possible. People usually regard money as a desirable commodity and prefer more of it to less of it. The utility measure of a large sum is normally greater than the utility measure of a small sum, and the utility function rises over any relevant range of money. We can describe a utility function as having a positive slope over this relevant range. The slope in this case is the ratio of an incremental change in the utility index $[\Delta U(M)]$ as a result of an incremental change in the stock of money (ΔM). The incremental changes will always have the same sign, so we may write:

$$\text{Slope} = \frac{\Delta U(M)}{\Delta M} > 0$$

This measure of the slope is called the **marginal utility of money** and, except for the algebraic sign, is an arbitrary measure. This follows from a utility function being unique only to a linear transformation.

The slope of a utility function is positive and probably does not vary in response to small changes in the stock of money. It follows that for small changes in the amount of money going to an individual, the utility function over that range has approximately a constant slope and may be regarded as linear. If the utility function is linear $[U(M)$ in Figure 6–1], the person maximizes expected utility by maximizing expected monetary value. Thus, expected monetary value may properly be used as a guide in decision making only when there is a reason to believe the pertinent utility function is linear over the range of possible outcomes. We have seen that for large variations in the amount of money, this is a most unlikely condition. At the extremes, for large losses and large gains, the utility function is almost certain to approach upper and lower limits. The slope of the curve usually will increase sharply as the amount of the loss increases, implying that the disutility of a large loss is proportionately more than the disutility of a small loss, but the curve will flatten as the loss becomes very large. Similarly, for large stocks of money, the slope of the utility function grows

Figure 6–1   Linear Utility for Money

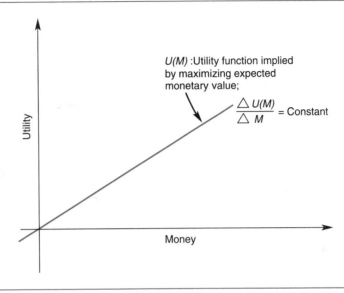

smaller with further additions to that stock. These observations are consistent with the traditional "diminishing marginal utility" view of consumer psychology. They are also consistent with the notion of "risk aversion," which pervades most business decision problems. An example of a risk averse utility function is shown in Figure 6–2. If an individual is risk averse, then the expected utility of a gamble is less than the utility of the expected monetary value.

It is possible for a decision maker to be risk preferring, at least over a range of the utility function. In this case, the expected utility of a gamble is more than the utility of the expected monetary value. A risk preferring utility function is also shown in Figure 6–2.

Assessing a Utility Function

The first step in actually deriving a utility function is to determine two values to use as reference points. For convenience, these can be the largest and smallest monetary values involved in the decision problem. The utility values corresponding to these monetary values are arbitrarily selected—for convenience we might assign utility values of 0 and 1 to these monetary values. For example, if the decision problem included monetary values ranging from $-\$10,000$ to $+ \$100,000$, we would assign a 0 utility to $-\$10,000$ and a utility of 1.0 to $\$100,000$. That is:

$$U(-\$10,000) = 0 \quad \text{and} \quad U(\$100,000) = 1.0$$

Figure 6–2   **Utility Functions**

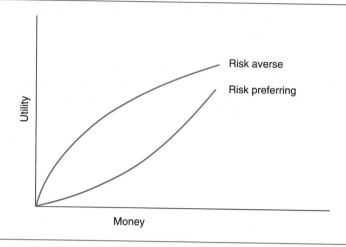

The selection of utility values of 0 and 1 is arbitrary. Values of -29 and $+132$ or other values could have been selected. In this sense, the utility scale is like that for temperature. Both the Celsius and Fahrenheit scales measure temperature but have different readings for the freezing point of water (0° and 32°, respectively) and for the boiling point (100° and 212°, respectively).

Next, formulate an alternative A_1 that offers a one-half chance at $-\$10,000$ and a one-half chance at $+\$100,000$. The expected utility of this alternative is the sum of the utility assignments to the possible events, weighted by the appropriate probabilities. In this case:

$$U(A_1) = \tfrac{1}{2}U(-\$10,000) + \tfrac{1}{2}U(\$100,000) = \tfrac{1}{2}(0) + \tfrac{1}{2}(1) = 0.5$$

Now formulate a second alternative (A_2) that yields some amount of money with certainty—say, \$25,000. You now have to choose between the two courses of action, A_1 and A_2. Say you choose A_2, or \$25,000 for certain. We infer that:

$$U(A_2) > U(A_1) = 0.5$$

or $U(\$25,000) > \tfrac{1}{2}U(-\$10,000) + \tfrac{1}{2}U(\$100,000) = 0.5$: that is, the utility of \$25,000 is greater than one half. Because the \$25,000 is preferred to A_1, we conclude that the utility index of A_2 is greater than one half. Assume next that you were offered \$5,000 for certain (A_3) and found that you preferred A_1 to A_3. This would imply that the utility index associated with \$5,000 should be less than one half. If your patience held out, you could continue proposing alternative acts yielding sums of money with certainty until you discovered one that was exactly as attractive as A_1. Suppose this offer was in the amount of \$15,000, so that we could infer that you were indifferent between $15,000 for certain and the original proposal. Thus, the utility assignment to $15,000 should be:

$$U(\$15,000) = \tfrac{1}{2}U(-\$10,000) + \tfrac{1}{2}U(\$100,000) = 0.5$$

We now have three points through which your utility function passes. Additional utility evaluations may be made in a similar manner. For example, pose an alternative that offers a 0.5 probability of $15,000 and a 0.5 probability of $100,000. Find the sum that must be offered with certainty to make you indifferent to the opportunity involving risk. Say this amount is $47,000. We could conclude that the appropriate utility assignment for $47,000 is:

$$U(\$47,000) = \tfrac{1}{2}U(\$15,000) + \tfrac{1}{2}U(\$100,000)$$
$$= \tfrac{1}{2}(0.5) + \tfrac{1}{2}(1.0) = 0.75$$

Next, pose the alternative involving a one-half chance at $15,000 and one-half chance at $-$10,000. You may consider this alternative unfavorable, and in fact be willing to pay some amount to be relieved of the alternative (in the same way that one buys insurance to be relieved of a risk). Suppose you are indifferent to $-$2,500 (that is, a payment of $2,500) and the opportunity involving risk. Then:

$$U(-\$2,500) = \tfrac{1}{2}U(-\$10,000) + \tfrac{1}{2}U(\$15,000)$$
$$= \tfrac{1}{2}(0) + \tfrac{1}{2}(0.5) = 0.25$$

You now have the five points of the utility function shown in Table 6–4 and Figure 6–3. These can be connected by a smooth curve to give an approximation for the utility function over the entire range: $-$10,000 to $100,000.

Note that:

$$U(\$15,000) = 0.5$$

and:

$$\tfrac{1}{2}U(-\$2,500) + \tfrac{1}{2}U(\$47,000) = \tfrac{1}{2}(0.25) + \tfrac{1}{2}(0.75) = 0.5$$

Hence, as a final check on your assessments, you should be indifferent between $15,000 for sure and an alternative involving a one-half chance at $-$2,500

Table 6–4 Assessed Utility Points

Monetary Value M	Utility Index $U(M)$
$- 10,000	0
-2,500	0.25
15,000	0.50
47,000	0.75
100,000	1.0

Figure 6–3   Assessed Utility Function

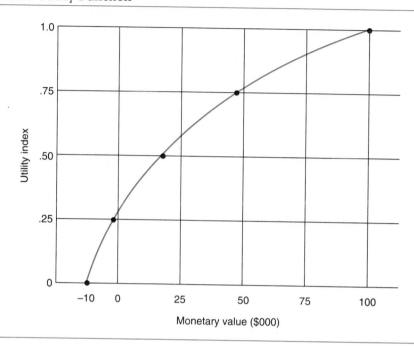

and one-half chance at $47,000. If this is not true, your assessments are not consistent and must be revised.

An alternative procedure for assessing the utility function is to pick a certain monetary value and then determine the probabilities that make a gamble involving the maximum and minimum values equivalent to the certain amount. For example, if we picked a certain amount L, we then formulate the equation:

$$pU(\$100,000) + (1 - p)U(-\$10,000) = U(L)$$

and we find the probability p that makes the decision maker indifferent between the two sides of this equation. As an illustration, if L were $25,000, the decision maker would have to assess a probability p such that he was indifferent between $25,000 for sure, and a p chance at $100,000 and a $(1 - p)$ chance at $-$10,000$. In this case p might be 0.60. Then:

$$U(L) = U(\$25,000) = 0.6U(\$100,000) + 0.4U(-\$10,000)$$
$$= 0.6(1) + 0.4(0) = 0.6$$

(because we have set $U(\$100,000) = 1.0$ and $U(-\$10,000) = 0, U(L) = p$). To obtain other values on the utility curve, other values of L would be selected and the p probability assessed. In this manner, a curve similar to that of Figure 6–3 could be obtained.

Using Utility Functions

A utility function represents the subjective attitude of a decision maker to risk. Hence, a utility function of a person can be used to evaluate decision alternatives involving uncertain outcomes.

Example Suppose a decision maker had to make a choice between two alternatives. Alternative A involved a contract in which the company was sure to make a profit of $20,000. Alternative B, on the other hand, was the introduction of a new product. The sales that the product would achieve, and hence the profit, were unknown. Management assigned the probabilities shown in Table 6–5 to the various profit possibilities.

The expected monetary value for alternative B is $25,000. On this basis, B would be preferred to A. On the other hand, if the decision maker were risk averse, the preference might change. Note that there is a 30 percent chance of no profit and a 10 percent chance of a loss with alternative B. If the decision maker had the utility function given in Figure 6–3, we would evaluate this alternative by using utility values instead of monetary values. By interpolating in Figure 6–3, we could find the utility values associated with each profit amount. These are given in Table 6–5. Using the probabilities in the same table, the *expected utility* would be calculated (by multiplying the probabilities by the utility amounts and summing). The expected utility is calculated as 0.524. Note that the utility of $20,000 is given in Table 6–5 as 0.55. Hence, the expected utility of alternative B is not as great as the utility of the contract involving $20,000 for sure, and the sure contract should be accepted.

Certainty Equivalents

The notion of a certainty equivalent has been presented several times in this chapter. Let us now consider its meaning more explicitly. Consider an uncertain decision situation, which may be represented by a lottery, L, with dollar out-

Table 6–5 **Probabilities, Payoffs, and Utilities for Alternative B**

Probability	Profit ($000s)	Utility
0.1	− $10	0
0.3	0	0.30
0.2	20	0.55
0.2	40	0.71
0.1	60	0.82
0.1	80	0.90
Expected values:	$25	0.524

comes A_1 and A_2, and corresponding probabilities p and $(1 - p)$. The **certainty equivalent** is a certain or sure dollar amount A^* which is equivalent, for the decision maker, to the lottery L.

The certainty equivalent can be interpreted as the maximum insurance that the decision maker would pay to be freed of an undesirable risk (for example, the maximum premium to guard against a fire in one's house). Or we might consider the certainty equivalent as the minimum certain amount one would be willing to accept for selling a desirable but uncertain set of outcomes.

Once we have obtained the utility function for a decision maker and also obtained the probabilities in a given decision situation, the certainty equivalent can be obtained directly by the methods described earlier. In our example above, the alternative of introducing the new product has an expected utility of 0.524. If $17,500 also has a utility of 0.524, we can say that the amount of $17,500 is the *certainty equivalent* of the alternative involving the new product introduction. When faced with an uncertain decision situation, it would be beneficial to determine the certainty equivalent directly by asking the decision maker. If this does not agree with the value computed using the utility function and the probabilities, then we have come up with an inconsistency; it may be due either to the utility curve or to the probabilities assigned to the outcomes. Hence, the use of the certainty equivalent is a check on the validity of our analysis.

The certainty equivalent also has another use in analyzing complex decision situations. Our procedure so far has called for obtaining probabilities of various outcomes and a utility function as separate inputs to the decision-making process. Since both of these often represent subjective judgments on the part of the decision maker, it is sometimes convenient to shortcut the analysis and come up with a certainty equivalent directly.

Example   A firm is bidding on a contract to supply 1,000 units of a certain electronic component. It has to decide its bid price. One uncertain factor in the decision process is the possibility of a strike by its workers. If they do strike, it will mean delays and penalties associated with meeting the deadline on the contract. To simplify the decision analysis, we might ask our manufacturer how much it would be willing to pay for insurance against losses due to the possible strike. It might answer, for example, $3,000. This amount is the certainty equivalent to the uncertain situation related to the strike (the dollar outcomes with and without a strike *and* the related probabilities). The decision maker may not actually be able to purchase insurance of this type, but the certainty equivalent provides a figure that we can use in our analysis to determine the proper bid to be made by the manufacturer.

Risk Premiums

Suppose an individual has a utility function $U(I)$ as shown in Figure 6–4. Consider first a gamble involving a one-half chance for the amount I_1 and a one-half

Figure 6–4   Utility Function

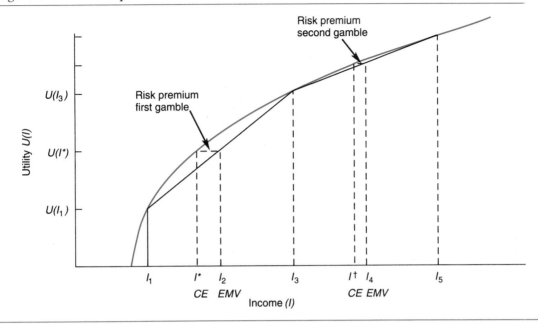

chance for the amount I_3. The expected monetary value (EMV) of this gamble is I_2. The certainty equivalent of the gamble is I^*, the certain amount that has the same utility as the expected utility of the gamble [i.e., $\frac{1}{2} U(I_1) + \frac{1}{2}U(I_3) = U(I^*)$]. The difference between the EMV and the certainty equivalent (CE) of the gamble (i.e., $I_2 - I^*$) is the **risk premium** associated with the gamble for that individual. The risk premium is a measure of how much risk aversion there is in a given portion of an individual's utility function. For two individuals presented with the same gamble, the one with the higher risk premium is the more risk averse.

For a given individual, the risk premium will generally not be the same at different parts of the utility function. Consider a second gamble involving a one-half chance at I_3 and a one-half chance at I_5, where I_5 is such that the distance from I_3 to I_5 is the same as that from I_1 to I_3 (i.e., $I_5 - I_3 = I_3 - I_1$). We can think of this second gamble as if it were composed of a sure amount of $(I_3 - I_1)$ plus the first gamble above involving I_1 and I_3. In this sense, the second gamble is the same as the first, except for a different starting point (I_3 versus I_1). The expected value is I_4, and the certainty equivalent is $I\dagger$. Note that the risk premium in the second gamble ($I_4 - I\dagger$) is less than the risk premium of the first gamble. Thus, the utility function shown in Figure 6–4 has the property of **decreasing risk aversion.** In other words, the individual becomes less risk averse as the money amount I increases.

This property of decreasing risk aversion is one that seems reasonable for most business and many personal decisions. The possibility of a loss of a given size becomes less significant the more wealth the investor possesses.

Utility Functions and Risk Preference

There is empirical evidence that for many individuals, their utility function actually has an area of risk preference.[5] In this area, the slope of the utility function increases up to a point of inflection and decreases thereafter (Figure 6–5 has two inflection points).

It is quite consistent for an individual with a utility function of this shape [$U(M)$ in Figure 6–5] to (1) pay a small premium for insurance against large losses, even when the premiums include a "loading" charge above the actuarial

Figure 6–5   Utility for Wealth

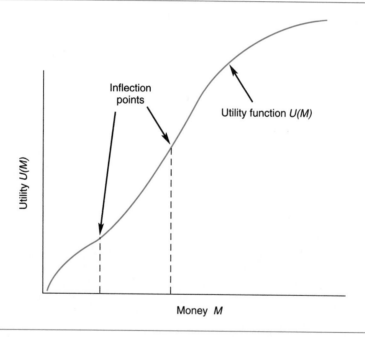

[5]The original conjecture was by Friedman and Savage, "The Utility Analysis of Choices Involving Risk," *Journal of Political Economy*, August 1948, supported by empirical observations that many people were willing to accept long-shot risky ventures (e.g., lotteries) at the same time that they insured against large losses. Since then, there has been some experimental support of this view.

cost of bearing the risk; and (2) simultaneously accept risky propositions that promise a chance at modest or large gains in return for small investments, even though the mathematical expectation may make the gamble unfair.

Example Consider the entrepreneur whose utility table contains the values shown in Table 6–6. Say that there are two decisions: (*a*) Is it desirable to pay a $100 premium to insure against a potential $10,000 fire loss when the probability of fire on the entrepreneur's property is 1 out of 200? (*b*) Is it desirable to invest $100 in an oil-drilling venture where a geologist has said there is only 1 chance in 200 of striking oil (with the expectation of $10,000 profit) and a 199/200 chance of losing the $100 investment? Let us analyze these decisions in terms of expectations calculated from the utility measures. The decision to insure or not is described in Table 6–7.

In Table 6–7, the expected utility of act 1 is less than the expected utility of act 2; the entrepreneur maximizes utility by taking act 2 (insuring).

Table 6–6

M	$U(M)$
$-\$10,000$	-800
-200	-2
-100	-1
0	0
$10,000$	250

Table 6–7 **Conditional and Expected Utility for Insurance**

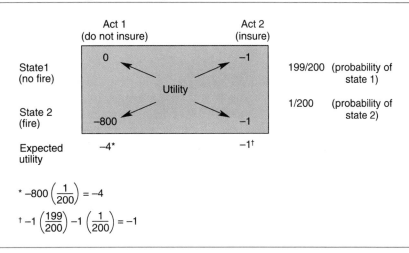

$$* -800\left(\frac{1}{200}\right) = -4$$

$$\dagger -1\left(\frac{199}{200}\right) -1\left(\frac{1}{200}\right) = -1$$

Table 6–8   **Conditional and Expected Utility for Investment**

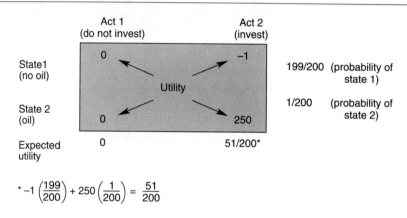

$$* -1 \left(\frac{199}{200}\right) + 250 \left(\frac{1}{200}\right) = \frac{51}{200}$$

The decision to invest or not may be analyzed in the same manner. The utility table shown in Table 6–8 may be constructed on the basis of the available information. It follows that the expected utility of act 1 is less than the expected utility of act 2. It is seen that the entrepreneur maximizes utility by taking act 2 (investing). The risky venture would be accepted at the same time the entrepreneur was insuring against a loss, contrary to the decisions indicated by expected monetary value.

SUMMARY

When risk considerations are important, maximizing expected utility may be more appropriate than maximizing expected monetary value. A utility function can be assessed using lotteries and indifference points, or by certainty equivalents. The decision alternative that maximizes expected utility is the preferred alternative.

Multiattribute Utility Functions

In some decision problems, there may be several important factors or *attributes* that affect the value of a given outcome. For example, various highway safety programs may reduce the number of fatal accidents and the amount of property damage. We will first consider a deterministic example (no risk) and then modify it to include risk considerations.

Example   Suppose there are five different proposals to improve highway safety, all with the same annual cost. Their anticipated outcomes are presented in Table 6–9.

An initial approach would be to try to reduce the multiple-attribute problem to a single-criterion problem by finding some way to make the attributes directly comparable. For example, suppose one studied a large number of past decisions

Table 6–9 **Alternative Safety Proposals**

Alternative	Annual Reduction in Fatalities	Annual Reduction in Property Damage ($ millions)
A	100	25
B	150	20
C	75	40
D	50	42
E	100	22

Table 6–10 **Dollar Outcomes (assuming one fatality = $250,000)**

Alternative	Annual Reduction in Fatalities	Value of Reduction in Fatalities ($ millions)	Annual Reduction in Property Damage ($ millions)	Total Reduction ($ millions)
A	100	25	25	50
B	150	37.5	20	57.5
C	75	18.75	40	58.75
D	50	12.5	42	54.5
E	100	25	22	47

involving the trade-off between fatalities and dollars spent to avoid them, and found that on the average, past decisions indicated that society was willing to spend $250,000 to avoid one accident fatality. Using the $250,000 estimate to convert fatalities to dollars, the dollar outcomes for the five alternatives are presented in Table 6–10.

From Table 6–10, alternative C has the highest dollar value if a fatality is evaluated at $250,000. This example illustrates how one might use trade-offs between different attributes so that the multiattribute problem becomes a single-attribute problem.

Noncomparable Attributes: Dominance

There will be attributes that cannot be compared directly. Suppose we cannot obtain agreement on placing a dollar value on an accident fatality in our example. The next step would be to look for any dominated alternatives. A **dominated alternative** is one that has all outcomes inferior to or at most equal to the outcomes of one other alternative. Reviewing Table 6–9, we can observe that alternative E is dominated by alternative A, which has the same fatality reduction and a more favorable property damage outcome. Thus, we can eliminate alternative E from further consideration.

If the decision alternatives are not mutually exclusive, and two or more of the alternatives may be used in any proportion, then it is useful to look for **weighted dominance.** We do this in our example by plotting the four remaining alternatives on a diagram with the attributes as axes (see Figure 6–6). We can connect the outcomes in Figure 6–6 that offer the highest amount of one attribute versus the other; thus, outcomes D, C, and B are connected by lines. These lines represent an **efficient frontier**; given the four alternatives, and given the opportunity to pursue more than one of them in some combination, the optimal point must lie on the efficient frontier.

Note the location of alternative A relative to the efficient frontier; it lies below the line connecting alternatives C and B. This means that a weighted-average mixture of B and C would outperform A, and hence A is dominated by alternatives C and B. To see this, consider a ⅓ weight for B and a ⅔ weight for C; this would correspond to spending one third of our budget on alternative B and two thirds on C. The weighted-average outcome would be:

Fatality reduction $\qquad (^1/_3)(150) + (^2/_3)(75) = 100$
Property damage reduction $\quad (^1/_3)(20) + (^2/_3)(40) = 33.33$

The point (100, 33.33) lies on the efficient frontier and is directly above alternative A, hence, dominating it.

The weighted-dominance concept makes sense only when the alternatives are not mutually exclusive and may be used in varying proportions. In our example,

Figure 6–6　　**Alternative Safety Proposals**

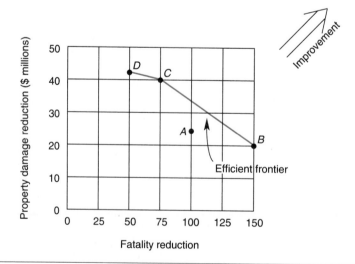

alternative B might be advertising for seat belt usage, while alternative C might involve building stronger guardrails on highway curves. Each of these alternatives could be pursued in a weighted-average manner, spending a fraction of our budget on B and the remainder on C, assuming the actual outcomes of the alternatives are proportional to the expenditures made.

Choice among Alternatives

In order to choose among points on an efficient frontier, we ask the decision maker to specify points of indifference between various outcomes. Consider Figure 6–7 with the attributes as axes. Suppose we present a specific outcome, X (100 fatalities and $40 million in property damage), to a decision maker. We pick another outcome, Y (with 125 fatalities and $35 million in property damage), and ask, "Is the first outcome X equal to the outcome Y?" If Y is preferred to X, we create an outcome Z with 125 fatalities and $20 million in property damage. Suppose X is preferred to Z. By varying the amount of property damage for the given 125 fatalities, we can eventually find a point of indifference such that the decision maker considers the two outcomes of equal value. Suppose for the outcome W (125 fatalities, $30 million property damage) the decision maker is indifferent between W and X; then we can draw an **indifference curve** between these two points. By continuing a series of similar questions, entire sets of indifference curves can be traced out, as shown in Figure 6–7.

Once a set of indifference curves has been obtained, it can be combined with the efficient frontier of Figure 6–6 to make an optimal decision. Figure 6–8 con-

Figure 6–7   Indifference Curves

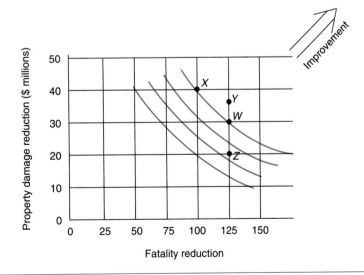

Figure 6–8   **Optimal Decision**

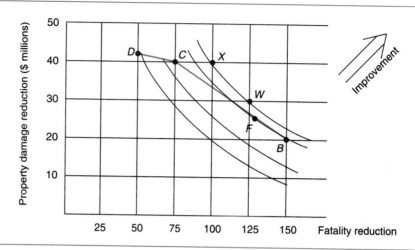

tains both the indifference curves and the efficient frontier. The optimal decision is to choose the point on the efficient frontier that attains the highest indifference curve. In Figure 6–8 the optimal decision is denoted by F; F represents approximately 128 fatality reduction and $26 million property damage reduction and is a weighted average of alternatives B and C.

Conjoint Analysis

For assessment of indifference curves among more than two attributes, a statistical technique called *conjoint analysis* is frequently used. It is becoming popular with marketing managers who need to assess the relative utilities of various product attributes to current and potential consumers of the product. While the statistical details of conjoint analysis are beyond the scope of this text, the output of such an analysis would be a set of importance weights for each attribute. For example, average importance weights for attributes of an automobile might be as illustrated in Table 6–11. Marketing managers may obtain such data for various segments of the potential buying population in order to perform market segmentation and design products with assortments of attributes that will appeal to various market segments.

SUMMARY

For riskless situations with multiple attributes, we first try to find trade-offs among the attributes that would allow the problem to be reduced to that of a single attribute, such as dollars. If agreement cannot be reached on such a trade-off, then we seek to eliminate dominated alternatives; and if the alternatives are not mutually exclusive, we also eliminate alternatives dominated by combina-

Table 6–11 **Conjoint Analysis Importance Weights**

Attribute	Weight
Performance	0.20
Reliability	0.20
Fuel economy	0.30
Safety	0.10
Features	0.20
Total	1.00

tions of other alternatives (the weighted dominance case). The remaining alternatives form an efficient frontier. Next, sets of indifference curves are constructed; and finally, combining the sets of indifference curves with the efficient frontier indicates the optimal decision (the one that lies on the highest indifference curve).

Risky Outcomes

We have just seen that analysis of a multiattribute decision problem is quite complex even when the outcomes are not uncertain. Analysis of the general problem with uncertain outcomes is a very complex problem. While conceptually the approach of finding indifference points would carry through to the case involving risk, in practice this is a very cumbersome and involved procedure.

There is one version of the risky problem that is reasonably straightforward to analyze; this is the situation in which the riskiness of the attributes can be dealt with *independently*. Independence of risky attributes does not mean the two attributes are unrelated; all it means is that our risk aversion preferences regarding one attribute are not a function of the level or riskiness of the other attribute. An example will help clarify this.

Example Consider our previous example, except suppose that there are only two alternatives, *B* and *C*, and that the outcomes of these alternatives are uncertain. Figure 6–9 describes the various outcomes and probabilities.

Now suppose the decision maker assesses two separate utility functions for fatality reduction and property damage reduction and agrees that the total utility is the sum of the two separate utility functions. If the total utility can be separated into two additive utility functions, then the problem can be analyzed in a reasonably straightforward manner.

For example, suppose the decision maker has a utility function U_1 for fatality reduction as given in Figure 6–10, and a corresponding utility function U_2 for property damage reduction as given in Figure 6–11.

Figure 6–9   **Uncertain Outcomes**

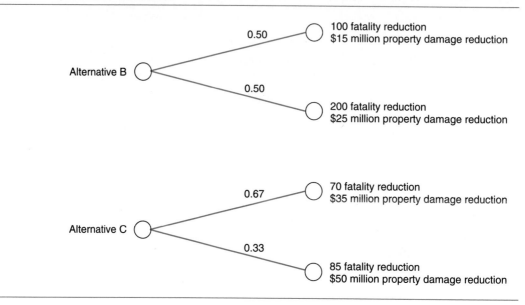

Figure 6–10   **Utility for Fatality Reduction**

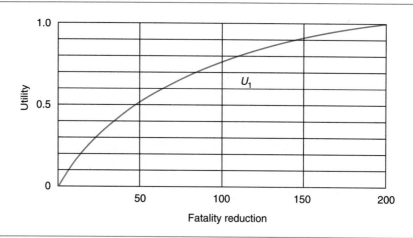

We can now use the utility functions with the risky outcomes to determine the total utility for each alternative, if the utility functions are additive.
For alternative *B*:

$$U(B) = 0.50\ U_1(100) + 0.50\ U_1(200) + 0.50\ U_2(15) + 0.50\ U_2(25)$$

Figure 6–11   **Utility for Property Damage Reduction**

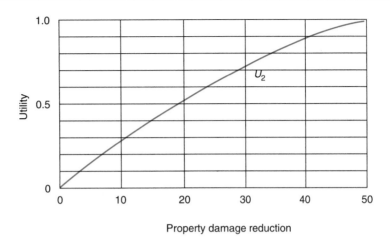

Reading utility values from Figures 6–10 and 6–11:

$$U(B) = 0.5(0.75) + 0.5(1.0) + 0.5(0.38) + 0.5(0.60)$$
$$= 1.365$$

For alternative C:

$$U(C) = 0.67 \, U_1(70) + 0.33 \, U_1(85) + 0.67 \, U_2(35) + 0.33 \, U_2(50)$$

Again reading utility values from the figures:

$$U(C) = 0.67(0.60) + 0.33(0.68) + 0.67(0.80) + 0.33(1.0)$$
$$= 1.4924$$

Thus, alternative C is preferred to alternative B.

A strong word of caution should be offered here; it may not be possible to represent the decision maker's preferences by separate additive utility functions. In that case, one must combine the indifference curve approach and assessment of preferences, and the analysis quickly becomes very cumbersome.[6]

SUMMARY

Risky multiattribute problems can be solved using utility functions if the utility of the outcomes can be represented by additive utility functions over each attribute.

---

[6]See C. A. Holloway, *Decision Making under Uncertainty: Models and Choices* (Englewood Cliffs, N.J.: Prentice Hall, 1979), Chapter 20.

Prospect Theory

Kahneman and Tversky are critical of expected utility theory because they have observed actions inconsistent with it. They offer an alternative framework called **prospect theory.**[7]

We will consider the types of problems that motivated Kahneman and Tversky. Consider two lotteries A and B:

Lottery	Outcomes	Probability
A	$4,000	0.8
	0	0.2
B	3,000	1.0

Which lottery would you choose? As might be expected, the largest percentage of persons faced with this choice picked B. The certainty of $3,000 seems to be preferred over an uncertain $4,000.

They also offered two other lotteries:

Lottery	Outcomes	Probability
C	$4,000	0.2
	0	0.8
D	3,000	0.25
	0	0.75

Now the decision makers tend to prefer C. Unfortunately for utility theory, the choice of C over D is inconsistent with the choice of B over A. Setting $U(0) = 0$, with B preferred over A, we have:

$$U(3,000) > .8U(4,000)$$

With C preferred over D, we have:

$$.2U(4,000) > .25U(3,000)$$

Multiplying both sides by 4, we have:

$$.8U(4,000) > U(3,000)$$

Having $U(3,000) > .8U(4,000)$ is inconsistent with $.8U(4,000) > U(3,000)$.

---

[7]D. Kahneman and A. Tversky, "Prospect Theory: An Analysis of Decision under Risk," *Econometrica,* March 1979, pp. 263–91. Also, Kahneman and Tversky, "The Framing of Decisions and the Psychology of Choice," *Science,* January 1981, pp. 453–58.

In the second set of lotteries, additional information was supplied (the possibility of a zero outcome for lottery D) that confuses the decision maker. An illusion takes place, and the decision maker falls into the trap and chooses C over D. To help the decision maker, we will change the method of presenting lotteries C and D, but will not change the lotteries.

Assume that there are three steps:

Step 1. A chance or random event. There is 0.75 probability of zero and 0.25 probability of proceeding to a choice involving lottery A and B.

Step 2. We have to choose between A and B.

Step 3. Determine the random outcome of A if A is chosen.

Note that the only decision to be made is to choose between A and B. We already know we prefer B to A. Figure 6–12 shows the decision tree for the three steps.

If we choose lottery B, we have:

Outcome	Probability
3,000	0.25
0	0.75

which is lottery D.

Figure 6–12

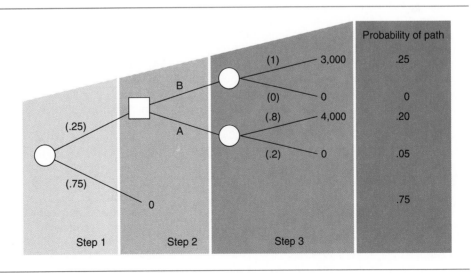

If we choose lottery *A*, we have:

Outcome	Probability
4,000	0.20
0	0.80

which is lottery *C*. Since we choose lottery *B*, we are choosing lottery *D* over lottery *C*. The example shows that by introducing additional information, we can confuse the decision maker.

Kahneman and Tversky make the very important point that the framing of the choices and information can strongly influence the decision. These observations are very important. They suggest that a decision maker has to realize that words and numbers have to be penetrated to their core to extract the basic elements of the decision. One has to realize that the statement "the glass is half full" is, in a decision context, exactly equal to the statement "the glass is half empty." We have to be indifferent to choosing between the two glasses. Not only are the outcomes and their probabilities important, but also important is the exact form in which they are presented.

Bibliography

Bunn, D. W. *Applied Decision Analysis*. New York: McGraw-Hill, 1984.

Edwards, W., and A. Tversky, eds. *Decision Making*. Baltimore: Penguin Books, 1967.

Fishburn, P. C. *Utility Theory for Decision Making*. New York: John Wiley & Sons, 1970.

Friedman, M., and L. J. Savage. "The Utility Analysis of Choices Involving Risk." *Journal of Political Economy*, August 1948.

Green, P. E., and Y. Wind. *Multiattribute Decisions in Marketing*. Hinsdale, Ill.: Dryden Press, 1973.

Holloway, C. A. *Decision Making under Uncertainty: Models and Choices*. Englewood Cliffs, N.J.: Prentice Hall, 1979.

IEEE Transactions on Systems Science and Cybernetics (Special Issue on Decision Analysis), vol. SSC–4, no. 3 (September 1968).

Kahneman, D., and A. Tversky. "Prospect Theory: An Analysis of Decision under Risk." *Econometrica*, March 1979, pp. 263–91.

———. "The Framing of Decisions and the Psychology of Choice." *Science,* January 1981, pp. 453–58.

Keeney, R. L., and H. Raiffa. *Decisions with Multiple Objectives*. New York: John Wiley & Sons, 1976.

Pratt, J. W.; H. Raiffa; and R. Schlaifer. "The Foundations of Decision under Uncertainty: An Elementary Exposition." *Journal of the American Statistical Association*, June 1964.

Savage, L. J. *The Foundations of Statistics*. New York: John Wiley & Sons, 1954.

Schlaifer, R. *Analysis of Decisions under Uncertainty*. New York: McGraw-Hill, 1969.

Swalm, R. O. "Utility Theory—Insights into Risk Taking." *Harvard Business Review,* November–December 1966.

Von Neumann, J., and O. Morgenstern. *Theory of Games and Economic Behavior*. Princeton: Princeton University Press, 1944.

Zeleny, M. *Multiple Criteria Decision Making*. New York: McGraw-Hill, 1982

Problems with Answers

6–1. Entrepreneur W has a utility index of 5 for a loss of $1,000, and 12 for a profit of $3,000. She says that she is indifferent between $10 for certain and the following lottery: a 0.4 chance at a $1,000 loss and a 0.6 chance at a $3,000 profit. What is her utility index for $10?

6–2. Entrepreneur X has a utility index for $-$2 of 0.50; his index for $500 is 0.60. He maintains that he is indifferent between $500 for certain and a lottery of a 0.8 chance at $-$2 and a 0.2 chance at $20,000. What is his utility index for $20,000?

6–3. Entrepreneur W has a utility index of 5 for a loss of $1,000 and a utility index of 6 for a loss of $500. What is the slope of her utility function between these points?

6–4. You have a date for the quantitative analysis ball; the admission is $10, which you do not have. On the day of the dance, your psychology instructor offers you either $8 for certain or a 50–50 chance at nothing or $12. Which choice would you make, assuming you had no other source of funds or credit? Why? If the utility of $8 is 20, and the utility of zero dollars is 0, what does this imply about the utility of $12?

6–5. Suppose that Smith has a utility function $U(x) = x^{2/3}$, where x is in dollars $(0 \leq x \leq 1,000)$. Smith is offered the following choices:

A: $8 for sure.
B: A lottery with a one-half chance for zero dollars and a one-half chance for $64.

Which lottery would you predict Smith will choose?

6–6. The Iota Engineering Company does subcontracting on government contracts. Iota is a small company with limited capital. The utility function is described as follows:

$$U(x) = -x/100 - x^2/5,000, x < -1,000$$
$$U(x) = x/100 - 170, -1,000 \leq x \leq 10,000$$
$$U(x) = \sqrt{x}, x > 10,000$$

a. Suppose Iota is considering bidding on a given contract. It will cost $2,000 to prepare the bid. If the bid is lost, the $2,000 cost is also lost. If Iota wins the bid, it will make $40,000 and recover the $2,000 bid preparation cost. Suppose Iota believes the probability of winning the contract is 0.5 if a bid is submitted. What should it do?

b. What would the probability of winning have to be before Iota would submit a bid?

6–7. The ABC Company wants its new product to be both aesthetically pleasing and inexpensive to produce. Cost engineers have evaluated five alternative designs for costs, and design experts have rated the designs aesthetically as follows:

Alternative	Unit Cost ($)	Aesthetic Appeal (10 = Best, 1 = Worst)
A	$100	5
B	80	7
C	110	8
D	125	9
E	150	10

The alternatives are mutually exclusive; only one can be selected.

a. Are there any dominated alternatives? Which are they, and why are they dominated?

b. Plot the remaining alternatives on a figure with the two attributes as axes.

c. Suppose the president of the company decides that one point of aesthetic appeal is worth $10 increased cost per unit. Draw a set of indifference lines on your figure with the slope representing

For Problem 6–8

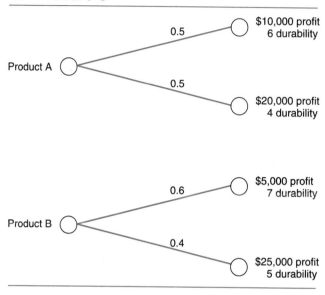

the president's trade-off. What is the preferred alternative?

6-8. The XYZ Company must select one of two new products to bring to market. Each product has a risky outcome regarding short-term profitability and long-term durability, as is illustrated above (durability is measured on a scale from 1 to 10, with 10 being best). The company thinks total utility is the sum of the utilities of profit and durability. For profit, the utility function is $U_1(p) = p^{2/3}$, where $p = \$000$s of profit. For durability, the utility function is $U_2(d) = d^{1/3}$, where $d = $ Durability scale.

a. Is either alternative dominated?

b. Evaluate both alternatives. Which is preferred?

Problems

6-9. Entrepreneur Y has a utility index of -108 for \$11,000, and -275 for zero dollars. He is indifferent between a 0.5 chance at \$11,000 plus a 0.5 chance at a \$20,000 loss and a certainty of zero. What is his utility index for a loss of \$20,000?

6-10. Entrepreneur Z has a utility index of 10 for \$18,750, 6 for \$11,200, and 0 for zero dollars. What probability combination of zero dollars and \$18,750 would make her indifferent to \$11,200 for certain?

6-11. Two economists, Alfred M. Noxie and J. Maynard K. Bampton, are arguing about the relative merits of their respective decision rules. Noxie says he always takes that act with the greatest expected monetary value; Bampton says he always takes the act with the greatest expected utility, and his utility function for money is $U(M) = 10 + 0.2M$. For decisions involving monetary payoffs, who will make the better choices?

6-12. You are a fire insurance sales representative confronted by a balky mathematician who argues that she should not insure her house against fire because of the small loading charge that provides the overhead for the insurance company. If her analysis is correct, what does this imply about the shape of her utility function?

6–13. Suppose the importance weights of Table 6–11 can be segmented into two different market segments, as follows:

Attribute	Segment A Weight	Segment B Weight
Performance	0.10	0.30
Reliability	0.30	0.10
Fuel economy	0.40	0.20
Safety	0.10	0.10
Features	0.10	0.30
Total	1.00	1.00

Describe in qualitative terms what the implications of these data are for each of the segments; that is, describe how the segments differ in their trade-offs among the multiple attributes presented.

6–14. You are the plant manager for a small manufacturing concern. The parking lot next to the factory must be repaved. A large contractor has told you that he will submit a bid at any time consisting of the expected full cost plus 10 percent profit. The only uncertainty in the cost calculation on this job is the weather. If it is clear, the incremental cost of the job will be $40,000. If it rains, the incremental cost will be $55,000. The weather bureau has informed you that the chance of rain for the relevant period is 1 out of 10, and that all contractors know and accept this information.

You know you will get two other bids on the job. Two small local contractors, Willie and Joe, have been engaged in a bitter rivalry ever since World War II. In recent years, the object of their rivalry has been to see who would be the first to enter the Six-Figure Club. Requirements for admission consist of making a profit of $100,000 or more for one year. You know that Willie has made profits this year of

$109,500, and Joe has made profits of $95,000. There is so little time left in the year that your job will be the last possible job for each of them. Also, they both have excess capacity and can undertake the job. What bids would you expect? How would you explain the bids?

6–15. Suppose a decision maker, when asked to find the certainty equivalents for the gambles shown in the first column below, responded with the answers in the second column.

Gamble	Assessed Certainty Equivalent
1. ½ chance at −$100,000 and ½ chance at $200,000	$ 10,000
2. ½ chance at $10,000 and ½ chance at $200,000	100,000
3. ½ chance at $10,000 and ½ chance at −$100,000	−55,000

a. Using graph paper, plot the utility points associated with the above gambles, and draw a smooth utility curve through the points.

b. Using this curve, find the certainty equivalent for the following gamble:

	Probability
−$ 80,000	0.2
0	0.4
80,000	0.2
160,000	0.2

6–16. The treasurer of a corporation is considering a decision to increase the deductible amount on the corporation's fire insurance from $2,000 per occurrence to $5,000 (meaning that the first $5,000 of fire loss would not be reimbursed under the policy). Such an increase in the deductible would lower the annual insurance premium from $2,500 to $1,400. Based on historical data, the treasurer estimates the probability of fire as follows:

Number of Fires in a Year	Probability
0	0.80
1	0.15
2	0.05
3 or more	0

If a fire occurs, the loss is certain to be above $5,000 because of the nature of the product produced.

When asked about risk aversion preferences, the following utility function was obtained:

Dollars	Utility
−$10,000	0.000
−4,000	0.300
0	0.490
1,000	0.537
3,000	0.620

Should the treasurer increase the deductible? Why or why not?

6–17. Refer to Problem 4–22 and the decision tree shown in Figure 4–13. Suppose QPC determines the following points on its utility function:

$ Millions	Utility
−4.00	0.0
−3.50	0.2
−2.00	0.4
0.75	0.6
5.00	0.8
10.00	1.0

Graph these points and draw a smooth curve through them. Then use this curve to determine what decision QPC should make in the decision tree given in Figure 4–13.

6–18. Refer to Problem 6–17. Suppose QPC has another venture that involves a 0.50 chance for a gain of $10 million and a 0.5 chance for a $4 million loss. Use the utility curve through the points given in Problem 6–17.

Several investors offer to join with QPC in this venture. In particular, Investor A offers to share 50 percent of both the gains and losses with QPC. Investor B offers to accept a 40 percent share of the losses in return for a 30 percent share of the gains. Investor C offers to pay QPC $2 million in return for a 50 percent share of the gains, but no share of the losses. Which, if any, of these offers should QPC accept?

6–19. Consider Figure 6–6 in the chapter. Suppose now that the alternatives there are mutually exclusive; only one can be selected.

a. Draw the efficient frontier for this situation.

b. Using the indifference curves of Figure 6–8 and outcomes of Figure 6–6, what is the best choice?

6–20. Four alternatives are available for investment. There are two criteria, with outcomes as follows (for each criterion, more is better):

Alternative	Criterion 1	Criterion 2
1	30	10
2	5	40
3	10	20
4	20	25

The alternatives are not mutually exclusive.

a. Are there any dominated alternatives? Which are they, and why are they dominated?

b. Plot the remaining alternatives, and show the efficient frontier.

For Problem 6–21

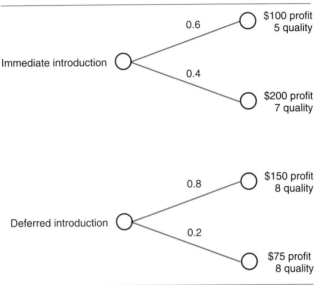

c. Now suppose that management decides that criterion 1 is twice as important as criterion 2, so that a unit on criterion 1 is equal to two units of criterion 2. Draw a set of indifference curves on your diagram, and indicate the optimal solution.

d. Now suppose that management decides the alternatives are mutually exclusive (only one can be selected). What is the optimal choice now?

6–21. A semiconductor products company has a new product, but it must decide on the timing of the introduction. Profitability will be greater if the introduction is immediate, but product quality (measured on a scale of 1 to 10, 10 is best) will be higher with a deferred introduction. Furthermore, each of these criteria has risky outcomes, as shown in the accompanying diagram above.

For the amounts of profits involved, the company's utility for profit is linear $[U(M) = M]$; but the company is quite concerned about the risk of low quality, and the utility function for quality is $U(q) = 100q^{1/2}$, where q = Quality index. The company's total utility is the sum of the two utilities for the separate criteria.

a. Is there a dominated alternative?

b. Evaluate both alternatives. Which is preferred?

More Challenging Problems

6–22. Refer to Problem 4–19. Suppose that the utility function for money for the drilling problem is the same as that assessed in Problem 6–15.

a. Should the company drill or sell the lease?

b. Suppose, before the company began drilling, another firm offered to buy the lease. What is the minimum price the company should accept?

c. Suppose, before drilling began, an outside syndicate of investors offered the following proposition: The syndicate would pay the company $20,000 for a 50 percent share in the costs and revenues associated with drilling. (That is, revenues to the company would be $20,000 plus one half of the values listed in Problem 4–19.) Should the company accept the offer?

6–23. Refer to Problem 4–35. Suppose the concessionnaire in that problem gave the following certainty equivalents for the gambles shown:

Gamble	Assessed Certainty Equivalent
1. ½ chance at −$20,000 and ½ chance at $40,000	−$ 5,000
2. ½ chance at −$5,000 and ½ chance at $40,000	13,000
3. ½ chance at −$5,000 and ½ chance at −$20,000	−16,000

a. Using these values, draw a utility function for the concessionnaire on graph paper.

b. How much food should the concessionnaire order to be consistent with this set of utility assessments?

6–24. Refer to Problem 4–38. Suppose that Little Electronics, after careful consideration, has assessed its utility function for the cash flows resulting from the lawsuit described in that problem. The utility function $U(X)$ can be described by the following function:

$$U(X) = 1 - \frac{1}{X + 2}$$

where X is the cash flow ($ millions) resulting from the lawsuit.

Develop the decision tree for Little's decision problem. Substitute the utility values in place of the cash flows at the ends of the tree. Analyze the tree using the utility values to determine what decision Little should make.

The Normal Probability Distribution and the Value of Information

This chapter presents an important probability concept called the *normal distribution,* which will subsequently be used in the evaluation of additional information in a decision problem.

Probability Distributions

There are discrete and continuous probability distributions. A discrete distribution is called a **probability mass function** (p.m.f.), and a continuous probability function is called a **probability density function** (p.d.f.). With a probability mass function (discrete distribution), the random variable is allowed to take on only selected values (for example, 0.1, 0.2, or 0.3, but perhaps not 0.11, 0.21, or 0.31).

As an example, we could indicate the proportion of families that have X members. A family may have 4 members, but it cannot have 4.2 members; thus, X must be an integer. Sometimes, we classify the data so that we may use a discrete probability distribution where we could use a continuous distribution. For example, it is possible that any amount of product may be demanded, but we may classify the demand for a day as falling into classifications of tenths of a ton (i.e., 0.1, 0.2, and so on).

The binomial distribution, which is described in Chapter 3, is another example of a discrete probability distribution. The random variable, number of successes, can only take on zero and positive integer values from one to n (the number of trials).

A **continuous probability density function** is a distribution where the value of the random variable may be any number within some given range of values—say, between zero and infinity. For example, assuming a probability density function of the height of the members of a population, there would be a value of the density function of 5.3 feet, 5.324 feet, 5.32431 feet, and so on, but the height cannot be negative. The density function has a value for all possible values of the random variable within a stated range. Graphs of the two types of distributions are shown in Figures 7–1 and 7–2.

Figure 7–1   **Discrete Probability Distribution (probability mass function or p.m.f.)**

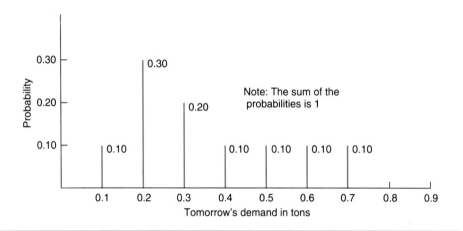

Figure 7–2   **Continuous Probability Distribution (probability density function or p.d.f.)**

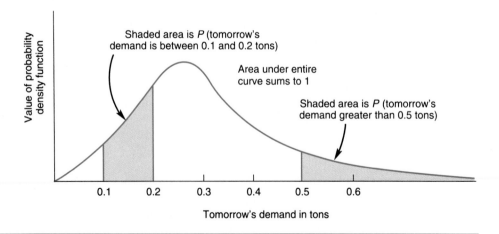

For a discrete distribution, the height of each line represents the probability for that value of the random variable. For example, 0.30 is the probability that tomorrow's demand will be 0.2 tons in Figure 7–1. For a continuous random variable, the height of the probability density function is *not* the probability for an event. Rather, the *area under the curve* over any interval on the horizontal axis represents the probability of taking on a value in that interval. For example, the shaded area on the left in Figure 7–2 represents the probability that tomorrow's demand will be in the *interval* between 0.1 and 0.2 tons.

Cumulative Mass Functions

Associated with probability mass functions are cumulative mass functions. A cumulative mass function shows cumulative probability. For example, consider the random variable S with the discrete probability mass function shown in Table 7–1.

In addition to being interested in the probability of S being equal to 2 [i.e., $P(S = 2) = 0.40$], we may wish to know the probability of S being equal to or less than 2 [i.e., $P(S \leq 2) = 0.60$]. The function giving values of this nature is called the *cumulative* mass function. The probability mass function and cumulative mass function of a "less than or equal to" type for the example in Table 7–1 are shown in Table 7–2 and Figure 7–3.

Table 7–1

s	$P(S = s)$
0	0.00
1	0.20
2	0.40
3	0.30
4	0.10
	1.00

Table 7–2

s	$P(S = s)$	$P(S \leq s)$
0	0.00	0.00
1	0.20	0.20
2	0.40	0.60
3	0.30	0.90
4	0.10	1.00

Figure 7–3 **Example of Probability Mass Function and Cumulative Mass Function**

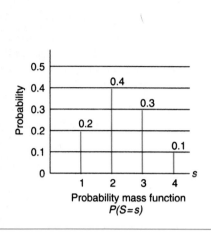
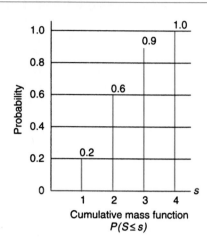

We may also wish to know the probability of S being greater than 2:

$$P(S > 2) = 1 - P(S \leq 2) = 1 - 0.60 = 0.40$$

Given the probability mass function, we can obtain the cumulative mass function and such variations as $P(S \geq 2)$ or $P(2 \leq S \leq 4)$.

Cumulative Distribution Functions

Cumulative distribution functions are associated with continuous probability density functions just as cumulative mass functions are associated with discrete probability mass functions.

We shall illustrate the cumulative distribution function using a rectangular or uniform probability distribution (look at Figure 7–4). If S is between a and b ($a \leq S \leq b$), then the value of the probability density function is $1/(b - a)$, and zero otherwise. If we sum the area under the probability density function:

$$f(S) = \frac{1}{b - a}$$

over the range from a to S for each value of S, we obtain the cumulative distribution, $F(S)$. We use $f(\cdot)$ to represent the probability density function and $F(\cdot)$ to represent the cumulative distribution function of the "less than or equal to" type (see Figure 7–5).

Figure 7–4   **Probability Density Function** $f(S) = \dfrac{1}{b-a}, a \le S \le b; f(S) = 0$ **Otherwise**

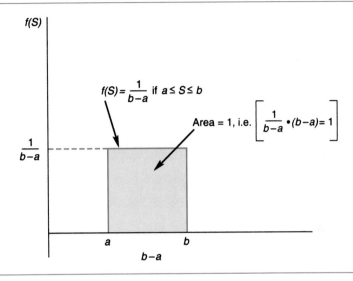

Figure 7–5   **$F(S)$, Cumulative Distribution Function for $f(S) = \dfrac{1}{b-a}$**

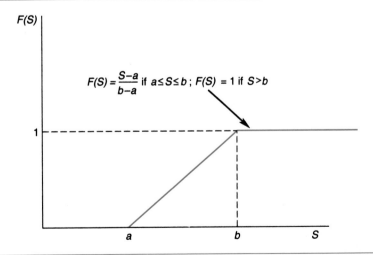

Figure 7–6

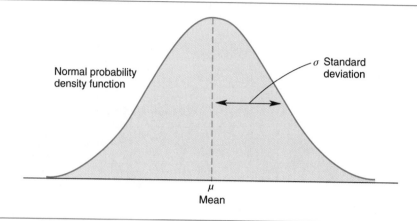

The Normal Probability Distribution

The **normal distribution,** sometimes called the **Gaussian distribution,** is an extremely important distribution. It is easier to manipulate mathematically than many other distributions and is a good approximation for several of the others. In many cases, the normal distribution is a reasonable approximation for a prior probability distribution for business decision purposes; and in the following chapters, we shall use the normal distribution in many of the applications. Despite its general application, it should not be assumed that every process can be described as having a normal distribution.

The normal distribution has a probability density function that is a smooth, symmetric, continuous, bell-shaped curve, as pictured in Figure 7–6. The area under the curve over any interval on the horizontal axis represents the probability of the random variable, X, taking on a value in that interval. As with any continuous probability density function, the area under the curve sums to 1.

A normal distribution is completely determined by its mean (denoted by μ) and standard deviation (σ); that is, once we know the mean and standard deviation, the shape and location of the distribution is set. The curve reaches a maximum at the mean of the distribution. One half of the area lies on either side of the mean. The greater the value of σ, the standard deviation, the more spread out the curve.[1] This is illustrated in Figure 7–7.

---

[1] The normal probability density function with parameters μ and σ is:

$$f_N(x) = \frac{1}{\sigma(2\pi)^{1/2}} e^{-(x-\mu)^2/2\sigma^2}, \quad -\infty < x < \infty$$

The normal cumulative distribution function is:

$$F_N(x) = \int_{-\infty}^{x} f_N(y)dy$$

Figure 7–7

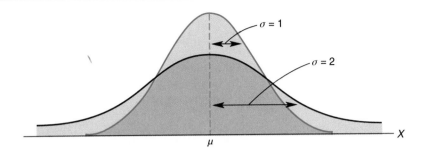

Figure 7–8

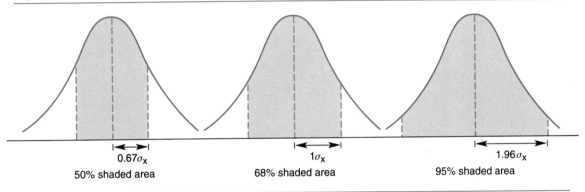

With any normal distribution, approximately 0.50 of the area lies within ± 0.67 standard deviations from the mean; about 0.68 of the area lies within ± 1.0 standard deviations; and 0.95 of the area lies within ± 1.96 standard deviations. See Figure 7–8.

Since the normal probability function is continuous (a probability density function), probability cannot be read directly from the graphs. We must consider the probability of the value of a random variable being in an interval (see Figure 7–9).

In Figure 7–9:

$$P(-2 \leq X \leq 0) = \text{Shaded area } A$$
$$P(X \geq 2) = \text{Shaded area } B$$
$$P(0 \leq X \leq 2) = \text{Area between } A \text{ and } B \text{ (also equal to the shaded area } A$$
$$\text{because of the symmetry of the normal curve)}$$

Figure 7–9

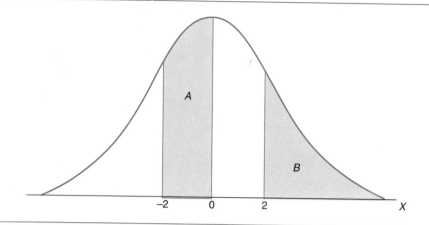

Figure 7–10

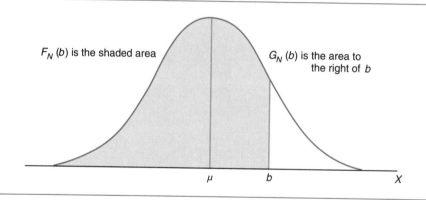

Right and Left Tails

The symbol F_N is used to represent a cumulative distribution function of a normal probability distribution. It is the area under the *left* tail of a normal probability density function. In Figure 7–10, the shaded area is the left tail of a normal curve; that is, $F_N(b)$. $F_N(b)$ is the probability of X being equal to or less than b; that is,

$$F_N(b) = P(X \le b) \qquad (7\text{–}1)$$

We now introduce a new symbol, G_N, which we define as the area under the *right* tail of a normal probability density function. In Figure 7–10, the unshaded area is the right tail of a normal curve; that is, $G_N(b)$.

$G_N (b)$ is the probability of X being greater than b; that is:

$$G_N (b) = P(X > b)$$

From Figure 7–10, it can be seen that $F_N (b)$ and $G_N (b)$ are related:[2]

$$G_N (b) = 1 - F_N (b) \qquad (7\text{–}2)$$

since the total area under the probability density function sums to 1 by definition.

The Standardized Normal Variable and Normal Probability Tables

A normal distribution with $\mu = 0$ (mean of 0) and $\sigma = 1$ (standard deviation of 1) is said to be a **standard normal distribution.** If a normal distribution has a mean other than 0 or a standard deviation other than 1, we may standardize the distribution. The ability to standardize normal distributions is one of the useful features of the distribution and allows us to look up normal probabilities in a relatively short table.

To standardize a normal random variable, we shall define a new **standardized normal variable,** Z, as follows:

$$Z = \frac{X - \mu}{\sigma} \qquad (7\text{–}3)$$

where X is the nonstandardized normal random variable we are concerned with, μ is the mean of this random variable, and σ is its standard deviation. In the above expression, Z is the distance of X from its mean, μ, measured in units of standard deviations. For example, if $Z = 4$, then:

$$4 = \frac{X - \mu}{\sigma}$$

so that:

$$4\sigma = X - \mu$$
$$X = \mu + 4\sigma$$

Thus, $Z = 4$ corresponds to a value of X that is four standard deviations larger than its mean. As a result of this operation, Z is a standardized, normally

---

[2]The basic mathematical relationships may be stated as:

$$F_N(b) = \int_{-\infty}^{b} f_N(X)dX$$

and

$$G_N(b) = \int_{b}^{\infty} f_N(X)dX$$

distributed random variable, which has a mean of 0 and a standard deviation of 1. Since we look up the probabilities in terms of Z, and all Zs have a mean of 0 and a standard deviation of 1, we need only one table of probabilities. Table A (in the appendix at the end of the text) is a table of cumulative normal probabilities. It should be noted that in Equation 7–3, we are transforming a value from one normal distribution into a value of a standard normal distribution. The value being transformed must come from a normal distribution.

Assume we are concerned with a normally distributed random variable, X, with mean $\mu = 8$ and standard deviation $\sigma = 3$. Let us find the following probabilities:

1. $P(X \leq 10)$.
2. $P(X > 10)$.
3. $P(10 < X \leq 15)$.

Example 1 We first standardize the random variable X for the value $X = 10$:

$$Z = \frac{X - \mu}{\sigma} = \frac{10 - 8}{3} = \frac{2}{3} = 0.67$$

We then look up the probability $P(Z \leq 0.67)$ in Table A and find it to equal 0.7486. The probability of X being less than 10 is 0.7486. [Note that $P(X \leq 10)$ is the same as $P(X < 10)$, since the probability of being exactly 10 is defined to be zero if the probability distribution is continuous.]

Example 2 From Example 1, we know that for $X = 10$, $Z = 0.67$, and:

$$P(X \leq 10) = P(Z \leq 0.67) = 0.7486$$

Then:

$$P(X > 10) = 1 - P(X \leq 10) = 0.2514$$

If the probability of X being less than 10 is 0.75, the probability of X being greater than 10 is 0.25. In terms of areas, if the area to the left of 10 is 0.75, and the total area under the density function is 1, then the area to the right of 10 is $(1 - 0.75)$, or 0.25.

Example 3 We want to determine area C of Figure 7–11. The area $C + D$ is $P(X > 10)$. Area D is $P(X > 15)$. The first step is to know $P(X > 10) = 0.2514$ from Example 2. To calculate area D or $P(X > 15)$, the first step is to compute Z for a value of $X = 15$.

$$Z = \frac{15 - 8}{3} = \frac{7}{3} = 2.33$$

In Table A (in the appendix at the end of the text), we find:

$$P(Z \leq 2.33) = 0.99010$$

Figure 7–11

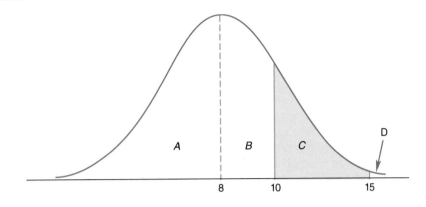

We can now calculate area D:

$$P(X > 15) = P(Z > 2.33) = 1 - P(Z \leq 2.33)$$
$$= 1 - 0.99010 = 0.00990$$

The probability of X being larger than 10 and less than 15 (or equivalently, Z being larger than 0.67 and less than 2.33) is area $C + D$ minus area D:

$$P(10 < X \leq 15) = P(X > 10) - P(X > 15)$$
$$= P(Z > 0.67) - P(Z > 2.33)$$
$$= 0.2514 - 0.0099 = 0.2415$$

SUMMARY

Discrete probability distributions have random variables that take on only specific values. The random variable for continuous distributions may be any value within a range. For a continuous probability distribution, probability is given by an area under the density function.

The normal distribution is a symmetric bell-shaped distribution that can be characterized by its mean and standard deviation. Normal probabilities are obtained by using the standardized normal variable Z and Appendix Table A.

Normal Prior Probabilities and the Value of Information

In the preceding sections, we described the general characteristics of the normal probability distribution. We shall now show the use of the normal distribution as a prior probability distribution. Our discussion here will follow closely the explanation of expected value contained in Chapter 4. The difference will be the use of continuous, rather than discrete, prior probabilities.

Suppose a company has an opportunity to buy a machine for $17,200. The machine, if successful, will save labor hours in a production process that now uses a large amount of hand labor. The physical life of this machine is one year. Assume the incremental cost of a labor hour to the company is $8; thus, if the machine will save more than 2,150 labor hours ($17,200/$8 = 2,150), the company will benefit from owning the machine.

Let us assume that the production engineer feels that the mean number of hours saved will be 2,300 and that there is a 50–50 chance that the actual hours saved could be less than 2,100 or more than 2,500 hours for the year.

With this description of the engineer's feelings, it is possible to assume that a specific normal distribution will fit the prior expectations. The mean of the distribution is 2,300. If we can determine the standard deviation, we have described the normal prior probability distribution.

In the normal distribution, roughly half the area (hence, half the probability) lies within ± 0.67 standard deviations of the mean. Figure 7–12 approximates the fit of a normal distribution to the engineer's estimates. The engineer has estimated a mean of 2,300 hours and has judged that the true value lies between 2,100 and 2,500 hours, with probability 0.50. Hence, half the area must lie outside these limits, 0.25 on the left side and 0.25 on the right side. Figure 7–12 shows that if we move in a positive direction of 200 units, we move out 0.67 σ. We can use this relationship to determine the standard deviation:

$$0.67\sigma = 200 \text{ hours}$$
$$\sigma = \frac{200}{0.67} = 300 \text{ hours}$$

The normal prior distribution has a standard deviation of approximately 300 hours.

Figure 7–12

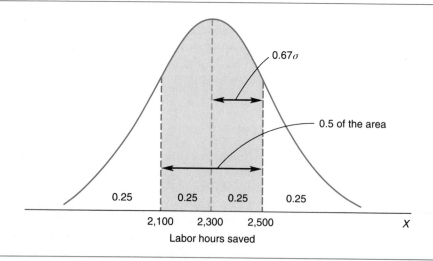

Note also that the normal distribution assigns probabilities to both large and small hour savings. This will be in accordance with the engineer's judgment that the probabilities are symmetrically distributed around the mean.

To summarize, we have taken the engineer's narrative description and converted it to a normal prior distribution with mean $\mu = 2,300$ hours and standard deviation $\sigma = 300$ hours. We also know that in order to break even, the machine must save at least 2,150 hours; and for every hour that actual savings differ from 2,150, the profit changes at a rate of $8 per hour.

Profits can be represented as a linear function of hours saved, with zero profit at 2,150 hours. Thus:

$$\text{Profits} = \pi = -17,200 + 8X$$

where X is the actual number of hours saved. Since this is a linear function, expected profits can be determined by replacing X by its expected value.[3]

$$E(\pi) = -17,200 + 8\mu$$
$$= -17,200 + 8(2,300) = 1,200$$

Whenever the estimate of mean savings is above the break-even point, expected profits are positive, and we should buy the machine. (Assume we are willing to buy the machine on a break-even basis; i.e., in this chapter, we shall ignore utility considerations and the interest return required for acceptable investments.) Even though the engineer's prior probability distribution is fairly tight (the standard deviation, $\sigma = 300$, is relatively small compared with the size of the mean, so that the engineer is fairly certain of the estimate of the mean), perhaps it would pay us to gather more information before we act. Hence, we are interested in the expected value of perfect information (EVPI).

Let us first define the conditional opportunity loss. The optimal action on an expected value basis is to buy the machine. Suppose we buy the machine and it turns out that the actual savings are less than 2,150 hours. In such a case, how much do we lose? If we let X_b stand for the break-even amount of 2,150 hours, the conditional loss will increase by $8 for every hour we fall short of the break-even point. If X is larger than X_b, the opportunity loss is zero if we buy the equipment. Thus, the conditional opportunity loss (assuming we buy the equipment) will be:

$$\begin{cases} \$8(X_b - X) & \text{if } X \leq X_b \\ 0 & \text{if } X > X_b \end{cases}$$

where X = the actual hours that are saved and $X_b = 2,150$, the hours required to break even. The conditional opportunity loss of buying the equipment is graphed in Figure 7–13.

Recall from Chapter 4 that the expected value of perfect information (EVPI) is a measure of the value of a perfect predictor or of perfect information. It is the expectation of the conditional value of perfect information.

---

[3] See Chapter 5.

Figure 7–13

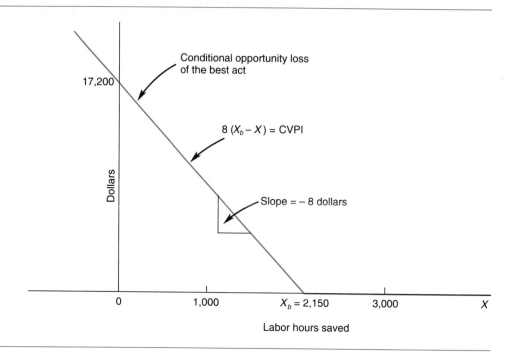

We have decided that our best act, based on present information and using the mean savings, is to buy the machine. If a perfect prediction device were to tell us the actual hour savings would be 2,852, or any number greater than 2,150, we would choose the same act as we would have chosen without this information, and the predictor would be of no value. However, if our predictor were to tell us the true hour savings would actually be 2,029, or any number less than 2,150, then we would not buy the machine, and we would avoid a loss. Hence, the predictor has value *only* if we change our decision when given the new information. The computation of **conditional value of perfect information** (CVPI) (assuming that without the information the equipment would be accepted) may be summarized as follows:

$$\text{CVPI} = \begin{cases} \$8(X_b - X) & \text{if } X \le X_b \\ 0 & \text{if } X > X_b \end{cases}$$

This functional relationship is also graphed in Figure 7–13, which shows that perfect information is worth nothing if the forecast of hours saved is greater than X_b and it increases linearly to the left of the break-even point (the hours saved are less than 2,150 and are decreasing). The CVPI is identical to the conditional opportunity loss of the best act.

The **expected value of perfect information** (EVPI) is calculated by weighting the conditional value of perfect information (CVPI) by the probability distribution. It is equal to the expected opportunity loss of the best act.

Figure 7–14 shows the prior normal probability distribution superimposed on the conditional value graph. The EVPI is the sum of the product of the normal curve and the CVPI line to the left of the break-even point. This results because CVPI $= 0$ for values of X greater than X_b (2,150 hours).

It can also be seen that the larger the standard deviation, σ, the higher the EVPI. This is because the larger the σ, the more spread out the normal curve, and the greater the probability weight given the larger losses (i.e., the higher values of the CVPI line). If the engineer were very close to being certain that the value of the mean was 2,300, there would be little or no expected value of perfect information. Figure 7–15 shows a situation where the value of information is very low. A σ of 50 hours would result in a situation of this nature.

The reason for perfect information being almost valueless in this latter situation is because the σ of the prior distribution is quite small compared with the distance from the mean to the break-even point. Note that the closer X_b is to μ (with a given σ), the higher will be the EVPI. This is shown graphically in Figure 7–16, where we first assume X_b is the break-even point and then assume X_c is the break-even point. If μ, the prior mean, is close to X_b, perfect information is more likely to change the decision as to which is the best act than if μ is relatively far from X_b. Remember that for perfect information to have any value, it is necessary for there to be a possibility that the optimum act will change in the light of the new information.

Summarizing, assuming a normal prior distribution, the EVPI depends on the following three factors:

1. The standard deviation, σ. This is a measure of how "uncertain" the estimator is about the prior mean.

Figure 7–14

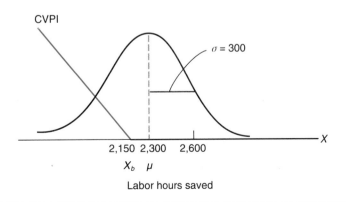

Figure 7–15

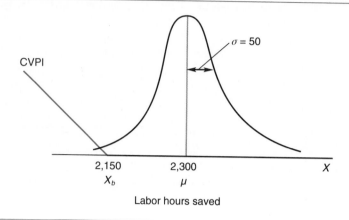

Labor hours saved

Figure 7–16

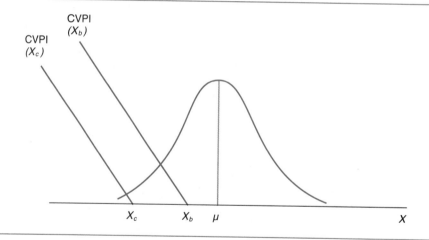

2. The distance of the prior mean from the break-even point $(X_b - \mu)$. This is important because it helps determine how likely the decision maker is to change the decision because of new evidence.

3. The absolute value of the slope of the CVPI line, C. The slope of the line is a measure of how rapidly the loss increases as the hours saved decrease below the break-even point.

It is at this point that we employ one of the more useful features of the normal distribution. The computation of the EVPI can be reduced to a straightforward formula calculation where the components of the formula are those listed above.

This formula is:[4]

$$EVPI = C \cdot \sigma \cdot N(D) \tag{7-4}$$

C is the absolute value of the slope of the CVPI line or the loss constant; σ is the standard deviation of the normal prior distribution; D of $N(D)$ is defined as follows:

$$D = \frac{|X_b - \mu|}{\sigma} \tag{7-5}$$

Thus, D is a measure of the distance of the mean from the break-even point, measured in units of standard deviations. The vertical bars in the formula for D should be read as "absolute value." The quantity $N(D)$ may be obtained from Table B (in the appendix at the end of the text). It is the **loss function** for the standard normal curve, valued for the distance measure D.

It should be noted that the higher the value of D, the lower the value of $N(D)$, and all other things being equal, the lower the EVPI.[5] The lower $N(D)$ results from the fact that the larger the distance $(X_b - \mu)$, the less likely it is that perfect information will change the optimum decision.

For the example of this chapter, EVPI is calculated as follows:

$$C = \$8$$
$$\sigma = 300$$
$$D = \frac{|2,150 - 2,300|}{300} = \frac{|-150|}{300} = \frac{1}{2} = 0.50$$
$$N(D) = N(0.50) = 0.1978 \text{ from Table B}$$
$$EVPI = C \cdot \sigma \cdot N(D)$$
$$EVPI = \$8 \cdot 300 \cdot 0.1978 = \$475$$

The reader may recall from Chapter 4 the difficulty of computing the EVPI for the discrete case. The use of the normal distribution simplifies computations substantially in most business applications. In the above example, we have computed the expected value of perfect information, $475 (which is also the opportunity loss of the best act), and the expected profit of the best act, $1,200. The sum of these two values, $1,675, may be defined as the **expected profit under certainty.**

If we had a perfect predictor available, we would be willing to pay up to $475 to use it. It is not likely that we have a *perfect* predictor; but in some instances,

---

[4]See R. Schlaifer, *Probability and Statistics for Business Decisions* (New York: McGraw-Hill, 1959), pp. 452–55.

[5]$N(D)$ is defined as follows:

$$N(D) = \int_{-\infty}^{-D} (-D - X)f^*(X)dX = \int_{D}^{\infty} (X - D)f^*(X)dX$$

where $f^*(X)$ is the standardized normal density function.

we shall be able to obtain helpful though imperfect information. The problems of determining optimum sample size and revising the prior normal distribution in the light of this additional information are introduced in the following chapter.

SUMMARY

When (a) uncertainty about an unknown variable can be represented by a normal distribution, (b) the decision involves selecting one of two alternatives, and (c) the profits or losses can be expressed as a linear function of the unknown variable, then the expected value of perfect information can be simply determined by Equation 7–4 and the use of Table B in the appendix.

Bibliography

Schlaifer, R. *Probability and Statistics for Business Decisions.* New York: McGraw-Hill, 1959.

Winkler, R. L. *Introduction to Bayesian Inference and Decision.* New York: Holt, Rinehart & Winston, 1972.

Also see the bibliographies of Chapters 3, 4, and 8.

Problems with Answers

7–1. Assume a normal distribution with mean of 12 and standard deviation of 4. Compute the following:
  a. $P(X \geq 15)$.
  b. $P(X < 10)$.
  c. $P(10 < X \leq 15)$.
  d. $P(X > 17)$.
  e. $P(15 < X \leq 17)$.

7–2. Given a random variable X normally distributed with mean of 15 and standard deviation of 3, determine the value of x in each case.
  a. $P(x \leq X) = 0.8413$.
  b. $P(X > x) = 0.2946$.
  c. $P(X > x) = 0.02275$.

7–3. In each case, a normal distribution is considered a good prior probability distribution. For each, determine the expected value of perfect information (EVPI).
  a. Mean is 100 units; standard deviation is 20 units; C, the loss constant, is $2,000 per unit; break-even point is 80 units.
  b. Mean is 100 units; standard deviation is 30 units; C, the loss constant, is $20,000 per unit; break-even point is 80 units.

7–4. Daily sales of a certain product are known to have a normal distribution of 20 per day, with a standard deviation of 6 per day.
  a. What is the probability of selling fewer than 16 on a given day?
  b. What is the probability of selling between 15 and 25 units on a given day?
  c. How many units would have to be on hand at the start of a day in order to have less than a 10 percent chance of running out?

7–5. The ABC Company is considering the sale of a new product. There are $1,750 of fixed costs associated with undertaking the project. The product will sell for $4 a unit, and the variable costs are $1.50. It is expected that 1,000 units will be sold, but the demand has a normal probability distribution with a σ of 150.
  a. How many units have to be sold to break even?
  b. What is the expected profit if the product is carried?
  c. What is the expected value of perfect information if the product is carried?

Problems

7–6. For the probability of sales given below, write out the required probability functions:

Sales (s) (in units)	Probability
1	0.10
2	0.15
3	0.20
4	0.30
5	0.20
10	0.03
15	0.02
	1.00

Required probability functions:

$$P(S \geq s)$$
$$P(S > s)$$
$$P(S < s)$$
$$P(S \leq s)$$

7–7. Find the following probabilities for a normally distributed random variable, X:

a. Mean of 0, standard deviation of 1:

$$P(X > 0.8)$$
$$P(X \leq 0.8)$$
$$P(X \geq -0.8)$$
$$P(-0.8 \leq X \leq 1.2)$$

b. Mean of 6, standard deviation of 2:

$$P(X > 8)$$
$$P(X \leq 8)$$
$$P(X \geq -8)$$
$$P(-8 \leq X \leq 12)$$

c. Mean of 6, standard deviation of 1:

$$P(X > 8)$$
$$P(X \leq 8)$$
$$P(X \geq 4)$$
$$P(4 \leq X \leq 12)$$

7–8. Find the value of the following normally distributed random variables, given each set of conditions:

a. X is normal; mean, 0; standard deviation, 1.

$$P(X > x) = 0.02068$$

What is x?

b. X is normal; mean, 8; standard deviation, 3.

$$P(Z > z) = 0.1587$$

What is x? (Z and z are the standardized values of X and x.)

c. X is normal; mean, 8; standard deviation, 3.

$$P(Z \leq z) = 0.7224$$

What is x?

d. X is normal; mean, 10; standard deviation, 2.

$$P(Z > z) = 0.2327$$

What is x?

7–9. Demand for a product is known to be normally distributed with mean of 240 units per week and standard deviation of 40 units. How many units should a retailer have in stock to ensure a 5 percent or less chance of running out during the week?

7–10. On a midterm exam, the scores were distributed normally with mean of 72 and standard deviation of 10. Student Body Wright scored in the top 10 percent of the class on the midterm.

a. Wright's midterm score was at least how much?

b. The final exam also had a normal distribution, but with mean of 150 and standard deviation of 15. At least what score should Wright get in order to keep the same ranking (i.e., top 10 percent)?

7–11. An investor wishes to invest in one of two projects. The returns for both projects are uncertain, and the probability distribution for returns can be expressed by a normal distribution in each case. Project A has a mean return of $240,000 with a standard deviation of $20,000. Project B has a mean return of $250,000 and a standard deviation of $40,000.

a. Consider a return of $280,000. Which project has a higher chance of returning this much or more?

b. Consider a return of $220,000. Which project has a higher chance of returning this much or more?

7-12. A manufacturer is considering a modification in a product, which will require a capital investment of $100,000. The product contributes an incremental profit of $5 per unit on a present value basis. Increased sales will result from the product modification by making the product attractive to 5,000 new retail stores. Without the modification, these retail stores would not handle the product. The sales manager feels that the mean sales per new store will be about six units and that there is a 50–50 chance that the mean sales could be less than five or more than seven units.

a. Fit a normal distribution to the above situation.

b. Calculate the expected profit of the best act. Should the investment be made?

c. Calculate the EVPI.

7-13. In the situation of Problem 7–12, suppose the sales manager thinks that the mean sales per store will be six units but that there is a 50–50 chance that the actual mean sales could be less than four or greater than eight units. Calculate the EVPI, and explain why it is greater than in Problem 7–12.

7-14. In each of the following situations, a normal distribution is considered to be a good prior probability distribution. However, in each case, different characteristics of the distribution are assumed.

a. Calculate the EVPI.

b. Explain the difference in EVPI between each situation and situation (1).

(1) Mean: 10 units.
   Break-even value: 7 units.

Standard deviation: 2 units.
   C, the loss constant: $5,000 per unit.

(2) Mean: 10 units.
   Break-even value: 7 units.
   Standard deviation: 5 units.
   C, the loss constant: $5,000 per unit.

(3) Mean: 10 units.
   Break-even value: 9 units.
   Standard deviation: 2 units.
   C, the loss constant: $5,000 per unit.

(4) Mean: 10 units.
   Break-even value: 7 units.
   Standard deviation: 2 units.
   C, the loss constant: $10,000 per unit.

7-15. A manufacturer is considering a capital investment necessary to enter a new market territory. The required investment is $100,000, and he feels that the mean present value of the cash flow is $150,000. However, he thinks there is a 50–50 chance that the actual present value could be less than $80,000 or more than $220,000. The $150,000, $80,000, and $220,000 figures are before subtracting the $100,000 investment.

a. Should the investment be made?

b. Calculate the EVPI, using a normal prior distribution.

7-16. The Bamonite Company is considering the lease of an "intelligent typewriter," which is expected to free 30 percent of a secretary's time for other needed tasks. The typewriter leases for $2,000 per year. The secretary works 2,000 hours per year and is paid $6 per hour. The manager estimates that there is a 50–50 chance that the actual saving in secretarial time will fall between 20 percent and 40 percent.

a. Should the company lease the typewriter?

b. What is the EVPI?

c. Suppose the manager could invest 10 hours of time (valued at $20 per hour) and determine exactly the amount of saving in secretarial time by a very thorough analysis. Now what should the manager do? Why?

7–17. The ABC Company is currently selling a product for $3 per unit. The incremental fixed costs associated with the product are $50,000. The variable costs are $2 per unit. There is excess capacity, and additional units can be produced with no additional fixed costs or changes in marginal costs.

The following schedule has been prepared for the purpose of analyzing a possible price change.

| | *Information for:* | | |
	Current Price	*Price after Decrease*	*Price after Increase*
Price	$3	$2.50	$4
Expected sales (000s)	100	250	60
Standard deviation of sales distribution (000s)	20	75	35

a. Compute the expected profit for each price.

b. Compute the break-even number of units for each price.

c. Compute the expected opportunity loss for each price.

7–18. A contractor considering the possibility of bidding on the construction of a new state highway has already decided that if she were to bid, she would do so at a price of $8.4 million. For the job to be worthwhile, she would need a profit of at least $0.4 million. Hence, she would not bid at all if estimated costs were above $8 million.

Based upon some preliminary calculations, the contractor has estimated cost of building the highway at $7.8 million. However, she knows that these preliminary calculations are often considerably in error. In a study of past jobs, it was found that the average of the preliminary estimates was close to the average actual cost. Furthermore, about two thirds of the preliminary estimates were within 10 percent of actual cost.

Assuming that the contractor is willing to base the decision on expected monetary value, which choice should she make? What is the EVPI?

More Challenging Problems

7–19. A mail-order firm is considering inserting color advertising in its catalog, which is mailed to 100,000 customers. Current purchases of those receiving black-and-white catalogs are $6 per customer. With the color catalog, management thinks that most probably sales would be increased to $7 per customer. However, there is considerable uncertainty about the effect of color, and management thinks that the estimate of $7 per customer might be off by as much as $1 in either direction with ⅔ chance. That is, the standard deviation is $1.

The company makes an average profit of 20 percent on a sale. It costs 25 cents more to print a color catalog than a black-and-white one.

a. Should the company use the color catalog?

b. What is the EVPI?

7–20. A construction company has a contract to complete a job in 180 days. It will have to pay a penalty of $10,000 per day for each day beyond 180 that it takes to complete the project. There is some uncertainty about how long it will take due to weather conditions, possible strikes, and so on. Management has assigned a normal probability distribution to the number of days necessary to complete the project. This distribution has a mean of 170 days and a standard deviation of 12 days.

a. What is the probability that the job will be completed on time?

b. What is the expected penalty cost?

7–21. A piece of equipment has a cost of $100,000. The expected benefits from its use are only $80,000, so the equipment is expected to cause a loss of $20,000 if purchased. The benefits are normally distributed with a standard deviation of $20,000.

a. The firm can buy perfect information as to performance of the equipment. What is the maximum amount it should be willing to pay, assuming it is considering the purchase of only one machine?

b. Now suppose that if the equipment is successful, the firm will buy 100 more units. Each unit will perform with the same economic results. Assume the only way to obtain information is to buy a piece of the equipment. Perfect information is then obtained. Should the one unit of equipment be purchased?

7–22. An electronics manufacturer is faced with a problem of deciding how to inspect integrated circuits as they come off the assembly line. A large percentage of the circuits are defective, and the manufacturer must choose between two inspection systems. Both inspection systems will give perfect performance on good circuits: that is, a good circuit will never be classified as defective. The two systems differ on classifying defectives. The first device, which is mechanical, will misclassify at an average rate of 10 percent, but the actual misclassification rate will be normally distributed about 0.10 with a standard deviation of 0.03 (this randomness is due to imperfect adjustment of the inspection machine at the beginning of each production run). A misclassification rate of 0.10 means that 0.10 of the *total*

lot remains defective after inspection, and so on. Because of the nature of the production run, once the inspection machine is adjusted, it cannot be readjusted until the next run.

The alternative inspection system is to place a worker on the assembly line, and the experience in the past has been that this system produces only 0.01 misclassifications. If the worker is used, the incremental cost over the machine will be $25 per production run (a run is 1,000 circuits). When a defective is classified as good, there is a cost of reworking the subassembly when the circuit is used. This cost is 50 cents per circuit misclassified.

Calculate the following (per production run):

a. The EMV of the best act.

b. The EVPI (concerning perfect information about the machine's rate of misclassification).

c. The expected cost under certainty.

7–23. Solve problem 7–22 assuming the mean machine misclassification rate is still 0.10 but the standard deviation is 0.05.

7–24. Solve problem 7–22 assuming the mean machine misclassification rate is 0.07 and the standard deviation is 0.03.

7–25. A manufacturer has decided to produce a new product. She may lease one of two production machines. Machine A has a leasing cost of $100,000 and a unit production cost (per unit produced) of $2; Machine B leases for $200,000 but has a unit production cost of only $1. The manufacturer feels that annual demand for the product will be "approximately 150,000 units"; she feels there is approximately ⅔ probability that demand will fall in the range between 100,000 and 200,000 units.

a. Compute the break-even value for demand (i.e., the demand value such that the manufacturer would be indifferent between the two machines).

b. Which machine should the manufacturer lease? Why? What is the saving in expected costs from the correct choice, as compared with the incorrect choice?

c. What is the CVPI?

d. What is the EVPI?

7–26. The purchasing agent for a large chain of bakeries is trying to decide the best way to purchase 100,000 bushels of wheat that the company will need in September. One alternative is to buy the wheat on the futures market at the current price for September wheat of $3.28 per bushel. This agrees with the agent's expectations for the price of wheat purchased in the open market in September (which is the other alternative). Past experience has indicated that the open market price may fluctuate considerably by September. The chances are two out of three that the price in September will be $0.25 above or below $3.28 (per bushel).

a. If the agent is risk averse, which alternative would he select: Buy the wheat on the futures market now, or on the open market in September?

b. What is the EVPI?

CHAPTER **8**

Revision of Normal Probabilities by Sampling

In Chapters 3 and 4, we discussed the idea of revising subjective probabilities in the light of new or experimental evidence. Chapter 3 introduced the revision of probabilities, and in Chapter 4, the general framework for including experimental or sample evidence was considered. It is the purpose of this chapter to extend this analysis and apply it in a specific decision situation using the normal probability distribution.

We shall use a problem to illustrate the concepts that are involved. Suppose a firm is considering manufacturing a new product. It will market this product through a chain of 5,000 stores. The firm is uncertain about the level of sales for the product and has not been able to decide whether or not to market it.

The first source of information the firm can tap in making this decision is its judgment and experience (including analysis of similar product introductions in the past). This experience may be represented by a subjective probability distribution for the mean sales of the new product per store. Suppose the management states that its subjective probability distribution for average sales per store is normal, with a mean of 400 units and a standard deviation of 30.

With no other evidence, the firm would make its decision using the above information. However, it may be able to experiment and obtain additional information. Experimentation could take the form, in this example, of a market research study in which a random sample is taken from the 5,000 stores. The new product could be test marketed in these selected stores and sales of the product measured. The results could then be used as estimates for all 5,000 stores.

The sample evidence itself is subject to some uncertainty. There may be a bias in the evidence.[1] In addition, there is random or sampling error, due to the

---

[1] We shall concern ourselves in this book only with sampling error. For a discussion of how some forms of bias may be treated, see R. Schlaifer, *Probability and Statistics for Business Decisions* (New York: McGraw-Hill, 1959), Chapter 31.

216

fact that we have experimented with a sample and not with the entire group of stores. Hence, we should not use sample evidence as the only basis for making this decision.

By revising probabilities, we can combine the subjective probabilities of the manufacturer with the sample evidence to give a *revised* or *posterior* subjective distribution. This posterior distribution is then the basis for decision making.

In this chapter we are concerned with the revision of the mean and the standard deviation of a normal prior distribution in the light of sample evidence. We shall also discuss whether or not it is desirable to obtain the sample evidence, assuming the sampling process has a cost.

We will first describe the several distributions encountered in the revision of the prior normal probability distribution.

The Probability Distributions

We shall use five probability distributions in the analysis:

1. The Population Distribution, Where σ_p = Standard Deviation and μ = Mean This distribution reflects the characteristics of the individual components of the population from which the sample is to be drawn. In our example, it is the probability distribution of sales per store for the population of all 5,000 stores. If all the data were available, we could array the number of stores making sales of different amounts and divide these numbers by the total number of stores, so that the sum of the proportions is equal to 1. A possible distribution of the sales of stores in the population is presented in Figure 8–1.

There would be a small proportion of stores with large sales (more than 800 units), but most stores are expected to sell less than 800 units. This distribution, as is typical of many distributions of economic data, is skewed to the right (i.e.,

Figure 8–1   **Population Distribution (distribution of sales per store)**

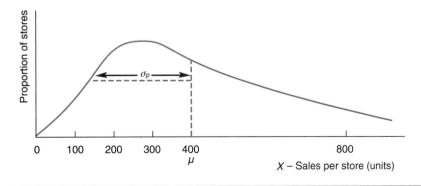

has a long right tail), and a normal distribution would be a poor approximation to the curve in Figure 8–1. The firm is assumed to have a reasonably good estimate of σ_p, the standard deviation of the distribution of store sales. It may be based on the data from past studies or from a sample. The true mean of the distribution is unknown.

Generally, μ and σ_p are unknown, and the mean and the standard deviation of the sample are used as estimates of μ and σ_p.

2. The Distribution in the Sample Suppose a random sample of n stores is selected. A frequency distribution, somewhat similar to that above, could be made for the elements in the sample; that is, a distribution of sales by store for those stores in the sample. Well-defined relationships exist between this distribution and the population distribution. In particular, let X_i be the sales of the ith store in the sample of n stores. Then the sample mean is:

$$\bar{X} = \frac{\sum_{i=1}^{n} X_i}{n} \tag{8-1}$$

and $\bar{X}$ is an unbiased estimate[2] of the population mean μ.

The sample variance[3] is:

$$\sigma_s^2 = \frac{\sum_{i=1}^{n} (X_i - \bar{X})^2}{n - 1} \tag{8-2}$$

and σ_s^2 is an unbiased estimate of the population variance σ_p^2. The sample standard deviation is σ_s and is an estimate of σ_p.

3. The Distribution of Sample Means There are many possible random samples that could be selected from a given population, and each sample will have a mean $\bar{X}$. Considering all possible samples, $\bar{X}$ itself is a random variable and has a probability distribution with mean $E(\bar{X})$ and standard deviation $\sigma_{\bar{x}}$. $E(\bar{X})$ and $\sigma_{\bar{x}}$ are unknown; however, the population distribution and the distribution of sample means are connected by the following relationships:

$$E(\bar{X}) = \mu \tag{8-3}$$

$$\sigma_{\bar{x}} = \frac{\sigma_p}{\sqrt{n}} \quad \text{or} \quad \sigma_{\bar{x}}^2 = \frac{\sigma_p^2}{n} \tag{8-4}$$

---

[2] A sample statistic is unbiased if the expected value of that statistic is equal to the corresponding population parameter. In particular, $E(\bar{X}) = \mu$ and $E(\sigma_s^2) = \sigma_p^2$. The sample mean is unbiased since, on the average, it will equal the population mean.

[3] In this book, we shall call σ_s^2, as defined above, the sample variance, although other writers may use that term to refer to the above formula with $n - 1$ replaced by n. Using n, the sample variance is not an unbiased estimate of the population variance σ_p^2.

It should be remembered that $\overline{X}$ represents the mean of a particular sample and $E(\overline{X})$ is actually an average of means of samples.

For large samples, even when the distribution of X is not normal, the distribution of sample means is approximately normal.[4] Normality of this distribution is important in subsequent analysis. We shall assume in this book that a large enough sample has been taken to assure normality of the distribution of sample means.[5]

4. The Prior Distribution of the Population Mean Before a sample is taken, there is a prior (or betting) distribution of the mean of the population. This is a subjective probability distribution of the decision maker. In our example, the management has a subjective prior distribution for mean sales per store. The parameters of the prior distribution are mean = 400 units (denoted by $\overline{\mu}_0$) and standard deviation = 30 units (denoted by σ_0). Note that σ_0 is the standard deviation of the prior probability distribution of the estimate of the population mean (it is *not* an estimate of the population standard deviation σ_p).

The random variable in the prior distribution (and also in the posterior distribution) is μ, the population mean. Although the actual population distribution has a given mean (as in Figure 8–1), this mean is unknown to the decision maker and is a (subjective) random variable.

The subscript 0 of the symbols $\overline{\mu}_0$ and σ_0 indicates a prior distribution. The subscript 1 will be used to indicate a posterior distribution.

5. The Posterior Distribution of the Population Mean After the sample is taken, the betting distribution of the population mean is updated to obtain the posterior distribution with $\overline{\mu}_1$, the mean, and σ_1, the standard deviation. If the prior distribution is normal, and if the distribution of the sample means is normal, then the posterior distribution will also be normal.

We now indicate how to update or revise the prior distribution using sample information to obtain the posterior distribution.

Revising the Prior Distribution

Assume the prior distribution of a population mean is normal and has a mean of $\overline{\mu}_0$ and a standard deviation of σ_0. A random sample of size n is taken; the sample mean is $\overline{X}$, and the standard deviation of the sample is σ_s (σ_s is an estimate of σ_p, the standard deviation of the population).

---

[4]This is the result of the Central Limit theorem of statistics. See any text on statistical theory, such as those listed at the end of the chapter.

[5]The question of how large a sample is necessary to assure normality of the sampling distribution of $\overline{X}$ is not simple. If the population is symmetric, very small samples are adequate. For extremely skewed distributions, very large samples are needed. For practical purposes, samples of 30 to 50 items are usually considered adequate. For more discussion of this point, see Schlaifer, *Probability and Statistics,* Chapter 17.

To simplify the formulas we shall use, we introduce the symbol I to represent the amount of **information** contained in a distribution and define I as being equal to the reciprocal of the corresponding variance; that is:

$$I_0 = \frac{1}{\sigma_0^2} \tag{8-5}$$

$$I_{\bar{x}} = \frac{1}{\sigma_{\bar{x}}^2} = \frac{n}{\sigma_p^2} \tag{8-6}$$

$$I_1 = \frac{1}{\sigma_1^2} \tag{8-7}$$

If the amount of information in a distribution is large, the amount of uncertainty is small, which is indicated by a tight distribution with small variance, and vice versa. Therefore, the variance of a distribution is inversely related to the amount of information.

The mean of the revised distribution, $\bar{\mu}_1$, is obtained by taking a weighted average of the prior mean and the sample mean, where the weights are the relative amounts of information of the distributions:

$$\bar{\mu}_1 = \left(\frac{I_0}{I_0 + I_{\bar{x}}}\right) \bar{\mu}_0 + \left(\frac{I_{\bar{x}}}{I_0 + I_{\bar{x}}}\right) \bar{X} \tag{8-8}$$

Equation 8–8 and Equation 8–10 (on page 222) for normal prior and sampling distributions are the equivalent of the probability revision procedure of Chapter 3. They determine the mean and the standard deviation of the posterior normal distribution.

Example　Our firm considering the introduction of a new product has a normal prior distribution of mean sales per store for the product with mean $\bar{\mu}_0 = 400$ units and a standard deviation of $\sigma_0 = 30$ units. There are 5,000 stores, and a sample of 100 stores is drawn at random. The product is introduced in the 100 stores, and sales records are kept. The average sales per store for the 100 stores is 420 units; that is, $\bar{X}$ (the sample mean) $= 420$. The sample standard deviation is 200 units; that is, $\sigma_s = 200$.

Using σ_s as an estimate of the standard deviation of the population σ_p, we can estimate $\sigma_{\bar{x}}$ using Equation 8–4:

$$\sigma_{\bar{x}} = \frac{\sigma_p}{\sqrt{n}} = \frac{\sigma_s}{\sqrt{n}} = \frac{200}{\sqrt{100}} = \frac{200}{10} = 20$$

The values of information are, from Equations 8–5 and 8–6:

$$I_0 = \frac{1}{\sigma_0^2} = \frac{1}{900}$$

$$I_{\bar{x}} = \frac{1}{\sigma_{\bar{x}}^2} = \frac{1}{400}$$

The revised mean, using Equation 8–8, is:

$$\bar{\mu}_1 = \left(\frac{1/900}{1/900 + 1/400} \right) \times 400 + \left(\frac{1/400}{1/900 + 1/400} \right) \times 420$$

$$= \frac{400/900 + 420/400}{1/900 + 1/400} = \frac{400 \times 400 + 420 \times 900}{400 + 900}$$

$$= \frac{538,000}{1,300} = 413.8$$

The mean of the prior distribution was 400, but since the standard deviation ($\sigma_0 = 30$) was relatively large compared with $\sigma_{\bar{x}}$, the amount of information in the prior distribution ($I_0 = 1/900$) was small. The mean of the sample was 420; and since the standard deviation of the sample mean was relatively small ($\sigma_{\bar{x}} = 20$), the amount of information in the sample ($I_{\bar{x}} = 1/400$) was relatively large. Thus, the revised mean, 413.8, is closer to the sample mean of 420 than the prior mean of 400. If the prior betting distribution has a relatively large standard deviation, the prior mean will be lightly weighted and will have less effect on the posterior (or revised) mean.

Note that from Equation 8–6:

$$I_{\bar{x}} = \frac{n}{\sigma_p^2}$$

Therefore, the amount of information in the sample is directly related to sample size. Since very large samples tend to be quite accurate, when n is large the prior distribution will tend to have little effect upon the posterior distribution and hence upon the decision.

On the other hand, for smaller samples, the prior distribution can have important effects, particularly if the population standard deviation (σ_p) is large.

Revision of the Standard Deviation

The information in the revised distribution is equal to the sum of the information in the prior distribution plus the information in the sample:

$$I_1 = I_0 + I_{\bar{x}} \tag{8–9}$$

Example In the example of the previous section, the values of I_0 and $I_{\bar{x}}$ were:

$$I_0 = \frac{1}{900}$$

$$I_{\bar{x}} = \frac{1}{400}$$

The value of I_1 is, by Equation 8–9:

$$I_1 = \frac{1}{900} + \frac{1}{400} = \frac{1,300}{360,000}$$

The standard deviation of the revised distribution may be computed using the definition of I_1 in Equation 8–7:

$$I_1 = \frac{1}{\sigma_1^2}$$

$$\frac{1}{\sigma_1^2} = \frac{1,300}{360,000}$$

$$\sigma_1^2 = \frac{360,000}{1,300} = 276.9$$

$$\sigma_1 = \sqrt{276.9} = 16.6$$

The revised standard deviation ($\sigma_1 = 16.6$) is smaller than that of either the standard deviation of the prior distribution ($\sigma_0 = 30$) or the standard deviation of the sample mean ($\sigma_{\bar{x}} = 20$). Thus, the posterior distribution, combining estimates from both sources (judgment and sample), has more information than either source has separately.

Instead of using the above formula, which makes use of I_1, we can develop a variation of the formula that uses only the relevant standard deviations:

$$\frac{1}{\sigma_1^2} = \frac{1}{\sigma_0^2} + \frac{1}{\sigma_{\bar{x}}^2}$$

$$\frac{1}{\sigma_1^2} = \frac{\sigma_{\bar{x}}^2 + \sigma_0^2}{\sigma_0^2 \times \sigma_{\bar{x}}^2}$$

$$\sigma_1^2 = \frac{\sigma_0^2 \times \sigma_{\bar{x}}^2}{\sigma_{\bar{x}}^2 + \sigma_0^2}$$

The revised standard deviation is equal to:

$$\sigma_1 = \sqrt{\frac{\sigma_{\bar{x}}^2 \times \sigma_0^2}{\sigma_0^2 + \sigma_{\bar{x}}^2}} \tag{8–10}$$

Using this equation to solve the example:

$$\sigma_1 = \sqrt{\frac{400 \times 900}{900 + 400}} = \sqrt{276.9} = 16.6$$

which agrees with the previous solution.

If σ_p, the standard deviation of the population, is known, then instead of estimating $\sigma_{\bar{x}}$ with:

$$\frac{\sigma_s}{\sqrt{n}}$$

Figure 8–2 **Prior and Posterior Distributions**

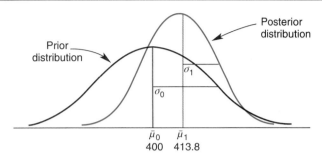

we can compute $\sigma_{\bar{x}}$ using the relationship:

$$\sigma_{\bar{x}} = \frac{\sigma_p}{\sqrt{n}}$$

Figure 8–2 compares the prior distribution with the posterior distribution.

SUMMARY

If (a) the prior uncertainty about an unknown variable can be represented by a normal distribution, and if (b) a sample is taken of sufficient size so that the distribution of sample means is approximately normal, then the revised (posterior) distribution for the unknown variable is also normally distributed, with mean and standard deviation given by Equations 8–8 and 8–10.

The Posterior Normal Distribution and Decision Making

The posterior distribution results from a combination of the prior subjective probabilities and sample evidence. The posterior distribution is itself a betting or decision-making distribution. Since it is normal, the techniques introduced in Chapter 7 are applicable. Let us briefly illustrate some of these points.

Suppose our firm that is considering the introduction of a new product has the following economic information. The cost of machinery and promotion for the new product is $520,000. The variable profit (or contribution) per unit sold is 25 cents, and the number of stores is 5,000.

After the sample is taken, the posterior random variable is μ_1—the mean sales per store. The profit equation, in terms of μ_1, is:

$$\text{Profit} = \pi = -520,000 + (0.25)(5,000)\mu_1$$
$$= -520,000 + 1,250\mu_1$$

The break-even value of mean sales per store, denoted by μ_b, is:

$$\mu_b = \frac{520,000}{1,250} = 416$$

Since the posterior mean $\bar{\mu}_1 = 413.8$ is still less than μ_b, the firm should not market the product.

We can determine the expected value of perfect information (EVPI) for the posterior distribution using Equation 7–4 from Chapter 7:

$$EVPI = C \cdot \sigma \cdot N(D)$$

where $\sigma = \sigma_1$; in this case:

$$\sigma = \sigma_1 = 16.6$$

$$C = (0.25)(5,000) = 1,250$$

$$D = D_1 = \frac{|\bar{\mu}_1 - \mu_b|}{\sigma_1} = \frac{|413.8 - 416|}{16.6} = 0.13$$

$$N(D_1) = 0.3373$$

$$EVPI = (1,250)(16.6)(0.3373) = \$7,000$$

SUMMARY

The posterior normal distribution can be used just as any normal distribution to make decisions and to determine the expected value of perfect information.

The Decision to Sample

Let us now consider whether sampling is appropriate and also how large a sample should be taken. The analysis in this section differs from that of the previous section in that it is *prior to* rather than *posterior to* the sample.

The Initial Situation

Management is considering investing in a new product. Assume the change in profit per unit resulting from a decision to invest is C (the profit function is linear) and the break-even amount is μ_b. The mean of the prior betting distribution on average sales is $\bar{\mu}_0$.

Figure 8–3 indicates the decision is not desirable. The mean $\bar{\mu}_0$ is to the left of μ_b, the break-even point; and the investment has a negative expected value equal to $-C(\mu_b - \bar{\mu}_0)$. However, there is a possibility that the true value of μ is to the right of μ_b.

The expected value of perfect information is:

$$EVPI = C \cdot \sigma_0 \cdot N(D_0)$$

Figure 8–3 **The Prior Distribution of the Population Mean**

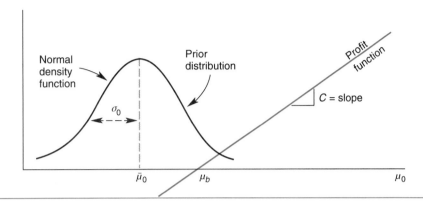

where:

$$D_0 = \frac{|\bar{\mu}_0 - \mu_b|}{\sigma_0}$$

Equation 8–11 also measures the expected opportunity loss for the decision not to invest, since not investing is the optimum decision. Before sampling, this value is based on the subjective feelings of the decision maker expressed in terms of a probability distribution for the population mean.

Example Consider the example used earlier in which a firm is investigating the introduction of a new product. There is a normal prior distribution of mean sales per store for the product with $\bar{\mu}_0 = 400$ units and a standard deviation of $\sigma_0 = 30$ units. There are 5,000 stores. The cost of machinery and promotion for the new product is $520,000. The variable profit (or contribution) per unit sold is 25 cents. The profit per unit change in μ, the mean sales per store, is:

$$C = 0.25 \cdot 5,000 = 1,250$$

The break-even value is $\mu_b = 416$ units.

The optimum act based on the prior probabilities is to reject the new product. However, the expected opportunity loss of the act of rejecting (the expected value of perfect information) is:

$$\text{EVPI} = C \sigma_0 N(D_0)$$

$$D_0 = \frac{|\bar{\mu}_0 - \mu_b|}{\sigma_0} = \frac{|400 - 416|}{300} = 0.53$$

$$N(D_0) = N(0.53) = 0.1887$$

$$\text{EVPI} = (\$1,250)(30)(0.1887) = \$7,076$$

Thus, we would be willing to pay up to $7,076 for perfect information about the true level of average store sales for the new product.

The Expected Posterior Distribution

Before taking a sample, we can estimate the change that will take place in the betting distribution. That is, we can obtain some idea of the posterior distribution before actually taking a sample and revising our prior betting distribution. We do not know beforehand the sample mean $\overline{X}$ and hence do not know exactly what the mean of the posterior distribution will be. However, if we can obtain some measure of the sample variance, we can estimate the posterior variance and the information in the posterior distribution. Recall that the sampling error (the standard deviation of the distribution of $\overline{X}$s) is:

$$\sigma_{\overline{x}} = \frac{\sigma_p}{\sqrt{n}}$$

Hence, we need a measure of the standard deviation of the population distribution (σ_p) to estimate the variance of a sample of a given size n. Such an estimate of σ_p could come from past studies, from an educated guess, or from a pilot sample of the population.

We shall use σ^{*2} to indicate the amount of reduction in the variance from the prior to the posterior distribution. That is:

$$\sigma^{*2} = \sigma_0^2 - \sigma_1^2 \tag{8-12}$$

$$\sigma_1^2 = \frac{\sigma_{\overline{x}}^2 \cdot \sigma_0^2}{\sigma_0^2 + \sigma_{\overline{x}}^2}$$

and substituting this into Equation 8–12:

$$\sigma^{*2} = \sigma_0^2 - \frac{\sigma_{\overline{x}}^2 \cdot \sigma_0^2}{\sigma_0^2 + \sigma_{\overline{x}}^2} = \frac{\sigma_0^2 \cdot \sigma_0^2}{\sigma_0^2 + \sigma_{\overline{x}}^2}$$

so that:

$$\sigma^* = \sqrt{\sigma_0^2 \cdot \frac{\sigma_0^2}{\sigma_0^2 + \sigma_{\overline{x}}^2}} \tag{8-13}$$

The Expected Value of Sample Information

The economic value of a sample results from the fact that it reduces the posterior expected loss. That is, the sample, by supplying additional information, reduces the probability of a wrong decision. The *expected value of sample information*—EVSI—is computed in a manner similar to the EVPI, with σ^* used as the standard deviation. Thus:

$$EVSI = C\,\sigma^* N(D^*) \tag{8-14}$$

where:

$$D* = \frac{|\mu_b - \bar{\mu}_0|}{\sigma^*}$$

The Sampling Decision

For the example above, let us consider the possibility of taking a sample of size $n = 100$. Recall that EVPI = \$7,076. Even if the cost of the sample is less than this, we are not sure that the sample is worthwhile, since the sample gives only imperfect information.

Assume that $\sigma_p = 200$ (we know this from past experience). With a sample size of 100, the standard deviation of sample means is:

$$\sigma_{\bar{x}} = \frac{\sigma_p}{\sqrt{n}} = \frac{200}{10} = 20$$

The value of σ^* is, from Equation 8–13:

$$\sigma* = \sqrt{\frac{\sigma_0^2 \times \sigma_0^2}{\sigma_0^2 + \sigma_{\bar{x}}^2}}$$

$$= \sqrt{\frac{30^2 \times 30^2}{30^2 + 20^2}} = \sqrt{\frac{810,000}{1,300}}$$

$$= 24.9 \text{ (approximately)}$$

From Equation 8–14

EVSI $= C \sigma* N(D*)$

$$D* = \frac{|400 - 416|}{24.9} = 0.64$$

$N(D*) = 0.1580$

EVSI $= (\$1,250)(24.9)(0.1580) = \$4,918$

In this situation, sampling of 100 units would not be undertaken if the cost of sampling 100 units were greater than \$4,918.

A Second Example Now, assume the break-even number of units is 402 (it was previously 416; it is now easier to make an incorrect decision). The expected value of perfect information using Equation 8–11 becomes:

EVPI $= C \sigma_0 N(D_0)$

$$D_0 = \frac{|400 - 402|}{30} = \frac{2}{30} = 0.07$$

$N(D_0) = N(0.07) = 0.3649$

EVPI $= (\$1,250)(30)(0.3649) = \$13,684$

From Equation 8–14, the expected value of sample information for a sample size of $n = 100$ is:

$$\text{EVSI} = C\,\sigma^*N(D^*)$$

$$D^* = \frac{|400 - 402|}{24.9} = 0.08$$

$$N(D^*) = N(0.08) = 0.3602$$

$$\text{EVSI} = (\$1{,}250)(24.9)(0.3602) = \$11{,}211$$

If the cost of sampling 100 units is less than \$11,211, then sampling is desirable.

The expected value of sample information has been made much larger in this second example by reducing the difference between the expected number of units and the break-even number of units. The expected value of sample information would also have been larger if σ_0 had been larger (hence, more uncertainty about the true μ), thus increasing the likelihood of making the wrong decision.

A Third Example   Now, assume σ_0 is 150 (it was previously 30) and σ_p is still 200. The computations would become:

$$\sigma_{\bar{x}} = \frac{\sigma_p}{\sqrt{n}} = \frac{200}{10} = 20$$

$$\sigma^* = \sqrt{\frac{\sigma_0^2 \times \sigma_0^2}{\sigma_0^2 + \sigma_{\bar{x}}^2}} = \sqrt{\frac{150^2 \times 150^2}{150^2 + 20^2}} = \sqrt{\frac{22{,}500 \times 22{,}500}{22{,}900}}$$

$$= \sqrt{22{,}107} = 148.7$$

Assuming the break-even number of units is still 402, the EVSI is now:

$$\text{EVSI} = C\,\sigma^*N(D^*)$$

$$D^* = \frac{|400 - 402|}{148.7} = \frac{2}{148.7} = 0.01344$$

$$N(D^*) = N(0.013) = 0.3923$$

$$\text{EVSI} = (\$1{,}250)(148.7)(0.3923) = \$72{,}919$$

The EVSI is now much higher than in either of the previous two illustrations. A value of 150 for σ_0 implied a great deal of uncertainty about our prior estimate $\bar{\mu}_0 = 400$. The sample considerably reduces this uncertainty; thus, it has great value.

If σ_p were smaller than 200 units, the sample would give more information, since the items would be picked from a less spread out population; σ^* would increase. This would tend to increase the EVSI. Moreover, the value of D^* would decrease, and the term $N(D^*)$ would thus increase, also increasing the expected value of sample information.

In many situation, σ_p will not be known. As estimate of σ_p can be obtained by taking a small preliminary sample and using the relationship:

$$\sigma_s = \sigma_{p \text{ est.}} = \sqrt{\frac{\Sigma(X - \overline{X})^2}{n - 1}} \qquad \text{(8-15)}$$

We can then determine whether further sampling is desirable, using σ_s to compute $\sigma_{\overline{x}}$:

$$\sigma_{\overline{x}} = \frac{\sigma_s}{\sqrt{n}} \qquad \text{(8-16)}$$

SUMMARY The expected value of sample information (EVSI) is the additional profit that the decision maker expects to make based upon acting optimally after observing the results of a sample of given size, compared with the profit that would be expected based upon the prior information alone. For problems involving (*a*) two alternatives, (*b*) linear profit functions, (*c*) normal prior distributions, and (*d*) approximately normal distribution of sample means, EVSI can be calculated by Equation 8–14.

Optimum Sample Size

The difference between the expected value of a sample of a given size (EVSI) and its cost is defined to be the **expected net gain** (ENG) from sampling. As the size of the sample increases, its value (EVSI) increases, but at a decreasing rate. The EVSI can never be greater than the expected value of perfect information (EVPI). The cost of sampling is related to sample size. In general, the larger the sample, the larger its cost. These relationships are graphed in Figure 8–4 for the case in which the cost of sampling is linear.

The expected net gain (ENG) rises at first and then declines. The value of n that maximizes ENG is the optimum sample size. A sample larger than this would have less net value; a sample smaller than this optimum could profitably be increased in size.[6]

A Comprehensive Example

Assume a manufacturer of toys is considering the production of a new toy. The investment necessary to undertake production and distribution of the toy is $500,000 for one year. The incremental profit (selling price minus variable cost) is $1 per toy. If the company is to break even, it must sell at least 500,000 units in the one year.

---

[6]Under certain circumstances, the determination of the optimum sample size can be reduced to a mathematical formula. See, for example, R. Schlaifer, *Probability and Statistics for Business Decisions* (New York: McGraw-Hill, 1959), Chapter 34. In this chapter, we shall determine approximate optima by trial and error.

Figure 8–4 Optimum Sample Size

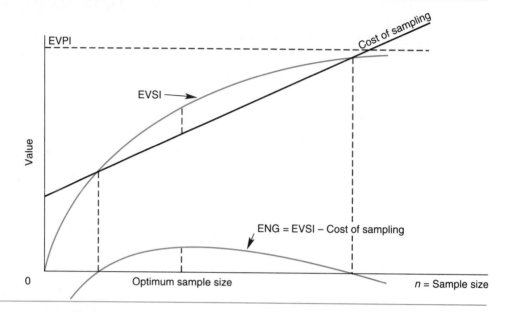

The product will be sold to 50,000 retail sport stores to which the company is selling its present products. The break-even sales per store, μ_b, is 10 units per store (500,000 ÷ 50,000). After careful thought, the manufacturer feels that the mean sales per store will be 12 units (i.e., $\bar\mu_0 = 12$), and assigns a 50 percent chance that mean sales per store will be less than 8 or greater than 16. If a normal distribution is accepted as an indication of prior subjective probabilities, the distribution may be roughly fitted as shown in Figure 8–5.

The mean of the distribution, $\bar\mu_0$, is equal to 12 units, and the standard deviation, σ_0, is 6 units. This is a distribution showing the likelihood of the different possible values of mean sales per store.

Under the above conditions, the best act is to introduce the new toy. This is because the required break-even sales per store, $\mu_b = 10$, is less than the estimated mean of 12. The cost of uncertainty, or the EVPI, is $76,650:

$$C = 1 \text{ toy} \times 50,000 \text{ stores} \times \$1 \text{ per toy}$$
$$= \$50,000$$

$$D_0 = \frac{|\bar\mu_0 - \mu_b|}{\sigma_0} = \frac{|12 - 10|}{6} = 0.333$$

$$N(D_0) = N(0.333) = 0.2555$$

$$\text{EVPI} = C\,\sigma_0\,N(D_0)$$
$$= \$50,000 \times 6 \times 0.2555$$
$$= \$76,650$$

Figure 8–5   **The Prior Subjective Distribution of Mean Sales per Store**

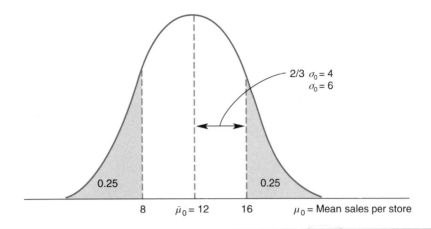

We must determine whether sampling is worthwhile, and if it is, how large a sample should be taken.

Let us first consider whether our action will be changed after we have obtained the sample information. If we take a sample and observe its mean, we shall then revise the mean of our prior subjective distribution. If the revised mean is greater than 10 (the break-even mean), we shall still choose to market the toy, and the sample information would turn out to have had zero value. On the other hand, if the sample mean is sufficiently below 10 so that the revised mean is also lower than 10, we would choose not to market the toy, and the sample would have value. Hence, the value of the sample depends to a great extent on the value of the revised mean.

The above discussion is illustrated in Figures 8–6 and 8–7. If the revised mean, $\bar{\mu}_1$, falls to the right of $\mu_b = 10$, we choose the same act as we would have chosen without the sample. On the other hand, if it has a value of t (see Figure 8–7), sampling would have avoided an expected loss of C^*. Before taking the sample, we do not know what $\bar{\mu}_1$ will be, so we shall treat it as a random variable. The best estimate of the revised mean is the mean of the prior distribution, since $\bar{\mu}_0$ is an unbiased estimate of $\bar{\mu}_1$.

Assume that $\sigma_p = 10$; that is, the standard deviation of the distribution of purchases of the many individual stores is 10. The standard deviation of the population, σ_p, is an important ingredient in the sample decision. If σ_p is large, it means the purchases of individual stores are widely dispersed from the mean sales of all stores. In such a case, a sample would not give as much information as if σ_p is small. To take an extreme case, if $\sigma_p = 0$, then a sample of one store will tell the manufacturer the amount of sales to each store in the population, for if $\sigma_p = 0$, then all stores in the population will purchase the same amount. On the other hand, if σ_p is very large, a small sample will give very little infor-

Figure 8–6

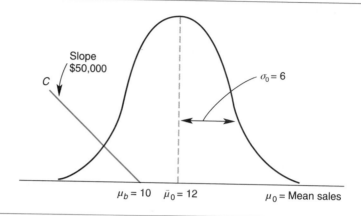

Figure 8–7

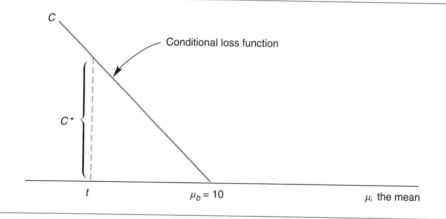

mation, since we may be obtaining observations from the extremes of the population distribution.

We must now compute σ^*, the square root of the change in the variance of the prior probability distribution. The manufacturer has estimated σ_p, the standard deviation of this population, to be 10. We first consider a sample size of $n = 25$. The standard deviation of sample means $\sigma_{\bar{x}}$ is:

$$\sigma_{\bar{x}} = \frac{\sigma_p}{\sqrt{n}} = \frac{10}{5} = 2$$

and:

$$\sigma_{\bar{x}}^2 = 4$$

We need to compute σ^*:

$$\sigma^* = \sqrt{\frac{\sigma_0^2 \cdot \sigma_0^2}{\sigma_0^2 + \sigma_{\bar{x}}^2}} = \sqrt{\sigma_0^2 \frac{\sigma_0^2}{\sigma_0^2 + \sigma_{\bar{x}}^2}}$$

where σ_0^2 is the prior variance; in our example, its value is 36, and $\sigma_{\bar{x}}^2$ is the variance of the sample means. The calculations are as follows:

$$\sigma^* = \sqrt{36 \cdot \frac{36}{36 + 4}} = \sqrt{36 \cdot \frac{36}{40}} = \sqrt{32.4} = 5.69$$

The estimate of σ^* is 5.69. Remember, this estimate is made before the sample is taken. With a sample size of 25, the expected value of the sample information is calculated as follows:

$$D^* = \frac{|12 - 10|}{5.69} = 0.351$$

$$N(D^*) = N(0.35) = 0.2481$$

$$\text{EVSI} = C \cdot \sigma^* \cdot N(D^*)$$

$$= \$50,000 \times 5.69 \times 0.248$$

$$= \$70,556$$

As can be seen from the above calculation, the EVSI with $n = 25$ is quite large. If the cost of sampling each store is $100, the cost of the sample is $2,500. The expected net gain (ENG) from sampling 25 units is the EVSI less the cost of sampling. Hence:

$$\text{ENG}_{25} = \text{EVSI} - \text{Cost of sampling}$$

$$= 70,556 - 2,500 = \$68,056$$

Since the ENG is positive, it is desirable to take a sample of 25. However, we may be able to increase the ENG by adjusting the sample size. We can approximate the optimal n by iterative procedures (trial and error), making calculations on either side of $n = 25$ and converging on the best n until we maximize the ENG. As we increase n, we shall increase the EVSI, but the sample cost will also increase. Hence, we must find the proper balance between the value of the additional information and the increased cost caused by increasing the sample size, n.

Table 8–1 shows the calculation of ENG from sampling for several sample sizes between 20 and 45. The ENG rises until the sample size reaches approximately 40 and then begins to decline. Therefore, we assume the optimal size is between 35 and 45. The change in the ENG is quite small even when the sample size is doubled. In this example, ENG is not very sensitive to changes in sample size in the 20-to-45 range.

Table 8–1　　　Calculation of Optimal Sample Size

Sample Size n	$\sigma_{\bar{x}}^2$ Variance of Sample Means $\sigma_p^2 = \dfrac{100}{n}$	σ^*	D^* $\dfrac{\lvert 12 - 10 \rvert}{\sigma^*}$	$N(D^*)$	$EVSI$ $50{,}000 \times \sigma^* N(D^*)$	Sample Cost	ENG $(EVSI -$ Sample Cost$)$
20	5.00	5.62	0.356	0.246	$69,126	$2,000	$67,126
25	4.00	5.69	0.351	0.248	70,556	2,500	68,056
35	2.85	5.75	0.346	0.250	72,125	3,500	68,625
40	2.50	5.77	0.345	0.251	72,739	4,000	68,739
45	2.22	5.80	0.344	0.251	73,099	4,500	68,599

SUMMARY　　The optimum sample size is the one that produces the greatest expected net gain (ENG); that is, the largest difference between EVSI and sample cost.

Conclusion

This chapter and the previous one have considered decision making with normal probabilities and linear loss functions. These assumptions of normality and linearity imply that we have considered a special case, but the applications appear to be widespread. Other methods have been developed for different distributions and loss functions; however, these methods are beyond the scope of this book. The normal distribution–linear loss function case illustrates well the concepts involved in decision making under uncertainty.

Bibliography

Jones, J. M. *Introduction to Decision Theory.* Homewood, Ill.: Richard D. Irwin, 1977.

Pratt, J. W.; H. Raiffa; and R. Schlaifer. *Introduction to Statistical Decision Theory.* New York: McGraw-Hill, 1965.

Raiffa, H., and R. Schlaifer. *Applied Statistical Decision Theory.* Boston: Division of Research, Harvard Business School, 1961.

Schlaifer, R. *Probability and Statistics for Business Decisions.* New York: McGraw-Hill, 1959.

Spurr, W. A., and C. P. Bonini. *Statistical Analysis for Business Decisions.* Homewood, Ill.: Richard D. Irwin, 1973.

Winkler, R. L. *Introduction to Bayesian Inference and Decision.* New York: Holt, Rinehart & Winston, 1972.

Problems with Answers

8-1. Given a normal prior distribution with $\bar{\mu}_0 = 10$ and $\sigma_0 = 2$. A sample of size $n = 36$ is taken, with $\bar{X} = 12$ and $\sigma_s = 6$. Compute the mean and the standard deviation of the posterior distribution.

8-2. An auditor believes the average credit card balance outstanding is probably over $10. More precisely, her feelings about the average balance can be represented by a normal distribution with a mean of 12 and a standard deviation of 2. A sample of 25 accounts is drawn at random, and the average balance on these accounts is $9. The standard deviation of the balances in the sample is $5. What should be the auditor's posterior distribution? What probability would she assign to the possibility that the average balance is less than $10?

8-3. A firm was considering introducing a new product into the market. The product was to be distributed through 5,000 independent wholesale merchants. Management expressed a prior judgment about the average sales per wholesaler in terms of a normal distribution with mean $\bar{\mu}_0 = 4$ cases per month and standard deviation $\sigma_0 = 1.5$ cases per month.

An experimental run of the new product was made. Then, a sample of 36 of the 5,000 wholesalers was contacted and persuaded to try the new product. The sales in the month in which the product was introduced were ignored, but the sales to each wholesaler for the second month were noted carefully. It was felt that the level of these repeat sales (i.e., second-month sales) would be a good indication of future sales.

In the sample of 36 wholesalers, the average sale per wholesaler was 3.6 cases for the second month, with a standard deviation of 2.4 cases per month.

a. After the sample, what posterior distribution should management assign to the average sales per month per wholesaler?

b. Suppose that to introduce the product to all the market would require $200,000 for purchase of new equipment and promotional effort. Because of certain financial considerations, management did not wish to undertake the introduction of the new product unless the profits would pay back this $200,000 cost within the first year. The firm would make a profit of $1 per case sold. After the sample, what decision should be made? What is the posterior EVPI?

8-4. Assume a normal prior distribution with $\bar{\mu}_0 = 20$ and $\sigma_0 = 10$. Also, $\sigma_p = 20$. The cost of a sample of size n is $10 + 2n$, $\mu_b = 15$, and $C = \$100$.

a. Compute the EVPI before the sample.

b. Compute the EVSI for $n = 10$, $n = 25$, and $n = 50$.

c. What is the optimum sample size (of the three choices above), and what is its ENG?

8-5. Refer to Problem 8-3. Suppose the firm had not yet taken the sample. However, based upon judgment and experience, the standard deviation of sales per wholesaler per month was estimated to be 2.5 cases per month.

a. Compute the EVSI for a sample of 36 wholesalers.

b. Suppose it costs $2,500 to make up, by special means, the product to be used in the sample test and an additional $1,000 in other fixed costs. The variable cost is $100 per wholesaler in the sample. Should the sample be taken? What is the ENG?

c. What is the ENG for a sample of 50 wholesalers?

d. What is the ENG for a sample of 75 wholesalers?

e. Based on (b), (c), and (d), what is the approximate optimum sample size?

Problems

8–6. Given a normal prior distribution with $\bar{\mu}_0 = 500$ and $\sigma_0 = 30$. A sample of size $n = 441$ is taken, with $\bar{X} = 450$ and $\sigma_s = 210$. Compute the mean and the standard deviation of the posterior distribution.

8–7. Which sample contains the most information:

a. A sample of 100 from a population with a standard deviation of 50? Or:

b. A sample of 64 from a population with a standard deviation of 40? Explain.

8–8. The controller of the ABC Machine Shop was complaining that unprofitable orders were being quoted by the company's salespeople. Top management believed that a reasonable profit standard was 15 percent of total invoice for each job. Management was confused by the controller's complaint since they thought they were close to their 15 percent target. Specifically, they had a normal prior distribution for "average percent profit" with a mean of 15 percent and a standard deviation of 2 percent.

A sample of 50 jobs were selected at random; of these, the average profit was 10 percent, and the standard deviation was 5 percent. Compute the appropriate posterior distribution after the sample.

8–9. Refer to Problem 7–16. Now suppose that the manager could sample 10 installations where the intelligent typewriter is being used. The sampling cost is $10 per observation ($100 for the sample of 10). Assume $\sigma_p = 400$ hours.

a. What is the EVSI?

b. What is the ENG?

c. What should the manager do?

8–10. Refer to Problem 7–19. Suppose that before making the decision as to which catalog to use, 100 color catalogs were printed and mailed to a sample of 100 customers. The average sale to these customers was then $7.40, with a standard deviation of $5. Utilizing this information and the prior probabilities of Problem 7–19, what decision should be made? What is the posterior EVPI?

8–11. Refer to Problems 7–19 and 8–10. Assume that the sample mentioned in Problem 8–10 has not yet been taken. Suppose that the mail-order firm can print a few color catalogs and mail them to a sample of customers. The purchases of these customers could be measured and some information about the effect of the color catalog obtained. From past experience, the standard deviation of customer purchases is known to be about $5. Suppose that the cost of sampling is $500 plus $5 per item sampled. What is the optimum sample size? [To simplify the problem, consider only the following values of n: $n = 0$ (no sample,) $n = 64$, $n = 100$, and $n = 225$.]

8–12. Refer to Problems 7–19, 8–10, and 8–11. Consider only a sample of size $n = 100$. Does the difference between the EVPI prior to the sample (Problem 7–19) and the EVPI posterior to the sample (Problem 8–10) equal the expected value of sample information (EVSI in problem 8–11)? Should it? Explain.

8–13. The National Paper Company (NPC) often purchases timber from independent landholders. Its buyers have a prior distribution for yield from an acre of loblolly pine with mean = 100,000 board feet and standard deviation = 10,000 board feet. One potential supplier has argued that his timber is better than average; a valid independent survey of 25 separate acres from his land has produced a mean of 110,000 board feet per acre, with a standard deviation of 5,000 board feet. The potential supplier will sell all his land to NPC at $1,080 per acre. NPC normally pays $1,000 per acre, thereby purchasing timber for 1 cent per board foot on average. Should NPC buy this supplier's land at $1,080 per acre?

8–14. The ACME Manufacturing Company is considering a more sophisticated inventory control procedure for its inventory of 10,000 different items. Management estimates that the average percent cost saving due to the improved methods would be 20 percent. Management feels that a normal prior distribution with a mean of 20 percent and a standard deviation of 8 percent adequately describes their feelings about the cost savings that would actually be produced.

Company analysts have explored cost savings in detail for a random sample of 100 items in the inventory. In the sample, percentage cost savings had an average value of 15 percent, with a standard deviation of 12 percent.

a. After the sample, what posterior distribution should management assign to the average percent savings to be obtained?

b. Suppose the new procedure will cost approximately 5 percent of the inventory-associated costs per year. Should the new procedure be implemented?

c. What is the EVPI for the prior distribution?

d. What is the EVPI for the posterior distribution?

8–15. Refer to Problem 8–14. Suppose now that the break-even percentage cost saving was 14 percent instead of 5 percent.

a. Should the new procedure be implemented now? Why?

b. What is the EVPI for the prior distribution?

c. What is the EVPI for the posterior distribution?

8–16. Refer to Problem 7–18. Suppose the contractor could make a detailed cost estimate before submitting the bid. The cost of making this detailed estimate is $18,000. Based on past experience with these detailed estimates, there is a two-thirds chance that a given estimate will be within 3 percent of the actual cost.

Should the contractor make the detailed estimate? What is the ENG?

Hint: Treat $(0.03)(7.80) = 0.234$ as $\sigma_{\bar{x}}$. Then proceed to calculate the EVSI.

More Challenging Problems

8–17. A specialty tool company is considering the introduction of a new product. Management thinks that each of the 1,000 distribution points for the company could sell 150 units on average; also, there is about a ⅔ probability that the average sales will be between 100 and 200 units.

The new tool would sell for $5 per unit. It could be manufactured by either of two machines. Machine A has a leasing cost of $100,000, and a unit production cost (per unit produced) of $2; machine B leases for $200,000 and has a unit production cost of $1.

In an attempt to estimate demand more accurately, the manufacturer has sent prototype tools out to 50 distribution points. Sales have averaged only 90 units

at each distribution point, with standard deviation of 60.

a. Before the sample information was gathered, what was the best decision the manufacturer could make? What was the EVPI?

b. After the sample, what is the posterior distribution of average demand per distribution point? What is the best action? What is the posterior EVPI?

c. Prior to the sample actually being collected, what was the EVSI?

8–18. Suppose that the total cost of taking a sample of any size was a fixed amount, K. What would be the optimum sample size?

8–19. In the example on pages 225–27, the EVPI is $7,076 (prior to sampling); the

EVSI is $4,918; but, as computed on page 224, for a sample of $n = 100$, the posterior EVPI $= \$7,000$. Resolve the apparent paradox here.

8–20. A major magazine publisher was considering publishing a hardcover volume of pictorial selections from its magazine. The pictoral volume would be sold largely by mail solicitation of the persons on the magazine's large mailing list. This list included not only subscribers but persons considered potential subscribers. Management felt that the volume would sell a considerable number of copies because of the reputation of the magazine and because the pictorial essays had received wide acclaim when they appeared in the magazine. In fact, many persons wrote in suggesting that a volume of this type be considered.

Some of the cost of publishing the volume had already been incurred when the photographs and text were prepared for the magazine. However, it was estimated that additional costs of $10,000 would be incurred. In addition, it was estimated that the cost of designing and printing the advertising material and the costs of the repeated mailings would amount to about $250,000. (The mailing list contained 2 million names—some, of course, were duplicates. Two mailings were contemplated, with a cost per individual name of 5 cents per mailing. In addition, there was about $50,000 involved in the development of the advertising material.)

The variable manufacturing cost of the proposed book was estimated to be $2 per volume. The selling price was fixed at $3.

Because of the high initial costs, management was undecided about the publishing venture. The best guesses centered at about 250,000 sold. Management believed (two chances out of three) that the sales would be somewhere between 200,000 and 300,000.

Management was somewhat reluctant to abandon the project completely be-

cause of the possible prestige value of such a volume. Therefore, the possibility of doing some market survey work prior to making the final decision was considered. It was a fairly simple task to select a sample of individuals from the mailing list and test the salability of the volume on these persons.

The mailing costs and other variable costs for each of the individuals in the sample amounted to 25 cents per person. However, it was necessary to design and print some special advertising literature, and this would cost about $13,000, regardless of the number of persons sampled. A sample of 2,000 persons was considered an appropriate sample size. The company statistician estimated that the standard error for the sample of 2,000 persons would be 10,000 books (that is, $\sigma_{\bar{x}} = 10,000$).

a. Based on the prior information only, what is the expected profit from publishing the volume? Disregarding any possibility of fringe benefits such as prestige value, should it be published? What is the expected value of perfect information (EVPI)?

b. What is the expected value of sample information (EVSI)? What is the expected net gain from sampling (EVSI − Cost of sample)? Should the sample be taken?

c. Suppose that spending the $13,000 on advertising literature would reduce the estimated development cost of $50,000 to $40,000 if the complete mailing is undertaken (i.e., $10,000 of the $13,000 is recoverable if the book is published). The break-even point is now 250,000 books. What is the EVSI in this case? What is the net gain from sampling? *Hint:* Note that if the sample is taken, the posterior profit function and hence the posterior break-even point are changed.

8–21. The Massachusetts Bay Transit Authority (MBTA) has been authorized by the state legislature to construct a rapid transit line from Route 128 to downtown Boston via Cambridge. The legislature has offered to subsidize the construction and operating costs of the line, but state law requires that the line not incur a loss (taking the subsidy into account). The MBTA has calculated that if 10,000 riders rode the line each weekday (round trip), they would just break even, given the subsidy. For each rider above or below the break-even point, the present value of the change in revenue is $150.

MBTA officials estimate that out of the 100,000 daily commuters currently commuting into Boston from the relevant area, approximately 12 percent (or 12,000) would ride the new line; however, they are not overly confident about their estimate of percent of ridership and feel that a prior distribution with $\bar{\mu}_0 = 0.12$ and $\sigma_0 = 0.04$ adequately describes their knowledge.

They plan to sample the appropriate commuter population to obtain better information. Samples are taken in groups of 100 and the standard deviation of sample proportions have been estimated as $\sigma_p = 0.08$ for each group of 100; for example, if 16 groups of 100 are sampled, the appropriate $\sigma_{\bar{x}} = 0.08/\sqrt{16} = 0.08/4 = 0.02$. The cost of interviewing each group of 100 commuters is $900.

a. Ignoring the state law against losses and assuming an immediate decision is required (sampling is not possible), should the MBTA construct the line or not? What is the expected opportunity loss of the best action?

b. Consider a sample of 16 groups (of 100 each). Prior to the sample actually being taken, what is the EVSI?

c. For (b), compute the ENG.

d. Now consider the following sample sizes (all referring to the number of groups of 100): 1, 9, 16. Compute the EVSI and the ENG. Which of those is the optimum sample size?

e. Will use of the optimal sample size *ensure* that if the line is constructed, it will not run at a loss? Comment on the effect of the state law on this type of decision.

8–22. Refer to Problem 8–21. Suppose the sample interviews are conducted in separate groups of 100, one after the other, and also suppose that the MBTA can stop interviewing at any time. For concreteness, suppose that the first four groups have been interviewed and the average percent ridership over the four groups is indicated to be 20 percent (0.20).

a. What are the parameters of the posterior distribution of fraction of ridership?

b. Given the posterior distribution, what is the EVPI?

c. Compare the current EVPI (from b) to the cost of interviewing the next 100 commuters. Without performing the EVSI calculation, can you guess whether it would be economic for the MBTA to cancel subsequent interviewing and make their decision now?

d. As of now, calculate the EVSI for the next single group (of 100 commuters). Is it larger or smaller than the sampling cost?

CHAPTER 9

Game Theory

We shall now develop a decision model that has, as its primary application, the relationships between two independent competing entities (i.e., individuals or organizations). This analysis is derived from the monumental work of J. von Neumann and O. Morgenstern, *Theory of Games and Economic Behavior*.[1]

Although game theory is not widely used in industry, a knowledge of the subject does give insights that are helpful in arriving at decisions. The assumptions of each game theory model should be carefully noted since they will frequently limit the application of the model.

Games

In the context of this chapter the word *games* is a generic term, incorporating conflict situations of a particular sort. In these situations, the success of one party tends to be at the expense of the others, so they are in a conflict, or competitive, relationship. However, any one of a wide range of agreements is preferable to no agreement, from the standpoint of all concerned, so it is in their mutual interest to cooperate. The essential characteristics are shared by many instances of social or business conflict, so the mathematics of games is of general interest.

We shall introduce a two-person zero-sum game and a two-person nonconstant-sum game in this chapter. Since the mathematics becomes difficult very quickly in response to minor modifications of the problem, we shall investigate relatively simple situations.

---

[1] J. Von Neumann and O. Morgenstern, *Theory of Games and Economic Behavior* (Princeton: Princeton University Press, 1944).

Two-Person Zero-Sum Games

In a two-person zero-sum game, the interests of the two opponents are opposed in such a manner that the sum of their utilities add to zero for every outcome of the game. An example of a zero-sum game would be two persons matching pennies, where each person has a linear utility function with respect to money for the range of feasible gains and losses. The sum of money (utility) won by one is the sum of money (utility) lost by the other.

An important solution to study is the **minimax solution,** which minimizes the maximum possible loss (or maximizes the minimum possible gain). It is a characteristic of two-person zero-sum games that there is a unique minimax solution. The prime advantage of a minimax solution in this situation is that *it is the best choice of the decision maker if the other participant has chosen a minimax solution*. Unlike a game against nature, where the sole advantage of a minimax solution is a form of conservatism, in a game against a thinking opponent, minimax is likely to be a desirable procedure. However, minimax may not lead to the best possible outcome if the opponent does not use a minimax solution.

We shall use a payoff table (Table 9–1) that shows the profits of the party whose strategies are listed down the left side of the table. The profits of the opponent (whose strategies or acts are listed across the top of the table) are not listed, since they are the negative values of the payoffs shown.

In the margins of the payoff table are the row minimums and column maximums. The minimax solution attempts to maximize a security level for the players (minimize the maximum possible loss, or maximize the minimum gain).

For each strategy of player I, we find the minimum gain we would make if faced by the best strategy of player II (these are the row minimums). For each strategy of player II, we find the maximum gain of player I (this is also the maximum loss of player II). These are the column maximums. Player I will choose the largest of the row minimums (in this case strategy 1), and player II will choose the smallest of the column maximums (in this case strategy 1). Since the maximum equals the minimax (both have values of 10), we have an equilibrium. The values are called an "equilibrium" pair. If one of the parties tried to move from this equilibrium while the other did not change position, the mover

Table 9–1   **Payoffs to Player I**

I \ *II*	*Strategy 1*	*Strategy 2*	*Minimum of Row*
Strategy 1	10	14	10
Strategy 2	7	12	7
Maximum of Column	10	14	

would arrive at an inferior position. A **pure strategy** (i.e., a choice of only one strategy by each player) leads to a strictly determined game when the maximum of the minimum values of a row is equal to the minimum of the maximum values of the columns.[2] The value 10 is called a **saddle point.**

It should be noted that the margins of Table 9–1 give the guaranteed minimum profits of player I or the guaranteed maximum costs of player II. Since the values listed in the table may be expectations, these may be guaranteed expected values.

An Example: Company versus Union

The labor contract between your company and the union will terminate in the near future. A new contract must be negotiated, preferably before the old one expires. You are a member of a management group charged with selecting the company representatives and a strategy for them to follow during the coming negotiations. After a consideration of past experience, the group agrees that the feasible strategies for the company are as follows:

C_1 = All-out attack; hard, aggressive bargaining
C_2 = A reasoning, logical approach
C_3 = A legalistic strategy
C_4 = An agreeable, conciliatory approach

Which strategy is best for the company? That depends on the strategy adopted by the union, and that knowledge is not available. However, assume the history of the union suggests that it is considering one of the following set of approaches:

U_1 = All-out attack; hard, aggressive bargaining
U_2 = A reasoning, logical approach
U_3 = A legalistic strategy
U_4 = An agreeable, conciliatory approach

We now must consider the consequences of each of our lines of action, conditional upon the union adopting any one of its available strategies. With the aid of an outside mediator, we construct Table 9–2.

If the company adopts strategy C_1 and the union adopts strategy U_1, the final contract will involve a 20-cent-per-hour increase in wages and benefits to the average worker. If the union adopts strategy U_2 in response to C_1, it will secure a 25-cent-per-hour increase; strategy U_3 is even better for the union against the company's C_1—it yields a 40-cent-per-hour raise. However, if the union adopts U_4 against C_1, it will end up with a 5-cent cut in wages. The other entries have a similar connotation. Both union and company must decide on the overall strategy before negotiations begin; an attitude cannot be taken and then changed

---

[2]This statement is valid as long as the decision maker whose positive gains are described in the payoff matrix has his strategies listed down the side of the matrix; otherwise, we would have to modify the description of a strictly determined game with pure strategies.

Table 9–2   Conditional Gains of Union (costs to company)

Union Strategies	Company Strategies				Row Minimums
	C_1	C_2	C_3	C_4	
U_1	+20¢	+15¢	+12¢	+35¢	+12¢ ←
U_2	+25	+14	+ 8	+10	+ 8
U_3	+40	+ 2	+10	+ 5	+ 2
U_4	− 5	+ 4	+11	0	− 5
Column maximums	+40¢	+15¢	+12¢	+35¢	

↑

when the other party commits itself. Assume the company's utility function is approximately linear in money, so that these figures may serve as the utility index for the company.[3] The mediator informs the management group that the union has also been considering alternative strategies and possible results of these lines of action. The mediator indicates that the union has constructed a table that does not vary significantly from Table 9–2, and the union has been provided with comparable information. Assume the union also has a linear utility function.

Given these conditions, what will the bargainers do? The company would prefer the union to be conciliatory (U_4) in response to its aggressive attack (C_1), with the result of a 5-cent reduction in wages. But if the company adopts C_1, it is quite possible the union will select a legalistic approach (U_3) and "sock" the firm for a 40-cent wage boost. The second best solution from the company's viewpoint would result from both the company and the union being agreeable (C_4, U_4). But if the company chooses C_4, the union might select an aggressive strategy (U_1) and win a 35-cent wage increase.

The union experiences the same difficulty: If it adopts U_3 in the hope of a 40-cent raise, the company may select a reasoning approach (C_2), which yields only 2 cents to the union. It is clear, however, that the union will never follow a conciliatory strategy (U_4), for it can gain more from U_1 no matter what strategy the company adopts. We may say that strategy U_1 *dominates* strategy U_4.

One rule the participants might adopt in such a situation is the minimax strategy. The company might adopt that strategy that minimizes the maximum wage increase it would have to grant, regardless of the action of the union. If the union adopted this rule, it would choose that strategy that maximized the minimum wage increase. In the case at hand, the minimax strategy for the company is C_3, with a maximum wage increase of 12 cents; the minimax strategy for the union is U_1, with a minimum wage increase of 12 cents. Since, in Table 9–2, 12

---

[3]In general, this will not be the case unless the wage costs are a relatively unimportant part of the firm's total costs and the negotiations do not have strong emotional or symbolic significance. Where the union and the company are both large and strong, this is not likely to be the situation, and the possible wage changes should be converted to utility terms.

cents is both the maximum of its C_3 column and the minimum of its U_1 row, it is the equilibrium solution of this situation. In game theory terms, 12 is designated as the value of the game. The pure strategies (U_1, C_3) provide equilibrium in this case, for if the company follows C_3, the U_1 is the union's best defense. If the union follows U_1, then C_3 is the company's best defense.[4]

Mixed Strategies

Not every conflict situation has a minimax equilibrium attainable by pure strategies. By changing one of the critical figures in Table 9–2, we can transform it into such a case. Say the intersection of C_3 and U_3 now is $+19$ cents rather than $+10$ cents, so that $+12$ cents is no longer the maximum of its column. This is shown in Table 9–3. Now C_2 is the strategy that minimizes the company's maximum loss; the union's maximum remains U_1. The intersection of these strategies is not an equilibrium point, however, because $+15$ cents is not the maximum of its column *and* the minimum of its row. If the union adopted strategy U_1, the company would prefer to have strategy C_3, not C_2. But if the company chose strategy C_3, the union would like U_3 better than U_1. If the union selected U_3, the company's optimum strategy would be C_2. Yet C_2 is the strategy against which the union would take U_1, as indicated initially. We have completed the full circle. The pure strategies (U_1, C_2) are not an equilibrium pair; they are not best against each other.

Let us reduce Table 9–3 to the strategies shown in Table 9–4. This is done by successive elimination of *dominated strategies*. Union strategy U_4 is dominated by U_1, so U_4 may be dropped. Then company strategy C_1 is dominated by either C_2 or C_3; thus, C_1 may be dropped. This leaves union strategy U_2 dominated by U_1, so that the only remaining union strategies are U_1 and U_3. At this point, company strategy C_4 is dominated by C_2, so the only pertinent strategies for the company are C_2 and C_3.

Our objective now is to derive some *probability mixture* of the strategies (that is, a **mixed strategy**) that will improve the position of both parties with respect to the available pure strategies. For example, assume that it is possible for the company to use strategy C_2, at random, one half of the time, the strategy C_3, at random, the other half. Then, if the union used strategy U_1, the expected wage increase would be:

$$\tfrac{1}{2}(+15\cent) + \tfrac{1}{2}(+12\cent) = +13\tfrac{1}{2}\cent$$

If the union used U_3, the expected wage increase would be:

$$\tfrac{1}{2}(+2\cent) + \tfrac{1}{2}(+19\cent) = +10\tfrac{1}{2}\cent$$

---

[4] A zero-sum game may have more than one equilibrium pair; however, all of the equilibrium pairs will have the same value, so the players will be indifferent among them.

Table 9–3 Conditional Gains to Union (costs to company)

Union Strategies	Company Strategies				Row Minimums	
	C_1	C_2	C_3	C_4		
U_1	+20¢	+15¢	+12¢	+35¢	+12¢	←
U_2	+25	+14	+ 8	+10	+ 8	
U_3	+40	+ 2	+19	+ 5	+ 2	
U_4	− 5	+ 4	+11	0	− 5	
Column maximums	+40¢	+15¢	+19¢	+35¢		

↑

Table 9–4 Undominated Strategies

Union Strategies	Company	
	C_2	C_3
U_1	+15¢	+12¢
U_3	+ 2	+19

Either of these is preferable from the company viewpoint to the +15 cents indicated by the minimax rule. The union, of course, also may adopt such a mixed strategy. One of von Neumann's great contributions was to prove that every two-person zero-sum game, regardless of the number of strategies available to the participants, has a unique equilibrium value. As a special case, the solution may involve pure strategies, as shown initially. If this is not the case, we still know that for some pair of *mixed* strategies an equilibrium exists.

Graphical Solution

A simple and instructive way to find the solution for the two-person two-strategy case is the geometric method suggested by Luce and Raiffa.[5] First, we shall derive the optimum mixed strategy for the company. Consider Figure 9–1, where possible mixed company strategies may be evaluated against the union's strategy U_1. On the vertical axes, the possible raises are plotted. The horizontal axis is scaled in terms of mixed strategies for the company from the limit of $(1.0C_2, 0C_3)$—the pure strategy C_2—to the limit $(0C_2, 1.0C_3)$, the pure strategy C_3. At the extremes, the payoffs are +15 cents and +12 cents, as shown in Table 9–4. The device of the mixed strategy enables us to select any point on the line

---

[5]R. D. Luce and H. Raiffa, *Games and Decisions* (New York: John Wiley & Sons, 1957).

Figure 9–1

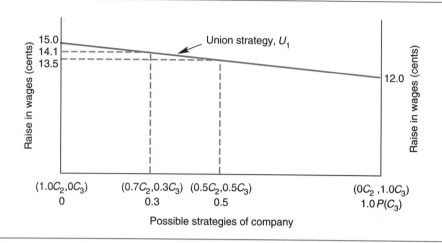

connecting $+15$ cents and $+12$ cents as a payoff to the union's strategy, U_1. For example, if we wanted to choose $+13.5$ cents in response to U_1, we would select the mixed strategy $(0.5C_2, 0.5C_3)$. If we chose the mixed strategy $(0.7C_2, 0.3C_3)$, the payoff would be $+14.1$ cents. Any point on the straight line in Figure 9–1 is feasible if the union follows strategy U_1.

Now, in Figure 9–2, we construct the appropriate mixed strategies payoff line for U_3, and consider it in conjunction with the U_1 line developed in Figure 9–1. The new line indicates the returns to the union for strategy U_3, assuming the company selects a mixed strategy between $(1.0C_2, 0C_3)$ and $(0C_2, 1.0C_3)$. For example, if the company adopts $(0.5C_2, 0.5C_3)$, the raise is 13.5 cents if the union adopts strategy U_1 and 10.5 cents if the union adopts U_3. From the company's standpoint, the maximum payoff for this strategy is 13.5 cents. For mixed strategies between $(1.0C_2, 0C_3)$ and $(0.35C_2, 0.65C_3)$, the maximum raise to the union is obtained if the union follows strategy U_1; for mixed strategies between $(0.35C_2, 0.65C_3)$ and $(0C_2, 1.0C_3)$, the maximum raise to the union is associated with union strategy U_3. The colored lines in Figure 9–2 indicate the set of maximum raises the company would have to provide, assuming the union always adopted the most favorable strategy available to it in response to any mixed strategy adopted by the company. If the company followed the rule of minimizing the maximum raise it would have to pay, it would adopt the mixed strategy $(0.35C_2, 0.65C_3)$ and give the union a raise of $0.35(15¢) + 0.65(12¢) = 13.05¢$ if it adopted strategy U_1, or $0.35(2¢) + 0.65(19¢) = 13.05¢$ if the union adopted U_3. Regardless of the union's action, it cannot get more than 13.05 cents per hour of expected wage increase (i.e., its best average increase is 13.05).

What strategy could we expect the union to follow? The minimax philosophy dictates that the union assume the company will erect the stoutest defense

Figure 9–2

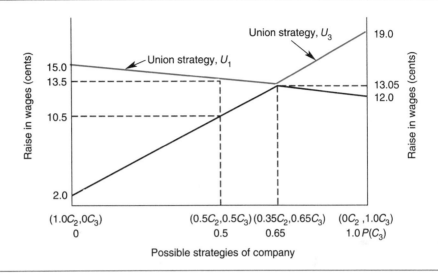

Figure 9–3

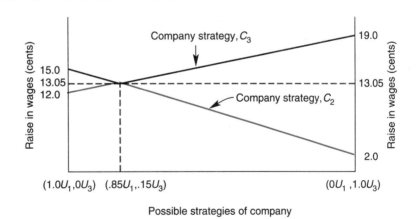

against any strategy it selects. We have sketched in Figure 9–3 the strategies available to the union and the set of minimum wage increases associated with those strategies. If the company adopts strategy C_3, the wage increases to the union in return for various mixed strategies are indicated by the line joining 12 cents and 19 cents. This line would indicate the minimum raise for strategies between $(1.0U_1, 0U_3)$ and $(0.85U_1, 0.15U_3)$. The line joining 15 cents and 2 cents defines the wage increases in response to various union mixed strategies if the company follows strategy C_2. This strategy provides the minimum wage boost for union action in the range $(0.85U_1, 0.15U_3)$ to $(0U_1, 1.0U_3)$. If the union wishes to maximize the minimum wage increase, it will adopt the strategy $(0.85U_1, 0.15U_3)$. This provides an expected increase of:

$$0.85(15¢) + 0.15(2¢) = 13.05¢$$

if the company adopts strategy C_2, and:

$$0.85(12¢) + 0.15(19¢) = 13.05¢$$

if the company adopts strategy C_3. The sum 13.05 cents is a saddle point in this game and provides the equilibrium solution.

It should be remembered that the example assumes that the monetary measures are also utility measures. The 13.05 is the expected utility of the cost to the company of following the mixed strategy, and it is also the expected utility of the wage increase to the union. If we fail to recognize that the 13.05 measures expected utility (as well as expected monetary value), then we may fall into the trap of thinking that the mixed strategy is not a minimax strategy because one possible event is a wage increase of 19 cents following the mixed strategy, but the maximum wage increase following C_2 is only 15 cents. For example, the expected utility of the cost to the company of U_3 is equal to:

$$0.35U(2¢) + 0.65U(19¢) = 0.35(2) + 0.65(19) = 13.05$$

The 13.05 is an expected utility measure and, as such, leads us to conclude that the mixed strategy results in minimum maximum cost for the company and maximum minimum wage increase to the union (in terms of expected utility or, equivalently in this example, expected monetary values).

Algebraic Solution

Instead of a graphical solution, we can solve algebraically for the probability that will cause the expected utility, from the point of view of the union, to be independent of the strategy of the company. Thus, no matter what strategy the company uses, the expected utility of the union strategy will be the same. Assume that the union uses a random device that leads to a probability of p for strategy U_1 and $(1 - p)$ for strategy U_3.

If the company uses strategy C_2, the union's expected utility is (see Table 9–4 for the source of the numbers):

$$E(U|C_2) = 0.15p + 0.02(1 - p)$$

If the company uses strategy C_3, the union has for its expected utility:

$$E(U|C_3) = 0.12p + 0.19(1 - p)$$

Set these two expected utilities equal, and solve for p:

$$0.15p + 0.02(1 - p) = 0.12p + 0.19(1 - p)$$
$$0.03p = 0.17(1 - p)$$
$$p = \frac{17}{20} = 0.85$$

The expected utility of the union's mixed strategy using a p of 0.85 is:

$$E(U|C_2) = E(U|C_3) = 0.15 \left(\frac{17}{20}\right) + 0.02 \left(\frac{3}{20}\right) = \frac{2.55 + 0.06}{20}$$
$$= \frac{2.61}{20} = 0.1305 \text{ or } 13.05¢$$

This expected value is larger than the minimum values that could result if either pure strategy is followed.

Solving the same problem from the point of view of the company, we now let p represent the probability that the *company* chooses strategy C_2. We have for the expected costs for the two strategies of the union:

$$E(C|U_1) = 0.15p + 0.12(1 - p)$$
$$E(C|U_3) = 0.02p + 0.19(1 - p)$$

Set these two expressions equal and solve for p:

$$0.15p + 0.12(1 - p) = 0.02p + 0.19(1 - p)$$
$$0.13p = 0.07(1 - p)$$
$$p = \frac{7}{20} = 0.35$$
$$1 - p = 0.65$$

With a p of $7/20$ for the company's mixed strategy, the expected cost to the company is equal to the expected value to the union:

$$E(C|U_1) = E(C|U_3) = 0.15 \left(\frac{7}{20}\right) + 0.12 \left(\frac{13}{20}\right) = \frac{1.05 + 1.56}{20}$$
$$= 0.1305 \text{ or } 13.05¢$$

This expected cost is independent of the union's strategy.

The algebraic solution method can be used to solve for mixed strategies when there are more than two possible acts, while the graphical solution shown earlier is limited to games in which at least one player has only two possible choices.

Linear Programming Solution

It is also possible to formulate the problem of finding the equilibrium mixed strategy as a linear programming problem. This has decided computational advantages if the number of pure strategies available to the players is large, since efficient computer programs exist for linear programming problems.

Evaluation of Minimax Strategy

Using minimax as a decision criterion in making decisions under uncertainty (games against nature) is not very desirable (see Chapter 5). However, in a two-person constant-sum game against a thinking opponent, it is reasonable, since it provides a participant with maximum security. It ensures a minimum outcome for you and a maximum for your opponent, regardless of the behavior of the opponent. You are indifferent to the strategy your opponent selects, for you are prepared for all contingencies.

Minimax has a particular appeal to students on academic scholarships who are preparing for exams, football coaches, and most credit officers and bankers. It is not a good strategy for those who think they can outguess their opponents and are willing to accept the risk of going on the offensive in nonzero-sum games.

The notion of using a mixed strategy for "one shot" business decisions is criticized by some analysts. You might imagine the reaction of a seasoned manager, for example, if you recommended the adoption of a marketing strategy against a competitor (price changes, advertising budget, etc.) by letting the decision depend on the spin of a roulette wheel or some other randomizing device.

While there is not a direct answer to this criticism, there are some insights gained from game theory that are relevant. Recall that one assumption of game theory implied perfect information for both opponents about the other's strategies and payoffs (or utilities). In this setting, a mixed strategy is a means of camouflaging your intentions. In the real world such perfect information is rarely available. Your opponent does not know exactly your payoffs and strategies. Hence, there is less need of camouflage. The uncertainty present serves somewhat the same purpose as randomizing.

Second, when there is no pure strategy solution, a game player is, in a sense, exploitable. That is, for any pure strategy you adopt, there is some strategy of your opponent that can hurt or exploit you. A mixed strategy can be viewed as a means of compromising or hedging against such exploitation.

Nonzero-Sum Games

For most two-person conflict situations, the utilities of the participants will not sum to a constant for all outcomes of the game. Some solutions will yield more joint satisfaction to the participants than others. These games are called nonzero-sum games. A famous type of example, originally called the "prisoner's dilemma" (see Problem 9–18), is given here.

Assume two firms are faced with a decision relative to whether or not they will advertise. They each have two possible decisions—no advertising, or advertising. The table of payoffs is as shown in Table 9–5.

The numbers in the table refer to the utilities of the two firms for each pair of decisions: firm I's utility is shown in black, and firm II's utility is shown in color. For example, if firm I advertises and firm II does not, firm I will have a utility of 5 and firm II a utility of −15.

No matter what firm I's decision is, firm II is better off if it advertises. That is, if firm I does not advertise, firm II will, for it prefers a payoff of five rather than a payoff of two. If firm I advertises, so will firm II, for it prefers a payoff of −10 to one of −15. Thus, the advertising strategy dominates the no-advertising strategy for firm II, and firm II is led to the decision to advertise. Exactly the same analysis holds for firm I, since the decision it faces is exactly the same as that of firm II. Firms I and II are both led by a rational decision process to advertise and incur a loss of −10 each. If they were not so "rational," they might each follow the dominated strategy of no advertising and receive a payoff of +2 each.

Of course, the above analysis assumes the two parties cannot cooperate (i.e., communicate their intentions), since this would change the nature of the game. It also assumes a one-shot playing of the game, with no learning by the parties concerned. It is possible that firms I and II would learn by the unhappy experience of their first try at this game and cooperate during a later playing of the game, even without actually communicating.

This example illustrates a two-person nonzero-sum game. Although there is a type of solution because the advertising decision dominates the no-advertising decision, it is not a very satisfactory solution. A pair of nonrational players may arrive at the more desirable solution where both parties do not advertise. Nonzero-sum games frequently do not have easily determined satisfactory solutions.

Table 9–5 **Payoff Table Showing Returns to Both Firms**

I \ II	No Advertising	Advertise
No Advertising	+2 / +2	+5 / −15
Advertise	−15 / +5	−10 / −10

Uncertain Payoffs

In the above example the payoffs were certain amounts. It is possible for the payoffs of a game to be subject to probability distributions. For example, instead of firm II knowing that its loss will be 10 if both firms advertise, it can be told that the payoff will be either a loss of 40 with a 0.5 probability or a gain of 20 with a probability of 0.5. The expected value is:

$$0.5(-40) + 0.5(20) = -10$$

When the payoffs are the result of a probabilistic process, it necessitates an additional computation. Before we analyze the possible decisions, the expected utility of each pair of decisions is computed and inserted into the table. It should be remembered that we are using expectations of utility and not expected monetary values.

Competitive Bidding: The Winner's Curse[6]

Imagine a small jar full of money (coins). Each member of the class can bid an amount of money for the privilege of owning the jar. The highest bid takes the jar. The bidders cannot collude. Professor Richard Thaler has conducted this experiment at Cornell University a number of times. Each time, the winning bid is larger than the value of the coins in the jar. This is an example of the winner's curse. The winner has a high likelihood of losing money in a bidding situation where the item's value is not known with certainty.

In the real world, firms bid for the right to drill oil wells. The most optimistic firm wins the bid. Firms also bid to take over other firms. Again, the most optimistic bidder wins.

The amount of the overbid is a function of the number of bidders. The larger the number of bidders, the more the winner will tend to overshoot the value of the asset that is being auctioned. Thus, oil companies will often join together and offer joint bids rather than each firm competing. The number of bids is thereby reduced by 50 to 75 percent.

Another strategy that is followed is for an estimated value to be determined, but then the bid amount is set substantially below the expected value. While the likelihood of winning is reduced, the likelihood of being happy if you do win (and ultimately making a net gain) is increased. The objective should be to make an economic gain, not to win the bid.

---

[6]For a theoretical discussion, see J. H. Kagel and D. Levin, "The Winner's Curse and Public Information in Common Value Auctions," *The American Economic Review,* December 1986, pp. 894–920.

Some firms active in the merger and acquisition business will not enter a competitive bidding situation. If a company is interested in selling out, this firm will make what it considers a fair bid only if the company selling out agrees to accept or reject the bid before it seeks a second bid. Naturally, the selling company might already have information regarding the population of prospective buyers and their likely bid prices. But it must make a decision on the bid without seeking out (or accepting) other offers. If the prospective buyer knows that other buyers have already made offers, it should reduce the amount it is willing to offer.

The winner's curse can be found in a wide range of situations. For example if, in a rapidly moving housing market, a house has been on the market for over a year, one would have to assume that many buyers have rejected the house at the asking price. Buying the house at the asking price would be a form of winner's curse, given the large number of buyers who have rejected it. It is possible that the house is unique and just what you want, while others do not like the unique features; it is also possible that the prospective buyers who rejected it knew what they were doing.

Conclusions

The reader should consider if there are any situations in the real world where two or more parties are competing with each other where the gains come close to being zero sum (what one person loses the other gains) or are nonzero sum. Are the results of such games always beneficial to society?

Examples of real life "games" range from wars (where one party can win only at the expense of the other and where both parties are likely to lose) to the automobile industry and college football, where escalation in "selling" expenditures sometimes results in all parties being worse off than they would have been with different strategies.

In the real world, exact solutions to game situations may not be applicable, so that the theories cannot be applied exactly. On the other hand, game theory helps us to learn how to approach and understand a conflict situation and how to improve the decision process.

SUMMARY

All two-person zero-sum games have an equilibrium minimax solution. This will be either a pair of pure strategies or a pair of mixed strategies. Nonzero-sum games can reach equilibrium solutions that may not be satisfactory.

The winner's curse suggests that when an item's value is uncertain, the highest bidder for it may overbid, with the amount of the overbid being an increasing function of the number of bidders.

Bibliography

Davis, M. D. *Game Theory, a Nontechnical Introduction.* New York: Basic Books, 1970.

Englebrecht-Wiggans, R. "Auctions and Bidding Models: A Survey." *Management Science,* February 1980.

————; P. R. Milgrom; and R. J. Weber. "Competitive Bidding and Proprietary Information." *Journal of Mathematical Economics* 11 (1983).

Kagel, J. H., and D. Levin. "The Winner's Curse and Public Information in Common Value Auctions." *The American Economic Review,* December 1986.

Luce, R. D., and H. Raiffa. *Games and Decisions.* New York: John Wiley & Sons, 1957.

Owen, G. *Game Theory.* Philadelphia: W. B. Saunders, 1968.

McDonald, J. *The Game of Business.* Garden City, N.Y.: Doubleday, 1975.

Shubik, M., ed. *Game Theory and Related Approaches to Social Behavior.* New York: John Wiley & Sons, 1964.

————. *Game Theory in the Social Sciences: Concepts and Solutions.* Cambridge, Mass.: MIT Press, 1983.

Vickrey, W. "Counterspeculation, Auctions, and Competitive Sealed Tenders." *The Journal of Finance,* March 1961.

Von Neumann, J., and O. Morgenstern. *Theory of Games and Economic Behavior.* Princeton: Princeton University Press, 1944.

Williams, J. D. *The Compleat Strategyst.* Rev. ed. New York: McGraw-Hill, 1966.

Wilson, R. B. "Competitive Bidding with Disparate Information." *Management Science,* March 1969; and "Competitive Bidding with Asymmetrical Information." *Management Science,* July 1967.

Problems with Answers

9–1. Prepare the payoff matrix for matching pennies, player 1 versus player 2. What does this assume about the utilities of players 1 and 2?

9–2. In matching pennies, is the minimax strategy a pure strategy?

9–3. If a player follows a pure strategy in matching pennies, what is the most the player can lose on a series of n plays?

9–4. Assume the following payoff matrix for two opponents, A and B, the amounts being the utility gained by A and lost by B for any given intersection of strategies:

	B_1	B_2
A_1	10	6
A_2	8	2

a. What strategy will A follow?

b. What strategy will B follow?

c. What is the "value" of the game?

d. Plot the payoffs from these strategies from player A's standpoint.

9–5. Say the following payoff matrix is appropriate for the merchandising strategies of two opponents:

Strategies of A \ Strategies of B	B_1	B_2
A_1	0 / 0	1 / 2
A_2	4 / 1	5 / 3

a. What strategy will A follow? Why?

b. What strategy will B follow? Why?

c. What outcome would you predict for this situation?

Problems

9–6. Assume the following payoff matrix for A and B, the amounts being the utilities gained by A and lost by B for any given intersection of strategies:

	B_1	B_2
A_1	10	6
A_2	8	12

a. What is the maximum minimum gain A can make for sure by following a pure strategy?

b. What is the minimum maximum loss B can incur for sure by following a pure strategy?

c. What is the mixed strategy for A?

d. Plot the mixed strategies for A and B.

e. If A and B follow mixed strategies, what is the value of the game?

9–7. What type of conflict situation is more likely—a zero-sum game or a nonzero-sum game?

9–8. Two firms, f and g, face the profit payoff for alternative merchandising strategies shown in the accompanying table.

a. What strategy will f follow? Why?

b. What strategy will g follow? Why?

c. What is the solution of the game?

d. Identify the equilibrium pair, if there is one.

Strategies of g \ Strategies of f	f_1	f_2
g_1	8 / 8	10 / 1
g_2	1 / 10	2 / 1

9–9. If Problem 9–8 were repeated daily for n days, where n is large, do you think the players would continue to follow an equilibrium strategy? What does this suggest?

9–10. The ABC Company and the XYZ Company are both currently distributing, through a subsidiary, automobiles in the country of Akro. The profits per year of the two subsidiaries are currently as follows: ABC, $10 million; and XYZ, $20 million.

The ABC Company is considering establishing a manufacturing plant in Akro. An analyst has projected a profit of $38 million after the plant begins operations (this assumes the XYZ Company continues to distribute automobiles, but not to manufacture them, in the country).

An analyst for the XYZ Company has heard of the plans of the ABC Company. If the plant is built by ABC, he projects XYZ's profits to fall to $4 million. If the XYZ Company builds a plant and the ABC Company does not, he anticipates profits of $38 million and a decrease in the profits of ABC to $4 million.

If both companies build plants, it is expected that they would both earn $5 million per year. What should the companies do?

9–11. Conduct the following experiment: Take a jar of coins and ask two people (separately) to estimate the value of the coins. Then ask four additional people to estimate the value. How does the highest estimate in the first sample ($n=2$) compare with the highest estimate in the second sample ($n=4$)? Did your experiment support or contradict the winner's curse?

More Challenging Problems

9–12. Two computer manufacturers, A and B, are attempting to sell computer systems to two banks, 1 and 2. Company A has four salespeople, company B has only three available. The computer companies must decide how many salespeople to assign to call on each bank. Thus, company A can assign four salespeople to bank 1 and none to bank 2, or three to bank 1 and one to bank 2, and so on.

Each bank will buy one computer system. The probability that a bank will buy from a particular computer company is directly related to the number of salespeople calling from that company relative to total salespeople calling. Thus, if company A assigned three people to bank 1, and company B assigned two people, the odds would be three out of five that bank 1 would purchase a company A computer system. (As a special case, if none call from either company, the odds are one half for buying either computer.)

Let the payoff be the expected number of computer systems that computer company A sells. (Then two minus this payoff is the expected number company B sells.)

What strategy should company A use in allocating its salespeople? What strategy should company B use? What is the value of the game to company A? What is the meaning of the value of the game in this problem?

9–13. Refer to Problem 9–12. Suppose that bank 1 is going to buy two computer systems, whereas bank 2 will buy only one. In this case, what is the optimum strategy for company A? For company B? What is the value of the game?

9–14. Refer to Problem 9–12. Suppose that each bank bought the computer system from the company sending the larger number of salespeople. (If both companies send equal numbers, the decision is made by the flip of a fair coin.) In this case, what is the optimum strategy for company A? For Company B? What is the value of the game?

9–15. Firms I and II are competing for business. Whatever I gains, II loses. The accompanying table shows the utilities to firm I for various market shares (assume the game is zero-sum). Find an equilibrium solution.

9–16. Companies A and B are in direct competition. Each has four alternative advertising campaigns; the table accompanying contains the gain to company A under each pair of campaigns chosen. (Since it is a zero-sum situation, gains to company B are the negative of gains to company A.) Find an equilibrium solution.

9–17. In a two-person zero-sum game, let the payoff to player I be denoted by X_{ij} where i represents the strategy of player I, and j

Firm I's Utility (for Problem 9–15)

I \ II	No Advertising	Medium Advertising	Large Advertising	Row Minimums
No Advertising	60	50	40	40
Medium Advertising	70	70	50	50
Large Advertising	80	60	75	60
Column Maximums	80	70	75	

Gains to Company A (for Problem 9–16)

Company A Alternatives	Company B Alternatives B_1	B_2	B_3	B_4
A_1	10	30	25	15
A_2	5	40	10	30
A_3	15	25	5	10
A_4	20	20	15	40

represents the strategy of player II. Suppose each player has three strategies, none of which are dominated. If p_i represents the optimal mixed-strategy probability that player I plays strategy i, write down three equations involving p_1, p_2, and p_3.

9–18. The name "prisoner's dilemma" for a class of game theory problems comes from the following story:

Two prisoners are arrested for a crime they committed together. However, the evidence against them is not very strong. The prosecutor separates the prisoners and offers each a deal: confess and agree to testify against your partner and you will get off free. Each prisoner knows that if he refuses to confess but his partner does and testifies against him, he will receive a very heavy sentence since the judge will interpret the refusal to confess as evidence that he is a hardened criminal. If both prisoners confess, there will be no need to have one testify against the other, and both will receive moderate sentences. If neither confesses, the prosecutor will be able to convict them on technical charges and they will receive light sentences.

Draw up the payoff table facing each prisoner. What should each prisoner do, assuming they cannot collaborate? What if they could collaborate?

PART III

Mathematical Programming

10

Introduction to Linear Programming

As described in earlier chapters in this book, managers build models to aid in the solution of decision problems. A linear programming model, or LP model, is a particular type of mathematical model in which the relationships involving the variables are linear, and in which there is a single performance measure or objective. An advantage of this type of model is that there exists a mathematical technique, called **linear programming**, that can determine the best or optimal decision even when there are thousands of variables and relationships. This chapter considers the formulation of linear programming models. The solution and interpretation of the results are treated in following chapters.

In the linear programming model, there is a set of **decision variables** X_1, X_2, ..., X_N. The linear programming model is designed to maximize (or minimize) an **objective function** of the form:

$$f = C_1X_1 + C_2X_2 + \ldots + C_NX_N$$

where f is some economic objective such as profits, production, costs, work-weeks, or tons shipped. More profits are generally preferred to less profits, lower costs are preferred to higher costs, and so on. The manager wishes to select values for the decision variables to achieve the most profit, or least cost, or most production, and so forth. All of the coefficients C_1, C_2, ..., C_N are constants, and all of the Xs are of the first power (i.e., no squares, cubes, for example). Thus, the function f is a **linear** function.

Generally, the manager cannot arbitrarily determine the values for the decision variables, the Xs. Rather, the choice is limited by a set of relationships or constraints. These relationships involving the Xs are also linear in form and are **linear inequalities** or **linear equalities:**

$$A_1X_1 + A_2X_2 + \ldots + A_NX_N \leq B_1$$

The A coefficients are constants. The constant B_1 restricts f, the objective function, as a result of restricting the decision variables, $X_1, X_2, \ldots, X_N$ (instead of $\leq$, we could have $\geq$ or an equality). The solution provided by linear programming is the set of values of the decision variables that achieves the desired maximum (or minimum) within the various constraints.

Linear programming does not allow for uncertainty in any of the relationships; there cannot be any probabilities or any random variables. Thus, the problem of maximizing the objective function subject to the various constraints is conceptually simple. Where there are only a few variables, common sense and some arithmetic will yield a solution, and decision makers have solved such problems for generations. However, as is often the case, intuition is of little use when the problem is more complex; when the number of decision variables is increased from three or four to hundreds or thousands, the problem defies rule-of-thumb procedures. Linear programming has made it possible to handle problems with large numbers of constraints in an orderly way.

This technique has exceptional power and generality. It is applicable to a variety of problems in a modern business organization and may be handled in a routine way with the aid of modern computers. It is one of the quantitative techniques that has provided management with a remarkable leverage on a set of problems that defied efficient solutions a relatively few years ago.

As a simple example, consider the following problem, which can be solved by the use of common sense or marginal analysis. Assume the incremental profit of product A is $5 per unit, the profit of product B is $2 per unit, and we can sell all we make of both products; further, either product may be produced with the same equipment. We can compute which product we should produce once we find out the capacity of our facilities in terms of A and B (see Table 10–1). The equipment can produce 100 units of A per day, or 600 units of B per day.

In this simple example, product B is obviously a more desirable product than A, since $1,200 of profits per day is better than $500. Now assume a more complicated problem where the plant is capable of making 20 different products in 15 different departments, and each product requires different production time in each department. If the difficulty of this problem is not impressive, assume that each department contains 10 processes, and each product requires different production time in each process. How do we determine the optimum product mix? A problem of this type is best solved by linear programming. The term **linear** is appropriate, since all profit and production relationships are assumed to be proportional or linear; that is, the highest degree of any variable is 1, and no variables are multiplied by any other variable.

Table 10–1

Product	Capacity (units per day)	Per Unit Profit	Total Incremental Profit per Day
A	100	$5	$ 500
B	600	2	1,200

There are several methods for solving linear programming problems. In Chapter 11, we shall introduce a graphical solution, and in Chapter 12 we introduce the simplex method, which is an algebraic method for deriving a solution.

In some of the examples to follow, the answers will be obvious; this is because the examples were constructed to be as simple as possible. In other examples, more complicated problems are treated, and some of the exercises are quite complex. The reader should keep in mind that we are attempting to illustrate a technique that may be applied to extremely complex problems. We apply it to simple situations for expository purposes. In practice, the computations in complex linear programming problems would be done on a computer. Prepared or "canned" computer programs to solve linear programming problems are now widely available even for personal computers.

Formulation of Linear Programming Problems

Before going into the details of learning how to solve linear programming problems, it is important to learn how to define the variables and equations—generally, how to set up a business problem in the form of maximizing (or minimizing) a linear function f, subject to linear constraints. We shall use the term **formulation** to mean translating a real-world problem into a format of mathematical equations. Formulation is often the most challenging part of analyzing a business problem.

We shall study several different problems, offering some experience in formulation and introducing some of the wide variety of problems that can be analyzed by linear programming.

Example 1: A Product Mix Problem

A manufacturing firm produces two products, A and B. Each of these products must be processed through two different machines. One machine has 24 hours of available capacity, and the second machine has 16 hours. Each unit of product A requires two hours of time on both machines. Each unit of product B requires three hours of time on the first machine and one hour on the second machine. The incremental profit is $6 per unit of product A and $7 per unit of product B, and the firm can sell as many units of each product as it can manufacture.

The objective of the firm is to maximize profits. The problem is to determine how many units of product A and product B should be produced within the limits of available machine capacities.

Formulation   Let:

X_1 = Number of units of product A to be produced
X_2 = Number of units of product B to be produced
P = Total incremental profit to the firm

The objective function is:

Maximize: $P = 6X_1 + 7X_2$

This equation states that the firm's total profit is made up of the profit from product A ($6 times the number sold) plus the profit from product B ($7 times the number sold).

The first constraint relates to the availability of time on the first machine. This can be expressed as:

$$2X_1 + 3X_2 \leq 24$$

Each unit of product A uses two hours of this machine, and each unit of product B uses three hours. Hence, the total hours used is expressed by the left-hand side of the expression above. This must be equal to or less than the total hours available on the first machine (24).

For the second machine, a similar constraint is:

$$2X_1 + 1X_2 \leq 16$$

In addition, implicit in any linear programming formulation are the constraints that restrict X_1 and X_2 to be nonnegative. In terms of the problem, this means that the firm can produce only zero or positive amounts.

The total formulation is:

Maximize: $P = 6X_1 + 7X_2$

Subject to: $2X_1 + 3X_2 \leq 24$
$2X_1 + X_2 \leq 16$
$X_1, X_2 \geq 0$

This example is simple, and one would not need linear programming to solve it. However, problems involving dozens of products and many different constraints cannot be solved intuitively, and linear programming has proved valuable in these cases.

Example 2: A Transportation Problem

A manufacturer of soap and detergents has three plants located in Cincinnati, Denver, and Atlanta. Major warehouses are located at New York, Boston, Chicago, Los Angeles, and Dallas. Sales requirements for the next year at each warehouse are given in Table 10–2.

There is some concern in the company about which factory should supply each warehouse. Factory capacity at each location is limited. Cincinnati has an annual capacity of 100,000 cases. Denver has a capacity of 60,000 cases, and Atlanta has a capacity of 50,000 cases.

The cost of shipping soap from each factory to each warehouse is given in Table 10–3. The company wishes to determine a shipping schedule that will minimize overall company transportation costs (denoted by C).

Table 10–2   **Warehouse Requirements**

Warehouse Location	Annual Sales (000s of cases)
New York	50
Boston	10
Chicago	60
Los Angeles	30
Dallas	20
Total	170

Table 10–3   **Cost of Shipping 1,000 Cases of Soap**

From \ To	New York	Boston	Chicago	Los Angeles	Dallas
Cincinnati	$120	$150	$ 80	$250	$180
Denver	210	220	150	100	110
Atlanta	150	170	150	240	200

Formulation   Let:

X_{11} = Number of cases shipped from first factory (Cincinnati) to first warehouse (New York), in thousands of cases

Similarly:

$X_{12}, X_{13}, X_{14}, X_{15}$ = Number of cases shipped from first factory (Cincinnati) to second, third, and so on, warehouses (Boston, Chicago, and so on)

$X_{21}, X_{22}, X_{23}, X_{24}, X_{25}$ = Number of cases shipped from second factory (Denver) to first, second, and so on, warehouses

$X_{31}, X_{32}, X_{33}, X_{34}, X_{35}$ = Number of cases shipped from third factory (Atlanta) to first, second, and so on, warehouses

Then the objective is to:

Minimize: $C = 120X_{11} + 150X_{12} + 80X_{13} + 250X_{14} + 180X_{15}$
$+ 210X_{21} + 220X_{22} + 150X_{23} + 100X_{24} + 110X_{25} +$
$150X_{31} + 170X_{32} + 150X_{33} + 240X_{34} + 200X_{35}$

The total cost is the sum of the products for each possible shipping route (from factory to warehouse) of the shipping cost from Table 10–3 times the number of thousands of cases shipped.

There are two sets of constraints for this problem. The first set guarantees that the warehouse needs will be met. Thus, for New York:

$$X_{11} + X_{21} + X_{31} = 50$$

This states that the sum of the cases shipped to New York from the first (Cincinnati), second (Denver), and third (Atlanta) factories must be 50,000 cases, the sales requirement for New York. For the other warehouses, we have:

$$\text{Boston:} \quad X_{12} + X_{22} + X_{32} = 10$$
$$\text{Chicago:} \quad X_{13} + X_{23} + X_{33} = 60$$
$$\text{Los Angeles:} \quad X_{14} + X_{24} + X_{34} = 30$$
$$\text{Dallas:} \quad X_{15} + X_{25} + X_{35} = 20$$

The second set of constraints guarantees that the factories do not exceed their capacities. Thus, for the Cincinnati factory:

$$X_{11} + X_{12} + X_{13} + X_{14} + X_{15} \leq 100$$

This expression indicates that the amount shipped from the first factory to the first, second, third, and so on, warehouses must not exceed the factory's capacity of 100,000 cases.

Similarly, for:

$$\text{Denver:} \quad X_{21} + X_{22} + X_{23} + X_{24} + X_{25} \leq 60$$
$$\text{Atlanta:} \quad X_{31} + X_{32} + X_{33} + X_{34} + X_{35} \leq 50$$

Finally, all the Xs must be greater than or equal to zero.

The solution of this linear programming problem will give the optimum (i.e., least-cost) shipping schedule for the company. This is an example of a special type of problem known, naturally enough, as the **transportation problem.** Chapter 13 is devoted to a special procedure for solving this type of problem.

In summary, the complete formulation of the problem is:

$$
\begin{aligned}
\text{Minimize:} \quad C = \ & 120X_{11} + 150X_{12} + 80X_{13} + 250X_{14} + 180X_{15} \\
& + 210X_{21} + 220X_{22} + 150X_{23} + 100X_{24} \\
& + 110X_{25} + 150X_{31} + 170X_{32} + 150X_{33} \\
& + 240X_{34} + 200X_{35}
\end{aligned}
$$

$$
\text{Subject to:} \quad
\left.
\begin{aligned}
X_{11} + X_{21} + X_{31} &= 50 \\
X_{12} + X_{22} + X_{32} &= 10 \\
X_{13} + X_{23} + X_{33} &= 60 \\
X_{14} + X_{24} + X_{34} &= 30 \\
X_{15} + X_{25} + X_{35} &= 20
\end{aligned}
\right\}
\begin{aligned}
&\text{Warehouse} \\
&\text{requirement} \\
&\text{constraints}
\end{aligned}
$$

$$
\left.
\begin{aligned}
X_{11} + X_{12} + X_{13} + X_{14} + X_{15} &\leq 100 \\
X_{21} + X_{22} + X_{23} + X_{24} + X_{25} &\leq 60 \\
X_{31} + X_{32} + X_{33} + X_{34} + X_{35} &\leq 50
\end{aligned}
\right\}
\begin{aligned}
&\text{Factory} \\
&\text{capacity} \\
&\text{constraints}
\end{aligned}
$$

$$X_{11}, X_{12}, \ldots, X_{35} \geq 0$$

Example 3: A Blending Problem

Various grades of gasoline are obtained by blending together certain blending gasolines that are the direct output of the refinery operations. In an actual refining operation, there are many blending gasolines, many final-product gasolines (e.g., various grades of aviation and motor gasoline), and many characteristics that are considered important in the chemical composition of the various grades of gasoline (including, for example, octane rating, vapor pressure, sulfur content, and gum content). In this simplified example, we assume that a refinery has available only two types of blending gasoline, whose characteristics are shown in Table 10–4.

These blending gasolines may be mixed to produce two final products, aviation gasoline and motor gasoline. The required characteristics of these final products are shown in Table 10–5.

When gasolines are mixed together, the resulting mixture has an octane and a vapor pressure in proportion to the volume of each gasoline mixed. For example, if 1,000 barrels of blending gasoline 1 were mixed with 1,000 barrels of blending gasoline 2, the resultant gasoline would have an octane rating of 99:

$$\frac{1,000 \cdot 104 + 1,000 \cdot 94}{2,000} = 99$$

and a vapor pressure of 7:

$$\frac{1,000 \cdot 5 + 1,000 \cdot 9}{2,000} = 7$$

The firm wishes to maximize revenue from the sale of final product gasoline.

Table 10–4 **Characteristics of Blending Gasolines**

Available Blends	Octane Rating	Vapor Pressure	Amount Available
Blending gasoline, type 1	104	5	30,000 barrels
Blending gasoline, type 2	94	9	70,000 barrels

Table 10–5 **Characteristics of Final-Product Gasolines**

Final Products	Minimum Octane Rating	Maximum Vapor Pressure	Maximum Sales	Selling Price (per barrel)
Aviation gasoline	102	6	20,000 barrels	$45.10
Motor gasoline	96	8	Any amount	32.40

Formulation Let:

X_1 = Number of barrels of blending gasoline 1 used in aviation gasoline
X_2 = Number of barrels of blending gasoline 2 used in aviation gasoline
X_3 = Number of barrels of blending gasoline 1 used in motor gasoline
X_4 = Number of barrels of blending gasoline 2 used in motor gasoline

The objective function is then to maximize P = Total revenue:

Maximize: $P = 45.10(X_1 + X_2) + 32.40(X_3 + X_4)$
$= 45.10X_1 + 45.10X_2 + 32.40X_3 + 32.40X_4$

Note that $X_1 + X_2$ is the total amount of aviation gasoline mixed (in barrels), and since it sells at \$45.10 per barrel, the revenue from this product is $45.10 (X_1 + X_2)$. Similarly, the revenue from motor gasoline is $32.40(X_3 + X_4)$, and the sum of these terms is the total revenue, P.

There are several kinds of constraints that affect how the refinery will blend its gasoline. The first is on the sales or demand size—the fact that no more than 20,000 barrels of aviation gasoline can be sold (see Table 10–5). This may be represented by the following expression:

$$X_1 + X_2 \leq 20,000$$

A second set of constraints relates to available amounts of blending gasolines (see Table 10–4). Thus, we have:

$$X_1 + X_3 \leq 30,000$$

Note that $X_1 + X_3$ represents the total amount of blending gasoline 1 (the sum of the amount used in aviation gasoline, X_1, and the amount used in motor gasoline, X_3). The equation above states that the amount of blending gasoline 1 used must not exceed the amount available—30,000 barrels. A similar constraint for blending gasoline 2 is:

$$X_2 + X_4 \leq 70,000$$

Another set of constraints relates to the octane ratings of the final-product gasolines. Recall that the total amount of aviation gasoline is $X_1 + X_2$. Its octane rating will be determined by the relative amounts of $X_1 + X_2$ according to the following formula:

$$\text{Octane rating of aviation gasoline} = \frac{104 \cdot X_1 + 94 \cdot X_2}{X_1 + X_2}$$

The numbers 104 and 94 are from Table 10–4 and are the octane ratings of blending gasoline 1 and blending gasoline 2, respectively. From Table 10–5, we note that the octane rating of aviation gasoline must be at least 102. So we have the following constraint:

$$\frac{104X_1 + 94X_2}{X_1 + X_2} \geq 102$$

Rearranging this expression in order to make it a linear constraint, we have:

$$104X_1 + 94X_2 \geq 102X_1 + 102X_2$$

or

$$(104X_1 - 102X_1) + (94X_2 - 102X_2) \geq 0$$

or

$$2X_1 - 8X_2 \geq 0$$

Similarly, for the octane rating for motor gasoline, we have:

$$104X_3 + 94X_4 \geq 96(X_3 + X_4)$$

or

$$8X_3 - 2X_4 \geq 0$$

A final set of constraints is related to the vapor pressure requirements of the final-product gasolines. For aviation gasoline, we have:

$$5X_1 + 9X_2 \leq 6(X_1 + X_2)$$

or

$$-X_1 + 3X_2 \leq 0$$

and the vapor pressure requirement of motor gasoline is:

$$5X_3 + 9X_4 \leq 8(X_3 + X_4)$$

or

$$-3X_3 + X_4 \leq 0$$

In summary, the total formulation of the linear programming model is:

Maximize: $P = 45.10X_1 + 45.10X_2 + 32.40X_3 + 32.40X_4$

Subject to: $X_1 + X_2 \leq 20,000$ Demand constraint

$\left. \begin{array}{l} X_1 + X_3 \leq 30,000 \\ X_2 + X_4 \leq 70,000 \end{array} \right\}$ Availability of blending gasoline constraints

$\left. \begin{array}{l} 2X_1 - 8X_2 \geq 0 \\ 8X_3 - 2X_4 \geq 0 \end{array} \right\}$ Octane rating constraints

$\left. \begin{array}{l} -X_1 + 3X_2 \leq 0 \\ -3X_3 + X_4 \leq 0 \end{array} \right\}$ Vapor pressure constraints

$X_1, X_2, X_3, X_4 \geq 0$

Gasoline blending was one of the very first applications of linear programming to business problems. Our example here is of course very much of an over-simplification of the real problem, but it captures the essential elements. The problem as formulated above is called the **blending problem.** Blending problems turn up in many contexts. One example of such a problem is in the production of feeds for animals. A feed mix for chickens, for example, may be made up of several different kinds of grains, and so forth. The feed mix manufacturer would like to use the cheapest grains available. However, the manufacturer is constrained by the fact that the feed mix must satisfy certain nutritional requirements (similar to the constraints on vapor pressure and octane rating in our gasoline example). In fact, certain aesthetic constraints also have to be added—the chickens will not eat the mixes determined solely by nutritional constraints.

The three examples so far have dealt with problems in one time period—often called **static** problems. Linear programming has also been applied to **dynamic** problems; that is, those extending over several time periods.[1] Consider the following example.

Example 4: A Scheduling Problem

A company faces a firm schedule of delivery commitments for a product over the next six months. The production cost varies by month due to anticipated changes in materials costs. The company's production capacity is 100 units per month on regular time and up to an additional 15 units per month on overtime.

Table 10–6 contains delivery requirements and production costs by month.

The cost of carrying an unsold unit in stock is $2 per month. The problem for the company is to determine the number of units to produce in regular time and overtime each month to meet requirements at minimum cost. The firm has no units on hand at the beginning of month 1 and wishes to have no units on hand at the end of month 6.

Formulation   Let:

$$X_1, X_2, X_3, X_4, X_5, X_6 = \text{Number of units produced in regular time each month}$$

$$Y_1, Y_2, Y_3, Y_4, Y_5, Y_6 = \text{Number of units produced in overtime each month}$$

$$I_1, I_2, I_3, I_4, I_5, I_6 = \text{Number of units in stock (unsold) at the end of each month}$$

Then the objective is to:

$$\text{Minimize: } C = 30X_1 + 30X_2 + 32X_3 + 32X_4 + 31X_5 + 32X_6 + 35Y_1 \\ + 35Y_2 + 37Y_3 + 37Y_4 + 36Y_5 + 37Y_6 + 2I_1 + 2I_2 + 2I_3 \\ + 2I_4 + 2I_5 + 2I_6$$

The first part of this expression is the regular-time production costs (from Table 10–6) times the amounts produced in regular time each month. The second part

---

[1] Dynamic programming also deals with dynamic problems (see Chapter 22). It is sometimes possible to formulate a problem as a linear programming problem and as a dynamic programming problem. See the exercises at the end of Chapter 22.

Table 10-6 **Requirements and costs**

	Month					
	1	*2*	*3*	*4*	*5*	*6*
Delivery commitments (units)	95	85	110	115	90	105
Cost per unit in regular time	$30	30	32	32	31	32
Cost per unit in overtime	$35	35	37	37	36	37

represents the overtime production costs times the amounts produced in overtime each month. The third part is the cost of carrying unsold units in stock times the number of unsold units each month.

The constraints on regular-time production are:

$$X_1 \leq 100$$
$$X_2 \leq 100$$
$$X_3 \leq 100$$
$$X_4 \leq 100$$
$$X_5 \leq 100$$
$$X_6 \leq 100$$

The constraints on overtime production are:

$$Y_1 \leq 15$$
$$Y_2 \leq 15$$
$$Y_3 \leq 15$$
$$Y_4 \leq 15$$
$$Y_5 \leq 15$$
$$Y_6 \leq 15$$

Finally, a group of *linking constraints* or balance constraints are needed to link the time periods together and ensure that delivery commitments are met. These constraints are of the form

$$(\text{Sources of units}) = (\text{Uses of units})$$

or

$$\begin{pmatrix} \text{Opening} \\ \text{Inventory} \end{pmatrix} + \begin{pmatrix} \text{Regular-time} \\ \text{production} \end{pmatrix} + \begin{pmatrix} \text{Overtime} \\ \text{production} \end{pmatrix} = \begin{pmatrix} \text{Delivery} \\ \text{commitments} \end{pmatrix} + \begin{pmatrix} \text{Ending} \\ \text{inventory} \end{pmatrix}$$

For month 1, this becomes:

$$0 + X_1 + Y_1 = 95 + I_1$$

since there is no initial inventory. Rearranging gives:

$$X_1 + Y_1 - I_1 = 95$$

Similarly, for month 2:

$$I_1 + X_2 + Y_2 = 85 + I_2$$

or

$$I_1 + X_2 + Y_2 - I_2 = 85$$

For the remaining months:

Month 3: $I_2 + X_3 + Y_3 - I_3 = 110$
Month 4: $I_3 + X_4 + Y_4 - I_4 = 115$
Month 5: $I_4 + X_5 + Y_5 - I_5 = 90$
Month 6: $I_5 + X_6 + Y_6 - I_6 = 105$

Since ending inventory should be zero, a final constraint is:

$$I_6 = 0$$

In summary, the formulation is:

Minimize: $C = 30X_1 + 30X_2 + 32X_3 + 32X_4 + 31X_5 + 32X_6 + 35Y_1$
$+ 35Y_2 + 37Y_3 + 37Y_4 + 36Y_5 + 37Y_6 + 2I_1 + 2I_2 + 2I_3$
$+ 2I_4 + 2I_5 + 2I_6$

Subject to:

$$\left.\begin{array}{l} X_1 + Y_1 - I_1 = 95 \\ I_1 + X_2 + Y_2 - I_2 = 85 \\ I_2 + X_3 + Y_3 - I_3 = 110 \\ I_3 + X_4 + Y_4 - I_4 = 115 \\ I_4 + X_5 + Y_5 - I_5 = 90 \\ I_5 + X_6 + Y_6 - I_6 = 105 \end{array}\right\} \begin{array}{l}\text{Inventory}\\ \text{balance}\\ \text{constraints}\end{array}$$

$$\left.\begin{array}{l} X_1 \leq 100 \\ X_2 \leq 100 \\ X_3 \leq 100 \\ X_4 \leq 100 \\ X_5 \leq 100 \\ X_6 \leq 100 \end{array}\right\} \begin{array}{l}\text{Regular-time}\\ \text{production}\\ \text{constraints}\end{array} \qquad \left.\begin{array}{l} Y_1 \leq 15 \\ Y_2 \leq 15 \\ Y_3 \leq 15 \\ Y_4 \leq 15 \\ Y_5 \leq 15 \\ Y_6 \leq 15 \end{array}\right\} \begin{array}{l}\text{Overtime}\\ \text{production}\\ \text{constraints}\end{array}$$

$$I_6 = 0 \quad \text{Ending inventory constraint}$$
$$X_1, X_2, X_3, X_4, X_5, X_6, Y_1, Y_2, Y_3, Y_4, Y_5, Y_6 \geq 0$$
$$I_1, I_2, I_3, I_4, I_5, I_6 \geq 0$$

Example 5: An Integrated Corporate Planning Model

This example deals with the formulation of a large-scale or system model, designed primarily for planning the integrated activities of a business firm. The example, diagrammed in Figure 10–1, is oversimplified and includes only two species of trees, two lumber and plywood products, and very few of the technological constraints involved in the production of lumber and plywood (see Table 10–7). The objective function is not shown in Table 10–7. It would be obtained by taking the prices of the finished products times the output of these products and subtracting the variable operating costs throughout the whole system.

Figure 10–1   Simplified Model of Wood Products Firm

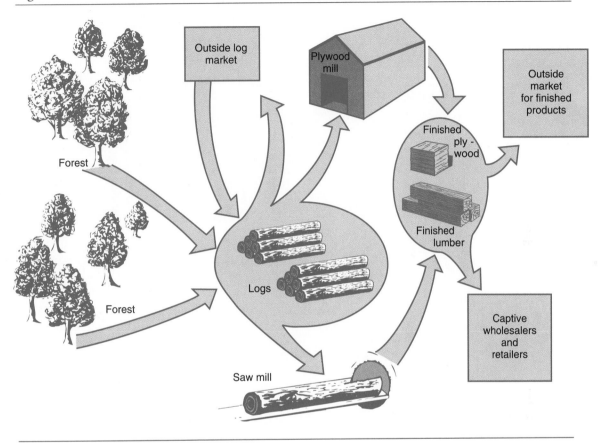

The Art of Formulating Linear Programming Models

Formulating any quantitative model means selecting out the important elements from the problem and defining how these are related. For real-world problems this is not an easy task and involves judgment and trial and error. In fact, it is more of an art than a systematic procedure. However, there are some steps that have been found useful in formulating linear programming models. These are:

1. Define in verbal terms the objective that you are trying to achieve in solving the problem. Select only one objective. For example, it might be "reduce cost" or "increase contribution to profit."

2. List verbally the decisions that are to be made as specifically as you can.

3. List verbally the constraining factors that affect these decisions. Try to be precise and complete. There are several general types of constraints listed

Table 10–7 Constraints for Wood Products Firm

	Availability of Lumber	Shipments of Lumber	Mill Constraints	Production Technology	Shipments to Markets	Market Demand
Fir	$X_1 \le A_1$	$X_7 + X_9 = X_1 + X_3 - X_5$	$X_7 + X_8 \le A_3$ $a_1X_7 + a_2X_8 \le A_4$ etc.	$X_{11} = a_5X_7 + a_6X_8$ $X_{12} = a_7X_7 + a_8X_8$	$X_{11} + X_{12} = X_{15} + X_{16}$	$X_{15} \le D_1$ $X_{16} \le D_2$
Pine	$X_2 \le A_2$	$X_8 + X_{10} = X_2 + X_4 - X_6$	$X_9 + X_{10} \le A_5$ $a_3X_9 + a_4X_{10} \le A_6$ etc.	$X_{13} = a_9X_9 + a_{10}X_{10}$ $X_{14} = a_{11}X_9 + a_{12}X_{10}$	$X_{13} + X_{14} = X_{17} + X_{18}$	$X_{17} \le D_3$ $X_{18} \le D_4$

Symbols (MBF stands for 000s of board feet):

X_1 = MBF of fir cut
X_2 = MBF of pine cut
X_3 = MBF of fir purchased from outside
X_4 = MBF of pine purchased from outside
X_5 = MBF of fir sold to outside
X_6 = MBF of pine sold to outside
X_7 = MBF of fir to sawmill
X_8 = MBF of pine to sawmill
X_9 = MBF of fir to plywood mill
X_{10} = MBF of pine to plywood mill
X_{11}, X_{12} = Production in MBF of two types of lumber (e.g., 2 × 4s and 2 × 6s)
X_{13}, X_{14} = Production in panels of two types of plywood (e.g., ½ inch and ⅜ inch)

X_{15} = Lumber sold to captive distributors
X_{16} = Lumber sold to outside market
X_{17} = Plywood sold to captive distributors
X_{18} = Plywood sold to outside markets
A_1 = MBF of fir available to cut
A_2 = MBF of pine available to cut
A_3 = Overall sawmill capacity
A_4 = Capacity of a particular part of sawmill (e.g., headrig saw)
A_5 = Overall plywood mill capacity
A_6 = Capacity of some particular part of plywood mill (e.g., lathe)
$a_1, a_2, \ldots, a_{12}$ = Technological coefficents
D_1, D_2, D_3, D_4 = Market demand limits

below. See if your problem has any of these conditions. Note that there may be other types of constraints as well. Any given problem will generally not have all of the types of constraints.

- *Capacity constraints.* These are limits because of the amount of equipment, space, or manpower available. The constraint relating to the time available on the machine in Example 1 is an illustration.
- *Market constraints.* These are limits (either lower or upper limits or both) on how much product can be sold or used. See the limit on sales of aviation gasoline in Example 3.
- *Availability constraints.* These are limits because of scarcity of raw materials, labor, funds, or other resources. See the constraints relating to the availability of blending gasoline in Example 3.
- *Quality or blending constraints.* These are constraints that put limits on mixes of ingredients, usually defining the quality of output products. See the blending constraints for octane and vapor pressure in Example 3.
- *Production technology or material balance constraints.* These are constraints that define the output of some process as a function of the inputs, often with a loss for scrap. See the constraints in Example 5 relating production of plywood panels to inputs of fir and pine lumber used.
- *Definitional constraints.* These are constraints that define a given variable. Often, such constraints come from accounting definitions. See the inventory balance constraint in Example 4.

4. Define specifically the decision variables. This is often the hardest step. What is needed is a list of variables, that is, the Xs and their definitions including specification of units of measurement. In some problems, there may be more than one way of defining the variables. One approach is to start by trying to define specific variables that fit with the list of decisions in step 2. For example, if your decision is to "decide on a product mix," then a likely set of variables might be:

X_1 for units of first product
X_2 for units of second product

And so on for all the products. Note that specifying values for all the Xs in effect defines the product mix.

Another approach that sometimes helps in defining the decision variables is to draw a flow diagram showing how the various parts of the problem are related. See Figure 10–1 as an example. Then variables are defined to represent flows of goods, materials, and so on between the various parts. Note how the variables in Table 10–7 are associated with the arrows in Figure 10–1. For example, one arrow shows logs flowing to the plywood mill. Variables X_9 (MBF of fir to plywood mill) and X_{10} (MBF of pine to plywood mill) are the decision variables corresponding to this flow of timber.

5. Specifically define the constraints, using the decision variables. Take the list of constraints defined in verbal terms in step 3 and use the decision variables from step 4 to produce detailed constraints. The result is a set of constraints such as those illustrated in all five examples in the chapter.

6. Define the objective function in detail. For each decision variable from step 4, a cost or profit coefficient must be defined. It is important to include only costs or profits that vary with the decisions under consideration. Fixed costs should always be excluded.

For example, labor cost per unit might seem a reasonable cost to include in a linear programming formulation defining what product mix a firm should produce. However, if the firm has a policy of paying employees for full-time work regardless of the actual time spent, then labor cost is really fixed. It does not vary with the product-mix decision and should be excluded from the objective function.

Although these six steps give a general outline for formulating linear models, there is no substitute for practice and experience. You should try several of the exercises at the end of the chapter to increase your ability to formulate models.

SUMMARY

A linear programming (LP) model is one in which a linear objective function is to be maximized or minimized subject to a set of linear constraints. All decision variables are nonnegative. Formulating an LP model means translating a business decision problem into LP terminology by defining variables, specifying an objective function, and writing all constraints as equalities or inequalities. The examples and steps given above are designed to help you formulate LP problems.

Limitations of Linear Programming

Although linear programming has proven to be a valuable tool in solving large and complex problems in business and the public sector, there are limitations.

First, there is no guarantee that linear programming will give integer-valued solutions. For example, a solution may call for 8.241 trucks. The manager can buy only 8 or 9 trucks—not 8.241. In many instances, rounding would give reasonably good solutions. In other situations, such answers may be poor. For example, in a decision about opening a new plant (a variable that can take on values of 0 or 1 only), a fractional answer would be useless. Fortunately, there are methods called *integer programming techniques* that can handle such problems. Chapter 14 discusses some of these techniques.

A second major limitation of linear programming is that uncertainty is not allowed. The model assumes known values for costs, constraint requirements, and so on, when in reality such factors may be unknown. Again, there are some approaches to dealing with this problem with techniques known as *linear programming under uncertainty* or *chance constrained programming*. Some of the advanced references in the chapter bibliography discuss these topics.

The third limitation is the assumption of linearity. Sometimes the objective or the constraints in real business problems are not linearly related to the variables. Again, advanced techniques under the title of *nonlinear programming* are available for dealing with problems of this type.

These limitations indicate that linear programming cannot be applied to all business problems. However, for those problems for which it is applicable, it has proven to be a useful and powerful tool.

SUMMARY

Linear programming is not useful for problems that require integer solutions, that involve uncertainty, or that have a nonlinear objective function or constraints, but it is applicable to a wide range of business decisions.

Bibliography

Baumol, W. J. *Economic Theory and Operations Analysis*. 4th ed. Englewood Cliffs, N. J.: Prentice Hall, 1977.

Bradley, S. P.; A. C. Hax; and T. L. Magnanti. *Applied Mathematical Programming*. Reading, Mass.: Addison-Wesley Publishing, 1977.

Charnes, A., and W. W. Cooper. *Management Models and Industrial Applications of Linear Programming*. 2 vols. New York: John Wiley & Sons, 1963.

Dantzig, G. B. *Linear Programming and Extensions*. Princeton, N. J.: Princeton University Press, 1963.

Eppen, G. D.; F. J. Gould; and C. Schmidt. *Quantitative Concepts for Management*. 3rd ed. Englewood Cliffs, N. J.: Prentice Hall, 1988.

Geoffrion, Arthur M. "Better Distribution Planning with Computer Models." *Harvard Business Review*. July–August 1976.

Hillier, F., and G. J. Lieberman. *Introduction to Operations Research*. 5th ed. New York: McGraw–Hill, 1990.

Savage, Sam L. *What's Best*. Oakland, Calif.: Holden-Day, 1986.

Schrage, L. *Linear, Integer and Quadratic Programming with LINDO*. 1989. 4th ed. South San Francisco, Calif.: Scientific Press, 1989.

Shapiro, R. O. *Optimization for Planning and Allocation: Text and Cases in Mathematical Programming*. New York: John Wiley & Sons, 1984.

Wagner, H. *Principles of Operations Research*, 2nd ed. Englewood Cliffs, N. J.: Prentice Hall, 1975.

Problems with Answers

10–1. A firm produces four products: A, B, C, and D. Each unit of product A requires two hours of milling, one hour of assembly, and $10 worth of in-process inventory. Each unit of product B requires one hour of milling, three hours of assembly, and $5 worth of in-process inventory. Each unit of C requires 2½ hours of milling, 2½ hours of assembly, and $2 worth of in-process inventory. Finally, each unit of product D requires five hours of milling, no assembly, and $12 of in-process inventory.

The firm has 120 hours of milling time and 160 hours of assembly time available. In addition, not more than $1,000 may be tied up in in-process inventory.

Each unit of product A returns a profit of $40; each unit of B returns a profit of $24; each unit of product C returns a profit of $36; and each unit of product D returns a profit of $23. Not more than 20 units of product A can be sold; not more than 16 units of product C can be sold; and any number of units of products B and D may be sold. However, at least 10 units of product D must be produced and sold to satisfy a contract requirement.

Formulate the above as a linear programming problem. The objective of the firm is to maximize the profit resulting from the sale of the four products. Do not attempt to solve this problem.

10-2. The U-Save Loan Company is planning its operations for the next year. The company makes five types of loans, listed below, together with the annual return (in percent) to the company.

Type of Loan	Annual Return (percent)
Signature loans	15
Furniture loans	12
Automobile loans	9
Second home mortgage	10
First home mortgage	7

Legal requirements and company policy place the following limits on the amounts of the various types of loans.

Signature loans cannot exceed 10 percent of the total amount of loans. The amount of signature and furniture loans together cannot exceed 20 percent of the total amount of loans. First mortgages must be at least 40 percent of the total mortgages and at least 20 percent of the total amount of loans. Second mortgages may not exceed 25 percent of the total amount of loans.

The company wishes to maximize the revenue from loan interest, subject to the above restrictions. The firm can lend a maximum of $1.5 million.

Formulate this problem as a linear programming problem. Do not solve it.

10-3. A company sells two different products, A and B. The selling price and incremental cost information is as follows:

	Product A	Product B
Selling price	$60	$40
Incremental cost	30	10
Incremental profit	$30	$30

The two products are produced in a common production process and are sold in two different markets. The production process has a capacity of 30,000 labor-hours. It takes three hours to produce a unit of A and one hour to produce a unit of B. The market has been surveyed, and company officials feel that the maximum number of units of A that can be sold is 8,000; the maximum for B is 12,000 units. Subject to these limitations, the products can be sold in any combination.

Formulate the above problem as a linear programming problem; that is, write the appropriate equations.

10-4. Mangus Electric Products Co. (MEPCO) produces large electric transformers for the electrical industry. The company has orders (Table 10-8) for the next six months. The cost of manufacturing a transformer is expected to vary somewhat over the next few months due to expected changes in materials costs and in labor rates. The company can produce up to 50 units per month on regular time and up to an additional 20 units per month using overtime. The costs for both regular and overtime production are shown in Table 10-8.

The cost of carrying an unsold transformer in stock is $500 per month. The company has 15 transformers in stock on January 1, and wishes to have no less than 5 in stock on June 30.

Formulate a linear programming problem to determine the optimal production schedule for MEPCO.

10-5. The Transvaal Diamond Company mined diamonds in three locations in South Africa. The three mines differed in terms of capacities, number, weight of stones mined, and costs. These are shown in Table 10-9.

Table 10–8

	Month					
	Jan.	*Feb.*	*Mar.*	*April*	*May*	*June*
Orders (units)	58	36	34	69	72	43
Cost per unit at regular time (in $000s)	$18.0	17.0	17.0	18.5	19.0	19.0
Cost per unit at overtime (in $000s)	$20.0	19.0	19.0	21.0	22.0	22.0

Table 10–9

Mine	*Capacity (M^3 of earth processed)**	*Treatment† Costs (rand per M^3)*	*Grade (carats per M^3)*	*Stone Count (number of stones per M^3)*
Plant 1	83,000	R0.60	0.36	0.58
Plant 2	310,000	R0.36	0.22	0.26
Plant 3	190,000	R0.50	0.263	0.21

*M^3 is cubic meters.
†Note mining costs are excluded from these figures. Assume that they are the same at each mine.

Due to marketing considerations, a monthly production of exactly 148,000 stones was required. A similar requirement called for at least 130,000 carats. (The average stone size was thus at least 130/148 = 0.88 carats.)

The problem for the company manager was to meet the marketing requirements at the least cost.

Formulate a linear programming model to determine how much should be mined at each location. Do not solve.

Problems

10-6. We want to select an advertising strategy to reach two types of customers: homemakers in families with over $10,000 annual income and homemakers in families with under $10,000 income.[2] We feel that

people in the first group will purchase twice as much of our product as people in the second, and our goal is to maximize purchases. We may advertise either on TV or in a magazine; one unit of TV advertising costs $20,000 and reaches approximately 2,000 people in the first group and 8,000 in the second. One unit of advertising in the magazine costs $12,000 and reaches 6,000 people in the

[2]This problem is adapted from F. M. Bass and R. T. Lonsdale, "An Exploration of Linear Programming in Media Selection," *Journal of Marketing Research* 3 (1966).

first group and 3,000 in the second.[3] We require that at least 6 units of TV advertising be used and that no more than 12 units of magazine advertising be used, for policy reasons. The advertising budget is $180,000.

Formulate this problem as a linear programming problem, defining all variables used.

10–7. The Super Sausage Company (SSC) has recently experienced drastic changes in raw material prices, and the manager has directed an analyst to reexamine the proportions in which SSC mixes ingredients to manufacture sausage.

Sausage manufacture involves meeting two key product requirements. The percentage of protein, by weight, must be at least 15 percent; and the percentage of fat, by weight, cannot exceed 30 percent (remaining weight is filler). SSC has the following four raw materials available for mixing, with the following characteristics:

Ingredient	Percent Protein	Percent Fat	Cost per Pound
A	40%	10%	$1.80
B	20	15	0.75
C	10	35	0.40
D	5	40	0.15

Formulate an LP that would aid SSC in determining its most desirable mixing schedule. (Do not solve this problem.)

10–8. Refer to Example 1 in this chapter. Suppose the firm has a third product, product C, which can be produced on either the first or the second machine. Producing it on the first machine requires one hour of time; producing it on the second machine requires two hours of time. Product C has an incremental profit of $9 per unit.

Modify the formulation of Example 1 to include product C.

10–9. The American Safety Council must allocate its national budget for the next fiscal year. Irrevocable decisions have already been made concerning various "program areas" and their total funding; for example, a total of $110,000 has been allocated to prevention of automobile fatalities and reduction of property damage. However, detailed allocation decisions must be made concerning specific *projects* designed to contribute to the program missions. In the case of automobile fatality prevention and reduction of property damage, Table 10–10 contains the projects recommended by council analysts, together with appropriate data. The decision makers of the council want you to help them make their budget allocation (or project choice and magnitude) decisions. In response to a question concerning which of their two specific missions is more important, they said: "That's a tough question! On the one hand, human life is sacred and cannot be purchased for any amount of money. On the other hand, if there are two competing ways to save the *same number of lives,* we would naturally prefer the project that also results in the lower amount of property damage."

When asked specifically what "trade-off" between lives saved and property damage would make them be indifferent, they said: "That's really a tough question! However, we are aware that a certain government agency has, for internal resource allocation purposes, an implicit dollar value for a human life saved of $300,000 (we think another agency also uses this number in making decisions about building additional safety into their equipment)."

Formulate an LP model whose solution would represent an optimal allocation of the budgeted $110,000, based on all the information above. Be sure to define all variables used. You need *not* solve the formulation.

[3] In this problem, it is assumed that the magazine's audience has no overlap with the TV audience.

Table 10–10

Project	Upper Limit of Expenditure on Project (measured in $)	Expected Fatalities Prevented per $1,000 Expended	Expected Reduction in Property Damage per $1,000 Expended
1. Seat belt advertising	$80,000	0.33	$ 0
2. Research in improved highway design	20,000	0.25	20,000
3. Research in improved automobile design	75,000	0.15	30,000
4. Dollars spent lobbying for tougher state "drunk driving" penalties	100,000	0.27	10,000

10–10. The Delight Dairy Company (DD) produces a broad line of dairy products. For production planning purposes, the products have been aggregated into two major classes: Ice Cream (many flavors, many package sizes) and Specialties (ice-cream sticks, ice-cream sandwiches, prepackaged ice-cream cones, etc.). Each class has its own distinct packaging equipment, but the two classes use a common, single ice-cream manufacturing machine; they also use the same pool of experienced labor to produce and package each class of product.

The Ice Cream class requires two hours of the ice-cream manufacturing machine, one hour on its own packaging line, and three labor hours to produce 1,000 gallons of finished product.

The Specialties class requires one hour of the ice-cream manufacturing machine, one hour on its own packaging line, and six labor hours to produce the equivalent of 1,000 gallons of finished product. One thousand gallons of Ice Cream can be sold by DD for $300; the equivalent of 1,000 gallons of Specialties can be sold for $500. (Raw material costs are approximately equal for 1,000 gallons of the two classes of product.)

The company currently works a one-shift operation (40 shop hours per week) and currently employs three full-time employees and one ¾-time employee for a total of $120 + 30 = 150$ labor-hours per week.

Formulate a linear programming model for production planning for Delight Dairy.

10–11. The Empire Abrasive Company (EAC) produces aluminum-oxide grit for use in grinding wheels and coated abrasives. There are two types of finished product: coarse grit and fine grit. There are also two types of input material, called Surinam Crude and Chinese Crude (for the country of origin of the bauxite from which the crude is processed). Finally, there are two processing modes, called *fast* and *slow,* which can be used with either input material to produce varying percentages of the finished products. Table 10–11 describes the percentages of each finished product resulting from the possible combinations of input material and processing mode.

Surinam Crude costs $300 per ton, and Chinese Crude costs $350. *Fast* processing costs $50 per ton, and *slow* processing costs $40. Coarse grit is sold

Table 10–11   Output Percentages for Coarse and Fine Grit

	Surinam Crude Input		Chinese Crude Input	
	Fast Process	Slow Process	Fast Process	Slow Process
Percent coarse grit	45	25	35	20
Percent fine grit	50	70	60	80
Loss in yield	5	5	5	0

Table 10–12

Type	Purchase Cost	Operating Cost (per ton-mile)	Capacity (ton-miles per month)
Trailer	$15,000	$0.28	10,000
Medium	8,000	0.32	8,000
Pickup	5,000	0.40	6,000

at a price of $500 per ton, and fine grit is sold for $325 per ton. EAC's plant can process 1,000 input tons of crude per week. There are no volume limits on amounts of finished product that can be sold.

Formulate a linear programming model of this problem that will indicate how EAC can obtain the most profitable situation. *Note:* EAC can use both types of crude and both types of processing modes; that is, fractional solutions are a distinct possibility.

10–12. The Consolidated Company has in the past contracted out the shipment of its products from its factory to its warehouses. The volume of deliveries is measured in ton-miles (the tons of product times the number of miles over which it is to be delivered). Consolidated has 400,000 ton-miles to be delivered each month.

Currently, Consolidated is paying Speedie Trucking Company 50 cents per ton-mile to deliver the product. Consolidated is considering purchasing a fleet of trucks to take over a part or all of this delivery service.

Three types of trucks are under consideration: large trailer-trucks, medium-sized trucks, and pickup trucks. Details of each are given in Table 10–12.

Speedie Trucking has indicated that it would be willing to continue to deliver any excess not delivered by Consolidated's own trucks at the rate of 50 cents per ton-mile.

Capital equipment funds are in short supply in Consolidated, and only $380,000 is available to purchase the equipment.

In addition to the budget limitation, there are other restrictions on the types of trucks purchased. The first involves dock loading space. Because of parking space and dock limitations, not more than 28 truck spaces are available. A trailer or medium truck would use one space. Two pickup trucks use one space.

Also, because of the types and sizes of deliveries, at least two thirds of the trucks purchased would have to be either trailers or medium trucks.

Formulate this as a linear programming problem. Do not solve. Be careful to specify the objective and define the variables.

10–13. The Gotham City School system has three high schools that serve the needs of five neighborhood areas. The capacities of the various schools are:

School	Capacity (maximum enrollment)
A	4,000
B	3,000
C	2,000
Total	9,000

The size (number of high school students) and ethnic mix of each neighborhood are as shown:

Neighborhood	Number of Students	Percent Minority Students
1	2,100	30
2	2,400	80
3	1,300	20
4	800	10
5	1,600	20
Total	8,200	

The distances (in miles) from each neighborhood to each school are as shown:

School	Neighborhood				
	1	2	3	4	5
A	1.2	0.4	2.6	1.4	2.4
B	0.8	2.0	0.5	0.7	3.0
C	1.3	2.2	1.6	2.0	0.2

A federal judge has ruled that no high school in the city can have more than 50 percent nor less than 30 percent minority enrollment. Assume that students bused from each neighborhood have the same ethnic mix as the whole neighborhood. You wish to devise a busing plan that will minimize the total number of student miles bused while meeting the judge's integration requirements, and at the same time guarantee that no student is bused more than 2.5 miles.

Formulate a linear programming model to solve this problem.

10–14. A manufacturer produces a product at three plants and distributes it through four market-service warehouses. The following data have been provided:

Warehouse	Selling Price (per unit)	Annual Demand (units)
1	$1.00	40,000
2	1.10	10,000
3	1.00	20,000
4	0.60	25,000

Plant	Unit Variable Production Cost	Annual Capacity (units)
A	$0.40	40,000
B	0.35	30,000
C	0.45	45,000

To	Warehouse			
From	1	2	3	4
Plant A	$0.20	$0.20	$0.30	$0.30
B	0.20	0.10	0.35	0.40
C	0.45	0.30	0.20	0.20

a. Suppose the *marketing* manager wishes to *meet all demands at minimum cost.* Write out a linear programming formulation of this problem that would produce optimal production and shipping decisions. Let X_{A2} be the amount produced at factory A for shipment to warehouse 2, and so on. *Do not solve* the problem.

b. Suppose the group vice president wishes to meet only those demands that are incrementally profitable. That is, the group vice president wishes to maximize profits, or revenues less production and transportation costs. Modify your linear programming formulation of (*a*) to solve this problem optimally. Do not solve the problem.

10–15. The Acme Skateboard Company manufactures three different models of skateboards: Regular, Super, and Deluxe. Data on costs, selling prices, and other information for each model are presented in Table 10–13.

Acme has a work force of five *salaried* individuals working up to 40 hours per week and paid $280 per week each (including fringe benefits) whether they work a full 40 hours or not. Acme desires to find the optimal weekly production plan that will maximize profit and contribution to fixed labor cost.

Formulate an LP that will maximize profit plus contribution to fixed costs.

10–16. The operations manager of Hervis Rent-A-Car Company thinks some type of mathematical model might be useful in weekly decisions on how to relocate rental cars from cities that have a surplus to cities where there is a deficit. Once a week, the manager collects data on the numbers of cars at each city; a comparison with a predetermined "target" number of cars for that city indicates the amount of surplus or deficit. (For example, if the Chicago Airport office has 67 cars currently, and its target is 80 cars, then it has a deficit of 13 cars.)

Each week the manager must determine how to relocate cars from the surplus cities to the deficit cities. Even though the target numbers do not change from week to week, the actual problem is different each week, due to more-or-less random aggregate patterns of rental clients. (For example, one week Chicago may have a deficit of 13 cars, as above; the next week, it may have 88 cars, or a surplus of 8 cars.)

The present approach to the problem is to start with the West Coast, and meet deficits using the *closest* cities having surpluses, if the manager hasn't already precommitted those surplus cars for

Table 10–13

Model	Regular	Super	Deluxe
Selling price per unit	$7	$15	$25
Raw material cost per unit	$3	$ 6	$10
Labor-hours required for assembly, finishing, and packaging per unit*	0.1	0.2	0.5
Demand upper limit on weekly sales	1,000	800	300

*For example, 10 Regular skateboards can be produced in one labor-hour; alternatively, five Super models can be produced, or two Deluxe models.

a different city. Nevertheless, the manager thinks there should be a more systematic way to attack the problem. At the beginning of each week, the status of each city (number of cars surplus or deficit) is known; the manager also knows the cost of relocating a car from city i to city j, denoted by C_{ij}. Hervis services 100 cities coast to coast, with a total fleet of 10,000 cars. The sum of all target quantities is also 10,000 cars; so deficits are precisely balanced by surpluses.

a. Formulate an LP to solve this problem.

b. The operations manager of Allegory Airlines (AA) has a problem similar to the Hervis car relocation problem. Each evening, each of AA's DC–9 aircraft terminates passenger flight operations at various cities; each morning, DC–9s are required at various cities to fly the next day's routes. Unfortunately, some cities end up with a DC–9 in the evening but don't need it in the morning, while the reverse occurs at other cities. AA's flight schedule remains unchanged for the seven days of the week, and in fact usually remains unchanged for three or four months. Thus, the problem faced by AA is *identical* every evening; for example, if Chicago has a surplus of two DC–9s tonight, it will have a surplus of two DC–9s every night until the next major schedule change.

AA has determined the cost to fly a plane from city i to city j, including such complexities as the cost to ferry the plane's crew and cabin attendants from city j back to their originating city (likely to be still a different city); this cost is denoted by C_{ij}.

Can your LP formulation for (a) of this question be used to solve AA's plane-relocation problem? (If yes, indicate changes in definitions of variables and any other required changes; if no, explain why not.)

More Challenging Problems

10–17. The Emory Aluminum Company rolls and sells aluminum foil in several widths. Customers can order rolls of foil 24 inches, 20 inches, 12 inches, or 8 inches wide. The foil is manufactured in a standard width of 54 inches, and the smaller widths are slit (cut) from the standard roll. There are many ways the smaller widths can be cut, as shown in Table 10–14.

For example, using method 3, one roll 24 inches wide, one roll 12 inches wide, and two rolls 8 inches wide are cut from the standard roll. This leaves 2 inches of scrap [54 − 24 − 12 − 2(8) = 2]. Because some scrap is generated by the

Table 10–14

Width	*Cutting Method*												
	1	*2*	*3*	*4*	*5*	*6*	*7*	*8*	*9*	*10*	*11*	*12*	*13*
24 inches	2	1	1	1	1								
20 inches		1				2	2	1	1	1			
12 inches			1	2		1		2	1		4	2	
8 inches			1	2	3		1	1	2	4		3	6
Scrap (inches)	6	2	2	6	6	2	6	2	6	2	6	6	6

slitting process, it is not possible to cut certain combinations (not shown). All rolls for cutting are a standard 54-inch width, and all orders are for the standard widths in the table. Furthermore, all orders are for a standard length (the length of a full roll).

Emory has received the following orders for the month of July:

Width	Rolls Ordered
24 inches	330
20 inches	120
12 inches	480
8 inches	160

How should Emory cut rolls to fill these orders? Formulate a linear programming model for the problem but do not solve it.

10–18. A rancher has 1,000 acres on which to grow corn or barley, or feed cattle. Information on the two crops under consideration is given below:

Item	Corn	Barley
Seed and other cash costs per acre	$100	$120
Labor-hours required per acre	10	8
Yield (bushel per acre)	120	100
Selling price ($ per bushel)	$4.25	$5.25
Purchase price ($ per bushel)	$4.50	—

The rancher can plant the land in any mix of the two crops; or the land can be used to raise young steers and feed them for a year. The steers cost $150 each and are sold for $800 after feeding. Each steer requires 20 hours of labor, one half acre of land, and 80 bushels of corn. The corn for the steers can be that grown on the ranch if enough is available, or it can be purchased.

The rancher can use either inexperienced labor, which costs $6 per hour, or experienced labor at a rate of $10 per hour. Each hour of inexperienced labor requires 0.15 hours of supervision, and each hour of experienced labor requires 0.05 hours of supervision. There are 2,000 hours of supervision available.

The rancher is limited to funds totaling $200,000 for buying seed and other cash costs for crops, for purchasing steers, and for paying labor.

Formulate as a linear programming model.

10–19. A manufacturer has contracted to produce 2,000 units of a particular product over the next eight months. Deliveries are scheduled as follows:

Month	Units
January	100
February	200
March	300
April	400
May	100
June	100
July	500
August	300
Total	2,000

The manufacturer has estimated that it costs her $1 to store one unit of product for one month. She has a warehouse capacity of 300 units.

The manufacturer can produce any number of units in a given month, since the units can be produced mostly with part-time labor, which can be easily obtained. However, there are costs of training new personnel and costs associated with laying off personnel who have been hired. The manufacturer has estimated that it costs approximately 75 cents per unit to increase the production level from one month to the next (e.g., if production in January is 200 and is increased to 300 in February, the cost is $75 for training the additional people required to produce at the 300-unit level). Similarly, it costs 50 cents per unit to reduce production from one month to the next. (At the end of eight months, all employees will be laid off, with the corresponding production-reduction costs.) Assume the production level before January is zero.

a. Formulate the above as a linear programming problem.

b. Suppose there is a limit on production of 300 units per month. Formulate the linear programming problem with this additional constraint.

10–20. The director of passenger services for Ace Air Lines was trying to decide how many new flight attendants to hire and train over the next six months. The requirements in number of flight attendant flight-hours needed were:

Month	Hours Needed
January	8,000
February	7,000
March	8,000
April	10,000
May	9,000
June	12,000

The problem was complicated by two factors. It took one month to train flight attendants before they could be used on regular flights. Hence, hiring had to be done a month before the need arose. Secondly, training of new flight attendants required the time of already trained attendants. It took approximately 100 hours of regular attendant time for each trainee during the month training period. In other words, the number of hours available for flight service by regular attendants was cut by 100 hours for each trainee.

The director of passenger services was not worried about January, because there were 60 attendants available. Company rules required that an attendant could not work more than 150 hours in any month. This meant that the director had a maximum of 9,000 hours available for January, 1,000 in excess of needs. (Attendants were not laid off in such cases; each merely worked fewer hours.)

Company records showed that 10 percent of the attendants quit their jobs each month for various reasons.

The cost to Ace Air Lines for a regular flight attendant was $1,500 per month for salary and fringe benefits, regardless of how many hours worked (of course, one could not work more than 150 hours). The cost of a trainee was $700 per month for salary and fringe benefits.

Formulate the above as a linear programming problem designed to solve the problem of the director of passenger services at minimum cost. Do not attempt to solve the programming problem. Be sure to identify all the symbols you use.

10–21. The land of Milkandhoney produced only three products—machinery, steel, and automobiles. All other goods were imported. The minister of the economy held the responsibility for economic planning, and he thought the welfare of the country could be served by maximizing the net dollar value of exports (that is, the value of the exports less the cost of the materials imported to produce those exports). Milkandhoney could sell all the steel, automobiles, or machinery it could produce on the world market at prices of $500 per unit for steel, $1,500 per unit for automobiles, and $2,500 per unit for machinery.

In order to produce 1 unit of steel, it took 0.05 units of machinery, 0.01 units of automobiles, 2 units of ore purchased on the world market for $100 per unit, and other imported materials costing $50. In addition, it took one-half worker-year of labor to produce each unit of steel. Milkandhoney's steel mills had a rated capacity of 100,000 units per year.

To produce 1 unit of automobiles, it took 1 unit of steel, 0.1 units of machinery, and 1 worker-year of labor. In addition, it took $300 worth of imported materials to produce each unit of automobiles. Automobile capacity was 700,000 units per year.

To produce 1 unit of machinery required 0.01 units of automobiles, 0.5 unit of steel, and 2 worker-years of labor, in addition to $100 for items imported from outside. The capacity of the machinery plants was 50,000 units per year.

The total personnel available for labor in Milkandhoney was 800,000 persons per year.

a. Assuming that no steel, automobiles, or machinery can be imported, formulate a linear programming model to determine the production mix that will maximize net exports (dollars). Be careful to define all variables and to state exactly all relationships among variables.

b. How would you formulate the linear programming problem if there were no restrictions on importation of any or all of automobiles, steel, or machinery at the prices given? Can you see an obvious solution to the problem thus formulated?

10–22. The Stateside Electric Company is planning construction of new facilities in its area for the next 10 years.[4] It is possible to construct four types of electric power facilities—steam plants using coal for energy, hydroelectric plants with no reservoir, hydroelectric plants with small reservoirs (enough water storage capacity to meet daily fluctuations), and hydroelectric plants with large reservoirs (with enough water storage to meet seasonal fluctuations in power demand and water flow).

Consumption of electricity is based on three characteristics. The first is the total annual usage—the requirement in the area is estimated to be 4,000 billion kilowatt-hours by the 10th year. The second characteristic is the peak usage of power—usually on a hot summer day at about 4 P.M. Any plan should provide enough peaking capacity to meet a projected peak need of 3,000 million kilowatts in the 10th year. The third characteristic is guaranteed power output—measured as the average daylight output in midwinter when the consumption is high and water levels for hydroelectric power are low. The 10-year requirement is for 2,000 million kilowatts of guaranteed power.

The various possible power plants vary in terms of how they can satisfy these characteristics. For example, hydroelectric plants with reservoirs are able to provide substantial peaking capacity, whereas steam plants and hydroelectric plants with no reservoirs are poor in this respect.

The characteristics of the various types of plants are shown in Table 10–15. Each is measured in terms of a unit of capacity. The unit of capacity is defined to be the capacity to produce 1 billion kilowatt-hours per year. Note that the types of plants vary substantially in their investment costs. The annual operating costs of the various types of plants also vary considerably. For example, the cost of coal makes the annual costs of the steam plants quite high, whereas the annual costs of operating

[4]This problem is based on the article "Application of Linear Programming to Investments in the Electric Power Industry," P. Masse and R. Gibrat, in *Management Science*, January 1957.

Table 10–15   Characteristics of Electric Plants per Unit (1 billion kilowatt-hours) of Annual Output

Type	Guaranteed Output (millions of kilowatts)	Peak Output (millions of kilowatts)	Investment Cost ($000s)	Discounted Total Cost ($000s)
Steam	0.15	0.20	$30	$65
Hydroelectric—no reservoir	0.10	0.10	40	42
Hydroelectric—small reservoir	0.10	0.40	60	64
Hydroelectric—large reservoir	0.80	0.90	100	110

Table 10–16

	Oct.	Nov.	Dec.	Jan.	Feb.	Mar.
Cars needed	380	360	300	360	330	340

the hydroelectric plants are relatively less. The final column in the table shows the discounted total costs, including both the investment cost and the discounted annual operating costs.

The company wants to develop a 10-year plan that would detail how much capacity of each type of plant to build. The objective is to minimize the total discounted cost. However, there is a restriction that no more than $350 million can be used for investment in plants over the 10 years.

Formulate this problem as a linear programming model.

10–23. In linear programming models, demand for a product is usually assumed known for certain. In reality, demand is often uncertain. This uncertain demand can sometimes be built into an LP model, as this exercise is designed to illustrate.

Refer to Problem 10–1 and its solution given at the end of the book. Consider product A, which is assumed in the problem to have an upper limit on demand of 20 units. Suppose instead that the upper demand limit for product A is uncertain, but you assess a 0.4 probability that at most 10 can be sold, and a 0.6 chance that the upper limit is 20. Suppose further, that if you produce more than 10 units and the upper limit of demand turns out to be only 10 units, you can sell the excess at a reduced price that would give you a profit of only $10 per unit. Your objective is to maximize expected profit. How would you modify the formulation for Problem 10–1 to accomplish this?

Hint: Define a new variable as the excess production of product A over 10 units, and consider the expected revenue to be received from the sale of any of these units.

10–24. The Premier Rent-a-Car Company operates a fleet of rental cars in a large western city. The company has forecast its demand for rental cars for the next six months as shown in Table 10–16.

The company obtains its cars by leasing them from an automobile manufacturer. Three leasing plans are available, involving leases of three, four, or five months' duration. Cars are leased

Table 10–17

	Type of Lease		
	Three Months	Four Months	Five Months
Total lease cost	$1,140	$1,360	$1,500
Cost per month	380	340	300

beginning on the first day of a month, and are returned to the manufacturer on the last day of the month at the end of the lease period. The costs for the three types of leases are shown in Table 10–17.

These costs include lease payments to the manufacturer and standard maintenance and repair expenses. A lease may be taken out in any month. The manufacturer has certain restrictions: At least 60 percent of the cars leased must be on the five-month lease, and no more than 20 percent can be on the three-month lease.

On September 30, the fleet consists of 300 cars. For 100 of these, the lease expires at the end of October; the lease on an additional 100 expires at the end of November; and the lease for the remaining 100 expires at the end of December. Premier would like to have between 300 and 350 cars remaining in the fleet at the end of March (after returning leased cars that are due to be returned that month).

Premier would like to minimize its leasing costs. Formulate a linear programming problem to solve this fleet-planning problem.

10–25. The Precision Pencil Company (PPC) produces wood pencils and the "lead" (actually graphite) that goes into the pencils. There are two major product classes: *regular* and *drafting* pencils. The production of lead for the two classes of product involves the same facilities, but for the higher-quality drafting lead, the various operations in the lead department require almost twice as much time per pound of lead produced as for the

less demanding regular lead. The fabrication department is highly automated, and in this phase of manufacture, the rate of fabrication for each product class is identical. The accompanying table summarizes the maximum production rate in output per hour for each department (lead and fabrication) *when the department is used only for one class of product.*

Maximum Production Rates for Each Product Separately

	Product Class	
Department	Regular (per hour)	Drafting (per hour)
Lead	500 pounds	300 pounds
Pencil fabrication	30 gross*	30 gross*

*One gross is 144 pencils.

Regular pencils use 10 pounds of regular lead per gross, and drafting pencils use 15 pounds of drafting lead per gross.

Demand for the drafting pencils is constant at 6,500 gross per quarter. Demand for the regular pencils is constant at 7,800 gross per quarter for the first quarter of the year, then jumps to 10,400 gross per quarter for the second and third quarters (due to back-to-school orders), and then drops back to 7,800 gross per quarter for the fourth quarter.

Each department (lead and fabrication) has available 520 hours per quarter of regular-time production. In addition, up to 78 hours per quarter of overtime production are available. Inventories of

Table 10–18   Fuel Requirements and Limits (1,000 gallons unless specified otherwise)

City Number	Flight Sequence	Minimum Fuel Required	Maximum Fuel Allowed	Regular Fuel Consumption if Minimum Fuel Boarded	Additional Fuel Burned per Gallon of Tankered Fuel (i.e., fuel above minimum—in gallons)	Price per Gallon (cents)
1	Los Angeles to Miami	23	33	12.1	0.40	82
2	Miami to Tampa	8	19	2.0	0.05	75
3	Tampa to La Guardia	19	33	9.5	0.25	77
4	La Guardia to Los Angeles	25	33	13.0	0.45	89
1	Los Angeles to Miami (etc.)					

both finished pencils and finished lead may be carried over from one quarter to the next.

The variable cost to manufacture a pound of lead is $0.10 for the regular lead and $0.15 for the drafting lead on regular-time production. The variable cost for a gross of pencils (including the lead cost) is $4 for the regular pencils and $4.50 for the drafting pencils on regular-time production. These costs are increased by 10 percent for overtime production. The total cost of holding inventory is 20 percent of the variable cost per year.

Formulate a linear programming model whose solution would indicate a production plan for PPC for the four quarters of the year. Do not attempt to solve it.

10–26. Nationwide Airlines,[5] faced with a sharply escalating cost of jet fuel, is in-

terested in optimizing its purchases of jet fuel at its various locations around the country. Typically, there is some choice concerning the amount of fuel that can be placed on board any aircraft for any flight segment, as long as minimum and maximum limits are not violated. The flight schedule is considered as a chain of flight segments, or legs, that each aircraft follows. The schedule ultimately returns the aircraft to its starting point, resulting in a "rotation." Consider the following rotation:

Los Angeles–Miami–Tampa–La Guardia–Los Angeles

The fuel for any one of these flight segments may be bought at its departure city, or it may be purchased at a previous city in the sequence and "tankered" for the flight. Of course, it takes fuel to carry fuel, and thus an economic trade-off between purchasing fuel at the lowest-cost location and tankering it all around the country must be made.

The data in Table 10–18 has been obtained.

[5]This problem has been adapted from D. Wayne Darnell and Carolyn Loflin, "National Airlines Fuel Management and Allocation Model," Interfaces, February 1977, pp. 1–16.

The column labeled "Regular fuel consumption" takes into account fuel consumption if the minimum amount of fuel is on board, and the column labeled "Additional fuel burned" indicates the additional fuel burned in each flight segment per gallon of "tankered" fuel carried; tankered fuel refers to fuel *above* the minimum amount.

Note that fuel originally carried into Los Angeles should equal fuel carried into Los Angeles on the next rotation, in order for the system to be in equilibrium.

An analyst has begun to formulate this problem as an LP. The following unknowns have been defined:

I_i = Leftover fuel inventory coming into city i (1,000 gallons)

X_i = Amount of fuel purchased at city i (1,000 gallons)

Thus, $(I_i + X_i)$ is the amount of fuel on board the aircraft when it departs city i.

Formulate as a linear programming problem.

10–27. Acme Injectors (AI) produces fuel injectors for automobiles.[6] The tolerance between a needle and an injector body is critical; and even the most modern machinery cannot grind needles and bodies to exactly this tolerance. AI produces

---

[6]This problem is taken from G. J. Gutierrez, W. H. Hausman, and H. L Lee, "Dynamic Control of Imperfect Component Production," paper presented at TIMS/ORSA meeting, Las Vegas, May 7–9, 1990.

groups of needles and bodies and then sorts them into 1 of 10 classes such that matching a needle of class i with a body of class i will meet the required tolerance.

Suppose that the grinding machines can be set at any class from 1 to 10 for both needles and bodies, and suppose that for each of those settings, the percentage of product output in all classes is known and specified by P_{ijN} and P_{ijB}; that is, P_{ijN} represents the percentage of needles produced in class j when the needle grinding machine is set at class i, and similarly for bodies. Classes $j = 0$ and $j = 11$ record defects (needles and bodies that are unusable). The grinding machines can be set to different values during different parts of a production run.

a. Formulate an LP model to determine grinding machine settings that maximize the percentage of needles and bodies that can be assembled into good injectors. Assume the production quantities are sufficiently large so that the output exactly matches the P_{ijN} and P_{ijB} percentages.

b. Now consider a highly simplified version of this problem, where needle grinding can be done perfectly; that is, $P_{ijN} = 1$ if $j = i$ and 0 if $j \neq i$. Also, for body grinding, assume $P_{i,i-1\ B} = 0.25$; $P_{i,i\ B} = 0.50$; and $P_{i,i+1\ B} = 0.25$ (all other values of P_{ijB} are zero). Can you solve this problem by inspection?

Case 10–28   The Impala Gold Company operated a gold mine in the Orange Free State, North Africa. The mining operation consisted of mining underground, at a depth of 4,000 feet, gold-bearing rock. The rock was transported up the mine shafts to a mill that crushed the rock and extracted the gold.

The Impala mine had three shafts. Information on these shafts is given in the following table. Note that the rock mined in each shaft area has a different gold content as well as different costs.

Rock mined from all three shafts was sent to the mill to be crushed and refined. The mill capacity depended upon how fine the rock was ground. If the rock was ground fine, mill capacity was 240,000 tons per month, and 95 percent of the gold was recovered in the operation. Rock from each shaft could be ground separately. The cost of milling a ton of rock ground fine was 1.12 Rand per ton. If the rock was ground coarse, mill capacity was 250,000 tons per month, but gold recovery dropped to 90 percent. The cost of milling a ton of rock ground coarse was 0.85 Rand. The mine could sell all the gold it produced at a price of 0.80 Rand per gram.

The mine manager was concerned about how much rock he should mine in each shaft area. He noted that the mill capacity was not sufficient to handle all three shafts operating at full capacity. The problem was further complicated by the legal requirements that a mine could not mine "above the average grade" of the ore reserves. In the Impala mine this average grade was 20 grams per ton. Thus, there was the legal restriction that the mix of rock from the three shafts could not exceed an average of 20 grams per ton in ore grade.

Formulate a linear programming model to maximize profit from operating the mine.

	Shaft 1	Shaft 2	Shaft 3
Hoist capacity of shaft (tons per month)	85,000	90,000	95,000
Ore grade (grams of gold per ton of rock)	25	20	15
Variable cost of mining rock (Rands per ton)	6	5	4

Case 10–29

The treasurer of Racy's department store is performing her financial planning for the next six months, September through February.[7] Because of the Christmas season, Racy's needs large amounts of cash, particularly in the months of November and December; and a large cash inflow occurs in January and February when customers pay their Christmas bills. These requirements are summarized in Table 10–19 (in $000s)

The treasurer has three sources of short-term funds to meet Racy's needs. These are:

1. *Pledge Accounts Receivable* A local bank will lend Racy's funds on a month-by-month basis against a pledge on the accounts-receivable balance at the beginning of a given month. The maximum loan is 75 percent of the receivables in a given month. The cost of this loan is 1.5 percent per month of the amount borrowed.

2. *Stretch Payment of Purchases* Payment of purchases can be delayed one month. Thus, for example, the $100,000 planned for payments for November could be delayed until December, and Racy's could use the funds to meet November

---

[7]This problem is based on A. A. Robichek, D. Teichroew, and J. M. Jones, "Optimal Short-Term Financing Decisions," *Management Science,* September 1965.

Table 10–19

	Sept.	Oct.	Nov.	Dec.	Jan.	Feb.
Accounts receivable balance (at beginning of month)	$70	$50	$70	$120	$100	$ 50
Planned payments of purchases (on assumption that discount is taken)	80	90	100	60	40	50
Cash needs for operations	—	30	60	90	—	—
Cash surplus from operations	20	—	—	—	30	150

needs. When purchase payments are thus stretched, Racy's loses the 3 percent discount it normally receives for prompt payment.

3. Use Short-Term Loan A bank is willing to lend Racy's any amount from $40,000 to $100,000 on a six-month basis. The loan would be taken out in full in the beginning of September for a fixed amount and paid back in full at the end of February. It would not be possible to add to the loan or to pay off part of the loan during the period. The cost of the loan would be 1 percent per month, payable each month.

In any period, if the firm has excess funds, they can be invested in short-term government securities that return 0.5 percent per month.

The objective of the treasurer is to minimize the net interest cost to Racy's while meeting the firm's cash needs.

Formulate the above short-term financing decision as a linear programming problem. Be sure to label all variables and to explain the relationships between variables.

Case 10–30

Daguscahonda Mines Corporation (DMC) operates a strip coal–mining operation in western Pennsylvania. Three mine sites (A, B, and C) currently are used, each producing coal of somewhat different sulfur and ash content. Coal from these sites is transported to a common crusher that grinds the coal into a finer mix. The coal is then "washed" to remove some of the sulfur and ash. In the washing process, the crushed coal is fed into a large tank containing a fluid. The cleaner coal floats and is removed for sale. Coal containing a heavier concentration of impurities sinks to the bottom and is discarded.

By using washing fluids of different densities (that is, having differing specific gravities), the amount of impurities removed can be controlled. Three fluids are currently in use, called here Light, Medium, and Heavy. With the Heavy fluid, a greater percentage of the coal is recovered (i.e., floats), but a smaller percentage of the impurities is removed. Refer to Table 10–20.

Table 10–20   Effects of Different Fluids on Coal Recovery and Impurities Remaining

Mine Source and Fluid Type	Tons of Coal Recovered per Ton Input	Percent Sulfur Content of Recovered Coal	Percent Ash Content of Recovered Coal
Mine A			
Light	0.40	0.62%	1.6%
Medium	0.50	0.91	1.9
Heavy	0.55	1.04	2.1
Mine B			
Light	0.70	0.22	1.9
Medium	0.90	0.35	2.3
Heavy	0.95	0.47	2.5
Mine C			
Light	0.62	0.42	1.5
Medium	0.75	0.50	1.8
Heavy	0.82	0.78	2.2

Table 10–21   Costs and Capacities of DMC Mines

Mine	Capacity (maximum tons mined per week)	Cost ($ per ton mined)
A	6,000	$25
B	2,300	45
C	5,000	40

For example, if the coal from mine A is washed using Light fluid, only 40 percent of the coal is recovered for sale. This recovered coal contains 0.62 percent sulfur and 1.6 percent ash. On the other hand, the use of Heavy fluid increases the yield to 55 percent, but the recovered coal contains 1.04 percent sulfur and 2.1 percent ash.

The crushing and washing operation is set up so that any combination of coal from the mines can be used in conjunction with any of the fluids. After the washing operation, all the recovered coal is mixed to make one blend, sold by DMC. Environmental requirements limit the blend to a maximum of 0.5 percent sulfur and 2.0 percent ash.

There are some other restrictions. The equipment available limits the amount that can be produced in each mine. See Table 10–21. The crusher can handle a maximum of 8,000 tons per week of unwashed coal on regular time, but can be worked overtime up to an additional 4,000 tons. The cost of the crushing operation is $5 per ton of *unwashed coal* on regular time and $7.50 per ton on overtime. The washing tank can handle up to 6,000 tons of *recovered coal* on regular time and an additional 3,000 tons on overtime. The cost of washing is $10 per ton of *recovered coal* on regular time and $15 on overtime.

The variable costs of operating each mine are also shown in Table 10–21. In addition, it costs $2 per ton of unwashed coal for Light fluid, $4 per ton of unwashed coal for Medium fluid, and $6 per ton of unwashed coal for Heavy fluid. DMC sells its coal blend for $100 per ton.

Formulate as a linear programming model.

Solution of Linear Programming Problems

In Chapter 10 we introduced a wide range of problems that can be formulated as linear programming models. In this chapter we address the solutions. Since real linear programming problems can be large and complex, sophisticated computer methods are used to solve them. These methods are of important interest to computer scientists and mathematicians, and the basic ideas of this technique—called the simplex method—are discussed in Chapter 12. Managers generally are more interested in the solutions themselves than in the mathematics of the solution methods. So why, you may ask, should you study this chapter? The answer is that the solutions to linear programming problems offer many insights about the decision problem. Chapter 2 discussed the value of sensitivity analysis and other insights that managers can obtain from models in general. The solutions to linear programming problems offer many such insights. And to properly understand these solutions, it is necessary to know something of the solution process. Hence, this chapter presents some basic algebraic and graphical solution ideas about linear programming and the insights that managers can achieve from these solutions.

Graphic Solution

It is usually not possible to solve linear programming problems graphically because of our inability to visualize more than three spatial dimensions. However, it is useful to see how a simple problem can be solved graphically since higher dimension problems have analogous solutions.

Situation   A firm manufactures two products, A and B. Each of these requires time on two machines. The first machine has 24 hours available, and the second has 16 hours available. Each unit of product A requires two hours of time on both machines. Each unit of product B requires three hours of time on the first machine and one hour on the second machine. The incremental profit is $6 per unit of A and $7 per unit of B, and the firm can sell as many of either product as it can manufacture.

Problem Assuming the objective is to maximize profit, how many units of product A and product B should be produced? This linear programming (LP) problem was discussed previously in Chapter 10. We shall briefly repeat its formulation.

Formulation Let:

X_1 = Number of units of product A to be produced
X_2 = Number of units of product B to be produced
P = Incremental profit

We can express the situation and the objective (to maximize profit) using the equations below:

Maximize: $P = 6X_1 + 7X_2$
Subject to: $2X_1 + 3X_2 \leq 24$
$2X_1 + X_2 \leq 16$
$X_1, X_2 \geq 0$

Solution In Figure 11–1, the two constraining equations are shown. The equation

$$2X_1 + 3X_2 \leq 24$$

is the constraint imposed by limitation of hours available (24) on the first machine, and all points to the left and below the line are possible (feasible) combinations of X_1 and X_2. Similarly,

$$2X_1 + X_2 \leq 16$$

is the constraint associated with the second machine, and the points to the left and below are feasible. We also have constraints $X_1 \geq 0$ and $X_2 \geq 0$, since we cannot have negative output.

Consider the point marked F inside the shaded region in Figure 11–1 involving production of five units of product A and four units of product B. This requires $2 \times 5 + 3 \times 4 = 22$ hours of time on the first machine. Since this is less than the 24 hours available, it satisfies the first machine constraint. Similarly, $2 \times 5 + 1 \times 4 = 14$ hours of time on the second machine are required, again less than the 16 available hours. Finally, both X_1 and X_2 are positive, satisfying the non-negativity constraints. Since the solution represented by point F does not violate any constraint, it is a **feasible** point. The colored region *ACDE* in Figure 11–1

Figure 11–1   LP Constraints and Feasible Region

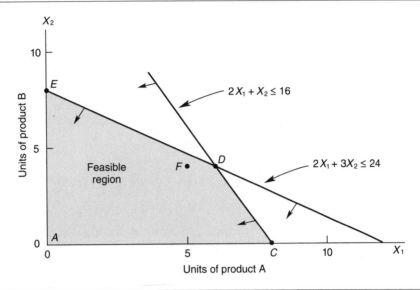

is the set of points that are feasible under all constraints, and it is called the **feasible region.**

Our aim is to find the point or points in the feasible region $ACDE$ that maximizes profit. We now show that *the optimum point will always be at a corner point of the feasible region.* The four corner points in $ACDE$ are the points A, C, D, and E. One of these points must be an optimum solution to the linear programming problem.[1]

To see intuitively why the optimum solution will always be at a corner point of the feasible region, we plot a set of profit functions. A *profit function* is a line containing all combinations of X_1 and X_2 that represent a constant amount of profit. In Figure 11–2, a series of profit functions for different profit levels are shown.

Consider the profit function for which $P = 42$. The equation of this line is:

$$P = 42 = 6X_1 + 7X_2$$

This line contains many feasible points (points within $ACDE$), all of which would give \$42 in profit. But the line $P = 54$ is better than $P = 42$, since it contains feasible points with profit of \$54. Note that the profit line $P = 54$ is parallel to the line $P = 42$; in LP problems, all profit lines will be parallel to one another. We continue considering lines parallel to line $P = 42$ until we

---

[1]We shall show shortly that two or more adjacent corner points can be alternative optimal solutions.

Figure 11–2   **Profit Functions $P = 6X_1 + 7X_2$**

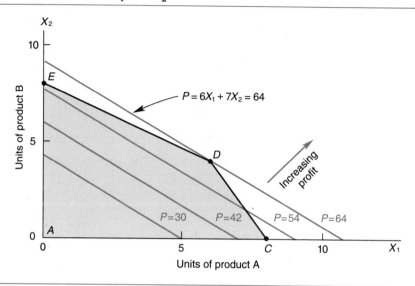

reach the line $P = 64$. Here, there is only one point in the $ACDE$ region—namely, D itself, and D (which is $X_1 = 6$, $X_2 = 4$) is the optimal solution. For larger values of P, there are no points in the $ACDE$ region.

The particular corner point that is the optimum solution depends on the slope of the profit function—that is, upon the relative profitability of products A and B. If, for example, product A were much more profitable per unit than B, say $8 per unit for A versus $2 per unit for B, then the objective function would be:

$$P = 8X_1 + 2X_2$$

The profit functions for this alternative case are shown in Figure 11–3. Note that point C now is the optimum solution. Similarly, if product B were much more profitable than A, and the objective function were, say,

$$P = 2X_1 + 8X_2$$

then point E would be the optimum. If the firm lost money on both products A and B, then point A, the origin with no production of either, would be the optimum.

Alternative Optimal Solutions   It is possible for the profit functions to have exactly the same slope as one of the constraint equations. For example, if the objective function were $P = 8X_1 + 4X_2$, it would represent a series of lines parallel to CD, as in Figure 11–4. In this case, there are multiple optimal solutions. Corner points C and D both are optimum points with profit of $64. But so are all the points lying on the line CD in Figure 11–4.

Figure 11–3   **Alternate Profit Functions** $P = 8X_1 + 2X_2$

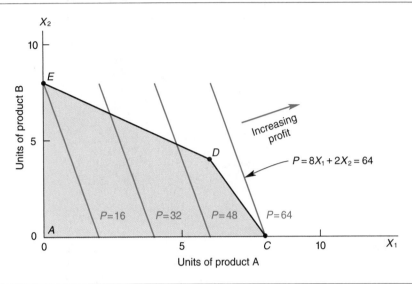

Figure 11–4   **Multiple Optimal Solutions** $P = 8X_1 + 4X_2$

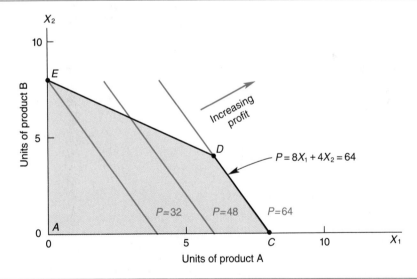

More Dimensions Visualize extending the LP problem to three dimensions, as shown in Figure 11–5. The constraints represent planes in three dimensional space, and the feasible region is a three-dimensional area bounded by these planes. The corner points A, B, . . . O represent places where these constraint planes intersect. The profit functions (not shown) are also planes. As in the

Figure 11–5   **Feasible Region in Three Dimensions**

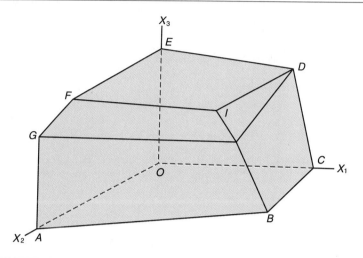

two-dimensional case, the optimal solution must be at one of the feasible corner points.

While we cannot visualize what a four or more dimensional problem would look like, the basic ideas can be extended to problems with many variables using algebraic methods.

SUMMARY

The optimal solutions to a linear programming problem always lie at a corner point of the feasible region. There may be alternative optimal solutions, involving adjacent corner points (and points on the line connecting them).

Sensitivity Analysis on the Constraints

As discussed in Chapter 2, finding the solution to a decision model is only the first step in analysis. It is also important for the manager to understand how sensitive that solution is to changes in assumptions and exogenous factors. This is true also for linear programming models, and one of the very nice features of LP models is that much of this sensitivity analysis comes directly from the solution to the problem. We shall address these ideas first graphically, and later in the chapter by interpreting the output of computer programs used to solve LP problems.

Let us expand slightly the problem we have been using as our example. Suppose that there is a market limit of six units on the number of units of product B that can be sold. The formulation now becomes:

Figure 11–6   **Feasible Region for Revised Problem**

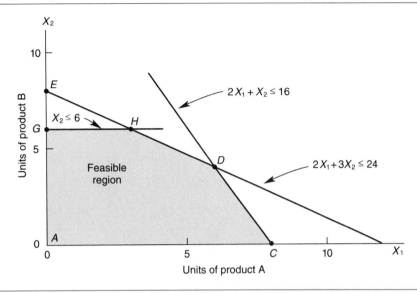

Maximize: $P = 6X_1 + 7X_2$
Subject to: $2X_1 + 3X_2 \leq 24$
$2X_1 + X_2 \leq 16$
$X_2 \leq 6$
$X_1, X_2 \geq 0$

and is graphed in Figure 11–6.

Dual Prices

Consider the constraint equation for machine 1, specifying that a maximum of 24 hours could be made available. In LP terminology, this capacity limit is often called the **right-hand side** (or simply **RHS**) value since it is on the right-hand side of the inequality sign. Suppose an extra hour could be made available so that the constraint now becomes

$$2X_1 + 3X_2 \leq 25$$

What happens to the solution?

This case is shown graphically in Figure 11–7. The new optimal solution moves to the point D', which has $X_1 = 5.75$ and $X_2 = 4.5.$[2] Since the old

---

[2]This solution can be found by simultaneously solving the two equations $2X_1 + X_2 = 16$ and $2X_1 + 3X_2 = 25$. Note that this is not an integer solution, but the Xs could be interpreted as rates of production.

Figure 11–7   **Sensitivity Analysis for Machine 1 Constraint**

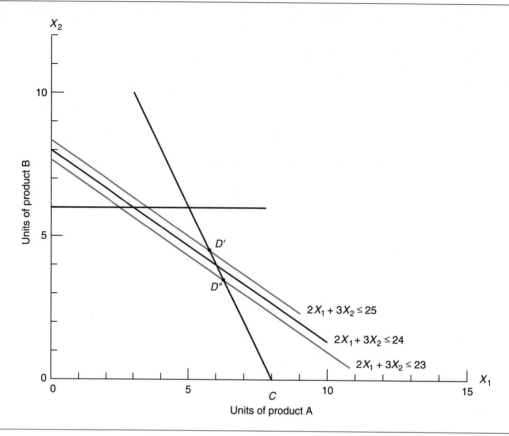

solution called for $X_1 = 6$ and $X_2 = 4$, an additional hour of time on machine 1 results in a reduction of 0.25 units of product A and an increase of 0.5 units of product B. The net change in the objective function P is thus:

$$-(0.25)\$6 + (0.50)\$7 = \$2$$

or an increase of \$2 in profit.[3] This is called the **dual price,** *marginal value,* or *shadow price.* It is the incremental change in profit per unit change in the RHS of a constraint.

Note that the dual price also holds for a decrease in the RHS value. For example, if only 23 hours were available on machine 1, the point D'' in Figure

---

[3]Another way to see this is to put the new values into the objective function $6X_1 + 7X_2$, giving a profit of \$66, versus \$64 previously, for an increase of \$2.

Figure 11–8 Sensitivity Analysis for Machine 2 Constraint

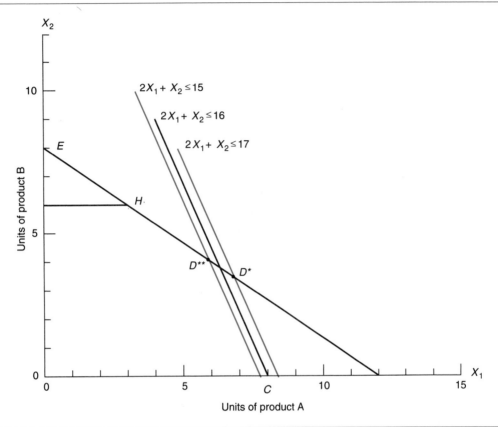

11–7 would be the optimal solution ($X_1 = 6.25$ and $X_2 = 3.5$), with a *decrease* in profit of $2. *Thus, the dual price, or marginal value, represents the incremental increase in profit when a constraint is relaxed by one unit, and the decrease in profit when a constraint is tightened by one unit.*

Exactly the same analysis can be applied to the constraint on machine 2. This is shown in Figure 11–8. When that constraint is relaxed by adding an additional hour, the constraint becomes:

$$2X_1 + X_2 \leq 17$$

and the optimum point is D^* with $X_1 = 6.75$ and $X_2 = 3.5$. This represents an increase of 0.75 in the units of product A and a decrease of 0.5 units of product B. The net effect on profit is:

$$+(0.75)\$6 - (0.5)\$7 = \$1$$

Figure 11–9   Sensitivity Analysis on Market Demand for Product B

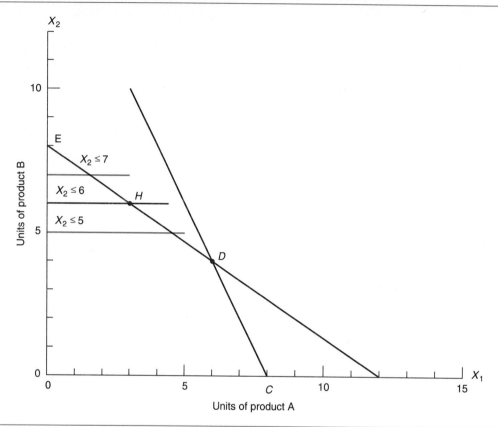

A similar reduction in the RHS (i.e., in the hours available) of constraint 2 results in a solution of $X_1 = 5.25$ and $X_2 = 4.5$ and a decrease in profit of $1. Thus, the dual price associated with the machine 2 constraint is $1.

Consider the third constraint, the limit on demand for product B:

$$X_2 \leq 6$$

A one-unit increase in this limit to $X_2 \leq 7$ and a one-unit decrease to $X_2 \leq 5$ are shown graphed in Figure 11–9. Note that neither change affects the solution at all because the constraint $X_2 \leq 6$ is not binding. The optimal solution called for only four units of product B, and so the market limit of six units doesn't matter. Thus, the dual price is zero. In fact, *the dual price of any non-binding constraint is always zero.*

Reduced Costs—Dual Prices for Non-Negativity Constraints   It is also possible to determine the marginal values associated with forcing at least one unit of a deci-

Figure 11–10   Sensitivity Analysis for Non-Negativity Constraint $X_2 \geq 0$

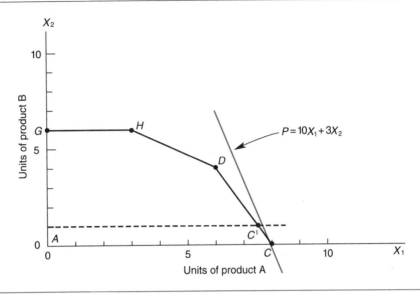

sion variable into the solution. Recall that the non-negativity constraints are $X_1 \geq 0$, $X_2 \geq 0$. Forcing one unit into the solution can be thought of as changing a non-negativity constraint to $X_1 \geq 1$ or $X_2 \geq 1$. The marginal values for doing this are called **reduced costs.**

Consider again our basic problem as graphed in Figure 11–9. The optimal solution calls for $X_1 = 6$ and $X_2 = 4$. Both of these are positive values, and hence, neither of the non-negativity constraints is binding. Thus, the marginal value (i.e., the reduced cost) associated with changing them is zero, just as for other non-binding constraints.

However, suppose the objective function were $P = 10X_1 + 3X_2$ as shown in Figure 11–10. Then point C is the optimum solution with $X_1 = 8$ and $X_2 = 0$ producing profit of $80. Note that since $X_2 = 0$, the non-negativity constraint $X_2 \geq 0$ is binding. Now suppose we must produce at least one unit of product B because of a commitment to a long-time customer, so that we change the constraint to $X_2 \geq 1$. This changes the optimum solution in Figure 11–10 to C', with $X_1 = 7.5$, $X_2 = 1$, and a profit of $78, a reduction of $2 from the previous level. Thus, in this case, the reduced cost or marginal value associated with the non-negativity constraint on X_2 is $2, the cost of keeping the goodwill of our customer.

Use of Dual Prices   These dual prices have important managerial uses. Although constraints and limits exist in the world, most of them are not absolute. For example, the manager who formulated the example LP problem determined the hours available on each machine under ordinary circumstances. But it may be possible to obtain additional hours by working overtime, by buying additional equipment, or by rescheduling other uses. The dual prices tell how much this is worth, at the margin, and thus help to identify key bottlenecks. In our example, the manager knows that it is twice as valuable ($2 versus $1) to obtain additional hours for machine 1 as it is for machine 2.

SUMMARY

A dual price represents the marginal value associated with a unit change in the RHS of a constraint. A reduced cost similarly represents the marginal value of forcing one unit of a decision variable into the solution. Reduced costs can be thought of as dual prices on the non-negativity constraints. If a constraint is not binding, its dual price is zero.

Right-Hand Side (RHS) Ranges

While the dual prices give the marginal value of making a small change in a constraint limit (i.e., in the RHS value), it would be a mistake to believe that these values would hold if capacity were changed arbitrarily. At some point, additional capacity becomes excess and has no value. Hence, there are limits on the range of capacity over which the marginal values hold.

Consider again the constraint of 24 hours for the time available for machine 1. Figure 11–11 shows what happens as additional hours are made available.

Figure 11–11   Range on Machine 1 Constraint

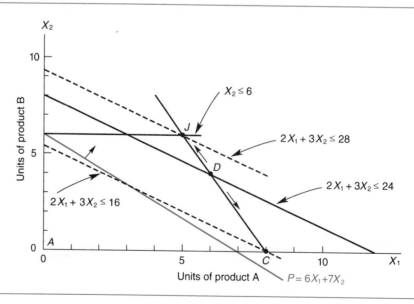

Recall from page 304 that each additional hour resulted in a reduction of 0.25 units of product A and an increase of 0.5 units of product B. The dual price associated with each incremental hour was $2. With 28 hours available, the optimal solution has moved from D to J. At J, the solution is $X_1 = 5$ and $X_2 = 6$. Beyond this point, additional hours on machine 1 will have no effect, since the constraint $X_2 \leq 6$ now becomes binding. Given the other constraints in the problem, 28 hours of time on machine 1 is the maximum that can be profitably used. Thus, this increase of 4 hours up to 28 hours available represents the upper limit on the range over which the dual price of $2 is valid.

Similarly, as hours of machine 1 time are reduced, the optimal solution moves down to point C in Figure 11–11, in which 16 hours of machine time are used. As hours are reduced, the decrease in profit comes from increasing units of product A and reducing units of product B. But at point C, no units of product B are being produced, so this substitution process is no longer possible. Thus, the lower limit on the range of the dual price of $2 for machine 1 time is a reduction of 8 hours (from 24 to 16).

For machine 2, a similar analysis can be done. Figure 11–12 shows the limits. As hours are added to the 16 available, the optimal solution moves from D to B. At this point, 8 hours have been added (from 16 to 24), and additional hours will add no value. When hours available are reduced by 4 (from 16 to 12), the optimal solution moves from D to H. Thus, the dual price of $1 holds over the range from 12 to 24 hours of time available on machine 2.

Figure 11–12   Range on Machine 2 Constraint

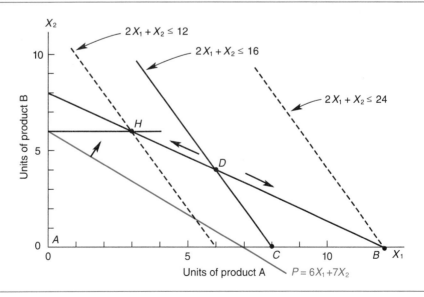

The constraint on market demand for product B, $X_2 \leq 6$, is somewhat different. Recall that this constraint is not binding and has a dual price of zero. The optimal solution calls for only four units of product B. Hence, the current demand limit could be increased indefinitely without any effect; if the constraint were $X_2 \leq 10$ or $X_2 \leq 100$, it would not matter. On the other hand, if the demand limit were to fall to four units so that the constraint were $X_2 \leq 4$, it would become binding. Any reduction below this four-unit limit would reduce profit. Hence, the range on the demand limit (i.e., the RHS) for the third constraint is from four units to infinity, and within this range the zero dual price holds.

For the three constraints, sensitivity analysis has produced the following ranges for the RHS values:

Constraint	Current Limit	Dual Price	Allowable Increase	Allowable Decrease
Machine 1 hours	24	$2	4	8
Machine 2 hours	16	$1	8	4
Demand for product B	6	0	Infinite	2

SUMMARY

The dual prices express the marginal value for changing the RHS of a constraint, but these values hold only over limited ranges.

Sensitivity Analysis—New Product Evaluation

Dual prices can be useful in identifying bottlenecks or constraints that are costly and might be profitably changed. Dual prices can also be useful in evaluating new products. Consider an extension of our example. The company's research and development department has created a new product, product C. It is very profitable, $10 per unit, but it requires four hours of time on machine 1 and three hours on machine 2. Should the company produce any units of product C?

Of course, we could reformulate the whole LP problem to add this new product. But a quick answer can be obtained by using the dual prices. Producing any of product C will require reducing the amounts of the other two products, since all products compete for time available on the two machines. Recall that the dual prices imply that an hour of time on machine 1 has a value of $2 and for machine 2, a value of $1. One unit of product C requires four hours and three hours on the two machines, respectively. Hence, the **opportunity cost** for a unit of product C is:

[(Dual price on machine 1 hours) × (Hours required on machine 1)] +
[(Dual price on machine 2 hours) × (Hours required on machine 2)]

or

$$\$2 \times 4 + \$1 \times 3 = \$11$$

This represents the cost of the lost opportunity to produce products A and B. Since the unit profit for product C is only $10, it should not be produced, since the opportunity cost exceeds the unit profit.

Another Example The same firm has another new item, product D, which requires one hour of time on each machine. It has a per unit profit of $5. Should any be produced?

The opportunity cost for this product is

$$\$2 \times 1 + \$1 \times 1 = \$3$$

Since the per unit profit of $5 exceeds the opportunity cost of $3, some of product D should be produced.

This analysis does not tell us exactly how many units of product D to make—only that we should include it in the product mix. The manager would reformulate the LP problem to include a new decision variable for product D, and re-solve the LP problem.

SUMMARY

The opportunity cost for a new product is calculated as the sum of the

(Dual price) · (Units required)

for all constraints affected. If the opportunity cost is less than the unit profit for the new product, then it is profitable and at least some of it should be included in the optimal solution. If the opportunity cost is greater than the unit profit, then the product should not be produced.

Sensitivity Analysis—Objective Function Coefficients

A manager may be interested in what happens to the solution of an LP problem if one of the coefficients of the objective function changes due to, for example, an increase in the price of a key raw material. We can do a graphical analysis similar to what was done for changes in RHS coefficients.

Suppose the per unit profit for product A is indeed fixed at $6 per unit, but the unit profit for B, while expected to be $7, might change. Figure 11–13 shows the profit functions as the unit profit of product B increases to $8, then $9, and then $10. When the objective function coefficient for X_2 is $8 (i.e., unit profit of $8 for product B), the profit function is $P = 6X_1 + 8X_2$ and point D is still the optimal solution. When the coefficient of X_2 increases to $9, the profit function slope is identical to that of the machine 1 constraint, and lies exactly on that constraint line. Hence, there are alternative optimal solutions (see page 300), and both D and H are optimal corner points. Suppose the coefficient of X_2 increases more, say to $10 per unit so that the profit function is $P = 6X_1 + 10X_2$, as shown in Figure 11–13. Note that there are points above this line (i.e., with higher profit) in the feasible region and hence the point D is no longer optimal. Point H now becomes the unique optimal solution. That is, when the coefficient of X_2 exceeds $9, the optimum jumps from point D to point H.

Figure 11–13 **Sensitivity Analysis: Increasing the per Unit Profit of Product B**

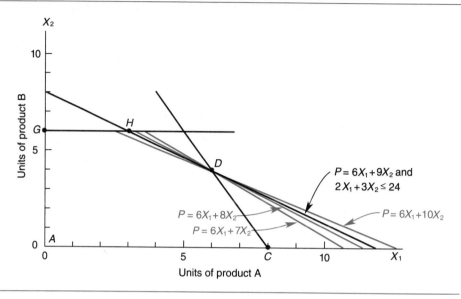

A similar analysis holds if the coefficient of X_2 falls. Figure 11–14 shows the profit function for values $5, $3, and $1 for the coefficient of X_2. For a coefficient of 3, the profit function is $P = 6X_1 + 3X_2$; now, the profit function lies exactly on the constraint for machine 2 and points D and C are both optimal. When the coefficient falls further, say to 1, the optimal point moves to C.

The same analysis can be done for the profit of A, holding the coefficient of X_2 constant and varying that for X_1. Although the graphical analysis is not shown, the results indicate that the coefficient for X_1 can fall from 6 to 4.67 before the optimal point shifts to H. Similarly, the coefficient can increase from 6 to 14 before the optimal point jumps to C.[4] These results can be summarized as:

Objective Function Coefficient Ranges
(range in which the basic solution
remains unchanged)

Variable	Current Coefficient	Allowable Increase	Allowable Decrease
Product A	6	8	1.33
Product B	7	2	4

---

[4]Actually, the analysis for X_1 is unnecessary since all that matters is the slope of the profit function. This is determined by the ratio of the two coefficients. When the ratio (coefficient of X_1)/(coefficient of X_2) is between ⅔ and 2.0, the optimal point is D. When the ratio is below ⅔, the optimal shifts to H; above 2.0, it shifts to C.

Figure 11–14   **Sensitivity Analysis: Decreasing the per Unit Profit of Product B**

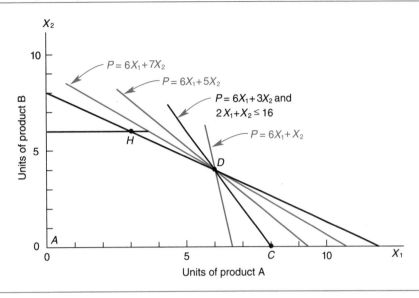

RHS Ranges versus Objective Coefficient Ranges   The sensitivity analysis ranges for the objective coefficients developed above and those for the RHS coefficients are similar in concept. However, there are also some important differences.

Within the range specified for the objective coefficient ranges, the optimal solution remains exactly the same—that is, the firm should produce six units of product A and four units of product B. Beyond the range, the optimal solution *jumps abruptly* to another corner point. The total profit, of course, varies with changes in the coefficients, but, to repeat, the solution stays fixed within the ranges.

In contrast, within the RHS ranges, the solution changes as the optimal point moves along one of the constraint lines. In our example, different amounts of products A and B are produced as the optimal point moves. At the limit of the range, a new corner point becomes the optimal solution.[5]

SUMMARY

The ranges, both for the RHS coefficients and for the objective function coefficients, provide important information in interpreting the LP solution. The RHS ranges determine the limits within which the dual price holds for each constraint. The objective coefficient ranges determine limits within which the solution remains the same.

---

[5]In the terms of the algebraic formulation to be discussed shortly, the basic variables remain the same within the range. At the limit, the set of basic variables changes.

Minimization

So far, our example has involved maximization of the objective function. Minimization is similar.

Example A company has two mills. The decision variables are the number of hours per week that each operates. The first mill can operate a maximum of 40 hours, and the second a maximum of 60 hours per week. Each hour of operation at the first mill results in 3 tons of finished product; each hour at the second mill produces 4 tons of product. The company has commitments to customers for at least 175 tons of finished product. It costs $20,000 for each hour of operation of the first mill and $40,000 per hour for the second; the company wishes to keep costs as low as possible. For policy reasons, the company wishes to operate at least as many hours at the second mill as at the first.

The LP formulation is:

Let: X_1 = Weekly hours at the first mill
      X_2 = Weekly hours at the second mill

Objective function:

$$
\begin{array}{lrcll}
\text{Minimize:} & C = 20X_1 + 40X_2 & & \text{(thousands of \$)} \\
\text{Subject to:} & X_1 & \leq & 40 & \text{(mill maximum)} \\
& X_2 & \leq & 60 & \text{(mill maximum)} \\
& 3X_1 + 4X_2 & \geq & 175 & \text{(customer requirements—tons)} \\
X_2 \geq X_1 \text{ or } & -X_1 + X_2 & \geq & 0 & \text{(policy requirement)} \\
& X_1 \geq 0, X_2 & \geq & 0 & \text{(non-negativity constraints)}
\end{array}
$$

The solution is graphed in Figure 11–15 with the feasible region shaded. The cost functions are in color. Since we seek a minimum value, the preferred lines (with smaller cost) are below. The optimum corner point occurs at X_1 = 25, X_2 = 25 with each mill operating at 25 hours per week, with a cost of $1,500 (thousand).

Note that the basic concepts of feasible region, corner points, and optimal solution are the same as in the maximization case. The basic ideas of sensitivity analysis and ranges are also similar and will be presented for this example later in the chapter in the section on interpretation of computer output.

Algebraic Approach

In Chapter 10, we considered the formulation of linear programming problems in algebraic terms. In this section, we shall extend the algebraic approach to demonstrate some important LP concepts.

Consider the original maximization problem that was solved at the beginning of this chapter. Recall that we had:

Figure 11–15   Graphic Analysis for Minimization Problem

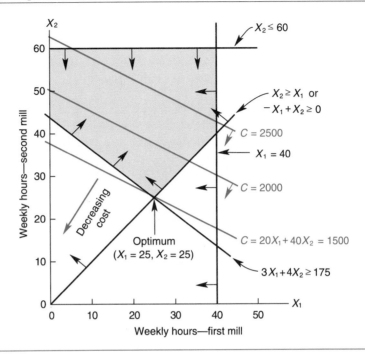

Maximize: $P = 6X_1 + 7X_2$
Subject to: $2X_1 + 3X_2 \leq 24$
$\qquad\quad 2X_1 + X_2 \leq 16$
$\qquad\qquad X_1, X_2 \geq 0$

The first step in our algebraic procedure is to convert the inequality expressions in the problem to equalities. This is done by adding two new variables, X_3 and X_4, called **slack variables.** The slack variables represent *unused capacity* in the first and second constraint, respectively. Thus, X_3 is the number of unused hours of capacity on machine 1 and X_4 is the number of unused hours on machine 2. It is always possible to convert the inequalities to equalities since there must be some amount—the unused capacity X_3—that, when added to $(2X_1 + 3X_2)$, will equal 24 (X_3 may be equal to or greater than zero).

The constraints of the problem are now rewritten as:

$2X_1 + 3X_2 + X_3 = 24$
$2X_1 + X_2 + X_4 = 16$
$X_1, X_2, X_3, X_4 \geq 0$

The objective function now becomes:

Maximize: $P = 6X_1 + 7X_2 + 0X_3 + 0X_4$

Figure 11–16   **Basic Solutions**

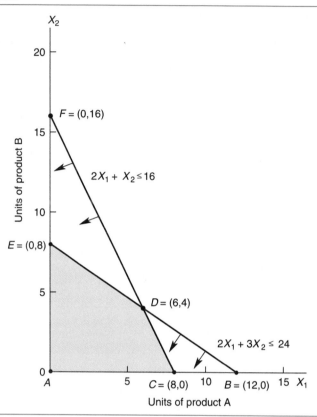

The slack variables introduce no profit, so their coefficients in the profit equation are zero.

Any values for X_1, X_2, X_3, and X_4 that satisfy the constraint equations are a feasible solution to the linear programming problem. The color shaded area in Figure 11–16 contains all the feasible solutions, as was discussed earlier in the chapter.

In the general linear programming problem, there are m constraint equations. After the slack variables have been added, there are more than m variables. You may recall from a course in algebra that one can find a single unique solution to a set of m linear equations if there are exactly m unknown variables. But with more than m variables, as in the LP case, there is no unique solution.

However, suppose we arbitrarily select any m variables and set the rest equal to zero, then solve the m equations for the selected m variables to obtain a solution. Such a solution is called a **basic solution**. The selected variables are called the **basic solution variables** or simply the **basis.** The variables set equal to zero are the **outside variables** or nonbasic variables.

In the example above, there are four unknown variables and two constraint equations.[6] To find a basic solution, we select any two variables and set the remaining two equal to zero. Suppose we arbitrarily select X_1 and X_3 as basic variables and set $X_2 = X_4 = 0$. The equations become:

$$2X_1 + 3(0) + X_3 = 24$$
$$2X_1 + 1(0) + 1(0) = 16$$

or

$$2X_1 + X_3 = 24$$
$$2X_1 = 16$$

The solution is $X_1 = 8$, $X_3 = 8$ (and recall that $X_2 = X_4 = 0$). This is one basic solution to the linear programming example. The other basic solutions can be obtained in a similar fashion and are given in Table 11–1. Note that some of the solutions call for negative values for one of the variables. These basic solutions are infeasible, since an LP problem does not allow negative values for any variables.

Each basic solution corresponds to an intersection of pairs of lines in Figure 11–16. Points A, C, D, and E correspond to the corner points of the feasible region. Points B and F are infeasible solutions. Thus, the *basic feasible* solutions correspond exactly with the corner points of the feasible region. Earlier in this chapter, we showed that the optimum solution to a linear programming problem must be a corner point. By the same token, *the optimum solution must be a basic feasible solution*.

In this simple problem, the optimum solution can be found by enumerating all the basic solutions, eliminating the infeasible ones, calculating the profit for each, and selecting the best, as is done in Table 11–1. However, a reasonably sized business problem may have thousands or millions of basic feasible

Table 11–1   **Basic Solutions**

Outside Variables (set equal to zero)	Solution Variables		Profit	Label in Figure 11–16
X_1 and X_2	$X_3 = 24,$	$X_4 = 16$	0	A
X_1 and X_3	$X_2 = 8,$	$X_4 = 8$	56	E
X_1 and X_4	$X_2 = 16,$	$X_3 = -24$	Infeasible	F
X_2 and X_3	$X_1 = 12,$	$X_4 = -8$	Infeasible	B
X_2 and X_4	$X_1 = 8,$	$X_3 = 8$	48	C
X_3 and X_4	$X_1 = 6,$	$X_2 = 4$	64	D

---

[6]For this purpose, we do not count the non-negativity constraints.

solutions, and this procedure would not be efficient. Instead, we rely on the simplex method, which is described in the next chapter.

The algebraic approach presented here is the foundation for the output presented in computer programs for solving LP problems. There are two important points to reiterate. The first is that slack variables are added to the formulation to represent unused capacity of some resource. If a constraint is of the greater-than-or-equal type, such as the one used to represent customer requirements in the example on page 314:

$$3X_1 + 4X_2 \geq 175$$

then a **surplus** variable is added, say X_3, so that

$$3X_1 + 4X_2 = 175 + X_3$$

or

$$3X_1 + 4X_2 - X_3 = 175$$

where X_3 represents the amount (in tons) by which the customer requirement is exceeded. These slack and surplus variables are important in interpreting linear programming solutions.

A second point is that *the number of variables in a basic solution (and hence in the optimal solution) is equal to the number of constraints in the LP problem* (not counting the non-negativity constraints).

Computer Solution of Linear Programming Problems

Computer codes are widely available for the solution of linear programming problems, not only on large computers, but even on personal computers. A very large problem involving thousands of variables and constraints requires the power of a large computer. However, such problems as the exercises in this book and moderate-sized real problems can be effectively solved on personal computers.

The simplex method is described in Chapter 12 and is the technique used in these computer programs, although generally modifications and refinements have been added to make the programs more accurate and efficient. Recently, a new approach to solving LP problems was announced by Dr. N. Karmarkar of Bell Labs that uses an approach different than the simplex method. Although this newer technique appears to have great potential, it is not known how widespread this method will become. In any case, the concepts developed in this chapter—basic solutions, interpretation of dual prices, sensitivity analysis, and parametric analysis—will remain important regardless of the solution procedure.

Table 11–2 is an illustration of the computer output for the solution to our example problem using the LINDO program (LINDO stands for Linear INter-

Table 11–2 LINDO Computer Solution

```
MAX      6 PRODA +  7 PRODB
SUBJECT TO
     2)  2 PRODA +  3 PRODB <= 24
     3)  2 PRODA +    PRODB <= 16
     4)    PRODB <=  6

END

LP OPTIMUM FOUND AT STEP     2

     OBJECTIVE FUNCTION VALUE

     1)   64.0000000

VARIABLE         VALUE          REDUCED COST
  PRODA         6.000000          .000000
  PRODB         4.000000          .000000

     ROW    SLACK OR SURPLUS     DUAL PRICES
     2)          .000000         2.000000
     3)          .000000         1.000000
     4)         2.000000          .000000

NO. ITERATIONS=    2

RANGES IN WHICH THE BASIS IS UNCHANGED:

                         OBJ COEFFICIENT RANGES
VARIABLE      CURRENT       ALLOWABLE      ALLOWABLE
               COEF         INCREASE       DECREASE
  PRODA      6.000000      8.000000       1.333333
  PRODB      7.000000      2.000000       4.000000

                         RIGHTHAND SIDE RANGES
     ROW      CURRENT       ALLOWABLE      ALLOWABLE
               RHS          INCREASE       DECREASE
     2       24.000000     4.000000       8.000000
     3       16.000000     8.000000       4.000000
     4        6.000000      INFINITY      2.000000
```

Comments

Formulation: PRODA and PRODB are decision variables
2) is a constraint on machine 1.
3) is a constraint on machine 2.
4) is a market demand constraint.

LP optimum found after examining two corner points.

Optimum profit is $64.

Optimal solution is 6 units of product A and 4 units of product B; reduced costs are both zero since some of each is produced.

No slack in constraints 2) and 3). Slack in constraint 4) implies unused demand for product B. Dual prices are shown.

Ranges in which the optimal solution remains the same.

Ranges in which the set of variables in the basic solution remains the same.

active Discrete Optimizer).[7] The decision variables can be given short names—here, they are PRODA and PRODB, for units of products A and B, respectively. The formulation as input to the computer is almost identical to that used in this chapter. The solution is given and comments are provided in Table 11–2. Note that the output includes not only the solution but also the reduced cost for each variable, the dual prices for the constraints, and the ranges for both the objective coefficients and the right-hand side values.

LINDO is an inexpensive and widely available software package for solving LP problems. It is available on both IBM-compatible and Macintosh personal computers as well as on large mainframes.

Another Example   Consider the example on page 314 of this chapter, involving a company that was trying to minimize the cost of operating two mills while meeting customer requirements. The LINDO formulation and solution are shown in Table 11–3. Variables MILL1 and MILL2 refer to the weekly hours at the first and second mills, respectively.

We shall use this example to review some of the points made in this chapter. First, note that there are four constraints, and hence there must be four basic variables in the solution. And indeed there are: MILL1 and MILL2, each with value 25, and there are 15 and 35 hours of slack in the constraints on capacities of each mill (rows 2 and 3). Secondly, note the dual price ($-\$8.57$) on the constraint requiring 175 tons of product to meet customer requirements. This is the marginal cost of an additional ton of production; producing 176 tons would cost $\$8.57$ (thousand) more than the cost of producing 175 tons. Also note that this marginal cost holds from the current requirement of 175 tons for an additional 105 tons up to a total of 280 tons (see right-hand side ranges in Table 11–3).

Linear Programming in Spreadsheet Packages

In addition to separate computer packages such as LINDO, linear programming capability has become available in recent years in popular spreadsheet packages, either as an add-on or as a part of the program. *What's Best*[8] is a program that is an add-on to Lotus 1-2-3, Excel, or other spreadsheet programs. Recently, *Quattro Pro*[9] and a new version of Lotus,[10] *Lotus 1-2-3/G,* have the ability to solve linear programming problems by a command from within the spreadsheet program. In these cases, the LP model is built right in the spreadsheet, and then optimized. The programs provide much of the same sensitivity analysis information (dual prices, reduced costs, etc.) as LINDO.[11] Because spreadsheet

[7]Linus Schrage, *Users Manual for LINDO* (Palo Alto, Calif.: The Scientific Press, 1984).
[8]Sam L. Savage, *What's Best* (Oakland, Calif.: Holden-Day, 1986).
[9]Borland International, *Quattro Pro,* (Scotts Valley, Calif.: Borland, 1989).
[10]Lotus Development Corp., *Lotus 1-2-3/G* (Cambridge, Mass.: Lotus, 1990).
[11]In fact, *What's Best* actually uses a version of LINDO to solve the LP problem.

Table 11–3 **LINDO Output for Second Example**

```
MIN       20 MILL1 + 40 MILL2
SUBJECT TO
       2)     MILL1 <=    40
       3)     MILL2 <=    60
       4)    3 MILL1 + 4 MILL2 >=    175
       5) -  MILL1 + MILL2 >=    0

LP OPTIMUM FOUND AT STEP      2

        OBJECTIVE FUNCTION VALUE

     1)    1500.00000

VARIABLE         VALUE       REDUCED COST
    MILL1      25.000000         .000000
    MILL2      25.000000         .000000

     ROW   SLACK OR SURPLUS   DUAL PRICES
      2)         15.000000        .000000
      3)         35.000000        .000000
      4)          .000000      -8.571428
      5)          .000000      -5.714285

NO. ITERATIONS =      2

RANGES IN WHICH THE BASIS IS UNCHANGED:

                        OBJ COEFFICIENT RANGES
VARIABLE           CURRENT        ALLOWABLE        ALLOWABLE
                   COEF           INCREASE         DECREASE
    MILL1       20.000000         9.999999        60.000000
    MILL2       40.000000         INFINITY        13.333330

                        RIGHTHAND SIDE RANGES
     ROW           CURRENT        ALLOWABLE        ALLOWABLE
                   RHS            INCREASE         DECREASE
      2         40.000000         INFINITY        15.000000
      3         60.000000         INFINITY        35.000000
      4        175.000000       105.000000       175.000000
      5          .000000        43.750000        26.250000
```

packages are so widespread and easy to use, this trend is bound to enable LP to be used more frequently in applications.

SUMMARY Computer packages such as LINDO provide not only the solution to LP problems, but also other sensitivity analysis information useful for managerial decision making.

Parametric Programming

Sensitivity analysis of the right-hand side values is concerned with defining a range of values about the optimum solution within which dual prices remain unchanged. Sometimes it is of interest to examine the changes in the linear programming solution as a given factor is changed over a wide range of values.[12] This type of analysis is called **parametric programming.**

An example will help to illustrate. Consider the following problem:

Maximize: $P = 5X_1 + 8X_2$

Subject to: $2X_1 + X_2 \leq 14$
$X_1 + 3X_2 \leq 12$
$X_2 \leq 3$

Let us suppose the first two constraints represent time used on machine 1 and machine 2, respectively, to produce units of products X_1 and X_2. The third constraint indicates that not more than three units of product X_2 can be sold. This set of constraints is shown graphically in Figure 11–17. The colored area represents the feasible region.

Figure 11–17

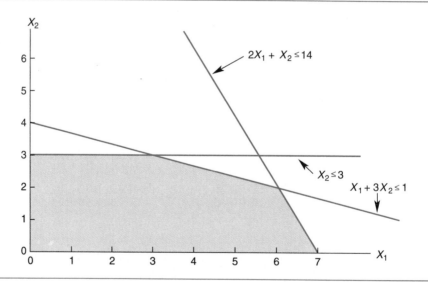

[12]We are concerned in this chapter only with variations in one variable at a time. The technique may be extended to consider variations in several variables—in fixed proportions to each other—all at the same time. See Harvey M. Wagner, *Principles of Operations Research*, rev. ed. (Englewood Cliffs, N.J.: Prentice Hall, 1975).

Suppose that we have an additional constraint on working capital, where X_1 and X_2 each require \$1 of working capital per unit:

$$X_1 + X_2 \leq K$$

This states that the total amount of working capital used must be less than an unspecified amount, K. We are interested in knowing how the solution to the problem changes as K varies from zero on up.

If $K = 0$, the only solution is that of no production and $X_1 = X_2 = 0$. As K increases, say up to 1, the first dollar of working capital is used to produce one unit of X_2, since X_2 is the more profitable product. Hence, at this stage, each unit of K (i.e., each dollar of working capital) produces \$8 of profit. This holds true until the situation described in Figure 11–18 is reached.

In Figure 11–18, three units of K are available, and all are used to produce units of X_2. However, at this point, the market constraint ($X_2 \leq 3$) becomes binding, and additional units of X_2 cannot be produced. Additional units of working capital now are used to produce units of X_1. Hence, at this stage, each dollar of working capital has an incremental value of \$5, the profit associated with selling one unit of X_1. This holds true until the situation described in Figure 11–19 is reached.

In Figure 11–19, the constraint on time available on machine 2 also becomes binding, at the point at which six units of K are available. Beyond this point, profit can be increased only by moving along the line $X_1 + 3X_2 = 12$, the equation of the constraint on machine 2. This means that for each one-unit reduction in X_2, three units of X_1 can be produced. The incremental value of K now drops

Figure 11–18

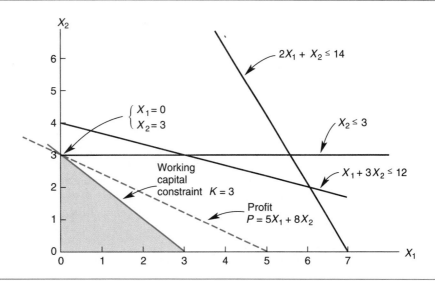

Figure 11–19

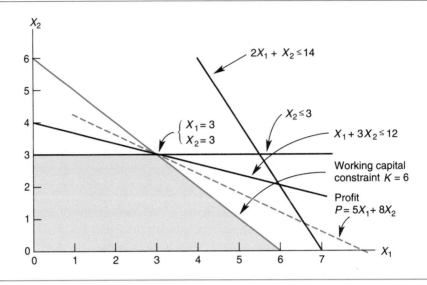

to \$3.50. (To see this, note that the substitution of one unit of X_2 for three units of X_1 produces \$7 additional profit—three times the \$5 profit from X_1 minus one times the \$8 profit from X_2, or \$7. Note also that this requires two units of working capital—three units for the new X_1 less one unit for reduced X_2. Hence, the marginal value of K is \$7/2, or \$3.50.)

Finally, the situation described in Figure 11–20 is reached. Here the constraints on both machine times are binding. Increasing the working capital, K, beyond this point would have no effect on the solution. The marginal value of K at this point becomes zero.

The effects of changes in the value of K are summarized in Figure 11–21. As K increases, the incremental value of additional units of working capital declines in a series of steps—as has been indicated above. The production of X_2 at first increases and later falls; the production of X_1 is zero at first, but then rises up to a level of six units.

An analysis of this sort would be useful to a firm that was trying to decide how much working capital to invest in this production operation. It is clear it would not invest more than \$8. However, it might invest somewhat less if it had profitable alternative uses for its funds. For example, if it could use the working capital elsewhere to return \$4 per unit, then it would not invest more than six units in this operation. Or if it could get a return of \$6 per unit elsewhere, it would not use more than three units in this operation.

In building a linear programming model of business systems, often a certain operation is found to be a binding constraint—a bottleneck. Management may

Figure 11–20

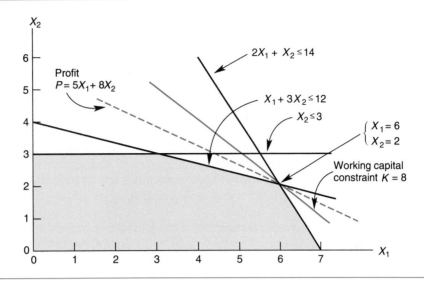

Figure 11–21

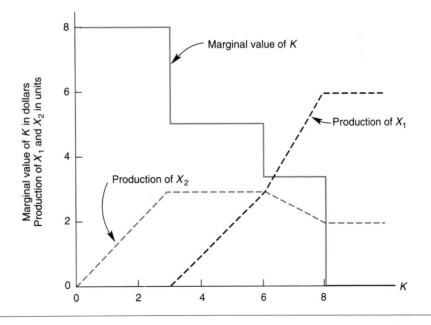

consider adding additional capacity. The question arises: How much additional capacity should be obtained? Parametric programming may help answer part of this question by showing what additional revenue or savings will result in adding different amounts of capacity. When the costs of adding this capacity are determined, then the answer can be obtained.

Parametric analysis may also be applied to the objective function to study the effects of changes in the price of a product or the cost of a raw material.

SUMMARY

Parametric programming analysis indicates the changes in an LP solution as a given factor is varied over a wide range. When applied to a resource constraint, it provides information on capacity changes. When applied to an objective function coefficient, it shows the effects of changes in prices or costs. Many LP computer programs will automatically perform sensitivity analysis and allow the user to do parametric programming analysis quickly and easily.

A Comprehensive Example

Let us consider a comprehensive example to review the LP concepts presented in this chapter. The Lazy Life of Leisure Company (LLL) produces patio furniture. The firm has three products: lounges, chairs, and picnic tables. It takes 60 minutes of labor to produce one lounge, 30 minutes for a chair, and 90 minutes for a table. In addition, it takes 6 units of lumber for a lounge, 6 units for a chair, and 12 units for a table. LLL has 9,000 minutes of labor and 600 units of lumber available. LLL can sell as many chairs and tables as it can produce. However, no more than 50 lounges can be sold. LLL makes a profit of $60 on each lounge, $40 on each chair, and $80 on each table. The LINDO formulation and solution of this case are shown in Table 11–4. The comments in the table describe the solution, the sensitivity analysis conclusions, and the parametric analysis.

An interesting feature of this solution is that an alternate optimum exists. Review page 300 and Figure 11–4 to see the meaning of this. We can see in the LP output that an alternate solution exists because one of the decision variables, TABLES, has a zero value in the solution, and also has a zero *reduced cost*.[13] This means that some number of tables can be introduced into the solution with zero effect on profit. From the LP output, we cannot determine the alternate basic solution, but we do know that one exists.

Suppose LLL were to consider another product, say SWINGS. Each SWING requires 200 minutes of labor, 9 units of lumber, and produces a profit of $100. Should any SWINGS be produced? The opportunity cost associated with one SWING is:

$$\text{(Dual price for labor)} \cdot \text{(Labor required)}$$
$$+ \text{(Dual price for lumber)} \cdot \text{(Lumber required)}$$
$$= 0 \times 200 + 6.67 \cdot 9 = \$60$$

---

[13]The indicators for an alternative optimal solution are:
A decision variable has zero value and the reduced cost is also zero (case in example), or
A slack or surplus variable has a zero value (constraint is binding) and the dual price is zero.

Since the profit of $100 exceeds this, some SWINGS should be produced. The problem would need to be reformulated and resolved to determine exactly how many SWINGS to produce.

Another feature shown in Table 11–4 is the parametric analysis. Note that the constraint on the amount of lumber available (600 units) was binding, and the dual price was $6.67 per unit. Suppose LLL could purchase additional lumber. How much should they purchase? The parametric analysis is designed to answer this. In particular, suppose that exactly 1,000 units could be purchased for $5,000. Should LLL make this purchase?

Note that the first additional 900 units (from 600 to 1,500) have a dual price of $6.67. The next 100 units have value (dual price) of $3.33. Hence, the total value of the 1,000 units is (900 × $6.67) + (100 × $3.33) = $6,333. Since this is greater than the $5,000 cost, the lumber should be purchased.

SUMMARY

This chapter presented the basic ideas in the solution of linear programming problems, first in the form of graphic solutions, and then in the output from computer software.

The optimal solution of an LP problem is a *corner point* of the feasible region. This corresponds, in algebraic terms, to a *basic feasible solution,* containing m basic variables (where m is the number of constraints).

Sensitivity analysis on the constraints involves first finding the *dual price,* the marginal value for a unit change in the right-hand side value of the constraint, and secondly, finding the range of values over which the dual price holds (the *RHS ranges*).

The *reduced cost* is a similar marginal value associated with introducing a unit of a decision variable into the optimal solution.

The *objective function coefficient ranges* provide additional sensitivity analyses. These ranges indicate the changes in the objective function coefficients within which the optimal solution remains the same.

Parametric analysis examines the changes in the solution and in the dual price as the RHS of a given constraint is varied over an extended range.

Computer software is widely available for solving LP problems, including some available within spreadsheets. The LINDO package is illustrated in this chapter, but other software output is similar.

The next three chapters continue the discussion of linear programming. Chapter 12 presents the details of the simplex method of solving LP problems. Chapter 13 considers special topics, and Chapter 14 considers integer programming, where the decision variables can take on only integer values.

APPENDIX   Interpreting LINDO Output

Output from LINDO is used in several exercises in this chapter. While the output is generally easy to interpret, there are a few aspects that can benefit from additional explanation.

Table 11–4   Computer Solution

```
:LOOK ALL

MAX    60 LOUNGES + 40 CHAIRS + 80 TABLES
SUBJECT TO
   2)   60 LOUNGES + 30 CHAIRS + 90 TABLES <= 9000
   3)    6 LOUNGES +  6 CHAIRS + 12 TABLES <=  600
   4)   LOUNGES <= 50
END

: GO
LP OPTIMUM FOUND AT STEP  2
      OBJECTIVE FUNCTION VALUE
   1)     5000.00000

VARIABLE        VALUE          REDUCED COST
LOUNGES       50.000000          .000000
CHAIRS        50.000000          .000000
TABLES          .000000          .000000

      ROW    SLACK OR SURPLUS    DUAL PRICES
       2)      4500.000000          .000000
       3)          .000000         6.666667
       4)          .000000        20.000000

NO. ITERATIONS =  2

DO RANGE (SENSITIVITY) ANALYSIS?
? YES
```

Comments

Formulation of the problem:

2) is a constraint on labor minutes available.
3) is a constraint on lumber.
4) is the sales limit on lounges.

GO starts the solution.

Solution profit is $5,000.

Rows correspond to constraint numbers (row 1 is objective function).

Solution calls for 50 lounges, 50 chairs, and no tables.

Note that the reduced cost for tables is zero, indicating that some tables could be produced without decreasing profit. This indicates that an alternative solution exists.

The value of an additional unit of lumber is $6.67 and $20 for an additional unit of demand for lounges.

Sensitivity analysis is requested.

```
RANGES IN WHICH THE BASIS IS UNCHANGED:

        OBJ COEFFICIENT RANGES

VARIABLE      CURRENT      ALLOWABLE     ALLOWABLE
               COEF        INCREASE      DECREASE

LOUNGES      60.000000     INFINITY     20.000000
CHAIRS       40.000000     20.000000      .000000
TABLES       80.000000       .000000     INFINITY

        RIGHTHAND SIDE RANGES
ROW           CURRENT      ALLOWABLE     ALLOWABLE
               RHS         INCREASE      DECREASE

 2)         9000.000000    INFINITY     4500.000000
 3)          600.000000    900.000000    300.000000
 4)           50.000000     50.000000     50.000000
: PARA
ROW:
3

NEW RHS VAL =
2000

VAR      VAR     PIVOT    RHS        DUAL        OBJ
OUT      IN       ROW     VAL      VARIABLE      VAL

SLK 2    SLK 4     2     1500.00    6.66667     11000.0
LOUNGES  SLK 3     4     1800.00    3.33333     12000.0
ART      ART       0     1800.00     .000000    12000.0
```

Ranges for the objective function coefficients. The program shows the increase or decrease (not the limit itself).

Ranges for constraints. As above, program shows the increase or decrease, not the limit.

PARA—request for parametric analysis. The program requests the row for this analysis. We select row 3, the constraint on lumber, and also select an upper limit of 2,000 units.

Three steps are found:

600 to 1,500 units—dual price = 6.67.
1,500 to 1,800 units—dual price = 3.33.
Above 1,800 units—dual price = 0.

LINDO Sign Convention

One aspect of LINDO that tends to be confusing is the convention used for the signs (plus or minus) on the dual prices and reduced cost values. The general rule is that tightening a constraint hurts (i.e., reduces profit or increases cost) while relaxing a constraint helps (increases profit or reduces cost). However, for equality constraints, it is sometimes unclear whether a constraint is being tightened or relaxed. The following table should help the interpretation.

Sign on Dual Price	Maximization or Minimization	Effect of a One Unit Increase of RHS Value
+	Maximization	Increase in profit
−	Maximization	Decrease in profit
+	Minimization	Decrease in cost
−	Minimization	Increase in cost

Reduced costs are either zero or have a positive sign. In minimization, the effect of forcing one unit into the solution is to increase cost. In maximization, the effect of forcing one unit into the solution is to reduce profit.

Degeneracy

Recall from the algebraic formulation in the chapter that, in an LP problem with m constraints, a basic solution will have exactly m basic or solution variables. We can determine the basic variables in LINDO output by simply identifying the decision variables or slack or surplus variables that are nonzero. Sometimes it happens (actually, frequently in large LP problems) that there are less than m nonzero variables in the optimal solution. This means that one or more of the basic variables just happens to turn out to be exactly zero. This is called *degeneracy*.

Generally, degeneracy is not really a problem, except that care is needed in interpreting some of the dual prices. In particular, when examining the right-hand side ranges, a particular dual price may have a zero allowable increase, a zero allowable decrease, or both. In other words, the dual price may hold only over a limited range, or no range at all. As long as this is recognized in interpreting LP output, degeneracy need not be a particular problem.

Alternate Solutions

Sometimes, an LP problem can have more than one optimal solution (see page 300 and Figure 11–4). When the solution is *not degenerate,* this case is easy to identify in LINDO output. If there is a decision variable that has a zero value and also a zero reduced cost, it indicates an alternate optimum. Similarly, a constraint with zero slack (or surplus) and a zero dual price also indicates an alternate optimum.

When the optimal solution is degenerate, determining if there are alternate solutions in LINDO output is not easily done and is not discussed here.

Bibliography

Schrage, Linus. *Linear, Integer and Quadratic Programming with LINDO*. 4th ed. South San Francisco, Calif.: Scientific Press, 1989.

Rubin, D. and H. Wagner. "Shadow Prices: Tips and Traps for Managers and Instructors." *Interfaces* (July–Aug. 1990), pp. 150–57.

See also the Bibliography of Chapter 10.

Problems with Answers

11-1. Solve the following problem graphically:

$$\text{Maximize:} \quad P = 2X_1 + 5X_2$$
$$\text{Subject to:} \quad X_1 + 3X_2 \leq 16$$
$$4X_1 + X_2 \leq 20$$
$$X_2 \leq 4$$
$$X_1, X_2 \geq 0$$

11-2. Refer to Problem 10–3 at the end of Chapter 10.

   a. Solve the problem graphically to find the optimal product mix.

   For (b) through (d) of this problem, consider each case separately. Also, convert all units to thousands. Solve graphically.

   b. Suppose the maximum number of units of product A that can be sold is actually 9 thousand units (rather than 8 thousand as in the base case). What effect does this have on the solution? What is the effect on the profit? What is the dual price for the constraint on the sales limit for product A?

   c. Suppose the maximum number of units of product B that can be sold is actually 13 thousand units (rather than 12 thousand as in the base case). What effect does this have on the solution? What is the effect on the profit? What is the dual price for the constraint on the sales limit for product B?

   d. Suppose there are 31 thousand labor hours available, rather than 30 thousand as in the base case. What effect does this have on the solution? What is the effect on the profit? What is the dual price for the constraint on the number of labor hours?

   e. Refer to (b), (c), and (d) above. Determine by graphic means the right-hand side ranges over which the dual prices hold for each of the three constraints.

11-3. Refer to Problem 10–1 at the end of Chapter 10. The problem formulation is given at the end of the book in answers to Chapter 10. If you have a computer and linear programming software available, solve the problem. If not, refer to the LINDO output given in the answers at the back of the book for this chapter. Then answer the following questions:

   a. What is the solution to the problem? How many units of each product are produced, and in which constraints is there slack or surplus? What is the optimum profit?

   b. What is the value of an additional hour of milling time? An additional hour of assembly time? An additional $1 in working capital for in-process inventory?

   c. Suppose the company could spend money on advertising that would have the effect of increasing the limit on demand for either product A or product C. How much should the company be willing to spend to increase the demand for product A by one unit? How much to increase the demand for product C by one unit?

d. Suppose that the contract for product D required 13 units (rather than 10). What effect would this have on the profit?

e. Suppose the profit per unit for product C were actually $46 (rather than $36). How would the solution change (i.e., how much of each product would be produced)? How much would the profit change?

f. A new product, product E, is under consideration. It requires 2 hours of milling time, 5 hours of assembly, and $20 in working capital. The profit per unit is $50. Should any units of product E be produced?

11–4. Refer to Problem 10–2 at the end of Chapter 10. The problem formulation is given at the end of the book in the answers to Chapter 10 problems. If you have access to a computer and linear programming software, solve the problem. If not, refer

to the LINDO output given in the answers at the back of the book for this chapter. Then answer the following questions:

a. What is the solution to the problem? How much of each type of loan should the company have? What is the total return expected from this plan?

b. If the company could raise additional funds beyond the $1.5 million currently available to lend, what would be the return on each additional dollar? Over what range would this value hold?

c. Suppose the annual return for second home mortgages were to increase from 10 percent to 12 percent. What effect would this have on the solution to the problem (i.e., on the loan portfolio)? What effect would it have on the total return? Suppose the rate for second mortgages went to 14 percent. What effect would this have? How high would the rate for second mortgages have to go before it had an effect on the loan portfolio?

Problems

11–5. Solve the following minimization problem graphically.

Minimize: $C = 4X_1 + 2X_2$
Subject to: $X_1 \geq 6$
              $X_1 + X_2 \geq 10$
              $X_1, X_2 \geq 0$

11–6. Refer to Problem 10–6 at the end of Chapter 10. Solve the problem graphically to find the optimal advertising strategy.

11–7. Refer to Problem 10–10 at the end of Chapter 10 (Delight Dairy Company problem).

a. Solve the problem graphically.

b. Suppose that 10 additional labor hours could be made available (by converting the ¾ time position to full-time). What does this do to the

solution? Show the result graphically. Calculate the dual price for an additional labor hour.

c. How many additional labor hours can be added before the dual price calculated in (*b*) changes? Show the result graphically.

d. Refer to the base case described in (*a*). Suppose competition has forced the price of ice cream down from $300 to $200 for 1,000 gallons. Would this change the production plan for DD? If so, what would be the new plan?

11–8. Refer to the gasoline blending problem, Example 3, on pages 267 to 270 in Chapter 10. The LINDO solution to this problem is given in Table 11–5. The variables are coded as: BLG1AV—barrels

Table 11–5   LINDO Computer Output for Gasoline Blending Problem (Problem 11–8)

```
MAX 45.1 BLG1AV + 45.1 BLG2AV + 32.4 BLG1MOT + 32.4 BLG2MOT
SUBJECT TO
        2) BLG1AV + BLG2AV <= 20000
        3) BLG1AV + BLG1MOT <= 30000
        4) BLG2AV + BLG2MOT <= 70000
        5) 2 BLG1AV - 8 BLG2AV >= 0
        6) 8 BLG1MOT - 2 BLG2MOT >= 0
        7)-BLG1AV + 3 BLG2AV <= 0
        8)-3 BLG1MOT + BLG2MOT <= 0


LP OPTIMUM FOUND AT STEP      5

        OBJECTIVE FUNCTION VALUE

        1)      3355455.00

VARIABLE            VALUE           REDUCED COST
   BLG1AV        7272.727000           .000000
   BLG2AV        1818.182000           .000000
   BLG1MOT      22727.270000           .000000
   BLG2MOT      68181.820000           .000000

     ROW     SLACK OR SURPLUS     DUAL PRICES
      2)        10909.090000          .000000
      3)             .000000        49.718180
      4)             .000000        26.627280
      5)             .000000        -2.309090
      6)        45454.550000          .000000
      7)         1818.182000          .000000
      8)             .000000         5.772726

NO. ITERATIONS =        5

RANGES IN WHICH THE BASIS IS UNCHANGED:

                          OBJ COEFFICIENT RANGES
VARIABLE            CURRENT         ALLOWABLE         ALLOWABLE
                     COEF           INCREASE          DECREASE
  BLG1AV          45.100000        73.225010         15.875000
  BLG2AV          45.100000       292.900000         16.933330
  BLG1MOT         32.400000        15.875000         73.225010
  BLG2MOT         32.400000        16.933330         24.408330

                          RIGHTHAND SIDE RANGES
     ROW            CURRENT         ALLOWABLE         ALLOWABLE
                     RHS            INCREASE          DECREASE
      2         20000.000000        INFINITY       10909.090000
     ,3         30000.000000      8000.000000       6666.667000
      4         70000.000000     20000.000000      24000.000000
      5              .000000     13333.330000       5000.000000
      6              .000000     45454.550000        INFINITY
      7              .000000        INFINITY        1818.182000
      8              .000000     16666.670000      20000.000000
```

of blending gasoline 1 used in aviation gasoline; BLG2AV—barrels of blending gasoline 2 used in aviation gasoline; BLG1MOT—barrels of blending gasoline 1 used in motor gasoline; and BLG2MOT—barrels of blending gasoline 2 used in motor gasoline.

a. What is the optimal solution to this problem?

b. Are there any alternative optimal solutions? How do you know?

c. Which of the constraints on octane rating and vapor pressure are binding?

d. Suppose the company could buy an additional 5,000 barrels of blending gasoline 1 for $200,000. Should the purchase be made? Why or why not?

e. A new product is proposed that would require blending exactly equal amounts of blending gasoline 1 and blending gasoline 2. Suppose the selling price for this new blend were $40 per barrel. Should any of this blend be made? Suppose the price were $35 per barrel; should any of the blend be made?

11-9. Refer to the transportation problem, Example 2 on pages 264 to 266 in Chapter 10. The LINDO output for this problem is given in Table 11–6. The decision variable CNY is the number of cases (in thousands) of soap shipped from the Cincinnati plant to the New York warehouse, variable DB is thousands of cases shipped from the Denver plant to the Boston warehouse, and so on. The first letter refers to the plant and the second (and third) letter refers to the warehouse location. Use the output in Table 11–6 to answer the questions below.

a. What is the optimal production and shipping plan for this company?

b. Suppose, for policy reasons, the company wanted to ship at least 1,000 cases from Cincinnati to Dallas. Would this increase the cost? By how much?

c. Suppose the company was considering a marketing program to increase the sales in the warehouse regions. If all else is equal (except shipping costs), which warehouse region would yield the most profit? Which would give the least profit?

d. Suppose the capacity of the Cincinnati plant can be increased by 10 percent by using overtime. The cost of this would be $1,000. Should this be done? Why or why not?

e. In the optimal plan, the Cincinnati plant is not shipping any soap to the Dallas warehouse. Suppose that the shipping department was able to negotiate a very favorable rate of $90 per 1,000 cases for the Cincinnati–Dallas route. Would this change the optimal shipping plan? How do you know?

11-10. A manufacturer of television sets made four models: (1) a portable black-and-white set called the Sport, (2) a regular black-and-white set called the Standard, (3) a portable color set called the Traveler, and (4) a regular color set called the Super. Each set required time to assemble and test. The assembly and testing requirements for each model are

(for Problem 11–10)

	Sport Model	Standard Model	Traveler Model	Super Model	Total Available
Assembly time (hours)	8	10	12	15	2,000
Test time (hours)	2	2	4	5	500
Marginal profit (dollars)	40	60	80	100	

Table 11–6   LINDO Output for Transportation Problem (Problem 11–9)

```
MIN    120 CNY + 150 CB + 80 CC + 250 CLA + 180 CD + 210 DNY +
       220 DB + 150 DC + 100 DLA + 110 DD + 150 ANY + 170 AB +
       150 AC + 240 ALA + 200 AD
SUBJECT TO
       2) CNY + DNY + ANY =    50
       3) CB + DB + AB =    10
       4) CC + DC + AC =    60
       5) CLA + DLA + ALA =    30
       6) CD + DD + AD =    20
       7) CNY + CB + CC + CLA + CD <=    100
       8) DNY + DB + DC + DLA + DD <=    60
       9) ANY + AB + AC + ALA + AD <=    50
END

LP OPTIMUM FOUND AT STEP 7

        OBJECTIVE FUNCTION VALUE

     1)     18000.0000

VARIABLE           VALUE        REDUCED COST
     CNY        40.000000           .000000
      CB          .000000         10.000000
      CC        60.000000           .000000
     CLA          .000000        180.000000
      CD          .000000        100.000000
     DNY          .000000         60.000000
      DB          .000000         50.000000
      DC          .000000         40.000000
     DLA        30.000000           .000000
      DD        20.000000           .000000
     ANY        10.000000           .000000
      AB        10.000000           .000000
      AC          .000000         40.000000
     ALA          .000000        140.000000
      AD          .000000         90.000000

     ROW    SLACK OR SURPLUS      DUAL PRICES
      2)          .000000       -150.000000
      3)          .000000       -170.000000
      4)          .000000       -110.000000
      5)          .000000       -100.000000
      6)          .000000       -110.000000
      7)          .000000         30.000000
      8)        10.000000           .000000
      9)        30.000000           .000000

NO. ITERATIONS =        7
```

(continued)

Table 11–6 (*concluded*)

```
RANGES IN WHICH THE BASIS IS UNCHANGED:

                         OBJ COEFFICIENT RANGES
    VARIABLE        CURRENT        ALLOWABLE        ALLOWABLE
                     COEF          INCREASE         DECREASE
      CNY         120.000000      10.000000        40.000000
      CB          150.000000      INFINITY         10.000000
      CC           80.000000      40.000000        INFINITY
      CLA         250.000000      INFINITY        180.000000
      CD          180.000000      INFINITY        100.000000
      DNY         210.000000      INFINITY         60.000000
      DB          220.000000      INFINITY         50.000000
      DC          150.000000      INFINITY         40.000000
      DLA         100.000000     140.000000        INFINITY
      DD          110.000000      90.000000        INFINITY
      ANY         150.000000      40.000000        10.000000
      AB          170.000000      10.000000        INFINITY
      AC          150.000000      INFINITY         40.000000
      ALA         240.000000      INFINITY        140.000000
      AD          200.000000      INFINITY         90.000000

                        RIGHTHAND SIDE RANGES
     ROW           CURRENT        ALLOWABLE        ALLOWABLE
                    RHS           INCREASE         DECREASE
       2           50.000000      30.000000        10.000000
       3           10.000000      30.000000        10.000000
       4           60.000000      30.000000        10.000000
       5           30.000000      10.000000        30.000000
       6           20.000000      10.000000        20.000000
       7          100.000000      10.000000        30.000000
       8           60.000000      INFINITY         10.000000
       9           50.000000      INFINITY         30.000000
```

shown in the accompanying table, together with the amount of time available for assembly and testing. In addition, due to a strike, there was a shortage of picture tubes. The supplier of picture tubes indicated that he would not be able to supply more than a total of 180 picture tubes in the next month; and of these, not more than 100 could be color picture tubes.

The problem is formulated and solved in Table 11–7. The decision variables SPORT, STANDARD, TRAVELER, and SUPER represent the number of units of that model produced.

Answer the following questions using the LINDO output in Table 11–7.

a. What is the optimum production schedule for the television manufacturer? Are there any alternative optimum schedules?

b. What is the marginal value of an additional hour of assembly time? Over what range of assembly time is this marginal value valid?

c. Suppose that 80 additional hours of test time could be obtained on the outside for $4 per hour. Should this be done? What will be the increase in profit?

Table 11–7   **LINDO Output for TV Manufacturer Problem (Problem 11–10)**

```
MAX 40 SPORT + 60 STANDARD + 80 TRAVELER + 100 SUPER
SUBJECT TO
        2)  8 SPORT + 10 STANDARD + 12 TRAVELER + 15 SUPER <= 2000
        3)  2 SPORT + 2 STANDARD + 4 TRAVELER + 5 SUPER <= 500
        4)  SPORT + STANDARD + TRAVELER + SUPER <= 180
        5)  TRAVELER + SUPER <= 100
END

LP OPTIMUM FOUND AT STEP 5

        OBJECTIVE FUNCTION VALUE

        1)  12500.0000

VARIABLE         VALUE        REDUCED COST
    SPORT       .000000        10.000000
 STANDARD    125.000000         .000000
 TRAVELER       .000000         .000000
    SUPER     50.000000         .000000

ROW     SLACK OR SURPLUS    DUAL PRICES
  2)          .000000        5.000000
  3)          .000000        5.000000
  4)         5.000000         .000000
  5)        50.000000         .000000

NO. ITERATIONS = 5

RANGES IN WHICH THE BASIS IS UNCHANGED:

                                OBJ COEFFICIENT RANGES
VARIABLE              CURRENT        ALLOWABLE        ALLOWABLE
                       COEF          INCREASE         DECREASE
    SPORT           40.000000       10.000000         INFINITY
 STANDARD           60.000000        6.666667        20.000000
 TRAVELER           80.000000         .000000         INFINITY
    SUPER          100.000000       50.000000          .000000

                                RIGHTHAND SIDE RANGES
ROW                  CURRENT        ALLOWABLE        ALLOWABLE
                      RHS           INCREASE         DECREASE
  2               2000.000000       33.333330       500.000000
  3                500.000000      100.000000        20.000000
  4                180.000000        INFINITY         5.000000
  5                100.000000        INFINITY        50.000000
```

d. What is the marginal value of an additional hour of test time? Over what range is this value valid?

e. Suppose that a price change is instituted that changes the marginal profit of the Sport model from $40 to $45. Would this change the optimum production plan? Suppose that the price of the Sport model changed from $40 to $55. In this case, would there be a change in the production plan?

f. How much would the price of the Standard model have to change before there would be a change in the production schedule?

g. Suppose that additional picture tubes can be obtained from another supplier, but at a cost of $2 more than the regular supplier's price for black and white and $5 more for color. Should any of these be purchased? How many?

h. Management is considering the introduction of a new color model called the Mate. The Mate model would require only 10 hours of assembly and 3 hours of test. The marginal profit from this new model would be $70. Should the new model be produced? If so, what will be the marginal value of producing one unit of the Mate model?

More Challenging Problems

11–11. Refer to the production scheduling model, Example 4 on pages 270 to 272 in Chapter 10. The problem is formulated and solved in Table 11–8. The decision variables are: JANRT, FEBRT, MARRT, and so on—number of units produced in regular time in January, February, March, and so forth; JANOT, FEBOT, and so on—number of units produced in overtime in January, February, and so forth; and INVJAN, INVFEB, and so on—number of units in inventory at the end of January, February, and so on.

Refer to Table 11–8 in answering the following questions:

a. What is the solution to the problem? That is, what should be the company's production schedule for the next six months? What is the cost of this plan?

b. After completing the production plan shown in Table 11–8, the company received an additional order for five units for January (increasing the commitments for that month from 95 to 100). The production manager argues that the marginal cost of producing these five units is $35 each (the overtime cost) since the plant is already scheduled to operate at full regular-time capacity. The sales manager argues that the marginal cost should only be $30 per unit, since previously only 95 units were the delivery commitment for January. What do you think will be the incremental cost of producing these five additional units? Why?

c. Suppose the company could temporarily increase the regular-time capacity for the month of April by 10 units. This would increase the cost of these extra 10 units from the regular-time cost of $32 per unit to $34 per unit. The cost of overtime units would continue to be $37 per unit. Should this change be made? How do you know?

d. Suppose that your accountant just informed you that a mistake had been made in estimating the regular-time per unit cost for the month of April. Instead of the $32 used in the analysis, the correct cost per unit should be $36. Would this change the production plan? Would it change the estimated total cost? By how much?

Table 11–8   **LINDO Output for Production Scheduling Example (Problem 11–11)**

```
MIN     30 JANRT + 30 FEBRT + 32 MARRT + 32 APRRT + 31 MAYRT
        + 32 JUNRT + 35 JANOT + 35 FEBOT + 37 MAROT + 37 APROT
        + 36 MAYOT + 37 JUNOT + 2 INVJAN + 2 INVFEB + 2 INVMAR
        + 2 INVAPR + 2 INVMAY + 2 INVJUN
SUBJECT TO
        2)    JANRT <=    100
        3)    FEBRT <=    100
        4)    MARRT <=    100
        5)    APRRT <=    100
        6)    MAYRT <=    100
        7)    JUNRT <=    100
        8)    JANOT <=    15
        9)    FEBOT <=    15
       10)    MAROT <=    15
       11)    APROT <=    15
       12)    MAYOT <=    15
       13)    JUNOT <=    15
       14)    JANRT + JANOT - INVJAN =      95
       15)    FEBRT + FEBOT + INVJAN - INVFEB =     85
       16)    MARRT + MAROT + INVFEB - INVMAR =    110
       17)    APRRT + APROT + INVMAR - INVAPR =    115
       18)    MAYRT + MAYOT + INVAPR - INVMAY =     90
       19)    JUNRT + JUNOT + INVMAY - INVJUN =    105
       20)    INVJUN = 0

        OBJECTIVE FUNCTION VALUE

        1)  18810.0000


VARIABLE          VALUE            REDUCED COST
   JANRT      100.000000             .000000
   FEBRT      100.000000             .000000
   MARRT      100.000000             .000000
   APRRT      100.000000             .000000
   MAYRT       95.000000             .000000
   JUNRT      100.000000             .000000
   JANOT         .000000            4.000000
   FEBOT         .000000            2.000000
   MAROT         .000000            2.000000
   APROT        5.000000             .000000
   MAYOT         .000000            5.000000
   JUNOT         .000000            4.000000
  INVJAN        5.000000             .000000
  INVFEB       20.000000             .000000
  INVMAR       10.000000             .000000
  INVAPR         .000000            8.000000
  INVMAY        5.000000             .000000
  INVJUN         .000000           35.000000
```

(continued)

Table 11–8 (*continued*)

```
ROW     SLACK OR SURPLUS      DUAL PRICES
 2)          .000000           1.000000
 3)          .000000           3.000000
 4)          .000000           3.000000
 5)          .000000           5.000000
 6)         5.000000            .000000
 7)          .000000           1.000000
 8)        15.000000            .000000
 9)        15.000000            .000000
10)        15.000000            .000000
11)        10.000000            .000000
12)        15.000000            .000000
13)        15.000000            .000000
14)          .000000         -31.000000
15)          .000000         -33.000000
16)          .000000         -35.000000
17)          .000000         -37.000000
18)          .000000         -31.000000
19)          .000000         -33.000000
20)          .000000            .000000
```

NO. ITERATIONS = 12

RANGES IN WHICH THE BASIS IS UNCHANGED:

```
                    OBJ COEFFICIENT RANGES
VARIABLE        CURRENT      ALLOWABLE     ALLOWABLE
                 COEF        INCREASE      DECREASE
  JANRT       30.000000      1.000000      INFINITY
  FEBRT       30.000000      3.000000      INFINITY
  MARRT       32.000000      3.000000      INFINITY
  APRRT       32.000000      5.000000      INFINITY
  MAYRT       31.000000      4.000000      1.000000
  JUNRT       32.000000      1.000000      INFINITY
  JANOT       35.000000      INFINITY      4.000000
  FEBOT       35.000000      INFINITY      2.000000
  MAROT       37.000000      INFINITY      2.000000
  APROT       37.000000      2.000000      1.000000
  MAYOT       36.000000      INFINITY      5.000000
  JUNOT       37.000000      INFINITY      4.000000
  INVJAN       2.000000      1.000000      4.000000
  INVFEB       2.000000      1.000000      2.000000
  INVMAR       2.000000      1.000000      2.000000
  INVAPR       2.000000      INFINITY      8.000000
  INVMAY       2.000000      4.000000      1.000000
  INVJUN       2.000000      INFINITY     35.000000
```

Table 11–8 (concluded)

```
                    RIGHTHAND SIDE RANGES
   ROW      CURRENT      ALLOWABLE      ALLOWABLE
             RHS         INCREASE       DECREASE
     2     100.000000    5.000000       5.000000
     3     100.000000    5.000000      10.000000
     4     100.000000    5.000000      10.000000
     5     100.000000    5.000000      10.000000
     6     100.000000    INFINITY       5.000000
     7     100.000000    5.000000       5.000000
     8      15.000000    INFINITY      15.000000
     9      15.000000    INFINITY      15.000000
    10      15.000000    INFINITY      15.000000
    11      15.000000    INFINITY      10.000000
    12      15.000000    INFINITY      15.000000
    13      15.000000    INFINITY      15.000000
    14      95.000000    5.000000       5.000000
    15      85.000000   10.000000       5.000000
    16     110.000000   10.000000       5.000000
    17     115.000000   10.000000       5.000000
    18      90.000000    5.000000      95.000000
    19     105.000000    5.000000       5.000000
    20        .000000     .000000        .000000
```

11–12. Co-Op Farm owns 1,000 acres of land on which it grows crops for sale to members of its grocery chain. Current plans call for the farm to grow corn and wheat on the land. Seed and other cultivation costs per acre are $100 for corn and $120 for wheat. Corn requires 10 labor hours per acre, while wheat requires 8 hours per acre. The yield at year-end in bushels per acre is 120 for corn and 100 for wheat. The farm can plant the land in any mix of the two crops. The farm receives $4.25 per bushel for corn sold and $5.25 per bushel for wheat sold to the grocery chain. The grocery chain can buy at most 100,000 bushels of corn and 175,000 bushels of wheat.

The farm is considering the possible raising of up to 2,000 steer cattle to sell beef to the grocery chain. To accomplish this, some of the land planned for corn or wheat can be dedicated as pasture to raise the young steers and feed them for one year. The steers cost $150 to pur-chase and are sold for $800 after feeding for one year. Each steer requires 20 hours of labor, one-half acre of land, and consumes 80 bushels of corn during its final fattening. The corn for the steers can be grown on the farm, if enough is available, or it can be purchased. If corn is purchased to feed the steers, it costs $4.50 per bushel.

The farm can use student labor, which costs $6 per hour, or experienced farmhands can be hired for $10 per hour. Each hour of student labor requires nine minutes (.15 hours) of supervision, and each hour of experienced farmhand labor requires three minutes (.05 hours) of supervision. There are 2,000 hours of supervision available.

The farm has $200,000 available to fund its farming operation. To efficiently operate the farm, the farm formulated its options as a linear program, using the following variable definitions:

Table 11-9   LINDO Output for Co-Op Farms Problem (Problem 11–12)

```
MAX - 120 W - 100 C + 5.25 WS + 4.25 CS + 650 S - 4.5 CPF - 6 SL - 10 EL

SUBJECT TO
      2) W + C + 0.5 S <=     1000                      Acreage limit.
      3) 8 W + 10 C + 20 S - SL - EL <=    0            Demand for labor.
      4) 0.15 SL + 0.05 EL <= 2000                      Upper limit on supervision hours.
      5) 120 W + 100 C + 150 S + 4.5 CPF
         + 6 SL + 10 EL <=  200000                      Budget constraint.
      6) - 80 S + CPF + CGF >=  0                       Demand for corn fed to steers.
      7) 120 C - CS - CGF >=   0                        Total usage of grown corn.
      8) 100 W - WS >=   0                              Wheat production.
      9) S <=   2000                                    Upper limit on steers.
     10) WS <=   175000                                 Upper limit on wheat sold.
     11) CS <=   100000                                 Upper limit on corn sold.

LP OPTIMUM FOUND AT STEP    7

     OBJECTIVE FUNCTION VALUE

     1)    358210.300

VARIABLE           VALUE          REDUCED COST
      W          793.357900          .000000
      C          118.081200          .000000
     WS        79335.800000          .000000
     CS             .000000          .055811
      S          177.121800          .000000
    CPF             .000000          .364393
     SL        11070.110000          .000000
     EL             .000000         4.151293
    CGF        14169.740000          .000000

ROW        SLACK OR SURPLUS        DUAL PRICES
      2)           .000000        350.645700
      3)           .000000          6.226938
      4)        339.483000          .000000
      5)           .000000           .037823
      6)           .000000         -4.305811
      7)           .000000         -4.305811
      8)           .000000         -5.250000
      9)       1822.878000          .000000
     10)      95664.200000          .000000
     11)     100000.000000          .000000
```

RANGES IN WHICH THE BASIS IS UNCHANGED:

OBJ COEFFICIENT RANGES

VARIABLE	CURRENT COEF	ALLOWABLE INCREASE	ALLOWABLE DECREASE
W	-120.000000	5.857180	6.368375
C	-100.000000	6.505330	10.250060
WS	5.250000	.058572	.063684
CS	4.250000	.055811	INFINITY
S	650.000000	151.24900	6.833376
CPF	-4.500000	.364493	INFINITY
SL	-6.000000	2.419982	.394233
EL	-10.000000	4.151293	INFINITY
CGF	.000000	1.890613	.085417

RIGHTHAND SIDE RANGES

ROW	CURRENT RHS	ALLOWABLE INCREASE	ALLOWABLE DECREASE
2	1000.000000	190.476200	278.787800
3	.000000	20476.190000	5333.332000
4	2000.000000	INFINITY	339.483300
5	200000.000000	23589.740000	32000.000000
6	.000000	90526.310000	13763.440000
7	.000000	90526.310000	13763.440000
8	.000000	79935.800000	95664.200000
9	2000.000000	INFINITY	1822.878000
10	175000.000000	INFINITY	95664.200000
11	100000.000000	INFINITY	100000.000000

C	=	Acres planted in corn
W	=	Acres planted in wheat
S	=	Steers purchased and sold
SL	=	Student labor hours used
EL	=	Experienced farmhand labor hours used
CPF	=	Bushels of purchased corn fed to steers
CGF	=	Bushels of grown corn fed to steers
CS	=	Bushels of corn sold
WS	=	Bushels of wheat sold

The formulation and LINDO output are given in Table 11–9. Answer (a) through (j) independently of the others.

a. What is the optimal farming schedule (i.e., the solution to the problem)? What is the total dollar payoff?

b. By how much would the price of corn sold have to change and in which direction (increase or decrease) for the farm to consider selling any corn to the Co-Op groceries?

c. What is the value of an additional hour of labor to the farm?

d. If the farm could borrow an additional $15,000 to help finance the farm's operation, what is the maximum interest rate (simple annual interest), if any, that the farm would be willing to pay?

e. A neighboring ranch has offered to lease 200 acres of land to Co-Op Farm for a fixed fee of $65,000, to be paid out of profits at year-end after crops and steers have been sold. Should the farm accept the offer?

f. By how much would the cost of "seed and other cultivation costs" of wheat have to increase before the farm would change the amount of acreage devoted to growing wheat?

g. The farm is contemplating the growing of tomatoes. Tomato plants can be acquired for $50 per acre. Tomatoes require 15 hours of labor per acre. An acre of tomatoes produces 40 bushels of salable tomatoes. Assuming tomatoes can be sold for $12 per bushel, should the farm devote any acreage to the growing of tomatoes?

h. For a fixed cost of $10,000, the farm can apply fertilizer to the land at the beginning of the planting season. The fertilizer is applied to all the land and increases the yield of corn to 130 bushels per acre and the yield of wheat to 110 bushels per acre. Would the farm find it profitable to apply the fertilizer?

i. The Co-Op would like to have some experienced farm labor on the farm. What would be the rate of change in payoff as experienced farmhand labor hours were added?

j. The dual price on constraint 3 (demand for labor) is 6.23. Yet the farm can hire unlimited student labor at $6.00 per hour. Explain this apparent contradiction.

12

Linear Programming
The Simplex Method

In the last chapter we demonstrated how to solve linear programming problems and do sensitivity analysis graphically, and also how to interpret the results of computer solutions. In this chapter we introduce an algebraic solution procedure called the simplex method to solve LP problems. This procedure, or variants of it, is coded into computer programs for solving very large LP problems, even those with thousands of variables and constraints.

Algebraic Formulation

The algebraic formulation was introduced in Chapter 11 (pages 314 to 318), and you should review that discussion before proceeding. Let us further consider the same problem that was formulated algebraically and solved graphically:

Maximize: $P = 6X_1 + 7X_2$
Subject to: $2X_1 + 3X_2 \leq 24$
$2X_1 + X_2 \leq 16$
$X_1, X_2 \geq 0$

where X_1 and X_2 represent the number of units of product A and product B, and the two constraints represent the limits (in hours) of capacity on two machines. Product A has an incremental profit of $6 per unit, and product B earns $7 per unit. Recall that the problem could be converted to a set of *equality* constraints by adding two *slack* variables, X_3 and X_4, representing the unused capacity on machine 1 and machine 2, respectively. Because the slack variables add nothing to profit, they will have zero coefficients in the objective function and the problem can be rewritten as:

345

$$\text{Maximize:} \quad P = 6X_1 + 7X_2 + 0X_3 + 0X_4$$
$$\text{Subject to:} \quad 2X_1 + 3X_2 + X_3 + 0X_4 = 24$$
$$2X_1 + X_2 + 0X_3 + X_4 = 16$$
$$X_1, X_2 \geq 0$$

In this problem there are now four variables and two constraints, not counting the non-negativity constraints. In a general linear programming problem with m constraints, there will be more than m variables once the slack or surplus variables are added. Recall that if we select some set of the m variables, set the rest equal to zero, and then solve for these m variables, we have a **basic solution.** The selected variables are called the **solution variables.** The variables set equal to zero are the **outside variables.** In the previous chapter, we found all the basic solutions for this problem, and showed how they related to corner points of the graphic solution (see Table 11–1 and Figure 11–16). Recall that some of the basic solutions are **infeasible**, since they involve negative values for one or more of the variables.

As an example, one basic solution involves selecting X_1 and X_2 as the solution variables and setting X_3 and $X_4 = 0$ (they are the outside variables). Solving the equations above results in $X_1 = 6$, $X_2 = 4$, and profit $P = 64$. This happens to be the optimal solution. Another basic solution selects X_3 and X_4 as the solution variables and $X_1 = X_2 = 0$, with profit $P = 0$.

The Simplex Method

The simplex method is a procedure that starts with an initial basic feasible solution. It then proceeds step by step to subsequent solutions, each of which: (1) is a basic feasible solution and (2) has greater profit than the previous solution.[1] Ultimately, we obtain a solution for which no improvement is possible, and the optimum has been found.

Example 1: Maximization of Costs   The process starts with the objective function and the constraint equations written in algebraic form. For our example, we have:

$$P = 6X_1 + 7X_2 + 0X_3 + 0X_4$$
$$2X_1 + 3X_2 + X_3 + 0X_4 = 24$$
$$2X_1 + X_2 + 0X_3 + X_4 = 16$$

The Simplex Table

It is convenient to do the calculations for the simplex procedure in the form of a table, such as Table 12–1.

---

[1]In some circumstances, it is possible for the profit to remain the same from one step to the next, but it cannot decrease.

Table 12–1   First Solution

C_j			0	0	6	7
	Solution Variables	Solution Values	X_3	X_4	X_1	X_2
		24	1	0	2	3
		16	0	1	2	1
	Z_j					
	$C_j - Z_j$					

Under each column heading (such as X_3, X_4, X_1, or X_2) of Table 12–1 are written the coefficients from the constraint equations of the variables found in the heading. Thus, under X_1 is written $\begin{pmatrix} 2 \\ 2 \end{pmatrix}$; under X_2 is written $\begin{pmatrix} 3 \\ 1 \end{pmatrix}$; under X_3 is written $\begin{pmatrix} 1 \\ 0 \end{pmatrix}$; and under X_4 is written $\begin{pmatrix} 0 \\ 1 \end{pmatrix}$. Under the column headed "Solution values," the constants or right-hand sides of the equations are listed. Each row in the table is thus one equation associated with a given constraint. It is convenient to place the columns containing the slack variables immediately after the solution column. The first row in the heading of the table contains the C_j's, or the profit per unit (the coefficients of the variables in the profit equation) for each variable X_1 through X_4.

Initial Solution

The initial basic solution in Table 12–1 consists of the slack variables X_3 and X_4 as solution variables, and variables X_1 and X_2 as outside variables. This is not a very profitable solution, with profit $P = 0$. It calls for no production of either product A or B. The terms X_3 and X_4 are entered in the simplex table under the "Solution variables" column, and their per-unit profits (the C_j's) are entered in the first column under the C_j heading (see Table 12–2).

The solution variables can be identified as those having columns under them containing one element with $+1$, and the remainder of the elements 0. Thus, column X_3 is $\begin{pmatrix} 1 \\ 0 \end{pmatrix}$, and column X_4 is $\begin{pmatrix} 0 \\ 1 \end{pmatrix}$. Also, the 1 must be in a different row than the 1 of any other column. Thus, X_3 has a 1 in the first row, and X_4 has a 1 in the second row. Note that this is equivalent to saying that we have solved the constraint equations in terms of X_3 and X_4:

$$X_3 = 24 - [2X_1 + 3X_2]$$
$$X_4 = 16 - [2X_1 + X_2]$$

(12–1)

Table 12–2   First Solution

C_j	Solution Variables	Solution Values	0 X_3	0 X_4	6 X_1	7 X_2
0	$\rightarrow X_3$	24	1	0	2	③
0	X_4	16	0	1	2	1
	Z_j	0	0	0	0	0
	$C_j - Z_j$		0	0	6	7

↑

Table 12–3

Solution Variables	X_1	X_2	$\ldots$	X_n
X_1	1	0	$\ldots$	0
X_2	0	1	$\ldots$	0
.	.	.	$\ldots$	.
.	.	.	$\ldots$	.
.	.	.	$\ldots$	.
X_n	0	0	$\ldots$	1

The variables omitted from the solution are currently X_1 and X_2; they are equal to 0. Thus, for this first trial solution, $X_3 = 24$ and $X_4 = 16$.

If there are n constraints in the problem, then the first n columns should appear as shown in Table 12–3.

Note that we have a diagonal of 1s, and the remainder of the numbers in the first n columns are 0s.

Substitution Coefficients   The coefficients in the columns of the body of the simplex table can be considered **substitution coefficients**. That is, they are the reductions in variables in the solution that will result from introducing one unit of each variable that is currently not in the solution. For example, in Table 12–2, $\binom{3}{1}$ is under column X_2. For every unit of product B (i.e., units of X_2) intro-

duced into the solution, three units of slack variable X_3 and one unit of slack variable X_4 must be removed from the solution in order to stay within the required constraints. Thus, the 3 and 1 are the amounts of X_3 and X_4 *substituted* for one unit of X_2. Similarly, for every unit of X_1 introduced into the solution, two units of X_3 and two units of X_4 must be removed. An inspection of our constraint equations (12–1) confirms the reasonableness of this interpretation.

Under each column of Table 12–2 is a Z_j total (where the j subscript refers to the specific column being totaled). The Z_j total of a column is the amount of profit given up by replacing some of the present solution mix with *one* unit of the item heading the column. It is found by multiplying the C_j of the row by the number in the row and jth column (the substitution coefficient), and adding. The computations of the Z_j's of Table 12–2 are as follows:

$$Z_3 = 1(0) + 0(0) = 0$$
$$Z_4 = 0(0) + 1(0) = 0$$
$$Z_1 = 2(0) + 2(0) = 0$$
$$Z_2 = 3(0) + 1(0) = 0$$

Similarly, a Z value can be calculated for the "Solution values" column (which we shall refer to hereafter as the 0th column):

$$Z_0 = 24(0) + 16(0) = 0$$

Z_0 represents the profit of the current solution.

Under the Z_j row is a row labeled $C_j - Z_j$. Subtract the Z_j total from the C_j amount at the very top of the column to find the *net* profit that is added by one unit of the product (if $C_j - Z_j$ is positive) or the amount of profit that will be lost (if $C_j - Z_j$ is negative). Thus, if one unit of X_2 is added to the solution (replacing some amounts of X_3 and X_4), $7 of net profit will be added.

The $C_j - Z_j$ row is in reality an equation, like the other rows in the linear programming table, and expresses the profit at that stage of the computations in terms of the outside variables. Thus, the $C_j - Z_j$ row is equivalent to:

$$\text{Profit} = 0X_3 + 0X_4 + 6X_1 + 7X_2$$

Finding a New Solution

The simplex method finds a new solution by replacing exactly one of the solution variables by one of the outside variables. This is accomplished in three steps:

1. Choose an entering variable that will increase the profitability of the solution.
2. Choose the leaving variable that will ensure a feasible basic solution.
3. Re-solve the constraint equations to find the new solution.

The Entering Variable Determine the variable that has the greatest net profit per unit. This is the one with the largest positive value in the $C_j - Z_j$ row at the bottom of the table. Variable X_2 (product B) contributes $7 per unit; this is greater than any other variable. Hence, X_2 is the variable that enters the solution. The column associated with X_2 is marked with an arrow in Table 12–2.

The Leaving Variable The next step is to determine which of the current solution variables (X_3 or X_4) is to leave the solution and be replaced by X_2. Consider adding units of X_2 into the solution one at a time. At some point one of the variables initially in the solution will be driven exactly to zero, hence, changing from a solution variable to an outside variable. We need to find out which solution variable will first be driven to zero as units of X_2 are introduced into the solution. Since variable X_1 will remain an outside variable with value zero, we can write the constraint equations as:

$$3X_2 + X_3 \qquad = 24$$
$$X_2 \qquad + X_4 = 16$$

If X_3 were to be the leaving variable (and hence become zero), we could solve the above equations for X_2 and X_4, obtaining $X_2 = 8$, $X_4 = 8$. This is a feasible solution.

If X_4 were to be the leaving variable (and hence become zero), solving the equations for X_2 and X_3 gives $X_2 = 16$, $X_3 = -24$. This is an infeasible solution, since it would require negative amounts of X_3. In other words, as units of X_2 are added, at the point $X_2 = 8$, the solution variable X_3 would be driven to zero; this is the first solution variable driven to zero (X_4, the other solution variable, is still positive at that point), so X_3 is the leaving variable.

The same result can be obtained using the table and a more mechanical rule. Divide each amount in the "Solution values" column by the amount *in the comparable row* of the entering X_2 column:

For X_3 row: $^{24}/_3 = 8$
For X_4 row: $^{16}/_1 = 16$

The smallest number obtained by this computation gives the maximum number of units of X_2, 8, which may be injected into the solution without driving some solution variable negative. If any of the amounts calculated by dividing are negative, they should be eliminated from consideration; otherwise, the *smallest* amount, as computed above, determines the leaving variable. In this case, the X_3 row has the smallest number (8), and X_3 is the leaving variable. The X_3 row is marked with an arrow in Table 12–2.

Note what we have done so far in the simplex procedure. First, we identified a variable that will increase profitability and indicated that it is to be included in the next solution. Then, we guaranteed that the next solution will be a basic feasible one by identifying a variable to be removed from the solution that will keep all variable values nonnegative. The third step is to determine the new solution.

Re-solving The actual replacement of X_3 by X_2 is accomplished making use of two techniques.

The element in the entering X_2 column and the leaving X_3 row is designated the **pivot element**. (In our example, the pivot element is circled in Table 12–2 and has a value of 3.) In order to obtain a new solution containing X_2, this element must be converted to a $+1$ and the other elements in the X_2 column converted to 0.

To convert the pivot element to $+1$ requires that we divide every element in the present X_3 row by the value of the pivot element (i.e., by 3). Recall that each row is in reality a constraint equation, and one may divide a whole equation by a constant.

The calculations are:

$$24/3 = 8$$
$$1/3 = 1/3$$
$$0/3 = 0$$
$$2/3 = 2/3$$
$$3/3 = 1$$

Thus, the new top row should be (8, 1/3, 0, 2/3, 1); and it is labeled X_2 in the second simplex solution (see Table 12–4).

The second part of the procedure is aimed at converting all the elements (except the pivot element) in the X_2 column to zero. In our example, the only other value in the X_2 column is a 1 in the X_4 row (circled in Table 12–4). This can be accomplished by multiplying the entire *new* X_2 row by the value in the X_2 column, X_4 row—that is, the circled value, 1—and subtracting the result from the old X_4 row. This is easier to illustrate than to describe (see Table 12–5).

The new values of the X_4 row are (8, − 1/3, 1, 4/3, 0).

To understand why the procedure described above is legitimate, recall that each row in the table is equivalent to an equation. Hence, we are simply

Table 12–4 **Second Solution–Partially Complete**

C_j			0	0	6	7
	Solution Variables	*Solution Values*	X_3	X_4	X_1	X_2
7	X_2 (new)	8	1/3	0	2/3	1
0	X_4 (old)	16	0	1	2	①
	Z_j					
	$C_j - Z_j$					

Table 12–5

Old X_4 Row	−	$\begin{pmatrix} Element\ in \\ Old\ X_4\ Row \\ and \\ X_2\ Column \end{pmatrix}$	·	*New X_2 Row*	=	*Values of New X_4 Row*
16	−	(1)	·	(8)	=	8
0	−	(1)	·	(1/3)	=	− 1/3
1	−	(1)	·	(0)	=	1
2	−	(1)	·	(2/3)	=	4/3
1	−	(1)	·	(1)	=	0

multiplying one equation by a constant (1 in this case) and subtracting it from another equation. The result is a new equation.

Table 12–6 shows the new solution. Recall that the table represents the solution of the constraint equations in terms of the new set of solution variables X_2 and X_4. Thus, we could write Table 12–6 as:

$$8 = \tfrac{1}{3} X_3 + 0X_4 + \tfrac{2}{3}X_1 + 1X_2$$
$$8 = -\tfrac{1}{3}X_3 + 1X_4 + \tfrac{4}{3}X_1 + 0X_2$$

or as:

$$X_2 = 8 - [\tfrac{1}{3}X_3 + \tfrac{2}{3}X_1]$$
$$X_4 = 8 - [-\tfrac{1}{3}X_3 + \tfrac{4}{3}X_1]$$

With X_3 and X_1 equal to zero, the new solution has eight units of product B ($X_2 = 8$) and eight units of slack in the second constraint ($X_4 = 8$).

Calculating the Z_j's　We first illustrate the calculation of the Z_j values for Table 12–6 by considering the X_1 column and Z_1. Recall that the coefficients $\tfrac{2}{3}$ and $\tfrac{4}{3}$ in the X_1 column are substitution coefficients indicating that one unit of X_1 would now replace $\tfrac{2}{3}$ of a unit of X_2 and $\tfrac{4}{3}$ of a unit of X_4. Since we are making a profit of $7 and $0 per unit of X_2 and X_4 respectively, the **opportunity cost** of introducing a unit of X_1 is:

$$Z_1 = \tfrac{2}{3} \times 7 + \tfrac{4}{3} \times 0 = \tfrac{14}{3}$$

In other words, it would cost us $\tfrac{14}{3}$ dollars to inject one unit of X_1 into the solution. But since X_1 has a profit of $6, the *net* profit from one unit of X_1 is $C_1 - Z_1 = 6 - \tfrac{14}{3} = \tfrac{4}{3}$.

The Z_j's for the other columns are calculated similarly:

$$Z_3 = 7(\tfrac{1}{3}) + 0(-\tfrac{1}{3}) = \tfrac{7}{3}$$
$$Z_4 = 7(0) \; + 0(1) \qquad = 0$$
$$Z_2 = 7(1) \; + 0(0) \qquad = 7$$

Table 12–6　　Second Solution

C_j			0	0	6	7
	Solution Variables	*Solution Values*	X_3	X_4	X_1	X_2
7	X_2	8	$\tfrac{1}{3}$	0	$\tfrac{2}{3}$	1
0	X_4	8	$-\tfrac{1}{3}$	1	$\tfrac{4}{3}$	0
	Z_j	56	$\tfrac{7}{3}$	0	$\tfrac{14}{3}$	7
	$C_j - Z_j$		$-\tfrac{7}{3}$	0	$\tfrac{4}{3}$	0

Finally, $Z_0 = 7(8) + 0(8) = 56$. This is the profit associated with the current (second) solution. It is an improvement over the previous solution.

Calculating the $C_j - Z_j$'s Once the Z_j values have been determined, the $C_j - Z_j$'s can be calculated next by subtracting the Z_j's from the C_j values at the top of the table. For example, in Table 12–6, in the X_1 column, C_1 is 6, Z_1 is $14/3$, and $C_1 - Z_1 = 6 - 14/3 = 4/3$. A positive $C_j - Z_j$ indicates that some amount of the given variable can profitably be included in the solution; a negative value indicates that the inclusion of the variable will reduce profit. Thus, we can further improve our solution by adding product A (i.e., X_1), increasing our profit by $4/3$ = $1.33 for each unit added.

There is an alternative method for calculating the $C_j - Z_j$ values directly, without first calculating the Z_j's. Recall that the $C_j - Z_j$ row in the table represents the profit equation, just as the other rows in the table represent constraint equations. Now, the same operations used on the other rows can be used on the $C_j - Z_j$ row. Table 12–7 is the second solution before the new Z_j and $C_j - Z_j$ rows have been calculated.

We would like to make the $C_2 - Z_2$ coefficient (circled number in Table 12–7) equal zero. The process of doing this is shown in Table 12–8; it is similar to the computations performed in Table 12–5.

Note that these are exactly the same values as each $C_j - Z_j$ obtained earlier. If there are many constraints, this method requires less effort than first calculating the Z_j's.

Table 12–7   Second Solution with Old Bottom Row

	C_j		0	0	6	7
	Solution Variables	Solution Values	X_3	X_4	X_1	X_2
7	X_2 (new)	8	$1/3$	0	$2/3$	1
0	X_4 (new)	8	$-1/3$	1	$4/3$	0
	$C_j - Z_j$ (old)		0	0	6	⑦

Table 12–8

Old $C_j - Z_j$ Row	−	Element in Old $C_j - Z_j$ Row and X_2 Column	·	New X_2 Row	=	Values of New $C_j - Z_j$ Row
0	−	(7)	·	($1/3$)	=	$-7/3$
0	−	(7)	·	(0)	=	0
6	−	(7)	·	($2/3$)	=	$4/3$
7	−	(7)	·	(1)	=	0

The Third Solution

The third solution is computed as follows:

1. Entering Variable The largest positive coefficient in the $C_j - Z_j$ row in Table 12–9 is $4/3$, associated with the X_1 column. Hence, X_1 is the entering variable. Each unit of X_1 will increase profit by \$1.33.

2. Leaving Variable This is determined as follows:

$$\text{For } X_2 \text{ row: } \frac{8}{2/3} = 12$$

$$\text{For } X_4 \text{ row: } \frac{8}{4/3} = 6$$

Each amount in the "Solution values" column is divided by the amount in the comparable row of the X_1 column. The 6 is the smaller amount and is from the X_4 row; thus, X_4 is the leaving variable.

The entering variable (X_1) and the leaving variable (X_4) are indicated by arrows in Table 12–9.

3. Re-solving The pivot element in the X_1 column, X_4 row (circled in Table 12–9) has a value of $4/3$. To convert this to 1, the old X_4 row is divided by $4/3$:

$$\frac{8}{4/3} = 6$$

$$\frac{-1/3}{4/3} = -1/4$$

$$\frac{1}{4/3} = 3/4$$

$$\frac{4/3}{4/3} = 1$$

$$\frac{0}{4/3} = 0$$

Table 12–9   **Second Solution**

	C_j			*0*	*0*	*6*	*7*
		Solution Variables	*Solution Values*	X_3	X_4	X_1	X_2
7		X_2	8	$1/3$	0	$2/3$	1
0	→	X_4	8	$-1/3$	1	$(4/3)$	0
		Z_j	56	$7/3$	0	$14/3$	7
		$C_j - Z_j$		$-7/3$	0	$4/3$	0

↑

The new X_1 row is $(6, -\frac{1}{4}, \frac{3}{4}, 1, 0)$ and is shown in Table 12–10.

The next step is to convert the circled value in Table 12–10 to zero. To do this, the new X_1 row is multiplied by $\frac{2}{3}$ and subtracted from the old X_2 row as shown in Table 12–11. The new X_2 row is $(4, \frac{1}{2}, -\frac{1}{2}, 0, 1)$, inserted in Table 12–12.

The computation of the Z_j's of Table 12–12 is as follows:

$$
\begin{array}{lllllll}
Z_0 &=& 7 & (4) &+& 6 & (6) &=& 64 \\
Z_3 &=& 7 & (\frac{1}{2}) &+& 6 & (-\frac{1}{4}) &=& 2 \\
Z_4 &=& 7 & (-\frac{1}{2}) &+& 6 & (\frac{3}{4}) &=& 1 \\
Z_1 &=& 7 & (0) &+& 6 & (1) &=& 6 \\
Z_2 &=& 7 & (1) &+& 6 & (0) &=& 7 \\
\end{array}
$$

The $C_j - Z_j$ values can be computed directly from these Z_j values. For illustrative purposes, we have also calculated them using the alternative method. These calculations are shown in Table 12–13. These values are identical to the values presented in Table 12–12.

Check for Optimality

Examine the $C_j - Z_j$ row in Table 12–12. All of the coefficients are either zero or negative, indicating that no variable can further increase profits if entered in

Table 12–10   Third Solution—Partially Complete

C_j			0	0	6	7
	Solution Variables	Solution Values	X_3	X_4	X_1	X_2
7	X_2 (old)	8	$\frac{1}{3}$	0	(②/₃)	1
6	X_1 (new)	6	$-\frac{1}{4}$	$\frac{3}{4}$	1	0
	Z_j					
	$C_j - Z_j$					

Table 12–11

Old X_2 Row	$-$	(Element in Old X_2 Row and X_1 Column	$\cdot$	New X_1 Row)	$=$	Values of New X_2 Row
8	$-$	$(\frac{2}{3})$	$\cdot$	(6)	$=$	4
$\frac{1}{3}$	$-$	$(\frac{2}{3})$	$\cdot$	$(-\frac{1}{4})$	$=$	$\frac{1}{2}$
0	$-$	$(\frac{2}{3})$	$\cdot$	$(\frac{3}{4})$	$=$	$-\frac{1}{2}$
$\frac{2}{3}$	$-$	$(\frac{2}{3})$	$\cdot$	(1)	$=$	0
1	$-$	$(\frac{2}{3})$	$\cdot$	(0)	$=$	1

Table 12–12   **Third Solution**

C_j			0	0	6	7
	Solution Variables	*Solution Values*	X_3	X_4	X_1	X_2
7	X_2	4	$\frac{1}{2}$	$-\frac{1}{2}$	0	1
6	X_1	6	$-\frac{1}{4}$	$\frac{3}{4}$	1	0
	Z_j	64	2	1	6	7
	$C_j - Z_j$		-2	-1	0	0

Table 12–13   **Calculation of $C_j - Z_j$ Row Using Alternative Method**

$\begin{array}{c}Old\\C_j - Z_j\,Row\end{array}$	$-$	$\left(\begin{array}{c}Element\ in\ Old\\C_j - Z_j\,Row\\and\ X_1\,Column\end{array}\right.$	$\cdot$	$\left.\begin{array}{c}New\\X_1\,Row\end{array}\right)$	$=$	$\begin{array}{c}Values\ of\ New\\C_j - Z_j\,Row\end{array}$
$-\frac{7}{3}$	$-$	$(\frac{4}{3})$	$\cdot$	$(-\frac{1}{4})$	$=$	-2
0	$-$	$(\frac{4}{3})$	$\cdot$	$(\frac{3}{4})$	$=$	-1
$\frac{4}{3}$	$-$	$(\frac{4}{3})$	$\cdot$	(1)	$=$	0
0	$-$	$(\frac{4}{3})$	$\cdot$	(0)	$=$	0

the solution. Hence, an optimal solution has been obtained. The optimal strategy is to produce four units of B and six units of A (that is, $X_1 = 6$, $X_2 = 4$ as seen in Table 12–12); this will result in $64 of profit. From the profit equation, we obtain:

$$P = \$6X_1 + \$7X_2 + 0X_3 + 0X_4 = (\$6 \cdot 6) + (\$7 \cdot 4) = \$64$$

The constraint equations are satisfied:

$$2X_1 + 3X_2 \le 24$$
$$12 + 12 \le 24$$

$$2X_1 + X_2 \le 16$$
$$12 + 4 \le 16$$

It should be noted that in this problem, we were maximizing an amount (profit) subject to constraints, all of which were in the form of a sum of variables equal to or less than a constant. This is important, since certain steps in the solution process will be modified as we change the description of the problem.

Example 2: Minimization of Costs   This example will differ from the previous example in several respects:

1. An amount is being minimized (rather than maximized).
2. There are three constraints—one equality and two inequalities.

Note that one of the inequalities is in the form of the variable being equal to *or greater than* a constant.

Situation The final product has a requirement that it must weigh exactly 150 pounds. The two raw materials used are A, with a cost of $2 per unit, and B, with a cost of $8 per unit. At least 14 units of B and no more than 20 units of A must be used. Each unit of A weighs 5 pounds; each unit of B weighs 10 pounds.

Problem How much of each type of raw material should be used for each unit of final product if we wish to minimize cost?

Formulation The first step is to formulate the problem by defining variables and specifying the objective function and the constraints. Let:

X_1 = Number of units of product A

X_2 = Number of units of product B

In the previous example, the objective function was the profit equation. In this example, it is the cost equation:

$$C = 2X_1 + 8X_2$$

Instead of finding the combination of X_1 and X_2 that minimizes the function $2X_1 + 8X_2$, we could solve the problem of maximizing $P = -2X_1 - 8X_2$. Both solutions would be the same, but to illustrate the procedure, we shall solve the minimization problem.

We must also set up the equations that establish the constraints. There are three (not counting non-negativity constraints):

$$5X_1 + 10X_2 = 150 \quad \text{(the total weight must be equal to 150 pounds)}$$
$$X_1 \leq 20 \quad \text{(no more than 20 units of A may be used)}$$
$$X_2 \geq 14 \quad \text{(at least 14 units of B must be used)}$$
$$X_1 \geq 0 \quad \text{(the amount of A used cannot be negative)}$$

Graphic Analysis To strengthen our understanding of the problem, we shall briefly illustrate again the graphic approach (see Figure 12–1).

Since the equation $5X_1 + 10X_2 = 150$ must be satisfied exactly, the solution must lie on the line *DEF*. And since the solution must satisfy the constraints $X_1 \geq 0$ and $X_2 \geq 14$, we can eliminate all but the line segment *DE*. Actually, we need examine only the points *D* and *E*, since the optimum must be a corner point. Note that the constraint $X_1 \leq 20$ is not binding; that is, it does not influence our choice of the optimum. The restrictions of the other constraints make the $X_1 \leq 20$ constraint unnecessary.

The objective function $C = 2X_1 + 8X_2 = 120$ is also known in Figure 12–1. This is not the optimum, since we can move the $C = 120$ line down to the left and decrease cost. The least cost will be reached at $C = 116$, which goes through the optimum point E $(X_1 = 2, X_2 = 14)$.

We shall now solve the same problem with the simplex procedure.

Figure 12–1

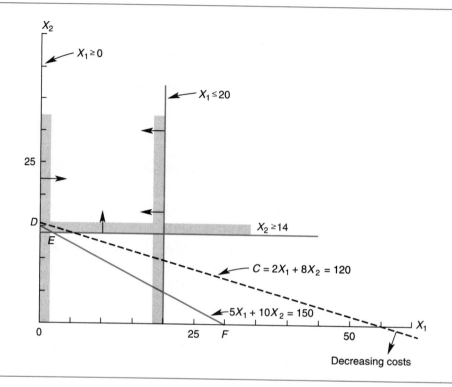

Algebraic Formulation　As in the previous example, the first step is to convert the inequality constraints to equations. For the constraint $X_1 \leq 20$, a slack variable—X_4, the unused amount of A—can be added. For the constraint $X_2 \geq 14$, a variable X_5, representing the excess or **surplus** amount of B, is added to the right side of the constraint, making $X_2 = 14 + X_5$. The other constraint is already in equation form.

The equations are thus:

$$
\begin{array}{rcl}
5X_1 + 10X_2 & = & 150 \\
X_1 \qquad\quad + X_4 & = & 20 \\
X_2 \qquad - X_5 & = & 14
\end{array}
$$

In the previous example we were able to find the first basic feasible solution by selecting the slack variables as the initial solution variables. This is not possible in this example, since there is no slack variable in the first constraint, and the sign of the surplus variable in the third constraint is negative.

To deal with this problem, **artificial** variables X_3 and X_6 are added to the first and third constraints, respectively. These artificial variables may be interpreted as the amounts by which the constraints are violated. Since we do not want to violate the constraints, we will attach a very large cost (or negative profit) to the artificial variables in the objective function. This will guarantee that they will be outside variables (and hence have value zero) in the final solution.

With the addition of the artificial variables, the constraints may now be expressed as:

$$
\begin{aligned}
5X_1 + 10X_2 + X_3 &= 150 \\
X_1 \qquad\qquad + X_4 &= 20 \\
X_2 \qquad\qquad - X_5 + X_6 &= 14
\end{aligned}
$$

The new cost function is:

$$C = 2X_1 + 8X_2 + MX_3 + 0X_4 + 0X_5 + MX_6$$

where M is a very large number.

To understand better the simplex table that follows (Table 12–14), we shall expand the constraint equations by adding Xs with zero coefficients to each constraint equation so that each equation has all the variables X_1 through X_6:

$$
\begin{aligned}
5X_1 + 10X_2 + 1X_3 + 0X_4 + 0X_5 + 0X_6 &= 150 \\
1X_1 + 0X_2 + 0X_3 + 1X_4 + 0X_5 + 0X_6 &= 20 \\
0X_1 + 1X_2 + 0X_3 + 0X_4 - 1X_5 + 1X_6 &= 14
\end{aligned}
$$

The first simplex table in this example (Table 12–14) is constructed from the coefficients of the variables of the constraint equations, the constants (150, 20, 14 in the "Solution values" column), and the cost coefficients of the cost equation.

Note that the calculation of the Z_j and then the $C_j - Z_j$ results in a bottom row that is somewhat different from the original objective function. This results from the inclusion of the artificial variables.

The first basic solution consists of the slack variable X_4 for the less-than-or-equals constraint and the artificial variables X_3 and X_6 for the equality and

Table 12–14   First Solution

C_j	Solution Variables	Solution Values	M X_3	0 X_4	M X_6	2 X_1	8 X_2	0 X_5
M	X_3	150	1	0	0	5	10	0
0	X_4	20	0	1	0	1	0	0
M	$\rightarrow X_2$	14	0	0	1	0	1	-1
	Z_j	$164M$	M	0	M	$5M$	$11M$	$-M$
	$C_j - Z_j$		0	0	0	$2 - 5M$	$8 - 11M$	M

$\uparrow$

greater-than-or-equals constraints. Each of these variables has a coefficient of 1 in one row and 0 in the other rows (check the X_3, X_4, and X_6 columns).

Entering Variable Since we are minimizing cost in this example, the variable with the most *negative* value in the $C_j - Z_j$ row is chosen as the entering variable. This is the variable that will reduce cost by the largest amount per unit. Variable X_2 wins this contest, since $8 - 11M$ is the most negative value (M is very large).

Leaving Variable The leaving variable is determined as in the first example, by calculating the ratio of the values in the "Solution Values" column to the coefficients in the entering variable column, and selecting the smallest nonnegative ratio. The leaving variable is X_6, since $14/1$ is less than $150/10$, and $20/0$ is not mathematically defined.

Re-solving The re-solving procedure is also exactly as illustrated in the first example.

1. Since there is already a 1 in the X_2 column of the old X_6 row, the pivot element is already 1, and nothing further has to be done to this row except to change its name to X_2.

2. The computations for the other rows and for the objective function are shown below. The second simplex table is Table 12–15.

X_3 Row	X_4 Row	$C_j - Z_j$ Row
$150 - (10) \cdot 14 = 10$	$20 - (0) \cdot 14 = 20$	
$1 - (10) \cdot 0 = 1$	$0 - (0) \cdot 0 = 0$	$0 \quad - (8 - 11M) \cdot 0 = 0$
$0 - (10) \cdot 0 = 0$	$1 - (0) \cdot 0 = 1$	$0 \quad - (8 - 11M) \cdot 0 = 0$
$0 - (10) \cdot 1 = -10$	$0 - (0) \cdot 1 = 0$	$0 \quad - (8 - 11M) \cdot 1 = -8 + 11M$
$5 - (10) \cdot 0 = 5$	$1 - (0) \cdot 0 = 1$	$2 - 5M \quad - (8 - 11M) \cdot 0 = 2 - 5M$
$10 - (10) \cdot 1 = 0$	$0 - (0) \cdot 1 = 0$	$8 - 11M \quad - (8 - 11M) \cdot 1 = 0$
$0 - (10) \cdot (-1) = 10$	$0 - (0) \cdot (-1) = 0$	$M \quad - (8 - 11M) \cdot (-1) = 8 - 10M$

Table 12–15   **Second Solution**

C_j			M	0	M	2	8	0
	Solution Variables	*Solution Values*	X_3	X_4	X_6	X_1	X_2	X_5
M	$\rightarrow X_3$	10	1	0	-10	5	0	⑩
0	X_4	20	0	1	0	1	0	0
8	X_2	14	0	0	1	0	1	-1
	Z_j	$112 + 10M$	M	0	$8 - 10M$	$5M$	8	$-8 + 10M$
	$C_j - Z_j$		0	0	$11M - 8$	$2 - 5M$	0	$8 - 10M$

$\uparrow$

Table 12–16   Third Solution*

C_j			M	0	M	2	8	0
	Solution Variables	Solution Values	X_3	X_4	X_6	X_1	X_2	X_5
0	→X_5	1	$\frac{1}{10}$	0	-1	$\frac{1}{2}$	0	1
0	X_4	20	0	1	0	1	0	0
8	X_2	15	$\frac{1}{10}$	0	0	$\frac{1}{2}$	1	0
	Z_j	120	$\frac{8}{10}$	0	0	4	8	0
	$C_j - Z_j$		$M - \frac{8}{10}$	0	M	-2	0	0

$\uparrow$

*Note that at this point, the artificial variables X_3 and X_6 are no longer in the solution. They could be eliminated in future tables.

Further Iterations The largest negative $(C_j - Z_j)$ column of Table 12–15 is X_5 (the $-10M$ is very large), and the leaving variable is X_3 ($\frac{10}{10}$ is chosen, since $\frac{20}{0}$ is not mathematically defined, and $\frac{14}{-1}$ is not eligible, since the ratio is negative).[2]

Table 12–16 is the third simplex table of this example. The new X_5 row is computed by dividing the old X_3 row by 10, the circled value in the X_5 column and X_3 row of Table 12–15. Computations of the X_4 row, the X_2 row, and the $C_j - Z_j$ row follow.

X_4 Row	X_2 Row	$C_j - Z_j$ Row
$20 - (0) \cdot \quad 1 = 20$	$14 - (-1) \cdot \quad 1 = 15$	
$0 - (0) \cdot \quad \frac{1}{10} = 0$	$0 - (-1) \cdot \quad \frac{1}{10} = \frac{1}{10}$	$0 \quad - (8 - 10M) \cdot \quad \frac{1}{10} = M - \frac{8}{10}$
$1 - (0) \cdot \quad 0 = 1$	$0 - (-1) \cdot \quad 0 = 0$	$0 \quad - (8 - 10M) \cdot \quad 0 = 0$
$0 - (0) \cdot (-1) = 0$	$1 - (-1) \cdot (-1) = 0$	$11M - 8 - (8 - 10M) \cdot (-1) = M$
$1 - (0) \cdot \quad \frac{1}{2} = 1$	$0 - (-1) \cdot \quad \frac{1}{2} = \frac{1}{2}$	$2 - 5M - (8 - 10M) \cdot \quad \frac{1}{2} = -2$
$0 - (0) \cdot \quad 0 = 0$	$1 - (-1) \cdot \quad 0 = 1$	$0 \quad - (8 - 10M) \cdot \quad 0 = 0$
$0 - (0) \cdot \quad 1 = 0$	$-1 - (-1) \cdot \quad 1 = 0$	$8 - 10M - (8 - 10M) \cdot \quad 1 = 0$

The largest negative $(C_j - Z_j)$ column of Table 12–16 is X_1 (X_3 is not negative, since M is very large). The leaving variable is X_5.

Table 12–17 is the fourth simplex table of this example. The new X_1 row is $(2, \frac{2}{10}, 0, -2, 1, 0, 2)$; that is, 2 times the old X_5 row. Computations of the X_4, X_2, and $C_j - Z_j$ rows follow.

[2]At this point, it would save several steps if we replaced row X_3 with variable X_1. The total saving from using X_1 is greater than the total saving from using X_5, but the simplex method bases its choice of entering variable on unit costs. Without working the problem, we do not know that X_1 is a better choice; thus, the use of the simplex method always leads to the correct solution, but not always via the shortest route.

Table 12–17 Fourth Solution

C_j	Solution Variables	Solution Values	M X_3	0 X_4	M X_6	2 X_1	8 X_2	0 X_5
2	X_1	2	$\frac{2}{10}$	0	-2	1	0	2
0	X_4	18	$-\frac{1}{5}$	1	2	0	0	-2
8	X_2	14	0	0	1	0	1	-1
	Z_j	116	$\frac{4}{10}$	0	4	2	8	-4
	$C_j - Z_j$		$M - \frac{4}{10}$	0	$M - 4$	0	0	4

X_4 Row	X_2 Row	$C_j - Z_j$ Row
$20 - (1) \cdot \quad 2 = \quad 18$	$15 - (\frac{1}{2}) \cdot \quad 2 = \quad 14$	
$0 - (1) \cdot \quad \frac{2}{10} = \quad -\frac{1}{5}$	$\frac{1}{10} - (\frac{1}{2}) \cdot \quad \frac{2}{10} = \quad 0$	$M - \frac{8}{10} - (-2) \cdot \quad \frac{2}{10} = M - \frac{4}{10}$
$1 - (1) \cdot \quad 0 = \quad 1$	$0 - (\frac{1}{2}) \cdot \quad 0 = \quad 0$	$0 \qquad - (-2) \cdot \quad 0 = 0$
$0 - (1) \cdot (-2) = \quad 2$	$0 - (\frac{1}{2}) \cdot (-2) = \quad 1$	$M \qquad - (-2) \cdot (-2) = M - 4$
$1 - (1) \cdot \quad 1 = \quad 0$	$\frac{1}{2} - (\frac{1}{2}) \cdot \quad 1 = \quad 0$	$-2 \qquad - (-2) \cdot \quad 1 = 0$
$0 - (1) \cdot \quad 0 = \quad 0$	$1 - (\frac{1}{2}) \cdot \quad 0 = \quad 1$	$0 \qquad - (-2) \cdot \quad 0 = 0$
$0 - (1) \cdot \quad 2 = \quad -2$	$0 - (\frac{1}{2}) \cdot \quad 2 = \quad -1$	$0 \qquad - (-2) \cdot \quad 2 = 4$

With Table 12–17, we have reached an optimum solution, since all of the values in the $C_j - Z_j$ row are positive or zero.

The optimum solution is to use 2 units (or 10 pounds) of A and 14 units (or 140 pounds) of B. This combination leads to a cost of $116, which is the least-cost combination of raw material consistent with the constraints. The end product weighs 150 pounds; there are two units of $X_1 \le 20$, 14 units of $X_2 \ge 14$; thus, the constraints are satisfied. Although we easily solved this problem earlier by graphic analysis, with a more complicated version of the problem (for example, 30 raw materials and 20 constraints), we would have to use the computerized simplex method to obtain an optimum solution.

SUMMARY

Summary of simplex procedure:

1. Modify the constraints:

Add a slack variable for each less-than-or-equal constraint.
Add an artificial variable for each equality constraint.
Add both an artificial and a surplus variable for each greater-than-or-equal constraint.
For each artificial variable, assign a very large cost (negative profit) in the objective function.

2. Identify the initial solution as composed of the slack and artificial variables.
3. Check for optimality. The current solution is optimal if:

For maximization, all coefficients in the $C_j - Z_j$ row are zero or negative.
For minimization, all coefficients in $C_j - Z_j$ row are zero or positive.
If optimum has been reached, stop simplex procedure.

4. Entering variable. This is the variable associated with the largest positive (for maximization) or largest negative (for minimization) coefficient in the $C_j - Z_j$ row.
5. Leaving variable. For each row, calculate the ratio of the values in the "Solution Values" column divided by the coefficients in the entering variable column. Ignore any ratios that are negative. The leaving variable is the one associated with the row having the smallest ratio.
6. Re-solve the equation as follows:
   a. Identify the pivot element as the coefficient in the entering variable column and leaving variable row.
   b. Divide all the coefficients in the leaving variable row by the pivot element.
   c. Modify the other rows, possibly including the objective function row, as:

$$\binom{\text{New}}{\text{row}} = \binom{\text{Old}}{\text{row}} - \binom{\text{Coefficient in entering}}{\text{variable column of row}} \cdot \binom{\text{Row obtained}}{\text{in step } 6(b)}$$

7.*Calculate the Z_j's. For the jth column: for each row, multiply the substitution coefficients by the C_j value for that row and sum. The total is Z_j. Repeat for all columns.
8.*Calculate the $C_j - Z_j$'s. Subtract the Z_j values from the original objective function coefficients (C_j's) at the top of the table.
9. Return to step 3.

Special Situations

We now illustrate some unusual situations that can sometimes be confusing. Each situation will be presented through an example.

Example 3: A Problem with an Unbounded Solution   In certain situations, it is possible that the linear programming problem does not have a finite solution. For example, assume that the third simplex table (Table 12–16), when developed in Example 2, appeared as shown in Table 12–18.

Variable X_1 is the entering variable. Column X_1 has been changed so that not only is $(C_j - Z_j)$ negative (as it was in Table 12–16) but all coefficients in the X_1 column are negative. In this situation, there is no finite optimum solution. If profit was being maximized, an analogous situation would occur if the $(C_j - Z_j)$ total were positive and all coefficients in the column were negative.

---

*These steps need not be done if the $C_j - Z_j$ row was calculated in step 6(c).

Table 12–18   Table 12–16 Modified

C_j	Solution Variables	Solution Values	M X_3	0 X_4	M X_6	-16 X_1	8 X_2	0 X_5
0	X_5	1	$\frac{1}{10}$	0	-1	$-\frac{1}{2}$	0	1
0	X_4	20	0	1	0	-1	0	0
8	X_2	15	$\frac{1}{10}$	0	0	$-\frac{1}{2}$	1	0
	Z_j	120	$\frac{8}{10}$	0	0	-4	8	0
	$C_j - Z_j$		$M - \frac{8}{10}$	0	M	-12	0	0

In Table 12–18 the negative $(C_j - Z_j)$ indicates that $12 of costs are saved for every unit of X_1 injected into the solution. However, the negative coefficients of $-\frac{1}{2}$, -1, and $-\frac{1}{2}$ indicate that for every unit of X_1 injected into the solution, say as a substitute for X_5, the ability to inject additional units will be increased. Thus, the desirable action would be to keep adding units of X_1. The more X_1 we use, the lower the costs; the problem does not have a finite optimum solution, since it contains no restriction on X_1.

If the above situation develops, the cause will frequently be a misstated constraint or incorrect data. Business situations properly described will not usually result in an unbounded solution as illustrated above.

Example 4:
Multiple
Solutions
There may be more than one optimal solution to a linear programming problem. In this case, two (or more) basic solutions[3] will have the same optimum profit (or cost).

Let us again modify the problem in Example 2 to illustrate this. Suppose that the cost of raw material A is $4 per unit rather than $2. Then Table 12–16 (with this modification and leaving out the artificial variables X_3 and X_6) would appear as Table 12–19.

No $C_j - Z_j$ value is negative, indicating an optimum has been reached. Note, however, that variable X_1 is not a solution variable and $C_1 - Z_1 = 0$. This indicates that variable X_1 can be brought into the solution without increasing or decreasing the cost. If variable X_1 is brought into the solution, the result is the same as that shown in Table 12–17 (except that total cost is $120, since X_1 now costs $4 per unit). The two solutions are:

	Solution 1	Solution 2
Raw material A	0	2
Raw material B	15	14
Total cost	$120	$120

---

[3]Also, any convex combination of these corner points is an optimum solution.

Table 12–19   Second Modification of Table 12–16

C_j	Solution Variables	Solution Values	0 X_4	4 X_1	8 X_2	0 X_5
0	X_5	1	0	½	0	1
0	X_4	20	1	1	0	0
8	X_2	15	0	½	1	0
	Z_j	120	0	4	8	0
	$C_j - Z_j$		0	0	0	0

Degeneracy

Recall that a basic solution to a linear programming problem with m constraints involves selecting m solution variables and then setting the remaining variables equal to zero. In general, when the equations are solved, the selected solution variables will have positive (nonzero) values. However, one or more of the solution variables may turn out to be zero. Such a situation is degenerate. There is **degeneracy** when there are fewer than m nonzero solution variables for m constraint equations. It is an indication that one or more of the constraint equations is redundant for the given solution.

Degeneracy results when two or more variables are tied in the selection of the leaving variable during the simplex procedure. Degeneracy is a potential problem, because it is theoretically possible for the simplex procedure to cycle back to former solutions and never reach the optimum. In actual practice, this cycling rarely occurs, and computer programs generally have no difficulty reaching the optimum even when degeneracy occurs. In doing the simplex by hand, when a tie occurs in the leaving variable, pick one arbitrarily. If cycling occurs and a solution reappears in the tables, then go back to where the tie occurred and select one of the other tied variables.

Degeneracy also causes some problems in interpretation of linear programming results. (See Chapter 11, Appendix, for further discussion.)

Example 5: No Feasible Solution   It is possible for the constraint equations to be inconsistent with any feasible solution. For example, suppose we had:

$$4X_1 + 2X_2 \leq 10$$
$$X_2 \geq 6$$
$$X_1 \geq 0$$

There are no values of X_1 and X_2 that will satisfy these three conditions.

In this example, the constraints are obviously contradictory, and it is easy to see that there is no feasible solution. In a more complicated problem, it may not be so obvious.

The lack of a feasible solution can be detected in the simplex table. At some point in the procedure, a solution occurs that would appear to be optimal (all the coefficients in the $C_j - Z_j$ row are nonpositive if maximizing, or nonnegative if minimizing). However, one of the solution variables is an artificial variable. Computer programs would stop at this point with a message that no feasible solution exists.

In a business situation, the lack of a feasible solution generally indicates an error in formulating the problem or in entering the data. If you are working some of the exercises in this book on a computer and you encounter the "no feasible solution" message, you should recheck your formulation and your data.

SUMMARY

Some special situations encountered in solving linear programming problems are:

- Unbounded solutions, where there is no limit on some entering variable, and hence there is unbounded profitability.
- No feasible solution, when constraints are so restrictive that there is no way of satisfying them.

Both of these can be detected during the simplex procedure. Both generally result from improper formulation of the problem or incorrect data.

Multiple solutions to linear programming problems are possible. This is indicated when one of the outside variables has a $C_j - Z_j$ value of zero in the optimal solution.

Degeneracy occurs when one or more of the solution variables equals zero.

Sensitivity Analysis

Linear programming models provide the manager not just with the optimal solution, but also with a variety of information that can provide additional economic insight about the problem being solved. This analysis is called **sensitivity analysis** and was discussed in some detail in Chapter 11. We return to it here to show how the information is derived from the simplex procedure.

Economic Interpretation of the $C_j - Z_j$ Values

First, consider the economic interpretation of the $C_j - Z_j$ values, the bottom row of the simplex table. Recall that Z_j is the opportunity cost of introducing one unit of variable j into the solution—the cost of replacing or substituting for other solution variables. Since C_j is the unit profit, the $C_j - Z_j$ value is the net profit (profit minus opportunity cost) resulting from introducing one unit of j into the solution.

As an illustration, let us return to Example 1 of this chapter, a problem with two products and constraints on the available time on two machines. The final tableau is given in Table 12–12, and is reproduced as Table 12–20. First, consider

Table 12–20 Final Tableau for Example 1

C_j	Solution Variables	Solution Values	0 X_3	0 X_4	6 X_1	7 X_2
7	X_2	4	½	$-$½	0	1
6	X_1	6	$-$¼	¾	1	0
	Z_j	64	2	1	6	7
	$C_j - Z_j$		-2	-1	0	0

the $C_j - Z_j$ value associated with a *slack variable*, such as variable X_3 in Table 12–20. Variable X_3 is the slack variable associated with the first constraint, the limit on time available for machine 1. In the optimal solution in Table 12–20, $C_3 - Z_3$ has a value of -2, meaning that introducing one unit of X_3 (i.e., one hour of slack time) into the solution will decrease profit by \$2. Note that introducing one unit of slack into the solution is effectively the same as reducing the capacity of machine 1 by one hour. Hence, the $C_j - Z_j$ values for slack variables associated with constraints can be considered as the *marginal values* associated with changes in capacity on that constraint. In the last chapter, we called these marginal values **dual prices.** Note that indeed the $C_j - Z_j$ values in Table 12–20 are (except for sign) exactly the dual prices developed both graphically and in the computer output in Chapter 11.[4]

When a decision variable is not included in the optimal solution, the $C_j - Z_j$ value represents the cost of forcing one unit into the solution. The term **reduced cost** was introduced in Chapter 11 to designate this cost.

Right-Hand Side Ranges

The interpretation of the dual price of X_3 in Table 12–20 is that one additional hour of machine time on machine 1 would be worth \$2. We might ask the following question: If we could buy additional hours of machine 1 time for less than \$2, could we increase our profit indefinitely by adding more hours?

We can answer this question by examining the X_3 column in Table 12–20. Recall the meaning of the coefficients in the table; if we were to introduce one unit of X_3, it would replace ½ unit of X_2 and $-$¼ unit of X_1 (i.e., it would actually add ¼ unit of X_1).

The question posed above, then, can be answered by considering how much X_3 can change before a change in the solution mix will occur.

---

[4]The graphic analysis and computer solution in Chapter 11 were performed on a modified version of Example 1, in which an additional constraint on the demand for product B was included. Hence, the sensitivity analysis results obtained in this section are not entirely comparable.

If we enter *positive* X_3 into the solution, the interpretation is that additional *slack* hours are made available on machine 1—and thus, those hours to be used for production are *reduced*. In the table, the process of introducing X_3 is the same as doing an iteration in the simplex procedure with X_3 as the entering variable. We divide the "Solution values" column by the amount in the comparable row of the X_3 column. The smallest nonnegative number thus obtained gives the number of units of X_3 that can enter. In our example:

	Solution Values	X_3	$\left(\dfrac{Solution\ Values}{X_3}\right)$
X_2	4	$\frac{1}{2}$	8
X_1	6	$-\frac{1}{4}$	-24

Here, the X_2 row is the only positive value and hence is also the smallest nonnegative value. This means that eight units of X_3 can be introduced before variable X_2 goes out of the solution. In terms of the problem, this means that we can cut back on a maximum of eight hours of those available on machine 1 before production of A stops.

We can also consider adding *negative* X_3. This means that we make additional hours available on machine 1. In order to consider introducing negative X_3 into our table, we can proceed as above, except that we must multiply all the values in the X_3 column by -1 before going to the next step in the simplex procedure. Thus, we would have:

	Solution Values	$(-1)X_3$	$\left(\dfrac{Solution\ Values}{(-1)X_3}\right)$
X_2	4	$-\frac{1}{2}$	-8
X_1	6	$\frac{1}{4}$	24

As before, the smallest nonnegative value determines how many units of negative X_3 can be introduced. Here, it is 24; after adding 24 additional hours of time (i.e., negative X_3) on machine 1, variable X_1 goes to zero and out of the solution.

The two steps can be combined into one. Look at the ratios of the "Solution values" column to the slack variable column. The smallest nonnegative ratio determines the amount of decrease; the smallest (in the sense of being closest to zero) nonpositive ratio determines the amount of the increase.[5]

---

[5]For purposes of this rule, a ratio of zero divided by a positive number is considered positive, and zero divided by a negative number is negative.

We have derived a range of values relative to the amount of time available on machine 1. We started out with 24 hours available. Then, we found that we could take away 8 hours before the solution mix changed, or we could add 24 hours before the solution mix changed. Hence, we have a range of 16 to 48 for hours available on machine 1, over which the basic solution mix does not change. Recall that the dual price for a marginal hour of machine 1 time was $2 (the $C_3 - Z_3$ value in Table 12–20). This value holds over the range we have just determined. In short, machine time on machine 1 has a value of $2 per hour over a range of available hours from 16 to 48 (assuming machine 2 hours remain fixed at 16).

Note that 16 to 48 hours is a range within which the solution *mix* remains the same. That is, the *list of solution variables* does not change. The actual solution *values* will change as more or less time is available on machine 1. Also, total profit will change at a rate of $2 per hour (the marginal value for X_3) for increments of machine 1 time.

We can do the same type of analysis on the time available on machine 2. Variable X_4 is the slack variable associated with machine 2. Look at the ratio of the "Solution Values" column to the slack variable column for X_4.

	Solution Values	X_4	$\left(\dfrac{Solution\ Values}{X_4}\right)$
X_2	4	$-\frac{1}{2}$	-8
X_1	6	$\frac{3}{4}$	8

As indicated above, the smallest nonnegative value determines the amount of decrease; the smallest (in the sense of being closest to zero) nonpositive ratio determines the increase. Machine 2 has 16 hours available and both the increase and decrease in this case is 8, or a range from 8 to 24 hours.

A summary of these results is shown in Table 12–21.

In some cases, all of the available capacity of a constraint is not used, and the slack variable will have a positive value in the solution. The dual price in

Table 12–21   **Sensitivity Analysis for First Example—Right-Hand Side Ranges**

Resource	Original Resource Constraint (machine-hours available)	Dual Price	Range over Which Dual Price Is Valid	
			Lower Limit	Upper Limit
Machine 1	24	$2	16	48
Machine 2	16	$1	8	24

such cases is zero—all of the available capacity is not being used, so additional capacity has no value. In that case, there is no upper limit on the range within which the zero dual price holds. But how much could the capacity be reduced before the solution changed? The answer is simple—if there are, for example, eight hours of slack in a given constraint, then capacity can be reduced by this eight hours before the solution is forced to change.

Changes in the Prices

Another major concern to managers is the sensitivity of the linear programming solution to changes in prices; that is, to changes in the per unit profits (or costs) of variables in the objective function.

In the case of variables that are not in the solution, determining this sensitivity is relatively easy. Recall that the Z_j measures the opportunity cost of introducing one unit of the particular variable into the solution. If the variable is not in the optimum solution, it means that its profitability (C_j) is not as great as the opportunity cost Z_j. In other words, $C_j - Z_j$ is negative.[6] To come into the solution, the profit must exceed Z_j. This is the upper limit before a change occurs. On the other hand, since the variable is not currently profitable enough to be in the solution, any decrease in per unit profit will not change its status.

In summary, for a variable not in the optimum solution, the price ranges are:

Lower Limit	Current Value	Upper Limit
No limit	C_j	Z_j

Within these limits, there is no change in the optimal solution.

For variables that are already in the solution, determining the sensitivity to per-unit profit changes is not so simple. The *dual* to a linear programming problem is a complementary problem, the details of which are explained in the appendix to this chapter. The same kind of analysis used to determine the right-hand side ranges can be used on the dual problem to determine the profit coefficient ranges.

Consider variable X_1, which had an original price of $6 and is a solution variable. We divide the coefficients of the $C_j - Z_j$ row in Table 12–20 by the coefficients of the X_1 row. This is the dual problem equivalent of dividing the "Solution values" column by the slack variable column used for right-hand side ranging. Then, the smallest nonnegative ratio obtained determines the amount of the increase in price, and the smallest nonpositive (closest to zero) ratio

---

[6]This is true if we are maximizing. If we are minimizing, then the variable will come into the solution if the cost drops below Z_j.

determines the decrease in price.[7] (Exclude the X_1 column from these calculations.)

	X_3	X_4	X_2
$C_j - Z_j$ row	-2	-1	0
X_1 row	$-\frac{1}{4}$	$\frac{3}{4}$	1
Ratio $(C_j - Z_j)$ row/X_1 row	8	$-\frac{4}{3}$	0

Thus, the possible profit increase is $8 and the decrease is $1.33 for variable X_1. That is, the per unit profit can range from ($6 $-$ $1.33) or $4.67 to ($6 + $8) or $14 without any change in the solution.

A similar analysis can be done for variable X_2. The results are summarized in Table 12–22.

Recall that the solution of this problem called for the production of six units of X_1 and four units of X_2. Table 12–22 indicates that this solution will not change unless the profit from a unit of X_1 drops below $4.67 per unit, or increases to above $14 per unit. Similarly, the solution will not change unless the X_2 profit per unit falls below $3 or increases above $9. Within the ranges specified by the objective function values, both the solution mix and the solution values remain the same. Total profit changes, however, when the unit profits (individual values) change.

The kind of information contained in sensitivity analysis is very valuable to management. The C_j's are usually subject to change from time to time. If a change is within the range determined by the sensitivity analysis, then there is

Table 12–22   **Sensitivity Analysis for First Example—Objective Function Coefficient Ranges**

		Range	
Price	Original Value	Lower Limit	Upper Limit
Price of X_1	$6	$4.67	$14
Price of X_2	7	3	9

---

[7]Note that the association of nonpositive ratio with decrease and nonnegative ratio with increase is the opposite from that used for right-hand side ranging. This is because of the way we have set up the $C_j - Z_j$ row in our tables.

no effect upon the optimum solution. If the change is outside the range, a new solution is needed, and the programming problem must be re-solved.

The linear programming problem is set up as a decision problem under certainty. Few problems in the real world are truly certain. Often, many factors are unknown and must be estimated using the best judgment available. The use of sensitivity analysis helps to show over what ranges the solution is and is not subject to change. As such, it is an important adjunct to the interpretation of the solution of a linear programming problem.

SUMMARY

Sensitivity analysis determines the range over which a given factor may vary without affecting the solution mix or the dual prices. Suppose we are maximizing.

For ranges of the right-hand side constants:

1. Identify the slack variable associated with the given constraint.
2. Divide the "Solution values" column of the final table by the column for the slack variable.
3. The limit on the decrease is the smallest nonnegative ratio determined in (2).
4. The absolute value of the smallest (closest to zero) nonpositive ratio calculated in (2) is the limit on the increase.

For objective function coefficient ranges:
If the variable is a solution variable, then:

1. Identify the row associated with the given variable in the final table. Ignore the column associated with the given variable.
2. Divide the $C_j - Z_j$ row by the row of (1).
3. The smallest nonnegative ratio calculated in (2) is the limit on the increase.
4. The absolute value of the smallest (closest to zero) nonpositive ratio calculated in (2) is the limit on the decrease.

If the variable is not a solution variable, then the limit on the increase is $Z_j - C_j$, and there is no limit on the decrease.

A Comprehensive Example

The previous examples in this chapter have involved only two dimensions. To illustrate the formulation and simplex solution of a linear programming problem in many dimensions, the following example is given.

A manufacturing firm makes equipment that utilizes many components. The assembly and testing of the complete unit are done by the firm; but it does not have enough capacity, technical personnel, nor funds to produce all the components in its own plants. Therefore, it must purchase many components from outside suppliers. Seven such components and their requirements are shown in Table 12–24 on page 374.

From Table 12–24, it can be seen that different parts require different amounts of resources and have different outside purchase costs. The question is: Which, if any, of these parts (and how many of each part) should be manufactured internally, and which should be purchased from outside?

We can express this as a linear programming problem in which we maximize savings from internal manufacture, subject to constraints on capacity, personnel, and funds. Let us suppose we have available the amounts of resources shown in Table 12–23. We can formulate the linear programming problem as follows:

Maximize:
$$P = 50X_1 + 100X_2 + 100X_3 + 50X_4 + 150X_5 + 100X_6 + 60X_7$$

where X_i is the amount of the ith part manufactured internally and the coefficients are the incremental per unit savings (purchase cost minus variable cost).

Subject to:
$$5X_1 + 2X_2 + X_3 + 3X_4 + X_5 + 0X_6 + 2X_7 \le 90$$
$$X_1 + X_2 + 4X_3 + 0X_4 + 5X_5 + 2X_6 + X_7 \le 97$$
$$0X_1 + 0X_2 + 2X_3 + 3X_4 + 2X_5 + 2X_6 + X_7 \le 200$$
$$X_1 + X_2 + 3X_3 + 2X_4 + 2X_5 + 3X_6 + X_7 \le 150$$
$$3X_1 + 5X_2 + X_3 + X_4 + 2X_5 + 2X_6 + 4X_7 \le 250$$

and:

$$X_1 \le 10 \qquad X_5 \le 10$$
$$X_2 \le 5 \qquad X_6 \le 5$$
$$X_3 \le 50 \qquad X_7 \le 20$$
$$X_4 \le 25 \qquad \text{and all} \quad X_j \ge 0, j = 1, 2, \ldots, 7$$

The initial simplex table is given in Table 12–25 including the slack variables X_8 through X_{19}.

Note that there are 12 constraint equations, and so the main part of Table 12–25 has 12 rows. The initial solution is given by using the slack variables. The initial solution indicates that nothing is manufactured internally and all requirements are purchased from outside suppliers. This is, of course, not the optimum, and it produces a saving of zero.

The simplex method can now be applied to Table 12–25. The entering variable is X_5, and the leaving variable is X_{17}. We do not intend to carry this problem through all the steps of the simplex procedure, since we wish merely to illustrate

Table 12–23   Available Resources

Hours of machining	90
Hours of assembly	97
Hours of testing	200
Engineering supervisor hours	150
Discretionary cash	$250

Table 12–24

Part Number	Variable Designation	Hours of Machining Required	Hours of Assembly Required	Hours of Test Required	Engineering Supervision Required	Working Capital Funds Required	Total Number of Units Needed	Price Quoted by Outside Manufacturer	Variable Cost of Materials, Direct Labor, etc.
182	X_1	5	1	0	1	3	10	$100	$ 50
184	X_2	2	1	0	1	5	5	150	50
193	X_3	1	4	2	3	1	50	200	100
197	X_4	3	0	3	2	1	25	100	50
284	X_5	1	5	2	2	2	10	250	100
629	X_6	0	2	2	3	2	5	200	100
845	X_7	2	1	1	1	4	20	100	40

the formulation of the problem. However, the final simplex table is shown as Table 12–26. The solution produces a saving of $4,450. The meanings of the solution variables are shown in Table 12–27.

For the slack variables corresponding to the resource constraints, we have:

Slack Variable		Amount	Meaning
X_8	=	0	All machine hours are used (i.e., slack = 0).
X_9	=	0	All assembly hours are used.
X_{10}	=	117	117 hours of test are not used.
X_{11}	=	63	63 hours of engineering supervision are not used.
X_{12}	=	103	$103 of working capital is not used.

Dual Prices and Reduced Costs

The bottom row $(C_j - Z_j)$ in Table 12–26 lists the dual prices associated with the constraints (i.e., with the slack variables) and the reduced costs associated with the decision variables. The variables X_8 through X_{12} are the slack variables associated with the constraints on resources (hours of capacity, personnel, and funds). When such slack variables have a zero dual price (as do X_{10}, X_{11}, X_{12}), we cannot increase profits by making more of the resources available. The resources are not fully utilized in the optimum solution (e.g., there are $X_{10} = 117$ hours of test unused). On the other hand, the dual prices associated with X_8 and X_9 give the increased profit associated with making one more unit of these resources available. For example, we could increase profits nearly $21 by making one more hour of assembly time available (i.e., $C_9 - Z_9 = -20\frac{5}{6}$). Profits would be decreased $20\frac{5}{6}$ by taking away one unit of assembly time.

The variables X_{13} through X_{19} are the slack variables associated with upper limits on production requirements. The dual prices refer to additional savings (from internal manufacture) if requirements are increased by one unit. If, for example, one more unit of part 284 (X_5) were required, the savings from internal manufacture would increase by $29.16 (the slack variable for requirements of part 284 is X_{17}, and $C_{17} - Z_{17} = -29\frac{1}{6}$). Conversely, if only 9 units of part 284 were needed instead of 10, then the savings from internal manufacture would decrease by $29.16. If all requirements for a part are not manufactured internally, then if the needs for this part were increased, this would merely increase the number of units purchased outside the firm, without affecting the savings from internal manufacture. In like manner, the needs for a part could decrease without the change affecting the savings (the number purchased outside the firm would simply decrease). In the example, X_4, part 197, has a requirement of 25 units, and of these, only 9 units are to be produced internally; and $C_{16} - Z_{16} = 0$. Savings, as measured by the linear programming model, would not be affected by a small change in the needs for X_4.

Table 12–25   **Initial Solution**

C_j	Solution Variables	Solution Values	0 X_8	0 X_9	0 X_{10}	0 X_{11}	0 X_{12}	0 X_{13}	0 X_{14}	0 X_{15}
0	X_8	90	1							
0	X_9	97		1						
0	X_{10}	200			1					
0	X_{11}	150				1				
0	X_{12}	250					1			
0	X_{13}	10						1		
0	X_{14}	5							1	
0	X_{15}	50								1
0	X_{16}	25								
0 →	X_{17}	10								
0	X_{18}	5								
0	X_{19}	20								
	Z_j	0	0	0	0	0	0	0	0	0
	$C_j - Z_j$		0	0	0	0	0	0	0	0

Table 12–26   **Final Solution**

C_j	Solution Variables	Solution Values	0 X_8	0 X_9	0 X_{10}	0 X_{11}	0 X_{12}	0 X_{13}	0 X_{14}	0 X_{15}
100	X_3	3		$1/4$					$-1/4$	
50	X_4	9	$1/3$	$-1/12$					$-7/12$	
0	X_{10}	117	-1	$-1/4$	1				$9/4$	
0	X_{11}	63	$-2/3$	$-7/12$		1			$11/12$	
0	X_{12}	103	$-1/3$	$-1/6$			1		$-25/6$	
0	X_{13}	10						1		
100	X_2	5							1	
0	X_{15}	47		$-1/4$					$1/4$	1
0	X_{16}	16	$-1/3$	$1/12$					$7/12$	
150	X_5	10								
100	X_6	5								
60	X_7	20								
	Z_j	4,450	$50/3$	$20/6$	0	0	0	0	$45/6$	0
	$C_j - Z_j$		$-50/3$	$-20/6$	0	0	0	0	$-45/6$	0

0	0	0	0	50	100	100	50	150	100	60
X_{16}	X_{17}	X_{18}	X_{19}	X_1	X_2	X_3	X_4	X_5	X_6	X_7
				5	2	1	3	1		2
				1	1	4		5	2	1
						2	3	2	2	1
				1	1	3	2	2	3	1
				3	5	1	1	2	2	4
					1					
					1					
							1			
1								1		
	1							1		
		1							1	
			1							1
0	0	0	0	0	0	0	0	0	0	0
0	0	0	0	50	100	100	50	150	100	60

$\uparrow$

0	0	0	0	50	100	100	50	150	100	60
X_{16}	X_{17}	X_{18}	X_{19}	X_1	X_2	X_3	X_4	X_5	X_6	X_7
	$-5/4$	$-1/2$	$-1/4$	$1/4$		1				
	$1/12$	$1/6$	$-7/12$	$19/12$			1			
	$1/4$	$-3/2$	$5/4$	$-21/4$						
	$19/12$	$-11/6$	$11/12$	$-35/12$						
	$-5/6$	$-5/3$	$-19/6$	$7/6$						
				1						
					1					
	$5/4$	$1/2$	$1/4$	$-1/4$						
1	$-1/12$	$-1/6$	$7/12$	$-19/12$						
	1							1		
		1							1	
			1							1
0	$29 1/6$	$58 1/3$	$5 5/6$	$104 1/6$	100	100	50	150	100	60
0	$-29 1/6$	$-58 1/3$	$-5 5/6$	$-54 1/6$	0	0	0	0	0	0

Table 12–27

Part Number	Requirement	Manufactured		Purchased	
		Variable	Amount	Slack Variable	Amount
182	10	X_1 =	0	X_{13} =	10
184	5	X_2 =	5	X_{14} =	0
193	50	X_3 =	3	X_{15} =	47
197	25	X_4 =	9	X_{16} =	16
284	10	X_5 =	10	X_{17} =	0
629	5	X_6 =	5	X_{18} =	0
845	20	X_7 =	20	X_{19} =	0

The $C_j - Z_j$ values for X_1 through X_7 are the reduced costs and indicate the opportunity loss if one unit of a given part must be included in the solution. For X_2 through X_7, the opportunity losses are zero, and each of these variables is in the solution. $C_1 - Z_1 = -54\frac{1}{6}$ indicates that management would reduce its profit by this much if it required that one unit of X_1 (part 182) must be produced internally.

Addition of New Products

As we have seen, dual prices give the opportunity costs of using scarce resources in a linear programming problem. In our examples, availability of time on machines has been the scarce factor. It is also possible to use dual prices to evaluate the value of adding new products or new production processes. Suppose a new part is introduced and the question is raised whether it should be manufactured internally or purchased outside. The new part requires two hours of machine time, one hour of assembly time, two hours of test time, one-half hour of supervisory time, and 50 cents of working capital. The variable savings from manufacturing the new part internally are $50 per unit.

The opportunity cost of producing this part internally can be determined by multiplying the dual prices by the resource requirements, as shown in Table 12–28.

Since the opportunity cost is greater than the incremental savings ($50), the part should not be produced internally. Had the opportunity cost been less than $50, it would have been profitable to produce at least some units of the new part.

There is a danger in interpreting dual prices too literally. If a particular constraint is binding and has a high dual price, management may add capacity to reduce the bottleneck. As capacity is added, at some point another resource will suddenly become an additional bottleneck, and the dual prices will change.

Table 12–28   **Evaluation of Opportunity Cost for New Product**

	(1) *Scarce Resource*	(2) *Dual Price*	(3) *Amount Required*	(4) *Opportunity Cost (2) · (3)*
Machine time		$16.67	2	$33.33
Assembly time		20.83	1	20.83
Test time		0.00	2	0.00
Supervisory time		0.00	½	0.00
Working capital		0.00	½	0.00
Total opportunity cost				$54.16

Table 12–29   **Determining Limits on Reduction and Addition of Assembly Hours**

Solution Variables	*Solution Values*	X_9	$\left(\dfrac{Solution\ Values}{X_9}\right)$
X_3	3	¼	12
X_4	9	− 1/12	− 108
X_{10}	117	− ¼	− 468
X_{11}	63	− 7/12	− 108
X_{12}	103	− ⅙	− 618
X_{13}	10	0	—
X_2	5	0	—
X_{15}	47	− ¼	− 188
X_{16}	16	1/12	192
X_5	10	0	—
X_6	5	0	—
X_7	20	0	—

Right-Hand Side Ranges

The dual prices, indicating the value of changing a constraint, hold only over a limited range. Earlier, the procedure for determining these ranges from the simplex table was shown. Let us now illustrate this procedure again with the problem whose final table is given in Table 12–26. As an example, the ranges associated with variable X_9—unused assembly time—are determined in Table 12–29.

The smallest non-negative value in the fourth column of Table 12–29 is 12, associated with variable X_3. Thus, assembly hours can be reduced 12 hours, from the currently available 97 to 85, before the solution mix changes.

The smallest (in absolute value) nonpositive value in column 4 of Table 12–29 is 108, associated with both X_4 (part 197) and X_{11} (engineering supervision hours). Thus, assembly hours can be increased from 97 to 205 before the solution mix changes. Over this range, 85 to 205 hours, the dual price of $20.83 is valid.

For another example, consider the slack variable X_{10} associated with testing hours. In the final solution, $X_{10} = 117$, implying that 117 hours of testing time remain unused. The dual price is zero. In this case, adding additional test hours will have no effect, so there is no upper limit on adding hours. And if the 117 unused hours were removed, the constraint would become binding. So the lower limit is the available amount, 200, minus 117, or 83 hours.

The detailed calculations are not shown for the other variables in this problem, but the complete set of ranges are shown in Table 12–30.

Care must be used in applying the results of sensitivity analysis, since all of the results relate to "one at a time" changes. For example, we have found that assembly hours can be reduced to 85 or increased to 205 hours without the solution mix changing. This is true only if no other changes are made (i.e., if all other resources are at their initial levels). If more than one change in resource levels is made, then the ranges will generally be different from those found using sensitivity analysis. In such situations, it may be simplest to rerun the LP with different sets of resource levels to study the effect on profitability.

Table 12–30

Variable Name	Associated Slack Variable	Amount Available	Amount Used in Optimum Solution	Dual Price	Range over Which Dual Price Is Valid	
					Lower Limit	Upper Limit
Resource constraints:						
Machine time	X_8	90	90	$16.67	63	138
Assembly time	X_9	97	97	20.83	85	205
Test time	X_{10}	200	83	0.00	83	No limit
Supervisory time	X_{11}	150	87	0.00	87	No limit
Working capital	X_{12}	250	147	0.00	147	No limit
Requirement constraints:						
Part 182	X_{13}	10	0	0.00	0	No limit
Part 184	X_{14}	5	5	45.83	0	17
Part 193	X_{15}	50	3	0.00	3	No limit
Part 197	X_{16}	25	9	0.00	9	No limit
Part 284	X_{17}	10	10	29.17	0	12.4
Part 629	X_{18}	5	5	58.33	0	11
Part 845	X_{19}	20	20	5.83	0	32

Objective Function Coefficient Ranges

As described earlier, the value of the objective function coefficient—the per unit profit or cost—can vary within a range without changing the LP solution. An instance in which this is easy to see, and which was not illustrated earlier, is when a decision variable is not included in the final solution. For example, consider variable X_1 in Table 12–26. No X_1 (units of part 182) are to be manufactured internally. The current objective function coefficient for part 182 is $50, the per unit savings from internal manufacture. Since none are included in the solution, this savings could fall without limit and still none would be manufactured.

The $C_j - Z_j$ value for X_1, called the reduced cost, is $54.17. If the savings were to increase by this much or more, it would pay to introduce some of X_1 into the solution. Hence, the upper limit on the range is $50 + $54.17 = $104.17. Within the range thus defined, the LP solution as given in Table 12–26 will remain the same.

APPENDIX   **Linear Programming: The Dual Problem**

Every linear programming problem we have solved has been of the type designated as *primal,* the primal being the first problem to which our attention is generally directed. Each primal problem has a companion problem called the *dual.* The dual has the same optimum solution as the primal, but it is derived by an alternative procedure. The analysis of this procedure may be instructive for several types of decision problems.

Frequently, the economic problem being solved as the primal involves the maximization of an objective function (for example, profits), subject to constraints that are frequently of a physical nature (such as hours of machine time). In this type of situation, the dual involves the minimization of total opportunity costs, subject to the opportunity cost (or equivalently, the value) of the inputs of each product being equal to or greater than the unit profit of the product. We shall discuss further the economic interpretation of the dual after investigating a specific example.

Example: The Primal   Assume that two products, A and B, are manufactured on two machines, 1 and 2.

Product A requires three hours on machine 1 and one-half hour on machine 2.

Product B requires two hours on machine 1 and one hour on machine 2.

There are six hours of available capacity on machine 1 and four hours on machine 2.

Each unit of A produces a net increase in profit of $12, and each unit of B an incremental profit of $4.

Let:

X_1 = Number of units of product A to be produced
X_2 = Number of units of product B to be produced
P = Profit

The objective function (or profit function) to be maximized is:

$$P = 12X_1 + 4X_2$$

The constraints are:

$3X_1 + 2X_2 \leq 6$ (There are six hours available on machine 1. Each unit of A requires three hours; B requires two hours per unit.)

$\frac{1}{2}X_1 + X_2 \leq 4$ (There are four hours available on machine 2. Each unit of A requires one-half hour; B requires one hour per unit.)

$X_1 \geq 0, X_2 \geq 0$ (The Xs cannot be negative. We cannot produce a negative amount of product.)

After slack variables are introduced to convert the inequalities into equalities, we have:

$$3X_1 + 2X_2 + X_3 + 0X_4 = 6$$
$$\frac{1}{2}X_1 + X_2 + 0X_3 + X_4 = 4$$

The final simplex table is shown in Table 12–31.

In Table 12–31 all the $C_j - Z_j$'s are ≤ 0; thus, an optimal solution has been reached. Two units of A should be produced, and this will result in a profit of $24. No other combination of products will result in as high a profit. For example, producing one unit of A and 1.5 units of B results in a profit of $12 · 1 + $4 · 1.5, or $18. We cannot produce one unit of A and two units of B since this would require more hours than are available on machine 1. The inclusion of three units of X_4 in the solution indicates that machine 2 will be idle for three hours.

Example:
The Dual

We will now construct the dual to this problem. There are five steps to obtain the dual from the primal problem:

Table 12–31   **Final Primal Simplex Table**

C_j	Solution Variables	Solution Values	0 X_3	0 X_4	12 X_1	4 X_2
12	X_1	2	$\frac{1}{3}$	0	1	$\frac{2}{3}$
0	X_4	3	$-\frac{1}{6}$	1	0	$\frac{2}{3}$
	Z_j	24	4	0	12	8
	$C_j - Z_j$		-4	0	0	-4

1. If the objective function is *maximized* in the primal, the objective function of the dual is *minimized*. In this example, the objective function of the primal is a profit equation, so the objective function of the dual will be a cost equation.
2. The coefficients of the variables of the cost equation (the dual objective function) are the right-hand side constants of the primal constraints. In this example, they are six and four and represent the hours of each machine available. The variables U_1 and U_2 of the cost equation of the dual are the respective costs per hour of using machine 1 and machine 2.[8] The cost equation (or dual objective function) is:

$$C = 6U_1 + 4U_2$$

3. The constants for the dual constraints are obtained from the profit function (the objective function) of the primal. Thus, the constants will be 12 and 4.
4. The dual constraints are formed by *transposing* the coefficients used in the primal. In the primal, the equations and coefficients were:

Primal Constraints	Coefficients	
$3X_1 + 2X_2 \leq 6$	3	2
$\frac{1}{2}X_1 + X_2 \leq 4$	½	1

The transposition is as follows (A^T indicates that A has been transposed):

$$A = \begin{pmatrix} 3 & 2 \\ \frac{1}{2} & 1 \end{pmatrix}$$

$$A^T = \begin{pmatrix} 3 & \frac{1}{2} \\ 2 & 1 \end{pmatrix}$$

The first column of A becomes the first row of A^T, and the second column of A becomes the second row of A^T.

5. If we are maximizing a primal objective function and if the constraints of the primal are "less than or equal to," the constraints of the dual will be "greater than or equal to." Thus, the dual constraints are:

$$3U_1 + \frac{1}{2}U_2 \geq 12$$
$$2U_1 + U_2 \geq 4$$

If this entire procedure is performed on the dual, the original (primal) problem will be obtained. Thus, the dual of the dual is the primal.

These rules require the primal problem to be either a maximization problem with all "less than or equal to" constraints, or a minimization problem with all "greater than or equal to" constraints. If an LP problem does not

---

[8]The U_1 and U_2 are opportunity cost measures and are not related to conventional accounting costs.

have one of these forms, multiplying the objective function or the constraints by -1 and writing equality constraints as two inequality constraints will enable it to be placed in one of the forms required by the rules listed above.

Interpretation of Dual Constraints

The interpretation of the dual constraints should help clarify the relationship between the primal and dual problems. The first inequality states that the time to produce product A on machine 1 (three hours) times the opportunity cost per hour of using machine 1 (U_1) plus the time to produce product A on machine 2 (one-half hour) times the cost per hour of using machine 2 (U_2) is greater than or equal to $12. The $12 is the net profit of a unit of A (see the profit function of the primal). Thus, the opportunity cost of producing A is going to be either equal to the net profit (in which case A will be produced) or greater than the net profit (in which case no units of A will be produced and the resources will be used elsewhere to attain higher profit).

The interpretation of the second constraint is similar. The total cost per unit of producing product B is $2U_1$ (cost of using machine 1) plus U_2 (cost of using machine 2). The total cost per unit is equal to or greater than $4, where $4 is the net increase in profit per unit of product B. Thus the cost of producing B is going to be either equal to the net profit per unit of B (in which case B will be produced) or greater than the net profit (in which case no units of B will be produced).

It should be noted that the form of solution does not allow the opportunity costs of producing either product to be less than the incremental profit of the product. This is reasonable, since the value of the machine-hours is measured by the profit they can produce. To have the total costs less than the profit would imply that we should produce more units of the product; but if the product is produced to the limit of productive capacity, the costs of the last unit will be equal to the profit. The only time the costs will be greater than the incremental profit will be when it is not desirable to produce any units of the product. Remember that these are opportunity, not accounting, costs.

The constraint equations, expanded to include slack variables and artificial variables, are:

$$3U_1 + \tfrac{1}{2}U_2 - U_3 + 0U_4 + U_5 + 0U_6 = 12$$
$$2U_1 + U_2 + 0U_3 - U_4 + 0U_5 + U_6 = 4$$

The expanded cost equation is:

$$C = 6U_1 + 4U_2 + 0U_3 + 0U_4 + MU_5 + MU_6$$

The large coefficient M is assigned to U_5 and U_6 in the expanded cost equation to drive these two variables from the solution; this is done because U_5 and U_6 are artificial variables.

Table 12–32 contains the final simplex solution to this dual LP.

Table 12–32   **Final Dual Simplex Table**

C_j	Solution Variables	Solution Values	M U_5	M U_6	0 U_3	0 U_4	6 U_1	4 U_2
0	U_4	4	$\frac{2}{3}$	-1	$-\frac{2}{3}$	1	0	$-\frac{2}{3}$
6	U_1	4	$\frac{1}{3}$	0	$-\frac{1}{3}$	0	1	$\frac{1}{6}$
	Z_j	24	2	0	-2	0	6	1
	$C_j - Z_j$		$M - 2$	M	2	0	0	3

The minimum of the cost equation is $24 (see Z_0 of Table 12–32 of the dual). This is equal to the maximum of the profit equation (see Z_0 of Table 12–31 of the primal). This will always be true; at the optimum solution, the primal objective function value will equal the dual objective function value.

Table 12–32 gives the optimal solution, since no variables have negative $C_j - Z_j$ values. U_1 has a value of $4, U_2 and U_3 both equal zero, and U_4 has a value of $4. In the next section, we shall study the significance of these values.

Dual Solution as Dual Prices

The economic interpretation of the dual solution is of considerable importance and usefulness. First, consider the dual variables U_1 and U_2. U_1 has a value of $4, which means an hour of time of machine 1 has a value of $4. How would the optimal solution change if there were an additional hour of machine 1 time available? Since the original solution was to produce 2 units of A ($X_1 = 2$) and none of B, the additional machine 1 time would be used to produce more units of A. Since one unit of product A takes 3 hours on machine 1, an additional hour will enable us to produce one third of a unit of A. The resulting change in profit is one third of $12, or $4. (Note that there is sufficient excess machine 2 capacity for this production.)

The actual cost of renting additional capacity of machine 1 may be greater or less than $4. If it is less (say $3), then the company should consider renting some additional capacity of machine 1. This is because for each additional hour of available capacity rented, the return is $4, whereas the cost is $3, resulting in an incremental gain of $1.

The value of U_2 is zero, which means the "opportunity cost" of an hour of time on machine 2 is zero. This is consistent with the fact that machine 2 has *idle hours* following the optimum schedule of production, and profit would not be increased by making more time on machine 2 available.

Note that this interpretation is exactly that attached to the dual prices introduced in Chapter 11. Now you understand the origin of that term. Dual prices are also called shadow prices or marginal values.

Dual prices can be interpreted as the "cost" of a constraint. We can say that a unit of slack of machine 1, which has only six hours available, "costs" at a rate of $4 per hour ($U_1$ has a value of $4 per unit). It would be worth $4 per hour in increased profitability to obtain an additional hour on machine 1 (e.g., use a second shift). Thus, *the dual price measures the value or worth of relaxing a constraint by acquiring an additional unit of that factor of production.*

Now consider the dual slack variables, U_3 and U_4. The dual slack variables measure the *opportunity loss* involved in production of the corresponding primal variable. Since U_3 is the slack variable in the first dual constraint, it corresponds to X_1 in the primal. Similarly, U_4 corresponds to X_2. U_4 has a value of $4; this means that the cost of forcing a unit of X_2 into the solution is $4.[9] U_3 has a value of zero, which means that there is no opportunity loss involved in producing X_1. Thus, X_1 is being produced in positive quantity in the optimal solution, whereas X_2 is not being produced. If there is a positive opportunity loss associated with a variable, it will have the value of zero in the optimal solution; conversely, if the opportunity loss associated with a variable is zero, the variable will take on some positive value in the optimal solution. In Chapter 11, we used the term **reduced costs** to refer to the dual solution variables interpreted in this fashion.

Note that the values of four for U_1 and U_4 are the same (except for the sign) as the $C_j - Z_j$ values for X_3 and X_2 in Table 12–31. This is not a coincidence. The U values of the dual solution are uniquely the $C_j - Z_j$ values of corresponding variables in the primal solution. By corresponding variables, it is meant that dual ordinary variables (U_1 and U_2) are associated with primal slack variables (X_3 and X_4, respectively), and dual slack variables (U_3 and U_4) are associated with primal ordinary variables (X_1 and X_2, respectively). These associations make sense, since the dual ordinary variable U_1 measures the opportunity cost per hour of using machine 1, and the primal slack variable X_3 represents the amount of unused capacity of machine 1. Similarly, the $C_j - Z_j$ values of the dual give the values of the corresponding variables in the primal solution. Thus, the simplex table for the primal solution provides both the primal solution and (through the $C_j - Z_j$ values) the values of the dual variables.

Based on the above analysis, we can state that the following products are always zero:

$$X_3 U_1 = X_4 U_2 = 0$$
$$X_1 U_3 = X_2 U_4 = 0$$

The first products are those of a primal slack variable and the corresponding dual ordinary variable. If a constraint is binding, the primal slack variable will

---

[9] If we forced a unit of X_2 to be produced, the constraint representing hours on machine 1 would force us to reduce production of X_1 to four thirds of a unit. Our profit would now be 12(4/3) + 4(1) = $20, a drop of $4 from the optimal profit of $24. Hence, U_4 is $4.

be zero (as is X_3 in our example), while if a constraint is not binding, then the dual price of that constraint (U_2 in our example) will be zero. The second products involve a primal ordinary variable and the corresponding dual slack variable. If a primal ordinary variable (here X_1) is positive, the opportunity loss (here U_3) associated with that product will be zero. If an opportunity loss is positive (here U_4), then the corresponding primal ordinary variable (X_2) will be zero. These relationships always hold at the optimum solution.

Bibliography

See the bibliography at the end of Chapter 10.

Problems with Answers

Some of the problems below are designed to give you practice in doing the simplex method. Calculating simplex tables involves a substantial amount of arithmetic. Since errors are cumulative, you should check your answers with those in the back of the book after you finish each part of a question. Make any corrections necessary, and then proceed to the next part. A pocket calculator is very useful for this work.

12–1. Assume two products, A and B, are manufactured on two machines, 1 and 2. Product A requires four hours on machine 1 and two hours on machine 2. Product B requires two hours on machine 1 and $8/3$ hours on machine 2. There are 10 hours of available capacity on machine 1 and 8 hours on machine 2. In addition, there is a maximum sales limit of six units on product A. Product A has an incremental profit of $4 for each unit and product B has an incremental profit of $3 per unit. Using X_1 for units of product A and X_2 for units of product B, the problem is formulated as:

Maximize: $P = 4X_1 + 3X_2$
Subject to: $4X_1 + 2X_2 \leq 10$
$2X_1 + 8/3X_2 \leq 8$
$0 \leq X_1 \leq 6$
$X_2 \geq 0$

Use the simplex method to find the values of X_1 and X_2 that maximize P.
a. Set up the first simplex table.

b. Determine the entering and leaving variables.
c. Re-solve to obtain the next simplex table.
d. Check to see if the solution is optimal.
e. Determine the next entering and leaving variables.
f. Re-solve to obtain the third simplex table.
g. Check to see if the solution is optimal. What is the solution?

12–2. Refer to Problem 12–1 and the optimal table given in the answer to (f) in the back of the book.
a. What is the dual price associated with machine 1? Over what range of hours is this value valid?
b. What is the dual price associated with machine 2? Over what range is this valid?
c. What is the dual price associated with the sales limit on product A? Over what range is this valid?

12–3. Refer to Problem 12–1 and the optimal table given in the answer to (f) in the back of the book.
a. How much would the per unit profit of product A have to change before the optimal solution would change?
b. Answer the same question for product B.

12–4. Refer to Problem 12–1 and the optimal table given in the answer to (f) in the back of the book. Suppose a new product is being considered that would require two hours on each machine. The per unit profit for this product is $3. Should the firm make any of this product?

12–5. Given:

$$3X_1 + 2X_2 \geq 12$$
$$\tfrac{1}{2}X_1 + X_2 \geq \$4$$
$$X_1 \geq 0$$
$$X_2 \geq 0$$

Use the simplex method to find the values of X_1 and X_2 that minimize the function $C = 6X_1 + 4X_2$.

a. Set up the first simplex table.
b. Determine the entering and leaving variables.
c. Re-solve to obtain the next simplex table.
d. Check to see if the solution is optimal. If not, repeat (b) and (c) until an optimal solution is obtained.

12–6. A cannery has formulated a linear programming model as an aid in planning how to can the current peach crop. There are two products—peach halves and peach slices. There are also two grades of peaches—grade A and grade B. Halves are canned entirely from A grade peaches, and slices can be made of a mixture of grade A and grade B peaches.

The decision variables are:

$X_1 =$ Number of pounds of grade A peaches used in halves
$X_2 =$ Number of pounds of grade A peaches used in slices
$X_3 =$ Number of pounds of grade B peaches used in slices

All units are measured in thousands of pounds.

The objective is to maximize the profit contribution from canning the current peach crop. The linear programming problem has been formulated as follows:

Maximize:
$$P = 0.15X_1 + 0.12X_2 + 0.12X_3$$
Subject to:

Halves demand:	X_1	≤ 180
Slices demand:	$X_2 + X_3$	≤ 125
Grade A available:	$X_1 + X_2$	≤ 225
Grade B available:	X_3	≤ 75
Slices quality mix:	$-4X_2 + X_3$	≤ 0

$$X_1 \geq 0$$
$$X_2 \geq 0$$
$$X_3 \geq 0$$

Slack variables X_4 through X_8 are added to the constraints.

The initial linear programming table is given as Table 12–33.

Table 12–33   (for Problem 12–6)

C_j			0	0	0	0	0	0.15	0.12	0.12
	Solution Variables	Solution Values	X_4	X_5	X_6	X_7	X_8	X_1	X_2	X_3
0	X_4	180	1					1		
0	X_5	125		1					1	1
0	X_6	225			1			1	1	
0	X_7	75				1				1
0	X_8	0					1		-4	1
	Z_j	0	0	0	0	0	0	0	0	0
	$C_j - Z_j$		0	0	0	0	0	0.15	0.12	0.12

a. Refer to Table 12–33. What is the entering variable? What is the leaving variable?

b. Calculate the next simplex table.

c. After a few iterations, Table 12–34 results. Calculate the Z_j and $C_j - Z_j$ values for this table. What is the next entering variable? What is the leaving variable?

d. Finally, Table 12–35 results. Is this solution optimal? How do you know? Are there any alternative optimal solutions? How do you know?

12–7. Refer to Problem 12–6 (and Table 12–35). Answer each of the following questions independently of each other.

a. What is the maximum price that the cannery would be willing to pay for additional grade A peaches? How much would be bought at that price?

b. What is the marginal value of additional grade B peaches? Over what range is this marginal value valid?

c. The marketing manager of the cannery has just revised the estimated demand for halves from 180,000 pounds to 200,000 pounds. Will this affect the solution to the canning problem? What will be the incremental profit associated with this change?

d. Suppose the marketing manager has revised his estimate of the demand

Table 12–34   (for Problem 12–6)

C_j			0	0	0	0	0	0.15	0.12	0.12
	Solution Variables	*Solution Values*	X_4	X_5	X_6	X_7	X_8	X_1	X_2	X_3
0.15	X_1	180	1					1		
0	X_5	80	1	1	−1					1
0.12	X_2	45	−1		1				1	
0	X_7	75				1				1
0	X_8	180	−4		4		1			1
	Z_j									
	$C_j - Z_j$									

Table 12–35   (for Problem 12–6)

C_j			0	0	0	0	0	0.15	0.12	0.12
	Solution Variables	*Solution Values*	X_4	X_5	X_6	X_7	X_8	X_1	X_2	X_3
0.15	X_1	180	1					1		
0	X_5	5	1	1	−1	−1				
0.12	X_2	45	−1		1				1	
0.12	X_3	75				1				1
0	X_8	105	−4		4	−1	1			
	Z_j	41.4	.03	0	0.12	0.12	0	0.15	0.12	0.12
	$C_j - Z_j$		−.03	0	−0.12	−0.12	0	0	0	0

for slices from 125,000 to 145,000 pounds. Will this affect the solution to the canning problem? What will be the incremental profit associated with this change?

e. How much would the price of peach halves have to change before the optimal solution changes?

f. The cannery is considering a new product, fancy slices, with a contribution of $0.14 per pound. A pound of fancy slices is composed of half a pound each of grade A and grade B peaches. Should any of this product be canned?

Problems

12–8. Solve the following problem by using the simplex method.

Maximize: $P = 3X_1 + 2X_2$
Subject to: $X_1 + 2X_2 \leq 6$
$2X_1 + X_2 \leq 6$
$X_1, X_2 \geq 0$

12–9. The ABC Company has the option of producing two products during periods of slack activity. For the next week, production has been scheduled so that the milling machine is free 10 hours, and skilled labor will have 8 hours of available time.

Product A requires four hours of machine time and two hours of skilled labor per unit. Product B requires two hours of machine time and two hours of skilled labor per unit.

Product A contributes $5 per unit to profit, and product B contributes $3 per unit to profit (not including skilled labor or machine time cost).

Use the simplex method to find the amounts of product A and product B that should be produced.

12–10. The Z company combines factors A and B to form a product that must weigh 50 pounds. At least 20 pounds of A and no more than 40 pounds of B can be used. A costs $25 per pound, and B costs $10 per pound.

Use the simplex method to find the amounts of factor A and factor B that should be used.

12–11. A firm's advertising department wishes to plan its advertising strategy to reach certain minimum percentages of high-

and low-income groups. Two alternatives are considered—television and magazines. Magazine advertising has an exposure for the high-income group of 2 percent per page, but only a 1 percent per page exposure for the low-income group. Television, on the other hand, exposes 3 percent of the low-income group per show and only 1 percent of the high-income group per show.

Magazine advertising costs $1,000 per page; television, $4,000 per show. If the firm wants a minimal exposure of 50 percent of the high-income group and 30 percent of the low-income group, what strategy should it use to minimize advertising cost? (*Note:* If a person views a show twice, or reads an advertisement twice, or views a show and reads an advertisement, this counts as double exposure. Exposure greater than 100 percent is thus possible.)

Formulate the above as a linear programming problem, and solve using the simplex method.

12–12. The Ajax Plywood Company is considering the production schedule for the next month. Ajax produces three types of plywood panels. Panels A and B can each be produced in two ways, requiring different amounts of pine, fir, and spruce. Limited quantities of these woods are available. Also, Ajax has limited capacity to dry the veneer for the panels. There is a limitation of 10 (thousand) panels on the overall capacity of the Ajax mill. These requirements are shown in Table 12–36.

Ajax wishes to maximize total contribution to profit. Adding slack variables:

X_6 = Unused pine (000 units)
X_7 = Unused fir (000 units)
X_8 = Unused spruce (000 units)
X_9 = Unused dryer time (000 minutes)
X_{10} = Unused overall capacity (000 panels)

The first simplex table is Table 12–37.

a. Assume that variable X_3 is to be the *entering* variable. What variable is the *leaving* variable? Why?

b. After two iterations, Table 12–38 results. What is the solution at this stage? Is the solution optimal? How

do you know? What is the entering variable? What is the leaving variable?

c. After three more iterations, Table 12–39 is obtained. Is this solution optimal? How do you know? Give a verbal description of the solution to the problem.

d. Are there any alternative solutions (see Table 12–39)? If so, give at least one.

Refer to Problem 12–12(c) (Table 12–39). Answer each of the following questions independently.

a. What is the marginal value (dual price) of an additional unit of pine?

Table 12–36 **(for Problem 12–12)**

		Requirements					
Product	*Variable*	*Pine (units)*	*Fir (units)*	*Spruce (units)*	*Drying Time (minutes)*	*Overall Capacity (each)*	*Profit Contribution ($ per unit)*
A–1	X_1	2	0	1	5	1	1.00
A–2	X_2	0	2	1	7	1	1.00
B–1	X_3	2	1	0	4	1	1.20
B–2	X_4	1	2	0	5	1	1.20
C	X_5	1	1	1	6	1	0.80
Total available (000)		12	15	6	60	10	

Table 12–37 **(for Problem 12–12)**

C_j			1.0	1.0	1.2	1.2	0.8	0	0	0	0	0
	Solution Variables	*Solution Values*	X_1	X_2	X_3	X_4	X_5	X_6	X_7	X_8	X_9	X_{10}
0	X_6	12	2		2	1	1	1				
0	X_7	15		2	1	2	1		1			
0	X_8	6	1	1			1			1		
0	X_9	60	5	7	4	5	6				1	
0	X_{10}	10	1	1	1	1	1					1
	Z_j	0	0	0	0	0	0	0	0	0	0	0
	$C_j - Z_j$		1.0	1.0	1.2	1.2	0.8	0	0	0	0	0

Table 12–38 (for Problem 12–12)

C_j			1.0	1.0	1.2	1.2	0.8	0	0	0	0	0
	Solution Variables	Solution Values	X_1	X_2	X_3	X_4	X_5	X_6	X_7	X_8	X_9	X_{10}
1.2	X_3	0		−1	1	0.5	−.5	0.5		−1		
0	X_7	15		3		1.5	1.5	−.5	1	1		
1.0	X_1	6	1	1			1			1		
0	X_9	30		6		3	3	−2		−1	1	
0	X_{10}	4		1		0.5	0.5	−.5				1
	Z_j	6	1	−0.2	1.2	0.6	0.4	0.6	0	−0.2	0	0
	$C_j - Z_j$		0	1.2	0	0.6	0.4	−0.6	0	0.2	0	0

Table 12–39 (for Problem 12–12)

C_j			1.0	1.0	1.2	1.2	0.8	0	0	0	0	0
	Solution Variables	Solution Values	X_1	X_2	X_3	X_4	X_5	X_6	X_7	X_8	X_9	X_{10}
1.2	X_3	5	2		1		1		−1			2
1.2	X_4	2	−2			1	−1	1	2			−4
0	X_8	3						1	1	1		−3
0	X_9	9						2	1		1	−9
1.0	X_2	3	1	1			1	−1	−1			3
	Z_j	11.4	1.0	1.0	1.2	1.2	1.0	0.2	0.2	0	0	0.6
	$C_j - Z_j$		0	0	0	0	−0.2	−0.2	−0.2	0	0	−0.6

Over what range is this marginal value valid?

b. What is the marginal value of an additional unit of fir? Over what range is this marginal value valid?

c. What is the marginal value of an additional unit of spruce? Over what range is this marginal value valid?

d. Suppose the firm is considering adding additional dryer time. Would this be profitable? What is the marginal value of an additional minute of dryer time? Over what range is this value valid?

e. What is the marginal value of an additional unit of overall capacity? Over what range is this value valid?

f. How much would the contribution of panel type C have to increase before Ajax would consider producing any of this type?

g. Consider product B − 1 (variable X_3). What are the limits on the increase and decrease in per-unit profit before the solution changes?

h. Suppose a new type of panel, type D, is being considered. This panel requires one unit each of pine, fir, and spruce, requires 10 minutes of dryer time, and has a contribution of $1.10. Should any of this panel be made?

12–14. A firm has a decision problem about how much of each of five products (X_1 to X_5) to produce. The problem has been formulated as a linear programming problem, and the first simplex table is shown as Table 12–40. Slack variables X_6, X_7, and X_8 are included.

a. What is the entering variable? What is the leaving variable?

b. A company analyst, Mr. Opt T. Mize, has applied the simplex procedure.

After iterating awhile, he arrives at Table 12–41. Identify the solution variables for this solution, and determine the values for the Z_j and $C_j - Z_j$ rows.

c. What is the next entering variable? What is the leaving variable?

d. After further iterations, Table 12–42

Table 12–40 (for Problem 12–14)

C_j			0	0	0	10	10	20	15	12
	Solution Variables	Solution Values	X_6	X_7	X_8	X_1	X_2	X_3	X_4	X_5
0	X_6	120	1			3	6	9		
0	X_7	108		1			3	6	6	6
0	X_8	36			1			3	3	9
	Z_j	0	0	0	0	0	0	0	0	0
	$C_j - Z_j$		0	0	0	10	10	20	15	12

Table 12–41 (for Problem 12–14)

C_j			0	0	0	10	10	20	15	12
	Solution Variables	Solution Values	X_6	X_7	X_8	X_1	X_2	X_3	X_4	X_5
		4	⅓		−1	1	2		−3	−9
		36		1	−2		3			−12
		12			⅓			1	1	3
	Z_j									
	$C_j - Z_j$									

Table 12–42 (for Problem 12–14)

C_j			0	0	0	10	10	20	15	12
	Solution Variables	Solution Values	X_6	X_7	X_8	X_1	X_2	X_3	X_4	X_5
10	X_1	40	⅓			1	2	3		
0	X_7	36		1	−2		3			−12
15	X_4	12			⅓			1	1	3
	Z_j	580	3.3	0	5	10	20	45	15	45
	$C_j - Z_j$		−3.3	0	−5	0	−10	−25	0	−33

Table 12–43   (for Problem 12–15)

C_j			40	60	80	100	0	0	0	0
	Solution Variables	Solution Values	X_1	X_2	X_3	X_4	X_5	X_6	X_7	X_8
0	X_8	50	-0.2		0.2		0.1	-0.5		1
60	X_2	125	0.5	1			0.25	-0.75		
0	X_7	5	0.3		0.2		-0.15	0.25	1	
100	X_4	50	0.2		0.8	1	-0.1	0.5		
	Z_j	12,500								
	$C_j - Z_j$		-10.0	0	0.0	0	-5.0	-5.0	0	0

results. What is the solution? Is it optimal?

12–15. Refer to Problem 11–10 and Table 11–7. The final simplex table is shown as Table 12–43, with variables X_1, X_2, X_3, and X_4 representing the number of Sport, Standard, Traveler, and Super models respectively, and variables X_5, X_6, X_7, X_8 representing slack in the constraints.

 a. Compare the solution to that obtained in the LINDO output in Table 11–7. Are the results the same? Should they be?

 b. The right-hand side ranges and objective function ranges are shown in Table 11–7. Use the simplex table to verify these results.

12–16. The following problems from Chapters 10 and 11 are of moderate size and can be solved by hand by the simplex method.

 a. Problem 10–3.

 b. Problem 10–8.

 c. Problem 10–10.

 d. Problem 11–1.

More Challenging Problems

12–17. The Ajax Nut Company sells mixed nuts of two quality levels. The more expensive mix has a higher proportion of cashews, whereas the cheaper mix contains more peanuts.

The prices of nuts purchased by Ajax are: cashews, 50 cents a pound; and peanuts, 20 cents a pound. The two mixes sold by Ajax and their prices are: mixture A, 80 cents a pound; mixture B, 40 cents a pound. Ajax can sell any amount of each of these mixtures but, due to a shortage of nuts, can obtain no more than 200 pounds of cashews and 400 pounds of peanuts.

Management has decided that mixture A should not contain more than 25 percent peanuts nor less than 40 percent cashews. Mixture B should have no more than 60 percent peanuts and no less than 20 percent cashews.

How should Ajax mix its nuts? That is, how many pounds of mixture A should be produced (and what should be its composition), and how many pounds of mixture B (and its composition)? Formulate the simplex table and solve.

12–18. The Paul Bunyan Lumber Company produces pine and fir saw lumber and two types of plywood. The company has a profit contribution of 4 cents a board foot (bf) for pine and 6 cents a bf for fir. Type 1 plywood contributes $1.20 per panel, and type 2 earns $1.50 per panel.

For the month of December, the company has 2,580 thousand bf (MBF) of pine available for either saw lumber or plywood. Similarly, 2,040 MBF of fir are available. One panel of type 1 plywood requires 16 bf of pine and 8 bf of fir. One panel of type 2 plywood requires 12 bf of each species.

Saw lumber is restricted only by the capacity of the headrig saw. The saw can handle 400 MBF per month of any species.

The plywood mill can be restricted by either the peeler or the dryer. During the month, no more than 250 thousand panels of lumber may be peeled, and there are 920 thousand minutes of dryer time available. Each type 1 panel requires four minutes of dryer time, and each type 2 panel requires six minutes of dryer time.

Market conditions limit the number of type 1 panels sold to no more than 120 thousand and the number of type 2 panels to no more than 100 thousand. Any amounts of saw lumber can be sold.

The company formulated a linear programming model of their operations as follows:

Let:

P = Profit contribution in thousands of dollars
X_1 = MBF of pine saw lumber sold
X_2 = MBF of fir saw lumber sold
X_3 = Thousands of panels of type 1 plywood sold
X_4 = Thousands of panels of type 2 plywood sold

Maximize:

$$P = 0.04 X_1 + 0.06X_2 + 1.20X_3 + 1.50X_4$$

Subject to:

$$X_1 \qquad + 16X_3 + 12X_4 \leq 2,580 \text{ (availability of pine)}$$
$$X_2 + \ 8X_3 + 12X_4 \leq 2,040 \text{ (availability of fir)}$$
$$X_1 + X_2 \qquad\qquad \leq \ 400 \text{ (sawmill capacity)}$$
$$X_3 + \quad X_4 \leq \ 250 \text{ (peeler capacity)}$$
$$4X_3 + \ 6X_4 \leq \ 920 \text{ (dryer capacity)}$$
$$X_3 \qquad \leq \ 120 \text{ (market demand, type 1 plywood)}$$
$$X_4 \leq \ 100 \text{ (market demand, type 2 plywood)}$$

Adding appropriate slack variables, the first simplex table is presented in Table 12–44. After several iterations, Table 12–45 is obtained.

Table 12–44 **Paul Bunyan Lumber Co.—Initial Table (for Problem 12–18)**

C_j	Solution Variables	Solution Values	0 X_5	0 X_6	0 X_7	0 X_8	0 X_9	0 X_{10}	0 X_{11}	0.04 X_1	0.06 X_2	1.20 X_3	1.50 X_4
0	X_5	2,580	1							1		16	12
0	X_6	2,040		1							1	8	12
0	X_7	400			1					1	1		
0	X_8	250				1						1	1
0	X_9	920					1					4	6
0	X_{10}	120						1				1	
0	X_{11}	100							1				1
	Z_j	0	0	0	0	0	0	0	0	0	0	0	0
	$C_j - Z_j$		0	0	0	0	0	0	0	0.04	0.06	1.20	1.50

a. What is the solution in the second table? Is it optimal? What is the total profit? Are there alternative optimal solutions?
b. Suppose one more unit (thousands of minutes) of dryer time could be made available. What effect would this have on the solution (i.e., what would be the new values of X_1, X_2, X_3, X_4)?
c. What is the incremental profit associated with adding one more unit (thousands of minutes) of dryer time? Over what range is this incremental profit valid?
d. What is the value of additional capacity at the headrig saw in the sawmill?

How much is the increase or decrease in this capacity before there is a basic change in the solution variables?
e. Suppose the demand for type 2 plywood could be increased by one unit (thousand panels). What would be the incremental profit of this? Over what range is this valid?
f. A third type of plywood panel is proposed. This would have a profit contribution of $1.60. It would require 8 bf of pine and 16 bf of fir. In addition, the drying time would be eight minutes. Should any of this type of panel be produced? What would be its incremental profit?

Table 12–45   Paul Bunyan Lumber Co.—Final Table (for Problem 12–18)

C_j	Solution Variables	Solution Values	0 X_5	0 X_6	0 X_7	0 X_8	0 X_9	0 X_{10}	0 X_{11}	0.04 X_1	0.06 X_2	1.20 X_3	1.50 X_4
0.04	X_1	100	1				−4.0		12.0	1			
0.06	X_2	200		1			−2.0				1		
0	X_7	100	−1	−1	1		6.0		−12.0				
0	X_8	70				1	−0.25		0.5				
1.20	X_3	80					0.25		−1.5			1	
0	X_{10}	40					−0.25	1	1.5				
1.50	X_4	100							1.0				1
	Z_j	262	0.04	0.06	0	0	0.02	0	0.18	0.04	0.06	1.20	1.50
	$C_j - Z_j$		−0.04	−0.06	0	0	−0.02	0	−0.18	0	0	0	0

13

Linear Programming
Special Topics

In this chapter we present two special topics related to linear programming. The first of these is a specialized case called the *transportation problem,* and the second deals with multiple objectives and goal programming.

The Transportation Problem

There is a type of linear programming problem that may be solved using a simplified version of the simplex technique.[1] Because of its major application in solving problems involving several product sources and several destinations of products, this type of problem is frequently called the **transportation problem**. Although the formation can be used to represent more general assignment and scheduling problems as well as transportation and distribution problems, we will illustrate it by an example involving distribution of product from factories to warehouses.

Example Let us assume there are three factories (F_1, F_2, and F_3) supplying three warehouses (W_1, W_2, and W_3). Factory capacities and warehouse requirements are given in Table 13–1. The costs of shipping from each factory to each destination are given in the body of Table 13–2. In the margins of the table are the amounts available at the factories and the requirements of the warehouses.

It is necessary to prepare an initial feasible solution, which may be done in several different ways; the only requirement is that the warehouse needs be met

---

[1]The coefficients of all variables in the constraint equations are either 0 or 1, and they follow a particular pattern. See the appendix to this chapter.

Table 13–1   Factory Capacities and Warehouse Requirements

Factories	Amount Available	Warehouses	Amount Needed
F_1	20	W_1	5
F_2	15	W_2	20
F_3	10	W_3	20
Total	45	Total	45

Table 13–2   Costs of Shipping and Supply/Demand Data

Source \ Destination	W_1	W_2	W_3	Units Available
F_1	$0.90	$1.00	$1.30	20
F_2	$1.00	$1.40	$1.00	15
F_3	$1.00	$0.80	$0.80	10
Units Demanded	5	20	20	45

within the constraint of factory production. One popular method is to start in the upper left-hand corner (the "northwest" corner), first supplying the needs of W_1, then W_2, then W_3. Another procedure (the one we shall employ) starts in Table 13–2. We try to find a box that has the lowest cost in both its row and its column. The logic here is that each factory must ship out its product, and the lowest cost in each row is the least expensive shipment from each factory. Similarly, the lowest cost in a column is the least expensive way to ship the product into a warehouse. This approach will not generally produce the optimal solution, but it usually gives a good starting point.

The 80 cents of costs in F_3W_2 is equal to the 80 cents of F_3W_3.[2] We could take either value, but we shall arbitrarily choose F_3W_2. Since the factory (F_3) can supply only 10 units, even though the warehouse (W_2) needs 20 units, we place a 10 in the F_3W_2 box of Table 13–3. In Table 13–3, the costs are in the upper left corner of each box and the units shipped are in the lower right corner (in color).

Since we have exhausted the capacity of factory 3, we can place zeros in the remaining boxes of row 3.

Returning to Table 13–2, the 90 cents in box F_1W_1 is also the lowest amount in its row and the lowest amount in its column. Since the warehouse only needs

---

[2] F_3W_2 indicates that factory 3 is supplying warehouse 2.

Table 13–3 First Solution

Source \ Destination	W_1	W_2	W_3	Units Available
F_1	$0.90 5	$1.00 10	$1.30 5	20
F_2	$1.00 0	$1.40 0	$1.00 15	15
F_3	$1.00 0	$0.80 10	$0.80 0	10
Units Demanded	5	20	20	45

5 units, even though the factory can supply 20 units, we place a 5 in the F_1W_1 box of Table 13–3. Since warehouse 1's requirements are now fully satisfied, we can place zeros in the remaining boxes in column 1.

At this point, we cannot find any more boxes that are minimums of both their rows and their columns (this is why the procedure doesn't usually reach the optimum solution). To place the remainder of the units, we proceed in a commonsense manner, making certain that no more is taken from a factory than it can produce and no more is sent to a warehouse than it needs. There are 15 units remaining from F_1; we shall assign 10 units to F_1W_2 and 5 units to F_1W_3. The needs of warehouse 2 are satisfied with this allocation, since we have already assigned 10 units to W_2 from F_3.

The 15 units of F_2 are assigned to F_2W_3, since warehouse 3 is now the only location that has unfilled needs. We have now assigned all factory output, and all warehouse requirements are met in this initial trial solution.

A requirement of the initial solution is that the number of routes used must equal the sum of the number of factories, F, plus the number of warehouses, W, minus 1; that is:

$$\text{Routes used} = F + W - 1$$

This number of routes corresponds to a basic solution (see Chapters 11 and 12).[3] If more than this number of boxes are used, the solution should be adjusted by making arbitrary changes consistent with the needs of the warehouses and the production capacity of the factories to reduce the number of routes.

Table 13–3 shows the first trial solution. Note that five routes are used, and $F + W - 1$ equals 5 (i.e., $3 + 3 - 1 = 5$). It would be a coincidence if the

---

[3]There are F equations for factory capacities and W equations for warehouse demands; but since the sum of factory capacities must equal the sum of warehouse requirements, one of these equations is redundant, so the number of independent equations is $F + W - 1$.

trial solution happened to be the optimum solution; but the closer the first solution is to an optimum solution, the less work is required.

Testing Alternate Routes

We must now test to see if costs can be reduced by some rearrangement of routes. From Table 13–3, total shipment costs for the first solution are:

$$5(0.90) + 10(1.00) + 10(0.80) + 5(1.30) + 15(1.00) = \$44$$

We shall proceed to test the relative cost advantage of alternative routes. Consider an unused route, such as shipping to warehouse 1 from factory 2 (i.e., box F_2W_1 has a zero entry in its lower right corner). The "direct" cost of using this route is the amount in the upper left corner of the box, $1; this amount is to be contrasted with the current costs of the indirect route from F_2 to W_1. The **indirect route** is identified as the path a unit would have to follow from a given factory to a given warehouse, using only established channels (i.e., the shipment must avoid zero boxes; otherwise, we are shipping from a box that has no units, or introducing two new boxes into the solution instead of one).

Indirect costs are obtained by tracing out an indirect route and accumulating costs. Considering box F_2W_1, the indirect route is: $+ F_2W_3, - F_1W_3, + F_1W_1$. This means that we could send a unit from F_2 to W_3, reduce the existing shipment from F_1 to W_3 by one unit, and send the unused F_1 unit from F_1 to W_1. The net result of these transactions is that all supplies and requirements are still met. The indirect cost is:

Charge for shipping from F_2W_3	+$1.00
Every unit F_2 sends to W_3 saves the cost of supplying W_3 from F_1	− 1.30
Charge for shipping from F_1 to W_1	+ 0.90
Indirect cost	+ 0.60

The cost of presently avoiding box F_2W_1 is 60 cents (the additional outlay of $1 for using F_2W_3, the saving of $1.30 resulting from not using F_1W_3 to as large an extent as possible, and the 90-cent cost of using box F_1W_1). Compared with this total indirect cost, 60 cents, is a cost of $1, which would result from using the direct route F_2W_1; thus, the indirect route is to be preferred.

There can be only one indirect route for each zero box, unless the previous trial solution contained more than $F + W - 1$ direct routes.

The other zero boxes may be evaluated in a comparable manner. For example, the indirect shipment from F_2 to W_2 is the charge from F_2 to W_3 ($1) less the F_1W_3 charge ($1.30) plus the F_1W_2 charge ($1) = 70 cents. Again, this is less than the cost of direct shipment ($1.40), so the current indirect route should be continued. The F_3W_1 box is also found to have a 70-cent cost for the indirect shipment; and again, this is less than the direct route cost ($1). However, the evaluation of the last unused route, F_3W_3, yields a cost for the indirect route of:

Table 13–4

Unused Route	Cost of Direct Route	Cost of Indirect Route
F_2W_1	$1.00	$0.60
F_3W_1	1.00	0.70
F_2W_2	1.40	0.70
F_3W_3	0.80	1.10

$$\$0.80 - \$1.00 + \$1.30 = \$1.10$$

and this is greater than the direct route cost of 80 cents. The direct route F_3W_3 should be used rather than the indirect route of

$$F_3W_2 - F_1W_2 + F_1W_3$$

since a saving of

$$\$1.10 - \$0.80 = \$0.30$$

per unit can be made by using the direct route. (See Table 13–4).

How many units can be shifted from the indirect route to the direct route F_3W_3? The answer is the minimum number in any of the connections of the indirect route that must supply units for the transfer. This is five units, from box F_1W_3. Thus, we ship five units by the direct route F_3W_3; since F_3 produces only 10 units, this imposes a reduction in the F_3W_2 box to five. An additional five units now are required at warehouse 2. This deficiency is met readily by factory 1, which has been forced to reduce its shipment to W_3 by exactly five units as a result of W_3's new source of supply. The new pattern is shown in Table 13–5.

All of the unused routes, identified by the zero entries in Table 13–5, must again be evaluated to see if a further reduction in cost is possible. This may be done as described above; the results are shown in Table 13–6.

In every case, the cost of the indirect route is less than the cost of the direct route, indicating that we have obtained an optimal solution minimizing the shipment costs. From Table 13–5, the total cost of shipment from factories to warehouses is:

$$(5)(\$0.90) + (15)(\$1.00) + (15)(\$1.00)$$
$$+ (5)(\$0.80) + (5)(\$0.80) = \$42.50$$

Note that the final solution uses five direct routes, where:

$$F + W - 1 = 5$$

F plus W may be generalized and called the sum of the number of margin requirements, since we may be dealing with entities other than warehouses and factories.

Table 13–5   Second Solution

Source \ Destination	W_1	W_2	W_3	Units Available
F_1	$0.90 5	$1.00 15	$1.30 0	20
F_2	$1.00 0	$1.40 0	$1.00 15	15
F_3	$1.00 0	$0.80 5	$0.80 5	10
Units Demanded	5	20	20	45

Table 13–6

Unused Route	Cost of Using Direct Route	Cost of Using Indirect Route
F_1W_3	$1.30	$1.00
F_2W_1	1.00	0.90
F_2W_2	1.40	1.00
F_3W_1	1.00	0.70

Integer Solutions

If all of the numbers representing factory availabilities and warehouse requirements are integers, then the optimum solution to a transportation problem will
contain all integers. This result follows from the fact that the procedure involves
only additions and subtractions of integers, and an initial integer solution will
remain integer until the optimal solution is reached. In the general linear programming problem covered in Chapters 10–12, integer solutions were not
guaranteed.

Degeneracy

In some programming situations, the problem of degeneracy appears. Degeneracy is caused by less than $F + W - 1$ boxes being used, which makes it impossible to evaluate a zero box by the direct methods described above.[4]

---

[4]For example, degeneracy may occur where a factory ships its entire output to one warehouse
and satisfies the total needs of that warehouse.

To resolve the degeneracy case, record some very small amount, say d, in one of the zero boxes. We shall treat d as if it were a standard quantity, and therefore an eligible node for evaluating indirect routes. In the final solution, the d is assigned a value of zero if it is still present in the calculations.

Supply Not Equal to Demand

If supply is not equal to demand, a "dummy" source or destination may be added to remove the discrepancy. For example, suppose the supply available $(F_1 + F_2 + F_3)$ exceeded the total warehouse requirements $(W_1 + W_2 + W_3)$ by 10 units. Then we would create a dummy warehouse 4 with requirement $W_4 = 10$ units, and shipments from any of the three factories to warehouse 4 would have a zero cost in the objective function. The factories supplying the dummy warehouse would actually reduce their production by the amount going to warehouse 4.

Computer Solutions

Just as an ordinary linear programming problem is solved in practice by using a computer program to perform the necessary steps, computer software exists to solve the less complicated transportation problem. These "Transportation LP" computer codes operate much faster than standard LP codes, since they can take advantage of the special structure of the transportation problem. The steps of these methods have been demonstrated so that a better understanding of the problem and the solution may be obtained.

Economic Interpretations

The Costs of Indirect Routes

The costs of the indirect routes are equivalent to the Z_j values (see Chapter 12) in standard linear programming and can be used in the same way.[5] Suppose, for example, after completing our analysis in Tables 13–5 and 13–6, we were informed that the requirements for W_2 had increased one unit and that the capacity of F_2 would be expanded to handle this increase. What would be the incremental increase in the shipping costs?

The cost of the indirect route for $F_2 W_2$ immediately gives us the answer. The direct route would cost $1.40, and the indirect only $1. Hence, the incremental cost of shipping this unit is simply $1. Table 13–7 shows how the original solution would be modified. Note that up to five units could be shipped using this indirect route.

---

[5] The $C_j - Z_j$ values, which represent the **reduced costs**, are the difference between the costs for the direct and indirect routes.

Table 13–7   **Effect of One Additional Unit for F_2 and W_2**

Source \ Destination	W_1	W_2	W_3	Units Available
F_1	5	15		20
F_2			15 + 1	15 + 1
F_3		5 + 1	5 − 1	10
Units Demanded	5	20 + 1	20	45 + 1

Changes in Shipping Costs

We can also examine the sensitivity of the solution to changes in shipping costs. For example, if the shipping cost from F_1 to W_3 (which is now $1.30) were to change, would our solution change? Note that the cost of the indirect route for F_1W_3 is $1. The shipping cost would have to fall below $1 before the direct route was used; that is, before the solution in Table 13–5 changed.

Locational Advantages

Suppose one unit was added to the requirements of W_1 (from five units to six units). Which factory should be expanded to meet this requirement? Using the method presented above, we can find the cost of supplying one unit to W_1 for each factory:

Factory	Route Used	Cost
F_1	Direct	$0.90
F_2	Indirect	0.90
F_3	Indirect	0.70

Note that it costs $0.20 less (considering only shipping costs) to supply the additional unit from F_3 than from either F_1 or F_2. There is a **locational advantage** for F_3 of $0.20. Actually, this same advantage holds even if the additional unit is required at W_2 or W_3.[6]

The same method can be used to examine the locational advantages of the warehouses. Suppose factory F_1 is to be expanded by one unit of capacity. A

---

[6]Just as with dual prices in standard linear programming, the locational advantage is a marginal value. It holds only over a limited range of changes in capacity or requirements.

sales campaign is to be undertaken in one of the warehouse regions to increase demand by one unit. Considering only the transportation costs, in which region should the campaign be undertaken? The costs of supplying each warehouse from F_1 is:

Warehouse	Route Used	Cost
W_1	Direct	$0.90
W_2	Direct	1.00
W_3	Indirect	1.00

This demonstrates that W_1 has a $0.10 locational advantage over the other two warehouses. This means that it would cost $0.10 less to satisfy one unit of additional demand in the W_1 region than in either of the others.

Knowledge of these locational advantages can be quite useful in management decisions about which of several plants to expand, or about the regions in which to attempt to increase sales.

SUMMARY The transportation problem is a special case of the general linear programming problem. For problems that fit its structure, a simplified solution method is available. An initial feasible solution with $F + W - 1$ routes is first found; then each unused route is evaluated by calculating its indirect cost. If the direct cost is less than the indirect cost, then the direct route should be added. The process is repeated until no unused routes are favorable. When supply is not equal to demand, dummy sources of supply or demand must be created.

Multiple Objectives and Goal Programming

In linear programming, a single objective is maximized or minimized subject to constraints. In many important problems, particularly in the public sector, there are several objectives that the decision maker is trying to achieve. In Chapter 6, decision making with multiple objectives was discussed for general problems. Here we specifically treat multiple objectives in linear programming problems.

Consider as an example the manager of a state forest. State law may specify that the forest manager must manage the forest so as to enhance timber growth, increase cover and food for forest animals, and of course do this at as low a cost as possible.

Suppose our manager has two activities that can be undertaken—thinning the forest (cutting out undergrowth) and cutting fire lanes. Let:

X_1 = Acres of land thinned
X_2 = Kilometers of fire lanes cut

Table 13–8   Costs and Benefits for Forest Activities

	Activity	
	Thinning (variable X_1, per acre)	Fire Lanes (variable X_2, per kilometer)
Costs:		
Cost (dollars)	$500	$500
Labor required (hours)	150	50
Benefits:		
Timber growth (units)	10	−5
Animal cover (units)	−10	60

Each of these activities has a cost and requires labor. In addition, each produces benefits (possibly negative) in terms of timber growth and animal cover.

As shown in Table 13–8, thinning costs $500 per acre, requires 150 labor hours per acre, results in timber growth of 10 units, but reduces animal cover by 10 units for each acre thinned. Cutting fire lanes costs $500 per kilometer cut, requires 50 labor hours per kilometer cut, reduces timber growth by 5 units per kilometer cut, and increases animal cover by 60 units per kilometer cut.

The decision problem for the forest manager is to determine X_1 and X_2; that is, how many acres to thin and how many kilometers of fire lanes to cut. The manager has available only 90,000 hours of labor. In addition, forest conditions limit the cutting of fire lanes to no more than 300 kilometers. The manager has a budget of $350,000.

The constraints for the problem can be expressed as:

$$150X_1 + 50X_2 \le 90{,}000 \quad \text{(labor hours)}$$
$$X_2 \le 300 \quad \text{(limit on fire lanes)}$$
$$500X_1 + 500X_2 \le 350{,}000 \quad \text{(budget)}$$

Three goals are to be satisfied simultaneously. The manager should achieve as much timber growth as possible, should provide as much animal cover as possible, and should reduce costs below budget as much as possible. There are several approaches for incorporating all these multiple objectives; we describe each in turn.

Approach 1: Single Objective with Others as Constraints

The manager may decide that one objective is of such importance that it overrides the others. The other objectives may be built in as constraints at some minimal level. The problem then becomes an ordinary linear programming problem of maximizing an objective function subject to constraints.

For example, our manager may decide that timber growth is most important. The objective then becomes:

Maximize: $10X_1 - 5X_2$

where the coefficients 10 and -5 from Table 13–8 are the effects on timber growth of thinning and cutting fire lanes, respectively. The constraints on labor hours, fire lanes, and budget, as shown above, would apply. The manager may also specify that there must be at least a minimal level of 1,000 units of animal cover with the additional constraint:

$$-10X_1 + 60X_2 \geq 1,000$$

where the coefficients of -10 and 60 represent the effects of thinning and cutting fire lanes on animal cover (see Table 13–8).

Figure 13–1 graphs this problem. The color-shaded region is the feasible region satisfying all the constraints including that on animal cover. The objective

Figure 13–1   Solution to Example Problem with Maximization of Timber Growth Objective

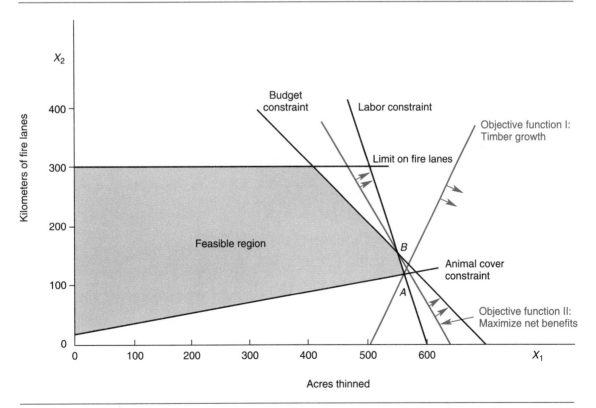

of maximizing timber growth is obtained at the point $X_1 = 563$ and $X_2 = 111$, with 5,080 units of timber growth (see point A in Figure 13–1).

It would have been possible for the manager to choose to maximize animal cover, while setting a minimum level for timber growth as a constraint. Or minimal levels for both animal cover and timber growth could be specified, and cost minimized. A major difficulty with this approach is that it does not involve any balancing or *trade-offs* of the various objectives. The manager might be more satisfied with more animal cover and less timber, but there is no direct way to achieve this. The manager could try different sets of constraints until a satisfactory solution emerges, but this is an awkward approach.

Approach 2: Define Trade-Offs among Objectives

In Chapter 6, one approach to multiobjective problems was to specify the trade-offs among the objectives. In the present example, one would specify how much a unit of timber growth was worth, and how much a unit of animal cover was worth, both in dollar terms. Then these objectives could be traded off with each other and with dollars of cost. By this process, the total net benefits in dollars could be maximized.

For example, suppose the manager decided that a unit of timber growth was worth $600 and a unit of animal cover was worth $100. This implies that the manager would be indifferent between obtaining an additional unit of timber growth or six units of animal cover, or $600 savings.

Given these values, we can compute the net benefit for each of the decision variables X_1 and X_2. Recall that each unit of X_1 (acre thinned) produces 10 units of timber (worth $600 each), removes 10 units of animal cover (at $100 each), and costs $500. Hence, the net benefit of a unit of X_1 is:

$$10(\$600) - 10(\$100) - \$500 = \$4,500$$

Similarly, the net benefit of a kilometer of fire lanes is computed as $-5(\$600) + 60(\$100) - \$500 = \$2,500$. Then the linear programming problem to maximize net benefits is:

Maximize: $4,500X_1 + 2,500X_2$

Subject to:
$$150X_1 + 50X_2 \leq 90,000$$
$$X_2 \leq 300$$
$$500X_1 + 500X_2 \leq 350,000$$

The optimal solution to this linear programming problem results in values of $X_1 = 550$ and $X_2 = 150$ (see point B in Figure 13–1). This can be converted into units of timber and animal cover, resulting in 3,750 units of timber and 3,500 units of animal cover.

The success of using this approach lies in being able to define the necessary trade-offs. As indicated in Chapter 6, this is not an easy task. Our manager may find it very difficult to attach a dollar value to a unit of animal cover. Some people would balk at even trying to provide such a value.

Approach 3: Goal Programming

A third approach is that of *goal programming*. The decision maker specifies desirable goals for each objective. Then the problem is formulated so as to minimize the shortfall related to obtaining these goals. The goals are usually specified at desirable (high) levels, so that it is not possible to satisfy all simultaneously.

Suppose the manager in our example set as desirable goals the production of 5,000 units of timber and 6,000 units of animal cover. The constraints then become:

$$
\begin{array}{lrcll}
\text{Timber:} & 10X_1 - 5X_2 + U_1 - E_1 & = & 5,000 & \\
\text{Animal Cover:} & -10X_1 + 60X_2 + U_2 - E_2 & = & 6,000 & \\
\text{Cost:} & 500X_1 + 500X_2 + U_3 - E_3 & = & 350,000 & \textbf{(13--1)} \\
\text{Labor:} & 150X_1 + 50X_2 & \leq & 90,000 & \\
\text{Fire lanes:} & X_2 & \leq & 300 &
\end{array}
$$

The variables U_1, U_2 represent the amounts by which the plan fails to achieve the timber goal of 5,000 units and the animal cover goal of 6,000 units. Thus, these can be described as the shortfall or *underage*. The variable U_3 is the savings in dollars below the budget level.

The variables E_1, E_2, and E_3 represent the amounts by which the specified goals are *exceeded*—that is, the overage.

One method of forming the objective function in goal programming is to minimize the shortfall. Thus, the objective might be to minimize $(U_1 + U_2 - U_3)$. This would minimize the amounts by which timber growth and animal cover fell below the goals and maximize the cost underage (by minimizing the negative of U_3) subject to the constraints above. The simplicity of this approach is appealing. But there is a major assumption, that one unit savings in dollars has the same value as a unit shortfall in timber and a unit shortfall in animal cover. The objective function has given equal weight to each.

A better approach is to define specifically the trade-offs among the various objectives. Suppose our manager decides that one unit in shortfall for timber is worth 600 times as much as a dollar savings and that a unit shortfall in animal cover is worth 100 times a dollar savings. Then the objective function would be:

Minimize: $600U_1 + 100U_2 - U_3$

again subject to the constraints (13–1).

This objective function attaches zero value to exceeding any of the goals of timber growth or animal cover. The manager might decide that there is some value to these overages and attach weights to the E variables also. For example, exceeding the timber goal may have value of $50 per unit, and exceeding the animal cover value may be worth $25 per unit. Also, each dollar over the cost budget (E_3) may be five times as important as a dollar saved (U_3). Then the objective function becomes:

Minimize: $600U_1 + 100U_2 - U_3 - 50E_1 - 25E_2 + 5E_3$

Minimizing the negative values for U_3, E_1, and E_2 is equivalent to maximizing.

One optimum solution to this linear programming problem requires thinning 550 acres and cutting 150 kilometers of fire lanes. The budget is met exactly. There are shortfalls of 250 units for the timber goal and 2,500 units for the animal cover goal. There is an alternative optimum basic solution, requiring 537 acres thinned, 189 kilometers of fire lanes cut, and 579 unit shortfall on timber but no shortfall on animal cover. However, this requires exceeding the budget by $13,160.

We can now observe that goal programming differs from Approach 2 (directly defining the trade-offs) in two respects:

1. Specific goals are incorporated and a different value is attached to the shortfall and excess of the goal. In Approach 2, a single weight was attached to each objective, and this applied over the entire range of possible values.
2. The objective function is defined in terms of the objectives themselves. In Approach 2, the net benefits for each activity had to be calculated, and these net benefits were then included in the objective function. The goal programming approach makes it easier to see the relative value attached to each of the multiple objectives.

Approach 4: Priority Programming

Suppose the manager in our example balks at assigning specific trade-offs among the various multiple objectives, but is willing to assign priorities to each, indicating the order in which each is to be satisfied. For example, suppose the goal constraints are specified as:

Timber growth: $10X_1 - 5X_2 + U_1 - E_1 = 3,000$
Animal cover: $-10X_1 + 60X_2 + U_2 - E_2 = 1,000$
Cost: $500X_1 + 500X_2 + U_3 - E_3 = 350,000$

The manager lists priorities as:

1. Minimize the shortfall of timber growth (U_1).
2. Minimize the shortfall of animal cover (U_2).
3. Minimize budget excess (E_3).
4. Maximize excess timber growth (E_1).
5. Maximize excess animal cover (E_2).
6. Maximize budget savings (U_3).

The priority programming approach is to attempt to achieve each objective *sequentially*, rather than *simultaneously*. We will illustrate the approach graphically.

Figure 13–2   **Steps in Priority Programming Example**

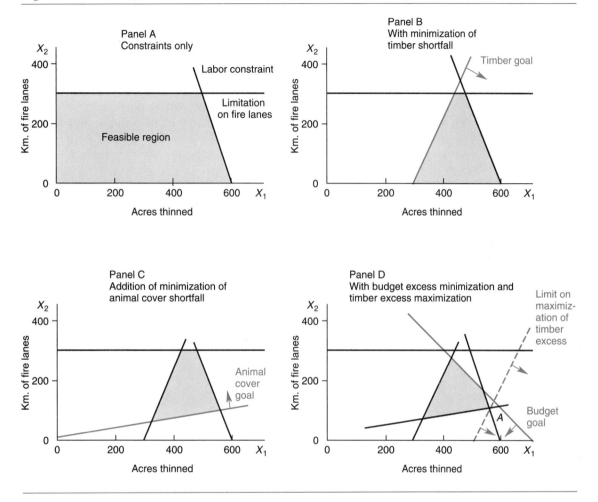

Consider Figure 13–2. Panel A shows the feasible region, considering only the constraints on labor and the limit on fire lanes. The manager's first priority is to minimize the shortfall in timber growth. In Panel B, this is minimized until there is no shortfall, and the remaining feasible region is shown as the color-shaded area. If there were no feasible region remaining, the priority programming process would stop, having achieved only as much as possible of the highest priority goal.

Since there is some feasible region left, the next highest priority is considered, namely minimization of shortfall in animal cover. This is shown in Panel C, and this can also be minimized until there is no shortfall, with the remaining feasible region shown in color.

The third priority goal of minimizing budget excess is shown in Panel D. This also may be achieved in total. Finally, the fourth-order priority goal of maximization of excess timber growth is invoked. This results in the solution, shown as point A in Panel D, of 563 acres thinned (X_1) and 111 kilometers of fire lanes cut (X_2). Since there is no feasible region remaining, it is not possible to proceed to the fifth- and sixth-order priority goals.

Special computer programs have been developed for priority programming. For a two-variable problem, of course, the solution can be obtained graphically, as we have illustrated. But more realistic problems involve many dimensions, and graphic solutions are not possible. The reader who is interested in the priority programming algorithm is referred to the references given at the end of this chapter.

SUMMARY

There are several methods of incorporating multiple objectives in linear programming problems. Simple approaches involve converting to a single-objective function by weighting the objectives or by incorporating the secondary objectives as constraints. Goal programming involves defining goals and including variables for deviations from these goals (either shortfalls or excesses). The objective function is defined to minimize the (possibly weighted) deviations. Priority programming defines goal constraints similarly, but involves satisfying the goals in sequential order, rather than simultaneously.

APPENDIX

The Transportation Problem Expressed in Conventional LP Form

In this appendix we present the transportation problem in standard LP notation.

- F_1, F_2, and F_3 are the production capacities of three factories.
- W_1, W_2, and W_3 are the needs of three warehouses.
- C_{11}, C_{12}, . . . , C_{ij}, . . . , C_{33} are the unit costs associated with factory i supplying warehouse j.
- The total transportation cost is f (we want to minimize f).
- X_{ij} is the amount transferred from the ith factory to the jth warehouse.

The LP formulation of the transportation problem is:

Minimize: $f = C_{11}X_{11} + C_{12}X_{12} + \ldots + C_{ij}X_{ij} + \ldots + C_{33}X_{33}$
Subject to:

$$
\begin{array}{llllll}
X_{11} + X_{12} + X_{13} & & & & & = F_1 \\
& X_{21} + X_{22} + X_{23} & & & & = F_2 \\
& & X_{31} + X_{32} + X_{33} & & & = F_3 \\
X_{11} & + X_{21} & + X_{31} & & & = W_1 \\
X_{12} & + X_{22} & + X_{32} & & & = W_2 \\
X_{13} & + X_{23} & + X_{33} & & & = W_3
\end{array}
$$

All $X_{ij} \geq 0$. Note that the coefficients of all X_{ij} in the constraint equations will be either 0 or 1, and they form a distinct pattern. If all variables and constraints in a linear programming problem fit the pattern shown above, then the problem is a transportation problem, and the special procedure of this chapter can be used to solve it. (The problem need not necessarily deal with transportation or distribution.)

Bibliography

Ignizio, J. P. *Goal Programming and Extensions*. Lexington, Mass.: Lexington Books, 1976.
————. *Linear Programming in Single and Multiple Objective Systems*. Englewood Cliffs, N.J.: Prentice Hall, 1982.

Lee, S. M. *Goal Programming for Decision Analysis*. New York: Van Nostrand Reinhold, 1973.
Also see the bibliography at the end of Chapter 10.

Problems with Answers

13–1. Using the transportation method, prepare a table of optimum allocation of shipments from the factories to the warehouses:

Factories	Amount Available
F_1	10
F_2	20
F_3	30
Total	60

Warehouses	Amount Needed
W_1	15
W_2	28
W_3	17
Total	60

The unit costs of shipping are:

	W_1	W_2	W_3
F_1	$0.90	$0.95	$1.30
F_2	1.00	1.40	0.95
F_3	1.05	0.85	1.10

13–2. Using the transportation method, prepare a table of optimum allocation of shipments from the factories to the warehouses:

Factories	Amount Available
F_1	20
F_2	15
F_3	30
Total	65

Warehouses	Amount Needed
W_1	10
W_2	26
W_3	29
Total	65

The unit costs of shipping are:

	W_1	W_2	W_3
F_1	$1.10	$1.12	$1.20
F_2	1.20	1.00	1.05
F_3	1.10	0.90	0.95

13–3. Using the transportation method, attempt to prepare a table of optimum allocation of shipments from the factories to the warehouses. Use the data and initial solution given below.

Unit Costs and Units Supplied and Demanded

Destination / Source	W_1	W_2	W_3	Units Available
F_1	$0.80	$0.85	$1.45	10
F_2	$0.90	$0.70	$1.05	20
F_3	$1.00	$0.60	$1.15	30
Units Demanded	10	28	22	60

First Solution

Destination / Source	W_1	W_2	W_3	Units Available
F_1	10			10
F_2		20		20
F_3		8	22	30
Units Demanded	10	28	22	60

13–4. A firm produces two products, A and B. The profit contribution and resource usages for a unit of each product are shown below.

	Product A	Product B
Profit contribution ($ per unit)	15	10
Resource usages:		
Machine time (hours per unit)	4	5
Raw material (tons per unit)	5	4
Skilled labor (hours per unit)	1	5
Unskilled labor (hours per unit)	2	0

The firm has available a maximum of 100 hours of machine time and 30 hours of unskilled labor.

There is a shortage of raw material. The firm has received an allocation of 100 tons from its headquarters, with instructions to use as little as possible, returning any excess for use in other divisions. More than the 100 tons allocated could be obtained, but only if "absolutely necessary."

The firm has a skilled labor force with 75 hours available on regular time. These skilled workers are reluctant to work overtime but will if necessary. Management wants to utilize the skilled workers during regular time as fully as possible.

The firm has a $300 profit goal, which it hopes to meet or exceed.

a. Define the decision variables, and define the constraints on machine time and unskilled labor.

b. Formulate the goal constraints on skilled labor, raw material, and profit. Allow for both underages and excesses in these constraints.

c. Assume that management attaches costs of $15 per ton to using raw material in excess of the allocation, $10 per hour to overtime for skilled workers, and $5 per hour to idle time for skilled workers. In addition, raw material unused (below the allocation) has a value of $5 per ton. A dollar of profit has the same value, regardless of whether or not the profit goal is exceeded.

Formulate the goal programming objective function.

d. Before going on with this part, check to see that your formulation is correct (by looking at the answers at the end of the book).

Now graph the decision problem. First, include the constraints on unskilled labor and machine time. Next, draw in the lines representing the skilled labor and raw material goals. Finally, include the profit goal.

e. Evaluate the following possible solution points. Find each point on your

graph. For each one, substitute in each of the goal equations to determine the underage or excess. Then substitute these values in the objective functions of (c). Find the optimal solution (with lowest value). The points are:
(1) Product A = 8.33 units; product B = 13.33 units.

(2) Product A = 11.11 units; product B = 11.11 units.
(3) Product A = 15 units; product B = 8 units.
(4) Product A = 15 units; product B = 6.25 units.

Problems

13–5. Instead of using the first solution as given in Problem 13–3, solve Problem 13–3 starting from the solution given below:

Alternative First Solution

Source ╲ Destination	W_1	W_2	W_3	Units Available
F_1	5	5		10
F_2	5		15	20
F_3		23	7	30
Units Demanded	10	28	22	60

13–6. Three classifications of workers (P_1, P_2, and P_3) may be used on three jobs (J_1, J_2, and J_3). Each worker has a different cost for each job, as shown in the following table. The number of workers required on each job and the number of workers available are also given in this table.

Direct Costs

Worker ╲ Job	J_1	J_2	J_3	Workers Available
P_1	$1.00	$1.10	$1.20	10
P_2	$0.90	$0.80	$1.10	15
P_3	$0.80	$0.85	$1.15	20
Workers Needed	5	10	30	45

Use the transportation method to find the optimum allocation.

13–7. A firm has two factories that ship to three regional warehouses. The unit costs of transportation are:

Unit Transportation Costs

		Warehouse	
Factory	W_1	W_2	W_3
F_1	$2	$2	$5
F_2	4	1	1

Factory 2 is old and has a variable manufacturing cost of $2 per unit. Factory 1 is modern and produces for $1 per unit. Factory 2 has a capacity of 25 units, and factory 1 has a capacity of 40 units. The needs at the warehouses are:

Warehouse	Units Needed
W_1	20
W_2	10
W_3	25

How much should each factory ship to each warehouse?

Hint: Add the manufacturing cost to the transportation cost to obtain a "unit delivered" cost. Minimize this. Also, set up a dummy warehouse to handle the excess capacity.

13–8. The ABC Company has four factories shipping to five warehouses. The shipping costs, requirements, and capacities are shown on the next page:

Shipping Costs ($ per case)

	W_1	W_2	W_3	W_4	W_5
F_1	1	3	4	5	6
F_2	2	2	1	4	5
F_3	1	5	1	3	1
F_4	5	2	4	5	4

Miles from Terminals to Plants

Terminals \\ Plants	E	F	G	H	I
A	20	47	17	41	62
B	74	13	52	40	32
C	60	31	51	71	68
D	39	41	37	21	38

Requirements (000s of cases)		*Factory Capacities (000s of cases)*	
W_1	80	F_1	100
W_2	50	F_2	60
W_3	50	F_3	60
W_4	30	F_4	50
W_5	40		

The company was considering closing down the fourth factory (F_4) because of high operating costs. If this were done, 30 units of capacity would be added to factory 3. The transportation manager was worried about the effect of this move on the company's transportation costs. He noted that warehouse 2 (W_2) received about 30 thousand cases from F_4. Since the shipping cost from F_3 to W_2 was $5 (compared with $2 from F_4 to W_2), the transportation manager estimated that the effect of closing F_4 would be a $90,000 increase in transportation costs. Do you agree with the transportation manager? What effect do you think closing F_4 will have on transportation costs?

13–9. Refer to Problem 10–14.
  a. Is (*a*) of that problem a transportation LP? Why or why not?
  b. Is (*b*) of that problem a transportation LP? Why or why not?

13–10. The Genesee Trucking Co. has four terminals, A, B, C, and D. At the beginning of each day, there are eight, six, four, and seven tractors available at the respective terminals. During the previous night, trailers were loaded at plants E, F, G, H, and I in the quantities three,

six, five, six, and five, respectively. The mileage between the terminals and the plants are given in the table, "Miles from terminals to plants."

From which terminals should the dispatcher send how many tractors to which plants if the total number of miles traveled by all tractors in picking up the trailers is to be minimized?

13–11. The dean of a business school is planning enrollment in the school's two major programs, an undergraduate course leading to a BBA degree, and a graduate program leading to the MBA. The dean has available 36 senior faculty and 42 junior faculty. To teach the courses for each BBA candidate, .02 senior faculty and .03 junior faculty are required. In other words, for every 100 BBAs, the school needs two senior faculty and three junior faculty. For every 100 MBAs, six senior faculty and four junior faculty are required.

The dean's problem is to determine the number of MBA and BBA students to enroll. Tuition for an MBA is $15,000 per year and $12,000 per year for a BBA. The university provost has decreed that the enrollment in the MBA program is limited to no more than half the enrollment in the BBA program.

The dean has three objectives. The first is tuition income and the dean has set a goal of $15 million. A second objective is to satisfy the needs of local business for BBAs, and a goal of an enrollment level of 1,000 BBAs has been set. The third objective is to satisfy the demand for MBAs, and the goal of 400 MBAs has been set. Assume that the dean wishes to meet the demand for BBAs and MBAs as closely as possible, with excesses and underages both to be avoided if possible. Also, the dean wishes to obtain as much tuition income as possible.

a. Formulate the constraints for the dean's problem as a goal-programming problem. Allow both underages and excesses for the goal constraints.

b. Formulate the objective function, assuming the following weights for each underage or excess.

Weight ($ equivalents)	Objective
15	Tuition underage
30,000	Shortfall in meeting BBA demand
24,000	Shortfall in meeting MBA demand
3	Tuition excess
9,000	BBA goal excess
6,000	MBA goal excess

c. Graph the problem. First, graph only the nongoal constraints. Then draw in the goal equations. Find the solution that is optimal. You may need to try several points to find which one is optimal. Consider points that are intersections of the various constraints and goal equations.

d. Assume that the dean wishes to assign priorities to the various goals in the order shown under (b). That is, minimizing tuition underage is the highest priority, minimizing the shortfall in BBA demand is next, and so on. Use the priority programming approach, and graphically solve the problem.

More Challenging Problems

13–12. A company manufactures two lines of its products, regular and super. The products are subject to seasonal sales fluctuations. In order to keep costs low, the company produces during low-volume months and stores the goods as inventory for the high-volume months. The projected sales of the two lines of product are given in the accompanying table.

The production facility of the factory has a capacity of 10,000 cases per month on the regular shift. Overtime can be used up to a capacity of 8,000 cases per month. However, it costs $1.20 per case more to produce on the overtime shift than on the regular shift.

Inventory of the finished product can be stored for any number of months. However, it costs 80 cents per case to store the regular product for one month, and the cost to store the super product is $1 per case per month.

What production schedule for the company minimizes the total overtime production and inventory storage costs?

Month	Sales (000s of cases)		
	Regular Line	Super Line	Total
January	4	2	6
February	6	2	8
March	6	6	12
April	8	10	18
May	8	12	20
June	4	8	12
Totals	36	40	76

Hint: Treat the different shifts each month as the sources; the product requirements in the different months are the destinations. Then solve as a transportation problem.

13–13. The Zeta Products Company has four factories that supply five warehouses. The variable costs of manufacturing and shipping of one ton of product from each factory to each warehouse are shown as numbers in the upper left-hand corner of the boxes in the accompanying table. The factory capacities and warehouse requirements in thousands of tons are shown in the margins of the table. Note that there is a dummy warehouse (labeled *slack*) to account for the difference between total capacity and total requirements.

After several iterations, a solution is obtained (the color numbers in the table). Answer each of the following questions independently.

a. Is this solution optimal? If so, what is the total cost?

b. Is there an alternative optimum? If so, what is the alternative optimum solution?

c. Suppose some new equipment was installed that reduced the variable operating cost by $2 per ton in the second factory (F_2). Is the shipping schedule still optimal? If not, what is the new optimum solution?

d. Suppose the freight charge from F_1 to W_1 was reduced by $2. Would this change the shipping schedule? If so, what would be the new optimum solution?

e. How much would the manufacturing cost have to be reduced in factory 1 before production would be increased above 55 (thousand) tons?

f. Suppose that new estimates indicated that requirements at W_2 would be 25 rather than the 20 originally estimated. What would be the total incremental cost if:
   (1) No expansion of any plant were undertaken?
   (2) F_3 was expanded by five to meet the additional requirements?

g. A program to increase sales in one of the warehouse districts is about to be undertaken. If the effectiveness of this program were the same in all districts, in which district would you suggest that the program be undertaken? Why? (Assume the selling price is the same in each warehouse district.)

Sources / Destinations	W_1	W_2	W_3	W_4	W_5	Slack	Capacities
F_1	17	9	14 / 25	10 / 30	14	0 / 20	75
F_2	13 / 10	6 / 20	11 / 15	11	12	0	45
F_3	8 / 30	17	9	12	12	0	30
F_4	15	20	11 / 10	14	6 / 40	0	50
Requirements	40	20	50	30	40	20	200

13–14. A company has three factories that supply three market areas. The transportation costs of shipping from each factory to each warehouse are given in boxes in the upper left corners of the table below. Factory capacities and market area requirements are shown in the margin.

After several iterations, the solution shown is obtained. (Solution is given in color.) Answer each of the following questions independently.

a. Is there a solution as good as or better than the one shown in the table below? If so, find it.

b. Suppose that demand at destination W_1 is increased by two units. Which factory will supply the additional units? What is the additional transportation cost in the system? What is the new solution?

c. Suppose 15 additional units are needed by destination W_3. Which factory or factories would supply the additional units? What would be the additional transportation costs in the system?

d. What would be the savings in transportation cost if the capacity of source F_3 could be increased by 10 units?

e. Suppose that the transportation cost from source F_1 to destination W_3 dropped to $2 instead of $4. Would this change the solution? What would be the cost reduction in the system?

13–15. A firm makes four products, labeled A, B, C, and D. The executive committee is meeting to decide on the product mix. The controller wants the mix that achieves the most profit; the sales manager wants to obtain the largest market share, and the production manager wants to balance the production facility. The president must mediate these potentially conflicting objectives.

The information on the four products is shown in Table 13–9.

The table shows the hours required per unit for each product in assembly, test, and machine time, as well as time in departments 1 and 2.

The profit per unit for each product is also shown in Table 13–9. The controller thinks the firm should emphasize products B and C, since they produce the most profit per unit. The controller would like to see the firm have a profit of $10,000.

The marketing manager views each product as a sale and hence, counting as one point in market share. A point in market share is a 0.01 percent share. The goal for the marketing manager is 800 share points (that is, 8 percent of the total market).

The production manager notes that the firm has 3,000 hours of assembly time available, 1000 hours of test time available, and 7,500 hours of machine time available. There are no limits on

Sources \ Destinations	W_1	W_2	W_3	Slack	Capacities
F_1	2	1 _10_	4	0 _10_	**20**
F_2	1 _10_	2	3 _10_	0 _10_	**30**
F_3	2	1 _10_	2	0	**10**
Requirements	**10**	**10**	**20**	**20**	**60**

Table 13–9   (for Problem 13–15)

	Product			
	A	*B*	*C*	*D*
Resources:				
Assembly time (hours)	4	15	5	2
Test time (hours)	2	2	2	1
Machine time (hours)	6	2	10	12
Department 1 (hours)	1	2	1	*
Department 2 (hours)	½	1	2	*
Goals:				
Profit ($)	10	50	20	5
Market share (points)	1	1	1	1

*Product D requires two hours of time, but this can be done either in department 1 or department 2, or split between them as desired.

hours for departments 1 and 2. However, it is the balancing of the hours worked in these departments that is of concern. The production manager would like the hours worked in each of departments 1 and 2 to be as nearly equal as possible.

The president has decided that a weighting must be given to each objective. A dollar profit is worth the same, regardless of whether above or below the controller's goal of $10,000. A point of market share is worth $10 below the 800 goal, but worth only $5 above it. A one-hour imbalance in production departments has a cost of $10.

Formulate this as a goal-programming problem. Solve on a computer, if possible.

13–16. Refer to Problem 10–16.
     a. Is (*a*) of that problem a transportation LP? Why or why not?
     b. Is (*b*) of that problem a transportation LP? Why or why not?

13–17. Refer to Problem 10–26. Is that problem a transportation LP? Why or why not?

13–18. One way to obtain an initial feasible solution to a transportation problem is to use routes that are both the lowest cost in the row and the lowest cost in the column. Prepare a small example (two sources and two destinations) showing that the optimum solution need not use such a route.

CHAPTER 14

Integer Programming and Branch and Bound Procedures[1]

Many business problems could be suitably formulated and solved by linear programming, except for one drawback—they require solutions that are integers. For example, a variable X in a linear programming model may refer to whether or not a new plant is built. If $X = 1$, the plant is to be built; $X = 0$ means no plant; and a value of X anywhere in between ($X = 0.56$, for instance) makes no sense. There is no guarantee that the standard solution procedures for linear programming will give such an integer solution.[2]

To deal with this problem, a set of techniques has been developed called **integer programming.** Some problems may require that all variables in the problem be integers—the **all-integer solution.** A special case of the all-integer solution occurs when all the variables can take on values of only 0 or 1. The most general case of integer programming is that in which some variables are required to be integers, but others can take on any values. This is called the **mixed-integer programming** problem.

The first part of this chapter will illustrate how integer programming formulations can represent a number of important business problems. In the second part, solution procedures for integer problems will be described. The appendix to this chapter describes how these procedures can be extended to other com-

---

[1] Chapters 10 and 11, dealing with linear programming, should be covered prior to studying this chapter.

[2] An important exception to this is the solution of network problems by LP, which do give integer solutions. The transportation problem and critical-path problem are examples of such network problems, and these are discussed in Chapters 13 and 20, respectively.

binatorial problems. Before we proceed, we will first illustrate a simple two-variable integer programming problem.

Example Consider the following integer programming problem:

Maximize: $P = 4X_1 + 5X_2$
Subject to: $\frac{2}{3}X_1 + X_2 \le 1$
$X_1 \le 1$
$X_1, X_2 \ge 0$
X_1, X_2 integer

The constraints and the objective function are plotted in Figure 14–1. Possible integer solutions are noted by small colored dots.

If we attempt to solve this problem ignoring the integer restrictions, the optimal linear programming solution is $X_1 = 1$, $X_2 = \frac{1}{3}$, denoted as A, producing a profit of \$5.67. However, this solution is not an integer solution, since $X_2 = \frac{1}{3}$. We might try to round the LP solution to the closest integer solution; in Figure 14–1, the closest integer solution to point A is $X_1 = 1$, $X_2 = 0$, producing a profit of \$4. However, such rounding can sometimes produce a solution that is infeasible; for example, if our second constraint were $X_1 \le 0.95$ instead of $X_1 \le 1$, then the solution $X_1 = 1$, $X_2 = 0$ would not satisfy the constraints.

More important, the rounded solution may not be optimal. In our example, consider the solution $X_1 = 0$, $X_2 = 1$; this solution is feasible and produces a larger profit (\$5), although it is not the "closest" integer solution to the answer

Figure 14–1

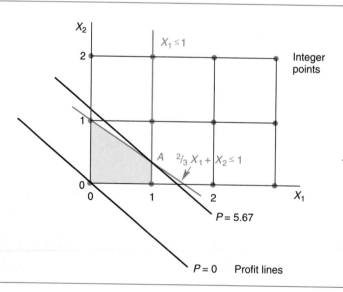

found using ordinary LP. As more dimensions are added to the problem, the rounding approach to solution becomes less and less desirable, and a systematic approach to finding a solution is necessary.

Before we describe ways of solving integer linear programming problems, we will first illustrate a variety of problems that can be formulated in this manner.

Formulation of Integer Programming Problems

In general, integer programming problems are formulated in much the same way as the standard linear programming problems discussed in Chapter 10, with the added proviso that one or more variables must assume integer values. That is, we establish a linear objective function that is maximized or minimized subject to linear constraints. However, there are some uses of zero/one variables that are unique to integer programming. A **zero/one** or **binary** variable is one that can take on only values of 0 or 1. The value 1 can be used to indicate the presence of something (a factory, for example); 0 indicates its absence. The use of binary variables is illustrated below.

The Fixed Charge Problem

Suppose a given product, if it is produced, contributes $5 per unit to profit. However, a one-time expense of $100 is incurred in setting up the machinery for a production run. This cost is zero if no units are produced.

Let X be the number of units produced. Then we could formulate the problem so that:

$$\text{Contribution} = \begin{cases} 5X - 100 & \text{if } X > 0 \\ 0 & \text{if } X = 0 \end{cases}$$

To rewrite the formulation in a linear form, we introduce a new variable Y, which takes on only the integer values of 0 or 1. Then we maximize $(5X - 100Y)$ subject to whatever other constraints we have plus the following two:

$$Y \leq 1 \qquad \text{and } Y \text{ is an integer}$$
$$\text{and } X \leq MY \qquad \text{where } M \text{ is some very large number}$$

Note that when $Y = 0$, the second constraint forces X to be 0 and the contribution $(5X - 100Y)$ is 0 also; when $Y = 1$, there is no practical limit on X; moreover, the fixed charge amount $100 is deducted from the profit. Hence, the use of the zero/one or binary integer variable Y allows us to formulate this type of problem with linear constraints.

The fixed-charge type of problem is common in business. There is an investment cost to build a new plant before any production can occur. There are usually fixed costs that have to be incurred if a second shift is undertaken or a new warehouse is opened.

Note in the above example that the objective function value and constraints are *linear*. That is, they involve only a constant times a variable (no squares or products of variables). One mistake that is sometimes made in integer programming formulations is to use nonlinear functions. For example, the fixed charge problem could be formulated by maximizing $5XY - 100Y$ with Y a zero/one variable as above. Note that this satisfies the requirements, since there is no profit or cost if $Y = 0$, and the profit is $5X - 100$ if $Y = 1$. However, the term $5XY$ is nonlinear because it involves the product of the two variables X and Y. Hence, this formulation would not be a valid integer linear programming problem.

Batch Size Problem

A similar problem is one in which some minimum level is required before an activity is undertaken. For example, a firm may have to buy a minimum quantity of at least 50 units of a certain product. Let X be the number of units bought. Then either $X = 0$ or $X \geq 50$.

This situation can be formulated with a zero/one integer variable Y by using constraints as follows:

$$X \leq MY \quad (M \text{ is a very large number})$$
$$X \geq 50Y$$

Note that if $Y = 0$, then, by the first constraint, X must be 0. If $Y = 1$, then, by the second constraint, X must be at least 50.

Either-Or Constraints

Sometimes, in a decision situation, either one or another constraint must hold, but not both. For example:

$$\text{Either:} \quad 5X_1 + 2X_2 \leq 10$$
$$\text{Or:} \quad 3X_1 - 4X_2 \leq 24$$
$$\text{But not both}$$

We can handle this in integer programming with the use of a zero/one Y variable by using both of the following modified constraints:

$$5X_1 + 2X_2 \leq 10 + MY$$
$$3X_1 - 4X_2 \leq 24 + M(1 - Y)$$

Note that when $Y = 0$, the first constraint is binding, but the right-hand side of the second becomes very large and hence is not binding. And conversely, when $Y = 1$, the second constraint binds but the first does not because MY is very large.

Examples of Integer Formulations

A Capital Budgeting Problem

Suppose that a firm has N projects ($i = 1, 2 \ldots N$) in which to invest capital. For each project i, let:

P_i = Net present value (the return of project i above cost, expressed in dollars of present value)[3]

C_i = Capital outlay at time zero for project i

R_{1i} = Cash flow in year 1 for project i

R_{2i} = Cash flow in year 2 for project i

.

.

.

R_{ti} = Cash flow in year t for project i

where each of the P, C, and R values is a known constant.

The firm wishes to select a *set* of projects to maximize net present value. A project is either undertaken in total, or rejected; that is, the firm cannot select some fraction of the project. The constraints may be of several kinds. For example:

1. A limited amount of funds available for investment at time zero—call this amount K.
2. Minimum required positive cash flows in future years 1, 2, . . . Call these requirements F_t.

For each project, we define a zero/one integer variable Y_i, where $Y_i = 1$ if the ith project is to be undertaken, and $Y_i = 0$ if not. We can then formulate this capital budgeting illustration as an integer programming problem as follows:

Maximize total net present value achieved:

$$P_1Y_1 + P_2Y_2 + P_3Y_3 + \ldots + P_NY_N$$

Subject to:
Capital available to invest:

$$C_1Y_1 + C_2Y_2 + \ldots + C_NY_N \leq K$$

Cash flow required in first period:

$$R_{11}Y_1 + R_{12}Y_2 + \ldots + R_{1N}Y_N \geq F_1$$

---

[3]To calculate the net present value, funds received in the future are discounted at an appropriate interest rate. The determination of this rate is not a trivial problem. See the appendix to Chapter 2.

Cash flow required in second period:

$$R_{21}Y_1 + R_{22}Y_2 + \ldots + R_{2N}Y_N \geq F_2$$

In general, cash flow required in t^{th} period:

$$R_{t1}Y_1 + R_{t2}Y_2 + \ldots + R_{tN}Y_N \geq F_t$$

In addition to these constraints, there may be restrictions on specific combinations of projects. For example, projects 3 and 4 may be mutually exclusive alternatives so that the firm would want either project 3 or 4 (or possibly neither), *but not* both included in the set of projects. The following constraint can be added that would achieve this:

$$Y_3 + Y_4 \leq 1$$

Note that this constraint would allow project 3 ($Y_3 = 1$) or project 4 ($Y_4 = 1$) but not both.[4] If exactly one of the two projects were required, there would be an equality:

$$Y_3 + Y_4 = 1$$

However, if the projects were such that at least one must be included (and possibly both), the constraint would become:

$$Y_3 + Y_4 \geq 1$$

As another example, suppose projects 5 and 6 were such that project 5 must be included if project 6 is included, but not necessarily the reverse. For example, project 5 might be building a factory in New England. Project 6 might be adding a second production line to this new factory. Obviously, the second line cannot be added if there is no factory, but the factory can be built without adding the second line. The following constraint will satisfy these requirements:

$$Y_6 \leq Y_5$$

Note that Y_5 can take on values of 0 or 1; however, Y_6 can be 1 only if Y_5 is also 1. Thus, the requirements are met.

The solution to this integer programming problem would result in a subset of Y variables, each equal to 1. The projects associated with these Y variables are selected for the capital budget. They satisfy all the constraints and maximize the objective function (highest total present value). The other Y variables would have values of 0; these are the rejected projects. This is an example in which all variables are binary (0 or 1).

---

[4] A brief word of caution is in order. These types of constraints often seem to be formulated easily by such expressions as $Y_3 \cdot Y_4 = 0$, which would require $Y_3 = 0$ or $Y_4 = 0$ or both. However, such a constraint is nonlinear because it involves the product of two variables. Integer linear programming requires linear constraints, and a linear objective function.

The maximum net present value of the problem should be compared to the solution that would result with a relaxation of one or more of the constraints so that the cost of the constraints can be estimated. If desired, the model can be modified to include investments of future years and their cash flows. Keep in mind that expanding the scope of the model also expands the amount of inputs that are required and the reliability of these inputs is apt to be low.

A Capacity Expansion Problem

Many firms having products with growing demand are faced with the decision of when to add new production capacity and how much to add. Consider, as an example, an electric utility that has estimated the demand for power in its region over the next nine years. Let D_t be the projected demand for the tth year ($t = 1, 2, \ldots 9$) above the current level. Let us suppose that three different size electric generating plants can be built with designation i ($i = 1, 2, 3$). Let K_i be the capacity and C_i the construction cost of the ith size of facility.

The utility wishes to minimize the discounted cost of new facilities, subject to having sufficient capacity to meet demands. Let α_t be the present value factor for year t (α_t is a number, less than 1, from a present value table). Let Y_{it} be a zero/one variable that has a value of 1 if a size i facility is built in year t. Thus, $Y_{25} = 1$ implies that a size 2 facility is to be added in year 5. Then, our objective function is:

Minimize:
$$\alpha_1[C_1Y_{11} + C_2Y_{21} + C_3Y_{31}] + \alpha_2[C_1Y_{12} + C_2Y_{22} + C_3Y_{32}]$$
$$+ \alpha_3[C_1Y_{13} + C_2Y_{23} + C_3Y_{33}] + \ldots + \alpha_9[C_1Y_{19} + C_2Y_{29} + C_3Y_{39}]$$

The first term in brackets represents the cost of any facility added in the first year, the second term is the same for the second year, and so on. The constraints require that sufficient capacity be added to meet expected additional demand. For the first year:

$$K_1Y_{11} + K_2Y_{21} + K_3Y_{31} \geq D_1$$

For the second year, any capacity added in the first year (above) plus that added in the second year is available to satisfy second year demand D_2:

$$[K_1Y_{11} + K_2Y_{21} + K_3Y_{31}] + [K_1Y_{12} + K_2Y_{22} + K_3Y_{32}] \geq D_2$$

Similarly, for the third year:

$$[K_1Y_{11} + K_2Y_{21} + K_3Y_{31}] + [K_1Y_{12} + K_2Y_{22} + K_3Y_{32}]$$
$$+ [K_1Y_{13} + K_2Y_{23} + K_3Y_{33}] \geq D_3$$

and so on for each year.

Note that each of the above constraints requires that the *accumulated* capacity equals or exceeds demand for a given year.

There may be additional constraints on the number of different sizes of facilities based on technical or other considerations. For example, if no more than four of the first size of facility can be built, a constraint can be added as follows:

$$Y_{11} + Y_{12} + Y_{13} + \ldots + Y_{19} \leq 4$$

Factory Size and Location

Suppose a firm is introducing a new product and must decide on the location and size of the factories to manufacture the product. The firm wishes to minimize the costs of manufacturing and distribution, as well as the costs for construction and operation of the facilities.

Three sites are available. Either a small or a large factory can be built on each site. At one of the sites, it is also possible to construct an extra large (huge) factory. Table 14–1 shows the costs and capacities for these alternatives. The annual cost in Table 14–1 includes the overhead for the facility as well as an annualized cost for the construction.

The firm must supply product to four regions. The distribution cost from each factory site to each region and the requirements for the regions are shown in Table 14–2.

The firm's problem is to decide which sites to use, how large a factory to build on the sites selected, and how much each factory should ship to each region.

The variables can be defined as:

A1 = Shipments (in 000s of units) from site A to region 1
A2 = Shipments (in 000s of units) from site A to region 2
.
.
.
C4 = Shipments (in 000s of units) from site C to region 4
PAS = Production (in 000s of units) at Small plant at site A
PAL = Production (in 000s of units) at Large plant at site A
.
.
.
PCL = Production (in 000s of units) at Large plant at site C
YAS = Integer zero/one variable that is 1 if a Small plant is to be constructed on site A, and 0 otherwise.
YAL = Integer zero/one variable that is 1 if a Large plant is to be constructed on site A, and 0 otherwise.
.
.
.
YCL = Integer zero/one variable that is 1 if a Large plant is to be constructed on site C, and 0 otherwise.

Table 14–1   **Costs and Capacities**

Location	Size	Annual Cost ($000s)	Capacity (000s of units)	Manufacturing Costs ($/Unit)
A	Small	1,000	600	5.00
	Large	1,500	1,200	4.00
B	Small	1,200	600	5.00
	Large	1,600	1,200	4.00
	Huge	2,000	2,000	3.50
C	Small	900	600	6.00
	Large	1,400	1,200	5.00

Table 14–2   **Distribution Costs ($/unit) and Requirements**

From Factory Site \ To	Region 1	Region 2	Region 3	Region 4
A	1	2	3	4
B	2	3	2	3
C	4	3	2	1
Requirements at Region (000s of units)	500	200	700	800

The formulation of this model is shown in Figure 14–2, using the LINDO package described earlier in Chapter 10.[5] LINDO is a software product available on both microcomputers and large computers for solving linear and zero/one integer programming problems. The solution of this problem will be illustrated in a later section of this chapter.

The objective function to be minimized contains the annual cost times the zero/one variables (for example, 1,000 YAS), the distribution costs times the units shipped on the given route (for example, 2 A2), and the manufacturing costs times the units manufactured (for example, 5 PAS). The first set of constraints (numbered 2 through 5 in Figure 14–2) guarantees that regional requirements are met. For example:

$$A1 + B1 + C1 = 500$$

requires that shipments to region 1 from sites A, B, and C equal the region's requirements of 500 units.

---

[5]See Linus Schrage, *Linear, Integer, and Quadratic Programming with LINDO*, 4th ed. (South San Francisco, Calif.: Scientific Press, 1989).

Figure 14–2   Factory Size and Location Model: LINDO Formulation

```
MIN          1000 YAS + 1500 YAL + 1200 YBS + 1600 YBL + 2000 YBH
             + 900 YCS + 1400 YCL + A1 + 2 A2 + 3 A3 + 4 A4
             + 2 B1 + 3 B2 + 2 B3 + 3 B4 + 4 C1 + 3 C2 + 2 C3
             + C4 + 5 PAS + 4 PAL + 5 PBS + 4 PBL + 3.5 PBH
             + 6 PCS + 5 PCL
SUBJECT TO
              2)     A1 + B1 + C1 = 500
              3)     A2 + B2 + C2 = 200
              4)     A3 + B3 + C3 = 700
              5)     A4 + B4 + C4 = 800
              6)  -  600 YAS + PAS <= 0
              7)  - 1200 YAL + PAL <= 0
              8)  -  600 YBS + PBS <= 0
              9)  - 1200 YBL + PBL <= 0
             10)  - 2000 YBH + PBH <= 0
             11)  -  600 YCS + PCS <= 0
             12)  - 1200 YCL + PCL <= 0
             13)     A1 + A2 + A3 + A4 - PAS - PAL            <= 0
             14)     B1 + B2 + B3 + B4 - PBS - PBL - PBH <= 0
             15)     C1 + C2 + C3 + C4 - PCS - PCL            <= 0
             16)     YAS + YAL          <= 1
             17)     YBS + YBL + YBH <= 1
             18)     YCS + YCL          <= 1
END
INTEGER-VARIABLES = 7
```

The second set of constraints (6 through 12) limit the production capacity. For example, constraint 6 is obtained from:

$$PAS \le 600\ YAS$$

or

$$-600\ YAS + PAS \le 0$$

This guarantees that the production at site A with a Small factory does not exceed 600 units if YAS = 1 (i.e., if a Small factory is constructed at site A) and is 0 if YAS = 0.

The next set of constraints (13 through 15) are balance constraints. For example:

$$A1 + A2 + A3 + A4 \le PAS + PAL$$

or

$$A1 + A2 + A3 + A4 - PAS - PAL \le 0$$

requires that the total shipments from location A (i.e., A1 + A2 + A3 + A4) are less than or equal to the production from either a small or large facility (PAS + PAL).

The final set of constraints (16 through 18) limits each site to only one facility. For example:

$$YBS + YBL + YBH \leq 1$$

requires that at most one of the three variables can be 1. That is, either a Small plant, a Large plant, a Huge plant, or none at all can be built at site B.

LINDO reorganizes the objective function and constraints so that the integer (zero/one) variables are the first (i.e., leftmost) variables. The last statement in Figure 14–2 indicating that there are seven integer variables implies that the first seven variables (the Y variables) are the integer ones.

SUMMARY An integer linear programming model is a linear programming model with the additional requirement that some or all of the variables must be integers. Formulating an integer linear programming model is similar to formulation of LP models, except that the integer restriction allows one to include fixed charges, either-or constraints, and related concepts.

Solution of Integer Programming Problems

The simplex procedure of Chapter 12, used to solve *linear* programming problems, does not generally produce *integer* solutions. Hence, it is not directly useful in solving integer programming problems. Sometimes, of course, a noninteger LP solution can be rounded off appropriately to give an integer solution. If the rounded solution is feasible and has a profit close to that obtained for the noninteger problem, then the rounding procedure is likely to be adequate. However, for many very important problems, this procedure will not work. In particular, if the problem contains zero/one variables of the type illustrated in the formulations earlier in this chapter, rounding will generally give infeasible solutions or ones that are not close to optimal, as was illustrated in Figure 14–1. Hence, a solution procedure specifically designed for integer problems is required. A number of such procedures have been developed.

One such technique is called the **cutting-plane** method. It is a variant of the simplex method, and in fact starts with the simplex solution to the linear programming problem, ignoring integer requirements. Then new constraints (*cutting planes,* or simply *cuts*) are added to the problem, which (1) make infeasible the previous noninteger optimal solution but (2) do not exclude any feasible integer solutions. A new LP solution is obtained and the process repeated (i.e., new cuts added) until an integer solution is found. This procedure has certain theoretical features (it can be proved that an integer solution will ultimately result). Sometimes there are computational difficulties, altnough recent research using sophisticated cutting-plane approaches has shown promising results.[6] However, we will present an alternative solution method called *branch and bound,* which is useful both for integer programming problems and other kinds of combinatorial problems. The branch and bound procedure has proven computationally feasible for a wide range of problems.

The Branch and Bound Algorithm

When a problem is required to have an integer solution, this means that there are a finite number of possible solution points. It is theoretically possible to use *complete enumeration* and evaluate every possible solution to find the optimum. If there are only a few integer variables, enumeration may be feasible and the most efficient solution procedure. However, for most realistic problems, it would be computationally cumbersome to enumerate all solutions. Complete enumeration might not be necessary if we could find ways of eliminating whole groups of solutions from consideration. The branch and bound technique is a method for doing this.

The Tree of Solution Possibilities

With integer problems, there are a finite number of possible solutions, and it is possible to represent them by a **tree diagram.** This can best be shown by an example. Consider the following integer programming problem:

$$
\begin{aligned}
\text{Maximize:} \quad & P = 6X_1 + 3X_2 + X_3 + 2X_4 \\
\text{Subject to:} \quad & X_1 + X_2 + X_3 + X_4 \le 8 \\
& 2X_1 + X_2 + 3X_3 \le 12 \\
& 5X_2 + X_3 + 3X_4 \le 6 \\
& X_1 \le 1 \\
& X_2 \le 1 \\
& X_3 \le 4 \\
& X_4 \le 2 \\
& X_1, X_2, X_3, X_4 \text{ all integers}
\end{aligned}
$$

Note that the constraints $X_1 \le 1$ and $X_2 \le 1$ in effect mean that X_1 and X_2 are zero/one integer variables. Variable X_3 can take on five values (0, 1, 2, 3, 4), and variable X_4 can have three values. Hence, considering only the last four constraints, there are $2 \cdot 2 \cdot 5 \cdot 3 = 60$ possible solutions. The enumeration of these 60 possible solutions is shown graphically in the tree in Figure 14–3. The order of variables in the tree is arbitrary, but the end of the tree must have 60 branches, one for each possible solution. Note that many of these solutions are infeasible; that is, they do not satisfy the first three constraints.

---

[6]See H. Crowder, E. L. Johnson, and M. Padberg, "Solving Large-Scale Zero-One Linear Programming Problems," *Operations Research,* September–October 1983.

Figure 14–3   Tree Showing All Possible Integer Solutions for $X_1 \le 1, X_2 \le 1, X_3 \le 4, X_4 \le 2$

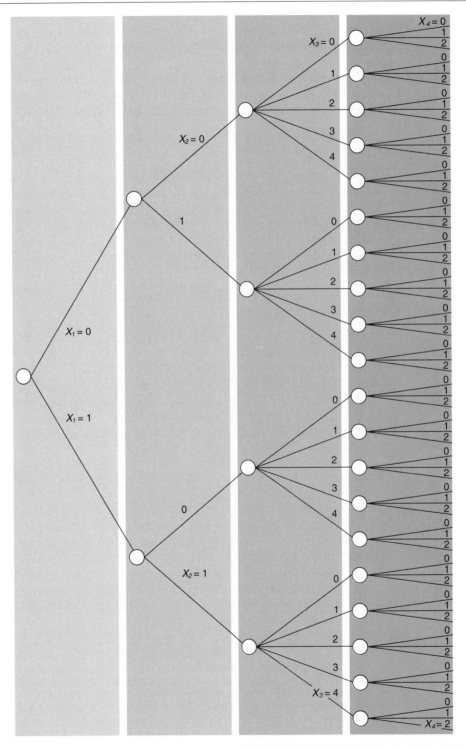

For such a small problem as this one, a computer could evaluate all 60 possibilities very quickly. However, as the problems grow in size, a complete evaluation becomes impractical.[7]

The **branch and bound** approach is designed to reduce the search by chopping off whole branches or limbs of this tree of possibilities and hence limiting the number of possibilities investigated. The key idea in eliminating branches is:

A branch can be eliminated if it can be shown to contain no feasible solution better than one already obtained.

The effective use of the branch and bound procedure requires a procedure to *bound* or find an *upper limit* for all the possible solutions in a given branch (a *lower limit* is needed when minimizing). The solution to the equivalent ordinary linear programming problem provides one convenient bound.

Consider our problem above, and solve it as a linear programming problem using the simplex method (that is, ignore the integer requirements). The solution is:

$$X_1 = 1, X_2 = 0, X_3 = 3.33, X_4 = 0.89$$

which is not an integer solution.[8] The profit is $P = 11.11$. This is the maximum profit that can be obtained, given the first three constraints. We know that there is no solution, and hence no integer solution, that can have a profit higher than 11.11. Thus, the value 11.11 is a *bound* on all the solutions in the problem. For any branch, we can find a bound (upper limit) in exactly the same way.

The steps in the branch and bound procedure are illustrated in Figure 14-4 for the example problem. The numbers in circles indicate the sequence of rounds for the development of the tree and for the branch and bound procedure.

Branch and Bound Solution of Example

Round 1 The first step is to solve the problem as an ordinary linear programming problem. If we are very lucky, the solution may turn out to be integer, but even when it is not, the initial LP solution is a good place to start. The LP solution to our example is $X_1 = 1, X_2 = 0, X_3 = 3.33, X_4 = 0.89$, and the profit is $P = 11.11$. This is not an integer solution, so we must proceed further.

Before proceeding, note that there is one obvious integer solution, $X_1 = X_2 = X_3 = X_4 = 0$, with profit $P = 0$. It is unlikely that this is the optimal solution, but it gives an initial "best so far" solution.

[7]To see this, consider a problem with 10 integer variables, each of which can take on five integer values (0, 1, 2, 3, or 4). The number of possible solutions is $5^{10} = 9,765,625$. Enumeration and evaluation of this many possible solutions would be a long and cumbersome way to proceed. Thus, we need a way of limiting the search to some smaller set of possible solutions.
[8]The ordinary LP problem has "relaxed" or omitted the integer constraints; this is sometimes called the *LP relaxation* of the integer programming problem.

Figure 14–4   **Summary of Steps in Solution of First Example Problem**

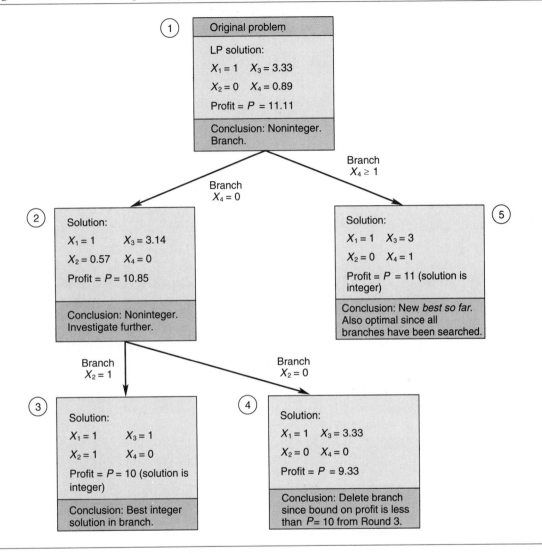

Round 2
Step 1. Begin The initial feasible integer solution is $X_1 = X_2 = X_3 = X_4 = 0$, with profit $P = 0$.
Step 2. Branch We must now select a variable and construct *branches*. The variable to be selected is arbitrary. A procedure that seems to work well is to branch on variables that are noninteger at the current stage. From round 1, both X_3 and X_4 are noninteger and let us arbitrarily select X_4 for branching. The

previous solution has $X_4 = 0.89$. Hence, a sensible pair of branches would require either $X_4 = 0$ or $X_4 \geq 1$. Note that this branching divides all the possible solutions into *two groups,* those for which $X_4 = 0$, and those for which $X_4 \geq 1$. Since X_4 must be an integer, it is not possible for X_4 to be between 0 and 1. This procedure defines the first pair of branches shown in Figure 14–4. Let us arbitrarily select the branch $X_4 = 0$ for initial investigation. To represent this branch, we replace the last constraint ($X_4 \leq 4$) in the example problem by the constraint $X_4 = 0$. Then the problem becomes:

$$
\begin{aligned}
\text{Maximize:} \quad & P = 6X_1 + 3X_2 + X_3 + 2X_4 \\
\text{Subject to:} \quad & X_1 + X_2 + X_3 + X_4 \leq 8 \\
& 2X_1 + X_2 + 3X_3 \leq 12 \\
& \quad\quad 5X_2 + X_3 + 3X_4 \leq 6 \\
& X_1 \leq 1 \\
& \quad\quad X_2 \leq 1 \\
& \quad\quad\quad X_3 \leq 4 \\
& \quad\quad\quad\quad X_4 = 0
\end{aligned}
$$

Step 3. Bound   The LP solution to this problem is $X_1 = 1$, $X_2 = 0.57$, $X_3 = 3.14$, $X_4 = 0$. The profit is $P = 10.85$ and this profit value is a *bound* on all the solutions on the branch $X_4 = 0$ (that is, for all the solutions for which $X_4 = 0$).

Step 4. Compare   Compare the best solution so far to the bound just generated. The best integer solution so far has profit $P = 0$, while the bound is $P = 10.85$; thus, we cannot yet eliminate this branch, and we investigate further down the branch.

Round 3

Step 2. Branch   Select a new variable to branch—say, X_2 (see Figure 14–4). Note that X_2 is noninteger in the LP solution above. Variable X_2 can only take on values of 0 or 1, so there are only two possible branches: $X_2 = 0$ or $X_2 = 1$. That is, we subdivide the possible solutions into two groups, those that have $X_2 = 0$, and those with $X_2 = 1$. (Recall that we are still working under the branch $X_4 = 0$, so that we are also dealing only with the possible solutions for which $X_4 = 0$.)

We arbitrarily select the branch $X_2 = 1$ and substitute this constraint in the problem above in place of $X_2 \leq 1$. The new problem is:

$$
\begin{aligned}
\text{Maximize:} \quad & P = 6X_1 + 3X_2 + X_3 + 2X_4 \\
\text{Subject to:} \quad & X_1 + X_2 + X_3 + X_4 \leq 8 \\
& 2X_1 + X_2 + 3X_3 \leq 12 \\
& \quad\quad 5X_2 + X_3 + 3X_4 \leq 6 \\
& X_1 \leq 1 \\
& \quad\quad X_2 = 1 \\
& \quad\quad\quad X_3 \leq 4 \\
& \quad\quad\quad\quad X_4 = 0
\end{aligned}
$$

Step 3. Bound The LP solution to this problem is: $X_1 = 1$, $X_2 = 1$, $X_3 = 1$, $X_4 = 0$, with a profit $P = 10$. Note that the solution happens to be integer.

Step 4. Compare This integer solution is better than our *best solution so far* ($P = 0$). It becomes the new "best so far" solution. Also, we do not have to investigate further down in this branch as we have the optimum for this branch. That is, for the set of possible solutions for which $X_4 = 0$ and $X_2 = 1$, there is none better than the one just obtained. However, there are other branches to review.

Round 4

Step 2. Branch Move back to the branch $X_2 = 0$ (see Figure 14–4), and select it for investigation. That is, we now consider the set of possible solutions for which $X_2 = 0$ (still within the set for which $X_4 = 0$). The problem to solve is the same as above (Round 3, Step 2) with the constraint $X_2 = 0$ replacing $X_2 = 1$.

Step 3. Bound The LP solution to this problem is: $X_1 = 1$, $X_2 = 0$, $X_3 = 3.33$, $X_4 = 0$, with profit $P = 9.33$.

Step 4. Compare This bound is *less than* the previous best so far ($P = 10$ from Round 3, Step 3). Hence, we can eliminate this branch from further consideration. It cannot contain an integer solution with profit greater than 10, since the best unrestricted solution has a profit of only 9.33.

Round 5

Step 2. Branch Move back up the tree to the branch $X_4 \geq 1$, which we created in Round 2, Step 2 (see Figure 14–4).

Step 3. Bound We solve the same LP problem as in Step 2 of Round 2 with the constraint $X_4 \geq 1$ replacing $X_4 = 0$. The solution is $X_1 = 1$, $X_2 = 0$, $X_3 = 3$, $X_4 = 1$, and the profit $P = 11$. Again, note that this is an integer solution.

Step 4. Compare The solution above is integer and is better than the previous best solution. It thus becomes the new *best so far*. It is a bound on all solutions below the branch ($X_4 \geq 1$) so we do not need to investigate further down that branch.

Step 5. Completion All branches have been investigated, and hence, the best so far solution obtained in Step 3 of Round 5 is the optimal integer solution, with profit $P = 11$.

We have completed the example problem. Since all branches have been investigated, the optimum solution is our current *best so far:*

$X_1 = 1$
$X_2 = 0$
$X_3 = 3$
$X_4 = 1$
$P = 11$

The summary of the procedures is given in Figure 14-4. Note that we did not have to investigate many branches—in fact, only five—to obtain the best solution from the 60 possibilities given in Figure 14-3.

The general series of steps for the branch and bound solution procedure is given in the Summary below.

SUMMARY

1. *Begin.* Find an *initial feasible integer* solution. (If it is difficult to find an initial solution, this step may be omitted.)
2. *Branch.* Select a variable and divide the possible solutions into two groups. Select one branch, that is, one of the groups, to investigate.
3. *Bound.* Find a *bound* for the problem defined by the branch selected. In our case, we use the LP solution to the integer problem as the bound. Note that the bound represents the upper limit for all possible solutions in a given branch.
4. *Compare.* Compare the bound obtained for the branch being considered with the *best solution so far* for the previous branches examined. If the bound is less than the best so far, delete the whole new branch. Then go on to branches not yet examined.[9]

   If the bound of this new branch is greater than the best solution so far, and if the solution is *integer,* then it becomes the new *best solution so far;* next, go on to examine other branches not yet considered.

   If the bound of the new branch is greater than the best solution so far, but the solution is *not integer,* there may be better solutions further down in the tree. Therefore, move one level down in the tree and branch (that is, go to Step 2).
5. *Completion.* When all branches have been examined, the *best solution so far* is the optimal solution.

Discussion

It is useful in solving problems by the branch and bound procedure to sketch a tree, as in Figure 14-4, to keep track of which branches have been investigated and which remain. The order in which branches are selected for analysis is arbitrary. We could have started by branching first on variable X_3, rather than variable X_4. As indicated earlier, a procedure that seems to work efficiently is to select branches that round off a given noninteger solution. For example, if a given solution is $X = 2.23$ for some variable, the branches $X \leq 2$ and $X \geq 3$ are often good branches to investigate.[10]

---

[9]It is possible that the LP problem formed by a given branch has no feasible solution. In this case, the given branch can be deleted, since obviously it contains no solutions, integer or otherwise.

[10]Computer programs that are in use on real problems have complex *heuristics* (rules of thumb) about how to develop the tree and which branches to investigate first.

Computer Solution

As an example of computer solution of a mixed integer linear programming problem, consider the factory size and location example discussed earlier in the chapter (see Figure 14–2 for the formulation). The problem is solved using the LINDO software package, which has the capability to solve linear and integer programming problems with zero/one integer variables.

Recall that in this example, there are seven zero/one variables relating to whether or not a factory of a given size is located at a specified site. For example, YBH refers to whether or not a Huge factory is located at site B. There are $2^7 = 128$ possible integer combinations, each of which involves the solution of a linear programming problem.

The solution is shown as Figure 14–5, and has been abridged to eliminate some of the less important output. Figure 14–6 shows the solution procedure in tree form. The circled numbers next to the output in Figure 14–5 correspond to the solution steps in Figure 14–6. (Note: Figure 14–6 contains additional information about the various steps beyond what is shown in the computer output.)

The initial solution, indicated as ⓪ in both Figures 14–5 and 14–6, gives the linear programming solution without regard to the integrality of the size/location variables. Note, for example, that YAL has a value of .583. This solution has a cost of $C = \$14,858$ and puts a lower bound on what might be possible.

Numbers ① through ④ in Figures 14–5 and 14–6 show the program branching repeatedly, first setting YBH to 1, then YCL to 0, then YAL to 0, then YCS to 0. At none of these stages is an integer solution found. Finally, the program sets YAS to 1 and the first integer solution, shown as ⑤, is found. This solution has cost $C = \$16,200$ and has YBH and YAS equal 1. That is, a Huge factory is to be built at site B and a Small factory at site A.

The program now starts moving back up the tree, and at ⑦, a new integer solution is found. This calls for a Huge factory at B and a Small factory at C (YBH and YCS = 1). The Huge factory produces 2,000 units (PBH = 2,000) and the small one only 200 (PCS = 200). This solution is the *new best-so-far* solution, with a cost of $C = \$16,100$.

Steps ⑧ and ⑨ move back up the tree, eliminating branches (an alternative optimum exists at ⑨, although it is not indicated in the LINDO output). Steps ⑩ through ⑱ explore other branches all with cost greater than the best-so-far of $16,100, until finally the program announces "ENUMERATION COMPLETE" and that the last solution (the one shown as ⑦) is the "BEST FOUND." Note that branches are eliminated either when the cost exceeds the best-so-far cost of $16,100 or when the branch has no feasible solution.

Discussion

The formulation of integer programming problems is an extension of linear programming ideas. In fact, many important real-world problems are of the mixed-integer type, with some variables restricted to integer values (often zero/one)

Figure 14–5   LINDO Solution for Factory Size and Location Example

```
: GO
LP OPTIMUM FOUND AT STEP 17
        OBJECTIVE FUNCTION VALUE
  1)            14858.3300
⓪
VARIABLE          VALUE         REDUCED COST
    YAS           .000000         850.000000
    YAL           .583333            .000000
    YBS           .000000        1200.000000
    YBL           .000000        1000.000000
    YBH           .350000            .000000
    YCS           .000000         800.000100
    YCL           .666667            .000000
     A1        500.000000            .000000
     A2        200.000000            .000000
     A3           .000000           1.750000
     A4           .000000           2.083333
     B1           .000000            .250000
     B2           .000000            .250000
     B3        700.000000            .000000
     B4           .000000            .333333
     C1           .000000           3.916667
     C2           .000000           1.916667
     C3           .000000           1.666667
     C4        800.000000            .000000
    PAS           .000000            .000000
    PAL        700.000000            .000000
    PBS           .000000            .500000
    PBL           .000000            .000000
    PBH        700.000000            .000000
    PCS           .000000            .000000
    PCL        800.000000            .000000

                  . . .


    NO. ITERATIONS = 17
    BRANCHES = 0
①      SET YBH TO 1 AT 1 BND =  -15233.330

②      SET YCL TO 0 AT 2 BND =  -15250.000

③      SET YAL TO 0 AT 3 BND =  -15500.000

④      SET YCS TO 0 AT 4 BND =  -15533.330

⑤      SET YAS TO 1 AT 5 BND =  -16200.000
```

(continued)

Figure 14–5 (*continued*)

```
NEW INTEGER SOLUTION OF 16200.0 AT BRANCH 5 PIVOT 45

          OBJECTIVE FUNCTION VALUE
  1)               16200.0000
     VARIABLE          VALUE
        YAS        1.000000
        YAL         .000000
        YBS         .000000
        YBL         .000000
        YBH        1.000000
        YCS         .000000
        YCL         .000000
         A1      200.000000
         A2         .000000
         A3         .000000
         A4         .000000
         B1      300.000000
         B2      200.000000
         B3      700.000000
         B4      800.000000

                  . . .

     NO. ITERATIONS = 45
     BRANCHES = 5
     BOUND ON OPTIMUM: 15250.00
     DELETE YAS AT LEVEL 5

     FLIP YCS TO 1 WITH BOUND -15500.00

NEW INTEGER SOLUTION OF 16100.0 AT BRANCH 5 PIVOT 47

          OBJECTIVE FUNCTION VALUE
  1)               16100.0000
   VARIABLE          VALUE
        YAS         .000000
        YAL         .000000
        YBS         .000000
        YBL         .000000
        YBH        1.000000
        YCS        1.000000
        YCL         .000000
         A1         .000000
         A2         .000000
         A3         .000000
         A4         .000000
         B1      500.000000
```

(*continued*)

Figure 14–5 (*concluded*)

```
    B2       200.000000
    B3       700.000000
    B4       600.000000
    C1          .000000
    C2          .000000
    C3          .000000
    C4       200.000000
   PAS          .000000
   PAL          .000000
   PBS          .000000
   PBL          .000000
   PBH      2000.000000
   PCS       200.000000
   PCL          .000000

                 . . .

     NO. ITERATIONS  =  47
     BRANCHES  =  5
     BOUND ON OPTIMUM: 15250.00
     DELETE YCS AT LEVEL 4
        FLIP YAL TO 1 WITH BOUND  -15250.00
(8)     DELETE YAL AT LEVEL 3
(9)     DELETE YCL AT LEVEL 2
(10)    FLIP YBH TO 0 WITH BOUND  -15441.67
(11)    SET YBL TO O AT 2 BND  =  -16050.000
(12)    SET YAL TO 1 AT 3 BND  =  -16066.670
(13)    SET YCL TO 0 AT 4 BND  =  -17600.000
(14)    DELETE YCL AT LEVEL 4
(15)    FLIP YAL TO 0 WITH BOUND  -16050.00
        DELETE YAL AT LEVEL 3
(16)    FLIP YBL TO 1 WITH BOUND  -15441.67
(17)    SET YCL TO 0 AT 3 BND  =  -16425.000
(18)    DELETE YCL AT LEVEL 3
        DELETE YBL AT LEVEL 2
        DELETE YBH AT LEVEL 1
        ENUMERATION COMPLETE. BRANCHES  =  9 PIVOTS  =  102
LAST INTEGER SOLUTION IS THE BEST FOUND
```

Figure 14–6   Steps in Solution of Factory Size and Location Example

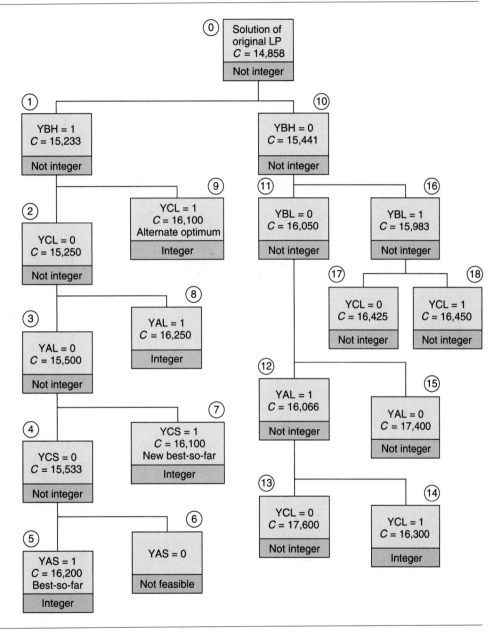

and others ordinary variables that can take on any nonnegative value. However, as we have seen, the solution procedures for integer problems are quite different than those for ordinary linear programming problems. The computations for integer problems are much more extensive, since they require solving many linear programming problems as a part of the process.

The field of integer programming is a good example of the progress that is being made in developing new quantitative techniques for the solution of business problems. Until recently, although integer problems could be formulated, only very small problems could be solved with reasonable amounts of computer time. Today, moderate-sized real problems, and even a few specialized very large problems, can be solved efficiently. This has resulted partly from the increase in size and speed of computers, but more important, from the development of good computer programs, generally utilizing variants of the branch and bound techniques described in this chapter. In the next few years, the remaining computation limits should recede further, and integer programming will become a more widely used technique. Already, examples are appearing. One good illustration is the problem faced by airlines in scheduling their flying crews (pilots, copilots, flight attendants, and so forth). This problem can be formulated as an integer programming one, and although it is quite a large one, it is being solved and used by airlines on a continuing routine basis.

APPENDIX   Branch and Bound Procedures for Combinatorial Problems

A **combinatorial problem** is one in which there is a large number of feasible solutions, each of which represents a variant or combination of different elements. Combinatorial problems can often be formulated using binary variables, and hence could be solved using the general integer programming techniques discussed in the chapter. In some cases, the special structure of the problem allows construction of special bounding procedures, which make the branch and bound procedure even more effective. This appendix is an example of one such procedure.

Example: An Assignment Problem[11]   A firm has four plants and four warehouses. Each plant must be uniquely assigned to one warehouse (and vice versa). The pairing (or assignment) of plants to warehouses will affect total shipping costs, and the goal is to obtain an assignment with the smallest total shipping cost. Table 14–3 contains annual shipping costs for each possible matching of a plant to a warehouse.

This problem is a combinatorial problem because there are a number of possible solutions, each one of which involves a yes or no answer to the question, "Is plant i assigned to warehouse j?" There are four possible ways in which plant

---

[11]We use an assignment problem for illustration here even though more specialized and efficient procedures exist to deal with this particular combinatorial problem. See F. Hillier and G. J. Lieberman, *Introduction to Operations Research,* 5th ed. (New York: McGraw-Hill, 1990).

Table 14–3   **Annual Shipping Costs ($000s)**

Plant \ Warehouse	1	2	3	4
A	10	33	41	30
B	24	17	50	60
C	39	32	62	39
D	22	27	39	37

A can be assigned: given an assignment for A, there are three possible ways in which plant B can be assigned; then two ways for C, and finally, D is paired with the remaining warehouse. Thus, the total number of possible assignments is $N! = (4)(3)(2)(1) = 4! = 24$. Although 24 is not too large a number, the same problem with 12 plants and 12 warehouses would contain $12! = 479,001,600$ possible solutions. This is the fundamental characteristic of a combinatorial problem; even a relatively small problem (12 plants and 12 warehouses) has a very large number of possible solutions.

The Bounding Procedure

We now need a way to find a lower limit of cost (i.e., a bound) on all the solutions. One simple way to do this is to assign, for each warehouse, that plant that has the *lowest* shipping cost to that given warehouse. Thus, for the first warehouse in Table 14–3, it is least costly to ship from plant A; for the second warehouse, it is cheapest to ship from plant B; for the third warehouse, plant D is cheapest; and for the fourth warehouse, plant A is cheapest. Note that this is not a feasible assignment, since it assigns plant A to both warehouses 1 and 4, and we require a unique assignment of plants to warehouses. However, the procedure is a convenient way of obtaining a lower bound, for the cost of any feasible assignment cannot be less than the cost obtained by this procedure. Moreover, if the assignment that results by this procedure happens to be a feasible one (i.e., a unique assignment of plants to warehouses), then it is optimal.

Mechanically, the procedure amounts to finding the minimum of each column. The numbers that are the column minimums are circled in Table 14–4.

The total of the column minimums is $96, which is a lower bound on cost.[12] There is no feasible assignment that costs less than $96.

---

[12] A better bounding procedure would be to calculate the row minimums as well as the column minimums, and then set the lower bound as Max (sum of column minimums, sum of row minimums). This procedure has not been used, in order to keep the illustration as clear as possible.

Table 14–4   **Obtaining Column Minimums for Example**

Plant \ Warehouse	1	2	3	4
A	⑩	33	41	㉚
B	24	⑰	50	60
C	39	32	62	39
D	22	27	㊴	37
Column Minimums	10	17	39	30

First Branch

Consider the example with cost data in Table 14–3. There are 24 possible solutions. Suppose we arbitrarily focus on the tentative assignment of plant *A* to warehouse 1 (or *not* that assignment). Then, our total set of 24 solutions is divided into two categories; those solutions with $(A,1)$ paired; and those solutions that do not match plant *A* with warehouse 1, denoted by $(\overline{A,1})$. This is our first "branch"; the process is depicted in Figure 14–7.

Lower Bounds

We now need to bound each category; that is, we need to calculate a lower limit on costs for the solutions in each category. Consider the category associated with the assignment $(A,1)$. The cost of this assignment is $10 plus the cost associated with the remaining plant-warehouse assignments. To find a bound on this, suppose we cross out the first row of Table 14–3 (since plant *A* is assigned) and the first column (since warehouse 1 is assigned). The new cost table is reproduced in Table 14–5.

Now we want to compute a lower bound on the assignment of the remaining plants *B, C, D* to the remaining warehouses, 2, 3, 4. To do this, we calculate the column minimums, as before (these are given and circled in Table 14–5). The total of these minimums is $93, and adding the $10 cost of the $(A,1)$ assignment, the total cost is $103. This is the lower bound on cost for this branch. Note that the solution indicated by the column minimums in Table 14–5 is not a feasible solution, since plant *D* is assigned to both warehouses 3 and 4.

Second Branch

Since we have not yet found a feasible assignment, we explore further down the tree. Consider the branch associated with assigning plant *B* to warehouse 2,

Figure 14–7   **First Branch of Example Problem**

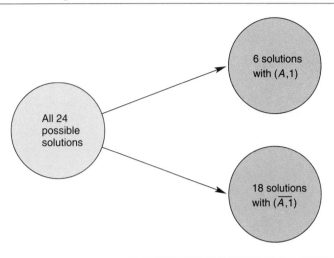

Table 14–5   **Remaining Shipping Cost, Given $(A, 1)$ Assignment**

Plant \ Warehouse	2	3	4
B	(17)	50	60
C	32	62	39
D	27	(39)	(37)
Column Minimums	17	39	37

denoted by $(B,2)$. Of the six cases for which we have $(A,1)$, two are associated with the further assignment of $(B,2)$, and the other four to the case in which B is not assigned to 2; that is, $(\overline{B,2})$. This branching is shown in Figure 14–8.

We now calculate the lower bound for the branch $(B,2)$. As before, we strike out the rows and columns for plants and warehouses already assigned. Thus, the A and B rows and the 1 and 2 columns are eliminated from Table 14–3, producing Table 14–6.

The lower bound on this branch is now the sum of the $10 cost of assignment $(A,1)$, the $17 cost of assignment $(B,2)$, and the total of the column minimums from Table 14–6, making a total of $103. Note that this is still not a feasible solution (as before, plant D is assigned to both warehouses 3 and 4.)

Figure 14–8   Second Branch of Example Problem

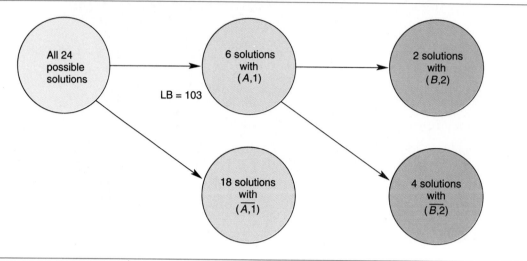

Table 14–6   Remaining Shipping Costs, Given $(A,1)$ and $(B,2)$ Assignments

Plant \ Warehouse	3	4
C	62	39
D	(39)	(37)
Column Minimums	39	37

Third Branch

The two solutions in the branch $(B,2)$ are now determined, and are drawn in Figure 14–9 to form a third set of branches. Each of these branches represents a feasible solution, with costs of $126 and $105, respectively. The allocation $(A,1)$, $(B,2)$, $(C,4)$ $(D,3)$, with cost $105, is the better one, and is the first *best-so-far* solution.

Branch $(\overline{B,2})$

We now move back up the tree to the branch $(\overline{B,2})$, which is the set of solutions in which B is not assigned to 2 [still all within the set $(A,1)$]. The costs for this case are given in Table 14–7. Note that an asterisk is placed in row B, column 2 to indicate that this possibility is not to be considered. The lower bound is cal-

Figure 14–9   **Third Branch of Example Problem**

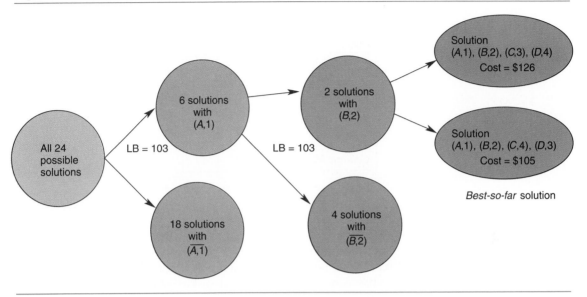

Table 14–7   **Shipping Costs Given $(A,1)$ and $(\overline{B,2})$ Assignments**

Plant \ Warehouse	2	3	4
B	*	50	60
C	32	62	39
D	(27)	(39)	(37)
Column Minimums	27	39	37

culated as before, by adding the cost ($10) of the $(A,1)$ assignment to the sum of the column minimums from Table 14–7, giving a total of $113.

This lower bound of $113 implies that there is no feasible solution in this branch with costs below $113. Since we already have a solution with a cost below this (the best-so-far solution with cost of $105), we can delete this whole branch without investigating further.

Branch $(\overline{A,1})$

We now move back up the tree to the one remaining uninvestigated branch, the one with 18 solutions that exclude the assignment of A to 1. As before, we make

Table 14–8   Shipping Costs, Given $(\overline{A,1})$ Assignment

Plant \ Warehouse	1	2	3	4
A	*	33	41	(30)
B	24	(17)	50	60
C	39	32	62	39
D	(22)	27	(39)	37
Column Minimums	22	17	39	30

a table of costs for this case (Table 14–8), with an asterisk placed in row A, column 1. The lower bound is obtained by summing the column minimums, giving a total of $108. Thus, none of the 18 solutions contained in this branch has a cost less than $108. Since our current best-so-far solution has a cost of $105, we can eliminate this entire branch and its 18 possible solutions from further consideration.

Since there are no more branches to investigate, the optimal solution is the current best-so-far: A–1, B–2, C–4, D–3, with a cost of $105.

SUMMARY

Applying the branch and bound procedure to a general combinatorial problem is similar to its use in solving integer linear programming problems. However, the way to calculate bounds must be determined for each specific application, and the branching process may be defined differently.

Bibliography

Bradley, S. P.; A. C. Hax; and T. L. Magnanti. *Applied Mathematical Programming.* Reading, Mass.: Addison-Wesley Publishing, 1977.

Crowder, H.; E. L. Johnson; and M. Padberg. "Solving Large-Scale Zero-One Linear-Programming Problems," *Operations Research,* September–October 1983.

Garfinkel, R. S., and G. L. Nemhauser. *Integer Programming.* New York: John Wiley & Sons, 1972.

Geoffrion, A. M., and R. E. Marsten. "Integer Programming Algorithms: A Framework and State-of-the-Art Survey." *Management Science,* March 1972.

Hillier, F., and G. J. Lieberman. *Introduction to Operations Research.* 5th ed. New York: McGraw-Hill, 1990.

Nemhauser, G. L., and L. A. Wolsey, *Integer and Combinatorial Optimization.* New York: John Wiley & Sons, 1988.

Plane, D. R., and C. McMillan, Jr. *Discrete Optimization.* Englewood Cliffs, N.J.: Prentice Hall, 1971.

Shapiro, R. D. *Optimization Models for Planning and Allocation: Text and Cases in Mathematical Programming.* New York: John Wiley & Sons, 1984.

Wagner, H. M. *Principles of Operations Research.* 2nd ed. Englewood Cliffs, N.J.: Prentice Hall, 1975.

Zionts, S. *Linear and Integer Programming.* Englewood Cliffs, N.J.: Prentice Hall, 1974.

Problems with Answers

14–1. A major movie studio plans to produce five specific movies over the next three years. Define a variable Y_{it} in which the subscript i refers to the particular movie ($i = 1,2,3,4,5$) and the subscript t refers to the year ($t = 1,2,3$). Y_{it} is a zero/one variable that has value 1 if the ith movie is produced in the tth year, and has value 0 otherwise. Consider each situation below separately, and formulate one or more linear integer constraints that satisfy the stated condition.

   a. No more than one movie may be produced in the first year.

   b. Movie 2 cannot be produced before movie 3. They may be produced in the same year, however.

   c. At least one movie must be produced each year.

   d. Movie 4 must be produced no later than year 2.

   e. Movies 1 and 5 cannot be produced in the same year.

14–2. Use the branch and bound procedure to solve the following problem:

   Maximize:
   $$2X_1 + X_2 + 4X_3 + 3X_4$$
   Subject to:
   $$3X_1 + 2X_2 + 5X_3 + 4X_4 \le 10$$
   $$- X_2 + X_3 \qquad \le 0$$

   All the variables X_1, X_2, X_3, X_4 are zero/one variables.

   The solution to the corresponding linear programming problem is:

   $$X_1 = 0; X_2 = 0.86; X_3 = 0.86; X_4 = 1$$

   with objective function value $Z = 7.3$. In solving the problem, proceed as follows:

   a. Define the possible branches. Then check your answer with that given at the end of the book. When there are several possible branches (as there often are), use the one given in the answers.

   b. Define the next linear programming problem to be solved, then check the answers for the solution to the LP problem.

   c. Determine if you have reached an optimum. Otherwise, go to (a) and define the next branch, and so on.

14–3. A research administrator in the Federal Science Foundation is trying to decide which projects to fund for the coming year. She has received the eight proposals listed below. After careful study, she has made a subjective estimate of the value of each project on a scale of 0 to 100. The research administrator wants to find a mix of projects having the greatest total value. However, there are several limitations. First, she has a budget of $320,000. Second, she must either accept or turn down a project (i.e., no partial funding). Third, certain projects are related. She does not wish to fund both projects G and H. Project D should not be funded unless A is also funded (but A can be funded without D).

   Formulate the administrator's problem as a linear (integer) programming problem.

Proposal	Cost ($000s)	Value
A	$ 80	40
B	15	10
C	120	80
D	65	50
E	20	20
F	10	5
G	60	80
H	100	100

14–4. The Bendigo company manufactures three products, ANZAs, BOZOs, and KARMAs. Bendigo has partially formulated its weekly product mix problem as a linear programming problem as follows:

Maximize: $100A + 120B$
Subject to:
$$3A + 7B + 2K \leq 1,000$$
(machine time available)
$$A + 1.5B + 2K \leq 300$$
(labor hours available)
$$23A + 18B + 25K = RMUSED$$
(raw material used)

where A, B, and K refer to the number of ANZAs, BOZOs, and KARMAs produced per week. At this point, Bendigo ran into trouble and turned to you to help complete the formulation.

For each of the parts below, add to or modify the formulation to incorporate the situation described. Formulate as a linear integer problem, using integer (including binary) variables as required. In each case, define any new variables, any new or modified constraints, and any additions or modifications to the objective function. Treat each part independently.

a. KARMAs are stamped on a special machine that is leased from the manufacturer. Up to 200 KARMAs can be stamped in a week. The lease specifies a fixed fee of $800 per week if any KARMAs are produced. However, there is no charge if the machine is not used in any week.

b. The cost of raw material is 25 cents per unit if less than 1,000 units are purchased. If 1,000 or more units are purchased, the cost is 20 cents per unit for all units purchased. An unlimited amount of raw material is available in any week, but it cannot be stored from one week to the next.

c. The sales revenue for a KARMA depends on the amount purchased. Bendigo receives $100 each for the first 20 units produced, $150 each for the next

50 units produced, and $120 each for any additional units up to a maximum of 200 total units produced.

d. The sales department estimates that the maximum sales are 100 units for ANZAs and 120 units for BOZOs. However, a selling campaign might be undertaken, at a cost of $5,000, on either product. The selling campaign would increase the demand by 50 units for the selected product. Because of the limited sales force, the campaign could be done for either ANZAs or BOZOs but not both.

14–5. (Note: This problem requires the solution technique discussed in the chapter appendix.) A firm has four plants and four warehouses. Each plant must be uniquely assigned to one warehouse (and vice versa). The pairing (or assignment) of plants to warehouses will affect total shipping costs, and the goal is to obtain an assignment with the smallest total shipping cost. The table below contains annual shipping costs for each possible matching of a plant to a warehouse.

Annual Shipping Costs ($000s)

Plant \ Warehouse	1	2	3	4
A	10	33	41	20
B	24	17	50	60
C	39	32	62	29
D	22	27	39	37

Use the branch and bound method to find the best pairing of plants to warehouses in order to minimize total shipping cost. (*Hint:* Once a branch has been made, a bound on the shipping cost of the unassigned facilities is the cost from the lowest-cost plant to each unassigned warehouse. Another bound is the cost to the lowest-cost warehouse from each unassigned plant.)

Problems

14–6. Consider the following problem:

Minimize: $Z = 8X_1 - 2X_2$
Subject to: $-X_1 + X_2 \leq 1.9$
$X_1 \qquad \leq 2$
$X_2 \leq 2$

where X_1 and X_2 are integers.

a. On a piece of graph paper, plot the constraints and note the integer points. Also, plot the objective function for one value of Z, and note its slope.

b. Use the branch and bound procedure to solve the problem. Define bounds, and then solve each linear programming problem by inspection from the graph. Branch first on variable X_2.

14–7. Use the branch and bound procedure to solve the following problem:

Maximize: $3X_1 + 6X_2 + X_3$
Subject to: $X_1 + X_2 + X_3 \leq 7$
$5X_1 + X_2 + X_3 \leq 15$
$X_1 + 4X_2 \qquad \leq 9$
$X_1 \leq 3; X_2 \leq 3; X_3 \leq 3$

All variables are integers.

14–8. Use the branch and bound procedure to solve the following problem:

Maximize:
$15X_1 + 3X_2 + 8X_3 - 10Y_1 - 10Y_2 - 2Y_3$
Subject to:
$3X_1 + 2X_2 + X_3 - 10Y_1 \qquad \leq 5$
$4X_1 - X_2 + 5X_3 \qquad - 12Y_2 \qquad \leq 6$
$X_1 + X_2 + X_3 \qquad - 4Y_3 \leq 0$

where the variables X_1, X_2, X_3 are not required to be integer, but Y_1 and Y_2 are zero/one variables, and $Y_3 \leq 3$ is also integer.

14–9. The chief of the Punxsutawney Police Department was trying to make up her budget request for the following year. A key element was the number of police personnel she would need for patrol duty. She had just received a study (see the accompanying table) that estimated how many patrols should be on the Punxsutawney streets during each four-hour period.

These estimates were based partly on past experience for requests for aid and for investigation of crimes, and partly on requirements for a new program of crime prevention. The new program stressed the visibility of patrol units on the streets during high potential crime times.

The chief's problem rose because she had to schedule police personnel on eight-hour shifts and not just for the four-hour segments shown in the table. The department was operating with the six staggered eight-hour shifts shown in the following table and the chief wanted to keep this policy.

Estimated Requirements for Police Patrols on Weekdays, by Time of Day

Time Period	Patrols Needed
10 P.M. to 2 A.M.	13
2 A.M. to 6 A.M.	1
6 A.M. to 10 A.M.	7
10 A.M. to 2 P.M.	6
2 P.M. to 6 P.M.	6
6 P.M. to 10 P.M.	17
Total	50

Punxsutawney Police—Staggered Shifts

Shift	Beginning Time	Ending Time
1	10 P.M.	6 A.M.
2	2 A.M.	10 A.M.
3	6 A.M.	2 P.M.
4	10 A.M.	6 P.M.
5	2 P.M.	10 P.M.
6	6 P.M.	2 A.M.

The chief's problem was to decide on the minimum number of personnel needed to meet the requirements. Assume that each patrol involved a single patrol-person. Also consider only the problem for weekdays. Formulate a linear integer programming problem to solve the chief's problem.

14–10. Refer to the illustration of the factory size and location problem in this chapter. The formulation given allows each region's requirements to be met partially from each of two or more factory sites. Suppose we wish to require that a region be supplied entirely from only one factory site. How would you formulate this problem?

14–11. The Snohomish Extrusion Company is planning its production schedule for the next quarter. Snohomish makes three products: alphas, betas, and gammas. The major factors used in manufacturing these products are labor-hours, raw material, and electric power. The requirements for each are shown below:

	Alphas	Betas	Gammas
Labor (hrs.)	5	2	1
Raw material (lbs.)	10	13	8
Power (kwh.)	300	180	120
Contribution per unit ($) excluding cost of labor, raw material, and power	170	240	120

Snohomish has up to 4,000 labor-hours available on its first shift operations (for the quarter), and the labor contract allows up to this amount at a rate of $10 per hour. Raw material (regular resin) costs $2 per pound, and up to 20,000 pounds can be purchased. Power costs 3 cents per kwh., and any amount can be purchased.

Snohomish has formulated the linear programming problem as follows:

Maximize:
$$170A + 240B + 120C - 10FSH - 2RMR - 0.03\,PA$$

Subject to:
$$5A + 2B + 1C = FSH$$
$$FSH \le 4{,}000 \text{ (labor requirements)}$$
$$10A + 13B + 8C = RMR$$
$$RMR \le 20{,}000 \text{ (raw material requirements)}$$
$$300A + 180B + 120C = PA \text{ (power requirement)}$$

where:

A = Number of alphas produced
B = Number of betas produced
C = Number of gammas produced
FSH = Number of labor-hours used on first-shift operations
RMR = Pounds of raw material (regular resin) used
PA = kwh. of power used at $0.03 price

Parts (a) through (c) below propose modifications of the above linear program. You should define whatever new variables are needed, including integer or binary integer (zero/one) variables. Also, show how you would modify any constraint and the objective function. Treat each case independently.

a. A second-shift operation is possible. This shift would allow an additional 2,000 labor-hours. Labor would cost $12 per hour on the second-shift operations. In addition, if the second shift is to operate, there will be fixed costs of $900 incurred (for supervision, overhead, and so on).

b. The price of power to Snohomish really depends on the amount used. The cost is $0.03 per kwh. for the first 30,000 kwh. The cost of additional power beyond this amount is $0.02 per kwh.

c. A new raw material, a special resin, has just been announced. This special raw material costs $4 per pound but

Planes Available for New Routes (for Problem 14–12)

Plane Type	Number Available	Seating Capacity	Operating Costs ($000s)	
			Chicago to Seattle and Return	Chicago to Denver and Return
A	1	320	108	101
B	2	250	90	88
C	3	130	66	62

would require considerably less per unit (only two pounds per unit for each of the three products). The use of this new raw material would require the lease of special-purpose equipment costing $8,000. In addition, there is a minimum order quantity of 2,000 pounds (and a maximum order quantity of 10,000 pounds) of this special raw material. Snohomish must decide which of the two raw materials to use. That is, Snohomish can use either the regular or the special resin, but not both.

14–12. Amazing Airlines (AA) is about to add two new cities to its route schedule. In particular, daily service is being inaugurated from Chicago to Seattle and return, and from Chicago to Denver and return. AA's decision problem involves what aircraft to assign to each of these two routes. AA has six planes available, with characteristics as shown in the accompanying table. A given aircraft will fly from Chicago to its destination and back daily. Any combination of aircraft types may be assigned to each route.

Amazing Airlines' market research department has done a careful study of demand on these routes, and the results are shown in the table below. These demand estimates are the maximum that AA would carry, assuming there was adequate seat capacity assigned to the given route.

Estimated Demand on New Routes

Route Leg	Estimated Daily Demand	One-Way Fare
Chicago to Seattle	310	$410
Seattle to Chicago	240	410
Chicago to Denver	290	350
Denver to Chicago	265	350

Formulate this problem as a linear integer programming problem.

14–13. The Rowbottom Sand and Gravel Company has the following amounts of materials to deliver to six customers:

Customer	Amount (tons)
A	¼
B	½
C	1½
D	½
E	¾
F	1

There are five trucks that can be used to make these deliveries. With the use of dividers, a truck can deliver a mix of loads up to its capacity. However, a customer's order cannot be split between trucks. Trucks available and their capacities are:

Truck	Capacity (tons)
1	1
2	2
3	1
4	2
5	1½

The costs associated with each truck delivering to the customer is given in the following table:

Costs (dollars) of Delivering Orders to Customers

Truck \ Customer	A	B	C	D	E	F
1	17	19	21	20	20	21
2	15	18	20	18	19	23
3	18	19	22	22	21	22
4	15	16	19	18	18	20
5	16	15	20	22	19	20

In addition to these costs, there is a fixed cost of $10 on trucks 1, 3, and 5 and $15 on trucks 2 and 4. These costs are incurred if the truck is used at all.

Finally, there is the restriction that the same truck cannot deliver to both customers A and B.

Formulate this as an integer programming problem.

14–14. A tire company has four plants located around the country. The company has recently decided to produce radial tires. Capital equipment to produce the new tires has an annual rental cost of $200,000 at each location at which the company wishes to produce radials. The company ships its tires to 15 warehouses around the country. The company must decide the number and location of plants (one or more) at which it will produce radials. Assume you know the following data:

P_i = Unit production cost at plant i (exclusive of rental cost)

C_{ij} = Unit shipping cost from plant i to warehouse j

D_j = Annual demand (in units) at warehouse j

K = The annual capacity (in units) for each capital equipment rental. (*Note: K is larger than ¼ of the sum of nationwide demands.*)

a. Formulate an integer programming model for this problem using zero/one integer variables as well as ordinary (noninteger) LP variables.

b. Describe in words how you could use the concept of branch and bound together with the concept of linear programming to obtain a solution to this model.

14–15. In a minimization of cost problem being solved by branch and bound, the "best solution so far" costs $65. A particular subset of solutions has just been evaluated using two different approaches to obtain lower bounds; the bounds obtained are $50 (this solution is infeasible) and $70 (this solution is feasible).

a. Can we eliminate that subset of solutions from further consideration (i.e., cut it off)? Explain.

b. Would your answer in (a) change if the $70 solution were infeasible rather than feasible? Explain.

14–16. The traveling salesrep problem requires a specified route in which each of n cities is visited once and only once, at minimum total distance traveled. The problem can be thought of as an assignment problem in which no item can be assigned to itself and subtours are not allowed. For example, suppose the distance between pairs of cities were as follows:

Miles between Cities

From \ To	A	B	C	D
A	0	13	41	20
B	24	0	50	60
C	39	32	0	29
D	22	27	39	0

Use the branch and bound method of the chapter appendix to obtain the optimum solution to this traveling salesrep problem.

14–17. List four problems arising in business that can be characterized (as a first approximation) as assignment problems.

14–18. List a business problem that can be characterized (as a first approximation) as a traveling salesrep problem (See Problem 14–16.).

14–19. A single machine is used to mix and package four flavors of ice cream (but not simultaneously). Productive time of the machine is lost while the machine is cleaned in preparation for production of the next flavor. The accompanying table shows the time required for changing from any flavor to any other flavor.

Suppose the flavors are demanded at equal rates, so that all flavors are produced once (and only once) in a "cycle." Find the optimum *sequence* of flavor production to minimize the changeover time lost from production.

Use the branch and bound technique to solve this problem. Be sure to *illustrate* your branching procedure and *explain* your bounding procedure. (See chapter appendix.)

Minutes Required for Changeover

From \ To	Van.	Choc.	Straw.	Rasp. Rip.
Vanilla	0	1	9	4
Chocolate	20	0	14	15
Strawberry	7	6	0	5
Raspberry Ripple	12	9	14	0

More Challenging Problems

14–20. The San Francisco office of the MBA Consulting Group is trying to schedule its consultants for the next four weeks. MBA has accepted four consulting jobs that must be completed during this time. The jobs, the required number of consultants, and the time requirements are as shown on the next page. MBA has a policy that once a consultant is assigned to a job, that person stays with the job until finished. Furthermore, once a job is begun, it is carried through to completion without interruption.

The San Francisco office has a permanent staff of four consultants. It was immediately obvious to the branch manager that the requirements could not be met with this staff. Additional consultants could be obtained from the national office in New York. However, the national office only assigns consultants on a monthly (i.e., four-week) basis. Hence, any consultants added must be added for all four weeks. Since the branch is charged for these national office consultants, the branch manager wants to minimize the number used while still meeting the job requirements.

Formulate this problem as an integer linear problem. (*Hint:* Let Y_{it} be a zero/one variable that is 1 if the ith job is started in period t, and 0 otherwise.)

Consulting Jobs (for Problem 14–20)

Job	Weeks Required for Job	Consultants Required Each Week
1	3	2
2	2	3
3	1	5
4	1	4

14–21. The Franchise Food Products Company operates two chains of ready-food stores, the Piazo Pizza chain and the Fisher Fish and Chips chain. The firm is expanding operations into Santa Clara County and is looking for sites to open new stores. Ten sites have been identified as potential sites, and the net revenue (in present-value terms) of each has been estimated for the use either as a Piazo Pizza parlor or a Fisher Fish and Chips restaurant. Let P_j ($j = 1, 2, \ldots,$ 10) be the net revenue for use of site j as a Pizza parlor and F_j ($j = 1, 2, \ldots, 10$) be the net revenue for the same site if it is used as a fish restaurant.

The company operates both chains of restaurants by franchising out the rights in a given region. According to the terms of the agreement with any Pizza franchise, the franchisee has the exclusive

rights within a two-mile radius of his restaurant. This means any sites selected for Pizza parlors must be at least four miles apart. A similar agreement exists in contracts with Fisher Fish franchises, but the exclusive rights are guaranteed within 2.5 miles; that is, the restaurants must be at least five miles apart. There are no restrictions on locations between the two chains (a Pizza parlor could be right next to a Fisher Fish restaurant, for example). A table of distances between sites is given below.

Each of the 10 potential sites may be developed as either a Pizza parlor or a Fish restaurant, but not both. Of course, it need not be developed at all.

Formulate the above as an integer programming problem to maximize the net revenue to Franchise Foods Products Company.

14–22. The Ininob Manufacturing Company produces three products: widgets, yamis, and zots. The company is trying to determine its production schedule for these products for the next month. The company sells widgets for $50 each, and zots for $40 each. At these prices, up to 200 widgets and 30 zots can be sold. The price for yamis has not yet been decided. Two prices are under considera-

Distance (miles) between Potential Restaurant Sites (for Problem 14–21)

From \ To	2	3	4	5	6	7	8	9	10
1	3.7	2.2	3.2	6.4	7.3	8.6	8.8	13.0	10.2
2		2.6	5.7	3.3	6.6	9.6	10.3	13.1	7.5
3			3.2	4.5	5.3	7.4	7.7	11.4	8.2
4				7.5	5.7	5.6	5.7	10.4	10.3
5					5.2	9.4	10.1	11.5	4.4
6						4.8	5.6	6.6	5.5
7							1.2	5.2	10.2
8								5.9	11.4
9									10.2

tion—$50 and $60. At the $50 price, up to 100 can be sold. At the $60 price, up to 60 can be sold.

Ininob purchases the raw material from which all three products are produced from a single firm. Widgets require 0.1 tons of raw material for each one produced. Yamis require 0.2 tons each; and zots require 0.3 tons each. Because of a shortage, there are only 50 tons of raw material available for production of all three products. The cost of the raw material is $20 per ton.

The first step in the production process for all three products is a molding and heating operation. This requires a special-purpose machine. A maximum of 400 hours are available on this machine. No additional hours can be obtained, since the machine is already operating three shifts. The variable cost of operating this machine is $8 per hour. Each widget requires one hour on the machine; each yami requires two hours; and each zot requires one-half hour.

After the molding and heating operation described above, each product is finished. Zots are finished on a zotting machine. It costs $500 to set up this machine and $10 per zot finished. If no zots ar produced there is, of course, no setup cost.

Widgets and yamis are finished on a widgeting machine. There is a cost of

$1,000 to set up this machine. However, once set up, the machine can finish either widgets or yamis or both. If neither yamis nor widgets are to be produced, the setup cost is not incurred. The variable cost of operating this machine is $10 per unit for either yamis or widgets.

Ininob has to decide its production schedule for all three products at the beginning of the month, and also to decide on the price of yamis.

Formulate the problem as an integer linear programming problem.

14–23. A firm has three factories that supply five sales regions. The transportation costs and sales requirements are shown in Table 14–9.

Each factory can operate at either one-shift or two-shift operations. The costs and capacities are shown in Table 14–10.

Note that the fixed costs for the first shift are large because the general overhead of the factory is included, whereas the fixed costs of the second shift include only those fixed costs associated with operating the second shift.

Management is considering adding an additional 400 units of capacity to factory 3 (200 units to each shift). The variable cost would be $1 per unit on the first shift and $1.50 per unit on the second shift. Additional fixed charges

Table 14–9   **Shipping Costs from Factories to Sales Regions (for Problem 14–23)**

Factories \ Sales Regions	1	2	3	4	5	Total Sales Requirements
1	$1	$1	$6	$3	$5	
2	2	1	4	1	6	
3	4	3	1	3	4	
Sales Requirements (units)	100	200	200	400	100	1000

Table 14–10   Factory Operating Costs and Capacities (for Problem 14–23)

	First Shift			Second Shift		
	Variable Cost (per unit)	Fixed Cost	Capacity (units)	Variable Cost (per unit)	Fixed Cost	Capacity (units)
Factory 1	$3.00	$200	100	$4.50	$50	100
Factory 2	1.50	500	300	2.00	70	300
Factory 3	1.00	400	200	1.50	70	200

would be $300 on the first shift and $50 on the second shift. (These amounts would include the required return on investment.)

It is company policy not to operate any second shift below 40 percent of capacity nor any first shift below 60 percent of capacity (i.e., a shift either operates at zero or above these limits).

The company wants to determine the optimum shipping schedule (factories to warehouses). In addition, it wishes to find out whether or not the additional capacity should be added to factory 3 and which, if any, shifts should be shut down in the various factories. (Note that the closing down of both shifts means closing down the factory.)

Formulate the problem as a mixed-integer linear programming problem. (One caution—be sure your formulation guarantees that the second shift doesn't operate without a first shift.) To make the formulation easier to write down, you may use symbols instead of the numbers given in Tables 14–9 and 14–10.

14–24. The city of Shamut has called for bids for construction of its new town hall. The call for bids lists five parts of the total job:

F — Foundation
S — Structure
P — Plumbing and heating
E — Electrical
I — Interior

The bid procedure specified that bids could be made on different parts or combinations of parts of the job, and multiple bids were allowed.

Five area contractors, each considered reliable by Shamut, have submitted various bids. The bids for the five contractors—Able, Baker, Charley, Dog, and Easy—are shown below.

In addition, Easy specified in its bid that it would give a discount of 10 percent from the stated single-part bid amounts if it received the contract for four or more parts of the job.

Your task as city manager is to award contracts in such a way as to minimize the cost to Shamut of getting the whole job done.

One complicating factor is that contractors Able and Baker are feuding with each other, and each has specified in the bids that they will not accept the contract for any part if the other does any part of the job.

Formulate a linear integer programming model to help the city manager decide on what bids to accept. Use no more than 25 decision variables. Make your formulation general; that is, do not arbitrarily delete bids just because you can see that they are not going to be accepted. Your formulation should be general enough so that it would hold up with different bid prices (of course, with changes in these numbers in the model).

(for Problem 14–24)

Contractor	Bid Number	Job Parts in Bid	Bid Amount ($000s)
Able	1	F only	$ 700
	2	$F + S$	3,800
	3	$F + S + P$	4,500
Baker	1	$P + E$	1,100
	2	$P + E + I$	1,900
	3	Whole job	5,800
Charley	1	P only	700
	2	E only	600
	3	I only	1,000
	4	$P + E$	1,200
Dog	1	$S + P$	3,600
	2	$S + P + E$	4,100
	3	$F + S + P + E$	4,600
Easy	1	F only	900
	2	S only	3,200
	3	P only	800
	4	E only	500
	5	I only	1,200

Case 14–25

The Allen Company is involved in the development of residential property. The figure shows a map of a new development in the planning stages.

Map of Wuthering Heights Development

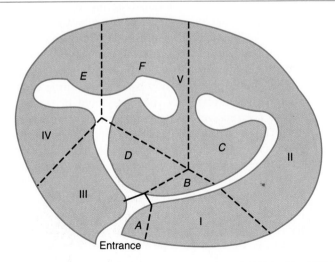

The access roads are shown in the map and are broken into segments labeled A through F. In addition, the area is broken into five subsections (labeled I through V on the map). Allen plans to develop this entire subdivision over an 18-month period.

The planning problem involves determining the order in which the roads and subsections are to be built. For planning purposes, the time is broken into three half-year periods. In any period (half year), any number of road segments can be constructed (subject to financial constraints described below). The only restriction is that a segment cannot be constructed before the roads leading to it. (For example, segment C could not be constructed before segment B. However, they could be constructed simultaneously.)

Houses can be constructed in any subsection no sooner than *one period after* the access roads to that section are completed. The table below gives the access roads that must be finished at least one period before the various subsections can be developed:

Subsection	Roads Required
I	A, B
II	A, B, C
III	A, D
IV	A, D, E
V	A, D, F

Any number of subsections can be developed in any period, and they can be completed in one period. The only restrictions on subsection development are road construction (discussed above) and financial (see below).

Suppose the cost of constructing the various road segments are: K_A, K_B, ..., K_F. Designate the cost of constructing the housing subsections as: C_I, C_{II}, ..., C_V. These costs represent the net amount funded by the Allen Company over and above the construction mortgages available from the bank. These costs are incurred in the period when a subsection is developed.

Designate the profit received from selling a subsection as P_I, P_{II}, ..., P_V. Again, these are net of the repayment of the mortgages on construction. The profits are received *one period after* development (that is, a one-period lag).

To finance this project, the Allen Company has available its own capital of $500,000. It also has the option of borrowing money from the bank (in addition to mortgage money). However, the bank insists on lending the full amount of the loan over the whole period of the project. That is, if an amount L is to be borrowed, it is obtained at the beginning of the project and paid back in full (with interest) at the end of two years. The two-year period is necessary so that profits from sales of property in the third period (and received in the fourth half year) can be used to repay the loan. The minimum loan is $1 million (that is, either zero or at least $1 million must be borrowed). The interest rate is 10 percent per year.

Formulate this problem as a mixed-integer linear programming problem. Assume that if a subsection is to be developed in any period, it will be fully finished (that is, no partial completions). The objective is to minimize the amount of interest on the bank loan.

Case 14–26

Jane Rodney, president of the Rodney Development Company, was trying to decide what types of stores to include in her new shopping center at Puyallup Mall. She had already contracted for a supermarket, a drug store, and a few other stores that she considered essential. However, she had available an additional 16,000 square feet of floor space yet to allocate. She drew up a list of the 15 types of stores she might consider (Table 14–11), including the floor space required by each. Rodney did not think she would have any trouble finding occupants for any type of store.

The lease agreements Rodney used in her developments included two types of payment. The store had to pay a certain annual rent, depending on the size and type of store. In addition, Rodney was to receive a small percentage of the store's sales if the sales exceeded a specified minimum amount. The amount of

Table 14–11   **Characteristics of Possible Lessees, Puyallup Mall Shopping Center**

Type of Store	Size of Store (000s of sq. ft.)	Annual Rent ($000s)	Present Value ($000s)	Construction Cost ($000s)
Clothing				
1. Men's	1.0	$ 4.4	$ 28.1	$ 24.6
2. Women's	1.6	6.1	34.6	32.0
3. Variety (both)	2.0	8.3	50.0	41.4
Restaurants				
4. Fancy restaurant	3.2	24.0	160.0	124.4
5. Lunch room	1.8	19.2	77.8	64.8
6. Cocktail lounge	2.1	20.7	100.4	79.8
7. Candy and ice-cream shop	1.2	7.7	45.2	38.6
Hardgoods				
8. Hardware shop	2.4	19.4	80.2	66.8
9. Cutlery and variety	1.6	11.7	51.4	45.1
10. Luggage and leather	2.0	15.2	62.5	54.3
Miscellaneous				
11. Travel agency	0.6	3.9	18.0	15.0
12. Tobacco shop	0.5	3.2	11.6	13.4
13. Camera store	1.4	11.3	50.4	42.0
14. Toys	2.0	16.0	73.6	63.7
15. Beauty parlor	1.0	9.6	51.2	40.0

annual rent from each store is shown in the second column of Table 14–11. In order to estimate the profitability of each type of store, Rodney calculated the present value of all future rent and sales percentage payments. These are given in the third column. Rodney wants to achieve the highest total *present value* over the set of stores she selects. However, she could not simply pick those stores with the highest present values, for there were several restrictions. The first, of course, was that she has available only 16,000 square feet.

In addition, a condition on the financing of the project required that the total annual rent should be at least as much as the annual fixed cost (taxes, management fees, debt service, and so forth). These annual costs were $150,000 for this part of the project. Finally, the total funds available for construction of this part of the project were $700,000, and each type of store required different construction costs depending on the size and type of store (fourth column in the table).

In addition, Rodney had certain requirements in terms of the mix of stores that she considered best. She wanted at least one store from each of the Clothing, Hardgoods, and Miscellaneous groups, and at least two from the Restaurant category. She wanted no more than two from the Clothing group. Furthermore, the number of stores in the Miscellaneous group should not exceed the total number of stores in the Clothing and Hardgoods groups combined.

Formulate Rodney's problem as an integer linear programming problem.

PART IV

Deterministic and Probabilistic Models

15

Inventory Control with Constant Demand

Inventory control represents an important management function that has been very successfully treated by quantitative methods. The concepts in this chapter and the two succeeding ones have been applied in numerous companies, large and small, with favorable results. Nevertheless, there are additional business situations (even in well-managed companies) where the insights gained from inventory control models can be extremely useful in seeking improved operating decisions.

In this chapter, we will assume that future demand for an item is known and constant; in succeeding chapters, we will allow demand to be uncertain.

In an ongoing inventory control system, there are two operating decisions to be made:

1. When to Place an Order We must find the optimum *order point,* so that when the inventory level falls to the order point,[1] we place a replenishment order. We shall assume the order point is determined by the units on hand rather than a passage of calendar time (for example, placing an order every month).

2. The Size of the Order The objective is to maximize the difference between revenue and cost associated with maintaining an inventory.

There are two general types of costs to be considered when demand is known and constant: (1) the cost of placing an order, and (2) the cost of carrying inventory in stock. The optimum order size and optimum order point will, in general, be a function of these two costs plus the intensity or rate of use (quantity used during a unit time period).

---

[1]If there is any inventory on order, then the total of inventory on hand plus that on order is compared with the order point.

467

Before we introduce specific models to solve for the optimum order size and order point, we will present a multi-item inventory classification technique called *ABC analysis* which is helpful in focusing management attention on the most important items in any multi-item inventory system.

ABC Analysis

Any significant inventory is always composed of more than one type of item. Each individual item requires analysis to compute its order size and order point, but it is useful at the outset to recognize that not all items are equally important to the organization. **ABC analysis** is a way of classifying items based on some measure of importance. Frequently, a readily available measure of importance is annual dollar sales for each item.

Figure 15–1 illustrates a typical ABC curve obtained by ranking each of a group of items by their dollar sales (in descending order) and then plotting the

Figure 15–1   **ABC Analysis Example**

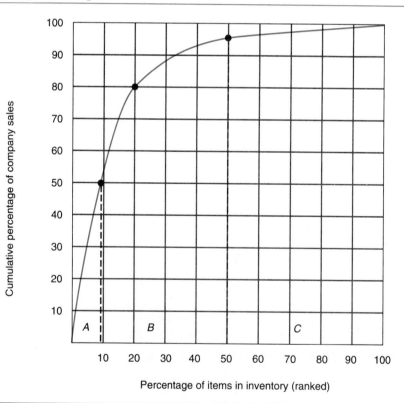

cumulative dollar sales versus the number of different items in the inventory. The well-known "20–80 rule" is demonstrated in this figure; 20 percent of the items are responsible for 80 percent of the total dollar sales of the company.

The shape of any ABC curve will be similar to that shown in Figure 15–1; this is because the items are *ranked* on the importance measure (annual dollar sales) before cumulating. It is impossible to avoid the type of curvature illustrated unless every item in a multi-item inventory system has exactly the same dollar-sales rate; this is highly unlikely.

The ABC curve is used by managers to determine where detailed analysis will pay off, and conversely, where improved accuracy at a large cost may be unwarranted. The usual procedure is to divide the curve into three regions or groups, as follows:

- A items—the top 50 percent of dollar sales.
- C items—the bottom 50 percent of items.
- B items—the items in between.

Figure 15–1 illustrates these three regions for the example. It should be emphasized that these particular breakdowns are not rigid; some companies divide their inventory into four groups (ABCD), and others use slightly different cutoffs for the various regions. The key point is that whatever the definitions, the typical A item is quite a bit more important than the typical B item, which in turn is more important than the typical C item.

For management purposes, the A items should receive the maximum analysis, monitoring, and review, since they rank highest on the importance measure. The B items should receive reasonable attention, but less than the A items. The C items represent many different items, but each individual C item has such low sales that C items can be managed more casually, with a tendency toward "high" inventory levels, since not much money is involved. If improved inventory control is being implemented in a company, the initial focus should be on the A items, since this is where the maximum leverage can be obtained.

Performing an ABC Analysis

The precise way to do an ABC analysis is to select a measure of importance and then rank all items in inventory on that measure, producing a curve similar to Figure 15–1. Alternatively, one can do an ABC analysis on a *sample* of items. Although the sample curve will not be 100 percent accurate, it is likely to be accurate enough for decision purposes. For example, a random sample of 200 items from a 20,000-item inventory could be selected and plotted cumulatively, as shown in Figure 15–2. Note that the vertical scale in Figure 15–2 is cumulative dollar sales; after all points have been plotted, we can add another scale (on the left) indicating percentages. In Figure 15–2, total dollar sales of all 200 items is $500,000; this quantity represents 100 percent of sales in the sample, thereby determining all other percentages (see added vertical scale in Figure 15–2).

Figure 15–2   **ABC Analysis of Random Sample of 200 Items**

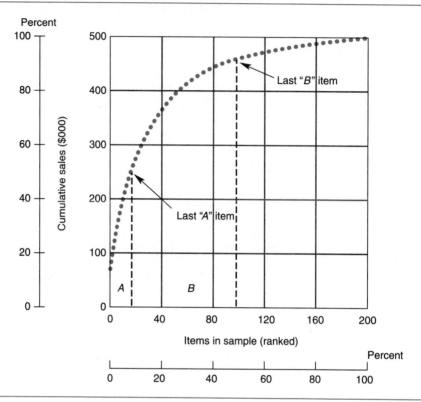

It is critical that the sample for the analysis be drawn *randomly,* so that there is a good likelihood that the outcome is representative. One way to do this would be to take every 100th item, for example, in a 20,000-item inventory listed by product number. This would produce a representative sample if there were nothing unusual about the 100th item, the 200th, and so on, in the listing by item number.

Once the sample is plotted, as in Figure 15–2, the ABC classifications can be made and the cutoff points determined as shown. If the ABC classifications described earlier are used, then the last A item is the one that brings cumulative dollar sales to the 50 percent mark. Suppose the actual dollar sales for that item were $8,561; then we might classify as an A item any item whose dollar sales exceeded $8,500. Similarly, the last B item is the item at the 50 percent point on the horizontal scale; suppose its dollar sales were $983. Then we could classify as a B any item with dollar sales below $8,500 but above $1,000. The C items would be items with sales below $1,000. In this manner, the information gained from our sample of 200 items can be applied to all 20,000 items in inventory, and the "error" caused by our sample not being perfect is likely to be very small.

Cautions Regarding ABC Analysis

There are two potential pitfalls in using ABC analysis. The first relates to the performance measure. Although dollar sales are frequently used as a performance measure, this is often due to the fact that this data is readily available in the computer. One should guard against selecting the wrong performance measure simply because it is easily available. Depending on the decision to be made, the performance measure should be selected as the scale that is the best available measure of importance for the decision. For instance, if one is concerned about decisions regarding inventory investment, the dollar-sales measure is likely to be appropriate; but if the decision will affect the company's ability to meet customer orders without delay, then some measure of profitability (rather than simply sales) may be more desirable.

The second problem is that often a company has items that ordinarily would be classified as C items on a dollar-sales measure but are highly important to the company's customers. An example is sales of spare parts for complex machinery. The dollar value of the sales of parts may be low compared with the sales of new machinery, but the spare parts are critical to the operation of the machinery already sold, and poor performance on customer orders for spare parts could have an extremely bad effect on future machinery sales. Thus, one should carefully consider other attributes of C items that might make them subject to more careful management, such as that given to B and A items.

SUMMARY ABC analysis classifies items based on a measure of importance. Management can then focus maximum attention on the A items and spend less effort on the B and C items. Taking a random sample of 100 or 200 items is often the simplest way to perform an ABC analysis.

The Economic Order Quantity with Known Demand

In the rest of this chapter, we shall investigate inventory control when we know the demand. We assume that both the replenishment lead time and the demand rate are known and constant. With this assumption, the computation of the other point is not complicated. If the usage rate is 3 units per day and the lead time for replenishment is 40 days, we set an order point of 40 times 3, or 120 units. This allows us no room for error, but it is consistent with the assumptions of known demand and known lead time. Figure 15–3 illustrates the inventory behavior of the system under our assumption of known and constant demand rate and lead time.

The optimum order size is determined by analyzing total costs. The total cost (TC) for a period will be equal to the sum of the ordering costs (or setup costs)

Figure 15–3   **Reordering and Known Demand**

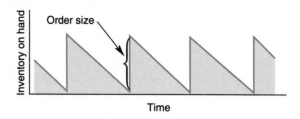

plus the costs of carrying the inventory during the period.[2] Assume that the units will be received all at once.

Let:

K = Incremental cost of placing an order (or setting up production)
k_c = Annual cost of carrying one unit of inventory
D = Annual total usage (demand) in units
Q = Optimum order size in units (the unknown)

Note that the annual number of orders placed depends on D and Q:

$$\frac{D}{Q} = \text{Annual number of orders}$$

Also:

$$\frac{Q}{2} = \text{Average inventory (assuming linear usage)}$$

Then:

$$\frac{Q}{2}k_c = \text{Annual cost of carrying inventory (average inventory times } k_c \text{, the annual holding cost per unit)}$$

$$\frac{D}{Q}K = \text{Annual cost of placing orders (annual number of orders, } D/Q \text{, times the cost of placing an order, } K\text{)}$$

The total annual cost is:

$$TC = \frac{Q}{2}k_c + \frac{D}{Q}K \qquad (15\text{--}1)$$

These costs are plotted as a function of order size in Figure 15–4. The minimum total cost of Figure 15–4 occurs when the slopes of the two cost components (ordering and carrying cost) are equal and opposite in sign. In this particular

---

[2]We need not consider shortage costs, since our assumptions of known demand and known lead time imply that shortages will not occur. The assumption of known demand will be relaxed in the next chapter.

Figure 15–4   **Inventory Costs**

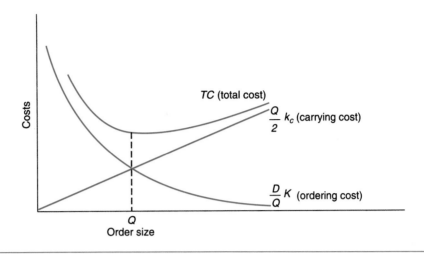

case, this occurs where the two cost components are equal (where the curves cross). We may use this fact to obtain a formula[3] for the optimal order quantity Q by setting the two costs equal and solving for Q. At the optimum:

$$\frac{Q}{2} k_c = \frac{D}{Q} K$$

or:

$$Q^2 = \frac{2KD}{kc}$$

so that:

$$Q = \sqrt{\frac{2KD}{k_c}} \qquad (15\text{–}2)$$

Equation 15–2 is often called the **economic order quantity** or **EOQ formula.**

---

[3]This formula may also be obtained by using calculus to minimize total cost with respect to Q. Take the first derivative of Equation 15–1 with respect to Q, set it equal to 0, and solve for Q:

$$TC = \frac{Q}{2} k_c + \frac{DK}{Q}$$

$$\frac{dTC}{dQ} = \frac{1}{2} k_c - \frac{DK}{Q^2} = 0$$

Solving:

$$Q = \sqrt{\frac{2KD}{k_c}}$$

Since $\dfrac{d^2TC}{dQ^2} = \dfrac{2DK}{Q^3} > 0$, this solution does produce a minimum TC.

Example 1   An example follows:

D = 3,000 units (expected annual demand)
k_c = $3 per unit per year
K = $5 per order

$$Q = \sqrt{\frac{2KD}{k_c}} = \sqrt{\frac{2 \cdot 5 \cdot 3,000}{3}} = \sqrt{10,000} = 100 \text{ units}$$

The optimum order size is 100 units. The total cost of using the optimal order size can be computed by substituting Q = 100 into the total cost Equation 15–1:

$$TC(Q = 100) = \frac{100}{2}(3) + \frac{3,000}{100}(5) = 150 + 150 = \$300$$

If D is measured in dollars instead of units, and if k_c is measured per dollar instead of per unit, the Q will also be in dollars. To illustrate this using the example above, let the price be $15 per unit. The annual demand in dollars is $15 · (3,000) = $45,000. Measuring k_c in dollars per dollar rather than dollars per unit, k_c is now $3/$15 = $0.20 per dollar per year. The formula is now:

$$Q \text{ (in \$)} = \sqrt{\frac{2 \cdot \$5 \cdot \$45,000}{\$0.20/\$}} = \$\sqrt{2,250,000} = \$1,500$$

The optimal order quantity in dollars is $1,500, corresponding to the optimal order quantity calculated above as 100 units (each unit is worth $15).

Even when the demand is not known with certainty, the above model is very helpful in approximating a solution for the problem of optimum order size.

Sensitivity of Costs to Errors in Q

It is possible to use the cost model of Equation 15–1 to demonstrate that total costs in this model are not very sensitive to errors in determining Q. For example, suppose in the example just considered the expected annual demand was incorrectly stated as 4,500 units instead of 3,000 units (a 50 percent overstatement). Then, using the optimal formula for Q, we would obtain the following (incorrect) order quantity:

$$Q = \sqrt{\frac{2 \cdot 5 \cdot 4,500}{3}} = \sqrt{15,000} = 123 \text{ units}$$

Note that because of the square root in the formula, a 50 percent error in estimating demand produces only a 23 percent error in the order size as compared with the optimal Q = 100. However, the true test of an error is how much it costs. Substituting Q = 123 into the total cost Equation 15–1 produces:

$$TC(Q = 123) = \frac{123}{2}(3) + \frac{3,000}{123}(5)$$
$$= 184.5 + 122 = 306.5$$

Comparing this total cost with the total cost of the optimal order size derived above ($TC = 300$), we see that the percentage increase in cost, or penalty for our error, is only $6.5/300 = 2.2$ percent. The same reasoning applies to a 50 percent error in either the order-processing cost or the inventory holding cost. Thus, as long as the costs and demand rate are reasonably estimated, it is likely that very little will be gained by making the estimates more precise.

Quantity Discounts

The preceding analysis ignored the possibility of quantity discounts (a lower price per unit if a larger quantity is purchased at one time). There are three basic elements to consider in evaluating whether or not to pursue a quantity discount.

1. The benefit of the discount in reduced purchase costs.
2. The cost of the discount in increased carrying costs.
3. The benefit of reduced numbers of orders per year.

It is always possible to evaluate quantity discounts by considering all possible alternatives, using the square root order quantity formula (15–2) and the equation for total cost (15–1) together with the stated discount. Incremental analysis can also be used to decide whether to take a discount or not. Consider the first example of this chapter. Suppose we were told by our supplier that a price discount of $1 per unit would be given if we purchased in quantities of 1,000 units or more. We would evaluate the *incremental* results of the three elements as follows:

1. Incremental benefit of discount:

($1 per unit) · (Annual demand of 3,000 units) = $3,000 per year

2. Incremental cost of higher inventory (assuming $Q = 1,000$ units)—Let:

$k_c' =$ Holding cost of items purchased with discount

Then, since the original price was $15 and the discount is $1, if the carrying cost is a function solely of the price, then $k_c' = (14/15)k_c = (14/15)\$3 = \$2.80$. The incremental cost of holding inventory is:

k_c' (new average inventory) $- k_c$ (old average inventory)

$$= \$2.80\left(\frac{1,000}{2}\right) - \$3\left(\frac{100}{2}\right) = \$1,400 - \$150 = \$1,250$$

3. Incremental benefit of reduced ordering costs:

$$K \cdot (\textit{Decrease} \text{ in annual orders}) = K \left(\frac{3,000}{100} - \frac{3,000}{1,000} \right)$$
$$= \$5(30 - 3) = \$5(27) = \$135$$

The net incremental benefit is $\$3,000 - \$1,250 + \$135 = \$1,885$. Since this value is positive, the discount should be taken.

Example 2   Annual demand for an item is 1,000 units. The item costs $10 per unit, and the annual inventory holding charge is 25 percent of the cost of the item. The order-processing cost is $50. If 500 or more units are ordered at once, a discount of $0.40 per unit will be given. What should the order quantity be?

We first compute the usual economic order quantity using Equation 15–2, noting that the holding cost $k_c = 0.25(\$10) = \$2.50$:

$$Q = \sqrt{\frac{2KD}{k_c}} = \sqrt{\frac{2 \cdot 50 \cdot 1,000}{2.50}} = \sqrt{40,000} = 200 \text{ units}$$

Now we evaluate the discount, using the three elements described:

1. Incremental price benefit: We assume that the discount, if taken, will be always taken. Thus, the annual benefit of the discount is:

$$(\$0.40 \text{ per unit})(1,000 \text{ units per year}) = \$400$$

2. Incremental holding cost: $k_c' = (\$9.60/\$10)k_c = \$2.40$, so that the incremental holding cost of ordering 500 units compared with ordering 200 units is:

$$\$2.40 \left(\frac{500}{2} \right) - \$2.50 \left(\frac{200}{2} \right) = \$600 - \$250 = \$350$$

3. Incremental benefit of reduced orders:

$$\$50 \left(\frac{1,000}{200} - \frac{1,000}{500} \right) = \$50(5 - 2) = \$150$$

The net incremental benefit is $\$400 - \$350 + \$150 = \$200$, and the discount should be taken. (Note that as soon as we discovered that the price break benefit more than compensated for the increased carrying costs, we could have opted for the discount then, without calculating the benefit of reduced orders.)

Blanket Orders

It may be possible to obtain a price discount by agreeing to purchase a specific level of annual volume from a supplier while maintaining the flexibility of frequent delivery of small quantities. This procedure is called a *blanket order*. In

Figure 15–5

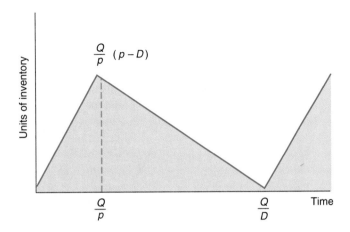

this chapter, we assumed that demand is known and constant; hence, blanket orders would always be favored, and the size of the delivery quantity could be calculated according to EOQ calculations (refer also to the just-in-time section below). In practice, when demand is not known and constant, there is some risk of accepting an annual commitment that would have to be balanced against the price discount available.

Assuming a Continuous Flow of Product

Instead of receiving the ordered units all at once, the firm may receive the product continuously over a period of time. For example, the units being produced may be sent into inventory one at a time instead of in a batch of size Q. Assume units are used at a rate D, that they are produced at a rate p, and that Q units are to be produced on each production run. Figure 15–5 shows the situation being considered.

It takes time Q/p for the entire Q to be produced. During this time, $(Q/p)D$ has been used. Hence, the amount available at the highest point in Figure 15–5 is:

$$Q - \frac{Q}{p}D = \frac{Q}{p}(p - D)$$

at the point in time Q/p.

The optimum production run size is:[4]

$$Q = \sqrt{\frac{2KD}{k_c} \cdot \frac{p}{p - D}} \qquad (15\text{--}3)$$

Example 3 It costs $50 to set up the production line for a product that sells 100,000 units per year. The carrying cost per unit is $5 per year. The rate of production is 200,000 units per year. What should be the size of the production run? From Equation 15–3:

$$Q = \sqrt{\frac{2KD}{k_c} \cdot \frac{p}{p - D}}$$

$$= \sqrt{\frac{2 \cdot 50 \cdot 100,000}{5} \cdot \frac{200,000}{100,000}}$$

$$= \sqrt{4,000,000} = 2,000 \text{ units}$$

In doing calculations of the type illustrated, one must be careful that the units are compatible. For example, if we were told that production *per day* was 800 units, we could not let p be equal to 800 and still use the demand rate of 100,000 units *per year* and the carrying cost of $5 *per year*. In this situation, we could convert the 800 units *per day* to an annual equivalent by multiplying by the number of workdays in a year (say there are 250 workdays in a year; this would give us the equivalent annual rate of 200,000 units per year).

Furthermore, this model assumes that all costs of holding inventory follow the pattern of Figure 15–5. However, if raw material cost for a manufactured product were a large fraction of the total product cost and raw material could not be purchased one unit at a time, then Figure 15–3 would better represent the situation and Equation 15–2 should be used.

Just-in-Time Inventory Systems

Recently, there has been much attention given to Japanese "just in time" or "Kanban" inventory systems. *Kanban* refers to a card that allows one department of the organization to produce some minimum quantity of items in response to another department's immediate requirement. The idea is to use very small order (or production) quantities, with relatively low order points so that replenishment inventory arrives "just in time."

The just-in-time concept strives for very low inventory levels, thereby lowering inventory holding cost. However, if order quantities are lowered below the economic order quantity level (see Equation 15–2), then ordering costs will in-

---

[4]See the appendix to this chapter for the derivation.

crease and the total cost will be higher than optimal (see Figure 15–4). Thus, in order to implement the just-in-time concept, it is necessary for the ordering (or setup) cost somehow to be lowered from its earlier value. An important contribution of the Japanese was to realize that K, the "setup cost," could be changed. We illustrate these concepts with an example based on Example 1.

Example 4   Consider Example 1, but suppose that the firm can lower its ordering cost from $5 per order to $1.25 per order by purchasing a membership in a special group buying club. The annual membership fee is $50. Should the firm join the buying club, and if so, in what quantities should it order?

First, assume the firm joins the buying club. Then:

$D = 3,000$ units
$k_c = $3 per unit per year
$K = $1.25 per order

From Equation 15–2:

$$Q = \sqrt{\frac{2KD}{k_c}} = \sqrt{\frac{2 \cdot 1.25 \cdot 3,000}{3}} = \sqrt{2,500} = 50 \text{ units}$$

The optimum order size has dropped from the earlier value of 100 units (when the ordering cost was $5 per order) to 50 units. The total cost of using this order size with the lower ordering cost can be computed by substituting $Q = 50$ into the total cost equation (15–1):

$$TC(Q = 50) = \frac{50}{2}(3) + \frac{3,000}{50}(1.25) = 75 + 75 = 150$$

The previous total cost (using the $5 per order cost) was calculated in Example 1 to be $300, so the annual saving in total cost is $300 − $150, or $150. Since this saving exceeds the membership cost of $50, the firm should join the buying club and purchase in quantities of $Q = 50$.

Inventory Turnover

A related concept sometimes used by management to monitor inventory levels is inventory *turnover*. Inventory turnover is the ratio of annual demand divided by average inventory. In symbols:

$$\text{Turnover} = \frac{\text{Annual demand}}{\text{Average inventory}} = \frac{D}{Q/2} \qquad \textbf{(15–4)}$$

For inventories involving multiple items, turnover is calculated using the aggregate cost of goods sold (COGS) and the aggregate value of inventory in dollars:

$$\text{Turnover} = \frac{\text{COGS}}{\$ \text{ inventory}}$$

It is sometimes suggested that if a firm's inventory turnover is lower than that of its competitors, then its inventory level is too high and should be reduced. The difficulty with this measure is that it focuses on only one type of cost, namely, inventory holding cost; it ignores ordering costs and shortage costs, as well as quantity discounts. In an environment in which quantity discounts are extremely important, a firm that takes appropriate advantage of them will certainly have higher average inventory and hence lower turnover than a firm that ignores such discounts. However, the first firm will also have lower *total* costs and hence higher profitability.

Thus, turnover is too narrow a measure of inventory performance; it omits important cost factors and may lead to unprofitable actions.

Example 5 Consider the quantity discount example based on Example 1 with $D = 3,000$ units. Let us compute the inventory turnover before and after the quantity discount is taken into consideration.

Before the quantity discount is offered, $Q = 100$. Using Equation 15–4:

$$\text{Turnover} = \frac{3,000}{100/2} = \frac{3,000}{50} = 60$$

Thus, initially there were 60 "turns" per year.

After the quantity discount is analyzed and found to be profitable, the order quantity changes to $Q = 1,000$ units in order to earn the discount. Now, the turnover becomes:

$$\text{Turnover} = \frac{3,000}{1,000/2} = \frac{3,000}{500} = 6$$

Hence, the turnover has been reduced from 60 turns a year to 6 turns a year. Using the "turnover" measure, this change sounds very unprofitable, but we have previously shown that the total cost has been reduced by $1,885 (see quantity discount example) by taking the discount. Therefore, the turnover measure is incomplete and misleading.

SUMMARY

Under constant demand, the economic order quantity (EOQ) formula will minimize order-processing plus inventory holding costs. Some deviation from the calculated EOQ is possible, since total costs are not very sensitive to the precise optimal value. Quantity discounts must be analyzed using incremental analysis. A modified formula applies when there is a continuous flow of product. Just-in-time inventory concepts must still deal with the fundamental costs of inventory: ordering and holding. Inventory turnover may be a misleading performance measure, since it deals with only one of these costs (the holding cost).

APPENDIX

Production Lot Size

How many units should be produced on one production run? This model assumes units are produced at a rate p and used at a rate D (see Figure 15–5).

$$Q = \text{Units of production (the unknown)}$$
$$p = \text{Annual production rate}$$
$$D = \text{Annual rate of demand}$$
$$p - D = \text{Net inventory increase rate (production less demand)}$$
$$\frac{Q}{p} = \text{Duration of production run}$$
$$\frac{Q}{D} = \text{Cycle time}$$
$$\frac{Q}{p}(p - D) = \text{Maximum inventory; } \frac{Q}{p} \text{ is duration of production run and}$$
$$(p - D) \text{ is inventory increase rate during production}$$
$$\frac{Q}{2p}(p - D) = \text{Average inventory}$$

The total annual cost of having a run size of Q units is:

$$TC = k_c \left[\frac{Q}{2p}(p - D) \right] + K \frac{D}{Q}$$

Taking the derivative of total cost with respect to Q:

$$\frac{dTC}{dQ} = k_c \left(\frac{p - D}{2p} \right) - \frac{KD}{Q^2}$$

Setting the first derivative equal to zero and solving for Q:

$$Q^2 = \frac{2KD}{k_c} \cdot \frac{p}{p - D}$$

$$Q = \sqrt{\frac{2KD}{k_c} \cdot \frac{p}{p - D}}$$

This is Equation 15–3 in this chapter.

Bibliography

Brown, R. G. *Decision Rules for Inventory Management*. New York: Holt, Rinehart & Winston, 1967.

————. *Materials Management Systems*. New York: John Wiley & Sons, 1977.

Buffa, E. S., and J. G. Miller. *Production-Inventory Systems: Planning and Control*. 3rd ed. Homewood, Ill.: Richard D. Irwin, 1979.

Hall, R. W. *Zero Inventories*. Homewood, Ill.: Dow Jones-Irwin, 1983.

Hillier, F., and G. J. Lieberman. *Introduction to Operations Research*. 5th ed. New York: McGraw-Hill, 1990.

McClain, J. O., and L. J. Thomas. *Operations Management: Production of Goods and Services*. 2nd ed. Englewood Cliffs, N.J.: Prentice Hall, 1985.

Nahmias, S. *Production and Operations Analysis*. Homewood, Ill.: Richard D. Irwin, 1989.

Schonberger, J. *Japanese Manufacturing Techniques*. New York: The Free Press, 1982.

Silver, E. A., and R. Peterson. *Decision Systems for Inventory Management and Production Planning*. 2nd ed. New York: John Wiley & Sons, 1985.

Tersine, R. J. *Principles of Inventory and Materials Management.* 2nd ed. N. Y.: Elsevier North-Holland, 1982.

Wagner, H. M. *Principles of Operations Research.* 2nd ed. Englewood Cliffs, N.J.: Prentice Hall, 1975.

Problems with Answers

15–1. Refer to Figure 15–1.
   a. What percentage of the items represents 40 percent of sales?
   b. What percentage of items represents 20 percent of sales?
   c. What percentage of sales is represented by the first 50 percent of the items?
   d. What percentage of sales is represented by the first 10 percent of the items?

15–2. A random sample of 10 items has been taken from a 20,000-item inventory. (Ten is too small a sample, but it keeps the arithmetic simple.) The 10 dollar-sales amounts are: 170, 320, 49, 94, 530, 125, 2, 70, 225, 30.
   a. Plot the ranked data on an ABC curve.
   b. Based on your sample, what is the percentage of total sales for the 20,000-item inventory that would be represented by the first 4,000 items?
   c. What percentage of sales is represented by the first 50 percent of the items?
   d. Suppose management wanted A items to represent the first 50 percent of sales, C items to represent the last 50 percent of items, and B items to be in between. What dollar-sales rates would you use to separate the A, B, and C ranges?

15–3. The costs of placing an order are $6. It is estimated that 1,000 units will be used in the next 12 months. The carrying cost per unit per year is $30. Compute the optimum order size.

15–4. The ABC Company uses 100,000 units per year of a product. The carrying cost per unit is $3 per year. The cost of ordering a batch is $60.
   a. What is the optimum order size?
   b. If the ordering costs were 60 cents per order, how many units should be ordered at one time?

15–5. Assume the same situation as in (a) of Problem 15–4, with the added information that the ordering cost can be reduced from $60 to $15 per batch if the company joins a cooperative buying organization with annual membership fee of $2,000.
   a. What would be the optimum order size if the company decided to join the cooperative buying organization?
   b. Should the company join the co-op?

15–6. The XYZ Company can turn out products at the rate of 14,000 units a day. Usage is 4,000 units a day. The cost of a setup for production is $1,000. The number of units used in a year is 1,440,000. The carrying cost per unit per year is $28. Assume a year consists of 360 days. Compute the optimum lot size for a production run.

15–7. Refer to Problem 15–3. Suppose the unit annual carrying cost of $30 is caused by a 20 percent holding cost rate per dollar tied up in inventory per year, multiplied by a unit variable cost of $150. Now suppose that the company can purchase units at a price of $148 each if they order in lots of 100 units each. Compute the total annual variable costs associated with both the original and the recently suggested purchase quantity (be sure to include the effect of the lower price). Should they buy in lots of 20 or 100 units?

Problems

15–8. A random sample of 10 items has been taken from a 40,000-item inventory. (Ten is too small a sample but it keeps the arithmetic simple.) The 10 dollar-sales amounts are: 350, 600, 120, 30, 175, 1100, 5, 50, 200, 90.

a. Plot the ranked data on an ABC curve.

b. Based on your sample, what is the percentage of total sales for the 40,000-item inventory that would be represented by the first 4,000 items?

c. What percentage of items would represent the first 25 percent of sales?

d. Suppose management wanted A items to represent the first 50 percent of sales, C items to represent the last 50 percent of items, and B items to be in between. What dollar-sales rates would you use to separate the A, B, and C ranges?

15–9. Select a random sample of 10 items from your refrigerator. Estimate your annual expenditures on each item, and then plot your ranked data on an ABC curve. Do you tend to pay more attention to the one or two items at the top of your ranking?

15–10. The costs of placing an order are $7.50. It is estimated that 256 units will be used in the next 12 months. The carrying cost per unit per month is $1.25. Compute the optimum order size.

15–11. The costs of placing an order are $150. It is estimated that 1,000 units will be used in the next 12 months. The carrying cost per unit per month is $2.50.

a. Compute the optimum order size.

b. Now suppose that the company could lower the ordering cost to $50; the cost of the effort to accomplish this change is $1,000. Assume the product will be sold only for the next two years. Compute the new optimal order quantity if the lower ordering cost were implemented, and determine if the company should invest $1,000 in the ordering-cost reduction program.

15–12. The ABC Company can turn out a product at the rate of 18,000 units a day. The cost of a setup for production is $2,250. The number of units used in a year is 2,880,000. The carrying cost per unit per year is 18 cents. Assume a year consists of 360 days. Compute the optimum lot size for a production run.

15–13. A company uses a certain part in the assembly of sets of electronic equipment at the rate of 8,000 per year. Each part has a value of $18. The company estimates that the cost of holding inventory is 20 percent of the value of the item per year.

The company can produce the part on either of two machines. Machine A has a setup cost of $200; machine B has a setup cost of only $100. However, it costs 10 cents more per unit to produce using machine B than it does using machine A.

Which machine should the company use? What is the optimum lot size?

15–14. A newly appointed inventory manager was given the following information for an item:

Annual usage in dollars = $100,000
Order-processing cost = $25
Carrying cost per dollar per year = 0.20

When asked to compute an optimal purchase amount for the item, the manager complained that he wasn't told the value per unit. Can you compute an optimal purchase amount for the item with the data provided? If so, do so; if not, explain why not.

15–15. Refer to (*a*) of Problem 15–4. Suppose the ABC Company was offered a discount of 12 cents per unit by its supplier if it ordered in lots of 10,000 units. Should ABC take the discount?

15–16. Father's Cookies produces chocolate-chip cookies in a large oven that holds up to 2,000 pounds of cookies at a time. Annual demand is constant at 200,000 pounds; variable cost is 25¢ per pound. Oven cleanout is required after the oven processes 2,000 or less pounds in a batch; the cleanout takes one hour's time for four workers, each of whom is paid $7 per hour. The inventory holding cost is 20 percent per dollar per year; spoilage occurs if inventory is held by Father's Cookies more than 12 months.

There is substantial unused oven capacity.

In what quantity should these cookies be produced? Why?

15–17. An item is consumed at the rate of 1,000 per year; ordering costs are $20 per order; and holding costs are 25 percent per year. Unit purchase cost is a function of quantity purchased at one time, as follows:

Quantity	Cost per Unit
1–100	$10.00
101–200	9.75
Above 200	9.50

What purchase quantity should be used for the item?

15–18. Refer to Problem 15–7.
   a. Compute the inventory turnover before the discount is offered.
   b. Compute the turnover if the discount is taken.
   c. From your answers to (a) and (b), can you decide if the discount should be taken or not? Explain.

More Challenging Problems

15–19. Consider Equation 15–1, total annual cost, and Equation 15–2, the economic order quantity formula. Suppose an error in data gathering creates an erroneous Q that is 20 percent smaller than the "true" Q^* (i.e., $Q_{error} = 0.80\ Q^*$). Substitute this error back into Equation 15–1 and find the percentage cost penalty that results from the 20 percent error in Q. (*Hint:* Use the fact that with the optimum Q^* the two terms of Equation 15–1 are equal, and each is one half of optimal (minimum) total annual cost.)

15–20. A company uses 2,000 units of a product each year (constant usage). The product is purchased from a supplier at a unit cost of $4; however, the company must pay the freight from the supplier's plant. Each unit weighs 5 pounds; the shipping cost is 20 cents per pound. The company estimates the order-processing cost is $25 per order; inventory holding costs are 20 percent per dollar per year.
   a. Find the optimal order quantity.
   b. Suppose that for shipments above 300 pounds, but less than 10,000 pounds, a flat charge of $50 *per shipment* (not per pound) is charged, while for shipments below 300 pounds the rate remains at 20 cents per pound. Now, what order quantity should be used to minimize the sum of all relevant variable costs?

15–21. The Bancroft Press publishes a wide variety of books. One of their steady sellers is *Imaginative Cooking,* now in its fourth edition. Bancroft expects that the next edition of this book will sell approximately 12,500 copies annually for the next few years.

In past years, Bancroft has always printed and bound a one-year supply of this type of book. Recently, increased inventory costs have forced a reconsideration of this policy. In particular, Bancroft is considering binding only half the printing quantity at the time of printing, and keeping the remaining printed sheets as unbound stock. When needed, the remaining half of the lot would be bound.

Costs are as follows (omitting typesetting costs, distribution costs, and other costs not affected by this decision):

	Printing	*Binding*
Setup cost	$5,000	$1,000
Variable cost per unit	4	2

Bancroft now charges inventory at 25 percent per dollar per year.

a. If a complete printing lot is bound at time of printing, what is the optimal quantity? What are the total annual costs?

b. If only half the printed quantity is bound, what is the optimal quantity to print? What are the total annual costs?

15–22. The ACME Dairy produces 15 flavors of ice cream, each of which is packaged in pints, quarts, and half gallons. Changeover time for package *size* is two hours, and the variable cost associated with this changeover is $80. Cleanout from one *flavor* to another takes 30 minutes, with a variable cost of $20. The amount of ice cream produced and packaged in one hour of run time is approximately 1,000 gallons (irrespective of flavor or package size), and the variable cost associated with that amount of product (materials plus direct labor) is $500. Inventory holding cost is 25 percent per dollar per year.

a. Should ACME produce all sizes of a given flavor before changing to the next flavor, or should it produce all flavors in a given size before changing to the next size? Why?

b. Suppose demand in gallons for each combination of flavor and size (45 products) is identical, equaling 40,000 gallons a year each. Assume there are 2,200 hours the dairy is in operation annually. What is the economic batch size in which all of the products should be produced?

c. The union has recently negotiated a new contract with ACME, which limits operating hours to 1,940 hours per

year (and no overtime is allowed). What effect will this restriction have, if any, on your answer to (b)? What cost, if any, has this restriction placed on ACME?

15–23. Ace Airlines has a need for about 100 new flight attendants per month as replacements for those who leave. Trainees are put through a four-week school. The fixed cost of running one session of this school is $15,000. Any number of sessions can be run during the year, but must be scheduled so that the airline always has enough flight attendants. The cost of having excess attendants is simply the salary that they receive, which is $1,500 per month. How many sessions of the school should Ace run per month, and how many flight attendants should be in each session?

15–24. Complex wood shapes used to form a bookcase are produced on an expensive automatic shaping machine. In order to set up the machine to produce the shapes, a cost of $500 is incurred. Once the machine is set up, it produces shapes at a rate of 200 bookcases per day at a cost of $5 (including raw material) per bookcase. After the shapes are produced, they must be assembled. The first-line supervisor feels there is some "setup" time involved in assembly, due to the learning curve phenomenon whereby each successive bookcase in an assembly batch is assembled more rapidly than the last. He estimates this effect can be represented by a $50 assembly setup charge. Once assembly of bookcases begins, the assembly rate is 100 bookcases per day; the cost of the finished bookcase is $15 (including the $5 cost of the shaped parts).

Annual demand for bookcases is constant at 2,500 bookcases. Holding cost is 20 percent per dollar per year.

a. Suppose the shaper department is separate from the assembly department and is separately controlled financially. If you were to set the production run size for the *shaper,* ignoring the fact that your product is only an intermediate one, how would you set it?

b. If you were to determine the *assembly* lot size without regard to the shaping department, how would you set it?

c. The supervisor has said, "Unassembled shaped pieces do us no good.

Whenever the shaper is run, we should run the entire quantity of shaped pieces through the assembly stage into finished-goods inventory so they will be useful to us." Given this suggested policy, what is the economic *quantity* in which shapes and assembled bookcases should be produced?

16

Inventory Control with Reordering and Uncertain Demand

In this chapter we expand the treatment of inventory control situations by allowing for uncertainty in demand.

Instead of assuming that the demand rate is known and constant, let us hypothesize that we know only the probability distribution of demand during the lead time, but not the actual demand during that period. When we set the order point, there is some probability that we shall run out of inventory and encounter a cost of shortage. We assume any leftover units can be used in the following period.

Figure 16–1 illustrates the behavior of inventory under this assumption. Note that an order of size Q is placed when inventory reaches a level R. Because of the uncertainty of demand during the lead time, a stockout sometimes occurs (such as during the third cycle in Figure 16–1). The annual expected cost of shortage will be affected by the choice of both the order point (R) and the order size (Q).

Before proceeding with the analysis, it is important to emphasize that the models of this chapter are appropriate only when the demand shown in Figure 16–1 comes from a reasonably large number of **independent** sources. Typically, this will occur for inventories of finished goods but will not occur for raw materials or purchased components in a manufacturing situation. In the latter case, for example, various sizes of electric motors may be purchased for assembly into air conditioners. Since the "demand" for motors is completely dependent on the assembly schedule for air conditioners, such demand is called **dependent** rather than independent. For dependent-demand situations, a schedule-planning

Figure 16–1   **Illustration of Inventory Pattern**

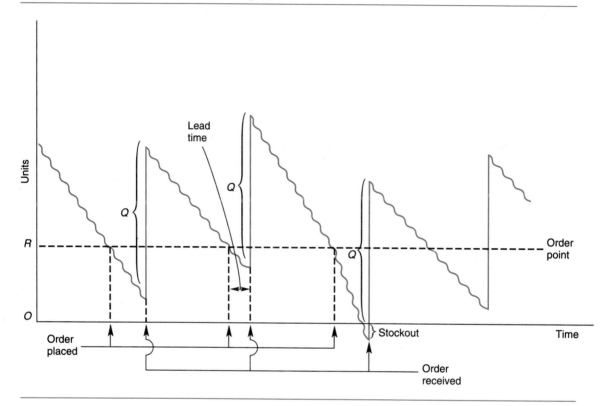

technique called **material requirements planning (MRP)** has been developed.[1] The models presented in this chapter should be used only in situations with independent demand.

We now wish to divide the inventory into two types: cycle stock and safety stock. **Cycle stock** is the inventory that was considered in Chapter 15: $Q/2$ on average. It is the inventory required to be carried as a function of the order size (Q). **Safety stock** refers to the difference between the order point (R) and the average demand during the replenishment lead time $(\overline{M})$. See Figure 16–2. The larger the safety stock (and the corresponding order point), the lower the chance that a stockout will occur, and vice versa.

It is interesting to look at the interaction between the various costs and the two variables (order point and order size) shown in Table 16–1.

---

[1]For a thorough treatment of MRP, see J. A. Orlicky, *Material Requirements Planning* (New York: McGraw-Hill, 1975).

Figure 16–2   **Cycle Stock and Safety Stock under Average Demand Rate**

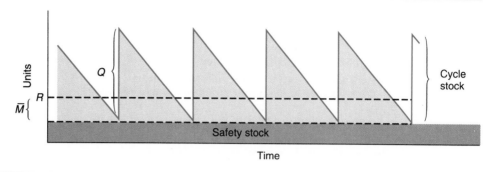

Table 16–1   **Actions and Results**

Action	Result
Decrease order point (i.e., place order when fewer units on hand).	Decrease carrying costs of safety stock and increase shortage cost.
Decrease order size.	Decrease carrying costs of cycle stock ($Q/2$), and increase shortage and ordering costs.
Increase order point.	Increase carrying costs of safety stock, and decrease shortage cost.
Increase order size.	Increase carrying costs of cycle stock, and decrease shortage and ordering costs.

A change in order size affects the frequency of reaching the ordering point (thus, the frequency of encountering a chance of shortage). A change in the order point affects the likelihood of shortages and affects the optimum number of times the order point should be encountered. Thus, the total cost is affected by both the order point and the order size, and the optimum order point and the optimum order size are related.

In order to model this inventory situation, we must decide how to evaluate shortages. Our first approach will be to assume we can estimate the cost of being out of stock one unit (the cost of shortage). While estimation of this type of cost is difficult and requires managerial assessment and judgment, frequently management is willing to set a range on this cost, such as "it is below $20" or "it is definitely above $5." Furthermore, once such a cost is estimated, every item will be consistently treated. Recognizing the potential difficulty of this approach, we will subsequently present an alternative model that allows management to specify the fraction of annual demand to be satisfied from stock.

Shortage Cost Model

Again, we want to minimize the total cost incurred during a given period. There are now three costs to consider:

K = Cost of placing one order
k_c = Cost of carrying one unit in inventory for one year
k_u = Cost of being out of stock one unit (cost of shortage)

The optimum order size and optimum order point will be, in general, a function of these three costs plus the average rate of demand over the lead time and the variability of demand over the lead time.

The Assumptions

We shall first assume that the replenishment lead time is known and constant. Second, the cost of shortage is assumed to be a cost per unit, independent of the duration of the out-of-stock position.[2] The third assumption is that M, the demand during the lead time, is normally distributed. This is the least essential of the assumptions and may be changed; it is chosen to simplify the computations. Next, we assume that the optimal order point R is larger than average lead time demand $\overline{M}$, so that the corresponding safety stock $(R - \overline{M})$ is positive. Finally, we assume safety stock, on the average, is always carried in inventory. We want to determine how much to order (Q) and when to order (R).

The Model

Let:

R = Order point (the total number of units on hand and on order that triggers the reorder)
Q = Order quantity (the number of units ordered at one time)
D = Average demand per year
K = Cost of placing one order
k_c = Cost of carrying one unit in inventory for one year
k_u = Penalty cost of being out of stock one unit (cost of shortage)
M = Number of units of demand over the replenishment lead time (a random variable)

---

[2] This measurement of shortage is most appropriate where sales are lost if inventory is not available. In this case, the cost of shortage would represent the opportunity cost of forgone profit plus any cost of ill will.

$\overline{M}$ = Average number of units demanded during the lead time

σ_M = Standard deviation of demand over the lead time

We want to determine the optimum order quantity (Q) and the optimum order point (R). We will assume that, as a reasonable approximation, the optimal order quantity for this situation (random demand) is the same as the economic order quantity (EOQ) for the case of constant demand covered in Chapter 15. That is, we will recommend use of the same square root EOQ formula derived there:

$$Q = \sqrt{\frac{2KD}{k_c}} \qquad \text{(16–1)}$$

This recommendation is made for two reasons. First, as shown in Chapter 15, the sum of annual order-processing costs plus annual inventory holding costs is not very sensitive to moderate errors in Q; as long as the order quantity is reasonably close to the optimal value, extreme precision is not required. Second, a number of studies have indicated that—although Q and R should theoretically be determined *simultaneously*—in most practical situations, no serious cost penalty occurs if Q is *independently* determined by the square root EOQ formula of Equation 16–1. Thus, we will advocate Equation 16–1 as the basic formula for Q, even when demand is probabilistic.[3]

Once Q is chosen, however, it is important to take its value into account in determining R, since the size of Q directly influences the number of times per year that we will be exposed to a possible stockout position.

Optimal Order Point—A Marginal Approach

It is possible to obtain the formula for the optimal order point by applying marginal analysis as follows. We start with some value of the order point R; for example, $R = \overline{M}$, average lead time demand. We then ask if it is worthwhile to increase R by one unit. That is, we compare the expected annual cost of adding another unit to R, versus the expected annual cost of *not* adding the additional unit.

The annual incremental cost of *adding* an additional unit to R is approximately equal to k_c, since the additional unit will be added to safety stock ($R - \overline{M}$) and therefore held in inventory almost all of the time.[4]

The annual incremental expected cost of *not adding* the additional unit to R will equal the probability that the additional unit (or more) will be demanded

---

[3]R. G. Brown has shown that the only time the penalty for using the EOQ formula above is serious occurs when the EOQ is less than the standard deviation of demand over the lead time (σ_M). In that case, an excellent heuristic is to simply set the order quantity equal to σ_M. For details, see R. G. Brown, *Materials Management Systems* (New York: John Wiley & Sons, 1977).

[4]This is a reasonable approximation, since the additional unit will always be represented in inventory except during stockout (which is a small part of the time).

during the lead time, multiplied by the unit stockout cost k_u, all multiplied by the number of inventory cycles per year (D/Q):

$$\begin{array}{c} \text{Incremental cost} \\ \text{of not adding} \\ \text{incremental unit} \end{array} = \text{Prob} \begin{bmatrix} \text{Next unit} \\ \text{(or more)} \\ \text{demanded} \end{bmatrix} \cdot k_u \cdot \begin{bmatrix} D \\ \overline{Q} \end{bmatrix}$$

Suppose we define $F(R)$ to be the probability that the demand (M) during the lead time will be less than or equal to our current value of R:

$$F(R) = \text{Prob}(M \le R)$$

Then the probability that the next unit (or more) will be demanded is $1 - F(R)$. The costs of adding and not adding the incremental unit are graphed in Figure 16–3.

Note that as R increases, the probability of the additional unit (or more) being demanded falls, and eventually the two lines cross in Figure 16–3. At this point, we stop adding units to R, since the cost of adding a unit exceeds the cost of not adding the unit. Where the lines cross, the two costs are equal:

$$k_c = [1 - F(R)] \cdot k_u \cdot \frac{D}{Q}$$

or:

$$[1 - F(R)] = \frac{k_c \, Q}{k_u \, D}$$

so that:

$$F(R) = 1 - \frac{k_c \, Q}{k_u \, D} \qquad\qquad \text{(16–2)}$$

Equation 16–2 may be used as follows to obtain the optimal value for R:

1. Compute Q from the square root EOQ formula (Equation 16–1).
2. Compute the right-hand side of Equation 16–2; this is the *desired* probability of lead time demand being less than or equal to R.
3. From normal tables, find the value of R for which the stated probability applies.

The term $F(R)$ in Equation 16–2 means: "Set R so that there is:

$$1 - \frac{k_c Q}{k_u D}$$

probability of M being equal to or less than R."[5]

---

[5] $F(R)$ is the *left* tail of a probability distribution; that is, the Prob $(M \le R)$. In most business situations, the shortage cost will be substantially higher than the carrying cost, so the ratio will usually be greater than 0.50, and safety stock $(R - \overline{M})$ will be positive.

Figure 16–3

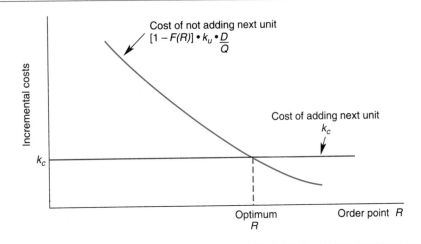

Figure 16–4

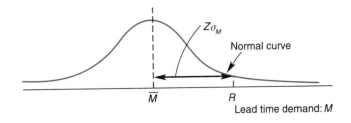

Let Z be the number of standard deviations[6] we must go from the mean sales, $\overline{M}$, before the probability is $F(R)$ that the demand, M, is equal to or less than R. We can obtain R, the optimum order point, as follows (see Figure 16–4):

$$R = \overline{M} + Z\sigma_M \qquad \textbf{(16–3)}$$

Note that by definition, the order point is equal to average lead time demand plus safety stock. Thus, the safety stock is $Z\sigma_M$.

Example 1　We assume that the order quantity, Q, has been determined, and our task is to find the optimum order point.

---

[6]See Chapter 7 for a discussion of this type of calculation.

Let:

$$D = 100 \text{ units per year}$$
$$Q = 50 \text{ units}$$
$$k_c = \$40 \text{ per unit per year}$$
$$k_u = \$80 \text{ for each unit short}$$
$$\overline{M} = 20$$
$$\sigma_M = 5$$

Then:

$$1 - \frac{k_c Q}{k_u D} = 1 - \frac{40 \times 50}{80 \times 100} = 1 - 0.25 = 0.75$$

$$F(R) = 0.75$$

Referring to a table of cumulative probabilities for the standard normal distribution (Table A in the appendix at the end of the text), we find $Z = 0.67$.
The optimum order point is:

$$R = \overline{M} + Z\sigma_M = 20 + (0.67)(5)$$
$$R = 20 + 3.35 = 23.35 \doteq 23$$

With an order point of 23 units, we shall not run out of stock approximately 75 percent of the time (remember, the mean demand is 20 units) during the ordering period. The safety stock is 3 units.

Example 2   The following example illustrates the computation of the optimum order size and order point.

- The amount expected to be used (D) is 1,800 units per year.
- The cost of making one order (K) is $10.
- The cost of carrying one unit for one year is 60 cents (this is k_c).
- The replenishment lead time is 20 days; and the mean usage, $\overline{M}$, during the lead time is 100 units, with a standard deviation of 30 units, and is normally distributed.
- The cost of shortage is $5 per unit out of stock (this is k_u).

Using Equation 16–1, we can determine Q:

$$Q = \sqrt{\frac{2KD}{k_c}} = \sqrt{\frac{2 \cdot 10 \cdot 1,800}{0.60}} = \sqrt{60,000} = 245 \text{ units}$$

From Equation 16–2 we obtain:

$$F(R) = 1 - \frac{k_c \, Q}{K_u \, D} = 1 - \frac{0.6(245)}{5(1,800)} = 0.98367$$

Referring to a table of cumulative probabilities for the normal distribution (Table A in the appendix at the end of the text), $F(R) = 0.98367$ is equivalent to:

$$Z = 2.14 \text{ standard deviations}$$

Thus:

$$R = 100 + 2.14 \cdot 30 = 164 \text{ units}$$

The safety stock in Example 2 is 64 units.

Note the difference in these two examples. In Example 2, both the shortage cost and the variability of demand during the lead time were significantly larger than in Example 1, leading to much higher safety stock.

Computing the Standard Deviation of Lead Time Demand (σ_M)

The replenishment lead time is usually different from the standard time period (for example, weekly or monthly) used to collect demand data. We need a way to compute σ_M from σ_1, where σ_1 refers to the standard deviation of demand over the standard time period (this value is easily obtained from the demand data; see Chapter 3). For example, suppose the lead time is three weeks and the standard time period is one week. Consider the lead time demand as the sum of three weekly random demands. Then, if the weekly demands are independent, the variance of the sum equals the sum of the variances (see Chapter 3):

$$\sigma_M{}^2 = \sigma_1{}^2 + \sigma_1{}^2 + \sigma_1{}^2 = 3\sigma_1{}^2$$

so that:

$$\sigma_M = \sqrt{3}\,\sigma_1$$

If L is the length of the lead time, then the general formula is:

$$\sigma_M = \sqrt{L}\,\sigma_1 \tag{16-4}$$

Example Suppose weekly demand for an item has a mean of 100 units and a standard deviation of 10 units ($\sigma_1 = 10$). If the lead time is four weeks, what is the mean ($\overline{M}$) and the standard deviation (σ_M) of lead time demand?

$$\overline{M} = 4(100) = 400$$
$$\sigma_M = \sqrt{4}(10) = 2(10) = 20$$

Total Expected Cost

The total cost for an inventory policy of (Q, R) is:[7]

$$\text{Total cost } (Q, R) = [K + k_u \sigma_M N(Z)]\frac{D}{Q} + \left[\frac{Q}{2} + (R - \overline{M})\right]k_c \tag{16-5}$$

---

[7] See the appendix at the end of this chapter for a derivation of this formula.

where $N(Z)$ refers to the unit-loss function for the standard normal distribution (Table B in the appendix at the end of the text), and Z is equal to R converted into standard deviation units from the mean demand over the lead time:

$$Z = \frac{R - \overline{M}}{\sigma_M}$$

Continuing with Example 2, the total cost of a policy of ordering 245 units at an order point of 164 units is:

$$TC(Q, R) = [K + k_u \cdot \sigma_M \cdot N(2.14)]\frac{D}{Q} + \left[\frac{Q}{2} + (R - \overline{M})\right]k_c$$

$$TC(Q, R) = [10 + 5 \cdot 30 \cdot 0.0058]\frac{1,800}{245} + \left[\frac{245}{2} + 164 - 100\right](0.6)$$

$$= (10.87)7.35 + (186.5)0.6$$

$$= 79.89 + 111.90 = 191.79$$

Recall that the above values for Q and R were determined using the square root EOQ formula (Equation 16–1) for Q. Let us now explore what the total cost is without this approximation. By trial and error, it is possible to find the precise pair of values for Q and R that minimizes the total cost; they are $Q = 255$ and $R = 164$. The (minimum) total cost of these optimal values is:

$$TC(Q, R) = [10 + 5 \cdot 30 \cdot 0.0058]\frac{1,800}{255} + \left[\frac{255}{2} + 164 - 100\right](0.6)$$

$$= (10.87)7.06 + (191.5)0.6 = 76.74 + 114.90 = 191.64$$

The more precise values result in an expected annual cost that is only 15 cents less (or 0.08 percent less) than the decision rule in which the order quantity is calculated independently of the order point.

For our example, the total cost is not very sensitive to the order quantity if an amount in the general magnitude of 250 units is ordered. Thus, we suggest using Equation 16–1 to obtain an approximate order quantity Q, and then using Equation 16–2 to solve for the corresponding order point R. Usually, the effect of this approximation on total cost is minor, as in our example.

Service Level Model

The previous model is recommended when the cost of a shortage (per unit) can be reasonably determined. As an alternative, it is possible to satisfy a specified fraction of demand (e.g., 95 percent) at minimum cost. Here, the burden of estimating a shortage cost is changed to the problem of assessing the desired service level, where service level is defined as the percentage of demand filled off-the-shelf (without backordering). Service levels may be set based on those provided by the competition (management may decide to meet or exceed the competition's service levels).

We will make the same assumptions as before and use the same notation, with one addition:

P = Service level (fraction of demand filled from stock)

It is recommended that the square root EOQ formula again be used to determine the order quantity, for the same reasons given previously. Regarding the order point, we first write down the expression[8] for the expected number of unfilled orders during a lead time as a function of Z, the number of standard deviations of protection:

$$\text{Expected unfilled orders in a lead time} = \sigma_M N(Z) \qquad \textbf{(16–6)}$$

where $N(Z)$ is the unit normal loss table presented in Table B in the appendix at the end of the book.

Next, we observe that average demand over a replenishment cycle must equal average supply in the long run, and since the amount supplied is Q, average demand over the cycle is also Q. Now we can write down the expected fraction of unfilled orders in a cycle:

$$\text{Fraction of unfilled orders per cycle} = \frac{\sigma_M N(Z)}{Q} = 1 - P \qquad \textbf{(16–7)}$$

Since our desired service level is P, Equation 16–7 can be set equal to $1 - P$, as shown. Rearranging, we obtain:

$$N(Z) = \frac{Q(1 - P)}{\sigma_M} \qquad \textbf{(16–8)}$$

Equation 16–8 is used as follows to obtain the optimal value for R:

1. Compute Q from the square root EOQ formula (Equation 16–1).
2. Compute the right-hand side of Equation 16–8.
3. From the unit normal loss table $N(Z)$ (Table B in the appendix at the end of the text), find the value of Z satisfying Equation 16–8.[9]
4. Then $R = \overline{M} + Z\sigma_M$.

Example 3   Consider Example 1 above, but instead of a shortage cost of $80 per unit short, suppose management desires that 97 percent of all demands be met from stock ($P = 0.97$). From Equation 16–8:

$$\frac{Q(1 - P)}{\sigma_M} = \frac{50 \cdot 0.03}{5} = 0.3$$

---

[8]See the appendix at the end of the chapter for a derivation of this formula.
[9]If the value of Equation 16–8 exceeds the highest value in the table (0.3989), then Z is set equal to zero, and the actual service level will exceed the specified value. This situation is due to a large value of Q relative to σ_M.

From Table B, the corresponding value of $Z = 0.22$, so that the optimal order point is:

$$R = \overline{M} + Z\sigma_M = 20 + (0.22)(5) = 21.10 = 21 \text{ units}$$

With an order point of 21 units, we shall satisfy approximately 97 percent of the demand.

It is important to note that the term *service level* defined here is *not* the same as the probability of no stockout in a lead time. Unfortunately, some writers use service level to refer to this probability. To illustrate the difference, consider Example 3, where the optimal $Z = 0.22$. Using Table A in the appendix at the end of the text, this value of Z will produce a probability 0.5871 of no stockout in a lead time. The reason that the percentage of demand filled off-the-shelf (our definition of service level) can be as high as 97 percent when the probability of no stockout in a lead time is only 59 percent relates to the size of the order quantity Q relative to the size of the standard deviation of lead time demand σ_M (see Equation 16–8). Intuitively, when stockouts do occur, the number of demands that are not met from stock is small, so that on average, 97 percent of all demands are met from stock.

When one reads or hears the expression "service level," one should ask how it is defined in order to avoid confusion and misunderstanding. The definition used here is more useful to management than the alternative definition.

Other Shortage Measures

In addition to a dollar cost per unit short and a stated percentage of service, a number of other measures of shortage performance have been modeled and "solved" for the corresponding formulas for optimal order points. The reader is referred to the bibliography at the end of this chapter for further information.

Just-in-Time Systems

The Japanese have developed inventory planning to a fine art. Their "just-in-time" (JIT) inventory policy is a very attractive alternative in concept.

Note that if the ordering or setup cost is driven toward zero, the inventory order quantity is driven as small as possible. (See the EOQ formula in Equation 16–1.) In that case, average cycle stock will be very small.

Also, if the lead time is close to zero (the setup or ordering time is extremely short), again the inventory level can be very low. If a unit is needed, it can be bought or produced in a very short time. Furthermore, if the expected sales during the lead time has a very small (almost zero) variance, then there is no need for a large safety stock.

Thus, there can be situations in which the just-in-time inventory policy is consistent with the models of this chapter. In particular, JIT policy is the special case when setup costs are very small and lead times are very short. However, if there is considerable uncertainty about the level of sales during the lead time, or if the lead time until replenishment is very uncertain, and there is a high cost of being short of inventory, there is sufficient justification for having safety stock inventory. One would not want a just-in-time policy if there were a large probability of being short, and if there were a large cost associated with being short.

In summary, the Japanese have done an excellent job of forcing us to consider ways of reducing inventory and inventory carrying costs. In Chapter 15 we discussed how the just-in-time (JIT) concept leads one to find ways of lowering the ordering cost. In this chapter, we see that if the replenishment lead time can be reduced, this will cause a reduction in the standard deviation of demand over the lead time (σ_M) and hence, a reduction in safety stock inventory. Again, one must always bear in mind all three types of costs in an inventory system: ordering costs, holding costs, and shortage costs.

SUMMARY

When demand is uncertain, we may continue to use the square root EOQ formula for order size. For the order point, we can either assess a shortage cost per unit, or a desired level of service can be specified. In either case, an optimal formula for the order point has been obtained.

APPENDIX

The Determination of the Optimum Order Point and Order Size

Let:

$$
\begin{aligned}
Q &= \text{Order size} \\
R &= \text{Order point} \\
D &= \text{Average demand per year} \\
M &= \text{Amount demanded during lead time } (\overline{M} = \text{Mean amount});\\
&\quad \text{a random variable} \\
f(M) &= \text{Probability density function for } M \\
R - \overline{M} &= \text{Safety stock} \\
\sigma_M &= \text{Standard deviation of demand over lead time} \\
R - M &= \text{Units unsold when new units are received (if } M < R) \\
M - R &= \text{Amount by which demand during lead time exceeds order point} \\
&\quad \text{(if } M > R) \\
K &= \text{Cost of placing order} \\
k_c &= \text{Carrying cost per unit per year} \\
k_u &= \text{Penalty cost for being out of stock one unit (cost of shortage)}
\end{aligned}
$$

The Total Annual Expected Cost

The total cost of a policy involving a specific order size, R, and a specific order quantity, Q, is equal to the sum of the costs of ordering, the costs of being out of stock, and the costs of carrying inventory:

$$\text{Total cost } (Q, R) = K\left(\frac{D}{Q}\right) + \left[k_u\int_R^\infty (M - R) f(M)dM\right]\frac{D}{Q}$$
$$+ \left[\frac{Q}{2} + (R - \overline{M})\right]k_c \qquad (16\text{-}9)$$

where $K(D/Q)$ is the cost of ordering; K is the cost per order; D/Q is the annual number of orders:

$$\left[k_u\int_R^\infty (M - R) f(M)dM\right]\frac{D}{Q}$$

is the cost of being out of stock; k_u is the cost per unit; the integral is the expected number of units out of stock per cycle; D/Q is the annual number of replenishment cycles—that is, the annual number of orders; $[(Q/2) + (R - \overline{M})]k_c$ is the cost of carrying inventory; and k_c is the cost of carrying one unit for one year. The remainder of the term is the average inventory; $Q/2$, the average inventory of cycle stock, plus the average safety stock $(R - \overline{M})$. The term $(R - \overline{M})$ only approximates the average level of safety stock, but the approximation is valid in most practical instances (see footnote 4 in this chapter).

The equations for Q and $F(R)$ are obtained from Equation 16–9, the equation for the total cost, by taking the partial derivatives with respect to R and with respect to Q and setting them equal to zero.[10]

$$\text{Total cost } (Q, R) = K\frac{D}{Q} + \left[\frac{Q}{2} + (R - \overline{M})\right]k_c + \left[k_u\int_R^\infty (M - R) f(M)dM\right]\frac{D}{Q}$$

$$= K\frac{D}{Q} + k_c\left[\frac{Q}{2} + (R - \overline{M})\right]$$

$$+ \frac{D}{Q}k_u\left[\overline{M} - \mathop{E}_{-\infty}^{R}(M) - R[1 - F(R)]\right]$$

Differentiating with respect to R:

$$\frac{\partial \text{ Total cost}}{\partial R} = k_c - \frac{D}{Q}k_u R f(R) + \frac{D}{Q}k_u[F(R) + R f(R) - 1]$$

$$= k_c - \frac{D}{Q}k_u + \frac{D}{Q}k_u F(R)$$

Setting the derivative equal to zero and solving for $F(R)$:[11]

$$F(R) = 1 - \frac{k_c Q}{k_u D} \qquad (16\text{-}2)$$

---

[10] The symbol $\mathop{E}\limits_{-\infty}^{R}(M)$ in the equations is the partial expectation. It equals $\int_{-\infty}^{R} Mf(M)dM$.

[11] Second-order conditions must also be checked.

Differentiating total cost with respect to Q:

$$\frac{\partial \text{ Total cost }(Q, R)}{\partial Q} = -\frac{KD}{Q^2} + \frac{k_c}{2} - \frac{D}{Q^2} k_u \int_R^\infty (M - R)f(M)dM$$

Setting the derivative equal to zero and solving for Q:

$$Q = \sqrt{\frac{2D\left[K + k_u \int_R^\infty (M - R)f(M)dM\right]}{k_c}} \qquad (16\text{-}10)$$

Equation 16–10 can be converted into a form that is more susceptible to computation. We make use of the fact that if M is normally distributed and if R is larger than the expected sales $(\overline{M})$ during the reorder period, then:

$$\int_R^\infty (M - R)f(M)dM = \sigma_M N(Z) \qquad (16\text{-}11)$$

where $N(Z)$ is the unit normal-loss integral valued for Z (R converted to standard deviations from the mean). The σ_M is the standard deviation of the distribution of demand during the lead time. Equation 16–11 is the expected number of unfilled orders in a lead time.

Equation 16–10 now becomes:

$$Q = \sqrt{\frac{2D[K + k_u \sigma_M N(Z)]}{k_c}} \qquad (16\text{-}12)$$

Note that R is in the above formula (Equation 16–10) for Q, and Q is in the Equation 16–2 for R. Theoretically, the two equations must be solved simultaneously. This can be done by the use of an iterative procedure, which starts with an estimate of Q, solves for R, then solves for a new Q, and repeats this process until a Q and an R are found to satisfy both equations. However, for practical purposes, it is sufficient to determine the value of Q by using the formula in the last chapter, where certain demand was assumed:

$$Q = \sqrt{\frac{2KD}{k_c}} \qquad (16\text{-}1)$$

The equation for total cost can be simplified (assuming $R > \overline{M}$) by making use of Equation 16–11. Substituting into Equation 16–9, we obtain:

$$\text{Total cost }(Q, R) = [K + k_u \sigma_M N(Z)]\frac{D}{Q} + \left[\frac{Q}{2} + (R - \overline{M})\right]k_c \qquad (16\text{-}13)$$

Bibliography

See the bibliography at the end of Chapter 15.

Problems with Answers

16–1. The following information relates to an item in inventory:

k_u = $2 cost per unit for sales lost
$\overline{M}$ = 50 mean sales during lead time
σ_M = 10 units
D = 1,000 units per year (estimated demand)
K = $6 per order (ordering costs)
k_c = $30 (cost of carrying a unit in inventory for one year)

The distribution of M is assumed to be normal.

a. Compute the approximate optimum order size.

b. Compute the approximate optimum order point.

16–2. The mean demand for an item in inventory for the coming year is 40,000 units. The lead time is 36 days, and the mean demand during the lead time is 4,000 units. The lead time demand is assumed to be normally distributed with σ = 500. The cost per unit of shortages is $10; the cost of placing an order is $64; and the cost of carrying a unit in inventory for one year is $2.

a. Compute the approximate optimum order size (round to the nearest whole unit).

b. Compute the approximate optimum order point.

c. Compute the total cost of the approximate order size and reorder point.

16–3. An oil company is drilling for oil in Alaska, and is concerned about its inventory of spare parts. It takes a month to receive orders. Consider part 8J2N. This part is expected to be needed at a rate of 100 per month (1,200 per year). Demand during the lead time (one month) is approximately normal with standard deviation 40. The order cost is $1,000 per order; the holding cost is $20 per year; and the shortage cost is $200 per unit. Determine the order size Q and the order point R.

16–4. Lead time demand for an item averages 100 units, with a standard deviation of 30. The order quantity is 200 units. Management desires that 99 percent of all demand be met from stock.

a. What is the optimal order point?

b. Suppose management wanted a 98 percent service level; what would the optimal order point be?

c. Suppose management wanted a 90 percent service level. Compute the optimal order point.

Problems

16–5. A retailer feels that the mean demand for an item in inventory for the coming year is 1,800 units. The lead time on orders is 20 days, and the mean demand during the lead time is 100 units. The lead time demand is assumed to be normally distributed, with σ = 30 (there is a 50–50 chance that the lead time demand could be less than 80 units or more than 120

units). The cost per unit of lost sales is $5, the cost of placing an order is $10, and the cost of carrying a unit in inventory for one year is $50.

a. Compute the approximate optimum order size (round to nearest whole unit).

b. Compute the approximate optimum order point.

16–6. The mean demand for an item in inventory for the next year is 4,000 units. The lead time on orders is 10 days. The demand for the product during the lead time is normally distributed and has a standard deviation of 30 units. The cost per unit of lost sales is $5, the cost of placing an order is $10, and the cost of carrying a unit in inventory for one year is 50 cents.

a. Compute the square root estimate of Q.

b. Compute the order point.

c. Compute the optimum order size after iterating (see the appendix at end of this chapter).

d. Compute the total cost of the initial order size and reorder point.

e. Compute the total cost of the optimum order size and reorder point.

16–7. The order-processing cost for an item is $50. Annual demand is 10,000 units. The item unit cost is $5; inventory holding cost is 20 percent per dollar per year.

a. Compute the economic order quantity in units.

b. Suppose the replenishment lead time is two weeks. Weekly demand averages 200 units (assume 50 weeks a year) with a standard deviation of 41 units; assume weekly demands are normally distributed and mutually independent. Management has determined that a unit backordered has a penalty cost of $3. Determine the optimal reorder point (R).

c. An analyst no longer with the company has previously recommended a reorder point of 603 units. What unit penalty cost (k_u) is implied by such a value for the reorder point?

16–8. An item is replenished 10 times per year, on the average. The annual unit holding

cost is one half the unit cost of being short. Weekly demand is normally distributed with a mean of 100 and a standard deviation of 20.

a. Compute the desired probability of not running out of stock during a lead time.

b. Suppose the replenishment lead time is *four* weeks. Compute the optimum order point.

16–9. Refer to Problem 16–8. Suppose that an error is made in estimating one of the values used to compute the order point. Specifically, suppose that a 50 percent error is made in estimating the shortage cost, with the result that the ratio k_c / k_u is erroneous.

a. Suppose the erroneous ratio is $k_c / k_u = 1.0$ instead of the true value of one half. Compute the probability of not running out of stock during a lead time and the associated order point.

b. Suppose the erroneous ratio is $k_c / k_u = 1/4$. Again, compute the probability of not running out, and the order point.

c. Comment on the relative sensitivity of the order quantity versus the order point.

16–10. An item averages 2,400 demands annually. The lead time is one month; the standard deviation of monthly demand is 50 units. The order quantity is 300 units; management desires that 99 percent of demands be met from stock.

a. What is the optimal order point?

b. Suppose management wanted a 98 percent service level. What is the optimal order point?

c. If management were satisfied with a 90 percent service level, what would the optimal order point be?

More Challenging Problems

16–11. A firm has a choice of manufacturing a part internally or purchasing it from an outside supplier. The variable cost per unit is the same in either case. However,

if the part is made internally, there is a setup cost of $100. If the part is purchased, there is a fixed order cost of $20. If the part is made internally, there is zero lead time; if purchased from outside, the lead time is 25 days (usage during the lead time is normally distributed with a mean of 100 units and a standard deviation of 20 units). The cost of carrying one unit in inventory is $2 per year. The cost of being short one unit is $18 (this is k_u). Annual requirements for this part are 1,000 units.

Should the firm make this part internally or purchase it on the outside? What other considerations besides inventory costs would actually go into a decision of this type?

16–12. The ABC Company has a machine that requires replacement of a certain part at random intervals when the part breaks. The lead time for ordering spares from the manufacturer is one month. The average number of breakdowns is one per month, and management accepts the premise that the breakdown of the part is consistent with the characteristics of a Poisson process.[12]

a. The current policy is to order five units of a part whenever a replenishment order is placed. If the management requires at least a 0.99 probability of the part being in stock during a replenishment lead time, what should the reorder point be?

b. If ordering costs are $10, and carrying costs are $2.40 per unit per year, what should the optimal order quantity be?

c. If the order quantity is changed, should management's goal of at least 0.99 probability of service during a lead time be revised? How should this

goal be set? What information would you need in order to make this decision?

16–13. A vaccine marketed by a drug company has a known and constant demand of 1,200 units per year (or 100 a month). The production cost is $120 per unit, the setup cost is $400 per batch, and the holding cost of inventory is 20 percent per year. Lead time for production is constant and known (one month).

a. What is the economic production quantity per batch?

b. The company has recently discovered that its vaccine has a shelf life of only 1.5 months. Determine the lowest-cost production strategy for this situation (i.e., that which minimizes total costs of setup, holding, and spoilage).

c. Now assume that the company's demand averages 100 units per month, but is no longer constant. The demand is normally distributed, with standard deviation of 20. The unit cost of a shortage is $640 (lost profit plus ill will). Ignoring the shelf-life problem of (b), what is the optimal inventory policy?

16–14. Consider Example 2 in the text. Suppose there is a quantity discount of $0.20 per item if 1,000 or more items are ordered. Should the company take advantage of this discount?

16–15. Aggregated Air Lines (AAL) maintains spare parts to repair jet engines, which fail randomly. As an example, consider part #7654, one of which is on each engine of a Boeing 747. When engines are brought to the maintenance base for disassembly, diagnosis, and repair, this part is examined carefully and is diagnosed as "needing repair" if necessary. Failures of this part per month occur according to a normal distribution with a mean of 5 and a standard deviation of 1.5.

The setup time for repair is very small compared with the value of the part itself, so whenever a part needs re-

---

[12]If the process is Poisson, then the probability of k occurrences during a unit time interval is:

$$P(k) = \frac{e^{-\lambda}\lambda^k}{k!}$$

where λ is both the mean or expected number of occurrences per unit of time and the variance of the number of occurrences per unit of time. See Appendix 1 in Chapter 18.

pair, it is sent to the repair shop (i.e., no "batching" takes place). Assume the repair shop takes exactly three months to repair this part. Suppose the airline has a target inventory of 30 spare parts; then the 30 parts must be able to cope with random demand over a three-month replenishment cycle or there will be a stockout.

AAL has determined that the cost of a shortage is $50 (this is the cost of expediting the delivery of a spare part from Boeing). You are asked to review their target number of 30 spares. How would you determine the optimal target quantity if the parts cost $125 each and annual inventory holding cost is 25 percent per year?

16–16. Refer to Problem 16–5. Apply R. G. Brown's heuristic (see footnote 3 in the chapter) and find the order quantity and the order point.

16–17. Refer to Problem 16–7. Suppose that for an annual fee of $100, it is possible to reduce the replenishment lead time from two weeks to one week to implement the just-in-time concept.

a. Assuming the fee is paid, compute the new economic order quantity (Q).

b. Assuming the fee is paid, compute the new optimal reorder point (R).

c. Compute the reduction in safety stock both in units and in dollars. Should the firm pay the fee? Explain.

16–18. The Friendly Computer Store currently orders packages of floppy disks from its supplier. Orders are received one month after they are placed. The unit cost of a package of disks is $3; annual inventory holding costs are 25 percent; the unit shortage cost for being stocked out of a package is assessed as $7. Monthly demand for packages of disks is a normally distributed random variable with a mean of 1,000 packages and a standard deviation of 200 packages.

a. A new employee has asked what the order-processing cost is to order disks; she is told it is $5. She then proposes that the company adopt a continuous review policy of the type described in this chapter. What would the optimal values for Q and R be for such a policy?

b. A second new employee discovers that the $5 order-processing cost can be reduced to $1 if the store is willing to invest $100 in a software package for order processing. Analyze whether or not the investment should be made.

16–19. An item has a unit cost of $20 when purchased under normal replenishment conditions involving a two-week lead time. If a stockout threatens, an immediate emergency replenishment can be obtained by paying $22 per unit (i.e., a $2 premium over the regular cost). The company has decided to pay the premium cost and order units as needed (one unit at a time) when inventory falls to zero. There is no order-processing cost when ordering emergency replenishments; the order-processing cost for normal replenishments is $20 per order. Carrying costs are 25 percent annually. Annual demand averages 10,400 units; weekly demand is normally distributed with a mean of 200 units and a standard deviation of 30 units.

a. Compute the desired replenishment quantity and reorder point for normal replenishments.

b. Suppose that the option of immediate emergency replenishment is no longer available. Also, suppose the company must satisfy 98 percent of demand off-the-shelf without backorder. What should the reorder point be now?

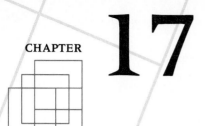

17

Inventory Control with Uncertainty and No Reordering

This chapter introduces methods of solving a "one shot" inventory problem when there is no opportunity for reordering and the item cannot economically be stored for future orders. This situation is faced by firms producing highly seasonal or style goods, goods that are perishable (flowers, foods), goods that become obsolete (magazines), and services that are perishable (for example, air-line seats on a given date). Chapter 4 suggested a method of solving this type of inventory problem, making use of conditional and expected value tables. In many situations, that method of analysis requires an excessive amount of clerical effort. An alternative procedure is to make use of marginal analysis and find the last unit worthy of being ordered.

It should be noted that this chapter deals with inventory control problems where the problems of order size, in conjunction with frequency and timing of order, are *not* present. We are concerned only with the problem of how much should be ordered if we are faced with a demand with known probabilities and *reordering is not possible*. (Chapters 15 and 16 considered the situation in which reordering is allowed).

We will assume that demand is uncertain but that the probability distribution of demand is known. This is analogous to knowing that a fair coin has a tail and a head but not knowing which will come up on the next toss.

Example 1   Let us assume that the demand for a product is known to have the distribution shown in Table 17–1. Assume that units cost $25 each and that leftovers may be sold for salvage for $5. The sales price is $55 per unit. We know the probability distribution of demand for our product, but we do not know before the period

Table 17–1 Demand Distribution

Demand	Probability
0	0.10
1	0.30
2	0.40
3	0.20
	1.00

Table 17–2 Computation of Expected Profit*

Event: Demand	Probability of Demand	Order One Unit		Order Two Units		Order Three Units	
		Conditional Profit	Expected Profit	Conditional Profit	Expected Profit	Conditional Profit	Expected Profit
0	0.10	$(20)	$ (2)	$(40)	$(4)	$(60)	$(6)
1	0.30	30	9	10	3	(10)	(3)
2	0.40	30	12	60	24	40	16
3	0.20	30	6	60	12	90	18
	1.00	Expected profit: $25			$35		$25

*Amounts in parentheses are negative.

begins how much will be demanded in this period. In this situation, how many units should be ordered?

One possibility would be to compute the different expected profits that would occur with different ordering plans. This is the procedure followed in Chapter 4. Table 17–2 presents this computation. Remember that if no units are purchased, no units may be sold; if one unit is purchased, no more than one unit may be sold, even if the amount demanded is greater.

Based on expected profit, the optimum act is to order two units, since the expected profit of $35 is higher than the expected profit resulting from any other strategy.

A Marginal Approach

In the above analysis, we computed the different total profits that would be expected following different ordering policies. A solution easier to compute uses a marginal approach. We compute the effect on profit of adding one more unit to the order size.

Let the probability of selling an additional unit (or more) be designated by p; then $(1 - p)$ is the probability of not selling the additional unit (or more). The values of p in our example are shown in Table 17–3.

Table 17-3

Demand	Probability of Demand	Cumulative Probabilities (p)
0	0.10	1.00
1	0.30	0.90
2	0.40	0.60
3	0.20	0.20
	1.00	

Table 17-4 **Conditional and Expected Costs**

Event: Demand for Next Unit (or more)	Probability of Event	Act	
		Do Not Order	Order
No	$1 - p$	0	c_o
Yes	p	c_u	0
Expected costs of acts		pc_u	$(1 - p)c_o$

The column headed "Cumulative probabilities" is p, since it indicates the probability of selling zero or more (1.00), one or more (0.90), two or more (0.60), or three or more (0.20) units. It is the *right tail* of the probability distribution.

Let c_o be defined as the unit **cost of overage;** that is, the cost of having one unit left over. For example, if a unit costs $25 and leftover units can be sold for $5, then the cost of overage is $20 per unit.

Let c_u be defined as the unit **cost of underage;** that is, the cost of not having any units to sell when a customer wants one. In our example, a unit costs $25 and sells for $55. Thus, the firm loses $30 of profit for each unit that it is short; that is, c_u is $30. We assume there is no cost beyond the present period because of the underage.

The relationship between the costs of overage and underage and the probability of demand for the next unit is shown in Table 17-4.

Table 17-4 shows that if a unit is ordered but there is no demand, the conditional cost is c_o. Similarly, if the unit is not ordered and there is a demand for it, the conditional cost is c_u. Note that the underage cost c_u is an **opportunity loss** (see Chapter 4).

The expected cost for the act "do not order" is pc_u; and that for the act "order" is $(1 - p)c_o$. The additional unit should be ordered provided the expected cost of doing so is less than the expected cost of not ordering. That is, order if:

$$(1 - p)c_o < pc_u$$

Table 17–5

(1) Policy: Go from Ordering	p	(2) Expected Cost of Ordering the Next Unit: $(1 - p)c_o$	(3) Expected Cost of Not Ordering the Next Unit: pc_u	(4) Net Incremental Cost of Ordering: (2) − (3)
0 to 1	0.90	$0.10 \cdot 20 = 2$	$0.90 \cdot 30 = 27$	−25
1 to 2	0.60	$0.40 \cdot 20 = 8$	$0.60 \cdot 30 = 18$	−10
2 to 3	0.20	$0.80 \cdot 20 = 16$	$0.20 \cdot 30 = 6$	10

Figure 17–1   Expected Costs of Acts

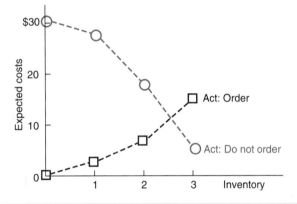

For example, consider initially ordering zero units, with the act "order" representing the order for one unit. Then:

$$\text{Expected cost (do not order)} = pc_u = (0.9)(\$30) = \$27$$

and:

$$\text{Expected cost (order)} = (1 - p)c_o = (0.1)(\$20) = \$2$$

The expected cost of ordering is less than the expected cost of not ordering, so the unit should be ordered. The same comparison must be made to see if the second unit should be ordered, and so on. Table 17–5 and Figure 17–1 illustrate these calculations.

A negative cost in column 4 of Table 17–5 is a net expected profit. Ordering the first unit increases profit by $25; ordering the second unit increases profit by $10 (to $35); and ordering the third unit decreases profit by $10 (to $25). It would not be desirable to stock three units, since there is an expected marginal cost of $10 associated with stocking the third unit.

Using this rule, the decision maker will keep adding additional units until the expected cost of "order" equals or exceeds the cost of "do not order." Recall that as more units are added, the probability of demand for the next unit (or more), p, will decline, and $(1 - p)$ will increase. Ultimately, the expected cost from ordering will exceed that of not ordering (see Figure 17–1).

Instead of completing a table such as Table 17–5 to find the optimal solution, there is an important shortcut we can use. Suppose we let p_c be the probability at which the cost of ordering *equals* the cost of not ordering. We call p_c the **critical probability** and can find it by solving the following equation:

$$(1 - p_c)\, c_o = p_c\, c_u$$

or:

$$p_c = \frac{c_o}{c_o + c_u} \qquad (17\text{--}1)$$

The ratio $c_o/(c_o + c_u)$ is called the **critical ratio.**

If the events are not continuous (for example, demand can be either 1,000 or 2,000 units, but not in between), it is not always possible to find the marginal sale with an exact probability of p_c. The following rules are useful in finding the optimum in the discrete case:

1. As long as the probability of selling one or more additional units is greater than p_c, the critical ratio, we should order that unit.
2. If the probability of selling the additional unit is equal to p_c, we are indifferent to including it in our order or leaving it out.
3. If the probability is less than p_c, do not order that unit.

In our example, c_o equals $20, and c_u is $30; thus:

$$p_c = \frac{c_o}{c_o + c_u} = \frac{20}{20 + 30} = \frac{20}{50} = 0.40$$

Referring to Table 17–3, we see that the decision maker would order two units (because $p = 0.60$ for the second unit, and this is greater than $p_c = 0.40$) but would not order the third unit (because $p = 0.20$ and this is less than 0.40).

Note that the inventory model that we have developed assumed linearity in the costs of overage and underage. That is, it has assumed that the per unit costs are the same for all units. In some cases, these assumptions are not realistic; and more appropriate, but more complex, functions for the marginal costs can be used.

Cost of Ill Will

Thus far, we have assumed that the only cost of an underage (i.e., of being out of stock) was the profit that was lost in the one period. But it is possible to modify the model to include customer ill will that might result from not finding the goods on hand. Estimating the cost of ill will can be a very difficult process. One approach is to assume you could buy a magic wand and use it to avoid one unit of stockout; how much would you be willing to pay for the magic wand? In any event it is necessary that an estimate of this factor be made in terms of the present value of future profits lost because of a unit underage. This amount can then be included in determining the critical ratio, and hence, in setting the optimal ordering policy.

Continuing Example 1 of this chapter, let us assume there is an additional ill will cost of $7.50 associated with every unit of demand not filled because of an inventory shortage. Consider these definitions and data:

c_o = Unit cost of overage = $20. The $20 is the difference between the cost per unit ($25) and the distress price ($5).

c_u = Unit cost of underage = $37.50. The $37.50 is equal to the sum of the profit lost by one unfilled demand ($55 − $25 = $30) and the cost of ill will ($7.50) for each unit of underage; that is, when there is demand and there are no units to sell.

The definition of the underage cost has been altered to include ill-will effects; however, the critical ratio equation still applies (Equation 17–1):

$$p_c = \frac{c_o}{c_o + c_u}$$

In our modified example:

$$p_c = \frac{c_o}{c_o + c_u} = \frac{20}{20 + 37.50} = 0.35$$

The increased penalty for not filling an order has had the same effect as an increase in the profit margin (i.e., an increase in the regret of not having a unit on hand when a unit is demanded), and it will tend to increase the size of the order by decreasing p_c.

Using a Continuous Probability Distribution

Instead of assuming that sales can take on only a few discrete values, we can make use of a continuous probability distribution. Such a distribution will make it possible to consider all feasible values of the random variable, demand. For illustrative purposes, assume that the random variable, tomorrow's demand, is normally distributed.

As in the previous section on the discrete case, we begin by computing p_c, where p_c is the critical ratio. This critical ratio is the probability at which the cost of ordering equals the cost of not ordering. In terms of the normal distribution, p_c can be represented by the colored area shown in Figure 17–2. It should be noted that p_c is the *right tail* of the distribution.

Figure 17–2

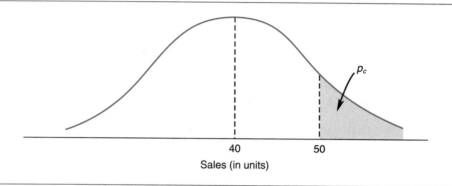

40   50

Sales (in units)

Figure 17–2 shows an optimum order of 50 units. If fewer than 50 units are ordered, p, the probability of selling an additional unit or more, will be greater than p_c; the same arguments presented for the discrete case hold in the continuous case.

In the computation of optimum order size, the first step is to find Z, the number of standard deviations from the mean, that will equate the right tail of the normal density function and p_c. It is then necessary to convert Z to units by multiplying Z by the standard deviation of the sales distribution. This number of units is then added to mean sales, if $p_c < 0.50$ (as shown in Figure 17–2), or subtracted, if $p_c > 0.50$. If $p_c = 0.50$, then $Z = 0$. This is the same process of standardizing a normal probability distribution as was introduced in Chapter 7.

Example 2   Assume that the distribution of demand is normal, c_o is equal to \$64, and c_u is equal to \$336. The critical ratio is:

$$p_c = \frac{c_o}{c_o + c_u} = \frac{64}{64 + 336} = 0.16$$

The 0.16 probability corresponds to the right tail of a normal distribution. Referring to Table A (in the appendix at the end of the text), we find that the left tails are given. The left-tail complement of a 0.16 right tail is 0.84, and this is approximately one standard deviation from the mean (with one standard deviation, the value in the table is 0.8413). If we move out one standard deviation to the right of the mean, the probability of making an additional sale or more will be equal to 0.16.

Assume mean sales for the coming period are 40 units and the standard deviation of the prior distribution is 10. We want to increase the order size until the probability of making an additional sale is equal to 0.16. We have to move

Figure 17–3

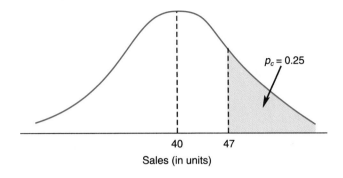

$p_c = 0.25$

40   47

Sales (in units)

one standard deviation to the right of the mean ($Z = 1$). In order to convert Z to units, we multiply by the standard deviation:

$$Z\sigma = 1 \cdot 10 = 10 \text{ units}$$

Since $p_c < 0.50$, we have to *add* 10 units to the mean sales to obtain Q, the optimum order size. We can write the following equation:

$$Q = \text{Mean sales} \pm Z\sigma$$
$$= 40 + 10 = 50$$

The sign is plus if $p_c < 0.50$ and minus if $p_c > 0.50$.

Example 3   Assume that demand has the same normal distribution as in Example 2. Suppose we have now computed p_c and found it to be 0.25. Figure 17–3 shows this situation.

The left-tail complement of a 0.25 right tail is 0.75; Table A shows that the Z value corresponding to $F(Z) = 0.75$ is approximately $Z = 0.67$. Then the optimal order size is:

$$Q = \text{Mean sales} + Z\sigma$$
$$= 40 + 0.67(10) = 46.7 \doteq 47$$

Example 4   Consider the same problem as Example 3, but now suppose that the forecast of sales is less certain; the standard deviation of the prior distribution is 25 instead of 10.

In Example 3, the critical ratio p_c was 0.25, and the corresponding Z value was approximately $Z = 0.67$. Using the larger standard deviation, the optimal order size is now:

$$Q = \text{Mean sales} + Z\sigma$$
$$= 40 + 0.67(25) = 56.75 \doteq 57$$

It is interesting to compare this result with that of Example 3, where the standard deviation of sales was 10. Note that as the forecast uncertainty increases (when the standard deviation increases), it is optimal to move even further away from the mean sales forecast of 40 units. This strategy may seem counterintuitive at first consideration, but it is a direct consequence of the critical ratio properly taking the costs of overage and underage into account. If we wish to have a 0.25 probability of underage, a higher standard deviation requires that a larger inventory be carried.

Relevant Costs

It is important to obtain correct estimates of relevant costs of overage and underage when using this solution procedure. These costs should be *incremental* or *marginal costs;* they should not contain any allocations of overhead or other fixed costs that would be unaffected by the decision under consideration. For example, suppose in Example 1 the unit cost of the item was as follows:

Raw materials	$20 ⎫	(variable costs)
Direct labor	5 ⎭	
Allocated overhead	25	(allocation of fixed cost)
Total	$50	

From an accountant's viewpoint, the fully allocated cost of the item is $50, but for decision-making purposes, the *incremental* unit cost is only $25 (the sum of raw material and direct labor, both of which are usually variable costs). We assume that the fixed overhead will not change whether or not we produce a marginal unit. Similarly, the unit underage cost should not contain any allocations of fixed costs.

Note that since the underage cost is an opportunity cost, it does not show up on the firm's profit-and-loss statement. Thus, a "conservative" management that focuses only on reported profit and loss may be missing significant opportunities for profit improvement if the underage cost is ignored.

SUMMARY

One-shot inventory problems can be analyzed by determining the underage cost, the overage cost, and the critical ratio p_c. The order size is increased until the probability of selling the next unit or more falls to p_c. If ill will is a consideration, it must be estimated and included in the unit cost of underage.

Bibliography

See the bibliography at the end of Chapter 15.

Problems with Answers

17-1. The probability distribution of the demand for a product has been estimated to be:

Demand	Probability of Demand
0	0.05
1	0.15
2	0.30
3	0.35
4	0.10
5	0.05
6	0.00
	1.00

Each unit sells for $50, and if the product is not sold, it is completely worthless. The purchase costs of a unit are $10.

a. Assuming no reordering is possible, how many units should be purchased?

b. If customer ill will is estimated to be $20 for every unit for which there is unfilled demand, how many units should be ordered?

17-2. Assume that our estimate of the demand for the next period is a normal distribution with a mean of 50 units and a standard deviation of 10 units. Reordering is not possible. Compute the optimum order sizes for the p_c's given below.

a. 0.60	e. 0.22
b. 0.50	f. 0.10
c. 0.45	g. 0.02
d. 0.40	

17-3. Given the following information, compute the optimum order size (reordering is not possible):

Sales price	$100
Incremental cost per unit sold (including purchase cost)	70
Purchase cost per unit	50
Salvage value (if not sold)	10
Loss in goodwill for each unit of demand not satisfied	50

The probability distribution of demand is normal; mean, 140; standard deviation, 20.

17-4. Refer to Problem 17-3. Recompute the optimum order size, assuming the standard deviation of the probability distribution is 50.

17-5. Refer to Problem 17-3. Recompute the optimum order size, assuming there is *no* loss in goodwill with unfilled orders.

a. Assume a standard deviation of 20.

b. Assume a standard deviation of 50.

c. Compare the above answers with those of Problems 17-3 and 17-4.

Problems

17-6. A wholesaler of stationery is deciding how many desk calendars to stock for the coming year. It is impossible to reorder, and leftover units are worthless. The following table indicates the possible demand levels and the wholesaler's prior probabilities:

Demand (in 000s)	Probability of Demand
100	0.10
200	0.15
300	0.50
400	0.25
	1.00

The calendars sell for $100 per thousand, and the incremental purchase cost is $70. The incremental cost of selling (commissions) is $5 per thousand.

a. Use the analysis of this chapter to find how many calendars should be ordered.

b. Check this calculation by preparing conditional and expected value tables and computing expected values for each act.

c. How much of an ill-will cost would have to exist to justify an order of 400,000 calendars?

17–7. Demand for a product is approximately normal with mean 40 units and standard deviation 12 units. The product costs $2 per unit and sells for $5. Unsold units have no value.

a. Assuming there is no goodwill loss due to unfilled demand, what is the optimum order size?

b. Suppose that the manager in charge of the product has usually ordered 60 units. She defends the policy on the ground that there is loss of customer goodwill associated with unfilled demand. What is the implied goodwill loss associated with the manager's policy?

17–8. List two inventory situations that you think would be reasonably represented by the model presented in this chapter. For each, describe what factors would be involved in the cost of overage, the cost of underage, and the goodwill loss.

17–9. A camera manufacturer makes most of its sales during the Christmas selling season. For each camera sold, it makes a unit profit of $20; if a camera is unsold after the major selling season, it must be sold at a reduced price, which is $5 less than the variable cost of manufacturing the camera. The manufacturer estimates that demand is normally distributed with a mean of 10,000 units and a standard deviation of 1,000 units.

a. Ignoring ill-will costs of a stockout, what is the optimum order size?

b. What ill-will cost per stockout would justify an order size of 11,500 units?

17–10. The Tail Ski Company sells skis for $50 a pair during the active selling season. Unsold skis at the end of the season can be sold through special outlets for $10 a pair or, alternatively, can be carried in inventory until the next regular selling season, when they could be sold for $15 a pair. Either of these alternatives can absorb large quantities of skis without affecting normal demand.

The manufacturing cost per pair of skis is as follows:

Direct materials	$10
Direct labor	5
Allocated overhead	10
	$25

The company has a 20 percent-per-dollar-per-year charge for holding inventory. Demand during the regular selling season is normal, with a mean of 10,000 and a standard deviation of 2,000 pairs. The company must determine its production prior to the selling season, due to limited production capacity.

What level of production is most desirable?

17–11. The Green Garden Store must order its allotment of spring plants by March 23 (there is no opportunity to reorder later in the season). Due to the impending drought, Green Garden has revised its sales forecast downward and now expects to sell about $100,000 (retail) worth of spring plants; the standard deviation of forecast error for this forecast is 15 percent (i.e., $15,000). Assume forecast errors are normally distributed.

For every $1 of retail sales, the store pays $0.30 for plants that it purchases wholesale. Leftover plants after the selling season cannot be sold; furthermore, Green Garden must pay to have them removed, at a cost of $0.05 per $1 retail sales value. All other costs of operating the store are unaffected by the sales volume that materializes.

In retail dollars' worth, how many dollars' worth of spring plants should the store order?

17–12. The Peninsula Pumpkin Store (PPS) purchases pumpkins for resale prior to Halloween. PPS sells pumpkins for $0.50 per lb., while its wholesale purchase cost is $0.30 per lb. Its suppliers require firm orders by September 1, so PPS must make a commitment before demand is known. As of September 1, PPS forecasts pumpkin demand at 10,000 lbs.; its forecast error is normally distributed with a standard deviation equal to 15 percent of its forecast. Forecasts have been unbiased, however. Leftover pumpkins (after Halloween) can be sold for an average of $0.20 per lb. without limit on volume. Customer orders that cannot be filled are assumed lost.

a. What total amount of pumpkins should PPS order on September 1?

b. Assume that PPS has found a backup supplier who will fill subsequent replenishment orders *immediately,* so that if PPS begins to run out of pumpkins, it can reorder in small quantities as needed from the second supplier. (PPS continues to use the original supplier for its initial order.) The new supplier charges $0.42 per lb. for this expedited service, and guarantees supply.

Now, what is the desired initial purchase order on September 1?

More Challenging Problems

17–13. The ACME Company produces air conditioners. Due to limited production capacity and the desire to maintain steady employment throughout the year, production of particular models must be determined prior to the heavy summer selling season. The junior model costs $60 to produce (incremental cost) and sells for $100, while the super model costs $120 to produce and sells for $210. Any units unsold at the end of the summer must be sold for a sacrifice price of 80 percent of the incremental production cost.

Seasonal demand for the junior model is estimated as normal, with a mean of 10,000 and a standard deviation of 3,000; for the super model, estimated demand is normal with a mean of 6,000 and a standard deviation of 2,000. The company feels that since the two models sell in different price ranges, the demands are independent.

a. Ignoring ill-will costs, compute optimal production sizes for the two models.

b. Suppose that the demands are no longer independent. As an extreme case, suppose that the number of units of the super model sold is precisely 60 percent of the number of units of the junior model sold. Also, suppose the mean sales of the junior model are estimated to be 10,000, with a standard deviation of 3,000 (ignore the other mean and standard deviation). Now, compute the optimal order size. (*Hint:* Given the strict dependence assumed, consider a *composite product* that contains 1 unit of the junior and 0.6 unit of a super.)

17–14. The Cox Photo Company is a mail-order firm specializing in 24-hour service on developing of negatives and making of prints. The general policy is that orders arriving in the morning mail must be finished and in the outgoing mail before the midnight mail pickup. This has usually involved little difficulty. Six full-time technicians work an eight-hour day from 8 A.M. to 5 P.M. and are paid at a rate of $8 per hour (including fringe benefits).

These technicians can process an average of five orders an hour. When on occasion more than about 240 orders arrive on a given day, one or more of the technicians work overtime at a rate of $12 per hour.

Cox Photo has recently bought out a competitor in the same community and plans to consolidate operations. Mr. Cox is undecided, however, on how many technicians to add to the six he now employs. By adding together the past order data of his competitor to his, Mr. Cox has the following frequency data to ponder.

Number of Incoming Orders	Fraction of Days
Under 220	0.03
220–39	0.03
240–59	0.09
260–79	0.16
280–99	0.18
300–19	0.20
320–39	0.15
340–59	0.10
360–79	0.05
380 and above	0.01
	1.00

One of the technicians at Cox Photo was taking a night course in statistics at a local college and tried her hand at analyzing the above data. She told Mr. Cox that the data closely fit a normal distribution, with a mean of 300 and a standard deviation of 40; but she was unable to answer the question of how many to employ.

a. How many technicians should Cox employ? What is the expected cost?

b. What additional factors should be included in making this decision?

17–15. The ABC Office Supply Company maintains a spare parts warehouse in Alaska to support its office equipment mainte-nance needs. Once every six months, a major shipment of replenishment parts is shipped from the contiguous United States to Alaska. Between these planned shipments, emergency air shipments are used as needed to resupply spare parts when inventory falls short of demand.

ABC must determine the optimal inventory level for its spare parts. As an example, part #123456 has exhibited demand over past six-month intervals that is normally distributed with a mean of 100 and a standard deviation of 10. The cost of overage per unit (representing the cost of inventorying the unneeded item for six months) is $5; the incremental production and shipping cost of the item is $40 per unit.

ABC is having difficulty determining its underage cost per unit, for two reasons. First, it prices spare parts at cost and does not take any markup on them. Second, it will always satisfy demand, using the emergency air shipments to resupply if demand exceeds inventory. Emergency air shipments have a cost per unit shipped of $25 above normal shipping costs.

What should the optimal target inventory for this part be?

17–16. You are in charge of the annual banquet for the Football Boosters Club at your college. Although a large attendance is expected, you will not know until the evening of the banquet exactly how many dinners will be served. Your arrangement with the hotel where the banquet is being held provides that one week before the banquet, you must make a commitment for the number of dinners. The price for these dinners will be $7 each. If fewer people show up than the committed number, you are still required to pay for the full number. If more people attend than your committed number, they will be served at a cost of $12 each. For example, if you commit for 200 people and 200 or fewer show up, you still have to pay $1,400. If more than 200 attend, you pay $1,400 plus $12 for each dinner in excess of 200.

Your judgment about the number attending can be described by a normal probability distribution with mean of 400 people and standard deviation of 100.

a. Suppose the cost of the banquet is being borne entirely by the Alumni Association, and your objective is to minimize the cost, given that all who attend will be served. How big a prior commitment for dinners should you make to the hotel?

b. Suppose there is a charge of $10 for every person attending. Your objective is to maximize the profit from the banquet. In this case, how large a prior commitment should you make to the hotel?

17–17. The Dresden Glass Company (DGC) produces high-quality decorative glass sculptures and distributes the products through department and specialty stores catering to the upper-income segment of the market. Virtually all their orders and shipments take place in October, in preparation for the retail Christmas-gift market. All items left unsold at the retailer level in January are returned to DGC for full credit, but the retailer pays the freight cost for the returns.

The economics for item #123C are as follows:

Standard manufacturing cost (per piece):	
Raw materials	$ 5.00
Direct labor	30.00
Variable overhead	5.00
Allocated overhead	15.00
Standard cost	55.00
Wholesale selling price from DGC to retailer	85.00
Retail selling price	170.00
Freight cost for returns from retailer to DGC (5 percent of $85)	4.25

If any retailer stocks out of this item, the unfilled orders are "lost" (as opposed to the customer waiting or buying a different gift item from the retailer). They are willing to ignore ill will but are not willing to ignore forgone profit.

What inventory level should a retailer have for DGC item #123C if mean seasonal demand is estimated at 100 units and the standard deviation is 20 units? (Assume a normally distributed random variable).

17–18. The Wyler Wine Company produces champagne fermented in the bottle. The fermentation process takes one year. The variable cost of initially producing a case of champagne (not including holding cost for the one-year fermentation period) is $10. The net selling price wholesalers pay is $18 per case. Cases unsold after their "target" year (year 1) are carried over into the next year, with no degradation in quality; however, money continues to be tied up in inventory. The company estimates inventory holding costs are 20 percent per dollar per year. Since the grapes ripen only once a year in the company's upstate New York location, they must make a production commitment once a year, for the entire amount of champagne they plan to produce.

Their decision for this year's production (for next year's sales) is approaching. The marketing forecast for next year's sales is 100,000 cases (σ = 8,000); anticipated inventory carryover is 15,000 cases. No ill-will costs are assessed for out-of-stock situations, but profit is forgone in those instances.

How many cases should the company plan to produce?

17–19. The Alpine Valley Ski Area (AVSA) must make a decision at 5 P.M. each afternoon whether to call in crews for snowmaking that evening or not. Snowmaking begins at 11 P.M. and continues until 3 A.M. However, snowmaking requires the temperature to be no higher than 27 degrees

Fahrenheit. If, at 11 P.M., the temperature is above 27 degrees, AVSA must pay its crews but does not make any snow; the cost to pay the crews is $1,000 per night. If AVSA decides at 5 P.M. not to make snow, but the temperature falls below 27 degrees at 11 P.M., AVSA recognizes that it has lost an evening's opportunity to make snow, which has a gross value estimated at $4,000, and a net value (after paying the crews) of $3,000.

AVSA uses the following forecasting rule: Forecasted temperature at 11 P.M. is equal to temperature at 5 P.M. less 10 degrees. A historical comparison of forecasted and actual 11 P.M. temperatures indicates that these forecasts are unbiased and that forecast errors are normally distributed with a standard deviation of 9 degrees.

What cutoff temperature at 5 P.M. should AVSA use in making its decision?

Hint: Find the desired probability (i.e., the optimal target gamble) that the crews will not be called when they would have been able to make snow.

17–20. An airline has found that the number of people not showing up for a flight (no-shows) is normally distributed with a mean of 20 and a standard deviation of 10. The airline estimates the opportunity cost of an empty seat to be $100; the ill-will and penalty costs associated with not being able to board a passenger holding a confirmed reservation are estimated to be $400.

The airline wishes to set a limit on "overbooking" for this flight. There are 150 seats. What should be its upper cutoff on confirmed reservations? Why?

18

Waiting Lines
Queuing Theory

Queues or waiting lines are very common in everyday life. There are few individuals in modern society who have not had to wait in line for a bus, a taxi, a movie ticket, a grocery check-out, a haircut, or registration material at the beginning of the school year. Most of us consider lines an unavoidable part of our civilized life, and we put up with them with more or less good humor. Occasionally, the size of a line we encounter discourages us, we abandon the project, and a sale is lost. This chapter is concerned with the decision-making process of the business firm (or government agency) that has charge of the operation and makes decisions relative to the number and capacity of service facilities that are operating.

Queuing theory or waiting-line theory is primarily concerned with processes characterized by random arrivals (i.e., arrivals at random time intervals); the servicing of the customer is also a random process. If we assume there are costs associated with waiting in line, and if there are costs of adding more channels (i.e., adding more service facilities), we want to minimize the sum of the costs of waiting and the costs of providing service facilities. The computations will lead to such measures as the expected number of people in line, the expected waiting time of the arrivals, and the expected percentage utilization of the service facilities. These measures can then be used in the cost computations to determine the number and capacity of service facilities that are desirable.

Queuing theory may be used to determine the optimum number of:

- Toll booths for a bridge or toll road.
- Doctors available for clinic calls.
- Repair persons servicing machines.
- Landing strips for aircraft.
- Docks for ships.

521

- Paramedic units available for emergency calls.
- Clerks for a spare-parts counter.
- Service windows for a post office.

The above are a few examples of the many different waiting-line situations encountered by managers.

Experience and Queues

Fortunately for the busy manager, reasonable queuing decisions can frequently be based on past experience or on the facts of the current situation. Thus, the management of a grocery chain knows approximately how many check-out counters should be installed in a new store by looking at the experience of comparable stores. At any time of the day, the store manager can tell how many of the installed counters should be open by noting the lengths of the queues and adding personnel from other chores, or sending the present check-out personnel to other tasks. Also, historical records (say of machine downtime) can indicate the amount of time that machines had to queue for repairs rather than relying upon the computations resulting from a mathematical model to determine the amount of downtime.

Although a number of problems encountered by an executive can be reasonably solved by the use of intuition or past experience, there will be many situations that are too complex for our intuition or where we desire a more accurate answer than we can expect to be supplied by intuition. In these situations, the problem can be approached by either simulation or a mathematical model procedure. In this chapter, we shall investigate several mathematical models of waiting-line situations; the next chapter demonstrates how simulation can be used to study more complex waiting-line problems.

Mathematical Models of Queuing

There are five major elements of any queuing situation.

Arrivals Customers come into the system for service. Customers may be people, machines needing repair, telephone calls to be answered, or fire alarms. How these customers arrive in the system is important. They may come singly or in batches; they may come evenly spaced in time or in a random pattern; they may come from an infinite (i.e., a very large) population of possible arrivals (for example, all the people in a city who might use a telephone), or they may come from a finite set (for example, the 10 machines in a shop that might break down and need repair).

Services Each customer must be serviced. This may mean giving the person a haircut, repairing a broken machine, making an airline reservation on the telephone, or dispatching fire trucks to put out a fire. How long it takes to complete a service is the second important element. It may take the same time for each customer, or service times may vary considerably in a random fashion.

Number of Servers There may be only one server or **channel** or many. A customer may be processed by only one server or several in turn. Servers may have different service rates (some machine repair technicians may be faster than others).

Queue Discipline While customers wait for service, they are in a waiting line or queue. There may be only one line or separate lines for each server. There may be a space limit on the waiting line, and customers who arrive when the line is full may turn away (called *balking*). The order in which customers are served is often by **FIFO**, or First In, First Out. But there may be express or priority service for some customers; an example is the express line at many supermarkets for customers with 10 items or less. Service may be in random order.

Measures of Performance There are various ways of judging how well a queuing system is performing. Results may be evaluated over a short period of time once the system opens, or based on the long run or *equilibrium* results. Generally, the time customers spend waiting is important, and we may look at the average waiting time or at a measure such as the percent of customers who have to wait longer than, say, 10 minutes. The average number of customers in line, the utilization rate of equipment, and the cost of operating the system are also measures of interest to managers. The manager would use these measures to determine the optimum number of servers and capacity for the queuing system.

A given queuing system can have any combination of the elements described above. Hence, there are a very large number of possible systems, and no one mathematical model can describe them all. In this chapter, we focus on a few simple models that have wide applicability, and that give us insight into queuing system behavior in general. Most queuing systems behave like the cases examined in this chapter. And the next chapter describes simulation, which can be used to model queuing and other systems in a very general way.

There are two important probability distributions that appear often in queuing models. The **Poisson** distribution assumes a very large (infinite) number of possible arrivals, with each having a small probability of occurrence. Arrivals are independent and the number of arrivals in one period of time does not affect the number in the next. The Poisson distribution is a good approximation for many processes that are considered "random," such as calls arriving at a switchboard, customers at a check-in counter, or fire alarms.

The random variable in the Poisson distribution is the *number of events* (e.g., arrivals) *in a unit of time*. The **exponential** distribution is a complementary distribution to the Poisson that has as the random variable *the time between events*. Both of these distributions are called **Markov** distributions. The details of these distributions are given in Appendix 1 to this chapter.

A Single-Server Queuing Model

For this model, we shall consider the case in which:

1. Arrivals are random, and come from the *Poisson* or *Markov* probability distribution.
2. Each service time is also assumed to be a random variable following the *exponential* or Markov distribution. Service times are assumed to be independent of each other and independent of the arrival process.
3. There is a single server or channel.
4. The queue discipline is FIFO, and there is no limit on the size of the line.
5. The average arrival and service rates do not change over time. The process has been operating long enough to remove effects of the initial conditions.

Notation It has become standard practice to denote queuing models by a shorthand notation as follows:

$$\frac{\text{Arrival time}}{\text{distribution}} \Big/ \frac{\text{Service time}}{\text{distribution}} \Big/ \frac{\text{Number of servers}}{\text{or channels}}$$

where:

M = Markov (or Poisson/exponential) distribution.
D = Deterministic (i.e., constant) times.
G = General distribution with specified standard deviation.

Using this notation, the model we are considering is an $M/M/1$ queuing model. Let:

λ = Average number of customers arriving in one unit of time
μ = Average number of customers the facility is capable of servicing in one unit of time, assuming no shortage of customers
L = Expected number of units being serviced and/or waiting in the system
L_q = Expected number in the queue (the number in the queue does not include the unit being serviced)
p_n = Probability of having n units in the system
W_q = Expected time an arrival must wait in the queue
W = Expected time an arrival spends in the system (both in queue and in service)

There are several relationships of interest:[1]

$$p_0 = 1 - \lambda/\mu \qquad \qquad \textbf{(18-1)}$$

$$p_n = (\lambda/\mu)^n p_0 \qquad \qquad \textbf{(18-2)}$$

$$p_n = (\lambda/\mu)p_{n-1} \qquad \qquad \textbf{(18-3)}$$

---

[1]See Appendix 2 at the end of this chapter for the derivation of Equation 18-2.

Since p_0 is the probability of the system being empty, it is the expected **idle time** of the system. Also, $(1 - p_0) = \lambda/\mu$ is the expected **busy time** of the system, or the expected **utilization** of the system.

The expected number in the waiting line and/or being serviced is:

$$L = \frac{\lambda}{(\mu - \lambda)} \qquad (18\text{--}4)$$

The expected number in the queue is:

$$L_q = \frac{\lambda^2}{\mu(\mu - \lambda)} \qquad (18\text{--}5)$$

The average waiting time (in the queue) of an arrival is:

$$W_q = \frac{L_q}{\lambda} = \frac{L}{\mu} \qquad (18\text{--}6)$$

Also, since the mean service rate is μ, the mean service time is $1/\mu$; hence, the average time an arrival spends in the system (both waiting and in service) is:

$$W = W_q + 1/\mu \qquad (18\text{--}7)$$

The probability that the number in the queue and being serviced is greater than k is:

$$P(n > k) = (\lambda/\mu)^{k+1} \qquad (18\text{--}8)$$

Equations 18–1 to 18–8 apply only if $(\lambda/\mu) < 1$. If the arrival rate, λ, is greater than the service rate, μ, the queue will grow without end unless one of the assumptions is changed.

Example 1 Assume patients for the medical office of a very large plant arrive randomly following a Poisson process. The office can process patients at an average rate of five patients an hour (one at a time); the service process is also Poisson. Patients arrive at an average of four per hour (we shall assume the process is Poisson, though this is not exact, since the population is not infinite, although it is very large.) The plant operates 24 hours a day.

$$\lambda = 4$$
$$\mu = 5$$

Since $(\lambda/\mu) < 1$, we can use the following relationships:

$$p_0 = 1 - \frac{\lambda}{\mu} = 1 - \frac{4}{5} = 0.20$$

On average, the office will be idle 20 percent of the time and busy 80 percent of the time.

$$L = \frac{\lambda}{(\mu - \lambda)} = \frac{4}{(5 - 4)} = 4$$

There will be an average of four persons in line and being serviced.

$$L_q = \frac{\lambda^2}{\mu(\mu - \lambda)} = \frac{4 \cdot 4}{5(5 - 4)} = \frac{16}{5} = 3.2$$

There will be an average of 3.2 persons in line.

$$W_q = \frac{L_q}{\lambda} = \frac{16/5}{4} = \frac{4}{5} = 0.8 \text{ hour}$$

The average waiting time of a patient is 0.8 of an hour.

$$W = W_q + 1/\mu = 0.8 + \frac{1}{5} = 1.0 \text{ hour}$$

The average time spent in the system (both waiting and obtaining service) is one hour.

All of the above measures assume the process has been operating long enough for the probabilities resulting from the physical characteristics of the problem to have made themselves felt; that is, the system is in equilibrium.

We now know:

1. The office will be 20 percent idle and 80 percent busy.
2. The average number of patients in the office is four.
3. The average number of patients waiting is 3.2.
4. A patient will wait for four fifths of an hour, on the average.
5. Total time (waiting and service) will average one hour.

If we assume a 24-hour workday, there will be an average of 96 patients arriving per day, and the expected total lost time of patients waiting will be:

$$T = \lambda \cdot 24 \text{ hours} \cdot W_q$$
$$T = 4 \cdot 24 \cdot 0.8 = 76.8 \text{ hours}$$

There will be a cost associated with these 76.8 hours. Assume the cost to the corporation is $20 for each hour lost by a worker waiting. The average cost per day from waiting is:

$$76.8 \cdot 20 = \$1,536$$

We can also compute the cumulative probability distribution of patients in the office from Equation 18–8. (See Table 18–1.)

It may be that we want to limit the probability of a given occurrence. For example, if we are willing to accept a 0.41 probability that more than three persons will be in the office (i.e., more than two waiting), then the current situation is acceptable.

Suppose that we could in some fashion increase the service rate from five to six per hour and thereby decrease the average time spent in service from 12 minutes to 10 minutes. What would be the effect of this change?

Table 18–1

More Than This Number in Office k	Probability $P(n > k) = \left(\dfrac{\lambda}{\mu}\right)^{k+1} = \left(\dfrac{4}{5}\right)^{k+1}$
0	0.8000
1	0.6400
2	0.5120
3	0.4096
4	0.3277
5	0.2621
6	0.2097

With $\mu = 6$, the expected number in the queue, L_q, is now 1.33 instead of the 3.2 found above. This can be calculated as follows:

$$L_q = \frac{\lambda^2}{\mu(\mu - \lambda)} = \frac{4 \cdot 4}{6(6 - 4)} = \frac{16}{12} = 1.33$$

The average wait for the patient is now:

$$W_q = \frac{L_q}{\lambda} = \frac{1.33}{4} = \frac{1}{3} \text{ hour}$$

Before the change, each patient spent an average of 12 minutes being served and 48 minutes waiting. After the change, each patient will spend an average of 10 minutes being served, and 20 minutes waiting. This can be verified by computing the total time in the system:

$$W = W_q + 1/\mu = \frac{1}{3} + \frac{1}{6} = \frac{1}{2} \text{ hour}$$

Each day there are 96 patients $(4 \cdot 24)$, and each patient will save one-half hour in total. At a cost of $20 per hour, the daily cost savings is:

$$96 \cdot \frac{1}{2} \cdot 20 = \$960$$

It would be worth $960 per day or $350,400 per year to the company to increase the service rate to six patients per hour.

Queuing System Behavior

The formulas presented for the single-channel case enable us to study system behavior as the arrival rate λ approaches the service rate μ. Recalling that (λ/μ) equals system utilization or the percentage of time the server is busy, we

Figure 18–1   Expected Number in System versus Utilization

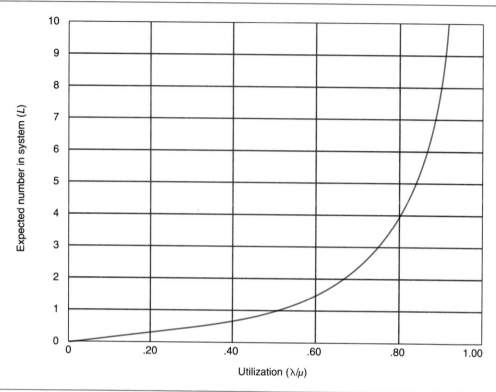

can plot the expected number in the system (L) as a function of utilization as in Figure 18–1.[2]

Reviewing Figure 18–1, it is striking how responsive the number in the system (L) is to the utilization. In a single-server queuing system, as the utilization rises much above 80 percent, the expected number in the system rises *ever more sharply*. The general implication is that if prompt service is desired in a single-channel system, there must be "excess" capacity (much less than 100 percent utilization) in order for one to avoid excessive waiting.

Although Figure 18–1 is directly applicable only under the stated assumptions, it is striking how many business situations behave in a qualitatively similar manner when utilization changes. Even in complex production facilities with many machines and alternative routings for parts, it has often been observed

---

[2]By dividing the numerator and denominator of Equation 18–4 by μ, it is possible to obtain L as a function of utilization, (λ/μ):

$$L = \frac{(\lambda/\mu)}{1 - (\lambda/\mu)}$$

that when increased demand leads to an increase in shop utilization, there is an even greater increase in the time an order spends in the shop (waiting time plus time being processed), fitting the general pattern of Figure 18–1.

There is pressure in most organizations to be efficient and to reduce idle time as much as possible. Managers do not like to see personnel or equipment standing idle. Yet with random arrivals and service times, we see the need to have excess capacity to avoid long lines and long waits for customers. This is a very important insight about queuing systems and one that is not obvious to most people.

General Service Times: The $M/G/1$ Model

Consider a single-server system with Poisson (or Markov) arrivals, and the FIFO queue discipline. But now suppose that the probability distribution of service times is an arbitrary or General distribution, with mean $1/\mu$ and standard deviation σ. In this situation, the following formulas apply:

$$W_q = \frac{\dfrac{\lambda}{\mu^2} + \lambda\sigma^2}{2\left(1 - \dfrac{\lambda}{\mu}\right)} \qquad (18\text{–}9)$$

$$W = W_q + \frac{1}{\mu} \qquad (18\text{–}10)$$

$$L_q = \lambda W_q \qquad (18\text{–}11)$$

$$L = \lambda W \qquad (18\text{–}12)$$

Equation 18–1 also applies here:

$$p_0 = 1 - \lambda/\mu \qquad (18\text{–}1)$$

Note that the variance of service time, σ^2, appears in the numerator of Equation 18–9. This implies that waiting time depends directly on the variability in service time.

Example 2   Consider a one-server situation as in Example 1, with average arrival rate of 4 per hour and an average service rate of 5 per hour. Note that a mean service rate of 5 per hour is equivalent to a mean service time of 12 minutes. Let us now suppose that the service time distribution is not exponential, but rather has the same mean service time of 12 minutes but a standard deviation of service time of 3 minutes. On a per hour basis, the standard deviation $\sigma = \frac{3}{60} = .05$ hours. Substituting into Equation 18–9:

$$W_q = \frac{(4/5^2) + 4(.05)^2}{2(1 - 4/5)} = \frac{.16 + .01}{.40} = 0.425 \text{ hour}$$

Other values of interest are calculated as follows:

$$W = W_q + \frac{1}{\mu} = 0.425 + 20 = 0.625 \text{ hour}$$

$$L_q = \lambda W_q = 4(0.425) = 1.70$$

and:

$$L = \lambda W = 4(0.625) = 2.50$$

Constant Service Times: The $M/D/1$ Model

Constant or Deterministic service times can also be modeled using Equations 18–9 through 18–12 by substituting a value of zero for the standard deviation σ. Then Equation 18–9 becomes:

$$W_q = \frac{\dfrac{\lambda}{\mu^2}}{2\left(1 - \dfrac{\lambda}{\mu}\right)} \tag{18-13}$$

and this equation can be used together with Equations 18–10 through 18–12 to calculate performance measures of interest for the $M/D/1$ model.

Example 3 Consider Examples 1 and 2, but now assume the service time takes exactly 12 minutes ($\mu = 5/\text{hour}, \sigma = 0$). From Equation 18–13:

$$W_q = \frac{4/5^2}{2(1 - 4/5)} = \frac{0.16}{0.40} = 0.40 \text{ hour}$$

And from Equation 18–11:

$$L_q = \lambda W_q = 4(0.40) = 1.6$$

It is of interest to compare the results of Examples 1, 2, and 3. The exponential (or Markov) service distribution[3] has a very high degree of variability and the standard deviation of service time equals the mean service time. That is, $\sigma = 1/\mu = 1/5 = 0.20$.

	Example 1	Example 2	Example 3
Standard deviation of waiting time distribution	$\sigma = 0.20$	$\sigma = 0.05$	$\sigma = 0$
Average waiting time—W_q	1.0	0.425	0.40
Average line length—L_q	3.2	1.7	1.6

---

[3]See Appendix 1 for details. Note that by inserting the variance of the Markov distribution in Equation 18–9, Equation 18–6 can be obtained.

Thus, we see that a reduction in the variability of service time from the exponential case produces significant improvement in system performance.

Role of Variability

The examples illustrate what we know from experience—unpredictability or variability is a major source of congestion in queuing systems. With variability, sometimes several arrivals occur faster than they can be served and the line grows. At other times, there are no arrivals and the system is idle. Similarly, recall how the line grows behind a customer who takes a long time to complete service in a supermarket or bank. Thus, variation in arrivals and service times is a key source of congestion in queuing systems, and the greater the variation, the more the congestion.

Figure 18–2 illustrates this by comparing the $M/M/1$ model with exponential service times with the $M/D/1$ model with constant service times. Note that at any given level of capacity utilization, exponential service times create an expected number in the system (L) that is exactly twice that obtained from constant service times. Hence, not only is it necessary to plan for less than 100 percent capacity utilization when either arrivals or service times are random, it is also very useful to reduce variability in service times.

Figure 18–2   **Effect of Variability on Number in System ($M/M/1$ versus $M/D/1$ queues)**

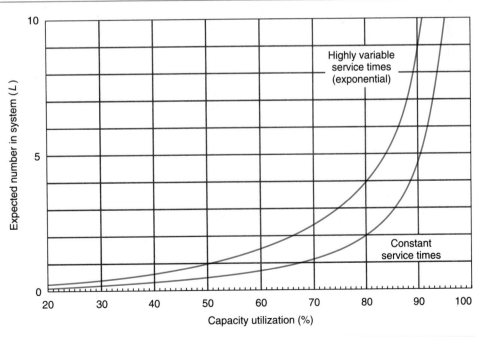

Multiple Servers: The $M/M/c$ Model

We shall now assume there are c channels and there is one waiting line if all the service facilities are busy. Each channel has the same service rate, μ. We shall again use n to represent the sum of the customers being served and in the waiting line.

The formulas below show the probability of zero customers in the system (p_0) and the probability of n customers in the system (p_n). These formulas are more complex than those for only one channel.

$$p_0 = \left[\frac{(\lambda/\mu)^c}{c!\left(1 - \dfrac{\lambda/\mu}{c}\right)} + 1 + \frac{(\lambda/\mu)^1}{1!} + \frac{(\lambda/\mu)^2}{2!} + \ldots + \frac{(\lambda/\mu)^{c-1}}{(c-1)!} \right]^{-1} \quad \textbf{(18–14)}$$

$$p_n = p_0 \frac{(\lambda/\mu)^n}{n!} \quad \text{if } n \le c \quad \textbf{(18–15)}$$

$$p_n = p_0 \frac{(\lambda/\mu)^n}{c!c^{n-c}} \quad \text{if } n > c \quad \textbf{(18–16)}$$

The capacity utilization in this system is $\dfrac{\lambda}{c\mu}$.

We can use the above equations if:

$$\frac{\lambda}{c\mu} < 1$$

If:

$$\frac{\lambda}{c\mu} > 1$$

then the waiting line grows larger and larger; that is, n becomes infinite if the process runs long enough.

When $c = 1$ (there is one service facility), Equations 18–15 and 18–16 reduce to Equation 18–2. From Equation 18–15, we have:

$$p_n = p_0 \frac{(\lambda/\mu)^n}{n!} \quad \text{if } n \le c$$

But n can only take on values of 0 or 1 if $n \le c = 1$. Thus:

$$p_n = p_0(\lambda/\mu)^n$$

If $c = 1$, Equation 18–16 also reduces to Equation 18–2.

With c service facilities, the average number of customers in the queue is:

$$L_q = \frac{(\lambda/\mu)^{c+1}}{c \cdot c!\left(1 - \dfrac{\lambda/\mu}{c}\right)^2} p_0 \quad \textbf{(18–17)}$$

The average number in the system (waiting plus in service) is:

$$L = L_q + \lambda/\mu \qquad (18\text{-}18)$$

The expected waiting time in the queue for an arrival is:

$$W_q = \frac{L_q}{\lambda} \qquad (18\text{-}19)$$

Similarly, the expected total time spent in the system (waiting plus service) is:

$$W = \frac{L}{\lambda} \qquad (18\text{-}20)$$

Example 4   Refer to the example of a medical office, Example 1, and consider the characteristics of the process if a second office is added. Each office can process five patients per hour, on average, and assume that the service times are exponential. Also, assume that there is a single common waiting line for both offices, served on a FIFO basis. Then this is an $M/M/c$ system with parameters:

$$\lambda = 4$$
$$\mu = 5$$
$$c = 2$$
$$\lambda/\mu = 0.8$$

We first calculate p_0, the expected idle time of the system, from Equation 18–14:

$$p_0 = \cfrac{1}{\cfrac{(\lambda/\mu)^c}{c!\left(1 - \cfrac{\lambda/\mu}{c}\right)} + 1 + \cfrac{(\lambda/\mu)^1}{1!} + \cdots + \cfrac{(\lambda/\mu)^{c-1}}{(c-1)!}}$$

$$p_0 = \cfrac{1}{\cfrac{(0.8)^2}{2(1 - 0.8/2)} + 1 + \cfrac{0.8}{1}} = \cfrac{1}{\cfrac{0.64}{1.2} + 1.8}$$

$$= \frac{1}{2.3} = 0.43$$

The expected number in the waiting line, from Equation 18–17, is:

$$L_q = \frac{(0.8)^3}{2 \cdot 2(1 - 0.8/2)^2} \cdot 0.43 = \frac{0.512 \cdot 0.43}{4 \cdot 0.36} = 0.153$$

The expected number in the system (waiting plus in service) is, by Equation 18–18:

$$L = L_q + \lambda/\mu = 0.153 + 0.8 = 0.953$$

The expected waiting time in the queue is:

$$W_q = \frac{L_q}{\lambda} = \frac{0.153}{4} = 0.038 \text{ hours}$$

We previously computed the expected time lost waiting in one day with one office to be 76.8 hours. The expected total time lost waiting is now:

$$T = \lambda \cdot 24 \text{ hours} \cdot W_q$$
$$= 4 \cdot 24 \cdot 0.038 = 3.65 \text{ hours}$$

Again assuming a cost of $20 for each hour, the average cost of waiting per day is:

$$3.65 \cdot \$20 = \$73$$

There has been a saving in expected cost of $1,463 (i.e., $1,536 − $73). If the cost of adding the second office is less than $1,463 per day, then the decision should be to go from one to two offices. We could also consider adding a third office; but since the expected cost of waiting is now only $73 per day, the adding of a third office is not likely to be worthwhile from an economic standpoint.

The calculations involved in Equations 18–14 through 18–20 can be tedious for more than two service channels. Table 18–2 can be used to calculate the expected waiting time, W_q, which is generally the most useful performance measure. The body of the table contains the value of the waiting time multiple (WTM)—the expected waiting time times the service rate.[4] Given values for λ, μ, and c, the value of W_q can be easily determined. In the example above, $\lambda = 4$, $\mu = 5$, and $c = 2$. The capacity utilization ratio is:

$$\lambda/(c\mu) = 4/(5 \cdot 2) = 0.40$$

Table 18–2   **Waiting Time Multiple (WTM) for M/M/C Queues**

Capacity Utilization $\dfrac{\lambda}{c\mu}$	Number of Service Channels					
	$c = 1$	$c = 2$	$c = 3$	$c = 4$	$c = 5$	$c = 10$
0.10	0.1111	0.0101	0.0014	0.0002	0.0000*	0.0000*
0.20	0.2500	0.0417	0.0103	0.0030	0.0010	0.0000*
0.30	0.4286	0.0989	0.0333	0.0132	0.0058	0.0002
0.40	0.6667	0.1905	0.0784	0.0378	0.0199	0.0015
0.50	1.0000	0.3333	0.1579	0.0870	0.0521	0.0072
0.60	1.5000	0.5625	0.2956	0.1794	0.1181	0.0253
0.70	2.3333	0.9608	0.5470	0.3572	0.2519	0.0739
0.80	4.0000	1.7778	1.0787	0.7455	0.5541	0.2046
0.90	9.0000	4.2632	2.7235	1.9694	1.5250	0.6687
0.95	19.0000	9.2564	6.0467	4.4571	3.5112	1.6512

*Less than 0.00005

---

[4]The waiting time multiple is the expected waiting time measured in units of expected service time:

$$\text{WTM} = W_q \cdot \mu$$

The corresponding WTM in Table 18–2 in the $c = 2$ column is 0.1905. Then:

$$W_q \mu = W_q(5) = 0.1905$$

and:

$$W_q = \text{WTM}/\mu = 0.1905/5 = 0.038$$

which agrees with the result calculated previously.

Example 5   Customers randomly arrive at an airport security station at an average rate of nine per minute ($\lambda = 9$). The station has four servers (i.e., four sets of X-ray and metal-detector units), and each server can process 2.5 persons per minute on average ($\mu = 2.5$). Assuming that arrivals and services are Poisson, what is the average line length and average waiting time?

We first calculate the capacity utilization as $\lambda/(c\mu) = 9/(4 \cdot 2.5) = 0.90$. From Table 18–2, the corresponding waiting time multiple in the $c = 4$ column is WTM = 1.9694.

$$\text{WTM} = 1.9694 = W_q \mu$$
$$W_q = 1.9694/\mu = 1.9694/2.5 = 0.78 \text{ minutes}$$

Thus, the average wait in line is 0.78 minutes, or 47 seconds. From Equation 18–19:

$$W_q = \frac{L_q}{\lambda}$$

or:

$$L_q = \lambda W_q = (9)(0.78) = 7.1 \text{ persons}$$

Thus, the average line length is 7.1 persons.

Pooled Facilities

Pooling refers to combining separate systems into a common pool or group. Suppose we have two separate queuing systems, each with one server (i.e., two $M/M/1$ systems), and separate waiting lines. What happens if we merge the two arrival streams into one and treat the system as an $M/M/2$ system?

Figure 18–3 illustrates how the waiting time multiple (WTM) is affected by pooling two independent units into a single "pooled" two-station server. At any given capacity utilization level, the WTM is much smaller under pooling. Intuitively, when systems are pooled, one avoids the situation where system A has a waiting line but system B is empty.

More extensive pooling provides even greater performance improvement. Figure 18–4 illustrates the effect of pooling five separate systems into one pooled system; note the very drastic reduction in WTM, particularly for higher capacity utilization levels.

Figure 18–3 **Effects of Pooling—$M/M/c$ Queues**
(two independent units versus one pooled unit)

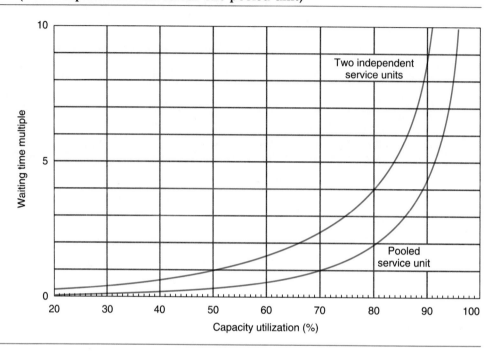

Example 6 Refer to the medical office example discussed in Examples 1 and 4. Suppose a second office is to be added but at a different location than the first, so that each will have its own waiting line. Suppose that roughly half the customers will be served by each office and arrive randomly as before. Now there are two independent $M/M/1$ queuing systems, each with:

$$\lambda = 2.0$$
$$\mu = 5.0$$

From Table 18–2, we can see that, for $c = 1$ and $\lambda/\mu = .40$, the WTM $= .6667$. Hence:

$$W_q = \text{WTM}/\mu = .1333 \text{ hour}$$

Compare this to the waiting time for the pooled facility in Example 4 in which the waiting time was .038 hour. Pooling, in this case, reduces the waiting time by about two-thirds.

Before we decide that pooling is always a virtue, one must bear in mind some of the costs of pooled systems. There may be administrative burdens, increased travel time by customers, and loss of organizational control. In our example, for instance, if the plant was spread over several buildings and the two separate

Figure 18–4   **Effects of Pooling—$M/M/c$ Queues**
(five independent units versus one pooled unit)

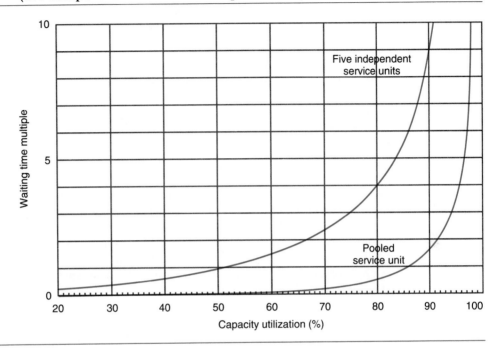

offices were located conveniently, the additional waiting time may be more than compensated for by savings in time taken by workers to get to the offices. Also note that most executives prefer to have their own secretary, rather than rely on a secretarial pool.

Conclusion

A number of more complex queuing models exist for queuing situations that do not fit the assumptions made above. However, not all assumptions can be analytically manipulated and solved for the information of interest. For the average situation, we may find it easier to use the technique of simulation (described in the next chapter) even when a theoretical model exists, since a simulation may easily be modified to include any specific characteristic of the problem setting (e.g., there may be space for only three trucks to wait at an unloading dock). Easy-to-use computer simulation languages and computer systems combine to make computer simulation more accessible at lower cost, so that simulation is being used to a greater degree to study specific queuing situations.

SUMMARY

For a single-channel facility, formulas are available for such important performance measures as mean wait time, mean number in the queue, and system utilization. For the multiple-channel case, tables are provided. Simulation should be considered as an alternative if the queuing assumptions are not appropriate.

There are three important managerial insights for queuing systems:

1. Plan for idle capacity—high capacity utilization implies long waits.
2. Variability is a culprit—lower variability (of arrivals or service times) is desirable.
3. Pooling reduces waiting time—other things being equal (but don't ignore administrative difficulties of pooling).

APPENDIX 1

The Poisson Process and Distribution

In a Poisson process, the probability of occurrence of an event is constant, and the occurrence of an event is independent of what has happened immediately preceding the present observation. We may be interested in what happens over a continuous interval. This interval may be a measure of distance—for example, a yard—or a unit of time such as a day. Printing errors per page of a book is an example of a process that may be Poisson; other examples are the manufacturing of textiles, rolled steel, pipe, wire, and so on, where there are X defects per unit measure of product.

The sales for a product may behave like a Poisson process. Suppose we have had 80 individual sales of one unit of product per person during the past 50 weeks, or an average sale of 1.6 units per week. We may wish to know the probability of different weekly sales in the next five weeks.

The Poisson probability distribution applied to a Poisson process gives the probability of a number of events in a measure of distance or time, given that we know (1) the expected number of events *per unit* of distance or time and (2) the length of distance or time. Suppose we use the symbol λ to be the expected number of events per unit measure; that is, the *rate* or *intensity* of the process. Examples of λ are 1.6 units of sales per week, 25 telephone calls per hour, 3 defects per 100 feet of pipe, and so forth. We shall let T be the unit of time or space during which events are to be counted. Then the Poisson probability of exactly r events occurring during time T, given the average number of events per unit of time is λ, is given as:[5]

$$P(R = r|\lambda,T) = \frac{e^{-\lambda T}(\lambda T)^r}{r!} \qquad (18\text{--}21)$$

In using the Poisson probability distribution, we may combine λ and T by multiplication to obtain m; that is, $m = \lambda T$, where m is the expected number of events in the specified time period. We *expect* m events in a specified time, T. For example, if $\lambda = 2$ (the average number of events per week) and $T = 5$ (the

[5]$e = 2.718 \ldots$, the base for natural logarithms.

time period is five weeks), the average number of events per five-week period is $2 \cdot 5 = 10$. A Poisson distribution has the special property that its variance is always equal to its mean, m, so the standard deviation is $\sqrt{m}$.

The Exponential Distribution

In connection with the Poisson process, we have discussed the Poisson probability distribution, which gives the probability of the number of occurrences of an event, given an intensity λ and a certain time period T. *For the same Poisson process,* we could ask about the waiting time between successive events (that is, the "interarrival time"). In other words, what is the probability distribution of time, t, *between* events? This probability distribution is called the **exponential distribution** (see Figure 18–5). The exponential probability density function is:

$$f(t) = \lambda e^{-\lambda t}, \qquad 0 \le t < \infty \qquad \textbf{(18–22)}$$

The mean of the exponential distribution is $E(t) = (1/\lambda)$ and the variance is $(1/\lambda)^2$.

The right-hand tail of the exponential distribution is:[6]

$$p(t > T) = e^{-m} \qquad \text{where } m = \lambda T$$

Figure 18–5   **Exponential Probability Density Function**

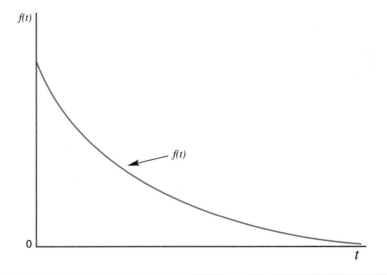

$$^6\int_{T}^{\infty} \lambda e^{-\lambda x} dx = -e^{-\lambda x}\Big|_{T}^{\infty} = 0 + e^{-\lambda T} = e^{-\lambda T} = e^{-m}$$

That is, the probability that the time between events (arrivals) is greater than T is e^{-m}. Note that this is also the value of a Poisson mass function for zero occurrences (arrivals) in a time period T.[7]

Thus, the Poisson distribution for arrivals per unit of time and the exponential distribution for interarrival times provide two alternative ways of describing the same thing. We can say that the number of arrivals per unit time is Poisson with mean rate $\lambda = 5$ per hour, for example, or alternatively, say that the interarrival times are exponentially distributed with mean interarrival time $(1/\lambda) = \frac{1}{5}$ hour; each statement implies the other.

APPENDIX 2

Derivation of Basic Queuing Formula

We want to derive the relationship:

$$p_n = (\lambda/\mu)^n p_0$$

Assume arrivals and services occur in accordance with a Poisson process. There is one service facility with a single "first come, first served" queue. Let:

λ = Average number arriving in one unit of time
μ = Average number the station can service in one unit of time
n = Number of units in the system either being serviced or waiting
$P_n(t)$ = Probability of having n units in the system at time t
p_n = Probability of having n units in the system, assuming equilibrium
λh = Probability of an arrival during time period h, when h is very small
μh = Probability of a service completion during time period h

We can reasonably assume that the probability of more than one change during time period h is very close to zero; to simplify the development, we shall assume it actually to be zero (i.e., the probability of two or more services or arrivals or a service and arrival is zero in a very small time interval). Thus:

$$1 - \lambda h - \mu h = \text{Probability of no changes}$$

We can reach state n (i.e., n units in the system) by one of four events, occurring as follows:

■ Event a: Be at n, and no change occurs.
■ Event b: Be at $n - 1$, and have an arrival take place.

---

[7]The Poisson mass function is:

$$P(R = r|\lambda,T) = e^{-m}\frac{m^r}{r!}$$

where $m = \lambda T$. If $r = 0$, then:

$$P(R = 0 \mid \lambda, T) = e^{-m}$$

That is, the probability of no arrivals in time T is e^{-m}.

- Event c: Be at $n + 1$, and have a service completion.
- Event d: Be at $n - y$ or $n + y$, and have y changes take place when $y > 1$ (we have assumed the probability of this event to be zero).

Since the events a, b, and c are mutually exclusive, we may add their probabilities:

$$P_n(t + h) = P(a) + P(b) + P(c), \qquad 1 \le n < \infty$$

$$P_n(t + h) = P_n(t)(1 - \lambda h - \mu h) + P_{n-1}(t)(\lambda h) + P_{n+1}(t)(\mu h) \qquad \textbf{(18-23)}$$

$$\frac{P_n(t + h) - P_n(t)}{h} = -(\lambda + \mu)P_n(t) + \lambda P_{n-1}(t) + \mu P_{n+1}(t) \qquad \textbf{(18-24)}$$

Rearranging terms and letting h approach zero:

$$\frac{dP_n(t)}{dt} = \lambda P_{n-1}(t) - (\lambda + \mu)P_n(t) + \mu P_{n+1}(t) \qquad \textbf{(18-25)}$$

In equilibrium:

$$\frac{dP_n(t)}{dt} = 0$$

and we obtain:

$$P_{n+1} = -\frac{\lambda}{\mu} P_{n-1} + \frac{\lambda + \mu}{\mu} p_n \qquad \textbf{(18-26)}$$

Returning to Equation 18-23:

$$P_n(t + h) = P_n(t)(1 - \lambda h - \mu h) + P_{n-1}(t)(\lambda h) + P_{n+1}(t)(\mu h) \qquad \textbf{(18-27)}$$

If we consider $P_0(t + h)$, then $n = 0$, $P_{n-1}(t) = 0$, and the term $-\mu h$ drops out because with zero customers, a service completion is impossible. We obtain:

$$P_0(t + h) = P_0(t)(1 - \lambda h) + P_1(t)(\mu h) \qquad \textbf{(18-28)}$$

Subtract $P_0(t)$ from both sides and divide by h:

$$\frac{P_0(t + h) - P_0(t)}{h} = -\lambda P_0(t) + \mu P_1(t) \qquad \textbf{(18-29)}$$

In equilibrium, this last equation is equal to zero as h goes to zero:

$$-\lambda p_0 + \mu p_1 = 0$$

$$p_1 = \frac{\lambda}{\mu} p_0 \qquad \textbf{(18-30)}$$

Using Equation 18-26, we obtain:

$$p_2 = -\frac{\lambda}{\mu} p_0 + \frac{\lambda + \mu}{\mu} p_1 \qquad \textbf{(18-31)}$$

Substituting $\frac{\lambda}{\mu}p_0$ for p_1:

$$p_2 = -\frac{\lambda}{\mu}p_0 + \frac{\lambda+\mu}{\mu}\left(\frac{\lambda}{\mu}p_0\right)$$

$$p_2 = \left(-\frac{\lambda\mu}{\mu^2} + \frac{\lambda^2+\lambda\mu}{\mu^2}\right)p_0 = \frac{\lambda^2}{\mu^2}p_0 = \left(\frac{\lambda}{\mu}\right)^2 p_0$$

Continuing this procedure, we find:

$$p_n = (\lambda/\mu)^n p_0 \qquad\qquad (18\text{--}32)$$

Bibliography

Feller, W. *An Introduction to Probability Theory and Its Applications*. Vol. I. 3rd ed. New York: John Wiley & Sons, 1968.

————. *An Introduction to Probability Theory and Its Applications*. Vol. 2. New York: John Wiley & Sons, 1966.

Gross, D., and C. M. Harris. *Fundamentals of Queueing Theory*. 2nd ed. New York: John Wiley & Sons, 1985.

Hillier, F., and G. J. Lieberman. *Introduction to Operations Research*. 5th ed. New York: McGraw-Hill, 1990.

Lee, A. M. *Applied Queueing Theory*. New York: Macmillan, 1966.

Newell, G. F. *Applications of Queueing Theory*. 2nd ed. London: Chapman & Hall, 1982.

Prabhu, N. U. *Queues and Inventories*. New York: John Wiley & Sons, 1965.

Wagner, H. M. *Principles of Operations Research*. 2nd ed. Englewood Cliffs, N.J.: Prentice Hall, 1975.

Wolff, R. W. *Stochastic Modeling and the Theory of Queues*. Englewood Cliffs, N.J.: Prentice Hall, 1989.

Problems with Answers

18–1. Ace Airline has one reservations clerk on duty at a time. He handles information about flight schedules and makes reservations. All calls to Ace Airline are answered by an operator. If a caller requests information or reservations, the operator transfers the call to the reservations clerk. If the clerk is busy, the operator asks the caller to wait. When the clerk becomes free, the operator transfers to him the call of the person who has been waiting the longest.

Assume that arrivals and services follow a Poisson process. Calls arrive at a rate of 10 per hour, and the reservations clerk can service a call in four minutes, on the average (i.e., $\mu = 15$ per hour).

a. What is the average number of calls waiting to be connected to the reservations clerk?

b. What is the average time a caller must wait before reaching the reservations clerk?

c. What is the average time for a caller to complete a call (i.e., waiting time plus service time)?

18–2. Refer to Problem 18–1. Suppose that the manager of Ace Airline is considering installing some visual display equipment and a new reservations system. One of the benefits of this system is that it will reduce the average time required to service a call from four to three minutes.

a. What would be the average number of calls waiting to be connected to the reservations clerk if this new system were installed?

b. What would be the expected waiting time before a caller was connected to the reservations clerk with the new system?

18–3. Refer to Problems 18–1 and 18–2. Suppose that instead of reducing the average time required to service a call, the new system will reduce the variability of service time. The service time distribution will have a mean of 4 minutes (as before), but a standard deviation of 2 minutes.

a. What is the average number of calls waiting to be connected to the reservations clerk?

b. What is the average time a caller must wait before reaching the reservations clerk?

c. Suppose the new system could reduce the variability in service times entirely, so that all calls could be serviced in exactly 4 minutes. Answer (a) and (b) for this case.

18–4. Refer to Problems 18–1 and 18–2. Suppose that instead of installing a new reservations system, Ace Airline was considering adding a second reservations clerk. The telephone operator could then refer calls to whichever clerk was free.

a. What would then be the average number of calls waiting to be connected to a reservations clerk?

b. What would then be the expected waiting time before a caller was connected to a reservations clerk?

18–5. Refer to Problem 18–4. Suppose that the cost of manning an additional station would be $50 per day. Ace Airline is undecided about incurring this additional cost.

a. If the goodwill cost of having a customer wait is 10 cents per minute spent waiting (before being connected to a clerk), should Ace Airline add the second clerk?

b. At what goodwill cost would Ace Airline be indifferent as to whether or not to add the second clerk?

c. What assumption is made about the expected number of calls for each hour of the day?

Problems

18–6. Two typists have identical jobs. Each types letters dictated by a manager. Suppose that letters to be typed arrive at random (following a Poisson process) at a rate of three per hour for each typist. Suppose that each typist can type four letters per hour, on the average (also a Poisson process).

a. Assuming that each typist does his or her own work, what is the expected waiting time for a letter (time before work is started on a letter)?

b. Suppose that the two typists are "pooled." That is, letters are sent to the two together and are done by whoever is free, in the order of arrival. What is the expected waiting time for a letter under this arrangement?

c. Comment on this example.

18–7. An integrated petroleum company is considering expansion of its one unloading facility at its Australian refinery. Due to random variations in weather, loading delays, and other factors, ships arriving at the refinery to unload crude oil arrive according to the Poisson distribution with average rate $\lambda = 5$ ships per week. Service time is also Poisson, with average service rate $\mu = 10$ ships per week.

a. What is the average number of ships waiting to deliver crude oil?

b. What is the average time a ship must wait before beginning to deliver its cargo to the refinery?

c. What is the average total time (waiting plus actual delivery) that a ship spends at the refinery?

18–8. Refer to Problem 18–7. The company has

under consideration a second unloading berth, which could be rented for $5,000 per week. The service time for this berth would also be Poisson, with the same rate $\mu = 10$ as the company's own berth. For each week of a ship spent idle waiting in line, the company loses $20,000.

a. If the second berth is rented, what will be the average number of ships waiting?

b. What would be the average time a ship would wait?

c. Is the benefit of reduced waiting time (in dollars) worth the rental cost for the second berth?

18–9. Refer to Problem 18–7. An alternative way to improve unloading facilities is for the company to rent a high-speed unloading device. With the new device, the service rate would be Poisson, with mean rate $\mu' = 15$ ships per week. The weekly rental cost of the new device is $5,000.

a. Compute the (new) average number of ships waiting if the device is installed.

b. Compute the (new) expected waiting time for ships.

c. Is the benefit of reduced waiting time (in dollars) worth the rental cost for the new device?

18–10. Refer to Problems 18–8 and 18–9. An analyst for the company, after studying the costs and benefits of the two suggested modifications, suggests, "In each case, the benefit exceeds the cost, so let's install *both* the high-speed unloading device on our own berth *and* rent the second berth." Unfortunately, there are no formulas in the chapter that are appropriate for a two-channel queue with differing service rates ($\mu_1 = 15$, $\mu_2 = 10$). Find a way to calculate an upper limit on the potential saving from avoidance of waiting delays, and use this limit to comment on the analyst's suggestion.

More Challenging Problems

18–11. Consider a single-channel queue with Poisson arrivals ($\lambda = 4$) and service ($\mu = 5$). Table 18–1 in the chapter presents probabilities that the number in the system exceeds k, for various values of k.

Now suppose we are dealing with a system in which there are trucks arriving at a loading dock, with space limited to one truck in service and, at most, two trucks waiting. If another truck arrives, the driver must double-park in the street, where an eager patrol officer will ticket the driver (no matter how short the stay). Can you use the data of Table 18–1 to estimate the average number of tickets written per hour? (*Hint:* Consider random arrivals to the system when it is in the steady state.)

18–12. The public works director for the city is examining a request for a new appointment as building inspector. The request

indicates that building inspections are expected to increase from 118 to 154 per month, a 30 percent increase. (Assume 22 working days in a month.) The department currently has four inspectors, and the proposal requests one additional, "only a 25 percent increase that will enable the department to maintain its policy of an average wait of less than one day for those requesting an inspector's services." The director knows that it takes about half a day, on the average, for an inspector to complete an inspection and file a report.

Assuming that requests for inspections and services (completions of inspections) are Poisson distributed, is the additional person necessary to meet the department policy?

18–13. Many banks and post offices have switched, in the last few years, from a system having a line at each teller or clerk to a single waiting line cordoned off by a set of ropes or chains. Examine this change by considering the following two cases:

a. *Case 1.* Customers arrive at a bank at an average rate of 80 per hour and form in a single line. There are five tellers, and the average service rate is 20 per hour for each teller. Assuming Poisson arrivals and services, how long is the average wait in line?

b. *Case 2.* Customers arrive at a teller's window at a rate of 16 per hour (with five tellers; this makes 80 arrivals per hour). There is a separate line at each window (with no switching between lines). As in Case 1, the average service rate for each teller is 20 per hour. How long is the average wait in line?

c. Comment on the results of Cases 1 and 2. What additional factors might affect waiting times in a real banking situation?

18–14. A tool crib in a factory is a room where special tools, jigs, and other equipment are stored for general use by mechanics. An attendant signs the equipment in and out as the mechanics request it or return it.

Assume that mechanics arrive at the crib at a rate of 60 per hour. It takes an attendant an average of 2.5 minutes to locate and sign out the equipment (or to check it in). Mechanics are paid at a rate of $16 per hour and attendants at a rate of $10 per hour (including fringe benefits). How many attendants should be hired to service the tool crib? (Assume arrivals and services are Poisson.)

18–15. For a single-server queuing system, suppose we redefine the time unit so that one unit of time equals the mean service time $(1/\mu)$. Under this definition of time, plot a graph of expected waiting time in the queue (W_q) versus utilization (λ/μ). Compare your figure to Figure 18–1. Why should they be similar?

18–16. Chicago's O'Hare International Airport uses two runways when demand is heavy. Assume that one runway is dedicated to takeoffs only, and the other is dedicated to landings only. Under this method of operation, the "service times" are exponentially distributed with a mean of two minutes per request on each of the runways. Assume no interference from one runway to the next, so that they can operate independently of one another. Assume requests for takeoff are Poisson, with a rate of 25 per hour, and requests for landings are also Poisson, with a rate of 25 per hour.

a. Calculate the average number of minutes spent waiting prior to service for takeoffs and for landings.

b. Suppose now that the O'Hare controllers can use both runways for takeoff and landings, interspersed; however, safety requirements under this mode of operation lengthen the average service time for both takeoffs and landings from 2 minutes to 2.16 minutes per request. (Actual service times are exponentially distributed, with mean = 2.16 minutes.) Pooling the two request arrival streams (takeoff requests and landing requests) results in Poisson arrivals with a rate of 50 per hour.

Now calculate average waiting time per request. Which arrangement is better—two separate systems or one pooled system?

18–17. The Santa Clon Transit System (SCTS) has 380 buses. On average, each bus requires maintenance (scheduled and unscheduled) once a month. Average maintenance time is two hours. SCTS has five skilled mechanics on duty to perform maintenance; they each work 160 hours per month. Assume arrivals (i.e., need for maintenance) and service times are Poisson processes.

a. What is the average time a bus spends waiting for maintenance to begin?

b. What is the average number of buses that are inoperable at any time (i.e., either waiting for service or in service)?

c. Suppose an analyst randomly observes the number of inoperable buses; the average number observed was 95. What might account for the discrepancy between this observation and your answer to (*b*)?

18–18. Consider the *M/G/*1 queue.

a. When services are Poisson, the standard deviation of the distribution of services times is $(1/\mu)$. Use this to show that Equation 18–9 is equivalent to Equation 18–6 for the case of Poisson services.

b. Refer to Problem 18–7. Assume that the average service rate is still 10 per week, but that there is no variation in service time. That is, it takes exactly .10 week to unload each ship. Determine the average wait for a ship, and the average number of ships waiting.

c. Again refer to Problem 18–7. Now assume that service time for unloading a ship is normally distributed, with mean service time of .10 week and a standard deviation of .05 week. Calculate the average waiting time and average line length in this case.

d. Compare the results of (*b*) and (*c*) with that obtained in Problem 18–7.

CHAPTER 19

Simulation

In recent years, techniques for testing the results of some business decisions before they are actually executed have been developed. The anticipated actual business processes are simulated on a computer. Computers have the advantage of being able to handle large amounts of data rapidly. However, the basic simulation procedure is independent of how the computations are made.

In a general way, any model of a business decision problem could be called a simulation model, since it represents or simulates some aspects of the real problem. For example, a linear programming model may be designed to represent a product-mix problem or a transportation-planning problem. We will refer to the models of Chapter 2 and those in this chapter as *simulation models*. These models differ from those considered elsewhere in two respects:

1. Simulation models are typically not designed to find optimal or best solutions, as in linear programming or decision analysis. Instead, several proposed alternatives are evaluated and a decision is made on the basis of a comparison of the results. In other words, they evaluate performance of a given prespecified system.
2. Simulation models generally focus on the detailed operations, either physical or financial, of the system. The system is studied as it operates over time, and the effects of one time period's results on the next are included.

To illustrate these differences, consider building a model of a factory that produces a series of products. A linear programming model might develop the optimal product mix. A more detailed simulation model might be concerned with the specifics of how the factory is scheduled to achieve the desired product mix, taking into account machine setup times, waiting time before processing, and other details that cannot be included in the linear programming formulation.

The case models of Chapter 2 are examples of *deterministic* simulations. Since they were treated extensively in that chapter, they will not be considered further. Rather, examples of simulations of queuing systems, of inventory models, and of risk analysis models are used to illustrate the *probabilistic* case, often called Monte Carlo simulation.

Probabilistic Simulation

In many situations, uncertainty plays a key part in the operations of the system, and it is important to take this randomness into account in the model. Waiting-line problems of the type discussed in the previous chapter can be analyzed by building such a simulation model. Where we can adequately solve the problem by mathematical methods, it is generally preferable to do so. However, there are many queuing (and other) situations that cannot be solved easily by mathematics, and hence, we resort to simulation.

Example 1   Consider a warehouse that has one dock used to unload railroad freight cars. Incoming freight cars are delivered to the warehouse during the night. It takes exactly half a day to unload a car. If more than two cars are waiting to be unloaded on a given day, the unloading of some of the cars is postponed until the following day.

Past experience has indicated that the numbers of cars arriving during the night have the frequencies shown in Table 19–1. Furthermore, there is no apparent pattern, so that the number arriving on any night is independent of the number arriving on any other night.

This is a one-channel queuing problem with an average service rate of two per day and an average arrival rate of 1.5 per day. However, it can be shown that the arrivals are not Poisson; hence, none of the queuing models presented in the previous chapter apply.

The first step in simulating this queuing process is to generate a history or time series of arrivals for a number of nights. This is done using a randomized

Table 19–1

Number of Cars Arriving	Relative Frequency
0	0.23
1	0.30
2	0.30
3	0.10
4	0.05
5	0.02
6 or more	0.00
	1.00

Average = 1.5 cars per night

or **Monte Carlo** process. One way to do this would be to take 100 chips and write the number 0 on 23 of them; the number 1 on 30 of them; the number 2 on 30 of them; and so on, corresponding to the frequencies in Table 19–1. We could then draw a chip from a hat, and the number on the chip would indicate the number of freight cars arriving in a given simulated period.

A simpler procedure is to use a table of random numbers, such as Table 19–2. Each entry in the table was drawn in such a way that each digit (zero through nine) had an equal chance of being drawn.

We could then assign two-digit random numbers to each of the possible outcomes (i.e., to the number of arrivals), as shown in Table 19–3.

There are 100 two-digit pairs of numbers. Note that 23 are assigned to the event "zero cars arrive"; 30 to the event "one car arrives"; 30 to the event "two cars arrive"; and so on. Since each two-digit number has a 1/100 chance of coming up, the probability that the event "zero cars arrive" will occur is 23/100, or 0.23, as desired.

We are now prepared to simulate the queuing process. This is done in Table 19–4.

Three days are used to start the process (marked x). For the first day, the random number (taken from Table 19–2) is 97. Since 97 corresponds to the event "four cars arrive" in Table 19–3, we list four in the third column. Of these four cars, two are unloaded, and the unloading of the other two is postponed until the following day. The random number for the second day is 02 (again from Table 19–2). This means zero cars arrive, and the two cars from the previous day are unloaded. We continue in the same fashion. However, we do not count the results of the first three days; this is the **initialization period.** The simulation starts with no freight cars, which is not typical. The initialization period gives the simulation a chance to reach typical or "steady state" behavior before results are counted.

Table 19–4 simulates 50 days of operation (in addition to the three days to get started). During most of the period, there is little delay. Note, however, that there is considerable delay starting around period 36. The average number of arrivals per day (1.58) over the sample period of 50 days is slightly larger than the expected number per day (1.50). On the average, 0.90 cars are delayed per day. For more accurate results, the simulation should be carried on for more days.

We could use the simulation model in much the same way that we used mathematical waiting-line models. That is, we can compare the effects of feasible alternatives upon waiting time and cost. For example, in this case we could compare delays under the current service rate of two per day with a service rate of three per day. Or we could introduce one or more additional channels.

Simulation and Computers

The calculations in Table 19–4 are tedious, and in an actual application of simulation they would be performed on a computer. The simplest computer implementation would be in a spreadsheet; many spreadsheet programs have the

Table 19-2   **Table of Random Digits**

97	95	12	11	90	49	57	13	86	81
02	92	75	91	24	58	39	22	13	02
80	67	14	99	16	89	96	63	67	60
66	24	72	57	32	15	49	63	00	04
96	76	20	28	72	12	77	23	79	46
55	64	82	61	73	94	26	18	37	31
50	02	74	70	16	85	95	32	85	67
29	53	08	33	81	34	30	21	24	25
58	16	01	91	70	07	50	13	18	24
51	16	69	67	16	53	11	06	36	10
04	55	36	97	30	99	80	10	52	40
86	54	35	61	59	89	64	97	16	02
24	23	52	11	59	10	88	68	17	39
39	36	99	50	74	27	69	48	32	68
47	44	41	86	83	50	24	51	02	08
60	71	41	25	90	93	07	24	29	59
65	88	48	06	68	92	70	97	02	66
44	74	11	60	14	57	08	54	12	90
93	10	95	80	32	50	40	44	08	12
20	46	36	19	47	78	16	90	59	64
86	54	24	88	94	14	58	49	80	79
12	88	12	25	19	70	40	06	40	31
42	00	50	24	60	90	69	60	07	86
29	98	81	68	61	24	90	92	32	68
36	63	02	37	89	40	81	77	74	82
01	77	82	78	20	72	35	38	56	89
41	69	43	37	41	21	36	39	57	80
54	40	76	04	05	01	45	84	55	11
68	03	82	32	22	80	92	47	77	62
21	31	77	75	43	13	83	43	70	16
53	64	54	21	04	23	85	44	81	36
91	66	21	47	95	69	58	91	47	59
48	72	74	40	97	92	05	01	61	18
36	21	47	71	84	46	09	85	32	82
55	95	24	85	84	51	61	60	62	13
70	27	01	88	84	85	77	94	67	35
38	13	66	15	38	54	43	64	25	43
36	80	25	24	92	98	35	12	17	62
98	10	91	61	04	90	05	22	75	20
50	54	29	19	26	26	87	94	27	73

Table 19–3

Number of Cars Arriving	Random Digits	Relative Frequency
0	00 to 22	0.23
1	23 to 52	0.30
2	53 to 82	0.30
3	83 to 92	0.10
4	93 to 97	0.05
5	98 and 99	0.02
		1.00

Table 19–4 Queuing System Simulation

Day Number	Random Number	Number of Arrivals	Total Number to Be Unloaded	Number Unloaded	Number Delayed to Following Day
x	97	4	4	2	2
x	02	0	2	2	0
x	80	2	2	2	0
1	66	2	2	2	0
2	96	4	4	2	2
3	55	2	4	2	2
4	50	1	3	2	1
5	29	1	2	2	0
6	58	2	2	2	0
7	51	1	1	1	0
8	04	0	0	0	0
9	86	3	3	2	1
10	24	1	2	2	0
11	39	1	1	1	0
12	47	1	1	1	0
13	60	2	2	2	0
14	65	2	2	2	0
15	44	1	1	1	0
16	93	4	4	2	2
17	20	0	2	2	0
18	86	3	3	2	1
19	12	0	1	1	0
20	42	1	1	1	0
21	29	1	1	1	0
22	36	1	1	1	0
23	01	0	0	0	0

(continued)

Table 19–4 (concluded)

Day Number	Random Number	Number of Arrivals	Total Number to Be Unloaded	Number Unloaded	Number Delayed to Following Day
24	41	1	1	1	0
25	54	2	2	2	0
26	68	2	2	2	0
27	21	0	0	0	0
28	53	2	2	2	0
29	91	3	3	2	1
30	48	1	2	2	0
31	36	1	1	1	0
32	55	2	2	2	0
33	70	2	2	2	0
34	38	1	1	1	0
35	36	1	1	1	0
36	98	5	5	2	3
37	50	1	4	2	2
38	95	4	6	2	4
39	92	3	7	2	5
40	67	2	7	2	5
41	24	1	6	2	4
42	76	2	6	2	4
43	64	2	6	2	4
44	02	0	4	2	2
45	53	2	4	2	2
46	16	0	2	2	0
47	16	0	0	0	0
48	55	2	2	2	0
49	54	2	2	2	0
50	23	1	1	1	0
Totals		79			45
Average		1.58			0.90

capability to generate random numbers. Appendix 2 to this chapter demonstrates some simulation techniques for spreadsheets, and spreadsheet add-in programs are available to facilitate Monte Carlo Simulation.[1] There are also general-purpose computer languages (e.g., GPSS, SIMSCRIPT, and SLAM) that have built-in routines to take care of various details common to most simula-

---

[1] See, for example, the program @RISK (Newfield, N.Y.: Palisade Corp., 1990).

tions. Finally, if one chooses, it is possible to program a simulation "from scratch" in any computer language.

In the rest of this chapter, we will continue to present concepts through hand simulation in order to communicate the ideas most clearly.

Simulation and Inventory Control

The use of simulation is not restricted to queuing processes. Many phases of business operations have been simulated with successful results. We shall illustrate by a brief example how simulation could be applied to the solution of an inventory problem.

Example 2 Suppose that the weekly demand of a certain product has the distribution shown in Table 19–5.

When an order is placed to replenish inventory, there is a delivery lag, which is a random variable, as shown in Table 19–6.

We should like to determine an order quantity, Q, and an order point, R. We can do this by trying several values of Q and R, and simulating to determine the best.

Table 19–5   **Probability Distribution for Weekly Demand**

Number Demanded	Probability	Random Numbers Assigned
0	0.10	00 to 09
1	0.40	10 to 49
2	0.30	50 to 79
3	0.20	80 to 99
	1.00	

Table 19–6   **Probability Distribution for Delivery Lag**

Number of Weeks from Order to Delivery	Probability	Random Numbers Assigned
2	0.20	00 to 19
3	0.60	20 to 79
4	0.20	80 to 99
	1.00	

Table 19–7 Inventory Simulation Illustration

Week Number	Receipts	Beginning Inventory	Random Number	Sales (units)	Ending Inventory	Lost Sales (outages)	Orders	Random Number for Orders	Number of Weeks Hence When Order Will Arrive
x		10	37	1	9				
x		9	51	2	7				
x		7	68	2	5		15	45	3
x		5	83	3	2				
x		2	56	2	0				
0	15	15	11	1	14				
1		14	91	3	11				
2		11	99	3	8				
3		8	57	2	6				
4		6	28	1	5		15	61	3
5		5	70	2	3				
6		3	33	1	2				
7	15	17	91	3	14				
8		14	67	2	12				
9		12	97	3	9				
10		9	61	2	7				
11		7	11	1	6				
12		6	50	2	4		15	86	4
13		4	25	1	3				
14		3	06	0	3				
15		3	60	2	1				
16	15	16	80	3	13				
17		13	19	1	12				
18		12	88	3	9				
19		9	25	1	8				
20		8	24	1	7				
21		7	68	2	5		15	37	3
22		5	78	2	3				
23		3	37	1	2				
24	15	17	04	0	17				
25		17	32	1	16				
26		16	75	2	14				
27		14	21	1	13				
28		13	47	1	12				
29		12	40	1	11				
30		11	71	2	9				
31		9	85	3	6				
32		6	88	3	3		15	15	2
33		3	24	1	2				
34	15	17	61	2	15				
35		15	19	1	14				
36		14	90	3	11				

Table 19–7 (concluded)

Week Number	Receipts	Beginning Inventory	Random Number	Sales (units)	Ending Inventory	Lost Sales (outages)	Orders	Random Number for Orders	Number of Weeks Hence When Order Will Arrive
37		11	24	1	10				
38		10	16	1	9				
39		9	32	1	8				
40		8	72	2	6	—			
Totals		412				0			
Average		10.3							

An illustration with $Q = 15$ and $R = 5$ is shown in Table 19–7. Note that the opening inventory is set to 10, and five weeks are used for initialization before the results are counted. We assume no backorders are allowed. If we established the cost of ordering, the cost of holding inventory, and the cost of being out of stock, we could estimate the cost of the inventory system under the rule $Q = 15$ and $R = 5$. Alternative rules could be compared to this. For example, the formulas for optimal order quantity and optimum reorder point (Equations 16–1 and 16–2 in Chapter 16) could be used, even though the assumptions needed for these formulas are not met in our example (the replenishment lead time is not constant). The amount of error introduced by using the formulas may be estimated by the simulation. Frequently, a method of solution may be operationally useful even when it is not strictly applicable theoretically.

SUMMARY

Probabilistic simulation models include random variables for uncertain events. Random numbers are assigned in accordance with the probabilities for the uncertain events, and the Monte Carlo process is used to generate a history of events for simulating the system under study. Queuing and inventory systems are examples of probabilistic simulation applications.

Risk Analysis

Consider the decision on a major capital investment such as the introduction of a new product. The profitability of the investment depends upon several factors that are generally uncertain. Estimates of total market for the product; the market share that the firm can attain; the growth in the market; the cost of producing the product; the selling price; the life of the product; and even the cost of the equipment needed—all are generally subject to substantial uncertainty.

One common approach would be to make single-number "best estimates" for each of the uncertain factors above and then to calculate a measure of profitability. This approach has two drawbacks:

1. There is no guarantee that using the "best estimates" will give the true expected profitability of the project.
2. There is no way to measure the risk associated with the investment. In particular, the manager has no way of determining the probability that the project will lose money or the probability that very large profits will result. For example, using only the one-number approach, a manager would not be able to distinguish between the two projects shown in Figure 19–1. And yet such information is necessary if techniques for dealing with risk, such as the utility measures of Chapter 6, are to be applied.

Risk analysis is a technique designed to circumvent these two disadvantages. The general approach is to assign a subjective probability distribution to each unknown factor and to combine these, using the Monte Carlo simulation approach, into a probability distribution for the project profitability as a whole. This can be shown with a simple example.

Example 3   Suppose we are considering marketing a new product. The investment required is $5,000. There are three uncertain factors: selling price, variable cost, and annual sales volume. The product has a life of only one year. Table 19–8 contains the various possible levels of these factors, together with the estimated probability of each. We will assume that the factors in Table 19–8 are statistically

Figure 19–1   Comparison of Two Projects

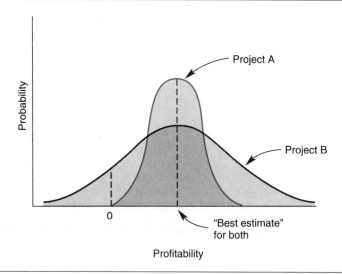

independent. (This is an important assumption. If it were not true, we would want to modify our simulation to include whatever probabilistic dependence we felt appropriate.)

Because this is a very simple example, it is possible to use the decision tree and probability tree techniques of Chapter 4 to calculate the various outcomes and probabilities. In this case, we have only $3 \cdot 3 \cdot 3 = 27$ possible distinct outcomes, but in a more realistic problem with many uncertain factors each having 10 or 20 levels, we could easily have a million possible outcomes. In these circumstances, the technique of simulation can be very useful in estimating both the average profitability of the investment and its "riskiness" as described by the probability of achieving various levels of profit.

We first need a way of generating random values for the elements of Table 19–8 according to the stated probabilities. As before, we associate various random numbers with various outcomes as in Table 19–9.

Now we can begin the simulation. We generate single-digit random numbers from the random number table (Table 19–2) and, in turn, determine a price, a cost, and a volume. Once these elements have been determined, profit is computed as follows:

$$\text{Profit} = (\text{Price} - \text{Cost}) \cdot \text{Volume} - \$5,000$$

Then the process is repeated a large number of times to generate a large number of profit outcomes. See Table 19–10 for a sample of 25 trials. Note that in the risk analysis type of simulation, each trial is separate from the rest; thus, there is no need for any initialization period.

Table 19–8 **Factors in Risk Analysis Example**

Selling Price	Probability	Variable Cost	Probability	Sales Volume (units)	Probability
$4	0.3	$2	0.1	3,000	0.2
5	0.5	3	0.6	4,000	0.4
6	0.2	4	0.3	5,000	0.4

Table 19–9 **Random Number Assignments in Risk Analysis Example**

Selling Price	Random Numbers	Variable Cost	Random Numbers	Sales Volume	Random Numbers
$4	0–2	$2	0	3,000	0, 1
5	3–7	3	1–6	4,000	2–5
6	8, 9	4	7–9	5,000	6–9

Table 19–10   **Risk Analysis Example—25 Trials**

Trial	Random Number	Price	Random Number	Cost	Random Number	Volume (000 units)	Profit ($000s)
1	8	$6	0	$2	6	5	15
2	0	4	4	3	3	4	−1
3	6	5	3	3	2	4	3
4	1	4	4	3	0	3	−2
5	3	5	6	3	0	3	1
6	5	5	6	3	9	5	5
7	1	4	6	3	7	5	0
8	3	5	8	4	6	5	0
9	2	4	8	4	8	5	−5
10	1	4	6	3	1	3	−2
11	5	5	7	4	3	4	−1
12	9	6	9	4	6	5	5
13	4	5	9	4	7	5	0
14	7	5	2	3	6	5	5
15	9	6	5	3	3	4	7
16	0	4	5	3	0	3	−2
17	1	4	1	3	8	5	0
18	0	4	6	3	4	4	−1
19	8	6	8	4	6	5	5
20	9	6	2	3	4	4	7
21	0	4	7	4	7	5	−5
22	0	4	0	2	8	5	5
23	4	5	0	2	1	3	4
24	6	5	5	3	8	5	5
25	4	5	0	2	1	3	4
						Average	= 2.08

Twenty-five trials is not enough to make a precise estimate of the average profitability or of the probability distribution of profits. If this process were programmed on a computer, several hundred trials could be easily simulated. However, for illustrative purposes, we will base our discussion on the results of these 25 trials.

Note that the average profit is 2.08 thousand or $2,080. It is interesting to compare this with simpler methods of analysis. For example, if we had used the one-number approach, and used the most likely value for each factor, our estimate of profit would have been:

$$\text{(Most likely profit)} = (\$5 - \$3) \cdot (4,000) - \$5,000 = \$3,000$$

Thus, the simple one-number approach, in this case, significantly overstates the expected profitability of the investment.

Figure 19–2   **Risk Analysis (sample cumulative probability function)**

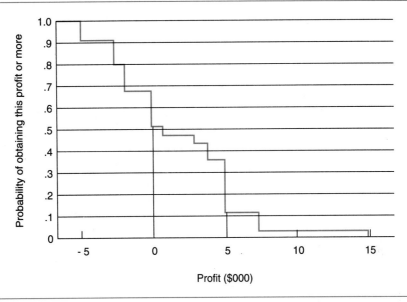

Because it is a simple case, computation of the expected profit (the profit of each of the 27 possible outcomes, weighted by the probabilities) can be performed;[2] this expected profit is $2,140. Thus, as one would expect, our sample average for 25 trials is not precisely equal to expected profit. However, the expected profit calculation sheds no light on the *risk* associated with the investment, whereas the set of 25 sample outcomes clearly indicates that one may actually incur a loss (for example, trial 2 in Table 19–10).

A convenient way to represent the results of a risk analysis is to list the outcomes by profitability and plot a graph of the sample cumulative probability function (see Figure 19–2). From Figure 19–2 we see that there is a 68 percent chance of making 0 profit or more (and a 32 percent chance of incurring a loss); there is a 36 percent chance of making $5,000 or more; and no chance of making more than $15,000. As larger numbers of trials are simulated, the curve of Figure 19–2 would smooth out somewhat (although it would continue to have the staircase shape because there is a finite number of alternative outcomes rather than an infinite number).

---

[2]In this case, since the factors are independent and related by simple multiplication and addition, we can compute the expected profit from the expected values of price, cost, and volume (see Chapter 4). If, however, these elements were not linearly related or independent, then the complete set of branches of the probability tree would have to be evaluated.

SUMMARY

Risk analysis is an application of simulation to evaluation of investment projects. Probability distributions are assessed for the uncertain factors involved in a project and combined, using the Monte Carlo process, to obtain the probability distribution for overall project profitability.

Simulation with Continuous Probability Distributions

In the risk analysis example above, the random variables were discrete (e.g., selling price took on only three distinct possible values: $4, $5, and $6). There may be situations in which we would like to assume that elements are random variables drawn from some continuous probability distribution. Suppose, for example, that we felt that annual sales volume in the risk analysis example would be normally distributed, with mean $\mu = 3,000$ units and standard deviation $\sigma = 500$ units. How can we generate random values of sales volume for use in a simulation?

Graphical Method

One way to generate random variables from continuous distributions is to plot the cumulative distribution function (see Chapter 7). For the normal distribution just mentioned, the cumulative distribution function is shown in Figure 19–3.

In order to use the cumulative distribution function, we first use a table of random numbers (like Table 19–2) to generate a random decimal between 0 and 1. This can be done by taking three random numbers from Table 19–2 and plac-

Figure 19–3   Cumulative Normal Distribution ($\mu = 3,000$, $\sigma = 500$)

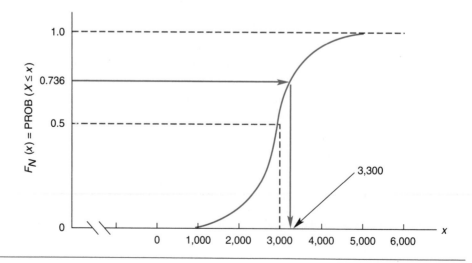

ing the decimal point in front of them. For example, if the random numbers 7, 3, and 6 were drawn, the corresponding decimal would be 0.736.

Then the cumulative curve of Figure 19–3 is *entered on the vertical axis* at the corresponding decimal value (0.736 in our example). Draw a horizontal line over to the cumulative curve, and when the line at height 0.736 hits the curve, drop straight down to the horizontal axis. Then read off the value reached; this value will be the particular random value desired. In our case, this value is approximately 3,300.

This method of generating random values works because the choice of a random decimal between 0 and 1 is equivalent to choosing a random *percentile* of the distribution. Then the figure is used to convert the random percentile (in our case, the 73.6 percentile) to a particular value (3,300). The method is general and can be used for *any* cumulative probability distribution, either continuous or discrete.

For a normal random variable, the process just described can be performed using standard normal tables (see Table A at the end of the text). We enter the table with the random decimal 0.736 and find the corresponding Z value is $Z = 0.63$. Then the random estimate of sales volume is:

$$\text{Sales volume} = \mu + Z\sigma = 3,000 + 0.63(500) = 3,315 \text{ units}$$

Sometimes it is possible to perform the above process algebraically. See Appendix 1 to this chapter for an illustration of the algebraic method.

Computer Generation of Random Variables

Computers have programs available to generate "equally likely" random decimals between 0 and 1. Also, computers have routines for generating standard normal random variables Z ($\mu = 0$, $\sigma = 1$) from which one can quickly generate values for normal random variables with any specified parameters by rearranging the transformation:

$$Z = \frac{X - \mu}{\sigma}$$

so that $X = \mu + Z\sigma$ as shown above.

A simple way of generating a random variable that approximates a standard normal variable is to sum 12 "equally likely" random decimals between 0 and 1, and then subtract 6. It can be shown that the mean of the resulting variable is 0 and the variance 1; and since 12 independent observations are being added to produce the variable, the statistical "central limit theorem" makes its distribution approximately normal.

SUMMARY

Simulation may be performed with continuous random variables either by graphic, tabular look-up, or computer generation using the appropriate cumulative probability distribution.

Simulation of Complex Systems

Although simulation is a useful tool in dealing with queuing, inventory, risk analysis, and other problems, perhaps its greatest contribution is in the analysis of complex systems. Many real-world problems involve systems made up of many component parts that are interrelated; the system may be dynamic and changing over time; and the system may involve probabilistic or uncertain events. Simulation may be the only technique for quantitative analysis of such problems.

We shall use an example to illustrate the use of simulation for these problems. Consider the operations of a barge line down the Ohio-Mississippi river system.[3] This barge company is a subsidiary of a steel company and receives barge loads of steel at its home port in Pittsburgh for shipment down the river to various ports, and to Gulf Coast ports by another barge line. Figure 19–4 sketches the operations of this system. Barge loads of steel arrive at the Pittsburgh port in a random fashion represented by a probability distribution in Figure 19–4. The destinations of these barges also vary from time to time, shown by the frequency distribution in the figure. If a barge is available, the steel is loaded. Otherwise, it must be shipped by another (i.e., a foreign) barge company. A tug will start with a tow of full barges (tow size is limited because of the locks in the river system) and calls on the various ports downstream. The number of ports is simplified to six in the illustration. At each port, barges designated for that port are dropped. At New Orleans, barges destined for Gulf ports of Pascagoula (P) and Orange (O) are transferred to another barge line and then the tug turns upstream and picks up available empty barges from the ports as it goes. These empty barges are available after a turnaround time (for unloading), which is a random event. Back at the home port, the tug returns to the available tug queue (after taking a short time for restocking, repairs, etc.) and the barges go to the empty barge queue, both ready to move back into the system again.

The company has 4 tugs and 127 barges, and at any one time these may be scattered throughout the system.

A simulation model of this system has been constructed and programmed on a computer. The probabilistic elements (arrivals of steel, destinations for barges, and turnaround times) are incorporated using the Monte Carlo simulation technique. The computer model must also keep track of time in the system; keep track of the barges, tugs, and physical limitations in the system; move the tugs and barges from port to port in accordance with travel distances (four days from Pittsburgh to Cincinnati, for example); and so on.

Once such a simulation model is developed, management can use it to try out possible alternative policies. Several scheduling rules might be tried including:

1. Having a tug leave Pittsburgh at fixed intervals—8 or 10 days apart—regardless of how many barges it has.
2. Having a tug leave when it has a tow of at least so many barges—16, for example.

---

[3]This example was adapted from G. G. O'Brien and R. R. Crane, "The Scheduling of a Barge Line," *Operations Research* 7 (1959), pp. 561–70.

Figure 19–4   Operations of Barge Company

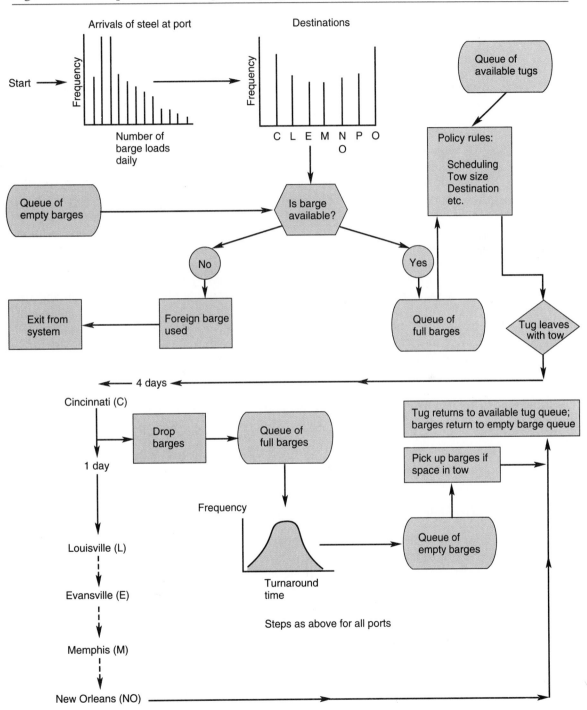

Other scheduling policies are, of course, possible. In addition, the company could examine the effects on the system of additional equipment—more barges or tugs, or faster tugs.

The simulation model allows the company to experiment with these and other changes without having to try them out on the real system. Besides the cost of disruption that would be incurred, it is difficult to evaluate results of an experiment in the real world because other external factors are constantly changing. It is hard to know if the observed results are attributable to the external factors or to the changes in the system. This problem does not exist in simulation models because the external factors can be controlled.

Simulation has been used extensively to deal with a great variety of problems. Simulation models have been built for transportation systems, factories, and airport operations; for the processing of defendants in court systems; for ambulance and fire services; for computer and communications systems; and for studying urban and world population and economic growth.

Although simulation models of complex systems can be very valuable, there are some disadvantages. They tend to be relatively costly to build. It may also be difficult to validate a complex simulation (i.e., ensure that the desired model framework is properly represented without any "bugs" in the computer program or logic). Also, one must determine an appropriate initialization period and run length for the simulation. Statistical methods can be useful in determining how long a simulation should be run in order to determine whether a particular result is due to chance or is a systematic result. And, of course, like all models, simulations are simplifications of the real world and may fail to adequately represent important elements or relationships.

SUMMARY

An important application of simulation is the study of complex operating systems that cannot be analyzed by optimization or other mathematical methods.

APPENDIX 1

Algebraic Method to Generate Random Variables

Suppose the cumulative distribution function of interest can be expressed in closed form (i.e., in a formula as a function of x without any integration signs); then the graphical process can be replaced by an equivalent algebraic relationship. For example, consider the exponential probability density function discussed in Appendix 1 of Chapter 18:

$$f(t) = \lambda e^{-\lambda t}, \quad 0 < t < \infty \tag{19-1}$$

The cumulative distribution function of the exponential distribution is:[4]

$$F(t) = 1 - e^{-\lambda t} \tag{19-2}$$

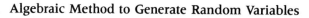

[4]See footnote 6 of Chapter 18.

Now we set a hypothetical random decimal (R.D.) equal to the cumulative distribution function and solve for t:

$$R.D. = 1 - e^{-\lambda t} \qquad (19\text{–}3)$$
$$e^{-\lambda t} = 1 - R.D.$$

Since our random decimal is between 0 and 1, so is $1 - R.D.$; thus, *this* quantity $(1 - R.D.)$ can be considered directly as a random decimal. So we can define:

$$e^{-\lambda t} = R.D. \qquad (19\text{–}4)$$

Taking natural logarithms:

$$-\lambda t = \log_e(R.D.) \qquad (19\text{–}5)$$

or:

$$t = -(1/\lambda)\log_e(R.D.) \qquad (19\text{–}6)$$

Equation 19–6 can be used directly to generate values from an exponential distribution with parameter λ. First, a random decimal (R.D.) is obtained from a random number table such as Table 19–2; then the particular value obtained is substituted into the right-hand side of Equation 19–6 and solved to produce a particular value for t. The value obtained will be a random draw from an exponential distribution with parameter λ.

For example, if $\lambda = 5$ and the random decimal were R.D. $= 0.475$, then from tables of natural logarithms, $\log_e (0.475) = -0.744$; and $t = -(1/5)(-0.744) = 0.1488$. This value would be a random draw from an exponential distribution with parameter $\lambda = 5$ (mean $1/\lambda = 1/5$).

APPENDIX 2

Monte Carlo Simulation on Spreadsheets

Spreadsheet programs are quite flexible. It is quite easy to use them to do simulation as described in this chapter, yet the manuals often do not illustrate this. This appendix is designed to be a short tutorial in building such models. It is designed for Lotus 1-2-3 and spreadsheets that are compatible with it such as VP Planner and Quattro. However, the ideas can be used in any spreadsheet.

The best way to use this tutorial is to sit down at a personal computer with a spreadsheet package and to work through the steps as instructed. The tutorial presumes you know at least the basics of spreadsheet usage.

Generating Random Values—the @RAND function

Before getting to the details, we need to provide a little background on Monte Carlo and generating random values from distributions. In particular, we shall explore the Lotus 1-2-3 function **@RAND**. To get started:

1. Boot up the computer and get into Lotus 1-2-3.
2. Move to any blank cell, say cell B2.

3. Type: **@RAND.**

Note what appears—it is a decimal greater than 0 but less than 1.0.

4. Copy cell B2 to cells B3 through B7.

(You should know how to do this by now. The commands are:

$$\text{/ C \{return\} B3.B7 \{return\}}$$

If all else fails, simply retype @RAND five times.)

Note that in each case, you get a different value, all between 0 and 1.0.

5. Now press the **Calc** key   (for Recalculation)

Note that the numbers change. Each time the spreadsheet is recalculated (by adding or modifying a cell or by using the **Calc** key), new values are determined for the @RAND function.

Because it is a little disconcerting to have the random numbers change each time we add to the model, let's turn off the automatic recalculation. To do this:

6. Type: **/ W G R M**   (command, Worksheet, Global Recalculation, Manual)

Now the spreadsheet will only recalculate when we press the **Calc** key.

The @RAND function generates uniform random numbers between 0 and 1. This means, for example, that there is a 10 percent chance of a value between .10 and .20, just as there is for the interval .80 to .90.

Simulating a Simple Queuing System

To make our analysis clear, let's work on a simple example. In fact, we shall use Example 1 of the chapter—a warehouse with one dock to unload railroad cars that arrive during the night. If you haven't already, you should read Example 1. Note that the company has assessed a probability distribution for arrivals of cars, Table 19–1. We want to generate a history of arrivals by random draws from this table, as was illustrated in Table 19–3.

Creating the @VLOOKUP Table

We first take Table 19–1 and from it, create a cumulative distribution as shown in Table 19–11.

We are now going to use the cumulative distribution and the Lotus **@VLOOKUP** function to complete our task.

1. Move to cell I1.
2. Type in the headings and values exactly as shown in Figure 19–5. The values come from the cumulative distribution in Table 19–11. The @VLOOKUP table is in the range I3 to J9. The first column is called the lookup column. The other column is the first column (to the right of the lookup column).
3. Move to cell A1 and erase the values in cells B2 to B7.
4. Next, type in the column headings and values as shown in Figure 19–6.

Table 19–11   Cumulative Distribution of Arrivals

Number of Cars Arriving (X)	Relative Frequency (probability of X arrivals)	Cumulative Probability (probability of less than X arrivals)
0	0.23	0
1	0.30	0.23
2	0.30	0.53
3	0.10	0.83
4	0.05	0.93
5	0.02	0.98
6 or more	0	1.00

Figure 19–5   The @VLOOKUP Table

```
        H     I         J        K
   1         Cumul.    No. of
   2         Prob.    Arrivals
   3           0                  0
   4         0.23                 1
   5         0.53                 2
   6         0.83                 3
   7         0.93                 4
   8         0.98                 5
   9           1                  6

            Lookup            First
            Column            Column
```

Figure 19–6   Headings for Columns of Model

```
         A          B         C          D          E         F
   1               Warehouse Simulation Model
   2    Dock Cap.        2
   3
   4    Day        Random    No. of     No. to    Actually   No.
   5               Number    Arrivals   Unload    Unloaded   Delayed
   6    --------   ------    --------   --------   --------   -------
   7        0                                                     0
   8
```

Note that the unloading capacity of the dock (two cars per day) is entered in cell B2. Also, there are no cars waiting as of day 0. (Enter the zeros in cells A7 and F7 as shown.)

5. Move to cell A8.
6. Type: $+A7+1$

This increments the day count by 1.

7. Move to cell B8.
8. Type: @RAND
9. Move to cell C8.
10. Type: @VLOOKUP(B8,I3.J9,1)

| Lookup | Lookup table | Column in |
| value | range | table |

This requires some explanation. The @VLOOKUP function uses the first argument—cell B8, which contains the random number—to search in the lookup column of the table—specified as I3 to J9—and finds the corresponding value in the first (and only, in this case) column of the table. Note the reference to the table I3 to J9 is made using absolute references by inserting the dollar sign ($) as shown. This is done so that when we copy (in a couple of steps), the table reference will always remain the same.

Stop and think for a minute about what we have done. If the random number in cell B8 is between 0 and less than 0.23, the first row of the lookup table is referenced and results in a value of 0—that is, zero arrivals. If the random number is 0.23 or above but less than 0.53, the second row of the table is referenced, giving one arrival. A random number between 0.53 and 0.83 results in two arrivals, and so on. This produces arrivals exactly as we wish—that is, with probabilities as given in Table 19–11.

11. Move to cell D8.
12. Type: $+F7+C8$

This indicates that the number of cars to be unloaded on a given day is the number delayed from the previous day plus the arrivals that night.

13. Move to cell E8.
14. Type: @MIN(B2,D8)

This indicates that the number of cars unloaded on a given day is the smaller of the dock's capacity (contained in cell B2) or the number available to be unloaded. This is not immediately obvious, so think about why this is so. Also note the absolute reference to cell B2 using the $. As before, this is because we want the reference to stay fixed when we copy, as we shall do shortly.

15. Move to cell F8.
16. Type: $+D8–E8$

The number of cars delayed to the following day equals the number to be unloaded less those actually unloaded.

You should pause at this point to survey what you have done—created the first day of our model. Be sure you understand it. Press the Calc key a few times and observe the results.

We are now going to copy the first day model 500 times in order to simulate 500 days of operation:

17. Move to cell A8.
18. Copy cells A8 . . . F8 to cells A9 . . . A507.

    If you are not sure exactly how to do this, follow the steps below:

    Type: / C A8.F8
    Press: **Return**
    Type: **A9.A507**
    Press: **Return**

    This will take a while, as it is a big copying job.

You have now created a simulation model. The company is concerned about the number of cars delayed because it is costly to have cars waiting. You now have a tool with which the management can study its operations.

You should study your model to make sure it is doing what you expected. Note that the C column shows the daily arrivals. Quickly scan it to see if it seems right—that is, if the arrivals seem "random" and in accordance with the probabilities in Table 19–11.

Column F contains the number of cars delayed. Note that on many days, none are delayed. But if you scan down the column, you will find periods in which the delays build up, with perhaps 10 or more railroad cars delayed. The delays may last for a period of several days, and then work down to zero again. This is exactly how queuing systems behave.

Summarizing the Results

To be useful, we need to summarize the results. We shall calculate the average number of cars delayed, and determine the cost of this delay. It would also be useful to produce a distribution showing how often each number of cars was delayed. Such a frequency distribution is easily produced using the 1-2-3 Data/Distribution command, which we shall illustrate. But first:

1. Move to cell L1 and type in the headings and other information shown in Figure 19–7.
2. Move to cell N1 and enter:

   @AVG(F8.F507)

   This calculates the average number of cars delayed per day.
3. Move to cell N2 and enter:

   100*365*N1

Figure 19–7   **Headings for Summary of Results**

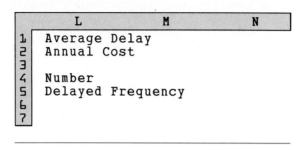

This calculates the annual cost (365 days) due to delayed cars, assuming that it costs $100 per day for each car delayed.

4. In column L, rows 7 through 27, enter the values:

    0, 1, 2, 3, . . . up to 20

    These are called the data "bins."
    (Note: The **Data/Fill** command is an easy way to do this.)

5. Type: / **D D**   (command, Data, Distribution)
    The computer asks for the data range. This is the range containing the values we wish to tabulate. This is column F of our model. So:

6. Specify the range by typing: **F8.F507**   then press: **Return**
    The computer next asks for the range for the bins.

7. Specify this range by typing: **L7.L27**   then press: **Return**
    After the computer finishes calculating, the distribution of values is shown in the table. This shows the number of days on which zero cars were delayed, the number of days on which one car was delayed, the number on which two cars were delayed, etc. Note that the average for this set of values is shown above.
    Pause at this point to look over the results.
    Suppose we want to save the results just calculated, and then calculate 500 more days. We'll simply move the results over one column.

8. Type: / **M M7.M27**   (command, Move, range M7.M27)
9. Press: **Return**
10. Type: **N7**   (to range starting at N7)
11. Press: **Return**
12. Press: **Calc**   (This may take awhile.)
13. Now type: / **D D**   (command, Data, Distribution)
14. Then press: **Return** *twice*
    A new distribution for another 500 days is shown together with the average delay and the cost of this delay.

Changing the Capacity

The results obtained above were based upon the assumption that the warehouse dock has the capacity to unload two railroad cars per day. Suppose the company could add new equipment that would increase the unloading capacity to three cars per day. This should reduce the delays. Let us see how much savings would result.

1. Write down the current estimated annual delay cost (it is in cell N2).
2. Move to cell B2.
3. Enter the number: **3** (the new capacity)
   (Don't forget to press **Return** after entering 3.)
4. Press: **Calc**
   This generates a new set of random numbers, and hence, a new simulation under the new condition (capacity of three cars per day).
5. Type: / **D D** (command, Data, Distribution)
6. Press: **Return** *twice*
   This calculates the delay distribution, the average number of cars delayed, and the cost of this delay.
7. Move to cell N2 to see the results.

By subtracting the result in cell N2 from what you recorded earlier, you have an estimate of the annual savings from increasing the capacity to three cars per day. This would have to be weighed against the cost of constructing the additional capacity.

Monte Carlo Risk Analysis

Spreadsheet software can also be used to do risk analysis, as described in the chapter. We shall redo the analysis of Example 3 to illustrate this. In Example 3, there was uncertainty about the price, variable cost, and sales volume for a new product. First, erase the previous example by typing / **W E Y.**

The probability distributions are given in Table 19–8. We need to set up a separate lookup table for each, just as we did earlier for the random arrivals in the example above.

1. Move to cell J1.
2. Fill in the table headings as shown in Figure 19–8. Note that you are creating three tables containing cumulative probability distributions.
3. Fill in the rest of the tables (rows 4 through 7) also as shown in Figure 19–8. Note that we are entering cumulative probabilities in columns J, M, and P.

Building the Monte Carlo Model

Let us now set up the Monte Carlo model for our example. As before, we want to turn off the automatic recalculation, so:

Figure 19–8   LOOKUP Tables for Risk Analysis Example

	J	K	L	M	N	O	P	Q
1	Cumul.	Selling		Cumul.	Variable		Cumul.	Sales
2	Prob.	Price		Prob.	Cost		Prob.	Volume
3	------	-------	-----	------	--------	-----	------	------
4	0	4		0	2		0	3000
5	0.3	5		0.1	3		0.2	4000
6	0.8	6		0.7	4		0.6	5000
7	1			1			1	
8								

Figure 19–9   Headings for Risk Analysis Example

	A	B	C	D	E	F	G
1	Random	Selling	Random	Variable	Random	Sales	Profit
2	number	price	number	cost	number	volume	dollars
3	------	------	------	------	------	------	------

1. Type: **/ W G R M**   (command, Worksheet, Global, Recalculation, Manual)
2. Move to cell A1 and type in the column headings for the model as shown in Figure 19–9.
3. Move to cell A4 and type: **@RAND**
4. In cell B4, type: **@VLOOKUP(A4,J4.K7,1)**
   The lookup for the selling price is contained in the range J4 through K7. The dollar signs are included to make the reference fixed when we copy the cell below.
5. In cell C4, type: **@RAND**
6. In cell D4, type: **@VLOOKUP(C4,M4.N7,1)**
   This is the lookup table for variable cost.
7. In cell E4, type: **@RAND**
8. In cell F4, type: **@VLOOKUP(E4,P4.Q7,1)**
   This is the lookup table for sales volume.
9. In cell G4, type: **(B4–D4)*F4–5000**
   This calculates the profit as:

$$(\text{Price} - \text{Variable cost}) \cdot (\text{Sales volume}) - \text{Fixed cost of } \$5,000$$

Before going on, you should go back and check your work in entering the formulas above.

We have completed the first trial of the model. In order to have a number of trials, say 100 trials, we simply copy it over into other cells.

10. Type: / **C A4.G4**   then press: **Return**   (command, Copy, from range A4 to G4)
11. Then type: **A5.A103**   then press: **Return**   (copy to range A5 to A103)
    This operation will take awhile, so be patient. It will result in 100 trials, with the profit values in column G. Pause and review the analysis. Scan up and down column G to see the range of profits resulting. Press the Calc key to get a new set of results.

At this point we could calculate an average and classify these profit values into a frequency distribution, just as we did in the warehouse unloading dock example earlier in this appendix. We shall not take you through the steps again. Rather, we shall illustrate another feature, graphing the risk profile—the cumulative frequency distribution for profit.

Graphing the Results

First, sort the results in order, from highest to lowest:

1. Move the cursor to cell G4.
2. Type: / **D S**   (command, Data, Sort)
    The **Sort** menu appears. The highlight is on **Data-Range,** and we need first to specify the range of values we wish to sort, so:
3. Press: **Return**
    The program asks us to specify the data range, so:
4. Type: **G4.G103**   (the range containing profit results)
    and press: **Return**
    The Sort menu returns. Next, we need to specify the primary key (you needn't know exactly what this means). To respond:
5. Type: **P**   (for primary key)
6. Type: **G3**   and press: **Return**
    The program now asks the order of the sort. We wish to have the profits from highest to lowest—descending order, so:
7. Type: **D**   and press: **Return**
    The program returns us to the Sort menu. We are now ready to perform the sort, so:
8. Type: **G**   (for Go)
    Note that cell G4 contains the largest (most positive) profit of the 100 trials, while cell G103 has the lowest profit. These are the values we wish to plot.
    We now need to define the probability scale, from 0 to 1.0 in units of .01 (since we had 100 trials). We shall put these in column H, using the Data/ Fill command.
9. Move to cell H4.
10. Type: / **D F**   (command, Data, Fill)
11. Type: **H4.H103**   (range to be filled)
    then press: **Return**
    We wish to start with 0, and the program suggests this, so:

12. Press: **Return**   (to set start at 0)
13. Type: **.01**   (for the Step)
    and press: **Return**
14. Type: **1.0**   (for the Stop)
    and press: **Return**
    Column H should now contain 0, .01, .02, and so on up to .99. Now we create the graph:
15. Type: / **G**   (command, Graph)
    The **Graph** menu appears.
16. Type: **T X**   (type of graph, XY type)
17. Type: **X G4.G103**   (to specify the data range for the X variable)
    and press: **Return**
18. Type: **A H4.H103**   (to specify the data range for the Y (or A) variable)
    and press: **Return**
19. Type: **O F A L Q**   (Options, Format, A-data set, Line, Quit)
    This last step merely tells Lotus that we wish to plot the data as a series of connected lines.
20. Type: **Q**   (again, to Quit the options menu)
    The graph menu returns. We are finished specifying the graph, so:
21. Type: **V**   (to view the graph)
    The graph should be compared to that shown in Figure 19–2. It will differ somewhat because this analysis is based on 100 trials (versus 25 in Figure 19–2) and, of course, it is based on a different set of random draws.
    When you have finished viewing the graph, press any key. Then:
22. Type: **Q**   (to quit the graph menu)

The examples illustrated in this appendix and in this chapter are simple examples, but the same methodology can be used to create quite complex Monte Carlo risk analysis models. And there exist Lotus add-in products that make all of this much easier by automatically sampling from a wide variety of distributions and by easing the creation of tables and graphs.[5]

---

[5] For example, @RISK (see footnote 1).

Bibliography

Bonini, C. P. *Building Monte Carlo Simulation Models Using Lotus 1-2-3*. Technical Report No. 19, Stanford University Graduate School of Business Computer Facility, 1985.

Boulden, J. B. *Computer-Assisted Planning Systems*. New York: McGraw-Hill, 1975.

Bratley, P.; B. L. Fox; and L. E. Schrage. *A Guide to Simulation*. New York: Springer-Verlag, 1983.

Gordon, G. *Systems Simulation*. 2nd ed. Englewood Cliffs, N.J.: Prentice Hall, 1978.

Hertz, D. B., and H. Thomas. *Risk Analysis and Its Applications*. New York: John Wiley & Sons, 1983.

———. *Practical Risk Analysis*. New York: John Wiley & Sons, 1984.

Hillier, F., and G. J. Lieberman. *Introduction to Operations Research*. 5th ed. New York: McGraw-Hill, 1990.

Maisel, H., and G. Gnugnoli. *Simulation of Discrete Stochastic Systems*. Chicago: Science Research Associates, 1972.

Meier, R. C.; W. T. Newell; and H. L. Pazer. *Simulation in Business and Economics*. Englewood Cliffs, N.J.: Prentice Hall, 1969.

Naylor, T. H. *Corporate Planning Models*. Reading, Mass.: Addison-Wesley Publishing, 1979.

Pritsker, A. A. B. *Introduction to Simulation and SLAM II*. 3rd ed. New York: John Wiley & Sons (Halsted Press), 1986.

Shannon, R. E. *Systems Simulation*. Englewood Cliffs, N.J.: Prentice Hall, 1975.

Wagner, H. M. *Principles of Operations Research*. 2nd ed. Englewood Cliffs, N.J.: Prentice Hall, 1975.

Watson, H. S. *Computer Simulation in Business*. New York: John Wiley & Sons, 1981.

Problems with Answers

19-1. *a.* Using the same history of arrivals shown in Table 19–4, simulate the waiting line process of the warehouse-railroad car example with a constant service rate of three per day.

b. Assuming that the warehouse company pays $20 per day for freight cars kept over one day, estimate the annual savings (250 days = 1 year) from a service rate of three per day (instead of two per day).

19-2. Continue Table 19–10 to 50 trials, using random numbers from Table 19–2. Plot your results on a diagram similar to Figure 19–2. Out of your sample of 25 trials, what is the probability of the profit being less than zero? What is the average profit for your sample of 25 trials? Compare your answer with those obtained in Table 19–10 and with the expected profit of $2,140; also, compute the *exact* probability of profit being less than zero and compare it to your sample outcome.

19-3. Refer to Problem 19–2. Suppose that the selling price and annual sales volume were *not* independent variables but were jointly distributed with the following probabilities. Note that the marginal probabilities are the same as in the chap-

Price \ Sales Volume	3,000	4,000	5,000	Row Sums
$4	0	0	0.3	0.3
$5	0	0.4	0.1	0.5
$6	0.2	0	0	0.2
Column Sums	0.2	0.4	0.4	1.0

ter; but now, the assumption of independence does not apply.

a. Simply by studying the accompanying joint probability table, can you predict whether expected profit under the new assumption will be higher or lower than previously? Why or why not?

b. Devise a scheme similar to Table 19–9 that uses random numbers to produce random values for price and volume when they are related as specified.

c. Use your scheme in (*b*) to generate 25 trials of the investment as in Table 19–10, but now assuming price and volume are dependent as specified.

d. Plot a figure similar to Figure 19–2 for your data in (*c*).

e. Compare your figure of (*d*) to Figure 19–2. Which investment would you prefer? Why?

Problems

19-4. Continue Table 19–7 to 100 periods, using random numbers from Table 19–2. Estimate the total annual cost (1 year = 50 weeks) if the cost of placing an order is $10, the cost of holding one unit of inventory is 50 cents per year, and the cost of outage is $3 per unit of lost sales. (Use average beginning inventory in determining cost of holding inventory.)

19–5. Pick an inventory rule that you consider good for the situation described in Problem 19–4. (That is, pick a number Q and a number R.) Simulate for 100 periods, and compare the cost of your rule with the cost in Problem 19–4.

19–6. Refer to Problem 18–7 in Chapter 18. Suppose now that arrivals are still Poisson, with average rate $\lambda = 5$ ships per week, but that service times are constant at 0.1 week. Simulate two weeks of operation, keeping track of the waiting time of each ship. (*Hint:* The times between arrivals are exponential random variables with parameter $\lambda = 5$. Starting from zero, generate random interarrival times as described in chapter Appendix 1.)

19–7. Refer to Problem 17–9. Describe the steps necessary to take random numbers, generate random demands according to the specified probability distribution, and evaluate costs for the policy $Q = 10,000$ units ordered.

19–8. An Idaho potato farmer is studying the risks associated with planting his potato crop. Based upon past experience, he assesses the following probabilities associated with potato prices per hundredweight (cwt.), yields in cwt. per acre, and costs (for fertilizer, water, seed, and labor) per acre.

The profit per acre is (Price · Yield) − Cost. Assume all probabilities are independent. Using the Monte Carlo method for 25 trials, estimate the expected profit per acre, and the probability distribution for profit per acre. What is the estimated probability that the farmer makes less than $100 per acre on his crop?

Price (per cwt.)	Probability	Yield (cwt. per acre)	Probability	Cost (per acre)	Probability
$2	0.10	210	0.10	$400	0.70
3	0.20	220	0.10	500	0.20
4	0.50	230	0.40	600	0.10
5	0.10	240	0.30		1.00
6	0.05	250	0.10		
7	0.05		1.00		
	1.00				

More Challenging Problems

19–9. Refer to Problem 19–8. In reality, the price and yield are not independent variables. A low yield generally means a shortage of potatoes, and the price rises; a high yield means low prices. However, this relationship is not exact, as there are other factors besides yields that affect prices. Suppose that the yield and cost per acre are the same as given in Problem 19–8 and are independent. Suppose, further, that price is related to yield by the following equation:

$$\text{Price} = 15.5 - 0.05(\text{Yield}) + D$$

where D is a random variable indicating a deviation from the equation. D has the following distribution (independent of yield and cost):

D	Probability
−$1.00	0.10
− 0.50	0.20
0	0.40
0.50	0.20
1.00	0.10
	1.00

Estimate the expected profit per acre and the distribution of profit per acre using the Monte Carlo method with 25 trials.

19–10. An analyst for International Widgets Corp. (IWC) was working on the corporate financial plan for the next year. IWC has two major divisions, one in the United States and the other in the United Kingdom. From the management of each division, the analyst had obtained an assessment of the probability distribution for net profit for the next year. These assessments are given below. Suppose it is reasonable to assume the distributions are independent.

a. Set up a procedure, using Monte Carlo methods, to estimate the probability distribution for combined net profit for IWC. Carry out the procedure for five Monte Carlo trials to illustrate how it is done.

b. Indicate how you would obtain the probability distribution of combined net profit from the Monte Carlo results.

c. Suppose the distributions were not considered independent (world economic conditions tend to affect all countries to some extent). To handle this problem, the analyst proposes to use the same random number in determining Monte Carlo sampled value both for U.S. and U.K. profit. Do you agree with the procedure? Comment briefly.

19–11.[6] The Acme Airline Company (AAC) is concerned about scheduling its engine repair shop. Under alternative A, engine repair times would be exponentially distributed with a mean time of 40 days. Under alternative B (a more complex procedure) engine repair times would be normally distributed with a mean of 40 days and a standard deviation of 5 days.

When an engine arrives for repair, a spare engine is sent out to take its place. The engine requiring repair is then sent to the shop; all engines under repair are worked on simultaneously.

---

[6]This problem requires knowledge of material in Appendix 1 to this chapter.

(for Problem 19–10)

U.S. Net Profit		U.K. Net Profit	
Amount ($ millions)	Probability of This Much Profit or Less	Amount (converted to $ U.S. in millions)	Probability of This Much Profit or Less
−$ 1.0	0.00	$0.5	0.00
3.0	0.10	0.7	0.10
6.0	0.25	0.9	0.25
8.0	0.50	1.0	0.50
10.0	0.75	1.3	0.75
15.0	0.90	2.0	0.90
20.0	1.00	3.0	1.00

When repairs have been completed, the repaired engine enters the "spares pool" to be used to satisfy a subsequent requirement. Engine arrivals for repair are Poisson with rate $\lambda = 0.5$ per day.

If an engine arrives when there are no spare engines to take its place, a spare engine is expedited from another location; this costs $10,000 per request. AAC has purchased 25 spare engines in order to keep the likelihood of expediting low.

Note that since engine repair times are not constant, engines may "cross" in time; that is, an engine that arrived at the repair facility later may actually be completed earlier.

Describe carefully how you would simulate this situation, including each of the following:

Random engine arrivals.
Random engine repair times (under each alternative).
The number of spares available at all times.
The number of occurrences of expediting.
Your initialization process.

19–12. *a.* Refer to Problem 18–1. Assume that the average service rate is still 15 per hour but that there is no variation in service time; that is, it takes exactly four minutes to service each call. Use the Monte Carlo method to simulate 25 trials.

b. Again refer to Problem 18–1. Now assume that service time for a call is normally distributed, with a mean service time of four minutes and a standard deviation of two minutes. Use the Monte Carlo method to simulate 25 trials.

c. Compare the results of (*a*) and (*b*) with that obtained in Problem 18–1.

19–13.[7] An Automatic Storage/Retrieval system (AS/RS) is a computer-controlled device for warehousing that can store pallets of material by picking one up at a conveyorized pickup/delivery point and moving both vertically and horizontally down an aisle until an open storage location for the pallet is found. When a retrieve request occurs, the AS/RS travels to the location in which the designated pallet is stored, pulls out the pallet, and delivers it to the pickup/delivery point.

The AS/RS can be described as a pallet loader that can be moved up or down a "mast," which rolls down a storage aisle. There are locations on either side of the aisle for storage. Consider an AS/RS with a single aisle.

a. Suppose arrivals of pallets to be stored are Poisson, as are requests for retrievals of pallets already stored. Also, suppose the "service times" (i.e., the time for the system to perform a store or a retrieve) are exponential. Suppose stores and retrieves are done separately, and suppose a single queue exists covering both stores and retrieve requests; also, priority is first-come, first-served. How would you *approach* the problem of analyzing such a system? (Note: the sum of two Poisson processes is again Poisson.)

b. Now suppose that two separate queues are maintained, one for stores and one for retrieve requests. Assume the operating policy is that stores and retrieves are now combined (as long as both queues are not empty) so that the AS/RS does not return to the pickup/delivery point empty. This combining of stores and retrieves naturally increases the performance of the system. Assume

---

[7]This problem is adapted from W. H. Hausman, S. C. Graves, and L. B. Schwarz, "Simulation Tests of Automatic Warehousing Systems," *AIIE Transactions,* September 1978.

service times are still exponentially distributed, but with a smaller mean. How would you approach the problem of analyzing this system?

c. Consider the situation in (b), but now assume that the AS/RS can select retrieve requests "out of order" in order to try to minimize wasted travel time. That is, given a decision to store a pallet in a given location, it may be more efficient to do one retrieve rather than another because of the location of the retrieves in the rack. How would you approach the problem of analyzing this system?

20

PERT
Program Evaluation and Review Technique

This chapter presents tools to manage the planning and control of major projects with many separate activities that require coordination. In many business situations, a number of different activities must be performed in a specified sequence in order to accomplish some major project. Some of the activities may be in series (for example, market research cannot be performed before the research design is planned), whereas others may be in parallel (for example, the engines for a ship can be built at the same time the hull is being constructed.) For a large, complex project, the complete set of activities will usually contain a combination of series and parallel elements. The technique of PERT (Program Evaluation and Review Technique) is designed to aid a manager in planning and controlling such a project. For planning purposes prior to the start of the project, the PERT technique allows a manager to calculate the expected total amount of time the entire project will take to complete. The technique highlights the bottleneck activities in the project so that the manager may either allocate more resources to them or keep a careful watch on them as the project progresses. For purposes of control after the project has begun, the technique provides a way of monitoring progress and calling attention to those delays in activities that will cause a delay in the project's completion date.

This chapter presents the basic concepts of PERT under conditions of both known and uncertain activity times.

Information Requirements

In order to use PERT, two types of information are needed for each activity in the project.[1] The *sequencing requirements* for an activity must be known. For example, we need to know the set of activities that must be completed prior to the beginning of each specific activity. In addition, we require an estimate of the *time* each activity will take.

Case I: Known Activity Times

In the first part of this chapter, we will assume that there is a precise, known amount of time that each activity in the project will take. In the second part, we will assume that the time to perform each activity is uncertain (i.e., a random variable).

Network Diagram

The **network diagram** is a graphical representation of the entire project. Each activity in the project is represented by a circle, and arrows are used to indicate sequencing requirements.[2]

Example Table 20–1 contains a list of six activities that constitute a project, together with the sequencing requirements and the estimated times for each activity. The immediate predecessor of activity B is activity A; this means that activity A must

Table 20–1

Activity	Immediate Predecessors	Estimated Time (days)
A	None	2
B	A	3
C	A	4
D	B, C	6
E	None	2
F	E	8

---

[1] A closely related procedure called CPM (Critical Path Method) also exists. In this chapter, the terminology of PERT is used, although the network diagram procedure follows the convention of CPM.

[2] In PERT, the arrows are used to represent activities; however, the CPM convention used here is easier to understand.

Figure 20–1   Network Diagram

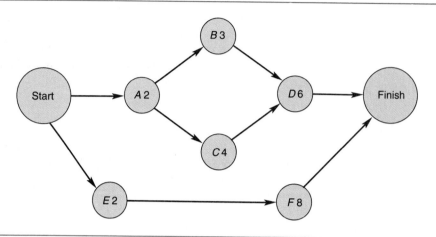

be completed before activity B can begin. Figure 20–1 shows the network diagram for our example, with the activities represented by circles. The arrows in the network diagram illustrate the sequencing requirements of the problem. For example, the arrow from circle A to circle B indicates that activity A must be completed before activity B can begin. Similarly, activities B and C must *both* be completed before activity D can begin.

The estimated time for each activity has been placed in the circle representing that activity. Once the network diagram is completed, it may be used to develop the critical path for the project.

The Critical Path

A **path** is defined as a sequence of connected activities in the project. In our example, there are only three possible paths: *ABD,* which has a length of 11 days; *ACD,* which has a length of 12 days; and *EF,* which has a length of 10 days. The **critical path** is the path that has the largest amount of time associated with it. In our example, it is *ACD,* with a length of 12 days. The length of the critical path determines the minimum time in which the entire project may be completed. The activities on the critical path are the bottleneck activities in the project.

The critical path is important for two reasons. First, the completion time for the project cannot be reduced unless one or more of the activities on the critical path can be completed in less time than the initial time estimate. The critical path highlights those activities that must be performed more rapidly if the total project completion time is to be reduced. Second, any delays in activities that are on the critical path will produce delays in completion of the project, whereas delays in noncritical activities may not actually delay the completion of the project. In our example, the estimated project completion time is 12 days. If we desire to reduce this time, we must reduce the time to complete one of the three activities on the critical path—A, C, or D. We obtain no benefit from reducing the time required to perform activities B, E, and F, since these activities are not on the critical path. Also, a delay of up to one day in the time required to perform activity B could be tolerated, since this would have no effect on the project completion time. On the other hand, any delay in activities A, C, or D would directly lengthen the project completion time. If activity C were delayed 3 days, the project would take 15 days rather than 12 to be completed.

For simple projects such as the one in our example, the critical path may be found by inspection of the network diagram. However, the PERT technique is typically used for planning and control of a large-scale, complex project (e.g., the construction of a 50-story building, the development and implementation of a new military defense system, or the design and installation of major new manufacturing processes). In such a situation, there may be hundreds or thousands of activities that must be performed to complete the project, and some systematic way of finding the critical path is needed.

Algorithm for Critical Path

An algorithm is a well-defined systematic procedure. The algorithm to find the critical path in a network is presented below. Let:

ES_i = Earliest start time for activity i

EF_i = Earliest finish time for activity i

where the earliest start time for an activity is the earliest possible time that the activity can begin, assuming that all of its predecessors also started at the earliest possible times. The earliest finish time for an activity is the sum of the earliest start time and the estimated time to perform the activity. The earliest finish time represents the earliest possible time that an activity could be finished, assuming all of its predecessors started at their earliest start times.

The ES and the EF for each activity in the network are obtained as follows: First, set the ES of the first activity equal to zero. Then add the estimated time to perform the first activity to its ES (zero), obtaining the EF for the first activity. Now consider any activity for which all its immediate predecessors have ES and EF values. The ES of such an activity is equal to the largest of the EF values of its immediate predecessors, because all have to be finished before that activity can be started. Again, the EF is obtained by adding the estimated time to perform the activity to its ES time.

Figure 20–2 contains ES and EF times for the activities in our first example. Activities A and E are the first activities, so ES for A and E is zero. Since activity A takes two days, the EF for activity A is 2. Similarly, the EF for activity E is 2. Then the ES for activities B and C is 2. The EF for B is $2 + 3$, or 5; and the EF for C is $2 + 4$, or 6. Since activity D requires both B and C to be completed before it can begin, the ES for activity D is the larger of 5 or 6;

Figure 20–2   **Earliest Start, Earliest Finish Time**

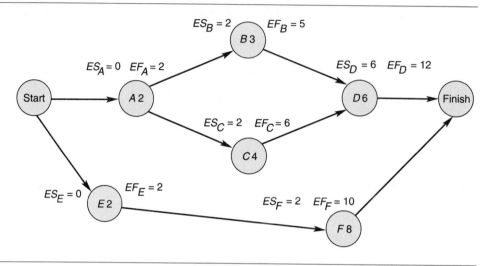

namely, 6. The EF for D is $6 + 6$, or 12. The ES for activity F is 2, and the EF for activity F is 10.

Continuing with our algorithm, define:

LS_i = Latest start time for activity i

LF_i = Latest finish time for activity i

where the latest finish time for an activity is the latest possible time an activity can finish without delaying the project beyond its deadline, assuming all of the subsequent activities are performed as planned. The latest start time for an activity is the difference between the latest finish time and the estimated time for the activity to be performed.

To obtain the LS and LF for each activity, we start at the end of the network diagram and first set the LF for the last activity equal to the EF for that activity.[3] Then we subtract the estimated time to perform the last activity from the LF to obtain the LS. Now consider any activity for which all of its immediate successors have LS and LF values. The LF of such an activity is equal to the smallest of the LS values of its immediate successors. Then the LS is obtained by subtracting the estimated time to perform the activity from its LF time. Figure 20–3 contains LS and LF times for the activities in our example, assuming the deadline for project completion is 12 days. Activities D and F are the last activities, so the LF for D and for F is set equal to the project deadline of 12

---

[3]In practice, the LF for the last activity is set equal to the project due date, or deadline. However, it is also instructive to set the LF of the last activity equal to its EF time, so that the critical path will have no slack.

Figure 20-3   Latest Start, Latest Finish Time

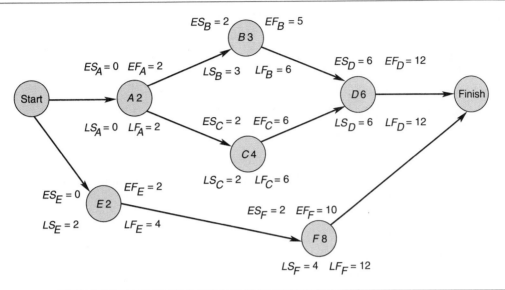

days. Since activity D takes 6 days, the LS for activity D is $12 - 6$, or 6. Activity F takes 8 days, so the LS for F is $12 - 8$, or 4. The LF for both B and C is 6, since they both have the same successor activity. The LS for activity B is $6 - 3$, or 3; and the LS for activity C is $6 - 4$, or 2. Activity A's LF is the smallest of the LS values of its immediate successors; the smaller of 3 and 2 is 2. Since activity A takes 2 days, the LS for A is $2 - 2$, or 0. Finally, the LF for activity E is 4, and its LS is 2.

Slack and Critical Path

Slack refers to the number of days an activity can be delayed without forcing the total project to be delayed beyond its due date. After the ES, EF, LS, and LF have been calculated for each activity in the project, the slack for each activity is calculated as the difference between the LS and the ES for that activity (or equivalently, the difference between the LF and the EF). In our example, we specified that the project deadline was the length of the critical path, or 12 days. Thus, there will be zero slack for those activities on the critical path. Table 20-2 presents the slack for each activity in our example. Activity B has slack of one day; activities E and F have slack of two days; and activities A, C, and D have zero slack. If the project deadline is set equal to the length of the critical path, then all activities with zero slack must be on the critical path, since the definition of the critical path implies that any delay in a critical activity will delay the total project. Conversely, any activity that has positive slack may be

Table 20–2   **Slack for Activities**

Activity	LS	ES	Slack
A	0	0	0
B	3	2	1
C	2	2	0
D	6	6	0
E	2	0	2
F	4	2	2

delayed beyond its ES by an amount of time up to the amount of slack, since such a delay will by itself have no effect on the duration of the total project.

The concept of slack for an activity assumes all other activities are completed in their planned times. Thus, if several activities are in series, any slack is "shared" among them. Once one such activity uses up its slack, the other activities in series will have zero slack. In our example, activities E and F share two days of slack.

The algorithm to compute slack and find the critical path for a network diagram has been programmed for computer calculations, and a number of software packages are available for both large computers and personal computers. These packages offer many options in addition to calculating the critical path. The program may, for example, display the network diagram on the screen or print it. Most of the programs also incorporate other aspects of project management, such as recording the budgets for the various tasks, designating who is responsible for each task, indicating whether or not the budgets have been met, and creating charts showing the time sequence of the projects.

SUMMARY

A network diagram shows the various tasks in a project, with arcs indicating which activities must precede others. The ES, LS, EF, and LF times are the early and late start and finish times for an activity. The ES and EF times are obtained by working through the network, starting from the first task. For each activity, ES is the largest of the EF times for all preceding activities, and EF is the ES plus the time for the activity itself. The EF of the last task is the minimum project completion time.

The LS and LF times are obtained by working backward through the network. For each activity, the LS is the LF minus the activity time, and the LF is the smallest LS of immediate successor activities.

Slack time is the difference between ES and LS for each activity. Activities with zero slack time are on the critical path.

Time-Cost Trade-Offs

In the analysis above, we have assumed that the time needed to complete any activity was fixed. Sometimes this is true; but more generally, management can alter the time needed to complete an activity by allocating more resources to

Table 20–3   Activity Times and Costs

	Time Required		Cost (dollars)	
Activity	Regular Program	Crash Program	Regular Program	Crash Program
A	2	1½	$ 100	$ 150
B	3	2	200	250
C	4	3	300	375
D	6	4½	500	740
E	2	1½	180	210
F	8	5½	1,000	1,200
			$2,280	$2,925

the task. For example, an activity—the painting of a house—may be assigned six days. However, this time can be shortened if more painters are assigned to the task or if they are scheduled to work overtime. The time for most activities may be thus shortened, usually at an increase in cost.[4] In this section, we shall examine how a manager might allocate resources to shorten the total project time.

To do this, let us consider the same example that we have been using. However, we shall allow the possibility that each activity may be done on a hurry-up or "crash" basis.[5] The times and costs for the regular and crash programs are given in Table 20–3.

Recall that the critical path is *ACD* and has a length of 12 days. This is under the assumption that the regular programs are used for each activity. In this case, the cost may be obtained by adding the figures in the fourth column of Table 20–3. The total is $2,280. Now, suppose that the manager of the project decides that 12 days is too long and that the project has to be completed in a shorter period. A shorter project completion time can be obtained by doing some of the activities on a crash basis, while incurring the additional cost of doing so. But which activities should be done on a crash basis?

The activities *not* on the critical path already have slack time. Cutting down the time needed for these activities would have no effect on the total project time. So the manager needs to examine only those activities *on* the critical path. Shortening the time of any activity on the critical path will shorten total project

---

[4]Note that the activity times are now assumed to be controllable but are still deterministic; that is, they still have no random components. Case II will consider the situation in which activity times are random variables.

[5]Here we assume an activity is either crashed or not. However, if activity crashing can occur proportionally (for example, a 40 percent crashing effort), then it is possible to formulate the deterministic time-cost trade-off problem (Case I) as a linear programming problem; see J. O. McClain and L. J. Thomas, *Operations Management: Production of Goods and Services*, 2nd ed. (Englewood Cliffs, N.J.: Prentice Hall, 1985), Chapter 3.

Table 20–4 **Incremental Costs for Crash Program**

Activity	Days Shortened by Crash Program	Incremental Cost of Crash Program	Incremental Cost per Day Shortened
A	½	$ 50	$100
C	1	75	75
D	1½	240	160

Figure 20–4 **Network with Activity C Shortened to Three Days**

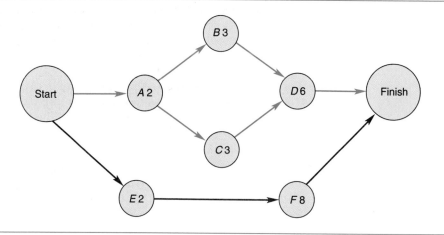

time. The three critical path activities, their incremental savings in days due to a crash program, and the incremental costs are shown in Table 20–4.

The last column of Table 20–4 contains the incremental cost per day shortened. This is obtained by dividing the incremental cost of the crash program for each activity by the number of days shortened. From Table 20–4, we can see that the activity that can be shortened most inexpensively on a per day basis is activity C. The cost per day for this is only $75, compared with $100 and $160 for activities A and D, respectively. If activity C is done on a crash basis, the total project completion time is cut by one day. The network now looks as shown in Figure 20–4. Both paths, *ACD* and *ABD,* are now critical, each being 11 days long. The cost of this crash program is $2,355, the additional $75 being the incremental cost of putting activity C on a crash basis.

If the manager wished to cut the project completion time further, more activities could be placed on a crash basis. The critical activities are now A, B, C, and D. Activity C cannot be shortened further. Shortening B would shorten the path *ABD* but would leave the path *ACD* unchanged at 11 days and hence, would not cut total project time. The project time can be cut only by reducing activities A or D. Referring to Table 20–4, we see that activity A is the less expensive.

Table 20–5   **Critical Paths and Costs for Alternative Programs**

Activities on:				
Regular Program	*Crash Program*	*Critical Path(s)*	*Project Completion Time*	*Project Total Cost*
All	None	*ACD*	12	$2,280
A, B, D, E, F	C	*ABD, ACD*	11	2,355
B, D, E, F	A, C	*ABD, ACD*	10½	2,405
B, C, E, F	A, D	*ACD, EF*	10	2,570
A, B, F	C, D, E	*ABD, ACD, EF*	9½	2,625
B, E	A, C, D, F	*ABD, ACD*	9	2,845

This reduction amounts to one-half day, with an additional cost of $50, making the total cost $2,405. The two reductions are summarized in the second and third rows of Table 20–5.

If the manager wished to reduce the project time even further, activity D would be placed on a crash basis. However, this would eliminate the need to have *both* A and C on a crash basis, since the critical path would shift to *EF;* path *EF* takes 10 days, whereas if A, C, and D are all crashed, path *ACD* takes only nine days. Thus, after deciding that activity D must be crashed to reduce the project time below 10½ days, the manager must review tentatively crashed activities A and C to ascertain which of these should be moved back to the regular program.

Assuming D and C are crashed (and A is not), then path *ACD* takes 9½ days, and path *EF* with 10 days is the critical path; the cost of crashing D and C is $2,280 + $75 + $240 = $2,595. However, suppose that D and A are crashed, and C is restricted to the regular program. Then path *ACD* takes 10 days, and there are two critical paths: *ACD* and *EF.* The cost of crashing A and D is $2,280 + $50 + $240 = $2,570. Thus, for a target of 10 project days, this alternative meets the target at lower cost. This example illustrates the complexity of making optimal time-cost trade-offs.

Since there are now two critical paths (*ACD* and *EF*), the manager must simultaneously shorten *both* of these paths in order to reduce further the project time. Consider each of these paths in turn. For path *EF,* activity E can be reduced by one-half day at a cost of $60 per day or activity F by 2½ days at a cost of $80 per day. Activity E is the less expensive, and the manager tentatively plans to crash activity E. Since this reduces path *EF* to 9½ days, the manager next considers ways to lower path *ACD* to 9½ days (or less). Path *ACD* will take precisely 9½ days if activities C and D are crashed. Now we must check to see whether any other paths have become critical. If activities C, D, and E are crashed, then path *ABD* becomes critical with time 9½ days. The fifth row in Table 20–5 shows this situation. All three paths are now critical; total project time is 9½ days, and total cost is $2,625.

Figure 20–5   **Time-Cost Trade-Offs**

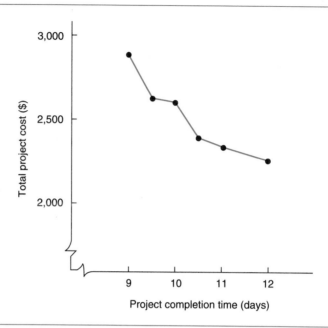

In order to reduce the total project time further, all three critical paths must be shortened simultaneously. This can be done by doing both activity A and activity F on a crash basis. Note that once activity F is crashed, activity E can be moved back to the regular program. The sixth line in Table 20–5 shows this situation. Total project time is nine days, with total cost of $2,845. It is not possible to reduce project time further. Activities B and E are at the regular program level; all others are on a crash basis.

Figure 20–5 summarizes the results of our analysis. The curve can be labeled a **time-cost trade-off curve,** indicative of the fact that the manager can have different project completion times, depending on how much the firm is willing to pay.[6]

The determination of the time-cost trade-offs above has been deliberately simplified in order to increase understanding of what is happening. But there is no reason why only two possible programs should be considered for each activity. There may be many alternative levels in addition to regular and crash programs. In fact, one could assume a continuum of possibilities, expressed by a straight line or other curve between the cost and time of the regular and crash

[6]Under our assumption that an activity is either crashed or not, only the points indicated in Figure 20–5 are feasible alternatives. The lines connecting the points are drawn only to give a proper graphic effect.

programs. Some PERT or critical path computer programs allow the user to find these resource-allocation or trade-off alternatives as a part of the solution of the critical path network.

SUMMARY

Management can allocate resources and incur additional costs to reduce total project time. By selectively reducing the time for critical path activities with the smallest incremental cost, the optimal trade-off function relating project time and cost can be developed.

Case II: Uncertain Activity Times

We now make a more realistic assumption concerning activity times; namely, that they are not known (or controllable) with certainty. Suppose activity times are treated as random variables. Then we need to obtain information concerning the probability density functions of these random variables before we may begin manipulating them. One technique to obtain such information is called the multiple-estimate approach.

Multiple Time Estimates for Uncertain Activity Times

Instead of asking for an estimate of expected activity time directly, three time estimates are requested, as follows:

a_i = Most optimistic time for activity i
b_i = Most pessimistic time for activity i
m_i = Most likely time for activity i (i.e., the mode)

Then Equation 20–1 is used to estimate the expected (mean) activity time:

$$t_i = (^1/_6)(a_i + 4m_i + b_i) \qquad \textbf{(20–1)}$$

where t_i is the expected activity time for activity i. For example, suppose the estimates for activity B are:

$$a_B = 1$$
$$b_B = 8$$
$$m_B = 3$$

Then the expected time for activity B is:

$$t_B = (^1/_6)(1 + 4 \cdot 3 + 8) = (^1/_6)(21) = 3.5$$

The most likely or modal estimate for activity B is 3, but the expected time for the completion is 3.5. This occurs because the pessimistic time estimate is quite large. The formula for expected time in Equation 20–1 is used because this formula approximates the mean of a beta distribution whose end points are a_i and b_i and whose mode is m_i. It is not possible to justify the use of the beta distribution in a rigorous sense, but the distribution has the following characteristics: It is unimodal, it is continuous, and it has a finite range. Intuitively, the formula in Equation 20–1 gives some weight to the end points (a_i and b_i) as well as the mode (m_i) in calculating the mean time for completion.[7]

The multiple-estimate approach is supposed to produce improved estimates of the expected time to complete an activity. In practice, it is not obvious that the multiple-estimate approach leads to a better expected value than the single-estimate approach; however, the multiple-estimate approach allows us to consider the variability of the time for completion of an activity. Equation 20–2 is used to estimate the standard deviation of the time required to complete an activity, based on the optimistic and pessimistic time estimates:

$$\sigma_i = (^1/_6)(b_i - a_i) \qquad\qquad (20\text{--}2)$$

where σ_i represents the standard deviation of the time required to complete activity i. Again, this formula is only an approximation used if the time to complete an activity is beta distributed. The value of the standard deviation is that it may be calculated for each activity on a path to obtain an estimate of the standard deviation of the duration of the path. For instance, suppose the multiple time estimates shown in Table 20–6 were made for the project in our example. The numbers in the table were chosen so that the estimated time, t_i, would be the same as the initial estimates in Figure 20–1. Thus, the critical path is still *ACD*, with an expected length of 12 days. Path *ABD* has an expected length of 11 days, and path *EF* has an expected length of 10 days. Table 20–6 contains the expected time for each activity and the standard deviation of time for each activity.

Some authors suggest computing the standard deviation of the length of each path. Starting with the critical path, if we assume that the activity times are independent random variables, then the variance of the time to complete the

Table 20–6   **Multiple Time Estimates**

Activity	a_i	b_i	m_i	t_i	$\sigma_i = (^1/_6)(b_i - a_i)$	σ_i^2
A	1	3	2	2	0.33	0.11
B	1	5	3	3	0.67	0.45
C	2	6	4	4	0.67	0.45
D	4	8	6	6	0.67	0.45
E	1	3	2	2	0.33	0.11
F	1	15	8	8	2.33	5.43

[7]Recently, Sasieni has demonstrated that the well-known formula in Equation 20–1 cannot be derived in general from the beta distribution; see M. W. Sasieni, "A Note on PERT Times," *Management Science* 32, no. 12 (December 1986), pp. 1652–53. Hence, Equation 20–1 should be interpreted as one reasonable way to estimate expected activity time from the three separate estimates a_i, b_i, and m_i.

critical path may be computed as the sum of the variances of the activities on the critical path.[8] In our example, the path ACD is the critical path. If we add the variances along this path, we obtain:

$$\sigma^2_{ACD} = 0.11 + 0.45 + 0.45 = 1.01$$

The standard deviation of the length of path ACD is:

$$\sigma_{ACD} = \sqrt{1.01} = 1.005$$

If there is a large number of independent activities on the critical path, the distribution of the total time for the path can be assumed to be normal.[9] Our example only has three activities, so the assumption of normality would not be strictly appropriate; but for illustration, our results may be interpreted as follows: The length of time it takes to complete path ACD is a normally distributed random variable with a mean of 12 days and a standard deviation of 1.005 days. Given this information, it is possible to use tables of the cumulative normal distribution to make probability statements concerning various completion times for the critical path.[10] For example, the probability of path ACD being completed within 14 days is:

$$F\left(\frac{X - \mu}{\sigma}\right) = F\left(\frac{14 - 12}{1.005}\right) = F(2) = 0.977 \text{ from Table A}$$

However, there is a major problem in performing this type of analysis on the critical path. Apart from the difficulties involved in assuming that all activity times are independent and beta distributed, it is not necessarily true that the longest *expected* path (i.e., the critical path) will turn out to be the longest *actual* path. In our example, the noncritical path EF has an expected length of 10 days. The variance of that path is:

$$\sigma^2_{EF} = 0.11 + 5.43 = 5.54$$

The standard deviation is:

$$\sigma_{EF} = \sqrt{5.54} = 2.35$$

If we assume that the distribution of the length of path EF is normal, then the probability of path EF being completed within 14 days is:

$$F\left(\frac{14 - 10}{2.35}\right) = F(1.70) = 0.955 \text{ from Table A}$$

---

[8]The variance of a sum of random variables equals the sum of the variances of each random variable if the variables are independent. See Chapter 3.

[9]The sum of n independent random variables with finite mean and variance tends toward normality by the central limit theorem as n tends toward infinity.

[10]See Chapter 7 for a review of the standardized normal variate:

$$Z = \frac{X - \mu}{\sigma}$$

Path *ACD* and path *EF* must both be completed within 14 days for the project to be completed within 14 days, since the project is not completed until all activities are completed. The probability that both paths (*ACD* and *EF*) are completed within 14 days is:

$$(0.977)(0.955) = 0.933$$

If we had considered only the critical path, the probability of not completing the project in 14 days would have been $1 - 0.977$, or 0.023. After path *EF* is also considered, the probability of not completing the project in 14 days is $1 - 0.933$, or 0.067, almost three times the probability of the critical path not being completed. Another way of describing the situation is to say that if the project takes more than 14 days, path *EF* has a larger chance of causing the delay than path *ACD* does.

A final difficulty remains. Path *ABD* may also turn out to be the most constraining path, and we could compute the variance of that path, as we did above for paths *ACD* and *EF*. However, there are two activities in common between path *ABD* and path *ACD* (activities A and D), and thus the lengths of the two paths are not independent variables. In order to calculate the probability that both path *ABD* and path *ACD* are completed in less than 14 days, we must deal with the joint probability of dependent events, and this is beyond the methods of calculation presented in this chapter. The problems we have encountered in a six-activity sample project are greatly magnified when a realistic project with hundreds of activities is considered. Thus, there is a serious danger in using the mean and variance of the length of the critical path to estimate the probability that the project will be completed within some specified time. Since some "non-critical" paths may in fact turn out to be constraining, the mean estimate of project completion time obtained by studying the critical path alone is *too optimistic* an estimate; it is biased and always tends to *underestimate* the average project completion time.

Fortunately, even though the analytical calculation of the distribution of the project completion time is exceedingly difficult in a real-size network, it is relatively easy to use the technique of Monte Carlo simulation (see Chapter 19) to obtain information about the likelihood of project duration when activity times are uncertain.

Simulation of PERT Networks

To overcome the problem described above, it is possible to simulate any PERT network. In general terms, the steps would proceed as follows:

1. Using (for example) a normal distribution of activity times for each activity, and using each activity's calculated mean and standard deviation from Equations 20–1 and 20–2, generate a random value (a realization) for the time to complete each activity in the network.
2. Treat the generated times as actual times for each activity, and use the critical path algorithm described earlier to find both the "actual critical path" (*ex post*) and the actual project duration.

3. Repeat steps 1 and 2 above for some large number of trials, recording a histogram of project completion times and the percentage of time each activity was on the *ex post* critical path.

Example Suppose a simulation were run 100 times for the sample network of the chapter, using means and standard deviations from Table 20–6. Figure 20–6 contains a representative histogram of the type that might be produced from the simulation. Although the information contained in Figure 20–6 would be useful in deciding whether or not the risk of project lateness were tolerable, it is of no direct help in deciding how to crash activities so as to speed the project. For this purpose, the simulation can record the percentage of times each activity was on the *ex post* critical path (that is, the path that actually turned out to be critical in a given simulation run). Table 20–7 is an example of such a record.

Activities E and F constitute one potentially critical path, and thus, have identical percentages in Table 20–7. Activities A and D are in series in two paths

Figure 20–6 Frequency Distribution for Project Duration

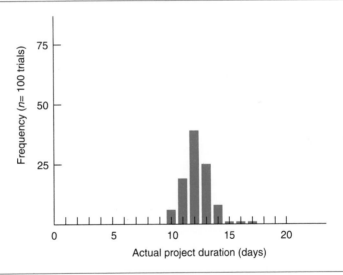

Table 20–7 Percentage of Time Activities Were Critical

A	71%
B	5
C	66
D	71
E	30
F	30

Table 20–8   Percentage of Time Activities Were Critical, Given Project
Duration > 12 Days

A	49%
B	3
C	46
D	49
E	54
F	54

(ABD and ACD), and hence, also have identical percentages. Activities B and C are in parallel, and thus, the sum of their percentages (5 percent + 66 percent) must add to 71 percent, which is the percentage for activities A and D in series with the B–C parallel link.[11]

Table 20–7 has been calculated using the entire simulation output. When considering which activities should be crashed to reduce the project completion time, it makes sense to consider only those simulation outcomes where the project was delayed beyond some desired target. Considering 12 days (the expected length of the "critical path") as our target, Table 20–8 contains illustrative data on the percentage of time each activity was critical, *given that the project took longer than 12 days to complete.* Note that these percentages will be different from those given in Table 20–7. Since we are less interested in "crashing" a project when it is completed prior to its expected date, the results of Table 20–8 would be more useful in determining which activity crashing would produce the largest reduction in delays beyond 12 days.

For a large network, a simulation of the regular program would produce a histogram like Figure 20–6. If the project performance needed to be improved, study of a table like Table 20–8 would indicate the set of activities that, on the average, were causing delays various percentages of the time. Then, after some of those "critical activities" were crashed, the simulation could be repeated to see whether or not project performance had been sufficiently improved.

SUMMARY   If the activity times in a PERT network are uncertain, then the length of the critical path calculated using deterministic estimates will understate the true expected project time. The probability distribution of the actual project time and the probability that each activity will be on the *ex post* actual critical path can be obtained by simulation. Conditional on the project being late, the simulation can also show the percentage of time each activity was on the actual critical path.

---

[11]This is true only if it is not possible for both paths ABD and ACD to be critical.

Evaluation of PERT

The PERT technique forces the planner to specify in detail the set of activities that constitute the project, and to estimate their times and state their sequencing requirements. The construction of the network diagram can often point out major problems in the project. If the critical path is longer than desired, the project can be replanned, with more resources committed to critical activities. Once the project has begun, the PERT technique may be used to provide periodic reports on the status of the project, including any changes in the critical path. If there is a path that is almost critical, the PERT technique can provide this information by pointing out activities with a small amount of slack.

The time estimates to perform activities constitute a major potential problem in the PERT technique. If the time estimates are poor, then the initial network diagram and initial critical path will have little real meaning after the project begins. Also, if there is uncertainty in how long it will take to complete the tasks, then this uncertainty must be taken into account in estimating the probability of project completion within any specified time. As we have seen, when activity times are random, one may compute the probability of the "critical path" being completed in any given time; but with random activity times, the actual *ex post* critical path may differ from the *ex ante* critical path. The best way of dealing with this complexity involves simulation of the network. In the simulation, both the probability of project lateness and the probability that each activity will be "critical" can be estimated, thereby providing guidance to the project planner.

Finally, the simple PERT technique does not consider the resources required at various stages of the project. For example, if a certain resource must be used to perform both activity B and C in our example, and if it can only be used for one activity at a time, then the diagram in Figure 20–3 is infeasible because activity C cannot be performed in parallel with activity B. Various extensions of the PERT technique have been developed that allow for resource constraints and that keep track of costs as well as time as the project progresses.

Many project managers experienced in using PERT and CPM now feel that the major advantages of the technique are in the planning stage of a project. Using PERT for active control of a project requires frequent updating and rerunning of the PERT calculations, whereas often a simple bar chart of progress to date can provide an adequate record for control purposes at much less cost.

Bibliography

Elmaghraby, S. E. *Activity Networks: Project Planning and Control by Network Flows.* New York: John Wiley and Sons, 1977.

Cleland, D. I., and W. R. King, eds. *Project Management Handbook.* New York: Van Nostrand Reinhold, 1983.

McClain, J. O., and L. J. Thomas. *Operations Management: Production of Goods and Services.* 2nd ed. Englewood Cliffs, N.J.: Prentice Hall, 1985.

Moder, J.; C. R. Phillips; and E. W. Davis, *Project Management with CPM, PERT, and*

PRECEDENCE Diagramming. 3rd ed. New York: Van Nostrand Reinhold, 1983.
Wiest, J. D., and F. K. Levy. *A Management*

Guide to PERT/CPM. 2nd ed. Englewood Cliffs, N.J.: Prentice Hall, 1977.

Problems with Answers

20–1. Consider the following data for the activities in a project:

Activity	Immediate Predecessors	Estimated Time (days)
A	—	5
B	A	4
C	—	7
D	B, C	3
E	B	4
F	D, E	2

    a. Draw a network diagram for the project.

    b. Compute the *ES, EF, LS,* and *LF* for each activity, assuming the *EF* and the *LF* for the last activity are the same. What is the minimum project completion time?

    c. List the activities that are on the critical path.

20–2. Consider the data in Problem 20–1, but suppose now that activity C takes nine days to complete rather than seven days.

    a. Does the critical path change?

    b. If activity C were to take 11 days to complete, would the critical path change?

20–3. You are given the following data concerning the activities in a project (numbers refer to days):

Activity	Immediate Predecessor	a_i	b_i	m_i
A	—	2	6	4
B	—	6	10	8
C	A	1	15	5
D	C	1	9	5
E	B	6	10	8

    a. Compute the expectation (t_i) and the variance (σ_i^2) of the time required to complete each activity.

    b. Draw a network diagram, and find the critical path by inspection. What is the expected length of the critical path?

    c. Assume the time required to complete a path is normally distributed. Compute the probability that path *ACD* will be completed in less than 16 days. Also compute the probability that path *BE* will be completed in less than 16 days.

    d. What is the probability that the project will be completed in less than 16 days?

Problems

20–4. The accompanying table contains a list of activities and sequencing requirements as indicated, which comprise necessary activities for the completion of a thesis.

    a. Draw a network diagram illustrating the sequencing requirements for the set of activities in the table. Be sure to portray activities by circles and sequencing requirements by arrows.

    b. Compute the *ES, EF, LS,* and *LF* for each activity, assuming the *EF* and the *LF* for the last activity are the same. What is the minimum project completion time?

(for Problem 20–4)

Activity	Description	Prerequisite Activity	Expected Time (weeks)
A	Literature search	None	6
B	Topic formulation	None	5
C	Committee selection	B	2
D	Formal proposal	C	2
E	Company selection and contact	A, D	2
F	Progress report	D	1
G	Formal research	A, D	6
H	Data collection	E	5
I	Data analysis	G, H	6
J	Conclusions	I	2
K	Rough draft (without conclusions)	G	4
L	Final copy	J, K	3
M	Oral examination	L	1

c. List the activities that are on the critical path.

20–5. Consider the following data for a project:

Activity	Immediate Predecessor	$t_i(days)$	σ_i
A	—	4.0	0
B	A	6.0	1.0
C	A	3.0	0
D	C	7.0	1.0
E	B, C	2.0	2.0

a. Draw a network diagram for the project.

b. Find the "critical path" (ex ante) by inspection. What is its expected length?

c. What is the probability that path ABE will be completed no later than day 15, assuming independence among activity times?

d. What is the probability that the entire project will be completed no later than day 15?

20–6. Consider the estimate of total project duration as calculated by the usual PERT algorithm (adding up expected time esti-

mates of all activities that are on the critical path).

a. Suppose you are dealing with a pure "series" network:

START → Ⓐ → Ⓑ → Ⓒ → . . .
Ⓧ → Ⓨ → Ⓩ → FINISH

Can you argue logically that the PERT estimate of total project duration is unbiased? (Hint: Recall that the expectation of a sum equals the sum of the expectations.)

b. Suppose you are dealing with a pure "parallel" network:

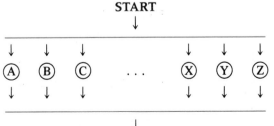

Assume that all activities in this network have the same expected time for completion. Can you argue logically that the PERT estimate of total project duration is biased in this case? In which direction is the estimate biased?

c. From your conclusion in (a) and (b), make a valid generalization about the bias (or lack thereof) inherent in a PERT project duration estimate when we have a large, complex network combining series and parallel portions.

20–7. A project is characterized by activities A through F. The predecessor activities and the times required, and costs for both a regular and a crash program for each ac-

tivity, are shown in the accompanying table.

a. Using only the times for the regular program activities, draw a PERT network for this problem. What is the critical path? How long will it take to complete the total project?

b. What is the cost of the project as given in (a)?

c. Find the time-cost trade-off points that are possible. What is the minimum time in which the project can be completed? What is the cost of this program?

(for Problem 20–7)

Activity	Predecessor Activities	Time (weeks)		Cost ($000s)	
		Regular Program	*Crash Program*	*Regular Program*	*Crash Program*
A (start)	—	0	—	0	—
B	A	5	3	10	22
C	A	2	1	6	15
D	B, C	3	2	6	15
E	B	4	2	10	25
F (finish)	D, E	0	—	0	—

More Challenging Problems

20–8. The Ocean Hardware Company was a chain of retail hardware and appliance stores. The company was considering the installation of a new computer system to do the payroll for the company, the sales accounting (paying for purchases and sending bills), and inventory record-keeping. The company controller was trying to lay out a schedule for the various tasks involved in putting the new computer system into operation.

The company planned to hire programmers to develop the payroll and accounting programs. However, an outside consulting firm was to be hired to do the inventory control program. Certain as-

pects of the inventory control program depended on the accounting program, and hence, it had to be developed after the accounting program was completed.

The job of completing each program involved preliminary work, final work, testing, revising, writing of manuals, and implementation. The new manager of the computer operations identified the list of tasks (activities) shown in the accompanying table that had to be performed, together with the times needed to accomplish each and the activities that had to be completed before the given activity could begin (the predecessor activities).

(for Problem 20–8)

Activity	Description	Predecessor Activity	Time to Complete (in months)
A	Analyze alternative computer systems, and order computer from the manufacturer	—	2
B	Wait for delivery of computer from manufacturer	A	4
C	Hire computer programmers	A	1
D	Do preliminary work on payroll program	C	1½
E	Do preliminary work on accounting program	C	2½
F	Do final work on both payroll and accounting programs	D, E	2
G	Hire outside consultant for work on inventory control program	A	1
H	Do preliminary work on inventory control program	E, G	2
I	Do final work on inventory control program	F, H	2
J	Do preliminary testing of payroll and accounting programs on rented machine	F	½
K	Revise payroll and accounting programs	J	½
L	Install and test computer upon delivery from manufacturer	B	½
M	Test payroll and accounting programs on installed computer	K, L	½
N	Prepare manuals describing payroll and accounting programs	J	1
O	Implement payroll and accounting programs	M, N	½
P	Test inventory control program on installed computer	I, L	½
Q	Prepare manuals describing inventory control programs	I	1
R	Implement inventory control program	P, Q	½
S	Done	O, R	0

a. How long will it take before the computer system with the three programs is completed? What activities are critical in achieving this time?

b. Suppose that management is concerned only with minimizing the time to get the accounting and payroll programs implemented. How long will this take? What activities are critical in this case?

20–9. Refer to Problem 20–3. Assume for purposes of this exercise that each activity time is equally likely between its a_i and b_i time estimates (i.e., ignore the m_i column, and consider activity times to be uniformly distributed over the appropriate range). Using the table of random digits (Table 19–2), perform a hand simulation of the network for 10 trials, recording for each trial the project completion time and the activities that were critical. Which

activities were critical the largest percentage of the time? Also compute the percentage of time each activity was critical, conditional on the project being delayed beyond 16 days.

20–10. A network for a project is shown in the accompanying figure. The t_i and σ_i attached to each node in parentheses represent the expected time and standard deviation respectively in months, of this segment of the project.

a. Identify the critical path, and calculate its expected length.

b. Assuming that the length of the "critical path" is normally distributed, calculate the probability that the *path* of (a) will be completed in less than 23 months.

c. Will the actual *project* be completed by 23 months:
(1) With the same probability as in (b)?

(for Problem 20–10)

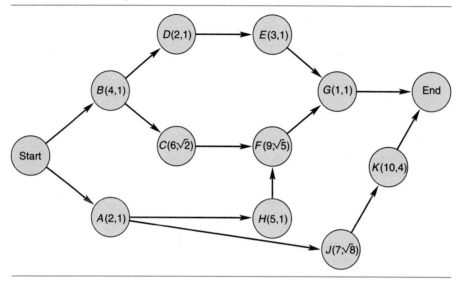

(2) With lower probability?

(3) With higher probability? Why?

d. Suppose you wish to reduce the probability that the project will take longer than 23 months. You can crash *one* of the following activities, and *only one*, by one month: A, C, E, or H. Which one would you choose to crash? Why? (*Note:* Assume that crashing will reduce the *mean* activity time by one month and leave the variance unchanged.)

20–11. In the project considered here, activity crashing can take place over a wide range of reduction times. The cost per day of reduction is given:

Activity	Immediate Predecessor	Normal Time (days)	Cost per Day to Crash	Lower Time Limit
A	None	3	$450	1
B	None	4	300	2
C	A	3	200	1
D	E	2	100	1
E	A, B	2	500	1
F	C, D	4	600	3

For example, activity C can be crashed from its normal time of three days down to as little as one day, or anywhere between; the cost per day to crash C is $200.

a. Draw a network diagram for this project. What is the critical path? How long will the project take, if no crashing takes place?

b. Determine the least-cost way to crash activities in order to complete the project in 11 days; in 10 days; in 9 days; in 8 days. Draw your results on a time-cost trade-off diagram.

c. Suppose the due date for the project is five days, and a penalty of $500 per day is assessed for each day late. What is the optimal number of days to crash the project? Why?

20–12. A firm is building a plant to produce a new frozen convenience food. The activities in the table on page 603 have been identified, the times estimated, and the precedence relationships established. How long will the project take? What activities are on the critical path(s)?

20–13. A project is composed of the five activities shown in the accompanying table. Probabilities have been assessed for the

(for Problem 20–12)

Activity	Description	Immediate Predecessors	Estimated Time (months)
A	Engineering design of building	None	1.5
B	Design of production line	None	1.0
C	Design of oven	B	2.0
D	Design of freezer	B	1.0
E	Design of packaging equipment	C, D	1.0
F	Order and manufacture of oven	C	9.0
G	Order and manufacture of freezer	D	8.0
H	Order and manufacture of packaging equipment	E	3.0
I	Submission and awarding of bids on building construction	A	2.0
J	Building construction (first phase)	I	9.0
K	Building construction (final phase)	J	1.5
L	Installation of oven	F, J	2.0
M	Installation of freezer	J, L	0.5
N	Installation of packaging equipment	H, J	0.5
O	Baking tests	K, L	1.0
P	Freezing tests	M, O	0.5
Q	Entire system test	N, P	0.5
R	USDA inspection	N, P	0.5

(for Problem 20–13)

	Time in Weeks							Expected Time	Predecessor Activities
Activity	4	5	6	7	8	9	10		
A	0.6	0.1	0.1	0.1	0.1			5	None
B		0.1	0.2	0.4	0.2	0.1		7	None
C		0.1	0.1	0.1	0.3	0.2	0.2	8	A, B
D	0.1	0.4	0.2	0.1	0.1	0.1		6	A, B
E	0.1	0.8	0.1					5	C, D

length of time in weeks that each activity will take, as shown in the table. Thus, for example, there is a 0.6 chance that activity A will take four weeks, a 0.1 chance that it will be completed in five weeks, a 0.1 chance that it will take six weeks, and so on.

a. Draw the network for this project. Note that there are four paths through the network. Using the expected times, calculate the time for each path. Which is the longest or critical expected path?

b. Assign random numbers to each out-

come (number of weeks) for each activity in accordance with the probabilities in the table (see Chapter 19).

c. Using the table of random numbers (Table 19–2), randomly select a time for each activity. Calculate the time for each of the four paths in the network, and record the time of the longest path and the activities on the longest path.

d. Repeat (c) 25 times (or the number of times assigned by your instructor). Calculate the average time for the longest path. Does it differ from that calculated in (*a*)? Why?

e. Calculate the percentage of time that each activity was on the longest path.

f. Conditional on the project being delayed beyond 21 days, compute the percentage of time that each activity was on the longest path.

20-14. This problem requires an understanding of linear programming problem formulation (see Chapter 10).

Consider Problem 20-11, in which activities may be crashed anywhere between the normal time and the lower time limit in a continuous fashion. Using the following notation, formulate Problem 20-11 as a linear programming problem.

Notation:

N_i = Normal time for activity i, $i = A, B, \ldots, F$

L_i = Lower time limit for activity i

z_i = Cost per day to crash activity i

X_i = Decision variable = Allowed time for activity i

ES_i = Earliest start time for activity i

ES_G = Project deadline (days) (treat this as a given constant)

21

Markov Processes

Some business situations can be modeled by describing separate classes, or states, with the system being in only one state at a time and switching among states being probabilistic. For example, a customer may purchase brand A, B, or C detergent, but any single purchase will involve only one brand. If the probability of the next purchase being brand A, B, or C depends only on the most recent purchase and not on earlier purchases, then the customer's purchase behavior can be modeled as a Markov process.

Markov processes can be analyzed to find both short-run and long-run future behavior, once the process has been specified. A simple Markov process is illustrated in Example 1.

Example 1   A machine that produces parts may either be in adjustment or out of adjustment. If the machine is in adjustment, suppose that the probability that it will be in adjustment a day later is 0.7, and the probability that it will be out of adjustment a day later is 0.3. If the machine is out of adjustment, the probability that it will be in adjustment a day later is 0.6, and the probability that it will be out of adjustment a day later is 0.4.[1] If we let state 1 represent the situation in which the machine is *in adjustment* and let state 2 represent its being *out of adjustment*, then the probabilities of change are as given in Table 21–1. Note that the sum of the probabilities in any row is equal to 1.

The process is represented in Figure 21–1 by two probability trees whose upward branches indicate moving to state 1 and whose downward branches indicate moving to state 2.

Short-Run Analysis

Suppose the machine starts out in state 1 (in adjustment). Table 21–1 and Figure 21–1 show there is a 0.7 probability that the machine will be in state 1 on the

---

[1]Assume the machine has a self-adjusting mechanism that functions imperfectly.

Table 21–1   **Probabilities of Change**

From \ To	In Adjustment (state 1)	Out of Adjustment (state 2)
In Adjustment (state 1)	0.7	0.3
Out of Adjustment (state 2)	0.6	0.4

Figure 21–1

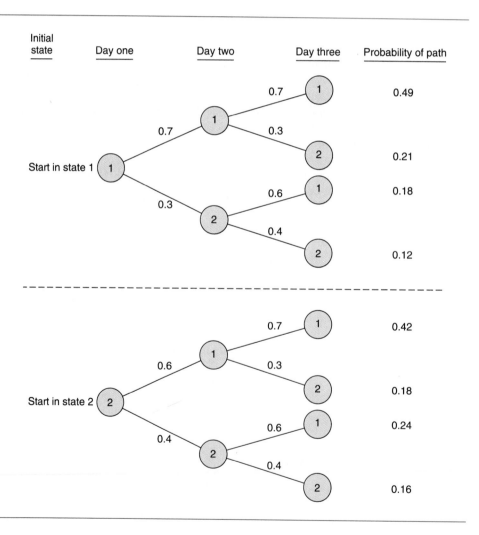

second day. Now, consider the state of the machine on the third day. The probability that the machine is in state 1 on the third day is $0.49 + 0.18 = 0.67$ (see the top half of Figure 21–1). This probability may also be computed as follows:

Let:

$$P\left(\begin{array}{c|c} \text{State 1} & \text{State 1} \\ \text{on day 3} & \text{on day 1} \end{array}\right) = \begin{array}{l} \text{Probability that the machine will} \\ \text{be in state 1 on day 3, } \textit{given } \text{that} \\ \text{it was in state 1 on day 1} \end{array}$$

Recognizing that:

$$P\left(\begin{array}{c|c} \text{State 1} & \text{State 1} \\ \text{on day 3} & \text{on day 2} \end{array}\right) = 0.7$$

and:

$$P\left(\begin{array}{c|c} \text{State 1} & \text{State 2} \\ \text{on day 3} & \text{on day 2} \end{array}\right) = 0.6$$

we have:

$$P\left(\begin{array}{c|c} \text{State 1} & \text{State 1} \\ \text{on day 3} & \text{on day 1} \end{array}\right) = (0.7)P\left(\begin{array}{c|c} \text{State 1} & \text{State 1} \\ \text{on day 2} & \text{on day 1} \end{array}\right)$$

$$+ (0.6)P\left(\begin{array}{c|c} \text{State 2} & \text{State 1} \\ \text{on day 2} & \text{on day 1} \end{array}\right) \qquad (21\text{--}1)$$

$$= (0.7)(0.7) + (0.6)(0.3)$$

$$= 0.49 + 0.18$$

$$= 0.67$$

The corresponding probability that the machine will be in state 2 on day 3, given that it started off in state 1 on day 1, is $0.21 + 0.12 = 0.33$ (see Figure 21–1). The probability of being in state 1 plus the probability of being in state 2 add to 1, since there are only two possible states in this example.

Given this information, the state probabilities on day 4 may be calculated as follows (see Figure 21–2):

$$P\left(\begin{array}{c|c} \text{State 1} & \text{State 1} \\ \text{on day 4} & \text{on day 1} \end{array}\right) = (0.7)P\left(\begin{array}{c|c} \text{State 1} & \text{State 1} \\ \text{on day 3} & \text{on day 1} \end{array}\right)$$

$$+ (0.6)P\left(\begin{array}{c|c} \text{State 2} & \text{State 1} \\ \text{on day 3} & \text{on day 1} \end{array}\right) \qquad (21\text{--}2)$$

$$= (0.7)(0.67) + (0.6)(0.33)$$

$$= 0.469 + 0.198$$

$$= 0.667$$

Figure 21–2

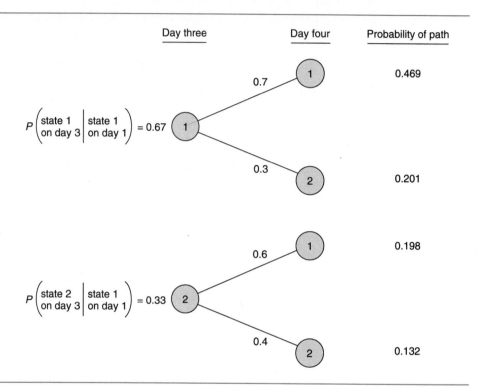

Table 21–2

Day number	Probability of Machine Being in State 1 on a Future Day, Given That It Started Off in State 1 on Day 1
1	1.0
2	0.7
3	0.67
4	0.667
5	0.6667
6	0.66667
7	0.666667
8	0.6666667

The corresponding probability that the machine will be in state 2 on day 4, given that it started off in state 1 on day 1, is $1 - 0.667 = 0.333$. This procedure may be continued to calculate the probability of the machine being in state 1 on any future day, given that it started off in state 1 on day 1. Table 21–2 contains the results of additional calculations.

Table 21–2 shows that the probability of the machine being in state 1 on any future day, given that it started off in state 1 on day 1, tends toward the value ⅔ as the day number increases.

Now, consider a related set of calculations for the probability of the machine being in state 1 on future days, given that it started out in state 2, the out-of-adjustment case. The probability that the machine will be in state 1 on day 3, given that it started off in state 2 on day 1, is $0.42 + 0.24 = 0.66$ (see the lower half of Figure 21–1); it may also be computed as follows:

$$P\left(\begin{array}{c}\text{State 1} \\ \text{on day 3}\end{array}\middle|\begin{array}{c}\text{State 2} \\ \text{on day 1}\end{array}\right) = (0.7)P\left(\begin{array}{c}\text{State 1} \\ \text{on day 2}\end{array}\middle|\begin{array}{c}\text{State 2} \\ \text{on day 1}\end{array}\right)$$

$$+ (0.6)P\left(\begin{array}{c}\text{State 2} \\ \text{on day 2}\end{array}\middle|\begin{array}{c}\text{State 2} \\ \text{on day 1}\end{array}\right) \qquad \textbf{(21–3)}$$

$$= (0.7)(0.6) + (0.6)(0.4)$$

$$= 0.42 + 0.24$$

$$= 0.66$$

The corresponding probability that the machine will be in state 2 on day 3, given that it started off in state 2 on day 1, is $0.18 + 0.16 = 0.34$ (see Figure 21–1). The state probabilities on day 4 may be calculated as follows, again assuming that the machine started off in state 2 on day 1:

$$P\left(\begin{array}{c}\text{State 1} \\ \text{on day 4}\end{array}\middle|\begin{array}{c}\text{State 2} \\ \text{on day 1}\end{array}\right) = (0.7)P\left(\begin{array}{c}\text{State 1} \\ \text{on day 3}\end{array}\middle|\begin{array}{c}\text{State 2} \\ \text{on day 1}\end{array}\right)$$

$$+ (0.6)P\left(\begin{array}{c}\text{State 2} \\ \text{on day 3}\end{array}\middle|\begin{array}{c}\text{State 2} \\ \text{on day 1}\end{array}\right) \qquad \textbf{(21–4)}$$

$$= (0.7)(0.66) + (0.6)(0.34)$$

$$= 0.462 + 0.204$$

$$= 0.666$$

The corresponding probability that the machine will be in state 2 on day 4, given that it started out in state 2 on day 1, is $1 - 0.666 = 0.334$. Table 21–3 contains the results of additional calculations.

Steady-State Analysis

Tables 21–2 and 21–3 show that the probability of the machine being in state 1 on any future day tends toward ⅔, *irrespective* of the initial state of the machine on day 1. This probability is called the long-run or **steady-state** probability of being in state 1; the corresponding probability of being in state 2 $(1 - ⅔ = ⅓)$

Table 21–3

Day number	Probability of Machine Being in State 1 on a Future Day, Given That It Started Off in State 2 on Day 1
1	0.0
2	0.6
3	0.66
4	0.666
5	0.6666
6	0.66666
7	0.666666
8	0.6666666

is called the steady-state probability of being in state 2. The steady-state probabilities are often significant for decision purposes. For example, if we were deciding to lease either this machine or some other machine, the steady-state probability of state 2 would indicate the fraction of time the machine would be out of adjustment in the long run, and this fraction ($\frac{1}{3}$ in our example) would be of interest to us in making the machine choice decision.

Calculation of Steady-State Probabilities

The steady-state probabilities for a Markov process may be derived in a more efficient manner than by completing such tables as Tables 21–2 and 21–3. We first write the general equation relating state probabilities for day n and the succeeding day $n + 1$, following the pattern of Equation 21–1:

$$P\left(\begin{array}{c}\text{State 1} \\ \text{on day } n+1\end{array}\middle|\begin{array}{c}\text{State 1} \\ \text{on day 1}\end{array}\right) = (0.7)P\left(\begin{array}{c}\text{State 1} \\ \text{on day } n\end{array}\middle|\begin{array}{c}\text{State 1} \\ \text{on day 1}\end{array}\right) \quad \text{(21–5)}$$
$$+ (0.6)P\left(\begin{array}{c}\text{State 2} \\ \text{on day } n\end{array}\middle|\begin{array}{c}\text{State 1} \\ \text{on day 1}\end{array}\right)$$

Next, we reason as follows: As the day number (n) increases to a very large number, the state probabilities for day n and for day $n + 1$ become nearly identical. As n approaches infinity, the probability of being in state 1 after n periods should be the same as the probability of being in state 1 after $n + 1$ periods. Thus, we write:

$$P\left(\begin{array}{c}\text{State 1} \\ \text{on day } n+1\end{array}\middle|\begin{array}{c}\text{State 1} \\ \text{on day 1}\end{array}\right) = P\left(\begin{array}{c}\text{State 1} \\ \text{on day } n\end{array}\middle|\begin{array}{c}\text{State 1} \\ \text{on day 1}\end{array}\right) \text{ as } n \to \infty \quad \text{(21–6)}$$

Substituting Equation 21–6 into Equation 21–5, we obtain:

$$P\left(\begin{array}{c}\text{State 1}\\\text{on day } n\end{array}\middle|\begin{array}{c}\text{State 1}\\\text{on day 1}\end{array}\right) = (0.7)P\left(\begin{array}{c}\text{State 1}\\\text{on day } n\end{array}\middle|\begin{array}{c}\text{State 1}\\\text{on day 1}\end{array}\right) \qquad (21\text{–}7)$$

$$+ (0.6)\left\{1 - P\left(\begin{array}{c}\text{State 1}\\\text{on day } n\end{array}\middle|\begin{array}{c}\text{State 1}\\\text{on day 1}\end{array}\right)\right\}$$

Solving:

$$P\left(\begin{array}{c}\text{State 1}\\\text{on day } n\end{array}\middle|\begin{array}{c}\text{State 1}\\\text{on day 1}\end{array}\right) = \frac{0.6}{1 - 0.7 + 0.6} = \frac{0.6}{0.9} = \frac{2}{3} \text{ as } n \to \infty \qquad (21\text{–}8)$$

It was not important that we assumed the machine started out in state 1; *in the steady state, the effects of the initial conditions disappear.* To demonstrate this fact, our computations are repeated, this time assuming that the machine started out in state 2:

$$P\left(\begin{array}{c}\text{State 1}\\\text{on day } n+1\end{array}\middle|\begin{array}{c}\text{State 2}\\\text{on day 1}\end{array}\right) = (0.7)P\left(\begin{array}{c}\text{State 1}\\\text{on day } n\end{array}\middle|\begin{array}{c}\text{State 2}\\\text{on day 1}\end{array}\right) \qquad (23\text{–}9)$$

$$+ (0.6)P\left(\begin{array}{c}\text{State 2}\\\text{on day } n\end{array}\middle|\begin{array}{c}\text{State 2}\\\text{on day 1}\end{array}\right)$$

and:

$$P\left(\begin{array}{c}\text{State 1}\\\text{on day } n+1\end{array}\middle|\begin{array}{c}\text{State 2}\\\text{on day 1}\end{array}\right) = P\left(\begin{array}{c}\text{State 1}\\\text{on day } n\end{array}\middle|\begin{array}{c}\text{State 2}\\\text{on day 1}\end{array}\right) \text{ as } n \to \infty \qquad (21\text{–}10)$$

Substituting Equation 21–10 into Equation 21–9, we obtain:

$$P\left(\begin{array}{c}\text{State 1}\\\text{on day } n\end{array}\middle|\begin{array}{c}\text{State 2}\\\text{on day 1}\end{array}\right) = (0.7)P\left(\begin{array}{c}\text{State 1}\\\text{on day } n\end{array}\middle|\begin{array}{c}\text{State 2}\\\text{on day 1}\end{array}\right) \qquad (21\text{–}11)$$

$$+ (0.6)\left\{1 - P\left(\begin{array}{c}\text{State 1}\\\text{on day } n\end{array}\middle|\begin{array}{c}\text{State 2}\\\text{on day 1}\end{array}\right)\right\}$$

Solving:

$$P\left(\begin{array}{c}\text{State 1}\\\text{on day } n\end{array}\middle|\begin{array}{c}\text{State 2}\\\text{on day 1}\end{array}\right) = \frac{0.6}{1 - 0.7 + 0.6} = \frac{0.6}{0.9} = \frac{2}{3} \text{ as } n \to \infty \qquad (21\text{–}12)$$

To simplify our notation, we shall let P_i represent the steady-state probability of being in state i. That is:

$$P_1 = P\left(\begin{array}{c}\text{State 1}\\\text{on day } n\end{array}\middle|\begin{array}{c}\text{State 1}\\\text{on day 1}\end{array}\right) = P\left(\begin{array}{c}\text{State 1}\\\text{on day } n\end{array}\middle|\begin{array}{c}\text{State 2}\\\text{on day 1}\end{array}\right) \text{ as } n \to \infty$$

$$P_2 = P\left(\begin{array}{c|c} \text{State 2} & \text{State 1} \\ \text{on day } n & \text{on day 1} \end{array}\right) = P\left(\begin{array}{c|c} \text{State 2} & \text{State 2} \\ \text{on day } n & \text{on day 1} \end{array}\right) \text{ as } n \to \infty$$

and so on.

Characteristics of a Markov Process

Example 1 demonstrates some properties of Markov processes. The basic assumption of a Markov process is that *the probabilities of going to each of the states depend only on the current state and not on the manner in which the current state was reached.* For example, if the machine is in state 1 on day 2, the probability of its changing to state 2 on day 3 is 0.3, irrespective of the state of the machine on day 1. This property is often called the property of *no memory.* There is no need to remember how the process reached a particular state at a particular period; the state of the process at a particular period of time contains all necessary information about the process and the likelihood of future changes.

A second characteristic of Markov processes is that there are initial conditions that take on less and less importance as the process operates, eventually "washing out" when the process reaches the steady state.[2] *The steady-state probabilities are the long-run probabilities of being in particular states,* after the process has been operating long enough to wash out the initial conditions. In deriving the steady-state probabilities for Example 1, we let the day number (n) tend toward infinity. In theory, the steady state would never be precisely reached, but the concept is useful. For example, if the initial state of the machine is unknown and the machine has been running for some time, then it is appropriate to assign initial-state probabilities that are equal to the steady-state probabilities. If the process is started by assigning steady-state probabilities to initial-state probabilities, then the probabilities of future states will all be equal to the steady-state probabilities.

It is important to distinguish between the steady-state probabilistic behavior of the process and the actual state values attained as the process operates. For

---

[2]We are assuming there are no "trapping states," where the probability of staying in a state is 1. With a trapping state, the initial state may be of importance. Also, we are assuming that the process is not cyclic. An example of a cyclic process is:

From \ To	1	2
1	0	1.0
2	1.0	0

Note that in this case, the process moves regularly back and forth between state 1 and state 2.

any particular set of days or time periods, the machine will take on a pattern of states, one on each day. When the process is analyzed before it is operated, however, then the steady-state probabilities are relevant. When one observes the machine and records the current state, this state becomes an initial state, and Tables 21–2 and 21–3 indicate the short-run probabilities of future changes. However, in the long run, the steady-state probabilities are of interest.

Example 1 has a discrete number of states (two), and potential changes occur once every time period (once a day in the example). We may describe these characteristics by saying that the process is discrete in state space (a discrete number of possible states) and in time (potential changes occur only once every time period). Sometimes the more precise label of *Markov chain* is used to distinguish this process from other Markov processes in which either the state space and/or the time periods between changes may be continuous instead of being discrete. In this chapter, we shall continue to use the general term *Markov process,* even though all of our examples will be discrete in state space as well as time periods between changes.

Steady-State Behavior of a Two-State Markov Process

For the case of a two-state Markov process, it is convenient to obtain general formulas for the steady-state probabilities in terms of the probabilities of change. Let:

p_{12} = Probability of going from state 1 to state 2
p_{21} = Probability of going from state 2 to state 1
P_i = Steady-state probability of being in state i

Then, following Equation 21–7, we may write:

$$P_1 = (1 - p_{12})P_1 + p_{21}(1 - P_1) \qquad (21\text{–}13)$$

Solving for P_1, we obtain:

$$P_1 = \frac{p_{21}}{p_{12} + p_{21}} \qquad (21\text{–}14)$$

Similarly, since $P_2 = 1 - P_1$, we can show:

$$P_2 = \frac{p_{12}}{p_{12} + p_{21}} \qquad (21\text{–}15)$$

Equations 21–14 and 21–15 are the general formulas for the steady-state probabilities of a two-state Markov process.

Example Consider Example 1 (at the start of this chapter) involving a machine that may be either in adjustment (state 1) or out of adjustment (state 2). The probabilities of change from one state to the other were given in Table 21–1. Substituting into Equation 21–14 to obtain the steady-state probability for state 1:

$$P_1 = \frac{p_{21}}{p_{12} + p_{21}} = \frac{0.6}{0.3 + 0.6} = \frac{2}{3} \qquad \textbf{(21–16)}$$

For state 2:

$$P_2 = 1 - P_1 = \frac{1}{3} . \qquad \textbf{(21–17)}$$

These answers are identical to the steady-state probabilities calculated earlier.

Use of Markov Processes in Decision Problems

Some decision problems can be solved by formulating a Markov process model of the situation and computing the steady-state probabilities from the probabilities of change. Let us extend our first example and assume that we have the alternative of leasing machine A (the one analyzed above) or machine B for the same annual cost. Suppose the probabilities of change for machine B are as shown in Table 21–4.

By comparing Table 21–4 with Table 21–1, we see that machine B has a lower probability of changing from the state of "In adjustment" to the state of "Out of adjustment" (0.2 versus 0.3). On the other hand, there is also a lower probability that the self-adjusting mechanism will correct itself and return to the in-adjustment state from the out-of-adjustment state (0.5 versus 0.6). It is not immediately clear which machine is more desirable to lease. However, let us calculate the steady-state probabilities for machine B. Using Equation 21–14, we obtain:

$$P_1 = \frac{0.5}{0.2 + 0.5} = \frac{0.5}{0.7} = \frac{5}{7} = 0.714 \qquad \textbf{(21–18)}$$

Now we may compare the steady-state probabilities of being in state 1 for machines A and B. Since machine B has a $5/7$ probability of being in adjustment in the steady state, whereas machine A has a $2/3$ probability, we would choose machine B (0.714 is greater than 0.667).

Table 21–4   **Probabilities of Change for Machine B**

From	*To*	*In Adjustment (state 1)*	*Out of Adjustment (state 2)*
In Adjustment (state 1)		0.8	0.2
Out of Adjustment (state 2)		0.5	0.5

Example 2 Suppose the manufacturer of a brand of coffee is considering an extensive advertising campaign designed to cause consumers to try that brand of coffee. From panel data obtained through market research, the firm has been able to estimate the current probabilities of consumers changing from "Our brand" to "Any other" and vice versa, as given in Table 21–5. Also, suppose that market researchers have estimated the corresponding probabilities that will exist after the advertising campaign has taken place, after taking into account any expected competitive reactions (see Table 21–6). Note that the probability of customers switching from "Any other" to "Our brand" has increased from 0.2 to 0.3, but the probability of retaining our current customers has not changed.

Suppose that the advertising campaign will cost $12 million per year, and that there are 50 million coffee purchasers in the market. For each customer, the average annual profit before taxes is $2. Should the manufacturer undertake the advertising campaign?

In order to solve this decision problem, we first calculate the steady-state probabilities that a customer will be buying our brand under the current conditions (no advertising campaign). Letting state 1 represent our brand and state 2 represent any other, using Table 21–5, the steady-state probabilities without advertising are calculated as follows, using Equation 21–14:

$$P_1 = \frac{0.2}{0.2 + 0.2} = \frac{0.2}{0.4} = \frac{1}{2} \tag{21-19}$$

Then, after the advertising campaign has taken place:

$$P_1 = \frac{0.3}{0.2 + 0.3} = \frac{0.3}{0.5} = \frac{3}{5} \tag{21-20}$$

Table 21–5   **Probabilities of Changing Brands of Coffee (no advertising campaign)**

From \ To	Our Brand (state 1)	Any Other (state 2)
Our Brand (state 1)	0.8	0.2
Any Other (state 2)	0.2	0.8

Table 21–6   **Probabilities of Changing Brands of Coffee (after advertising campaign)**

From \ To	Our Brand (state 1)	Any Other (state 2)
Our Brand (state 1)	0.8	0.2
Any Other (state 2)	0.3	0.7

The steady-state probabilities may be used to make an economic evaluation of the advertising campaign. If the campaign is undertaken, we shall incur $12 million of costs per year. The benefits of the campaign are that the steady-state probability that a purchaser buys our brand of coffee will increase from 50 percent to 60 percent.[3] If we have an additional 10 percent of the total market, that represents 5 million customers. Each customer represents average annual profit of $2, so that we shall obtain additional profits of $2 · 5 million = $10 million each year. The value of the benefits is less than the value of the costs ($12 million), and the advertising campaign should not be undertaken.

Extension of Example 2   Now, suppose the manufacturer were faced with an alternative campaign that also has $12 million of costs per year but would alter the probabilities of change as shown in Table 21–7. This advertising campaign increases the probability of retaining our own customers from 0.8 to 0.9, but leaves the probability of switching from any other brand to our brand unchanged.

In order to evaluate this second advertising campaign, we first compute the steady-state probabilities after the campaign, as follows, using Equation 21–14:

$$P_1 = \frac{0.2}{0.1 + 0.2} = \frac{0.2}{0.3} = \frac{2}{3} \qquad \textbf{(21–21)}$$

Since the steady-state probability that a purchaser buys our brand increases from ½ to ⅔, we expect to gain an additional ⅙ of the total market of 50 million people, or 8⅓ million people. A stream of payments of $16.67 million (i.e., $2 · 8⅓ million) per year is obtained. In this case, the value of the benefits ($16.7 million per year) exceeds the annual cost ($12 million), and the second advertising campaign is a profitable one to undertake.

Table 21–7   **Probabilities of Changing Brands of Coffee (after second advertising campaign)**

From \ To	*Our Brand (state 1)*	*Any Other (state 2)*
Our Brand (state 1)	0.9	0.1
Any Other (state 2)	0.2	0.8

[3]There is a problem in deciding how quickly the campaign will take effect. Here, we assume that the change is instantaneous; but if purchase decisions are made once a month, it could take three or four months of "transition" before we get close to the new steady state. The calculations could be modified to handle this complexity (see Tables 21–2 and 21–3 as examples of how to calculate short-run transition probabilities).

Example 3 A firm must decide whether or not to stock an infrequently demanded product. Each week, there may be demands for zero, one, or two units, each with the probabilities shown in Table 21–8.

If the firm stocks the product, it plans to use the following ordering policy: Order one unit when inventory on hand is zero. Assume that the carrying cost per unit per week is $100 and that the profit on a single sale is $500. Any demands that cannot be met from stock are lost. Units ordered at the end of one week arrive at the beginning of the next week. The firm needs to calculate the expected profits from stocking inventory in order to make the decision.

To solve this problem, we first specify the following state probabilities:

State 1: Zero units on hand at the end of the week and one on order; (0,1).
State 2: One unit on hand at the end of the week and zero on order; (1,0).

These two states exhaust the feasible alternatives if the firm follows its stated ordering policy; it would never have zero units on order when its inventory was zero, and it would never have more than one unit on hand. Now, using the probabilities of demand as given in Table 21–8, let us assume that it stocks the product. Then the probabilities of changing from one state to another from one week to the next are contained in Table 21–9. The reader should study the probabilities in Table 21–9 and determine how they are computed. For example, if we are in state 1 (zero on hand and one on order), then if zero units are demanded (probability 0.8), we shall have one unit on hand and zero units on order one week later (state 2). Thus, the probability of going from state 1 to state 2 is 0.8. If one unit is demanded (probability 0.1), then the unit on order will be used to satisfy that demand, and we shall have zero units on hand. However, our

Table 21–8

Units Demanded per Week	Probability
0	0.8
1	0.1
2	0.1

Table 21–9   **Probabilities of Change**

From \ To	State 1 (0, 1)	State 2 (1, 0)
State 1 (0, 1)	0.2	0.8
State 2 (1, 0)	0.2	0.8

decision rule is to place an order when inventory falls to zero. This action will take place if a demand for one unit occurs, and we shall return to state 1 (zero units on hand and one unit on order). Similarly, we shall return to state 1 if two units are demanded (probability 0.1), even though only one demand will be met. Thus, the probability of staying in state 1 is 0.1 + 0.1 = 0.2.

The change probabilities from state 2 are similar to those from state 1. Zero demand causes us to remain in state 2, while demand for either one or two units causes a move from state 2 to state 1.

Solution   The steady-state probabilities are obtained as follows:

$$P_1 = \frac{0.2}{0.8 + 0.2} = 0.2$$

The steady-state probabilities for state 1 and state 2 are 0.2 and 0.8, respectively.[4]

Now we may calculate the expected profit per week. When the process is in state 1, we have just sold one unit for a profit of $500. When the process is in state 2, we have just experienced zero demand, so we have incurred a carrying charge of $100. Thus, our weekly expected profit is:

$$EP = (0.2)(\$500) + (0.8)(-\$100) = \$100 - \$80 = \$20$$

Since the expected profit is positive, the manager should stock the product.

Steady-State Solution to Larger Problems

All the examples solved thus far in the chapter have involved only two different states. However, the same approach to a solution can be used for larger problems with three or more states. The only complication is that instead of having just one equation like that of 21–14, for larger problems there will be two or more simultaneous linear equations that, when solved, will produce the steady-state probabilities.[5]

Example 4   Consider the Markov process whose probabilities of change are contained in Table 21–10.

This is a three-state process; in order to find the steady-state probabilities, we write two equations that are similar in form to Equation 21–7:

---

[4]As shown in Table 21–9, the probabilities of going to state 1 and going to state 2 are the same in each row. Thus, these probabilities must be the steady-state probabilities. Whenever all rows of a transition probability table are identical, the steady-state probabilities may be obtained by inspection.

[5]The number of simultaneous equations to be solved will always equal one less than the number of states, since state probabilities sum to unity and therefore one of the unknown state probabilities can always be written as one minus the sum of all the others.

Table 21–10   **Daily Probabilities of Change**

To From	State 1	State 2	State 3
State 1	0.6	0.3	0.1
State 2	0.7	0.2	0.1
State 3	0.2	0.4	0.4

$$P\left(\begin{array}{c}\text{State 1}\\\text{on day }n\end{array}\middle|\begin{array}{c}\text{State 1}\\\text{on day 1}\end{array}\right) = (0.6)P\left(\begin{array}{c}\text{State 1}\\\text{on day }n\end{array}\middle|\begin{array}{c}\text{State 1}\\\text{on day 1}\end{array}\right)$$

$$+ (0.7)P\left(\begin{array}{c}\text{State 2}\\\text{on day }n\end{array}\middle|\begin{array}{c}\text{State 1}\\\text{on day 1}\end{array}\right) \quad \text{(21–22)}$$

$$+ (0.2)P\left(\begin{array}{c}\text{State 3}\\\text{on day }n\end{array}\middle|\begin{array}{c}\text{State 1}\\\text{on day 1}\end{array}\right)$$

$$P\left(\begin{array}{c}\text{State 2}\\\text{on day }n\end{array}\middle|\begin{array}{c}\text{State 1}\\\text{on day 1}\end{array}\right) = (0.3)P\left(\begin{array}{c}\text{State 1}\\\text{on day }n\end{array}\middle|\begin{array}{c}\text{State 1}\\\text{on day 1}\end{array}\right)$$

$$+ (0.2)P\left(\begin{array}{c}\text{State 2}\\\text{on day }n\end{array}\middle|\begin{array}{c}\text{State 1}\\\text{on day 1}\end{array}\right) \quad \text{(21–23)}$$

$$+ (0.4)P\left(\begin{array}{c}\text{State 3}\\\text{on day }n\end{array}\middle|\begin{array}{c}\text{State 1}\\\text{on day 1}\end{array}\right)$$

Equations 21–22 and 21–23 are two equations with three unknowns. However, since the sum of the probabilities must be 1.0, we may substitute for the third unknown as follows:

$$P\left(\begin{array}{c}\text{State 3}\\\text{on day }n\end{array}\middle|\begin{array}{c}\text{State 1}\\\text{on day 1}\end{array}\right) = 1 - P\left(\begin{array}{c}\text{State 1}\\\text{on day }n\end{array}\middle|\begin{array}{c}\text{State 1}\\\text{on day 1}\end{array}\right)$$

$$- P\left(\begin{array}{c}\text{State 2}\\\text{on day }n\end{array}\middle|\begin{array}{c}\text{State 1}\\\text{on day 1}\end{array}\right) \quad \text{(21–24)}$$

Letting P_1, P_2, and P_3 represent the steady-state probabilities, and substituting Equation 21–24 into Equations 21–22 and 21–23, we obtain:

$$P_1 = 0.6P_1 + 0.7P_2 + 0.2(1 - P_1 - P_2) \quad \text{(21–25)}$$

$$P_2 = 0.3P_1 + 0.2P_2 + 0.4(1 - P_1 - P_2) \quad \text{(21–26)}$$

which, collecting terms, are:

$$0.6P_1 - 0.5P_2 = 0.2 \qquad (21\text{--}27)$$

$$0.1P_1 + 1.2P_2 = 0.4 \qquad (21\text{--}28)$$

Equations 21–27 and 21–28 can be solved simultaneously to obtain the steady-state probabilities. Multiplying the second equation by six and subtracting it from the first to remove the P_1 term, we obtain:

$$-7.7P_2 = -2.2 \qquad (21\text{--}29)$$

or:

$$P_2 = \frac{2.2}{7.7} = \frac{2}{7}$$

and substituting $P_2 = \frac{2}{7}$ into Equation 21–27, we obtain:

$$0.6P_1 - 0.5(\tfrac{2}{7}) = 0.2 \qquad (21\text{--}30)$$

or:

$$0.6P_1 = {}^{24}/_{70}$$

so that:

$$P_1 = {}^4/_7$$

Finally, using the fact that the steady-state probabilities must sum to 1.0, we see that $P_3 = 1 - P_1 - P_2 = 1 - \frac{6}{7} = \frac{1}{7}$.

This same approach may be used in solving for the steady-state probabilities for Markov processes with a large number of states. The solution of simultaneous linear equations is a straightforward process even when the number of equations is quite large. Computers can solve such systems of equations rapidly.

SUMMARY In a Markov process, the probabilities of change depend only on the current state and not how the state was reached. Both short-run and long-run behavior can be analyzed and used to solve managerial decision problems. When more than two states are present, the long-run steady-state probabilities are obtained by solving sets of simultaneous linear equations.

Bibliography

Çinlar, E. *Introduction to Stochastic Processes.* Englewood Cliffs, N.J.: Prentice Hall, 1975.

Howard, R. A. *Dynamic Probabilistic Systems.* 2 vols. New York: John Wiley & Sons, 1971.

Karlin, S., and H. Taylor. *A First Course in Stochastic Processes.* Rev. ed. New York: Academic Press, 1975.

Kemeny, J. G.; A. Schleifer, Jr.; J. L. Snell; and G. L. Thompson. *Finite Mathematics with Business Applications.* 2nd ed. Englewood Cliffs, N.J.: Prentice Hall, 1972.

Ross, S. *An Introduction to Probability Models.* 3rd ed. New York: Academic Press, 1985.

Taylor, H., and S. Karlin. *An Introduction to*

Stochastic Modeling. New York: Academic Press, 1984.

Wolff, R. W. *Stochastic Modeling and the The-* *ory of Queues.* Englewood Cliffs, N.J.: Prentice Hall, 1989.

Problems with Answers

21–1. Two machines, A and B, are candidates for leasing. The two machines have differing probabilities of changing from an in-adjustment state (state 1) to an out-of-adjustment state (state 2), as shown below.

   Solve for the steady-state probabilities for each machine. Which machine would be the more desirable to lease?

21–2. The following transition probability table in the next column represents the behavior of department store customers in paying (or not paying) their monthly bills.

   a. What are the steady-state probabilities?

To / From	Paid (state 1)	Not Paid (state 2)
Paid (state 1)	0.95	0.05
Not Paid (state 2)	0.95	0.05

   b. Should the credit manager attempt to discontinue credit to those customers who have not paid previous bills? Why, or why not?

21–3. The Ajax Car Rental Company rents cars from three airports—A, B, and C. Customers return cars to each of the airports according to the following probabilities:

Probabilities of Change: Machine A (Problem 21–1)

To / From	In Adjustment (state 1)	Out of Adjustment (state 2)
In Adjustment (state 1)	0.9	0.1
Out of Adjustment (state 2)	0.6	0.4

Probabilities of Change: Machine B (Problem 21–1)

To / From	In Adjustment (state 1)	Out of Adjustment (state 2)
In Adjustment (state 1)	0.8	0.2
Out of Adjustment (state 2)	0.7	0.3

From \ To	A (state 1)	B (state 2)	C (state 3)
A (state 1)	0.8	0.2	0.0
B (state 2)	0.2	0.0	0.8
C (state 3)	0.2	0.2	0.6

a. Calculate the steady-state probabilities.

b. The Ajax Company is planning to build a maintenance facility at one of the three airports. Which airport would you recommend for this purpose? Why?

21–4. Consider Problem 21–3. Suppose there are 100 cars each at locations A, B, and C.

a. What will the expected distribution of cars be one time period later?

b. Two time periods later?

Problems

21–5. The ABC Ski Resort has found that after a clear day, the probability of stormy weather is 0.3, whereas after a stormy day, the probability of clear weather is 0.8. Write down the transition probability table. What are the steady-state probabilities for clear days and stormy days?

21–6. The following table contains various probabilities of a manager moving among three floors of a department store. Compute the steady-state probabilities.

From \ To	Floor 1	Floor 2	Floor 3
Floor 1	0.0	0.4	0.6
Floor 2	0.8	0.0	0.2
Floor 3	0.8	0.2	0.0

21–7. The Acme Company has obtained the following transition probability table for car rental customers:

From \ To	No. 1	Acme	All Others
No. 1	0.6	0.2	0.2
Acme	0.2	0.6	0.2
All Others	0.4	0.2	0.4

A typical customer rents a car once every six months. Solve for the steady-state probabilities.

21–8. The stock price for the XYZ Company has been observed for 100 days. Each day the price either goes up one point or falls by one point, according to the following probabilities:

From \ To	Up One (state 1)	Down One (state 2)
Up One (state 1)	0.4	0.6
Down One (state 2)	0.6	0.4

What are the steady-state probabilities?

21–9. Consider the XYZ Company stock in Problem 21–8. Suppose now that if the stock goes up on one day, the probability that it goes up the next day is 0.6; and if the stock goes down on one day, the probability that it goes down the next day is 0.5. Write down the transition probability table, and compute the steady-state probabilities.

21–10. Consider a Markov process with the following transition table:

From \ To	State 1	State 2	State 3
State 1	0.7	0.3	0.0
State 2	0.8	0.2	0.0
State 3	0.0	0.2	0.8

a. If the process starts in state 1, and a very large number of transitions occurs, what fraction of these transitions is from state 1 to state 2? (*Hint:* First, calculate the steady-state probability of being in state 1).

b. Repeat (*a*), assuming the process starts in state 2.

21–11. A cabdriver has found that if she is in town 1, there is a 0.8 probability that her next fare will take her to town 2 and a 0.2 probability that she will stay in town 1. If she is in town 2, there is a 0.4 probability that her next fare will take her to town 1 and a 0.6 probability that her next fare will keep her in town 2.

The average profit for each type of trip is as follows:

Within town 1: $1
Within town 2: $1
Between towns: $2

a. Write down the transition probability table for two states, and compute the steady-state probabilities for being in town 1 and town 2.

b. Use the two steady-state probabilities of (*a*) in conjunction with the transition probabilities to compute expected profit per fare.

c. Alternatively, set up the process as a four-state process by defining states as the type of trip encountered rather than the location. Write down the transition probability table for the four-state formulation. Is this approach an easier way to calculate the expected profitability than that of (*b*)?

More Challenging Problems

21–12. Refer to Problem 21–2. Suppose one set of customers (called "unpredictable") has the transition probability table of that problem, while another set (called "predictable") has the following:

Probabilities of Change—Predictable Customers

From \ To	Paid (state 1)	Not Paid (state 2)
Paid (state 1)	0.99	0.01
Not Paid (state 2)	0.49	0.51

a. What are the steady-state probabilities for the predictable customers? How do they compare to those of unpredictable customers?

b. Now suppose the department store has determined that it "breaks even" when the probability of payment is 0.949. If a new customer can be accurately classified as "unpredictable," should the store accept the customer for credit or not? Why?

c. Given the break-even probability of (*b*), should the store accept a new customer who is classified as "predictable" but whose state is unknown?

d. Given (*b*) and (*c*), suppose a new customer applies for credit and is predictable. Suppose also that the last state (paid or not paid) is known. Should the store accept the customer or not, depending on the last state? Why?

21–13. Refer to Example 3 in this chapter.

Consider the following order policy: Order two units if stock on hand is zero; otherwise, do not order. Set up the transition probability table for this case, and calculate the steady-state probabilities and the expected profit. [*Hint:* There are three states: (1) zero on hand and two on order; (2) one on hand and zero on order; and (3) two on hand and zero on order.]

21–14. Refer to Example 3 and to Problem 21–13. Consider the following policy: Order two units if stock on hand is zero; order one unit if stock on hand is one; order no units if stock on hand is two. Set up the transition probability table for this case, and calculate the steady-state probabilities and the expected profit.

21–15. Ajax Novelty Company is a mail-order shipper of a wide range of novelty and gift items. The company has a mailing list of 100,000 potential customers. Current policy calls for Ajax to mail its catalog to the complete list every six months. In the past, about 50 percent of previous customers order after any catalog mailing (a previous customer is one who placed an order in the past six-month period). On the other hand, only about 10 percent of persons who were previously noncustomers order. Typically, a customer places one order during a six-month period, and Ajax makes an average profit of $8 per order.

Ajax was considering changing current policies. Two new alternatives were considered for analysis.

The first possibility involved using a fancier catalog than previously. The cost of this would add 25 cents to the catalog cost (or $25,000 to the cost of a mailing). This change was not expected to affect the percentage of previous customers who reordered. However, the percentage of noncustomers who ordered was expected to increase from 10 to 15 percent.

A second alternative was to offer special discounts to previous customers. This would reduce the average profit from $8 to $7.50 for these customers, but the plan was expected to increase the number of customers from 50 percent to 60 percent. The plan would have no effect on previous noncustomers (the percent who order would remain at 10 percent, and profit would be $8 per order).

a. Consider the three plans presented above. Formulate each as a Markov process (i.e., define the states and give the transition probability table).

b. Estimate the profitability of each plan. Which should Ajax adopt?

21–16. A magazine made a profit of $2 on its regular one-year subscriptions. Eighty percent of subscriptions were renewed. The magazine was debating methods of obtaining new subscriptions. One method involved mail solicitation of po-

(for Problem 21–17)

From \ To	0 to 4 Years	5 to 8 Years	9 Years and More	Leaving Service
0 to 4 Years	.75	.05	0	.20
5 to 8 Years	0	.75	.10	.15
9 Years and More	0	0	.90	.10
Leaving Service	0	0	0	1.00

tential customers on selected mailing lists. The costs of mail solicitation would be $.25 per mailing. It was estimated that 5 percent of those mailed would become regular subscribers.

A second method involved personal solicitation of a selected group of potential customers. The cost of this would be $1 per solicitation, but 25 percent were expected to become regular customers. Which method should the magazine adopt? (*Hint:* Think about whether the steady-state probabilities or the transient probabilities are relevant to this problem.)

21–17. Suppose the Department of Defense has obtained estimates of the annual percentage of individuals reenlisting for longer tours of duty, as shown in the table on page 624.

In other words, each year, 75 percent of the individuals with 0 to 4 years of duty stay in that category, 20 percent leave, and 5 percent move to the 5–8 year category, and so on.

a. Compute the steady-state probabilities of each of the four states.

b. Given your answer in (a), can you suggest a modification of the Markov process formulation that would make the steady-state results of the model more useful for planning purposes?

21–18. Smokers and nonsmokers of various ages have been modeled as a Markov process, and the accompanying annual probabilities of change have been estimated.

a. Compute the steady-state probabilities of each of the five states.

b. Given your answer to (a), can you suggest a modification of the Markov process formulation that would make the steady-state results of the model more meaningful?

c. Suppose Stage 5 were redefined as "other" with row probabilities of change as follows: 1, 0, 0, 0, and 0. Explain what these numbers imply regarding the balance of births and deaths and the likelihood that a child turning age 10 is a smoker.

d. Compute the steady-state probabilities of the five states using the data as modified in (c).

e. An intensive advertising campaign discouraging smoking is aimed at teenagers; this campaign will alter the top row of probabilities to .85, .05, .1, 0, and 0. Compute the new steady-state probabilities (again with the last row as stated in (c)). Do you think that the implications of the row probabilities in (c) are still valid for (e)? Why or why not?

(for Problem 21–18)

From \ To	Stage 1	Stage 2	Stage 3	Stage 4	Stage 5
Stage 1: Nonsmokers, Age 10–19	.8	.1	.1	0	0
Stage 2: Smokers, Age 10–19	.05	.85	0	.1	0
Stage 3: Nonsmokers, ≥ Age 20	0	0	.98	0	.02
Stage 4: Smokers, ≥ Age 20	0	0	.10	.85	.05
Stage 5: Deceased	0	0	0	0	1

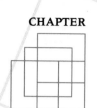

22

Dynamic Programming

In some decision problems, there may be a sequence of related decisions to make. Dynamic programming is a mathematical technique designed to solve such problems. The method of solution is to divide the total problem into a number of subproblems and to solve each subproblem in such a way that the overall optimal solution is obtained.

The basic ideas used in dynamic programming are illustrated by the following example.

Example 1: A Pricing Problem

Consider a problem involving pricing strategy. A firm must decide which price level to choose in pricing a new product over the next five years. It is considering four different prices: $5, $6, $7, or $8 per unit. After evaluating potential pricing moves by its competitors, it has constructed a payoff table, which relates its price in a given year to the present value of the profit expected that year. The payoff values are presented in Table 22–1.

Table 22–1   **Payoff Table ($millions)**

Price \ Year	1	2	3	4	5
$5	9	2	4	5	8
$6	7	4	8	2	1
$7	6	5	9	6	4
$8	8	7	1	7	3
	Decision 1	Decision 2	Decision 3	Decision 4	Decision 5

Figure 22–1   **Allowable Movements**

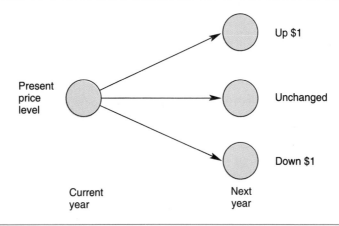

Under these circumstances, the firm should treat each year separately and choose the price in each year that maximizes the present value of its profit. However, suppose that the firm wishes to avoid making drastic changes in price from one year to the next, and it has decided that the change in price from one year to the next must not be greater than $1. For example, if the price in year 1 is $6, then in year 2 the price must be either $5, $6, or $7; it cannot be $8. Figure 22–1 illustrates the allowable price movements. The problem may be restated as follows: The firm must decide which way to move its price from one year to the next. The objective is to choose a set of prices over the five years that maximizes the present value of profits.[1] The basic concepts of dynamic programming can be used to solve this problem.

Basic Concepts

The three basic concepts used in dynamic programming are:

1. The total problem is divided into a number of subproblems.
2. Working backward from the natural end of the problem, each subproblem is solved in turn.

---

[1]This is a simplified example, and an alert reader might be able to obtain the correct answer merely by inspecting Table 22–1. To illustrate how complex even this small problem is, consider how the solution changes (if at all) if profits in year 2 with a price of $6 were 6 instead of 4. Or if profits in year 4 with a price of $5 were to be 7 instead of 5. Or make year 3's payoff with a price of $5, 7 instead of 4. It is difficult to determine the consequence of these changes without the use of the dynamic programming approach.

3. After each subproblem is solved, the answer is recorded, and the payoff (profit, cost, and so forth) from that stage on to the end of the problem is also recorded.

In order to apply the first concept to our example, our total problem is divided into a series of five subproblems. In our example, the five subproblems represent the five decisions on which way to move the price level. The bottom of Table 22–1 indicates the five decisions to be made on which way to move.

The second concept is applied by solving the last subproblem first, and working backward from the right-hand side to the left-hand side of the table. For example, the last subproblem is *which way to move when you are at one of the price levels in the fourth year*. This subproblem may be solved by studying each allowable move from each price level and choosing the move with the highest payoff. For example, from the $5 price level in year 4, it is better to move directly across to the payoff of 8 rather than down to the payoff of 1. From the $8 price level in year 4, it is better to move upward to the payoff of 4 rather than across to the payoff of 3.

The third concept is applied by recording a number in the upper left-hand corner of each box to represent the sum of the payoffs on the *best* path from that box onward. Consider the top box in the fourth year (the one containing five). Since the best move from this box is a move across to 8, we add 8 to 5 and record 13 in color in the upper left-hand corner of that box. Once that box is reached, the best path from that box onward to the end of the table has a sum of 13. We also record the best decision by drawing an arrow from that box across toward the value of eight. Table 22–2 shows this procedure carried out for all the boxes in column 4. For completeness, the numbers in column 5 have been placed in their respective upper left-hand corners.

Now we work backward and consider decision 4, the price to charge at the beginning of year 4. If this decision were approached without prior preparation, our answer might be the following: "It would depend on which way you planned to move after this move." But since the last decision has already been solved, the colored numbers in the upper left-hand corners of the boxes in column 4 may be used to represent the relative attractiveness of the various boxes in column 4. For example, consider the top box in column 3 (the one containing four). By studying the colored numbers in column 4, we see that it is better to move across and incur a payoff of 13 rather than down to a payoff of 10. Repeating our earlier recording procedure, the value of 13 plus 4, or 17, is recorded in color in the upper left-hand corner of the top box in column 3. We also record the best decision by an arrow from that box across toward the top box of column 4. By following this same procedure for the other boxes in column 3, we may solve decision 4. (See Table 22–2.)

Then we work backward again and begin to solve decision 3. Using the same procedure as above, the reader may fill in the upper left-hand corners of column 2 in Table 22–2 and draw arrows indicating the best move to make. The same procedure is used again for decision 2; and finally, decision 1 involves choosing

Table 22–2

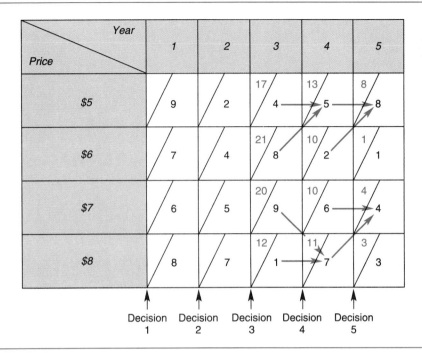

the largest of the values in the upper left-hand corners of the boxes in column 1. The completed solution is contained in Table 22–3. From Table 22–3, the optimal strategy is to begin with a price of $8 in year 1, keep it unchanged at $8 in year 2, change it to $7 in year 3, change it back to $8 in year 4, and change it to $7 in the fifth year. The profit from this strategy is recorded in color in the upper left-hand corner of the fourth box in the first column and amounts to 35. No other strategy results in a payoff this large. If for some reason the manager did not wish to set a price of $8 the first year, the next best alternative would be a price of $5. The payoff from starting with a $5 price and making optimal decisions from year 1 onward is 34, as recorded in color in the first box in column 1 of Table 22–3.

Formalizing the Dynamic Programming Technique

The dynamic programming technique is formalized by referring to stages, state variables, optimal decision rules, and optimal policies. **Stage** refers to the particular decision we are facing; in Example 1, there are five decision stages (see Table 22–1). A **state variable** is a variable defining the current situation at any stage. The state variable for Example 1 would be the current price level at a

Table 22–3

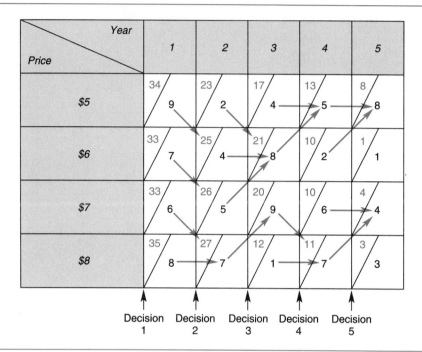

given stage. An **optimal decision rule** specifies which decision to make, as a function of the state variable and the stage number. The optimal decision rule for decision 5 (stage 5) in our example would specify: "Keep the price constant if the price is $5; lower the price if the price is $6; keep the price constant if the price is $7; and lower the price if the price is $8" (see Table 22–3). An **optimal policy** is a **set** of optimal decision rules that guides one's decisions through all stages of the entire problem. The optimal policy for Example 1 is the complete set of arrows in Table 22–3 that specifies the optimal moves to make through the five-year span of time.

Principle of Optimality

The principle behind the operation of the dynamic programming technique is called the **principle of optimality:**

> An optimal policy has the property that whatever the initial state and initial decision are, the remaining decisions must constitute an optimal policy with regard to the state resulting from the first decision.[2]

---

[2]R. E. Bellman, *Dynamic Programming* (Princeton: Princeton University Press, 1957), p. 83.

Table 22–4   Demand Requirements

Period n	Units Required D_n
1	2
2	3
3	2
4	4

The principle of optimality allows one to divide the total problem and solve the last decision stage, then work backward and solve the second-to-last decision, and so on, until the first decision is solved.

Example 2: An Inventory-Production Problem Suppose a firm is faced with demand for its product in each of the next four periods as shown in Table 22–4. It must decide upon a production schedule to meet these demands. In any period, the cost of production is $1 per unit plus a setup cost of $3. The setup cost is not incurred if zero units are produced. No more than six units can be produced in any period. The requirements can be summarized as:

$$\text{Production cost} = \begin{cases} \$3 + 1 \cdot X & \text{if } 0 < X \le 6 \\ 0 & \text{if } X = 0 \end{cases}$$

where X = Number of units produced.

In addition, there is an inventory holding cost of $.50 per unit per period. The firm has zero inventory on hand at the beginning of period 1 and wishes to have zero inventory at the end of period 4. The problem is to find a production schedule that will meet the demand requirements at minimum cost (production plus inventory costs).

Problem Formulation

We formulate this problem as a dynamic programming problem as follows:

Stages   Each period is a stage; $n = 1, 2, 3, 4$.

State Variable   The amount of inventory at the *beginning* of a period, designated by I_n.

Decision Variable   The production level each period, designated by X_n.

Optimal Decision Rule   (To be determined) This will specify the optimal production X_n^* as a function of beginning inventory. That is:

$$X_n^* = X_n(I_n)$$

for each period.

Note that the periods are linked by the inventory balance equation relating inventory in one period to that in the next:

$$I_{n+1} = I_n + X_n - D_n \qquad (22\text{--}1)$$

That is, opening inventory in the next period equals beginning inventory the period before plus production less demand for that period, where D_n is the demand in the nth period (Table 22–4).

The cost in any period is the sum of production and inventory costs:

$$\text{Period cost} = C_n(X_n, I_n) = \begin{cases} 3 + 1X_n & \text{if } X_n > 0 \\ 0 & \text{if } X_n = 0 \end{cases} + 0.5I_n \qquad (22\text{--}2)$$

Finally, let $f_n(I_n)$ represent the optimal (minimum) cost from the nth period to the end, given an inventory of I_n at the beginning of period n. For example, $f_2(3)$ would be the cost of the optimal production schedule from the second period through the fourth, given a beginning inventory of three units in period 2. This function $f_n(I_n)$ is called the **return function.**

Now we can write a series of equations defining the return function for each period. Let us begin at the last period of the process ($n = 4$):

$$f_4(I_4) = \text{Minimum } \{C_4(X_4, I_4)\}$$
$$0 \leq X_4 \leq 6 \qquad (22\text{--}3)$$
$$\text{and } X_4 + I_4 \geq D_4$$

Note the restrictions on X_n because of the production limitations ($0 \leq X_n \leq 6$) and because of the need to meet each period's demand from either production or inventory ($X_n + I_n \geq D_n$).

Backing up one period, the return function at period $n = 3$ is:

$$f_3(I_3) = \text{Minimum } \{C_3(X_3, I_3) + f_4(I_3 + X_3 - D_3)\}$$
$$0 \leq X_3 \leq 6 \qquad (22\text{--}4)$$
$$\text{and } X_3 + I_3 \geq D_3$$

For the general period n, the return function can be given as:

$$f_n(I_n) = \text{Minimum } \{C_n(X_n, I_n) + f_{n+1}(I_n + X_n - D_n)\}$$
$$0 \leq X_n \leq 6 \qquad (22\text{--}5)$$
$$\text{and } X_n + I_n \geq D_n$$

Problem Solution

This problem is solved starting with the last period and working backward. At each stage, the optimal decision is found, minimizing the cost for that period plus subsequent-period costs. This conforms to the principle of optimality stated above. Each stage involves finding an optimum value of X_n for each I_n.

To find the actual numerical solution to the problem, we start with period 4. Since the firm wishes to have no inventory at the end of the period, the production amounts are easily determined (Table 22–5). Recall that demand in period 4 is four units. Hence, only enough is produced to meet this need. Values of beginning inventory larger than four need not be considered.

We now turn to period three. Beginning inventory in period 3 can range from zero units on hand to six units. More than six units would be excess, since demand in periods 3 and 4 totals six units. We construct Table 22–6, which examines all feasible production plans.

Note that in Table 22–6, the optimum production amount is marked with an * for each level of beginning inventory. The costs under the "Subsequent costs" column are taken from Table 22–5.

The results of the analysis in Table 22–6 may be summarized in Table 22–7. Thus, for any beginning inventory, we have determined the optimal production schedule for periods 3 and 4.

We now turn to period 2. Beginning inventory can range from zero to four units. The four-unit upper limit results from the fact that at most, six units can be produced in period 1, and two of these must be used to satisfy period 1 demand. The analysis for period 2 is shown in Table 22–8. Note that the values in the column labeled "Subsequent costs" are the costs for periods 3 *and* 4, and are obtained from Table 22–7. A summary for period 2 is provided in Table 22–9.

Finally, we come to period 1. The analysis for this period is shown in Table 22–10. This table is short, since we have a known beginning inventory of zero units.

As can be seen from Table 22–10, the optimum production in period 1 is five units, and the total cost for all four periods is $20.5. The optimum schedule for periods 2, 3, and 4 can now be determined by working through Tables 22–9, 22–7, and 22–5:

Period	Beginning Inventory	Optimal Production	Ending Inventory = Beginning Inventory Next Period
1	0	5	3
2	3	0	0
3	0	6	4
4	4	0	0

We can check the cost of the optimal solution. There are two production runs (in periods 1 and 3) that cost (3 + 5) and (3 + 6), for a total of $17. Also, ending inventory holding charges (at the end of periods 1 and 3) are $0.50 \cdot 3$ and $0.50 \cdot 4$, for a total of $3.50. Thus, total production, setup, and holding costs are $17 + $3.50, or $20.50; this agrees with the optimal solution in Table 22–10.

Table 22–5   Period 4 Solution

Beginning Inventory I_4	Optimal Production $X_4^* = X_4(I_4)$	Cost		Total Cost $f_4(I_4)$
		Production	Inventory	
0	4	$7	$0	$7.0
1	3	6	0.5	6.5
2	2	5	1.0	6.0
3	1	4	1.5	5.5
4	0	0	2.0	2.0

Table 22–6   Period 3: Determination of Optimal Production

Beginning Inventory I_3	Possible Production Amounts X_3	Ending Inventory I_4	Cost in Period 3		Total $C_3(X_3,I_3)$	Subsequent Costs $f_4(I_4)$	Total Costs $C_3(X_3, I_3)$ $+ f_4(I_4)$
			Production	Inventory			
0	2	0	$5	$0	$5.0	$7.0	$12.0
	3	1	6	0	6.0	6.5	12.5
	4	2	7	0	7.0	6.0	13.0
	5	3	8	0	8.0	5.5	13.5
	6*	4	9	0	9.0	2.0	11.0*
1	1	0	4	0.5	4.5	7.0	11.5
	2	1	5	0.5	5.5	6.5	12.0
	3	2	6	0.5	6.5	6.0	12.5
	4	3	7	0.5	7.5	5.5	13.0
	5*	4	8	0.5	8.5	2.0	10.5*
2	0*	0	0	1.0	1.0	7.0	8.0*
	1	1	4	1.0	5.0	6.5	11.5
	2	2	5	1.0	6.0	6.0	12.0
	3	3	6	1.0	7.0	5.5	12.5
	4	4	7	1.0	8.0	2.0	10.0
3	0*	1	0	1.5	1.5	6.5	8.0*
	1	2	4	1.5	5.5	6.0	11.5
	2	3	5	1.5	6.5	5.5	12.0
	3	4	6	1.5	7.5	2.0	9.5
4	0*	2	0	2.0	2.0	6.0	8.0*
	1	3	4	2.0	6.0	5.5	11.5
	2	4	5	2.0	7.0	2.0	9.0
5	0*	3	0	2.5	2.5	5.5	8.0*
	1	4	4	2.5	6.5	2.0	8.5
6	0*	4	0	3.0	3.0	2.0	5.0*

*Indicates optimum for the given beginning inventory.

Table 22-7   **Summary for Period 3**

Beginning Inventory I_3	Optimal Production X_3^*	Ending Inventory I_4	Total Cost Periods 3 and 4 $f_3(I_3)$
0	6	4	$11.0
1	5	4	10.5
2	0	0	8.0
3	0	1	8.0
4	0	2	8.0
5	0	3	8.0
6	0	4	5.0

Table 22-8   **Period 2: Determination of Optimal Production**

Beginning Inventory I_2	Possible Production Amounts X_2	Ending Inventory I_3	Cost in Period 2			Subsequent Costs $f_3(I_3)$	Total Costs $C_2(X_2, I_2)$ + $f_3(I_3)$
			Production	Inventory	Total $C_2(X_2, I_2)$		
0	3	0	$6	$0	$6.0	$11.0	$17.0
	4	1	7	0	7.0	10.5	17.5
	5*	2	8	0	8.0	8.0	16.0*
	6	3	9	0	9.0	8.0	17.0
1	2	0	5	0.5	5.5	11.0	16.5
	3	1	6	0.5	6.5	10.5	17.0
	4*	2	7	0.5	7.5	8.0	15.5*
	5	3	8	0.5	8.5	8.0	16.5
	6	4	9	0.5	9.5	8.0	17.5
2	1	0	4	1.0	5.0	11.0	16.0
	2	1	5	1.0	6.0	10.5	16.5
	3*	2	6	1.0	7.0	8.0	15.0*
	4	3	7	1.0	8.0	8.0	16.0
	5	4	8	1.0	9.0	8.0	17.0
	6	5	9	1.0	10.0	8.0	18.0
3	0*	0	0	1.5	1.5	11.0	12.5*
	1	1	4	1.5	5.5	10.5	16.0
	2	2	5	1.5	6.5	8.0	14.5
	3	3	6	1.5	7.5	8.0	15.5
	4	4	7	1.5	8.5	8.0	16.5
	5	5	8	1.5	9.5	8.0	17.5
	6	6	9	1.5	10.5	5.0	15.5
4	0*	1	0	2.0	2.0	10.5	12.5*
	1	2	4	2.0	6.0	8.0	14.0
	2	3	5	2.0	7.0	8.0	15.0
	3	4	6	2.0	8.0	8.0	16.0
	4	5	7	2.0	9.0	8.0	17.0
	5	6	8	2.0	10.0	5.0	15.0

*Indicates optimum for the given beginning inventory.

Table 22–9 **Summary for Period 2**

Beginning Inventory I_2	Optimal Production $X_2{}^*$	Ending Inventory I_3	Total Costs Periods 2, 3, and 4 $f_2(I_2)$
0	5	2	$16.0
1	4	2	15.5
2	3	2	15.0
3	0	0	12.5
4	0	1	12.5

Table 22–10 **Period 1: Determination of Optimal Production**

Beginning Inventory I_1	Possible Production Amounts X_1	Ending Inventory I_2	Cost in Period 1			Subsequent Costs $f_2(I_2)$	Total Costs $C_1(X_1, I_1)$ + $f_2(I_2)$
			Production	Inventory	Total $C_1(X_1, I_1)$		
0	2	0	$5	$0	$5.0	$16.0	$21.0
	3	1	6	0	6.0	15.5	21.5
	4	2	7	0	7.0	15.0	22.0
	5*	3	8	0	8.0	12.5	20.5*
	6	4	9	0	9.0	12.5	21.5

*Indicates optimum for the given inventory.

Example 3:
A Breeding
Problem
Consider a decision faced by a cattle breeder. The breeder must decide how many cattle should be sold in the market each year and how many should be retained for breeding purposes. Suppose the breeder starts with a herd of 200 cattle. If cattle are bred, there will be 1.4 times as many cattle at the end of the year as at the beginning. The cost of breeding is $30 for each head of cattle not sold. Breeding takes one year, and the $30 cost includes all expenses of maintaining an animal and its offspring. Alternatively, the breeder may sell cattle in the market, at a price that depends on how many cattle are sold. If Y represents the number of cattle sold in a given year, then the price, P, is given by Equation 22–6:

$$P = 200 - 0.2Y, \quad 0 \le Y \le 1,000 \tag{22–6}$$

Assume that the breeder plans to sell the entire herd at the beginning of 10 years from now and retire, and that the buyer of the herd will pay $150 per head at that time. The breeder must decide how many cattle to sell in the market each year and how many cattle to breed so that profit is maximized. The time value of money is omitted in this example for clarity of exposition.

Formulation

This problem may be solved by dynamic programming. Define the following:

X_n = Size of herd at the beginning of year n (the state variable)

$f_n(X_n)$ = Maximum return from year n to year 10 when X_n cattle are in the herd at the beginning of year n and optimal decisions are made from year n to year 10 (the return function)

Y_n = Number of cattle to be sold at the beginning of year n (the decision variable)

$Y_n^*(X_n)$ = Optimal number of cattle to sell at the beginning of year n, given a herd size of X_n at that time (the optimal decision rule)

Note that n, the stage number, refers to the year in which a decision is being made; $n = 1, 2, \ldots , 10$. Also note that the maximum return, $f_n(X_n)$, is a function of both the stage number (n) and the current state variable (X_n), representing the size of the herd.

Starting at the end of the actual decision process, the size of the herd in year 10 is represented as X_{10}. Since the herd is to be sold at \$150 per head at the beginning of year 10, we may write:

$$F_{10}(X_{10}) = 150X_{10} \qquad (22\text{--}7)$$

Working backward, the decision at the beginning of year 9 and the corresponding maximum return from year 9 onward may be written as:

$$f_9(X_9) = \text{Max} \{\overbrace{(200 - 0.2Y_9) \cdot Y_9}^{\textit{Sell } Y_9} + \overbrace{[f_{10}(1.4(X_9 - Y_9)) - 30(X_9 - Y_9)]}^{\textit{Breed } (X_9 - Y_9)}\} \qquad (22\text{--}8)$$
$$0 \le Y_9 \le X_9$$

Equation 22–8 indicates that the maximum return available from year 9 onward, given a current herd size of X_9, is equal to the maximum amount that may be obtained by selling Y_9 cattle and breeding the remainder $(X_9 - Y_9)$. The terms in braces { } in Equation 22–8 represent the return from selling Y_9 cattle plus the gross return from breeding $(X_9 - Y_9)$ cattle, less the cost of breeding the $(X_9 - Y_9)$ cattle. Note that the gross return from breeding $(X_9 - Y_9)$ cattle is written as $f_{10}(1.4(X_9 - Y_9))$ and not $150(1.4)(X_9 - Y_9)$. This is done to emphasize that a **recurrence relation** is being developed between the maximum return at any stage (n) and the maximum return at the succeeding stage ($n + 1$). Figure 22–2 is an illustration of the decision at year 9. The optimal decision in year 9, denoted as $Y_9^*(X_9)$, will typically be a function of the herd size, X_9.

Working backward, a similar equation exists for the decision problem faced in year 8:

$$f_8(X_8) = \text{Max} \{\overbrace{(200 - 0.2Y_8) \cdot Y_8}^{\textit{Sell } Y_8} + \overbrace{[f_9(1.4(X_8 - Y_8)) - 30(X_8 - Y_8)]}^{\textit{Breed } (X_8 - Y_8)}\} \qquad (22\text{--}9)$$
$$0 \le Y_8 \le X_8$$

Figure 22–2

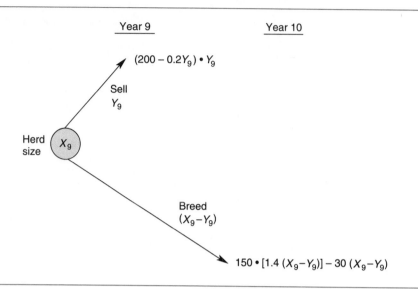

It is possible to write the equation in general for year n:

$$f_n(X_n) = \underset{0 \le Y_n \le X_n}{\text{Max}} \{\overbrace{(200 - 0.2Y_n) \cdot Y_n}^{\textit{Sell } Y_n} + \overbrace{[f_{n+1}(1.4(X_n - Y_n)) - 30(X_n - Y_n)]}^{\textit{Breed }(X_n - Y_n)}\} \quad \textbf{(22–10)}$$

$$\text{for } n = 1, 2, \ldots, 9$$

Equation 22–10 illustrates the basic recurrence relationship for our dynamic programming problem.

Solution

The set of equations represented in Equations 22–7 and 22–10 may be solved *recursively,* starting with Equation 22–7 and working backward. As each equation is solved, we must record both the optimal decision rule relating $Y_n{}^*$ to X_n and the maximum return obtained as a function of X_n.

First, solve Equation 22–7:

$$f_{10}(X_{10}) = 150X_{10}$$

We sell the entire herd at the beginning of year 10, regardless of its size. The solution to Equation 22–7 is trivial because the problem states that the breeder will sell his entire herd at year 10. Thus, $Y_{10}{}^*(X_{10}) = X_{10}$.

Next, consider Equation 22–8 for year 9; substituting the solution for Equation 22–7 into Equation 22–8:

$$f_9(X_9) = \text{Max } \{ \overset{\textit{Sell } Y_9}{\overline{(200 - 0.2Y_9) \cdot Y_9}} + \overset{\textit{Breed } (X_9 - Y_9)}{\overline{[150(1.4)(X_9 - Y_9) - 30(X_9 - Y_9)]}} \} \quad \textbf{(22–11)}$$
$$0 \le Y_9 \le X_9$$

or:

$$f_9(X_9) = \text{Max } \{200Y_9 - 0.2(Y_9)^2 + 210(X_9 - Y_9) - 30(X_9 - Y_9)\} \quad \textbf{(22–12)}$$
$$0 \le Y_9 \le X_9$$

Simplifying, we obtain:

$$f_9(X_9) = \text{Max } \{-0.2(Y_9)^2 + 20Y_9 + 180X_9\} \quad \textbf{(22–13)}$$
$$0 \le Y_9 \le X_9$$

The set of terms in the braces { } in Equation 22–13 is a quadratic equation. To find the value of Y_9 that maximizes our return, we may use calculus.[3] Take the first derivative and set it equal to zero:

$$\frac{d\{\ \}}{dY_9} = -0.2(2)Y_9 + 20 = 0 \quad \textbf{(22–14)}$$

so that:

$$Y_9{}^* = \frac{20}{0.4} = 50 \quad \textbf{(22–15)}$$

Thus, at year 9, the breeder should sell 50 head of cattle and breed the rest.[4] The maximum return from year 9 to year 10 may be calculated by substituting the optimal decision value into Equation 24–11:

$$\begin{aligned}
f_9(X_9) &= [200 - 0.2(50)] \cdot 50 + 210(X_9 - 50) - 30(X_9 - 50) \\
&= [190] \cdot 50 + 180(X_9 - 50) \quad \textbf{(22–16)} \\
&= 9{,}500 + 180X_9 - 9{,}000 \\
&= 180X_9 + 500
\end{aligned}$$

assuming X_9 is greater than 50. If less than 50 cattle are in the herd at year 9, then all should be sold.

Now consider the decision in year 8. We may write:

$$f_8(X_8) = \text{Max } \{ \overset{\textit{Sell } Y_8}{\overline{(200 - 0.2Y_8) \cdot Y_8}} + \overset{\textit{Breed } (X_8 - Y_8)}{\overline{[f_9(1.4(X_8 - Y_8)) - 30(X_8 - Y_8)]}} \} \quad \textbf{(22–17)}$$
$$0 \le Y_8 \le X_8$$

---

[3]We could also use trial and error, but calculus is much more efficient for this particular problem.
[4]Note that in this example, the optimal decision in year 9 is not a function of the herd size as long as $X_9 \ge 50$. The marginal revenue from selling the 50th animal is $180.20. The incremental benefit from not selling it in period 9 is $180 (that is, $1.4 \cdot \$150$ less $30). If $X_9 < 50$, then $Y_9{}^* = X_9$; that is, all cattle should be sold in year 9 if there are fewer than 50.

Since $X_9 = 1.4(X_8 - Y_8)$ and we have established that $f_9(X_9) = 180X_9 + 500 = 180(1.4)(X_8 - Y_8) + 500$ by Equation 22–16, we may substitute this[5] into Equation 22–17 to obtain:

$$f_8(X_8) = \text{Max} \{(200 - 0.2Y_8) \cdot Y_8 + [180(1.4)(X_8 - Y_8) + 500 - 30(X_8 - Y_8)\}$$
$$0 \le Y_8 \le X_8 \tag{22-18}$$

or:

$$f_8(X_8) = \text{Max} \{200Y_8 - 0.2(Y_8)^2 + 252(X_8 - Y_8) + 500 - 30(X_8 - Y_8)\}$$
$$0 \le Y_8 \le X_8 \tag{22-19}$$

Simplifying, we obtain:

$$f_8(X_8) = \text{Max} \{-0.2(Y_8)^2 - 22Y_8 + 222X_8 + 500\} \tag{22-20}$$
$$0 \le Y_8 \le X_8$$

Again, the value of Y_8 that maximizes the return is obtained by setting the derivative of the term in braces in Equation 22–20 equal to zero, and solving for $Y_8{}^*$:

$$\frac{d\{\ \}}{dY_8} = -0.2(2)Y_8 - 22 = 0 \tag{22-21}$$

so that:

$$Y_8{}^* = \frac{-22}{0.4} = -55 \tag{22-22}$$

The value of Y_8 that maximizes the return is negative, but negative values are not allowed. Thus, we set $Y_8{}^*$ equal to zero for maximum feasible return. Then:

$$f_8(X_8) = 222X_8 + 500 \tag{22-23}$$

The reason we find that we should not sell any of the cattle for $200 is that an animal retained will lead to 1.96 animals in two periods, which when sold will bring $294 (that is, $1.96 \cdot \$150$). The cost of maintaining the animal the first period is $30 and maintaining 1.4 animals the second period is $42. Thus, the benefit from not selling now is $294 - \$72 = \$222$, compared with $200 obtained from selling now.

The solution process could be continued for year 7 and earlier years, each time obtaining the optimal decision $Y_n{}^*$. In this manner, the optimal policy or set of decision rules would be obtained. For this example, the optimal policy involves breeding all the herd every year until year 9 and selling 50 head in that year. The value of $f_1(X_1)$ for X_1 equal to 200 would indicate the maximum profit available to the breeder, assuming the optimal policy is followed for the 10 years.

---

[5] Strictly speaking, Equation 22–16 is valid only for $X_9 \ge 50$. When X_9 is below 50, it is optimal to set $Y_9 = X_9$; and the return function for that range could be written down. It turns out that the same solution for Y_8 is reached as is obtained in Equation 22–22.

Formulation and Solution of Dynamic Programming Problems

In order to formulate a managerial decision problem as a dynamic programming problem, it is necessary to divide the problem into a number of subproblems or decision stages, as the examples have shown. It is also necessary to be able to describe the state of the system by a state variable.[6] Finally, one must be able to write the general recurrence relation between the maximum return at one stage and the maximum return at the next stage; see Equations 22–5 and 22–10 as examples. The stage often refers to a time period, but need not necessarily represent time.

The actual numerical solution to a dynamic programming problem is rarely worked out by hand; a computer is generally required to perform the calculations. Sometimes the particular structure of a problem will allow the maximization or minimization in the recurrence relation to be performed by calculus, as in our third example, or by other analytical methods. At other times, it may be necessary to program a computer to search over a grid of allowable values in order to determine the optimal decision by trial and error. This search procedure was used in our first and second examples, where we simply looked at all the available possibilities and chose the one with the highest payoff at each stage.

Although the basic concepts of dynamic programming are present in every dynamic programming formulation and solution, the actual numerical procedures used for solution may vary widely, depending on the problem being solved. For this reason, no prepared computer software exists for the solution of dynamic programming problems comparable to well-known software for solving linear programming problems. In fact, a dynamic programming problem is not nearly so well defined as a linear programming problem; all one knows is that decision stages are present, a state variable exists, and recurrence relations have been recorded. The complexity of the recurrence relations determines in large part whether the dynamic programming problem is easy to solve, hard to solve, or impossible to solve.

Dynamic Programming under Uncertainty

It is possible to expand the range of problems that may be formulated as dynamic programming problems to include problems where uncertainty exists (in the sense of a known probability distribution). The particular maximization or minimization in the recurrence relation may contain random variables. The following example illustrates the use of dynamic programming under uncertainty.

---

[6]The state variable may actually be more than one variable, but if its dimensionality exceeds two or three, then it is very difficult to obtain numerical solutions.

Example 4:
A
Purchasing
Problem
A firm must obtain a raw material in five weeks. The price of the raw material varies each week, according to the probabilities in the following table, but the price in any week is independent of that in other weeks. If the firm decides to purchase the raw material at the end of a week, it pays the price that prevails in that week.

Price	Probability
$500	0.3
600	0.3
700	0.4

If it chooses to delay its purchase, it must obtain the raw material in some future week, at whatever price prevails when it decides to purchase the material. If the firm has not purchased the material before week 5, it is forced to purchase it at the end of week 5, since the material is needed for production. The objective is to find a purchasing policy that will minimize the expected cost of the material.

Formulation

This problem may be solved by dynamic programming. Let:

$$n = \text{Week number; } n = 1, 2, \ldots , 5 \text{ (the stage number)}$$
$$X_n = \text{Price observed in week } n \text{ (the state variable)}$$
$$f_n(X_n) = \text{Minimum expected cost if price observed in week } n \text{ is } X_n \text{ and an optimal policy is followed from week } n \text{ to the end of the process (the return function)}$$

We work backward and consider the last week (week 5):

$$f_5(X_5) = X_5 \tag{22-24}$$

since the firm must purchase the material in week 5 if it has not already done so.

Now, in the next-to-last week (week 4):

$$f_4(X_4) = \text{Min} \{\underset{Act}{X_4}; \quad \underset{Wait}{(500) \cdot (0.3) + (600) \cdot (0.3) + (700) \cdot (0.4)}\} \tag{22-25}$$

That is, the firm may either act and obtain the price X_4, or wait and obtain the expected value of the price in the last week. Let us rewrite Equation 22-25 in terms of $f_5(X_5) = X_5$:

$$f_4(X_4) = \text{Min} \{\underset{Act}{X_4}; \quad \underset{Wait}{f_5(500) \cdot (0.3) + f_5(600) \cdot (0.3) + f_5(700) \cdot (0.4)}\} \tag{22-26}$$

Figure 22-3 illustrates the alternatives faced in week 4.

Figure 22–3

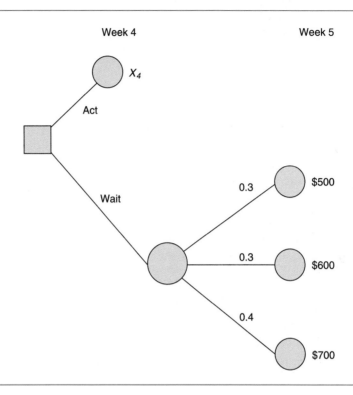

The situation in week 3 is:

$$f_3(X_3) = \text{Min}\{\overset{Act}{X_3};\ \overset{Wait}{f_4(500) \cdot (0.3) + f_4(600) \cdot (0.3) + f_4(700) \cdot (0.4)}\} \quad (22\text{–}27)$$

and in general in week n:

$$f_n(X_n) = \text{Min}\{\overset{Act}{X_n};\ \overset{Wait}{f_{n+1}(500) \cdot (0.3) + f_{n+1}(600) \cdot (0.3) + f_{n+1}(700) \cdot (0.4)}\} \quad (22\text{–}28)$$

$$n = 1, 2, \ldots, 4$$

Solution

Equations 22–24 and 22–28 may be solved recursively, starting with Equation 22–24 and working backward. At week 5, the material must be purchased if it has not been purchased earlier. At week 4, Equation 22–25 holds. To perform the minimization involved in Equation 22–25, we set the values of the two alternatives ("Act" versus "Wait") equal to each other and solve for the break-even value of X_4, represented by X_{4b}:

$$X_{4b} = 500(0.3) + 600(0.3) + 700(0.4) \tag{22-29}$$
$$= 150 + 180 + 280 = 610$$

If the price in week 4 is below $610, the purchase should immediately be made; whereas if the price is above $610, the purchase should be delayed. It is necessary to record the minimum expected cost at week 4:

$$f_4(X_4) = \begin{cases} 500 \text{ if } X_4 = 500 \\ 600 \text{ if } X_4 = 600 \\ 610 \text{ otherwise} \end{cases} \tag{22-30}$$

Equation 22–30 states that the minimum expected cost as of week 4 is $500 if the price is $500, $600 if the price is $600, or $610 if the price is $700. Note that the value of $610 represents the expected price in week 5.

Now, consider week 3:

$$f_3(X_3) = \text{Min} \{ \overset{Act}{X_3}; \; \overline{f_4(500)(0.3) + f_4(600)(0.3) + f_4(700)(0.4)}^{Wait} \} \tag{22-31}$$

Substituting Equation 22–30 into Equation 22–31:

$$f_3(X_3) = \text{Min} \{ \overset{Act}{X_3}; \; \overline{(500)(0.3) + (600)(0.3) + (610)(0.4)}^{Wait} \} \tag{22-32}$$

Again, we find the break-even value for X_3, represented as X_{3b}, at which the two alternatives have equal value:

$$X_{3b} = 500(0.3) + 600(0.3) + 610(0.4) \tag{22-33}$$
$$= 150 + 180 + 244 = 574$$

If the price in week 3 is below $574, the purchase should immediately be made; but if the price is above $574, the purchase should be delayed. The minimum expected cost at week 3 is recorded as follows:

$$f_3(X_3) = \begin{cases} 500 \text{ if } X_3 = 500 \\ 574 \text{ otherwise} \end{cases} \tag{22-34}$$

At week 2:

$$f_2(X_2) = \text{Min} \{ \overset{Act}{X_2}; \; \overline{(500)(0.3) + (574)(0.3) + (574)(0.4)}^{Wait} \} \tag{22-35}$$

Thus:

$$X_{2b} = 500(0.3) + 574(0.3) + 574(0.4) \tag{22-36}$$
$$= 150 + 172.2 + 229.6 = 551.8$$

and:

$$f_2(X_2) = \begin{cases} 500 \text{ if } X_2 = 500 \\ 551.8 \text{ otherwise} \end{cases} \qquad (22\text{--}37)$$

Finally, in week 1:

$$f_1(X_1) = \text{Min} \{X_1; \overbrace{}^{Act} \quad \overbrace{(500)(0.3) + (551.8)(0.3) + (551.8)(0.4)}^{Wait}\} \qquad (22\text{--}38)$$

Thus:

$$X_{1b} = 500(0.3) + 551.8(0.3) + 551.8(0.4) \qquad (22\text{--}39)$$
$$= 150 + 166.54 + 220.72 = 536.26$$

and:

$$f_1(X_1) = \begin{cases} 500 \text{ if } X_1 = 500 \\ 536.26 \text{ otherwise} \end{cases} \qquad (22\text{--}40)$$

The optimal policy for the purchasing manager may be summarized as follows: If the price in week 1, 2, or 3 is $500, make the purchase immediately; otherwise, wait. If the price in week 4 is either $500 or $600, make the purchase immediately; otherwise, wait. If no purchase has been made by week 5, the purchase must be made at the price prevailing in week 5. If the optimal policy is followed, Equation 22–40 indicates that the minimum expected cost is $500 if X_1 equals $500, and $536.26 if X_1 is greater than $500. Prior to knowing X_1, the minimum expected cost is $500(0.3) + 536.26(0.7) = $525.38.

SUMMARY

Dynamic programming can be used to solve problems involving sequences of related decisions. Formulation of a dynamic programming problem requires defining stages, state variables, return functions, and optimal decision rules. Working backward, each stage is solved, and the payoff and the optimal decision is recorded. The technique can also be applied to problems involving uncertainty.

Appendix

The Use of Dynamic Programming in Markov Processes[7]

It is possible to use the technique of dynamic programming to optimize the short-run behavior of a Markov process with decisions. The following example illustrates the use of dynamic programming to solve a Markov process model where the solution depends on the initial state. In this type of problem, the short-run behavior is relevant to the decision.

Example Consider the machine described in Example 1 at the beginning of Chapter 21. Suppose the machine moves from state 1 (in adjustment) to state 2 (out of adjustment), and vice versa, with probabilities of change as given in Table 22–11:

---

[7]Chapter 21 on Markov processes should be read before this appendix is studied.

Table 22–11

From \ To	In Adjustment (state 1)	Out of Adjustment (state 2)
In Adjustment (state 1)	0.9	0.1
Out of Adjustment (state 2)	0.7	0.3

Assume that when the machine is in state 1 for a day, a profit of $200 is gained; whereas if the machine is in state 2 for a day, a loss of $600 is incurred. If the decision maker is concerned with the long run, one would proceed as in Chapter 21 and calculate the steady-state probabilities as follows, using Equation 21–14:

$$P_1 = \frac{0.7}{0.1 + 0.7} = \frac{0.7}{0.8} = \frac{7}{8} \qquad (22\text{--}41)$$

The expected daily profit in the long run would be:

$$\text{Profit} = (\tfrac{7}{8})\$200 + (\tfrac{1}{8})(-\$600) = \$100$$

Now, you have the option to add a repair crew to repair the machine when it is observed in state 2 (out of adjustment). You observe the machine at the beginning of the day, and the repair crew performs its repairs very quickly, so that a full day's operation in state 1 is completed after repair. (Assume that after a repair, the machine functions perfectly for one full day.) Assume the state transitions occur at the end of the working day. The cost of having the machine repaired each time is $850. Should the repair crew be added?

Steady-State Solution

If we are interested in the long-run, steady-state behavior of the system, this problem can be solved by specifying the transition probability table that would represent the option of adding the repair crew (see Table 22–12).

Since the repair is in fact performed quickly, we interpret state 2 as earning the $200 normally earned in state 1, *less* the cost of repair ($850), for a net cost of $650. The steady-state probability of state 1 is now:

$$P_1 = \frac{1.0}{0.1 + 1.0} = \frac{10}{11} \qquad (22\text{--}42)$$

The expected daily profit in the long run, assuming the repairs are performed whenever needed, would be:

$$\text{Expected profit} = (\tfrac{10}{11})\$200 + (\tfrac{1}{11})(-650) = \$122.73$$

Table 22–12

From \ To	In Adjustment (state 1)	Out of Adjustment (state 2)
In Adjustment (state 1)	0.9	0.1
Out of Adjustment (state 2)	1.0	0

Since this exceeds the $100 obtained without the repairs, the repair crew should be added.

Now, suppose we are only concerned with the next five days of operation, after which (for example) we may be planning to sell the machine. Now we need to know the optimal use of the repair capability over the five-day period. We must take into account the fact that the incremental value of being in state 1 versus state 2 will be affected by future decisions to repair or not to repair. In this type of problem, dynamic programming often provides an answer.

Dynamic Programming Formulation

Let:

n = Day number; $n = 1, 2, \ldots, 5$ (the stage number)
X_n = State variable indicating the state of the process (1 or 2) on day n
$f_n(X_n)$ = Maximum profit earned from day n to day 5 when the process is in state X_n on day n and optimal decisions are made from day n to day 5 (the return function)

At day 5:

$$f_5(1) = 200$$

$$
\begin{array}{lcc}
 & Repair & Do\ not\ repair \\
f_5(2) = \text{Max} \{ & -850 + 200, & -600\} \\
 = \text{Max} \{ & -650, & -600\} \\
 = -600
\end{array}
$$
(22–43)

Let us record the optimal decision rule as a function of the state variable, and let the optimal decision on day n be represented by $Y_n^*(X_n)$. Repair is possible only when the machine is out of adjustment (state 2). If one represents "Repair" and zero represents "Do not repair," then:

$$Y_5^*(2) = 0$$
(22–44)

That is, we do not repair on day 5.

Working backward, on day 4 we write:

$$f_4(1) = 200 + (0.9)(200) + [1 - 0.9](-600) = 320$$

(22–45)

	Repair	Do not repair

$$f_4(2) = \text{Max} \left\{ \begin{array}{ll} -850 + 200 + 0.9(200) & -600 + (0.7)(200) \\ \quad + [1 - 0.9](-600), & \quad + [1 - 0.7](-600) \end{array} \right\}$$
$$= \text{Max} \{ -530, \qquad -640 \}$$
$$= -530$$

Recording the optimal decision rule as a function of the state variable, we write:

$$Y_4^*(2) = 1$$

(22–46)

Note that the decision to repair when the machine is out of adjustment was undesirable on day 5 but is desirable on day 4.

On day 3:

$$f_3(1) = 200 + (0.9)(320) + [1 - 0.9](-530) = 435$$

(22–47)

	Repair	Do not repair

$$f_3(2) = \text{Max} \left\{ \begin{array}{ll} -850 + 200 + 0.9(320) & -600 + (0.7)(200) \\ \quad + [1 - 0.9](-530), & \quad + [1 - 0.7](-530) \end{array} \right\}$$
$$= \text{Max} \{ -415, \qquad -535 \}$$
$$= \qquad -415$$

and:

$$Y_3^*(2) = 1$$

(22–48)

On day 2:

$$f_2(1) = 200 + (0.9)(435) + [1 - 0.9](-415) = 550$$

(22–49)

	Repair	Do not repair

$$f_2(2) = \text{Max} \left\{ \begin{array}{ll} -850 + 200 + (0.9)(435) & -600 + (0.7)(435) \\ \quad + [1 - 0.9](-415), & \quad + [1 - 0.7](-415) \end{array} \right\}$$
$$= \text{Max} \{ -300, \qquad -420 \}$$
$$= \qquad -300$$

and:

$$Y_2^*(2) = 1$$

(22–50)

Finally, on day 1:

$$f_1(1) = 200 + (0.9)(550) + [1 - 0.9](-300) = 665$$

$$f_1(2) = \text{Max} \begin{cases} \underline{Repair} & \underline{Do\ not\ repair} & \\ -850 + 200 + (0.9)(550) & -600 + (0.7)(550) & \\ \qquad + [1 - 0.9](-300), & \qquad + [1 - 0.7](-300) \end{cases} \tag{22-51}$$

$$= \text{Max}\{-185, \qquad\qquad -305\}$$

$$= \qquad -185$$

and:

$$Y_1{}^*(2) = 1 \tag{22-52}$$

The set of optimal decision rules $Y_1{}^*(2)$, $Y_2{}^*(2)$, . . . , $Y_5^*(2)$ constitutes an optimal policy with respect to the repair decision for a five-day horizon. Note that on day 5 it is not optimal to repair if the machine is out of adjustment, whereas on days 1 through 4 it is optimal to repair if the machine is out of adjustment. This situation occurs because the gain from repairing the machine has two components. First, the day's production is valued at $200 instead of − $600. Second, the machine is in state 1 at the end of the day rather than state 2, and future probabilities are more heavily weighted in favor of state 1. On day 5, the process stops, and the *future* value of ending day 5 in state 1 versus state 2 is worthless. On day 4, however, the future value of ending the day in state 1 has some value. A naive comparison of one-day benefits of $800 versus one-day costs of $850 would lead one to reject the repair alternative, whereas the dynamic programming analysis indicates precisely when the repair option should be taken.

Discussion

If the actual problem does not involve a finite horizon such as five days, then one may attempt to formulate the problem as two alternative Markov processes (as was done initially above with the repair option). If the dynamic programming problem cannot be formulated in this manner, there are two ways to modify our procedure. One way is to continue to work backward from some general day n to day $n - k$, and maximize the average daily return over the $k + 1$ days of operation. As we continue to work backward, eventually the maximum average daily return will approach a constant value, and the decision rule for the first day would be the appropriate one to use.

An alternative way to handle the infinite-horizon problem is to add discounting to the process. If the time value of money is taken into account, then each term representing future gains is discounted. As we work backward from n to day $n - k$, eventually the maximum present value of all returns will approach a constant value. Then the decision rule for the first day would be the appropriate one to use in the infinite-horizon case.

It should be noted that the first of these methods maximizes average daily return, and the second maximizes the present value of all future returns. If the discount factor is substantially less than 1, the two methods may produce different results, and the decision maker must decide which objective is appropriate.

Bibliography

Bellman, R. E. *Dynamic Programming*. Princeton: Princeton University Press, 1957.

Bellman, R. E., and S. E. Dreyfus. *Applied Dynamic Programming*. Princeton: Princeton University Press, 1962.

Denardo, E. V. *Dynamic Programming: Models and Applications*. Englewood Cliffs, N.J.: Prentice Hall, 1982.

Dreyfus, S. E., and A. M. Law. *The Art and Theory of Dynamic Programming*. New York: Academic Press, 1977.

Hillier, F., and G. J. Lieberman. *Introduction to Operations Research*. 5th ed. New York: McGraw-Hill, 1990.

Howard, R. A. *Dynamic Programming and Markov Processes*. Cambridge, Mass.: MIT Press, 1960.

Nemhauser, George L. *Introduction to Dynamic Programming*. New York: John Wiley & Sons, 1966.

Wagner, H. M. *Principles of Operations Research*. 2nd ed. Englewood Cliffs, N.J.: Prentice Hall, 1975.

Problems with Answers

22–1. A manager must decide on a pricing policy for a new product over the next four years. She is considering five different price levels: $12, $14, $16, $18, and $20 per unit. After evaluating potential price moves by her competitors, she has constructed the following payoff table, which relates her price in a given year to the present value of the profit expected that year.

Payoff Table

Price \ Year	1	2	3	4
$12	3	9	3	7
$14	2	1	2	2
$16	7	4	8	1
$18	9	2	6	4
$20	5	5	3	1

a. If there are no restrictions on price changes from year to year, state the optimal pricing strategy, and compute the maximum total profit.

b. Now suppose the manager wishes to avoid making price changes of more than $2 from one year to the next. Find the optimal policy, and compute the maximum total profit.

22–2. A cattle breeder has a herd of 400 cattle. He plans to sell his entire herd one year from now at $150 per head. He may sell cattle now at a price per head that is dependent on the number of cattle he chooses to sell. If Y represents the number he sells now, then the price he obtains per head will be:

$$P = 200 - 0.2Y, \quad 0 \le Y \le 1,000$$

Alternatively, any cattle not sold are bred at a cost of $30 per head, and the breeding ratio is 1.4 cattle resulting per head bred.

a. Compute the cattle breeder's profit if he sells all of his herd now.

b. Compute his profit if he sells none of his herd now.

c. Write down a general expression for his profit if he sells Y cattle now and breeds the remainder $(400 - Y)$. Simplify your expression as much as you can.

d. Substitute into your profit expression in (c) the value of $Y = 50$, and compute the profit when 50 cattle are sold now.

e. Now take the derivative of your expression in (c) with respect to Y, and set it equal to zero. Verify that the optimal number of cattle to sell now is 50.

f. This problem is a two-year version of the 10-year cattle-breeding problem discussed in this chapter. Equation 22–16 represents maximum total profit when there is one year left, as in our case:

$$f_9(X_9) = 180X_9 + 500 \quad \textbf{(22–16)}$$

where X_9 represents the size of the herd.

Substitute the herd size of 400 into Equation 22–16, and compute the maximum total profit for our problem. Your answer should be identical to the answer to (d).

g. Use Equation 22–16 to calculate the maximum total profit of a herd of 200 now.

22–3. Consider an inventory problem like that of Example 2 of this chapter. Suppose that the demand is as follows:

Month	Demand
January	4
February	5
March	3
April	2

The setup cost is $5, the variable production cost is $1, and the inventory holding cost is $1 per month. Further suppose that the beginning inventory on January 1 is one unit. What is the optimum production schedule for this problem?

22–4. A manager must hire an assistant in five days. The manager uses a testing procedure that results in each applicant being given a numerical rating. Assume that the best rating observed each day varies according to the probabilities in the table below:

Best Rating	Probability
10	0.2
9	0.4
8	0.4

If an applicant is not offered the job the day he or she applies, that applicant is lost. If the manager has not hired an assistant before day 5, the best applicant who applies on day 5 must be hired. The objective is to maximize the expected rating of the assistant.

a. Consider the situation on day 4, one day from the end. Compute the expected rating that will be obtained if the manager does not hire an assistant on day 4, but chooses to delay until day 5.

b. Use your result to state the optimal decision rule for day 4. For example, under what conditions should the manager delay choosing an assistant, and under what conditions should hiring occur immediately, assuming the best rating obtained on day 4 is known?

c. Now consider the situation on day 3. Compute the expected rating that will be obtained if the manager does not hire an assistant on day 3 but chooses to delay the decision. Remember that the manager need not necessarily hire the best applicant applying on day 4. The choice should be delayed if the best rating on day 4 is low, as found in (b).

d. Use your result in (c) to state the optimal decision rule for day 3.

22–5. Redo Problem 22–4, using the following notation:

n = Day number; $n = 1, 2, \ldots, 5$ (the stage number)

X_n = Best rating observed on day n (the state variable)

$f_n(X_n)$ = Maximum expected rating if best rating observed on day n is X_n and an optimal policy is followed from day n to the end of the process (the return function)

a. Consider the last day (day 5), and write an equation for $f_5(X_5)$.

b. Consider the next-to-last day (day 4), and write an equation for $f_4(X_4)$. Note that $f_4(X_4)$ equals the larger of the expected ratings under the two alternatives—"Act" and "Wait."

c. Set the two expected outcomes in (b) equal to find the break-even value of X_4, represented as X_{4b}. Then state the optimal decision rule at day 4. Verify that your rule is the same as the one obtained in (b) of Problem 22–4.

d. Using the optimal decision rule for day 4, write an equation for $f_3(X_3)$.

e. Now perform (c) and (d) alternatively to obtain $f_2(X_2)$ and $f_1(X_1)$. If the best rating on day 1 is 9, what action should the manager follow on day 1, and what is her maximum expected rating?

f. Suppose the personnel department says that it is able to guarantee an assistant with a "9" rating if it is given three days to do so. Decide whether the offer is helpful to the manager or not.

Problems

22–6. Suppose the cattle breeder in Problem 22–2 had an opportunity to invest money obtained from selling cattle now at an interest rate of 10 percent per year.

a. Calculate the present value of his profit if he sells none of his herd now. Assume his breeding costs are incurred immediately, whereas his profits from selling his entire herd next year are obtained one year hence.

b. Rewrite your general expression in (c) of Problem 22–2 to include the effect of the time value of money. Simplify your expression.

c. Now take the derivative of your expression in (b) with respect to Y and set it equal to zero. Verify that when the time value of money is added to the analysis, the optimal number of cattle to sell now increases.

22–7. A cattle breeder starts with a herd of 100 cattle and plans to sell the entire herd at the beginning of five years from now at $300 per head. If cattle are sold in market, the price P is given as follows:

$$P = 500 - 0.1Y, 0 \leq Y \leq 5{,}000$$

where Y represents the number of cattle sold in a given year. If cattle are bred, the cost is $50 per head, and the breeding ratio is approximately 1.8.

a. Write down the expression for the return function $f_n(X_n)$ for year 5.

b. Write down an expression for the return function in year 4, $f_4(X_4)$, using Y_4 to represent the number of cattle sold in the market in year 4. Simplify your equation by substituting in the expression for $f_5(X_5)$ obtained in (a).

c. Perform the maximization required in the equation in (b) by taking a derivative and setting it equal to zero.

d. Using the optimal decision at year 4 as obtained in (c), rewrite the value of the return function $f_4(X_4)$ in terms of X_4 alone.

e. Now consider year 3, and write the return function $f_3(X_3)$. Simplify your equation by substituting in the expression for $f_4(X_4)$ obtained in (d).

Note that your sequence of steps (c) and (d) may be repeated for each prior year; in this manner, the complete problem may be solved.

22–8. An investor has $10 million to invest sometime in the next five months. Each month, a new investment opportunity arises; the return each investment promises is a random variable distributed according to the probabilities in the table below:

Return on Investment	Probability
20%	0.6
30	0.3
100	0.1

At the beginning of each month, an investment opportunity is presented, with some actual return based on the probabilities in the table. The investor must either take that opportunity or reject it. Once rejected, the opportunity is withdrawn. If the investor has not invested money by the fifth month, it must be invested at the return available in the fifth month. Let:

X_n = Return available in month n

$f_n(X_n)$ = Maximum expected return if return of X_n is available in month n and optimal decisions are made from month n to month 5

a. Write an equation for the return in the fifth month, $f_5(X_5)$.

b. Now consider the situation in month 4. Write an equation for $f_4(X_4)$. Note that $f_4(X_4)$ equals the larger of the expected returns under the two alternatives— "Act" and "Wait."

c. Set the two expected profits in (b) equal to find the break-even value of X_4, represented as X_{4b}. Then state the optimal decision rule at month 4.

d. Using the optimal decision rule for month 4, write an equation for $f_3(X_3)$.

e. Now perform (c) and (d) alternatively to obtain $f_2(X_2)$ and $f_1(X_1)$. If the return available in month 1 is 30 percent, should the investor make the investment in month 1 or not? What is the expected return if the optimal decision is made?

22–9. A winemaker has produced the last barrel of wine before retirement. The winemaker must decide how many years to age the wine before bottling and selling it. The price obtained for the wine increases as the age of the wine increases, according to the accompanying table.

The winemaker will not age the wine more than six years. Let:

n = Year number (the stage number)

X_n = Age of wine in years (the state variable)

$f_n(X_n)$ = Maximum discounted revenue available when wine of age X_n exists at year n and optimal decisions are followed from year n to year 6 (the return function)

Age of Wine (in years)	Price of Wine
1	$56
2	59
3	67
4	75
5	82
6	84

Assume the discount rate is 10 percent per year.

Note that $X_n = n$ in this particular problem.

a. Write an equation for $f_6(X_6)$.

b. Write an equation for $f_5(X_5)$. Note that $f_5(X_5)$ equals the larger of the present values of the two alternatives—"Sell" or "Wait."

c. Find the optimal decision rule in year 5.

d. Write an equation for $f_4(X_4)$.

e. Now perform (*c*) and (*d*) alternatively to obtain $f_3(X_3)$, $f_2(X_2)$, and $f_1(X_1)$. How long should the winemaker age the wine, and what will the present value (in year 0) of the revenue be?

22–10. A ship's cargo capacity is 20 tons. There are three different types of cargo that may be carried in the ship—type 1, type 2, and type 3. The profit obtained from carrying a unit of each type of cargo is contained in the table below. The weight of a unit of each type is also included in the table.

Cargo Type	Profit per Unit	Weight per Unit (tons)
1	$ 40	5
2	220	10
3	360	15

a. By trial and error, find the cargo combination that maximizes profits and satisfies the weight constraint of 20 tons.

b. Now, let:

X_n = Available tons when the first n types of cargo are being considered (the state variable)

$f_n(X_n)$ = Maximum profit available when available capacity is X_n, n types of cargo are being considered, and optimal decisions are made

Y_i = Number of units of type i (i = 1, 2, and 3) included in the cargo combination (the decision variable)

Write an equation for $f_1(X_1)$. Note that $f_1(X_1)$ represents the maximum profit available when available capacity is X_1 and when only type 1 is considered for cargo. (*Hint:* Use the symbol [ ] to represent "greatest integer in.")

c. Now write an equation for $f_2(X_2)$ that uses the symbol Y_2 to indicate the number of units of type 2 to include. Note that $f_2(X_2)$ is the maximum profit that can be obtained when available capacity is X_2 and the first two types of cargo are considered.

d. Now write an equation for $f_3(X_3)$.

22–11. A concert hall is at the end of a dead-end street 10 blocks long. Paid parking at the hall itself costs $10; however, when Prof. H. arrives, the probability of observing an open place on the street is shown in the accompanying table.

Prof. H. estimates that each block walked has a cost of $1; for example, if a space is found in block 7, three blocks must be walked, with an imputed cost of $3. It is not possible to turn around and take a previously found space; moreover, if Prof. H. has not chosen a space on the street when block 10 is reached, $10 must be paid to park in the paid-parking lot.

Prof. H. needs a *decision rule* to help with the myriad parking choices every concert night. In the professor's words, "When I find myself in block i and see an open space, should I take it or drive on, hoping for something closer?"

The professor has already learned by experience to pass up open spaces on blocks 1 and 2 and to take an open

(for Problem 22–11)

Block Number	1	2	3	4	5	6	7	8	9	10	(concert hall)
Probability of an Open Space	0.9	0.8	0.7	0.6	0.5	0.4	0.3	0.2	0.1	0.0	

space in block 8 or 9 if available; however, help is needed in determining what to do in the other cases.

a. Formulate this problem as a dynamic programming problem by defining stages, a state variable, and a return function.

b. Solve your formulation. What is the first block in which an open space should be taken?

22–12. You have just purchased an apartment building. After deductions for depreciation, interest payments, and other expenses, you will receive the cash flows (after taxes) each year as shown in the first column of the accompanying table. If you decide to sell the building in any year, you will have the additional cash flow (after taxes) from the sales as shown in the second column. Of course, once you sell the building, cash flows cease.

Year	Cash Flow from Rentals Less Expenses and Taxes	Cash Flow at Year-End after Taxes from Sale
1	$90,000	$200,000
2	80,000	260,000
3	80,000	320,000
4	70,000	340,000
5	60,000	340,000
6	50,000	300,000
7	40,000	250,000
8	30,000	200,000
9	10,000	180,000
10	10,000	160,000

a. Assume you wish to maximize the total cash flow from owning the building. In what year should you sell it? (Ignore any discounting; that is, treat dollars received in any year as having the same present value.) Formulate this problem as a dynamic programming model and solve.

b. Suppose you wish to take into account the time value of money. Suppose that a dollar received in a year is worth only $0.90 in present value terms, a dollar received in two years is worth $0.9 \cdot 0.9 = \$0.81$ now, and so on. The 0.9 factor is called a *discount factor*. Using the discount factor to make dollars equivalent in present value terms, formulate and solve a dynamic programming model to decide when you should sell the building.

22–13. You are moving and can make at most three house-hunting trips, eight weeks apart, to find a house. You have decided that the probability of finding an "acceptable" house is shown in the following table. You must buy a house before you move. You have estimated the cost of one house-hunting trip at $2,000 (not reimbursed by your employer). You feel that in eight weeks' time there is enough turnover so that the three trips will be probabilistically independent in their outcomes.

Use the concepts of dynamic programming to obtain a *complete* optimal strategy that would tell you what to do after each visit to minimize your *expected cost* of finding and acquiring an acceptable house. Then apply your optimal strategy to the case in which you have just completed your first visit and have found an acceptable house at $140,000. Should you buy it or look further?

Price	Probability of Finding Acceptable House at This Exact Price	Cumulative Probability of Finding an Acceptable House at This Price or Lower
$130,000	0.5	0.5
140,000	0.3	0.8
160,000	0.2	1.0
	Sum = 1.0	

More Challenging Problems

22–14. An investor is considering buying into each of three ventures that have been proposed to him. He estimates the return on his investment in each (see the accompanying table). The projects have minimum investments of $60,000, $80,000, and $50,000, respectively. A fourth alternative of investment in government bonds is available for any amount invested, returning annually $4 per $100 invested.

Year	Operating Costs during Year	Sale Value at End of Year
1	$ 900	$6,800
2	1,200	6,200
3	1,600	5,800
4	2,200	5,000

If the investor has $200,000 available, how should he invest it to maximize his annual return? If he has $150,000? If he has $250,000? What is the annual return in each case?

22–15. You are considering your transportation costs over the next five years. The characteristics of the automobile you buy are listed in the table in the next column. In no case would you keep an automobile longer than four years. Purchase cost new is $8,000.

a. Suppose you consider buying only new cars. How often should you buy a new car if you wish to minimize transportation costs (purchase costs plus operating costs less sale value)?

b. Suppose you would consider buying a used car at the prices listed in the last column of the table (excluding, of course, the possibility of buying a four-year-old model). Does this change your optimal policy?

22–16. Refer to the flight attendant problem, Problem 10–20. Formulate this as a dynamic programming problem and solve.

22–17. At the beginning of each month, a firm places an order for a particular product, which is delivered at the end of the

(for Problem 22–14)

Project 1 (shopping center development)		Project 2 (housing development)		Project 3 (industrial firm)	
Investment Amount ($000s)	Annual Return ($000s)	Investment Amount ($000s)	Annual Return ($000s)	Investment Amount ($000s)	Annual Return ($000s)
$ 60	$ 6.0	$ 80	$ 6.0	$ 50	$4.0
70	8.0	90	8.0	60	4.8
80	9.0	100	10.0	70	5.6
90	10.0	110	12.0	80	6.4
100	11.0	120	13.0	90	7.2
110	11.5	130	13.8	100	8.0
120	12.0	140	14.2	110	8.8
(maximum investment)		150	14.5	120	9.6
		(maximum investment)		(maximum investment)	

month. The firm sells some product during the month from inventory on hand—ordered in previous months—because the amount ordered at the beginning of the current month will not arrive until the end of the month. The firm can sell any number of units in any month.

The purchase and selling prices of the product vary from month to month. The table below gives the projected prices for the next six months. The firm is limited in its operations by the size of its warehouse, which can hold a maximum of 100 units of the product.

The problem for the firm is to determine the number of units to buy and sell each month in order to obtain the most profit. The firm has no units on hand at the beginning of January and wishes to have no units on hand at the end of June. Formulate this as a dynamic programming problem and solve. (*Hint:* There are really only two possibilities—either a full or an empty warehouse at the end of each period.)

Purchase and Selling Price

Month	Purchase Price (beginning of month)	Selling Price (during month)
January	$50	—
February	50	$60
March	40	40
April	60	50
May	50	60
June	—	70

22–18. Reformulate Problem 22–10 (the cargo-loading problem) by letting X represent the number of tons available and letting $f(X)$ represent the maximum profit obtainable from all three types of cargo when optimal decisions are made. If we define $f(0) = 0$ and $f(X) = 0$ for all $X < 0$, verify that the following functional equation holds:

$$f(X + 1) = \text{Max } \{f(X) + f(1); \ 40 + f(X - 4); \\ 200 + f(X - 9); \ 360 + f(X - 14)\}$$

Compute $f(1)$ through $f(20)$.

22–19. In contrast to the backward algorithm described in this chapter, for some dynamic programming problems a *forward algorithm* may be used to solve the problem. In a forward algorithm, the return function would typically represent the maximum profit (or minimum cost) obtained from the beginning of the process up to stage n. The algorithm would start at the beginning, and work its way to the natural end of the problem.

a. Refer to Problem 22–1. Outline how a forward algorithm would work for this problem, and use it to solve the problem.

b. Do you think a forward algorithm would be successful in solving a dynamic programming problem with random variables? Why or why not?

22–20. A drug firm is trying to develop a cure for a particular ailment. Five possible compounds are under consideration. Each is considered to have a ¹⁄₁₀ chance to be effective as a cure (i.e., a ¹⁄₁₀ chance of success). To test each compound will take one month and costs $10,000. The drug firm has three months in which to test the five compounds.

The problem is to develop a testing strategy. A strategy involves determining how many compounds to test in each month. For example, one strategy is: Try one compound in month 1; if not successful, try a second in month 2; if still not successful, try the remaining three in month 3. Note that testing the compounds sequentially reduces the expected cost, since it reduces the probability that all five compounds will have to be tested before a success is found.

Assume that the probabilities are independent. Note that if k compounds are tried in any month, the probability of at least one success is $[1 - (0.9)^k]$.

a. Formulate a general dynamic recursion for N periods and M compounds to be tested. The objective is to minimize the expected cost of finding a success.

b. Apply your recursion to the data in the case above ($M = 5$ compounds, $N = 3$ months).

22–21. A firm uses a digger to mine coal in a certain mine. The mine has a life of 10 years. The company is currently using a digger that is two years old. A new digger costs $150,000. Maintenance, downtime, and other costs vary with the age of a machine as shown in the table below.

At any time, a machine may be rebuilt. This makes the machine equivalent to a two-year-old machine in terms of maintenance costs and so on. The cost of a rebuild is $60,000. The firm wishes to find an optimum policy (one that minimizes maintenance and equipment costs) for equipment replacement and rebuild over the 10-year period. Assume equipment has no value at the end of the 10 years. Note that in any year, the firm has three choices: (1) keep the current digger another year; (2) rebuild the digger; (3) replace the digger with a new one.

a. Formulate the dynamic recursion for this problem.

b. Solve the problem.

22–22. This problem requires an understanding of Markov processes (see Chapter 21).

Assume a machine moves from state 1 (in adjustment) to state 2 (out of adjustment), and vice versa, with the probabilities of changes as given in the table below.

Assume that when the machine is in state 1 for a day, a profit of $100 is gained; and if the machine is in state 2 for a day, a loss of $50 is incurred.

a. Compute the steady-state probabilities and the expected daily profit rate.

b. Now suppose the machine may be repaired at a cost of $200. You observe the machine at the beginning of the day, and the repairer performs repairs very quickly, so a full day's operation in state 1 occurs after repairing. Assume the state transitions occur at the end of the working day. If the manager is interested in only the next five days of operation, use dynamic programming to compute the optimal decision rules concerning the repair decision. What is the expected value of starting the five-day period with the machine in state 1?

Age of Machine at Beginning of Year	*Cost of Maintenance, etc., during Year*
New	$ 0
1 year	10,000
2	20,000
3	30,000
4	50,000
5	70,000
6	90,000
7	120,000
8	150,000
9	180,000

From \ *To*	*In Adjustment (state 1)*	*Out of Adjustment (state 2)*
In Adjustment (state 1)	0.5	0.5
Out of adjustment (state 2)	0.4	0.6

Appendix of Tables

Table A   **The Standardized Normal Distribution Function,* $F_N(Z)$**

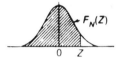

Z	0.00	0.01	0.02	0.03	0.04	0.05	0.06	0.07	0.08	0.09
0.0	0.5000	0.5040	0.5080	0.5120	0.5160	0.5199	0.5239	0.5279	0.5319	0.5359
0.1	0.5398	0.5438	0.5478	0.5517	0.5557	0.5596	0.5636	0.5675	0.5714	0.5753
0.2	0.5793	0.5832	0.5871	0.5910	0.5948	0.5987	0.6026	0.6064	0.6103	0.6141
0.3	0.6179	0.6217	0.6255	0.6293	0.6331	0.6368	0.6406	0.6443	0.6480	0.6517
0.4	0.6554	0.6591	0.6628	0.6664	0.6700	0.6736	0.6772	0.6808	0.6844	0.6879
0.5	0.6915	0.6950	0.6985	0.7019	0.7054	0.7088	0.7123	0.7157	0.7190	0.7224
0.6	0.7257	0.7291	0.7324	0.7357	0.7389	0.7422	0.7454	0.7486	0.7517	0.7549
0.7	0.7580	0.7611	0.7642	0.7673	0.7703	0.7734	0.7764	0.7794	0.7823	0.7852
0.8	0.7881	0.7910	0.7939	0.7967	0.7995	0.8023	0.8051	0.8078	0.8106	0.8133
0.9	0.8159	0.8186	0.8212	0.8238	0.8264	0.8289	0.8315	0.8340	0.8365	0.8389
1.0	0.8413	0.8438	0.8461	0.8485	0.8508	0.8531	0.8554	0.8577	0.8599	0.8621
1.1	0.8643	0.8665	0.8686	0.8708	0.8729	0.8749	0.8770	0.8790	0.8810	0.8830
1.2	0.8849	0.8869	0.8888	0.8907	0.8925	0.8944	0.8962	0.8980	0.8997	0.90147
1.3	0.90320	0.90490	0.90658	0.90824	0.90988	0.91149	0.91309	0.91466	0.91621	0.91774
1.4	0.91924	0.92073	0.92220	0.92364	0.92507	0.92647	0.92785	0.92922	0.93056	0.93189
1.5	0.93319	0.93448	0.93574	0.93699	0.93822	0.93943	0.94062	0.94179	0.94295	0.94408
1.6	0.94520	0.94630	0.94738	0.94845	0.94950	0.95053	0.95154	0.95254	0.95352	0.95449
1.7	0.95543	0.95637	0.95728	0.95818	0.95907	0.95994	0.96080	0.96164	0.96246	0.96327
1.8	0.96407	0.96485	0.96562	0.96638	0.96712	0.96784	0.96856	0.96926	0.96995	0.97062
1.9	0.97128	0.97193	0.97257	0.97320	0.97381	0.97441	0.97500	0.97558	0.97615	0.97670
2.0	0.97725	0.97778	0.97831	0.97882	0.97932	0.97982	0.98030	0.98077	0.98124	0.98169
2.1	0.98214	0.98257	0.98300	0.98341	0.98382	0.98422	0.98461	0.98500	0.98537	0.98574
2.2	0.98610	0.98645	0.98679	0.98713	0.98745	0.98778	0.98809	0.98840	0.98870	0.98899
2.3	0.98928	0.98956	0.98983	0.9^20097	0.9^20358	0.9^20613	0.9^20863	0.9^21106	0.9^21344	0.9^21576
2.4	0.9^21802	0.9^22024	0.9^22240	0.9^22451	0.9^22656	0.9^22857	0.9^23053	0.9^23244	0.9^23431	0.9^23613
2.5	0.9^23790	0.9^23963	0.9^24132	0.9^24297	0.9^24457	0.9^24614	0.9^24766	0.9^24915	0.9^25060	0.9^25201
3.0	0.9^28650	0.9^28694	0.9^28736	0.9^28777	0.9^28817	0.9^28856	0.9^28893	0.9^28930	0.9^28965	0.9^28999
3.5	0.9^37674	0.9^37759	0.9^37842	0.9^37922	0.9^37999	0.9^38074	0.9^38146	0.9^38215	0.9^38282	0.9^38347
4.0	0.9^46833	0.9^46964	0.9^47090	0.9^47211	0.9^47327	0.9^47439	0.9^47546	0.9^47649	0.9^47748	0.9^47843

For example: $F(2.41) = .9^22024 = .992024$.

*From A. Hald, *Statistical Tables and Formulas* (New York: John Wiley & Sons, 1952); reproduced by permission of Professor A. Hald and the publishers.

Appendix of Tables

Table B $N(D)$—Standard Normal Distribution Loss Function*

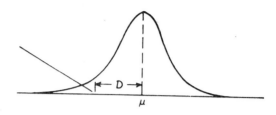

D or Z	.00	.01	.02	.03	.04	.05	.06	.07	.08	.09
.0	.3989	.3940	.3890	.3841	.3793	.3744	.3697	.3649	.3602	.3556
.1	.3509	.3464	.3418	.3373	.3328	.3284	.3240	.3197	.3154	.3111
.2	.3069	.3027	.2986	.2944	.2904	.2863	.2824	.2784	.2745	.2706
.3	.2668	.2630	.2592	.2555	.2518	.2481	.2445	.2409	.2374	.2339
.4	.2304	.2270	.2236	.2203	.2169	.2137	.2104	.2072	.2040	.2009
.5	.1978	.1947	.1917	.1887	.1857	.1828	.1799	.1771	.1742	.1714
.6	.1687	.1659	.1633	.1606	.1580	.1554	.1528	.1503	.1478	.1453
.7	.1429	.1405	.1381	.1358	.1334	.1312	.1289	.1267	.1245	.1223
.8	.1202	.1181	.1160	.1140	.1120	.1100	.1080	.1061	.1042	.1023
.9	.1004	.09860	.09680	.09503	.09328	.09156	.08986	.08819	.08654	.08491
1.0	.08332	.08174	.08019	.07866	.07716	.07568	.07422	.07279	.07138	.06999
1.1	.06862	.06727	.06595	.06465	.06336	.06210	.06086	.05964	.05844	.05726
1.2	.05610	.05496	.05384	.05274	.05165	.05059	.04954	.04851	.04750	.04650
1.3	.04553	.04457	.04363	.04270	.04179	.04090	.04002	.03916	.03831	.03748
1.4	.03667	.03587	.03508	.03431	.03356	.03281	.03208	.03137	.03067	.02998
1.5	.02931	.02865	.02800	.02736	.02674	.02612	.02552	.02494	.02436	.02380
1.6	.02324	.02270	.02217	.02165	.02114	.02064	.02015	.01967	.01920	.01874
1.7	.01829	.01785	.01742	.01699	.01658	.01617	.01578	.01539	.01501	.01464
1.8	.01428	.01392	.01357	.01323	.01290	.01257	.01226	.01195	.01164	.01134
1.9	.01105	.01077	.01049	.01022	$.0^2$9957	$.0^2$9698	$.0^2$9445	$.0^2$9198	$.0^2$8957	$.0^2$8721
2.0	$.0^2$8491	$.0^2$8266	$.0^2$8046	$.0^2$7832	$.0^2$7623	$.0^2$7418	$.0^2$7219	$.0^2$7024	$.0^2$6835	$.0^2$6649
2.1	$.0^2$6468	$.0^2$6292	$.0^2$6120	$.0^2$5952	$.0^2$5788	$.0^2$5628	$.0^2$5472	$.0^2$5320	$.0^2$5172	$.0^2$5028
2.2	$.0^2$4887	$.0^2$4750	$.0^2$4616	$.0^2$4486	$.0^2$4358	$.0^2$4235	$.0^2$4114	$.0^2$3996	$.0^2$3882	$.0^2$3770
2.3	$.0^2$3662	$.0^2$3556	$.0^2$3453	$.0^2$3352	$.0^2$3255	$.0^2$3159	$.0^2$3067	$.0^2$2977	$.0^2$2889	$.0^2$2804
2.4	$.0^2$2720	$.0^2$2640	$.0^2$2561	$.0^2$2484	$.0^2$2410	$.0^2$2337	$.0^2$2267	$.0^2$2199	$.0^2$2132	$.0^2$2067
2.5	$.0^2$2005	$.0^2$1943	$.0^2$1883	$.0^2$1826	$.0^2$1769	$.0^2$1715	$.0^2$1662	$.0^2$1610	$.0^2$1560	$.0^2$1511
3.0	$.0^3$3822	$.0^3$3689	$.0^3$3560	$.0^3$3436	$.0^3$3316	$.0^3$3199	$.0^3$3087	$.0^3$2978	$.0^3$2873	$.0^3$2771
3.5	$.0^4$5848	$.0^4$5620	$.0^4$5400	$.0^4$5188	$.0^4$4984	$.0^4$4788	$.0^4$4599	$.0^4$4417	$.0^4$4242	$.0^4$4073
4.0	$.0^5$7145	$.0^5$6835	$.0^5$6538	$.0^5$6253	$.0^5$5980	$.0^5$5718	$.0^5$5468	$.0^5$5227	$.0^5$4997	$.0^5$4777

$N(D)$ is defined as follows:

$$N(D) = \int_{-\infty}^{-D} (-D - X)\, f^*(X)dX = \int_{D}^{\infty} (X - D)\, f^*(X)dX$$

where $f^*(X)$ is the standardized normal density function, and D is positive.

*By permission from R. Schlaifer, *Probability and Statistics for Business Decisions* (New York: McGraw-Hill, 1959).

Table C Cumulative Binomial Distributions* $P(R \geq r \mid n, p)$

$n = 1$

p\r	01	02	03	04	05	06	07	08	09	10
1	0100	0200	0300	0400	0500	0600	0700	0800	0900	1000

p\r	11	12	13	14	15	16	17	18	19	20
1	1100	1200	1300	1400	1500	1600	1700	1800	1900	2000

p\r	21	22	23	24	25	26	27	28	29	30
1	2100	2200	2300	2400	2500	2600	2700	2800	2900	3000

p\r	31	32	33	34	35	36	37	38	39	40
1	3100	3200	3300	3400	3500	3600	3700	3800	3900	4000

p\r	41	42	43	44	45	46	47	48	49	50
1	4100	4200	4300	4400	4500	4600	4700	4800	4900	5000

$n = 2$

p\r	01	02	03	04	05	06	07	08	09	10
1	0199	0396	0591	0784	0975	1164	1351	1536	1719	1900
2	0001	0004	0009	0016	0025	0036	0049	0064	0081	0100

p\r	11	12	13	14	15	16	17	18	19	20
1	2079	2256	2431	2604	2775	2944	3111	3276	3439	3600
2	0121	0144	0169	0196	0225	0256	0289	0324	0361	0400

p\r	21	22	23	24	25	26	27	28	29	30
1	3759	3916	4071	4224	4375	4524	4671	4816	4959	5100
2	0441	0484	0529	0576	0625	0676	0729	0784	0841	0900

p\r	31	32	33	34	35	36	37	38	39	40
1	5239	5376	5511	5644	5775	5904	6031	6156	6279	6400
2	0961	1024	1089	1156	1225	1296	1369	1444	1521	1600

p\r	41	42	43	44	45	46	47	48	49	50
1	6519	6636	6751	6864	6975	7084	7191	7296	7399	7500
2	1681	1764	1849	1936	2025	2116	2209	2304	2401	2500

$n = 3$

p\r	01	02	03	04	05	06	07	08	09	10
1	0297	0588	0873	1153	1426	1694	1956	2213	2464	2710
2	0003	0012	0026	0047	0073	0104	0140	0182	0228	0280
3				0001	0001	0002	0003	0005	0007	0010

p\r	11	12	13	14	15	16	17	18	19	20
1	2950	3185	3415	3639	3859	4073	4282	4486	4686	4880
2	0336	0397	0463	0533	0608	0686	0769	0855	0946	1040
3	0013	0017	0022	0027	0034	0041	0049	0058	0069	0080

p\r	21	22	23	24	25	26	27	28	29	30
1	5070	5254	5435	5610	5781	5948	6110	6268	6421	6570
2	1138	1239	1344	1452	1563	1676	1793	1913	2035	2160
3	0093	0106	0122	0138	0156	0176	0197	0220	0244	0270

Note: For $p > 0.5$, the following identity holds:

$$P(R \geq r \mid n, p) = 1 - P(R \geq n - r + 1 \mid n, 1 - p)$$

For example, consider the probability of two or more heads in three tosses of a coin with P (head) = 0.60; this is identical to one minus the probability of two or more tails in three tosses, with P (tail) = 0.4, or $1 - 0.3520 = 0.6480$.

*By permission from R. Schlaifer, *Probability and Statistics for Business Decisions* (New York: McGraw-Hill, 1959).

Table C (*continued*)

p r	31	32	33	34	35	36	37	38	39	40
1	6715	6856	6992	7125	7254	7379	7500	7617	7730	7840
2	2287	2417	2548	2682	2818	2955	3094	3235	3377	3520
3	0298	0328	0359	0393	0429	0467	0507	0549	0593	0640

p r	41	42	43	44	45	46	47	48	49	50
1	7946	8049	8148	8244	8336	8425	8511	8594	8673	8750
2	3665	3810	3957	4104	4253	4401	4551	4700	4850	5000
3	0689	0741	0795	0852	0911	0973	1038	1106	1176	1250

$$n = 4$$

p r	01	02	03	04	05	06	07	08	09	10
1	0394	0776	1147	1507	1855	2193	2519	2836	3143	3439
2	0006	0023	0052	0091	0140	0199	0267	0344	0430	0523
3			0001	0002	0005	0008	0013	0019	0027	0037
4									0001	0001

p r	11	12	13	14	15	16	17	18	19	20
1	3726	4003	4271	4530	4780	5021	5254	5479	5695	5904
2	0624	0732	0847	0968	1095	1228	1366	1509	1656	1808
3	0049	0063	0079	0098	0120	0144	0171	0202	0235	0272
4	0001	0002	0003	0004	0005	0007	0008	0010	0013	0016

p r	21	22	23	24	25	26	27	28	29	30
1	6105	6298	6485	6664	6836	7001	7160	7313	7459	7599
2	1963	2122	2285	2450	2617	2787	2959	3132	3307	3483
3	0312	0356	0403	0453	0508	0566	0628	0694	0763	0837
4	0019	0023	0028	0033	0039	0046	0053	0061	0071	0081

p r	31	32	33	34	35	36	37	38	39	40
1	7733	7862	7985	8103	8215	8322	8425	8522	8615	8704
2	3660	3837	4015	4193	4370	4547	4724	4900	5075	5248
3	0915	0996	1082	1171	1265	1362	1464	1569	1679	1792
4	0092	0105	0119	0134	0150	0168	0187	0209	0231	0256

p r	41	42	43	44	45	46	47	48	49	50
1	8788	8868	8944	9017	9085	9150	9211	9269	9323	9375
2	5420	5590	5759	5926	6090	6252	6412	6569	6724	6875
3	1909	2030	2155	2283	2415	2550	2689	2831	2977	3125
4	0283	0311	0342	0375	0410	0448	0488	0531	0576	0625

$$n = 5$$

p r	01	02	03	04	05	06	07	08	09	10
1	0490	0961	1413	1846	2262	2661	3043	3409	3760	4095
2	0010	0038	0085	0148	0226	0319	0425	0544	0674	0815
3		0001	0003	0006	0012	0020	0031	0045	0063	0086
4						0001	0001	0002	0003	0005

p r	11	12	13	14	15	16	17	18	19	20
1	4416	4723	5016	5296	5563	5818	6061	6293	6513	6723
2	0965	1125	1292	1467	1648	1835	2027	2224	2424	2627
3	0112	0143	0179	0220	0266	0318	0375	0437	0505	0579
4	0007	0009	0013	0017	0022	0029	0036	0045	0055	0067
5				0001	0001	0001	0001	0002	0002	0003

p r	21	22	23	24	25	26	27	28	29	30
1	6923	7113	7293	7464	7627	7781	7927	8065	8196	8319
2	2833	3041	3251	3461	3672	3883	4093	4303	4511	4718
3	0659	0744	0836	0933	1035	1143	1257	1376	1501	1631
4	0081	0097	0114	0134	0156	0181	0208	0238	0272	0308
5	0004	0005	0006	0008	0010	0012	0014	0017	0021	0024

Table C (continued)

p r	31	32	33	34	35	36	37	38	39	40
1	8436	8546	8650	8748	8840	8926	9008	9084	9155	9222
2	4923	5125	5325	5522	5716	5906	6093	6276	6455	6630
3	1766	1905	2050	2199	2352	2509	2670	2835	3003	3174
4	0347	0390	0436	0486	0540	0598	0660	0726	0796	0870
5	0029	0034	0039	0045	0053	0060	0069	0079	0090	0102

p r	41	42	43	44	45	46	47	48	49	50
1	9285	9344	9398	9449	9497	9541	9582	9620	9655	9688
2	6801	6967	7129	7286	7438	7585	7728	7865	7998	8125
3	3349	3525	3705	3886	4069	4253	4439	4625	4813	5000
4	0949	1033	1121	1214	1312	1415	1522	1635	1753	1875
5	0116	0131	0147	0165	0185	0206	0229	0255	0282	0313

$$n = 6$$

p r	01	02	03	04	05	06	07	08	09	10
1	0585	1142	1670	2172	2649	3101	3530	3936	4321	4686
2	0015	0057	0125	0216	0328	0459	0608	0773	0952	1143
3		0002	0005	0012	0022	0038	0058	0085	0118	0159
4					0001	0002	0003	0005	0008	0013
5										0001

p r	11	12	13	14	15	16	17	18	19	20
1	5030	5356	5664	5954	6229	6487	6731	6960	7176	7379
2	1345	1556	1776	2003	2235	2472	2713	2956	3201	3446
3	0206	0261	0324	0395	0473	0560	0655	0759	0870	0989
4	0018	0025	0034	0045	0059	0075	0094	0116	0141	0170
5	0001	0001	0002	0003	0004	0005	0007	0010	0013	0016
6										0001

p r	21	22	23	24	25	26	27	28	29	30
1	7569	7748	7916	8073	8220	8358	8487	8607	8719	8824
2	3692	3937	4180	4422	4661	4896	5128	5356	5580	5798
3	1115	1250	1391	1539	1694	1856	2023	2196	2374	2557
4	0202	0239	0280	0326	0376	0431	0492	0557	0628	0705
5	0020	0025	0031	0038	0046	0056	0067	0079	0093	0109
6	0001	0001	0001	0002	0002	0003	0004	0005	0006	0007

p r	31	32	33	34	35	36	37	38	39	40
1	8921	9011	9095	9173	9246	9313	9375	9432	9485	9533
2	6012	6220	6422	6619	6809	6994	7172	7343	7508	7667
3	2744	2936	3130	3328	3529	3732	3937	4143	4350	4557
4	0787	0875	0969	1069	1174	1286	1404	1527	1657	1792
5	0127	0148	0170	0195	0223	0254	0288	0325	0365	0410
6	0009	0011	0013	0015	0018	0022	0026	0030	0035	0041

p r	41	42	43	44	45	46	47	48	49	50
1	9578	9619	9657	9692	9723	9752	9778	9802	9824	9844
2	7819	7965	8105	8238	8364	8485	8599	8707	8810	8906
3	4764	4971	5177	5382	5585	5786	5985	6180	6373	6563
4	1933	2080	2232	2390	2553	2721	2893	3070	3252	3438
5	0458	0510	0566	0627	0692	0762	0837	0917	1003	1094
6	0048	0055	0063	0073	0083	0095	0108	0122	0138	0156

$$n = 7$$

p r	01	02	03	04	05	06	07	08	09	10
1	0679	1319	1920	2486	3017	3515	3983	4422	4832	5217
2	0020	0079	0171	0294	0444	0618	0813	1026	1255	1497
3		0003	0009	0020	0038	0063	0097	0140	0193	0257
4				0001	0002	0004	0007	0012	0018	0027
5								0001	0001	0002

Table C (*continued*)

p r	11	12	13	14	15	16	17	18	19	20
1	5577	5913	6227	6521	6794	7049	7286	7507	7712	7903
2	1750	2012	2281	2556	2834	3115	3396	3677	3956	4233
3	0331	0416	0513	0620	0738	0866	1005	1154	1313	1480
4	0039	0054	0072	0094	0121	0153	0189	0231	0279	0333
5	0003	0004	0006	0009	0012	0017	0022	0029	0037	0047
6					0001	0001	0001	0002	0003	0004

p r	21	22	23	24	25	26	27	28	29	30
1	8080	8243	8395	8535	8665	8785	8895	8997	9090	9176
2	4506	4775	5040	5298	5551	5796	6035	6266	6490	6706
3	1657	1841	2033	2231	2436	2646	2861	3081	3304	3529
4	0394	0461	0536	0617	0706	0802	0905	1016	1134	1260
5	0058	0072	0088	0107	0129	0153	0181	0213	0248	0288
6	0005	0006	0008	0011	0013	0017	0021	0026	0031	0038
7					0001	0001	0001	0001	0002	0002

p r	31	32	33	34	35	36	37	38	39	40
1	9255	9328	9394	9454	9510	9560	9606	9648	9686	9720
2	6914	7113	7304	7487	7662	7828	7987	8137	8279	8414
3	3757	3987	4217	4447	4677	4906	5134	5359	5581	5801
4	1394	1534	1682	1837	1998	2167	2341	2521	2707	2898
5	0332	0380	0434	0492	0556	0625	0701	0782	0869	0963
6	0046	0055	0065	0077	0090	0105	0123	0142	0164	0188
7	0003	0003	0004	0005	0006	0008	0009	0011	0014	0016

p r	41	42	43	44	45	46	47	48	49	50
1	9751	9779	9805	9827	9848	9866	9883	9897	9910	9922
2	8541	8660	8772	8877	8976	9068	9153	9233	9307	9375
3	6017	6229	6436	6638	6836	7027	7213	7393	7567	7734
4	3094	3294	3498	3706	3917	4131	4346	4563	4781	5000
5	1063	1169	1282	1402	1529	1663	1803	1951	2105	2266
6	0216	0246	0279	0316	0357	0402	0451	0504	0562	0625
7	0019	0023	0027	0032	0037	0044	0051	0059	0068	0078

$$n = 8$$

p r	01	02	03	04	05	06	07	08	09	10
1	0773	1492	2163	2786	3366	3904	4404	4868	5297	5695
2	0027	0103	0223	0381	0572	0792	1035	1298	1577	1869
3	0001	0004	0013	0031	0058	0096	0147	0211	0289	0381
4			0001	0002	0004	0007	0013	0022	0034	0050
5							0001	0001	0003	0004

p r	11	12	13	14	15	16	17	18	19	20
1	6063	6404	6718	7008	7275	7521	7748	7956	8147	8322
2	2171	2480	2794	3111	3428	3744	4057	4366	4670	4967
3	0487	0608	0743	0891	1052	1226	1412	1608	1815	2031
4	0071	0097	0129	0168	0214	0267	0328	0397	0476	0563
5	0007	0010	0015	0021	0029	0038	0050	0065	0083	0104
6		0001	0001	0002	0002	0003	0005	0007	0009	0012
7									0001	0001

p r	21	22	23	24	25	26	27	28	29	30
1	8483	8630	8764	8887	8999	9101	9194	9278	9354	9424
2	5257	5538	5811	6075	6329	6573	6807	7031	7244	7447
3	2255	2486	2724	2967	3215	3465	3718	3973	4228	4482
4	0659	0765	0880	1004	1138	1281	1433	1594	1763	1941
5	0129	0158	0191	0230	0273	0322	0377	0438	0505	0580
6	0016	0021	0027	0034	0042	0052	0064	0078	0094	0113
7	0001	0002	0002	0003	0004	0005	0006	0008	0010	0013
8									0001	0001

Table C (*continued*)

p	31	32	33	34	35	36	37	38	39	40
r										
1	9486	9543	9594	9640	9681	9719	9752	9782	9808	9832
2	7640	7822	7994	8156	8309	8452	8586	8711	8828	8936
3	4736	4987	5236	5481	5722	5958	6189	6415	6634	6846
4	2126	2319	2519	2724	2936	3153	3374	3599	3828	4059
5	0661	0750	0846	0949	1061	1180	1307	1443	1586	1737
6	0134	0159	0187	0218	0253	0293	0336	0385	0439	0498
7	0016	0020	0024	0030	0036	0043	0051	0061	0072	0085
8	0001	0001	0001	0002	0002	0003	0004	0004	0005	0007

p	41	42	43	44	45	46	47	48	49	50
r										
1	9853	9872	9889	9903	9916	9928	9938	9947	9954	9961
2	9037	9130	9216	9295	9368	9435	9496	9552	9602	9648
3	7052	7250	7440	7624	7799	7966	8125	8276	8419	8555
4	4292	4527	4762	4996	5230	5463	5694	5922	6146	6367
5	1895	2062	2235	2416	2604	2798	2999	3205	3416	3633
6	0563	0634	0711	0794	0885	0982	1086	1198	1318	1445
7	0100	0117	0136	0157	0181	0208	0239	0272	0310	0352
8	0008	0010	0012	0014	0017	0020	0024	0028	0033	0039

n = 9

p	01	02	03	04	05	06	07	08	09	10
r										
1	0865	1663	2398	3075	3698	4270	4796	5278	5721	6126
2	0034	0131	0282	0478	0712	0978	1271	1583	1912	2252
3	0001	0006	0020	0045	0084	0138	0209	0298	0405	0530
4			0001	0003	0006	0013	0023	0037	0057	0083
5						0001	0002	0003	0005	0009
6										0001

p	11	12	13	14	15	16	17	18	19	20
r										
1	6496	6835	7145	7427	7684	7918	8131	8324	8499	8658
2	2599	2951	3304	3657	4005	4348	4685	5012	5330	5638
3	0672	0833	1009	1202	1409	1629	1861	2105	2357	2618
4	0117	0158	0209	0269	0339	0420	0512	0615	0730	0856
5	0014	0021	0030	0041	0056	0075	0098	0125	0158	0196
6	0001	0002	0003	0004	0006	0009	0013	0017	0023	0031
7						0001	0001	0002	0002	0003

p	21	22	23	24	25	26	27	28	29	30
r										
1	8801	8931	9048	9154	9249	9335	9411	9480	9542	9596
2	5934	6218	6491	6750	6997	7230	7452	7660	7856	8040
3	2885	3158	3434	3713	3993	4273	4552	4829	5102	5372
4	0994	1144	1304	1475	1657	1849	2050	2260	2478	2703
5	0240	0291	0350	0416	0489	0571	0662	0762	0870	0988
6	0040	0051	0065	0081	0100	0122	0149	0179	0213	0253
7	0004	0006	0008	0010	0013	0017	0022	0028	0035	0043
8			0001	0001	0001	0001	0002	0003	0003	0004

p	31	32	33	34	35	36	37	38	39	40
r										
1	9645	9689	9728	9762	9793	9820	9844	9865	9883	9899
2	8212	8372	8522	8661	8789	8908	9017	9118	9210	9295
3	5636	5894	6146	6390	6627	6856	7076	7287	7489	7682
4	2935	3173	3415	3662	3911	4163	4416	4669	4922	5174
5	1115	1252	1398	1553	1717	1890	2072	2262	2460	2666
6	0298	0348	0404	0467	0536	0612	0696	0787	0886	0994
7	0053	0064	0078	0094	0112	0133	0157	0184	0213	0250
8	0006	0007	0009	0011	0014	0017	0021	0026	0031	0036
9				0001	0001	0001	0001	0002	0002	0003

p	41	42	43	44	45	46	47	48	49	50
r										
1	9913	9926	9936	9946	9954	9961	9967	9972	9977	9980
2	9372	9442	9505	9563	9615	9662	9704	9741	9775	9805
3	7866	8039	8204	8359	8505	8642	8769	8889	8999	9102
4	5424	5670	5913	6152	6386	6614	6836	7052	7260	7461
5	2878	3097	3322	3551	3786	4024	4265	4509	4754	5000
6	1109	1233	1366	1508	1658	1817	1985	2161	2346	2539
7	0290	0334	0383	0437	0498	0564	0637	0717	0804	0898
8	0046	0055	0065	0077	0091	0107	0125	0145	0169	0195
9	0003	0004	0005	0006	0008	0009	0011	0014	0016	0020

Table C (continued)

$$n = 10$$

p r	01	02	03	04	05	06	07	08	09	10
1	0956	1829	2626	3352	4013	4614	5160	5656	6106	6513
2	0043	0162	0345	0582	0861	1176	1517	1879	2254	2639
3	0001	0009	0028	0062	0115	0188	0283	0401	0540	0702
4			0001	0004	0010	0020	0036	0058	0088	0128
5					0001	0002	0003	0006	0010	0016
6									0001	0001

p r	11	12	13	14	15	16	17	18	19	20
1	6882	7215	7516	7787	8031	8251	8448	8626	8784	8926
2	3028	3417	3804	4184	4557	4920	5270	5608	5932	6242
3	0884	1087	1308	1545	1798	2064	2341	2628	2922	3222
4	0178	0239	0313	0400	0500	0614	0741	0883	1039	1209
5	0025	0037	0053	0073	0099	0130	0168	0213	0266	0328
6	0003	0004	0006	0010	0014	0020	0027	0037	0049	0064
7			0001	0001	0001	0002	0003	0004	0006	0009
8									0001	0001

p r	21	22	23	24	25	26	27	28	29	30
1	9053	9166	9267	9357	9437	9508	9570	9626	9674	9718
2	6536	6815	7079	7327	7560	7778	7981	8170	8345	8507
3	3526	3831	4137	4442	4744	5042	5335	5622	5901	6172
4	1391	1587	1794	2012	2241	2479	2726	2979	3239	3504
5	0399	0479	0569	0670	0781	0904	1037	1181	1337	1503
6	0082	0104	0130	0161	0197	0239	0287	0342	0404	0473
7	0012	0016	0021	0027	0035	0045	0056	0070	0087	0106
8	0001	0002	0002	0003	0004	0006	0007	0010	0012	0016
9							0001	0001	0001	0001

p r	31	32	33	34	35	36	37	38	39	40
1	9755	9789	9818	9843	9865	9885	9902	9916	9929	9940
2	8656	8794	8920	9035	9140	9236	9323	9402	9473	9536
3	6434	6687	6930	7162	7384	7595	7794	7983	8160	8327
4	3772	4044	4316	4589	4862	5132	5400	5664	5923	6177
5	1679	1867	2064	2270	2485	2708	2939	3177	3420	3669
6	0551	0637	0732	0836	0949	1072	1205	1348	1500	1662
7	0129	0155	0185	0220	0260	0305	0356	0413	0477	0548
8	0020	0025	0032	0039	0048	0059	0071	0086	0103	0123
9	0002	0003	0003	0004	0005	0007	0009	0011	0014	0017
10								0001	0001	0001

p r	41	42	43	44	45	46	47	48	49	50
1	9949	9957	9964	9970	9975	9979	9983	9986	9988	9990
2	9594	9645	9691	9731	9767	9799	9827	9852	9874	9893
3	8483	8628	8764	8889	9004	9111	9209	9298	9379	9453
4	6425	6665	6898	7123	7340	7547	7745	7933	8112	8281
5	3922	4178	4436	4696	4956	5216	5474	5730	5982	6230
6	1834	2016	2207	2407	2616	2832	3057	3288	3526	3770
7	0626	0712	0806	0908	1020	1141	1271	1410	1560	1719
8	0146	0172	0202	0236	0274	0317	0366	0420	0480	0547
9	0021	0025	0031	0037	0045	0054	0065	0077	0091	0107
10	0001	0002	0002	0003	0003	0004	0005	0006	0008	0010

$$n = 11$$

p r	01	02	03	04	05	06	07	08	09	10
1	1047	1993	2847	3618	4312	4937	5499	6004	6456	6862
2	0052	0195	0413	0692	1017	1382	1772	2181	2601	3026
3	0002	0012	0037	0083	0153	0248	0370	0519	0695	0896
4			0002	0007	0016	0030	0053	0085	0129	0185
5					0001	0003	0005	0010	0017	0028
6								0001	0002	0003

Table C (*continued*)

p	11	12	13	14	15	16	17	18	19	20
r
1	7225	7549	7839	8097	8327	8531	8712	8873	9015	9141
2	3452	3873	4286	4689	5078	5453	5811	6151	6474	6779
3	1120	1366	1632	1915	2212	2521	2839	3164	3494	3826
4	0256	0341	0442	0560	0694	0846	1013	1197	1397	1611
5	0042	0061	0087	0119	0159	0207	0266	0334	0413	0504
6	0005	0008	0012	0018	0027	0037	0051	0068	0090	0117
7		0001	0001	0002	0003	0005	0007	0010	0014	0020
8							0001	0001	0002	0002

p	21	22	23	24	25	26	27	28	29	30
r
1	9252	9350	9436	9511	9578	9636	9686	9730	9769	9802
2	7066	7333	7582	7814	8029	8227	8410	8577	8730	8870
3	4158	4488	4814	5134	5448	5753	6049	6335	6610	6873
4	1840	2081	2333	2596	2867	3146	3430	3719	4011	4304
5	0607	0723	0851	0992	1146	1313	1493	1685	1888	2103
6	0148	0186	0231	0283	0343	0412	0490	0577	0674	0782
7	0027	0035	0046	0059	0076	0095	0119	0146	0179	0216
8	0003	0005	0007	0009	0012	0016	0021	0027	0034	0043
9			0001	0001	0001	0002	0002	0003	0004	0006

p	31	32	33	34	35	36	37	38	39	40
r
1	9831	9856	9878	9896	9912	9926	9938	9948	9956	9964
2	8997	9112	9216	9310	9394	9470	9537	9597	9650	9698
3	7123	7361	7587	7799	7999	8186	8360	8522	8672	8811
4	4598	4890	5179	5464	5744	6019	6286	6545	6796	7037
5	2328	2563	2807	3059	3317	3581	3850	4122	4397	4672
6	0901	1031	1171	1324	1487	1661	1847	2043	2249	2465
7	0260	0309	0366	0430	0501	0581	0670	0768	0876	0994
8	0054	0067	0082	0101	0122	0148	0177	0210	0249	0293
9	0008	0010	0013	0016	0020	0026	0032	0039	0048	0059
10	0001	0001	0001	0002	0002	0003	0004	0005	0006	0007

p	41	42	43	44	45	46	47	48	49	50
r
1	9970	9975	9979	9983	9986	9989	9991	9992	9994	9995
2	9739	9776	9808	9836	9861	9882	9900	9916	9930	9941
3	8938	9035	9162	9260	9348	9428	9499	9564	9622	9673
4	7269	7490	7700	7900	8089	8266	8433	8588	8733	8867
5	4940	5223	5495	5764	6029	6288	6541	6787	7026	7256
6	2690	2924	3166	3414	3669	3929	4193	4460	4729	5000
7	1121	1260	1408	1568	1738	1919	2110	2312	2523	2744
8	0343	0399	0461	0532	0610	0696	0791	0895	1009	1133
9	0072	0087	0104	0125	0148	0175	0206	0241	0282	0327
10	0009	0012	0014	0018	0022	0027	0033	0040	0049	0059
11	0001	0001	0001	0001	0002	0002	0002	0003	0004	0005

$$n = 12$$

p	01	02	03	04	05	06	07	08	09	10
r
1	1136	2153	3062	3873	4596	5241	5814	6323	6775	7176
2	0062	0231	0486	0809	1184	1595	2033	2487	2948	3410
3	0002	0015	0048	0107	0196	0316	0468	0652	0866	1109
4		0001	0003	0010	0022	0043	0075	0120	0180	0256
5				0001	0002	0004	0009	0016	0027	0043
6							0001	0002	0003	0005
7										0001

p	11	12	13	14	15	16	17	18	19	20
r
1	7530	7843	8120	8363	8578	8766	8931	9076	9202	9313
2	3867	4314	4748	5166	5565	5945	6304	6641	6957	7251
3	1377	1667	1977	2303	2642	2990	3344	3702	4060	4417
4	0351	0464	0597	0750	0922	1114	1324	1552	1795	2054
5	0065	0095	0133	0181	0239	0310	0393	0489	0600	0726
6	0009	0014	0022	0033	0046	0065	0088	0116	0151	0194
7	0001	0002	0003	0004	0007	0010	0015	0021	0029	0039
8					0001	0001	0002	0003	0004	0006
9										0001

Table C (*continued*)

p	21	22	23	24	25	26	27	28	29	30
r										
1	9409	9493	9566	9629	9683	9730	9771	9806	9836	9862
2	7524	7776	8009	8222	8416	8594	8755	8900	9032	9150
3	4768	5114	5450	5778	6093	6397	6687	6963	7225	7472
4	2326	2610	2904	3205	3512	3824	4137	4452	4765	5075
5	0866	1021	1192	1377	1576	1790	2016	2254	2504	2763
6	0245	0304	0374	0453	0544	0646	0760	0887	1026	1178
7	0052	0068	0089	0113	0143	0178	0219	0267	0322	0386
8	0008	0011	0016	0021	0028	0036	0047	0060	0076	0095
9	0001	0001	0002	0003	0004	0005	0007	0010	0013	0017
10						0001	0001	0001	0002	0002

p	31	32	33	34	35	36	37	38	39	40
r										
1	9884	9902	9918	9932	9943	9953	9961	9968	9973	9978
2	9256	9350	9435	9509	9576	9634	9685	9730	9770	9804
3	7704	7922	8124	8313	8487	8648	8795	8931	9054	9166
4	5381	5681	5973	6258	6533	6799	7053	7296	7528	7747
5	3032	3308	3590	3876	4167	4459	4751	5043	5332	5618
6	1343	1521	1711	1913	2127	2352	2588	2833	3087	3348
7	0458	0540	0632	0734	0846	0970	1106	1253	1411	1582
8	0118	0144	0176	0213	0255	0304	0359	0422	0493	0573
9	0022	0028	0036	0045	0056	0070	0086	0104	0127	0153
10	0003	0004	0005	0007	0008	0011	0014	0018	0022	0028
11				0001	0001	0001	0001	0002	0002	0003

p	41	42	43	44	45	46	47	48	49	50
r										
1	9982	9986	9990	9990	9992	9994	9995	9996	9997	9998
2	9834	9860	9882	9901	9917	9931	9943	9953	9961	9968
3	9267	9358	9440	9513	9579	9637	9688	9733	9773	9807
4	7953	8147	8329	8498	8655	8801	8934	9057	9168	9270
5	5899	6175	6443	6704	6956	7198	7430	7652	7862	8062
6	3616	3889	4167	4448	4731	5014	5297	5577	5855	6128
7	1765	1959	2164	2380	2607	2843	3089	3343	3604	3872
8	0662	0760	0869	0988	1117	1258	1411	1575	1751	1938
9	0183	0218	0258	0304	0356	0415	0481	0555	0638	0730
10	0035	0043	0053	0065	0079	0095	0114	0137	0163	0193
11	0004	0005	0007	0009	0011	0014	0017	0021	0026	0032
12				0001	0001	0001	0001	0001	0002	0002

$n = 13$

p	01	02	03	04	05	06	07	08	09	10
r										
1	1225	2310	3270	4118	4867	5526	6107	6617	7065	7458
2	0072	0270	0564	0932	1354	1814	2298	2794	3293	3787
3	0003	0020	0062	0135	0245	0392	0578	0799	1054	1339
4		0001	0005	0014	0031	0060	0103	0163	0242	0342
5				0001	0003	0007	0013	0024	0041	0065
6						0001	0001	0003	0005	0009
7									0001	0001

p	11	12	13	14	15	16	17	18	19	20
r										
1	7802	8102	8364	8592	8791	8963	9113	9242	9354	9450
2	4270	4738	5186	5614	6017	6396	6751	7080	7384	766.
3	1651	1985	2337	2704	3080	3463	3848	4231	4611	4983
4	0464	0609	0776	0967	1180	1414	1667	1939	2226	2527
5	0097	0139	0193	0260	0342	0438	0551	0681	0827	0991
6	0015	0024	0036	0053	0075	0104	0139	0183	0237	0300
7	0002	0003	0005	0008	0013	0019	0027	0038	0052	0070
8			0001	0001	0002	0003	0004	0006	0009	0012
9								0001	0001	0002

Table C (continued)

p	21	22	23	24	25	26	27	28	29	30
r										
1	9533	9604	9666	9718	9762	9800	9833	9860	9883	9903
2	7920	8154	8367	8559	8733	8889	9029	9154	9265	9363
3	5347	5699	6039	6364	6674	6968	7245	7505	7749	7975
4	2839	3161	3489	3822	4157	4493	4826	5155	5478	5794
5	1173	1371	1585	1816	2060	2319	2589	2870	3160	3457
6	0375	0462	0562	0675	0802	0944	1099	1270	1455	1654
7	0093	0120	0154	0195	0243	0299	0365	0440	0527	0624
8	0017	0024	0032	0043	0056	0073	0093	0118	0147	0182
9	0002	0004	0005	0007	0010	0013	0018	0024	0031	0040
10			0001	0001	0001	0002	0003	0004	0005	0007
11									0001	0001

p	31	32	33	34	35	36	37	38	39	40
r										
1	9920	9934	9945	9955	9963	9970	9975	9980	9984	9987
2	9450	9527	9594	9653	9704	9749	9787	9821	9849	9874
3	8185	8379	8557	8720	8868	9003	9125	9235	9333	9421
4	6101	6398	6683	6957	7217	7464	7698	7917	8123	8314
5	3760	4067	4376	4686	4995	5301	5603	5899	6188	6470
6	1867	2093	2331	2581	2841	3111	3388	3673	3962	4256
7	0733	0854	0988	1135	1295	1468	1654	1853	2065	2288
8	0223	0271	0326	0390	0462	0544	0635	0738	0851	0977
9	0052	0065	0082	0102	0126	0154	0187	0225	0270	0321
10	0009	0012	0015	0020	0025	0032	0040	0051	0063	0078
11	0001	0001	0002	0003	0003	0005	0006	0008	0010	0013
12							0001	0001	0001	0001

p	41	42	43	44	45	46	47	48	49	50
r										
1	9990	9992	9993	9995	9996	9997	9997	9998	9998	9999
2	9895	9912	9928	9940	9951	9960	9967	9974	9979	9983
3	9499	9569	9630	9684	9731	9772	9808	9838	9865	9888
4	8492	8656	8807	8945	9071	9185	9288	9381	9464	9539
5	6742	7003	7254	7493	7721	7935	8137	8326	8502	8666
6	4552	4849	5146	5441	5732	6019	6299	6573	6838	7095
7	2524	2770	3025	3290	3563	3842	4127	4415	4707	5000
8	1114	1264	1426	1600	1788	1988	2200	2424	2659	2905
9	0379	0446	0520	0605	0698	0803	0918	1045	1183	1334
10	0096	0117	0141	0170	0203	0242	0287	0338	0396	0461
11	0017	0021	0027	0033	0041	0051	0063	0077	0093	0112
12	0002	0002	0003	0004	0005	0007	0009	0011	0014	0017
13							0001	0001	0001	0001

$$n = 14$$

p	01	02	03	04	05	06	07	08	09	10
r										
1	1313	2464	3472	4353	5123	5795	6380	6888	7330	7712
2	0084	0310	0645	1059	1530	2037	2564	3100	3632	4154
3	0003	0025	0077	0167	0301	0478	0698	0958	1255	1584
4		0001	0006	0019	0042	0080	0136	0214	0315	0441
5				0002	0004	0010	0020	0035	0059	0092
6						0001	0002	0004	0008	0015
7									0001	0002

p	11	12	13	14	15	16	17	18	19	20
r										
1	8044	8330	8577	8789	8972	9129	9264	9379	9477	9560
2	4658	5141	5599	6031	6433	6807	7152	7469	7758	8021
3	1939	2315	2708	3111	3521	3932	4341	4744	5138	5519
4	0594	0774	0979	1210	1465	1742	2038	2351	2679	3018
5	0137	0196	0269	0359	0467	0594	0741	0907	1093	1298
6	0024	0038	0057	0082	0115	0157	0209	0273	0349	0439
7	0003	0006	0009	0015	0022	0032	0046	0064	0087	0116
8			0001	0001	0002	0003	0005	0008	0012	0017	0024
9							0001	0001	0002	0003	0004

Table C (*continued*)

p	21	22	23	24	25	26	27	28	29	30
r										
1	9631	9691	9742	9786	9842	9852	9878	9899	9917	9932
2	8259	8473	8665	8837	8990	9126	9246	9352	9444	9525
3	5887	6239	6574	6891	7189	7467	7727	7967	8188	8392
4	3366	3719	4076	4432	4787	5136	5479	5813	6137	6448
5	1523	1765	2023	2297	2585	2884	3193	3509	3832	4158
6	0543	0662	0797	0949	1117	1301	1502	1718	1949	2195
7	0152	0196	0248	0310	0383	0467	0563	0673	0796	0933
8	0033	0045	0060	0079	0103	0132	0167	0208	0257	0315
9	0006	0008	0011	0016	0022	0029	0038	0050	0065	0083
10	0001	0001	0002	0002	0003	0005	0007	0009	0012	0017
11						0001	0001	0001	0002	0002

p	31	32	33	34	35	36	37	38	39	40
r										
1	9945	9955	9963	9970	9976	9981	9984	9988	9990	9992
2	9596	9657	9710	9756	9795	9828	9857	9881	9902	9919
3	8577	8746	8899	9037	9161	9271	9370	9457	9534	9602
4	6747	7032	7301	7556	7795	8018	8226	8418	8595	8757
5	4486	4813	5138	5458	5773	6080	6378	6666	6943	7207
6	2454	2724	3006	3297	3595	3899	4208	4519	4831	5141
7	1084	1250	1431	1626	1836	2059	2296	2545	2805	3075
8	0381	0458	0545	0643	0753	0876	1012	1162	1325	1501
9	0105	0131	0163	0200	0243	0294	0353	0420	0497	0583
10	0022	0029	0037	0048	0060	0076	0095	0117	0144	0175
11	0003	0005	0006	0008	0011	0014	0019	0024	0031	0039
12		0001	0001	0001	0001	0002	0003	0003	0005	0006
13										0001

p	41	42	43	44	45	46	47	48	49	50
r										
1	9994	9995	9996	9997	9998	9998	9999	9999	9999	9999
2	9934	9946	9956	9964	9971	9977	9981	9985	9988	9991
3	9661	9713	9758	9797	9830	9858	9883	9903	9921	9935
4	8905	9039	9161	9270	9368	9455	9532	9601	9661	9713
5	7459	7697	7922	8132	8328	8510	8678	8833	8974	9102
6	5450	5754	6052	6344	6627	6900	7163	7415	7654	7880
7	3355	3643	3937	4236	4539	4843	5148	5451	5751	6047
8	1692	1896	2113	2344	2586	2840	3105	3380	3663	3953
9	0680	0789	0910	1043	1189	1348	1520	1707	1906	2120
10	0212	0255	0304	0361	0426	0500	0583	0677	0782	0898
11	0049	0061	0076	0093	0114	0139	0168	0202	0241	0287
12	0008	0010	0013	0017	0022	0027	0034	0042	0053	0065
13	0001	0001	0001	0002	0003	0003	0004	0006	0007	0009
14										0001

$n = 15$

p	01	02	03	04	05	06	07	08	09	10
r										
1	1399	2614	3667	4579	5367	6047	6633	7137	7570	7941
2	0096	0353	0730	1191	1710	2262	2832	3403	3965	4510
3	0004	0030	0094	0203	0362	0571	0829	1130	1469	1841
4		0002	0008	0024	0055	0104	0175	0273	0399	0556
5			0001	0002	0006	0014	0028	0050	0082	0127
6					0001	0001	0003	0007	0013	0022
7								0001	0002	0003

p	11	12	13	14	15	16	17	18	19	20
r										
1	8259	8530	8762	8959	9126	9269	9389	9490	9576	9648
2	5031	5524	5987	6417	6814	7179	7511	7813	8085	8329
3	2238	2654	3084	3520	3958	4392	4819	5234	5635	6020
4	0742	0959	1204	1476	1773	2092	2429	2782	3146	3518
5	0187	0265	0361	0478	0617	0778	0961	1167	1394	1642
6	0037	0057	0084	0121	0168	0227	0300	0387	0490	0611
7	0006	0010	0015	0024	0036	0052	0074	0102	0137	0181
8	0001	0001	0002	0004	0006	0010	0014	0021	0030	0042
9					0001	0001	0002	0003	0005	0008
10									0001	0001

Table C (continued)

p / r	21	22	23	24	25	26	27	28	29	30
1	9709	9759	9802	9837	9866	9891	9911	9928	9941	9953
2	8547	8741	8913	9065	9198	9315	9417	9505	9581	9647
3	6385	6731	7055	7358	7639	7899	8137	8355	8553	8732
4	3895	4274	4650	5022	5387	5742	6086	6416	6732	7031
5	1910	2195	2495	2810	3135	3469	3810	4154	4500	4845
6	0748	0905	1079	1272	1484	1713	1958	2220	2495	2784
7	0234	0298	0374	0463	0566	0684	0817	0965	1130	1311
8	0058	0078	0104	0135	0173	0219	0274	0338	0413	0500
9	0011	0016	0023	0031	0042	0056	0073	0094	0121	0152
10	0002	0003	0004	0006	0008	0011	0015	0021	0028	0037
11			0001	0001	0001	0002	0002	0003	0005	0007
12									0001	0001

p / r	31	32	33	34	35	36	37	38	39	40
1	9962	9969	9975	9980	9984	9988	9990	9992	9994	9995
2	9704	9752	9794	9829	9858	9883	9904	9922	9936	9948
3	8893	9038	9167	9281	9383	9472	9550	9618	9678	9729
4	7314	7580	7829	8060	8273	8469	8649	8813	8961	9095
5	5187	5523	5852	6171	6481	6778	7062	7332	7587	7827
6	3084	3393	3709	4032	4357	4684	5011	5335	5654	5968
7	1509	1722	1951	2194	2452	2722	3003	3295	3595	3902
8	0599	0711	0837	0977	1132	1302	1487	1687	1902	2131
9	0190	0236	0289	0351	0422	0504	0597	0702	0820	0950
10	0048	0062	0079	0099	0124	0154	0190	0232	0281	0338
11	0009	0012	0016	0022	0028	0037	0047	0059	0075	0093
12	0001	0002	0003	0004	0005	0006	0009	0011	0015	0019
13					0001	0001	0001	0002	0002	0003

p / r	41	42	43	44	45	46	47	48	49	50
1	9996	9997	9998	9998	9999	9999	9999	9999	10000	10000
2	9958	9966	9973	9979	9983	9987	9990	9992	9994	9995
3	9773	9811	9843	9870	9893	9913	9929	9943	9954	9963
4	9215	9322	9417	9502	9576	9641	9697	9746	9788	9824
5	8052	8261	8454	8633	8796	8945	9080	9201	9310	9408
6	6274	6570	6856	7131	7393	7641	7875	8095	8301	8491
7	4314	4530	4847	5164	5478	5789	6095	6394	6684	6964
8	2374	2630	2898	3176	3465	3762	4065	4374	4686	5000
9	1095	1254	1427	1615	1818	2034	2265	2510	2767	3036
10	0404	0479	0565	0661	0769	0890	1024	1171	1333	1509
11	0116	0143	0174	0211	0255	0305	0363	0430	0506	0592
12	0025	0032	0040	0051	0063	0079	0097	0119	0145	0176
13	0004	0005	0007	0009	0011	0014	0018	0023	0029	0037
14			0001	0001	0001	0002	0002	0003	0004	0005

$$n = 16$$

p / r	01	02	03	04	05	06	07	08	09	10
1	1485	2762	3857	4796	5599	6284	6869	7366	7789	8147
2	0109	0399	0818	1327	1892	2489	3098	3701	4289	4853
3	0005	0037	0113	0242	0429	0673	0969	1311	1694	2108
4		0002	0011	0032	0070	0132	0221	0342	0496	0684
5			0001	0003	0009	0019	0038	0068	0111	0170
6					0001	0002	0005	0010	0019	0033
7							0001	0001	0003	0005
8										0001

p / r	11	12	13	14	15	16	17	18	19	20
1	8450	8707	8923	9105	9257	9386	9493	9582	9657	9719
2	5386	5885	6347	6773	7161	7513	7830	8115	8368	8593
3	2545	2999	3461	3926	4386	4838	5277	5698	6101	6482
4	0907	1162	1448	1763	2101	2460	2836	3223	3619	4019
5	0248	0348	0471	0618	0791	0988	1211	1458	1727	2018
6	0053	0082	0120	0171	0235	0315	0412	0527	0662	0817
7	0009	0015	0024	0038	0056	0080	0112	0153	0204	0267
8	0001	0002	0004	0007	0011	0016	0024	0036	0051	0070
9			0001	0001	0002	0003	0004	0007	0010	0015
10							0001	0001	0002	0002

Table C (continued)

r \ p	21	22	23	24	25	26	27	28	29	30
1	9770	9812	9847	9876	9900	9919	9935	9948	9958	9967
2	8791	8965	9117	9250	9365	9465	9550	9623	9686	9739
3	6839	7173	7483	7768	8029	8267	8482	8677	8851	9006
4	4418	4814	5203	5583	5950	6303	6640	6959	7260	7541
5	2387	2652	2991	3341	3698	4060	4425	4788	5147	5501
6	0992	1188	1405	1641	1897	2169	2458	2761	3077	3402
7	0342	0432	0536	0657	0796	0951	1125	1317	1526	1753
8	0095	0127	0166	0214	0271	0340	0420	0514	0621	0744
9	0021	0030	0041	0056	0075	0098	0127	0163	0206	0257
10	0004	0006	0008	0012	0016	0023	0031	0041	0055	0071
11	0001	0001	0001	0002	0003	0004	0006	0008	0011	0016
12						0001	0001	0001	0002	0003

r \ p	31	32	33	34	35	36	37	38	39	40
1	9974	9979	9984	9987	9990	9992	9994	9995	9996	9997
2	9784	9822	9854	9880	9902	9921	9936	9948	9959	9967
3	9144	9266	9374	9467	9549	9620	9681	9734	9778	9817
4	7804	8047	8270	8475	8661	8830	8982	9119	9241	9349
5	5846	6181	6504	6813	7108	7387	7649	7895	8123	8334
6	3736	4074	4416	4759	5100	5438	5770	6094	6408	6712
7	1997	2257	2531	2819	3119	3428	3746	4070	4398	4728
8	0881	1035	1205	1391	1594	1813	2048	2298	2562	2839
9	0317	0388	0470	0564	0671	0791	0926	1076	1242	1423
10	0092	0117	0148	0185	0229	0280	0341	0411	0491	0583
11	0021	0028	0037	0048	0062	0079	0100	0125	0155	0191
12	0004	0005	0007	0010	0013	0017	0023	0030	0038	0049
13		0001	0001	0001	0002	0003	0004	0005	0007	0009
14								0001	0001	0001

r \ p	41	42	43	44	45	46	47	48	49	50
1	9998	9998	9999	9999	9999	9999	10000	10000	10000	10000
2	9974	9979	9984	9987	9990	9992	9994	9995	9997	9997
3	9849	9876	9899	9918	9934	9947	9958	9966	9973	9979
4	9444	9527	9600	9664	9719	9766	9806	9840	9869	9894
5	8529	8707	8869	9015	9147	9265	9370	9463	9544	9616
6	7003	7280	7543	7792	8024	8241	8441	8626	8795	8949
7	5058	5387	5711	6029	6340	6641	6932	7210	7476	7728
8	3188	3428	3736	4051	4371	4694	5019	5343	5665	5982
9	1619	1832	2060	2302	2559	2829	3111	3405	3707	4018
10	0687	0805	0936	1081	1241	1416	1607	1814	2036	2272
11	0234	0284	0342	0409	0486	0574	0674	0786	0911	1051
12	0062	0078	0098	0121	0149	0183	0222	0268	0322	0384
13	0012	0016	0021	0027	0035	0044	0055	0069	0086	0106
14	0002	0002	0003	0004	0006	0007	0010	0013	0016	0021
15					0001	0001	0001	0001	0002	0003

$$n = 17$$

r \ p	01	02	03	04	05	06	07	08	09	10
1	1571	2907	4042	5004	5819	6507	7088	7577	7988	8332
2	0123	0446	0909	1465	2078	2717	3362	3995	4604	5182
3	0006	0044	0134	0286	0503	0782	1118	1503	1927	2382
4		0003	0014	0040	0088	0164	0273	0419	0603	0826
5			0001	0004	0012	0026	0051	0089	0145	0221
6					0001	0003	0007	0015	0027	0047
7							0001	0002	0004	0008
8										0001

r \ p	11	12	13	14	15	16	17	18	19	20
1	8621	8862	9063	9230	9369	9484	9579	9657	9722	9775
2	5723	6223	6682	7099	7475	7813	8113	8379	8613	8818
3	2858	3345	3836	4324	4802	5266	5711	6133	6532	6904
4	1087	1383	1710	2065	2444	2841	3251	3669	4091	4511
5	0321	0446	0598	0778	0987	1224	1487	1775	2087	2418
6	0075	0114	0166	0234	0319	0423	0548	0695	0864	1057
7	0014	0023	0037	0056	0083	0118	0163	0220	0291	0377
8	0002	0004	0007	0011	0017	0027	0039	0057	0080	0109
9		0001	0001	0002	0003	0005	0008	0012	0018	0026
10							0001	0001	0002	0003	0005
11										0001

Table C (continued)

p r	21	22	23	24	25	26	27	28	29	30
1	9818	9854	9882	9906	9925	9940	9953	9962	9970	9977
2	8996	9152	9285	9400	9499	9583	9654	9714	9765	9807
3	7349	7567	7859	8123	8363	8578	8771	8942	9093	9226
4	4927	5333	5728	6107	6470	6814	7137	7440	7721	7981
5	2766	3128	3500	3879	4261	4643	5023	5396	5760	6113
6	1273	1510	1770	2049	2347	2661	2989	3329	3677	4032
7	0479	0598	0736	0894	1071	1268	1485	1721	1976	2248
8	0147	0194	0251	0320	0402	0499	0611	0739	0884	1046
9	0037	0051	0070	0094	0124	0161	0206	0261	0326	0403
10	0007	0011	0016	0022	0031	0042	0057	0075	0098	0127
11	0001	0002	0003	0004	0006	0009	0013	0018	0024	0032
12			0001	0001	0002	0002	0003	0005	0007
13								0001	0001

p r	31	32	33	34	35	36	37	38	39	40
1	9982	9986	9989	9991	9993	9995	9996	9997	9998	9998
2	9843	9872	9896	9917	9933	9946	9957	9966	9973	9979
3	9343	9444	9532	9608	9673	9728	9775	9815	9849	9877
4	8219	8437	8634	8812	8972	9115	9241	9353	9450	9536
5	6453	6778	7087	7378	7652	7906	8142	8360	8559	8740
6	4390	4749	5105	5458	5803	6139	6465	6778	7077	7361
7	2536	2838	3153	3479	3812	4152	4495	4839	5182	5522
8	1287	1426	1642	1877	2128	2395	2676	2971	3278	3595
9	0492	0595	0712	0845	0994	1159	1341	1541	1757	1989
10	0162	0204	0254	0314	0383	0464	0557	0664	0784	0919
11	0043	0057	0074	0095	0120	0151	0189	0234	0286	0348
12	0009	0013	0017	0023	0030	0040	0051	0066	0084	0106
13	0002	0002	0003	0004	0006	0008	0011	0015	0019	0025
14				0001	0001	0001	0002	0002	0003	0005
15										0001

p r	41	42	43	44	45	46	47	48	49	50
1	9999	9999	9999	9999	10000	10000	10000	10000	10000	10000
2	9984	9987	9990	9992	9994	9996	9997	9998	9998	9999
3	9900	9920	9935	9948	9959	9968	9975	9980	9985	9988
4	9610	9674	9729	9776	9816	9849	9877	9901	9920	9936
5	8904	9051	9183	9301	9404	9495	9575	9644	9704	9755
6	7628	7879	8113	8330	8529	8712	8878	9028	9162	9283
7	5856	6182	6499	6805	7098	7377	7641	7890	8122	8338
8	3920	4250	4585	4921	5257	5590	5918	6239	6552	6855
9	2258	2502	2780	3072	3374	3687	4008	4335	4667	5000
10	1070	1236	1419	1618	1834	2066	2314	2577	2855	3145
11	0480	0503	0597	0705	0826	0962	1112	1279	1462	1662
12	0133	0165	0203	0248	0301	0363	0434	0517	0611	0717
13	0033	0042	0054	0069	0086	0108	0134	0165	0202	0245
14	0006	0008	0011	0014	0019	0024	0031	0040	0050	0064
15	0001	0001	0002	0002	0003	0004	0005	0007	0009	0012
16							0001	0001	0001	0001

n = 18

p r	01	02	03	04	05	06	07	08	09	10
1	1655	3049	4220	5204	6028	6717	7292	7771	8169	8499
2	0138	0495	1003	1607	2265	2945	3622	4281	4909	5497
3	0007	0052	0157	0333	0581	0898	1275	1702	2168	2662
4		0004	0018	0050	0109	0201	0333	0506	0723	0982
5			0002	0006	0015	0034	0067	0116	0186	0282
6				0001	0002	0005	0010	0021	0038	0064
7						0001	0003	0006	0012
8								0001	0002

p r	11	12	13	14	15	16	17	18	19	20
1	8773	8998	9185	9338	9464	9566	9651	9719	9775	9820
2	6042	6540	6992	7398	7759	8080	8362	8609	8824	9009
3	3173	3690	4206	4713	5203	5673	6119	6538	6927	7287
4	1282	1618	1986	2382	2798	3229	3669	4112	4554	4990
5	0405	0558	0743	0959	1206	1482	1787	2116	2467	2836

Table C (continued)

r	p=11	12	13	14	15	16	17	18	19	20
1	8908	9119	9291	9431	9544	9636	9710	9770	9818	9856
2	6342	6835	7277	7669	8015	8318	8581	8809	9004	9171
3	3488	4032	4568	5089	5587	6059	6500	6910	7287	7631
4	1490	1867	2275	2708	3159	3620	4085	4549	5005	5449
5	0502	0685	0904	1158	1444	1762	2107	2476	2864	3267
6	0135	0202	0290	0401	0537	0700	0891	1110	1357	1631
7	0030	0048	0076	0113	0163	0228	0310	0411	0532	0676
8	0005	0009	0016	0026	0041	0061	0089	0126	0173	0233
9	0001	0002	0003	0005	0008	0014	0021	0032	0047	0067
10				0001	0001	0002	0004	0007	0010	0016
11							0001	0001	0002	0003

r	p=21	22	23	24	25	26	27	28	29	30
1	9887	9911	9930	9946	9958	9967	9975	9981	9985	9989
2	9313	9434	9535	9619	9690	9749	9797	9837	9869	9896
3	7942	8222	8471	8692	8887	9057	9205	9333	9443	9538
4	5877	6285	6671	7032	7369	7680	7965	8224	8458	8668
5	3681	4100	4520	4936	5346	5744	6129	6498	6848	7178
6	1929	2251	2592	2950	3322	3705	4093	4484	4875	5261
7	0843	1034	1248	1487	1749	2032	2336	2657	2995	3345
8	0307	0396	0503	0629	0775	0941	1129	1338	1568	1820
9	0093	0127	0169	0222	0287	0366	0459	0568	0694	0839
10	0023	0034	0047	0066	0089	0119	0156	0202	0258	0326
11	0005	0007	0011	0016	0023	0032	0044	0060	0080	0105
12	0001	0001	0002	0003	0005	0007	0010	0015	0021	0028
13				0001	0001	0001	0002	0003	0004	0006
14									0001	0001

r	p=31	32	33	34	35	36	37	38	39	40
1	9991	9993	9995	9996	9997	9998	9998	9999	9999	9999
2	9917	9935	9949	9960	9969	9976	9981	9986	9989	9992
3	9618	9686	9743	9791	9830	9863	9890	9913	9931	9945
4	8856	9022	9169	9297	9409	9505	9588	9659	9719	9770
5	7486	7773	8037	8280	8500	8699	8878	9038	9179	9304
6	5641	6010	6366	6707	7032	7339	7627	7895	8143	8371
7	3705	4073	4445	4818	5188	5554	5913	6261	6597	6919
8	2091	2381	2688	3010	3344	3690	4043	4401	4762	5122
9	1003	1186	1389	1612	1855	2116	2395	2691	3002	3325
10	0405	0499	0608	0733	0875	1035	1213	1410	1626	1861
11	0137	0176	0223	0280	0347	0426	0518	0625	0747	0885
12	0038	0051	0068	0089	0114	0146	0185	0231	0287	0352
13	0009	0012	0017	0023	0031	0041	0054	0070	0091	0116
14	0002	0002	0003	0005	0007	0009	0013	0017	0023	0031
15			0001	0001	0001	0002	0002	0003	0005	0006
16									0001	0001

r	p=41	42	43	44	45	46	47	48	49	50
1	10000	10000	10000	10000	10000	10000	10000	10000	10000	10000
2	9994	9995	9996	9997	9998	9999	9999	9999	9999	10000
3	9957	9967	9974	9980	9985	9988	9991	9993	9995	9996
4	9813	9849	9878	9903	9923	9939	9952	9963	9971	9978
5	9413	9508	9590	9660	9720	9771	9814	9850	9879	9904
6	8579	8767	8937	9088	9223	9342	9446	9537	9615	9682
7	7226	7515	7787	8039	8273	8488	8684	8862	9022	9165
8	5480	5832	6176	6509	6831	7138	7430	7706	7964	8204
9	3660	4003	4353	4706	5060	5413	5762	6105	6439	6762
10	2114	2385	2672	2974	3290	3617	3954	4299	4648	5000
11	1040	1213	1404	1613	1841	2087	2351	2631	2928	3238
12	0489	0518	0621	0738	0871	1021	1187	1372	1575	1796
13	0146	0183	0227	0280	0342	0415	0500	0597	0709	0835
14	0040	0052	0067	0086	0109	0137	0171	0212	0261	0318
15	0009	0012	0016	0021	0028	0036	0046	0060	0076	0096
16	0001	0002	0003	0004	0005	0007	0010	0013	0017	0022
17				0001	0001	0001	0001	0002	0003	0004

Table C (*continued*)

r \ p	11	12	13	14	15	16	17	18	19	20
6	0102	0154	0222	0310	0419	0551	0708	0889	1097	1329
7	0031	0034	0054	0081	0118	0167	0229	0306	0400	0513
8	0005	0006	0011	0017	0027	0041	0060	0086	0120	0163
9		0001	0002	0003	0005	0008	0013	0020	0029	0043
10					0001	0001	0002	0004	0006	0009
11								0001	0001	0002

r \ p	21	22	23	24	25	26	27	28	29	30
1	9856	9886	9909	9928	9944	9956	9965	9973	9979	9984
2	9169	9306	9423	9522	9605	9676	9735	9784	9824	9858
3	7616	7916	8187	8430	8647	8839	9009	9158	9288	9400
4	5414	5825	6218	6591	6943	7272	7578	7860	8119	8354
5	3220	3613	4012	4414	4813	5208	5594	5968	6329	6673
6	1586	1866	2168	2488	2825	3176	3538	3907	4281	4656
7	0645	0799	0974	1171	1390	1630	1891	2171	2469	2783
8	0217	0283	0363	0458	0569	0699	0847	1014	1200	1407
9	0060	0083	0112	0148	0193	0249	0316	0395	0488	0596
10	0014	0020	0028	0039	0054	0073	0097	0127	0164	0210
11	0003	0004	0006	0009	0012	0018	0025	0034	0046	0061
12		0001	0001	0002	0002	0003	0005	0007	0010	0014
13						0001	0001	0001	0002	0003

r \ p	31	32	33	34	35	36	37	38	39	40
1	9987	9990	9993	9994	9996	9997	9998	9998	9999	9999
2	9886	9908	9927	9942	9954	9964	9972	9978	9983	9987
3	9498	9581	9652	9713	9764	9807	9843	9873	9897	9918
4	8568	8759	8931	9083	9217	9335	9439	9528	9606	9672
5	7001	7309	7598	7866	8114	8341	8549	8737	8907	9058
6	5029	5398	5759	6111	6450	6776	7086	7379	7655	7912
7	3111	3450	3797	4151	4509	4867	5224	5576	5921	6257
8	1633	1878	2141	2421	2717	3027	3349	3681	4021	4366
9	0720	0861	1019	1196	1391	1604	1835	2084	2350	2632
10	0264	0329	0405	0494	0597	0714	0847	0997	1163	1347
11	0080	0104	0133	0169	0212	0264	0325	0397	0480	0576
12	0020	0027	0036	0047	0062	0080	0102	0130	0163	0203
13	0004	0005	0008	0011	0014	0019	0026	0034	0044	0058
14	0001	0001	0001	0002	0003	0004	0005	0007	0010	0013
15						0001	0001	0001	0002	0002

r \ p	41	42	43	44	45	46	47	48	49	50
1	9999	9999	10000	10000	10000	10000	10000	10000	10000	10000
2	9990	9992	9994	9996	9997	9998	9998	9999	9999	9999
3	9934	9948	9959	9968	9975	9981	9985	9989	9991	9993
4	9729	9777	9818	9852	9880	9904	9923	9939	9952	9962
5	9193	9313	9418	9510	9589	9658	9717	9767	9810	9846
6	8151	8372	8573	8757	8923	9072	9205	9324	9428	9519
7	6582	6895	7193	7476	7742	7991	8222	8436	8632	8811
8	4713	5062	5408	5750	6085	6412	6728	7032	7322	7597
9	2928	3236	3556	3885	4222	4562	4906	5249	5591	5927
10	1549	1768	2004	2258	2527	2812	3110	3421	3742	4073
11	0686	0811	0951	1107	1280	1470	1677	1902	2144	2403
12	0250	0307	0372	0449	0537	0658	0753	0883	1028	1189
13	0074	0094	0110	0147	0183	0225	0275	0334	0402	0461
14	0017	0022	0029	0038	0049	0063	0079	0100	0125	0154
15	0003	0004	0006	0007	0010	0013	0017	0023	0029	0036
16		0001	0001	0001	0001	0002	0003	0004	0005	0007
17									0001	0001

n = 19

r \ p	01	02	03	04	05	06	07	08	09	10
1	1738	3188	4394	5396	6226	6914	7481	7949	8334	8649
2	0153	0546	1100	1751	2453	3171	3879	4560	5202	5797
3	0009	0061	0183	0384	0665	1021	1439	1908	2415	2946
4		0005	0022	0061	0132	0243	0398	0602	0953	1150
5			0002	0007	0020	0044	0085	0147	0235	0352
6				0001	0002	0006	0014	0029	0051	0086
7						0001	0002	0004	0009	0017
8								0001	0001	0003

Table C (*continued*)

n = 20

p	01	02	03	04	05	06	07	08	09	10
r										
1	1821	3324	4562	5580	6415	7099	7658	8113	8484	8784
2	0169	0599	1198	1897	2642	3395	4131	4831	5484	6083
3	0010	0071	0210	0439	0755	1150	1610	2121	2666	3231
4		0006	0027	0074	0159	0290	0471	0706	0993	1330
5			0003	0010	0026	0056	0107	0183	0290	0432
6				0001	0003	0009	0019	0038	0068	0113
7						0001	0003	0006	0013	0024
8								0001	0002	0004
9										0001

p	11	12	13	14	15	16	17	18	19	20
r										
1	9028	9224	9383	9510	9612	9694	9759	9811	9852	9885
2	6624	7109	7539	7916	8244	8529	8773	8982	9159	9308
3	3802	4369	4920	5450	5951	6420	6854	7252	7614	7939
4	1710	2127	2573	3041	3523	4010	4496	4974	5439	5886
5	0610	0827	1083	1375	1702	2059	2443	2849	3271	3704
6	0175	0260	0370	0507	0673	0870	1098	1356	1643	1958
7	0041	0067	0103	0153	0219	0304	0409	0537	0689	0867
8	0008	0014	0024	0038	0059	0088	0127	0177	0241	0321
9	0001	0002	0005	0008	0013	0021	0033	0049	0071	0100
10			0001	0001	0002	0004	0007	0011	0017	0026
11							0001	0002	0004	0006
12									0001	0001

p	21	22	23	24	25	26	27	28	29	30
r										
1	9910	9931	9946	9959	9968	9976	9982	9986	9989	9992
2	9434	9539	9626	9698	9757	9805	9845	9877	9903	9924
3	8230	8488	8716	8915	9087	9237	9365	9474	9567	9645
4	6310	6711	7085	7431	7748	8038	8300	8534	8744	8929
5	4142	4580	5014	5439	5852	6248	6625	6981	7315	7625
6	2297	2657	3035	3427	3828	4235	4643	5048	5447	5836
7	1071	1301	1557	1838	2142	2467	2810	3169	3540	3920
8	0419	0536	0675	0835	1018	1225	1455	1707	1982	2277
9	0138	0186	0246	0320	0409	0515	0640	0784	0948	1133
10	0038	0054	0075	0103	0139	0183	0238	0305	0385	0480
11	0009	0013	0019	0028	0039	0055	0074	0100	0132	0171
12	0002	0003	0004	0006	0009	0014	0019	0027	0038	0051
13			0001	0001	0002	0003	0004	0006	0009	0013
14							0001	0001	0002	0003

p	31	32	33	34	35	36	37	38	39	40
r										
1	9994	9996	9997	9998	9998	9999	9999	9999	9999	10000
2	9940	9953	9964	9972	9979	9984	9988	9991	9993	9995
3	9711	9765	9811	9848	9879	9904	9924	9940	9953	9964
4	9092	9235	9358	9465	9556	9634	9700	9755	9802	9840
5	7911	8173	8411	8626	8818	8989	9141	9274	9390	9490
6	6213	6574	6917	7242	7546	7829	8090	8329	8547	8744
7	4305	4693	5079	5460	5834	6197	6547	6882	7200	7500
8	2591	2922	3268	3624	3990	4361	4735	5108	5478	5841
9	1340	1568	1818	2087	2376	2683	3005	3341	3688	4044
10	0591	0719	0866	1032	1218	1424	1650	1897	2163	2447
11	0220	0275	0350	0434	0532	0645	0775	0923	1090	1275
12	0069	0091	0119	0154	0196	0247	0308	0381	0466	0565
13	0018	0025	0034	0045	0060	0079	0102	0132	0167	0210
14	0004	0006	0008	0011	0015	0021	0028	0037	0049	0065
15	0001	0001	0001	0002	0003	0004	0006	0009	0012	0016
16							0001	0001	0002	0002	0003

p	41	42	43	44	45	46	47	48	49	50
r										
1	10000	10000	10000	10000	10000	10000	10000	10000	10000	10000
2	9996	9997	9998	9998	9999	9999	9999	10000	10000	10000
3	9972	9979	9984	9988	9991	9993	9995	9996	9997	9998
4	9872	9898	9920	9937	9951	9962	9971	9977	9983	9987
5	9577	9651	9714	9767	9811	9848	9879	9904	9924	9941

Table C (*concluded*)

p	41	42	43	44	45	46	47	48	49	50
6	8921	9078	9217	9340	9447	9539	9619	9687	9745	9793
7	7780	8041	8281	8501	8701	8881	9042	9186	9312	9423
8	6196	6539	6868	7183	7480	7759	8020	8261	8482	8684
9	4406	4771	5136	5499	5857	6207	6546	6873	7186	7483
10	2748	3064	3394	3736	4086	4443	4804	5166	5525	5881
11	1480	1705	1949	2212	2493	2791	3104	3432	3771	4119
12	0679	0810	0958	1123	1308	1511	1734	1977	2238	2517
13	0262	0324	0397	0482	0580	0694	0823	0969	1133	1316
14	0084	0107	0136	0172	0214	0265	0326	0397	0480	0577
15	0022	0029	0038	0050	0064	0083	0105	0133	0166	0207
16	0004	0006	0008	0011	0015	0020	0027	0035	0046	0059
17	0001	0001	0001	0002	0003	0004	0005	0007	0010	0013
18						0001	0001	0001	0001	0002

Solutions to Selected Problems

Chapter 1

1-1. *a*. Set $1,000 = (1 - .40)X$, and solve for X: $X = 1000/.60 = 1,667$ units.
 b. Total cost $= \$5,000 + \$30(1,667) = \$5,000 + \$50,000 = \$55,000$
 c. Since revenue is only $50,000, under these circumstances the contract should be rejected (a loss of $5,000 would result if the contract were accepted).

1-2. *a*. The annual saving from the plastic gear is (50¢) (80,000 units) $= \$40,000$. Since the annual cost of conversion is only $20,000, the company should convert to the plastic gear.
 b. Additional annual costs of the plastic gear due to higher failures are ($40) $(2/1000)(80,000) = \$6,400$. Thus, total costs are $20,000 + $6,400 $= \$26,400$. This is still less than the saving of $40,000, so the company should still convert to plastic.

Chapter 2

2-1. *a*. Decision variable: PRICE.
 Exogenous variables: UNIT SALES, FIXED COSTS (both manufacturing and marketing), VARIABLE COST/UNIT.
 Performance measure: PROFIT
 Intermediate variables: SALES (dollars), MANUFACTURING COST, MARKETING COST, GROSS MARGIN (optional).
 Policies/constraints: None.
 b. Relationships:
 SALES (dollars) = UNIT SALES * PRICE
 MANUFACTURING COST = 80,000 + 300 * UNIT SALES
 GROSS MARGIN = SALES (dollars) − MANUFACTURING COST
 MARKETING COST = 10,000 + .10 * SALES (dollars)
 PROFIT = GROSS MARGIN − MARKETING COST
 [If variable GROSS MARGIN is not used, then PROFIT = SALES (dollars) − MANUFACTURING COST − MARKETING COST.]

c. Using the format given in the problem, and assuming the labels are in column A and numbers and formulas in column B, we have:

```
                    A                              B
  1 UNIT SALES                                   100
  2 PRICE                                        1600
  3 VARIABLE COST/UNIT                            300
  4
  5        PROJECTED INCOME STATEMENT
  6            MYOWN COMPANY, 1992
  7
  8 SALES (dollars)                      +B1*B2
  9 MANUFACTURING COST         (80000 + (B3*B1))
 10                                      --------
 11 GROSS MARGIN                         +B8-B9
 12
 13 MARKETING COST             (10000 + (.10*B8))
 14                                      --------
 15 PROFIT BEFORE TAX                    +B11-B13
                                         --------
```

d. (1) The break-even point occurs at a unit sales of about 79.
   (2) The three alternatives and their profits are:
       Base case: Price = 1,600; Unit sales = 100; Profit = $24,000
                  Price = 1,400; Unit sales = 130; Profit = $34,800
                  Price = 1,200; Unit sales = 150; Profit = $27,000
   Looking only at profit, the $1,400 price is best.

Chapter 3

3–1. The possible outcomes are: (Outcomes are independent.)

HHH	⅛	THH	⅛
HHT	⅛	TTH	⅛
HTT	⅛	THT	⅛
HTH	⅛	TTT	⅛

Total = ⁸⁄₈ = 1

a. P(three heads) = ⅛ or P(three heads) = $P(H) \cdot P(H) \cdot P(H)$
   = ½ · ½ · ½ = ⅛.

b. P(two or more heads):
       HHH ⅛
       HHT ⅛
       HTH ⅛
       THH ⅛
       ────
        ½

c. P(one or more tails):

HHT	$\frac{1}{8}$
HTT	$\frac{1}{8}$
HTH	$\frac{1}{8}$
THH	$\frac{1}{8}$
TTH	$\frac{1}{8}$
THT	$\frac{1}{8}$
TTT	$\frac{1}{8}$

$\frac{7}{8}$ or $1 - P(\text{HHH}) = 1 - \frac{1}{8} = \frac{7}{8}$

d. P(the last toss being a head):

HHH	$\frac{1}{8}$
HTH	$\frac{1}{8}$
THH	$\frac{1}{8}$
TTH	$\frac{1}{8}$

$\frac{1}{2}$

Note: Since outcomes are independent, this is P(heads) on one toss of fair coin, which is $\frac{1}{2}$.

3–2.

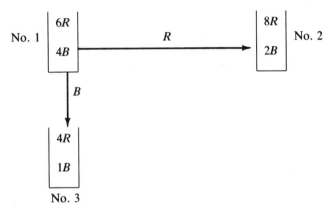

a. P(red on second|red on first) $= \frac{8}{10} = \frac{4}{5}$
b. P(black on second|red on first) $= \frac{2}{10} = \frac{1}{5}$
c. P(red on second|black on first) $= \frac{4}{5}$
d. P(black on second|black on first) $= \frac{1}{5}$
e. P(black on second) $= P(B_2|R_1) \cdot P(R_1) + P(B_2|B_1) \cdot P(B_1)$

$$= \frac{1}{5} \cdot \frac{3}{5} + \frac{1}{5} \cdot \frac{2}{5} = \frac{1}{5}$$

f.

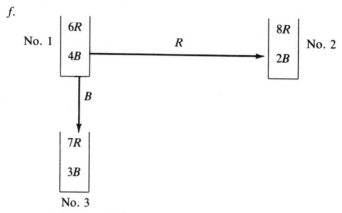

No. 3

a. P(red on second|red on first) = $\frac{8}{10}$ = $\frac{4}{5}$

b. P(black on second|red on first) = $\frac{2}{10}$ = $\frac{1}{5}$

c. P(red on second|black on first) = $\frac{7}{10}$

d. P(black on second|black on first) = $\frac{3}{10}$

e. $P(B_2) = P(B_2|R_1) \cdot P(R_1) + P(B_2|B_1) \cdot P(B_1)$

$$= \frac{1}{5} \cdot \frac{3}{5} + \frac{3}{10} \cdot \frac{2}{5} = .24$$

In the first instance, the conditioning event was not important because the proportions of reds and blacks in urns nos. 2 and 3 are the same. Thus, independence exists. In the second case, the proportions are not the same, so the conditioning event is important.

3–3. *a.* $n = 2$ P(heads) = .4 P(tails) = .6

  (1) P(2 heads) = .16

  (2) P(2 tails) = .36

  (3) P(1 head) = .48

  (4) P(1 head) + P(2 heads) = .48 + .16 = .64

  (5) P(1 tail) = .48

       P(1 tail) + P(2 tails) = .48 + .36 = .84

  (6) $P(R \leq 1) = 1 - P(R > 1) = 1 - .36 = .64$

A partition of the event, two tosses, is:

					Probability
P(1 head) =	.48	or	HH =		.16
P(2 heads) =	.16		HT =		.24
P(2 tails) =	.36		TH =		.24
	1.00		TT =		.36
					1.00

b. $n = 3$

  (1) P(3 heads) = .064

  (2) P(2 heads) = .288

(3) $P(1 \text{ head}) = .432$

(4) $.064 + .288 + .432 = .784$

3-4. *a.* $P(\text{under } 55) = \frac{9}{30} = .30$. This is a marginal or simple probability.

b. $P(55 \text{ or older, Marketing}) = \frac{5}{30} = .167$. Joint probability.

c. $P(\text{under } 55|\text{Finance}) = \frac{4}{18} = .222$. Conditional probability.

d. No. Note that $P(\text{under } 55)$ does not equal $P(\text{under } 55|\text{Finance})$, which would be necessary for independence. Generally, the "Other" category executives are younger than their counterparts who were in Finance and Marketing.

3-5.

Value of the Random Variable X_i (percent defective)	$P(X_i)$ $P(event)$	$X_i P(X_i)$	Squared Deviations from the Mean of $3.8; [X_i - E(X)]^2$		Squared Deviations Weighted by the Probability: $P(X_i) \cdot [X_i - E(X)]^2$
1	.10	.10	$(2.80)^2 =$	7.84	.784
2	.15	.30	$(1.80)^2 =$	3.24	.486
3	.20	.60	$(.80)^2 =$	.64	.128
4	.30	1.20	$(-.20)^2 =$	.04	.012
5	.20	1.00	$(-1.20)^2 =$	1.44	.288
10	.03	.30	$(-6.20)^2 =$	38.44	1.153
15	.02	.30	$(-11.20)^2 =$	125.44	2.509
	1.00	3.80 percent			5.360

Expected percent defective is 3.80. Variance of random variable is 5.360. Standard deviation of the random variable is $\sqrt{5.36} = 2.32$.

3-6. *a.* $P(R \geq 4|.5, 10) = .8281$

$P(R \geq 5|.5, 10) = .6230$

$P(R = 4|.5, 10) = .8281 - .6230 = .2051$

b. $P(R > 4|.5, 10) = P(R \geq 5|.5, 10) = .6230$

c. $P(R \geq 4|.4, 8) = .4059$

d. $P(R < 4|.2, 10) = 1 - P(R \geq 4|.2, 10) = 1 - .1209 = .8791$

e. $P(R = 0|.3, 10) = 1 - P(R \geq 1|.3, 10) = 1 - .9718 = .0282$

f. $P(R \geq 5|.6, 10) = 1 - P(R \geq 6|.4, 10) = 1 - .1662 = .8338$

3-7. *a.* $P(R = 0|p = .1, n = 20)$ $= .1216$

b. $P(R = 1)$ $= .2701$

c. $P(R \geq 4)$ $= .1330$

d. $P(R > 4)$ $= .0432$

e. $P(R = 4)$ $= .0898$

3-8. $P(\text{head and } A_1) = (.8)(.5) = .40$

$P(\text{head and } A_2) = (.2)(.9) = .18$

$P(\text{head}) = .58$

$P(A_1|\text{head}) = .40/.58 = .690$

$P(A_2|\text{head}) = .18/.58 = .310$

Chapter 4

4–1. *a.* **Expected Monetary Value**

Event	P(Event)	Act 1	Act 2	Act 3
A	.35	1.4	1.05	.70
B	.45	1.8	2.70	2.25
C	.20	.8	1.20	1.60
	EMV:	4.0	4.95*	4.55

*Optimum act.

b. **Expected Opportunity Loss**

Event	Act 1	Act 2	Act 3
A	0	.35	.70
B	.90	0	.45
C	.80	.40	0
EOL:	1.70	.75*	1.15

*Optimum act.

c.

Event	Conditional Value under Certainty
A	4
B	6
C	8

d.

Event	P(Event)		Conditional Value		Expected Value under Certainty
A	.35	·	4	=	1.40
B	.45	·	6	=	2.70
C	.20	·	8	=	1.60
				EMV:	5.70

e. Expected monetary value under certainty   5.70
Expected monetary value of optimum act   4.95
EVPI (also the EOL of the optimum act)   .75

4-2. *a.* Since there is no penalty loss for unsold copies, the operator should order at least 14 or more copies to make certain all demand is satisfied.

b.

Expected Value Table

						Acts: Stock					
			10		*11*		*12*		*13*		*14*
Event	*P(Event)*	*CV*	*EV*	*CV*	*EV*	*CV*	*EV*	*CV*	*EV*	*CV*	*EV*
Demand 10	.10	2.00	.20	1.70	.17	1.40	.14	1.10	.11	.80	.08
11	.15	2.00	.30	2.20	.33	1.90	.29	1.60	.24	1.30	.195
12	.20	2.00	.40	2.20	.44	2.40	.48	2.10	.42	1.80	.36
13	.25	2.00	.50	2.20	.55	2.40	.60	2.60	.65	2.30	.575
14	.30	2.00	.60	2.20	.66	2.40	.72	2.60	.78	2.80	.84
EMV:	1.00		2.00		2.15		2.23		2.20		2.050

The best act under conditions of zero salvage value is "Stock 12."

c. \$2.23.

4-3. *a.* **Expected Value Table**

			Acts		
			Introduce	*Do Not* *Introduce*	
Event	*P(Event)*	*CV**	*EV*	*CV*	*EV*
30,000 demand	.05	(200,000)	(10,000)	0	0
40,000 demand	.10	(100,000)	(10,000)	0	0
50,000 demand	.20	0	0	0	0
60,000 demand	.30	100,000	30,000	0	0
70,000 demand	.35	200,000	70,000	0	0
	1.00	EMV:	80,000		0

*Calculation of CV:

$30,000 \cdot \$10 - 500,000 = (200,000)$
$40,000 \cdot \$10 - 500,000 = (100,000)$
$50,000 \cdot \$10 - 500,000 = 0$
$60,000 \cdot \$10 - 500,000 = 100,000$
$70,000 \cdot \$10 - 500,000 = 200,000$

Expected Profit is \$80,000.
The best act is to introduce the product.

b. **Expected Loss Table**

		Acts			
		Introduce		*Do Not Introduce*	
Event	*P(Event)*	*CL*	*EL*	*CL*	*EL*
30,000 demand	.05	200,000	10,000	0	0
40,000 demand	.10	100,000	10,000	0	0
50,000 demand	.20	0	0	0	0
60,000 demand	.30	0	0	100,000	30,000
70,000 demand	.35	0	0	200,000	70,000
	1.00		20,000		100,000

The EVPI is 20,000; the EOL of the best act.

c. The EVPI would increase from 20,000 to 30,000 and the EV of the best act would decrease from 80,000 to 60,000. The profit under certainty would be 90,000 instead of 100,000. EVPI increases because the possible expected loss associated with introducing the product is more serious.

4–4. The optimal strategy is to introduce product A; set a low price if there is a time delay; set a high price if there is no time delay. The expected net profit is $3.28 million. The development of the tree is shown in the diagram.

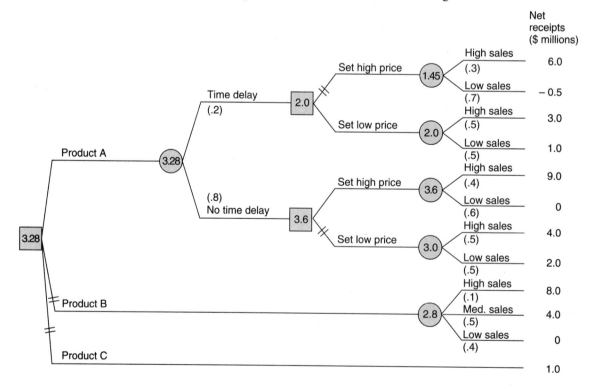

4–5. *a.*

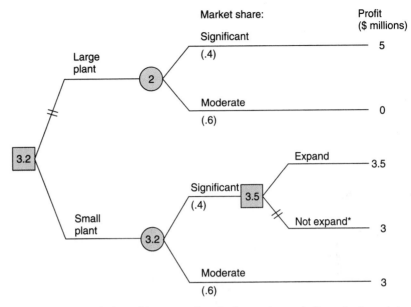

*The assumption here is that, without expansion, the firm can keep only the moderate market share.

b. The firm should build the small plant and expand it if the promotion effort captures a significant share of the market. The expected net profit is $3.2 million.

4–6. With a prior probability of 0.4 for a recession, you would not sell. That is:

$$.4(\$.8 \text{ million}) + .6(\$1.3 \text{ million}) = \$1.10 \text{ million}$$

which is greater than $1.0 million.

To revise the prior probability: (let B = Bad debts rising)

State	Prior (p)	P(B|p)	P(B, p)	Posterior P(p|B)
Recession	.4	.8	.32	.64
Normal	.6	.3	.18	.36
			$p(B)$ = .50	

Now it would be wise to sell. That is:

$$.64(\$.8 \text{ million}) + .36(\$1.3 \text{ million}) = \$.98 \text{ million}$$

which is less than $1.0 million.

688 Solutions to Selected Problems

4–7. The probability of the test result (the two rolls with neither a 7 nor an 11) is 5/9·5/9 if the dice are loaded, and 7/9·7/9 if they are not. Call the test result S and the state (loaded or not) p. Then:

State (p)	Prior	P(S|p)	P(S, p)	P(p|S)
Loaded	.7	$\left(\frac{5}{9}\right)^2=\frac{25}{81}$	$\frac{17.5}{81}$	.54
Unloaded	.3	$\left(\frac{7}{9}\right)^2=\frac{49}{81}$	$\frac{14.7}{81}$	.46
		$P(S)=$	$\frac{32.2}{81}$	

If the dice are loaded, the expected payoff per play is $\frac{4}{9}(-\$3)+\frac{5}{9}(\$1)$
$=\$-\frac{7}{9}$; if not $\frac{2}{9}(-\$3)+\frac{7}{9}(\$1)=\$\frac{1}{9}$
$E(V)=.54\left(-\frac{7}{9}\right)+.46\left(\frac{1}{9}\right)=-\$.37$. Don't play.

4–8. The joint probability table is:

Level of Sales	Survey Prediction			Marginal Probability
	Success	Inconclusive	Failure	
High	.09	.15	.06	.30
Low	.14	.35	.21	.70
Marginal probability	.23	.50	.27	1.00

and the posterior probabilities are:

$P(H|S)=\frac{.09}{.23}=.39 \quad P(L|S)=.61$

$P(H|I)=\frac{.15}{.50}=.30 \quad P(L|I)=.70$

$P(H|F)=\frac{.06}{.27}=.22 \quad P(L|F)=.78$

The decision tree is then:

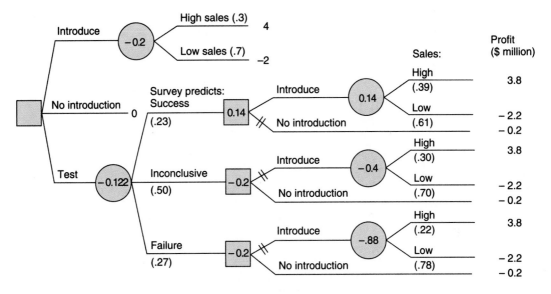

The survey should not be taken, since the net value is negative (-0.122). Thus, the cost of the survey of $0.2 million exceeds the expected value (which is $0.2 - 0.122$ or $.078 million).

4-9. The joint probability table is:

Potential Level of Sales	Survey Prediction			Marginal Probability
	Success	*Inconclusive*	*Failure*	
High	0.20	0.20	0.10	0.5
Low	0.05	0.25	0.20	0.5
Marginal probability	0.25	0.45	0.30	

The posterior probabilities are:

$$P(H|S) = .20/.25 = 0.80 \quad P(L|S) = .05/.25 = 0.20$$
$$P(H|I) = .20/.45 = 0.44 \quad P(L|I) = .25/.45 = 0.56$$
$$P(H|F) = .10/.30 = 0.33 \quad P(L|F) = .20/.30 = 0.67$$

The tree is then:

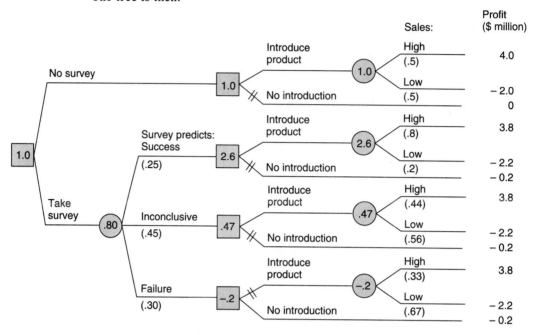

a. See upper branches of tree. Without the survey, the product should be introduced. The expected profit is $1.0 million.

b. Zero. As can be seen, the survey never changes the decision to introduce the product (in the case of failure prediction, either action has the same expected value). Hence, the survey has no value. The company would be wasting the $.2 million cost.

Chapter 5

5–1. a. Act d_6, with a calculated value of 3.75.

b. Acts d_1, d_4, and d_6, all of which have minimum profits of zero.

c. Act d_5 for which the value is 5 (associated with event q_3).

d. Act d_4, with expected value of 3.4.

5–2. a. Both d_4 and d_6 dominate d_1 by outcome dominance.

b. Act d_4 dominates d_3 by event dominance. Also, of course, d_4 and d_6 dominate d_1 by event dominance, since they dominate by outcome dominance.

c. To investigate probabilistic dominance, the information must be rearranged as in the table below. We need not consider acts d_1 and d_3, since we found that they were dominated by outcome or event dominance. Acts d_4, d_5, and d_6 all dominate d_2 by probabilistic dominance. Also, act d_4 dominates d_5.

d. This leaves acts d_4 and d_6 as undominated. The dominance criterion does not give us a choice between them.

					Acts			
	d_2		d_4		d_5		d_6	
Profit X	$P(X)$	$P(X$ or more$)$	$P(X)$	$P(X$ or more$)$	$P(X)$	$P(X$ or more$)$	$P(X)$	$P(X$ or more$)$
-4	0	1.0	0	1.0	0	1.0	0	1.0
-3	.2	1.0	0	1.0	0	1.0	0	1.0
-1	0	.8	0	1.0	.2	1.0	0	1.0
0	.2	.8	.2	1.0	0	.8	.4	1.0
2	.4	.6	0	.8	.2	.8	0	.6
3	0	.2	.4	.8	.2	.6	0	.6
5	.2	.2	.2	.4	.4	.4	.6	.6
6	0	0	.2	.2	0	0	0	0

5–3. *a.* The expected value of B is $(5 \cdot .1 + 6 \cdot .5 + 7 \cdot .4 = 6.30)$

Profit $= 20Q - (10,000 + QB)$

$E(\text{Profit}) = 20 \cdot 1,000 - (10,000 + 6.30 \cdot 1,000)$

$= 20,000 - 16,300 = \$3,700$

b. Expected sales is 500 units.

$E(\text{Profit}) = 20E(Q) - (10,000 + E(BQ))$

$= 20 \cdot 500 - (10,000 + 500 \cdot 6.30)$

$= 10,000 - 13,150 = -\$3,150$

5–4. The expected value of X, $E(X)$, is calculated as:

$(.10)(50) + (.3)(100) + \ldots + (.05)(300) = 150$. Profit $= -500 + 5X$

Hence, $E(\text{Profit}) = -500 + (5)(150) = \$250$

5–5. *a.* There are four strategies:

(1) Do not introduce the product.

(2) Introduce the product; if a competitive product is introduced, set a high price (if no competitive product, set a high price).

(3) Introduce the product; if a competitive product is introduced, set a medium price (if no competitive product, set a high price).

(4) Introduce the product; if a competitive product is introduced, set a low price (if no competitive product, set a high price).

b. Strategy 1 has a 1.0 probability for zero profit. For the remaining strategies:

Profit ($000s)	Strategy 2		Strategy 3		Strategy 4	
X	$P(X)$	$P(X$ or more$)$	$P(X)$	$P(X$ or more$)$	$P(X)$	$P(X$ or more$)$
-200	.16	1.00	0	1.00	0	1.00
-100	0	.84	0	1.00	.56	1.00
-50	0	.84	.24	1.00	0	.44
0	.40	.84	0	.76	0	.44
50	0	.44	0	.76	.16	.44
100	0	.44	.48	.76	.08	.28
150	.24	.44	0	.28	0	.20
250	0	.20	.08	.28	0	.20
500	.20	.20	.20	.20	.20	.20

c. Strategy 3 (set medium price) dominates strategy 4 (set low price). Every value for the cumulative probability $P(X$ or more) in the table above is at least as large or larger for strategy 3. This can also be seen in the plots shown in the accompanying diagram. There is no other dominance.

d.

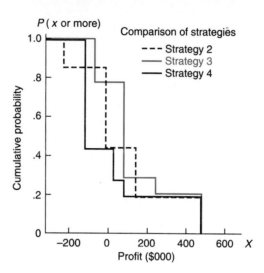

Chapter 6

6–1. $.4(5) + .6(12) = 2 + 7.2 = 9.2$

6–2. $.60 = .2x + .8(.50); x = 1.0$

6–3. $\dfrac{\Delta(u)}{\Delta M} = \dfrac{1}{500} = .002$

6–4. Most subjects would take the lottery, implying that their utility for \$12 is more than double that of \$8. The utility of \$12 is 40 or more: $\frac{1}{2}U(12) + \frac{1}{2}U(0) \geq U(8)$. $\frac{1}{2}U(12) \geq 20.\ U(12) \geq 40$.

6–5. $U(A) = 8^{2/3} = 4$

$U(B) = \frac{1}{2}U(0) + \frac{1}{2}U(64) = \frac{1}{2} \cdot 0^{2/3} + \frac{1}{2} \cdot 64^{2/3} = 0 + \frac{1}{2} \cdot 16 = 8$

Therefore, alternative A (the \$8 for sure) is less preferable than the lottery.

6–6. *a.* Alternative 1: Do not bid.

$U(\$0) = -170$

Alternative 2: Bid.

$U(\text{Bid}) = \frac{1}{2}U(-2{,}000) + \frac{1}{2}U(40{,}000) = \frac{1}{2}(-780) + \frac{1}{2}(200)$
$= -390 + 100 = -290$

$U(\text{Bid}) < U(\$0)$

Therefore, do not bid.

b. Let p be the probability of winning.

$$(1 - p)(-780) + p(200) = -170$$
$$-780 + 780p + 200p = -170$$
$$980p = 610$$
$$p = .622$$

6–7. *a.* Alternative A has outcomes strictly inferior to those of alternative B; hence, B dominates A.

b–c.

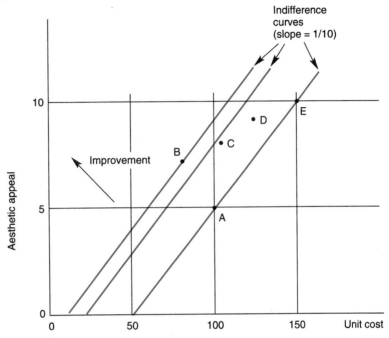

Alternative B reaches the highest attainable indifference curve, so it is the preferred alternative.

6–8. *a.* No.

b. For product A:

$$U(A) = .5(10)^{2/3} + .5(20)^{2/3} + .5(6)^{1/3} + .5(4)^{1/3}$$
$$= .5(4.64) + .5(7.37) + .5(1.82) + .5(1.59)$$
$$= 7.71$$

For product B:

$$U(B) = .6(5)^{2/3} + .4(25)^{2/3} + .6(7)^{1/3} + .4(5)^{1/3}$$
$$= .6(2.92) + .4(8.55) + .6(1.91) + .4(1.71)$$
$$= 7.01$$

Thus, product A is preferred.

Chapter 7

7–1. *a.* $Z = (15 - 12)/4 = .75$; $P(Z \geq .75) = 1 - .7734 = .2266$

b. $Z = (10 - 12)/4 = -.50$; $P(Z \leq -.50) = P(Z \geq .50) = 1 - .6915 = .3085$

c. $P(10 < X \leq 15) = 1 - P(X < 10) - P(X \geq 15) = 1 - .3085 - .2266 = .4649$

$d.$ $Z = (17 - 12)/4 = 1.25; P(Z > 1.25) = 1 - .8944 = .1056$

$e.$ $P(15 < X \le 17) = P(X > 15) - P(X > 17) = .2266 - .1056 = .1210$

7-2. $a.$ From the table, $P(Z \le 1.0) = .8413$; hence, $x = 15 - (1)(3) = 12$

$b.$ $P(X > x) = 1 - P(x \le X) = 1 - .2946 = .7054; P(Z \le .54) = .7054$; hence, $x = 15 + (.54)(3) = 16.62$

$c.$ $P(X \ge x) = 1 - P(x \le X) = 1 - .02275 = .97725$

$P(Z \le 2.0) = .97725$ from Table A; hence $x = 15 + 2(3) = 21.0$

7-3. $a.$ $D = |X_b - \mu|/\sigma = |80 - 100|/20 = 1.0$. From Table B in the appendix, $N(1.0) = .08332$. EVPI $= C\sigma N(D) = (2000)(20)(.08332) = \$3,333$

$b.$ $D = |80 - 100|/30 = .67; N(D) = .1503$

EVPI $= (20,000)(30)(.1503) = \$90,180$

7-4. Note: No correction is made in computations for the fact that only integral units could be sold. With this interpretation, it would be appropriate to write probability of sales less than 16 as $P(X \le 15.5)$.

$a.$ $P(X < 16) = P(Z < \frac{2}{3}) = .2514$

$b.$ $P(15 \le X \le 25) = P(-.83 \le Z \le .83) = .7967 - .2033 = .5934$

$c.$ $P(X \ge x) = .10$. Solve for x. $P(Z \ge z) = .10$ for $z = 1.28$

$x = 20 + 1.28(6) = 27.7$ or 28 units

7-5. $a.$ $\dfrac{\$1,750}{4 - 1.50} = 700$ units

$b.$ $\$2.50(1,000 - 700) = \$750$ or $\$2.50(1,000) - \$1,750 = \$750$

$c.$ $D = \dfrac{1,000 - 700}{150} = 2$

$N(D) = N(2) = .008491$

EVPI $= C\sigma_x N(D)$

$= \$2.50 \cdot 150 \cdot .008491 = \$3$

Chapter 8

8-1. $I_0 = \dfrac{1}{2^2} = .25; I_{\bar{x}} = \dfrac{n}{\sigma_s^2} = \dfrac{36}{36} = 1.0$

$\bar{\mu}_1 = \dfrac{\mu_0 I_0 + \overline{X} I_{\bar{x}}}{I_0 + I_{\bar{x}}} = \dfrac{10(.25) + 12(1.0)}{1.25}$

$= \dfrac{14.5}{1.25} = 11.6$

$I_1 = I_0 + I_{\bar{x}} = 1.25$

$\sigma_1^2 = \dfrac{1}{1.25} = .80; \sigma_1 = \sqrt{.80} = 0.9$

8-2. $\mu_0 = 12; \sigma_0 = 2; I_0 = .25; \overline{X} = 9; \sigma_s = 5; I_{\overline{x}} = \dfrac{n}{\sigma_p^2} = \dfrac{25}{25} = 1$

when σ_s is used to estimate σ_p.

$$\overline{\mu}_1 = \frac{\dfrac{12}{4} + \dfrac{9}{1}}{1.0 + .25} = \frac{12}{1.25} = 9.6$$

$I_1 = .25 + 1 = 1.25$

$\sigma_1^2 = \dfrac{1}{I_1} = \dfrac{1}{1.25} = .80; \sigma_1 = \sqrt{.80} \approx .9$

$Z = \dfrac{10 - 9.6}{.9} = \dfrac{.4}{.9} = .44$

From the normal table, the probability that the average balance is less than $10 is .67.

8-3. a. $\overline{\mu}_0 = 4.0; \sigma_0 = 1.5; I_0 = \dfrac{1}{2.25} = .4444$

$\overline{X} = 3.6; \sigma_s = 2.4; I_{\overline{x}} = \dfrac{1}{0.16} = 6.25; \sigma_{\overline{x}} = \dfrac{2.4}{\sqrt{36}} = 0.4$

$I_1 = 6.69$

$$\overline{\mu}_1 = \frac{(.4444)4.0 + (6.25)(3.6)}{6.69} = \frac{24.27}{6.69} = 3.63$$

$\sigma_1^2 = \dfrac{1}{6.69} = .150; \sigma_0 = .38$

Normal distribution with mean 3.63 cases and standard deviation .38 cases.

b. μ_b is the break-even point; $1 \cdot 5{,}000 \cdot 12$ months $\cdot \mu_b = 200{,}000$

$\mu_b = \dfrac{200{,}000}{60{,}000} = 3.33$

Posterior decision should be to go ahead, since $\overline{\mu}_1 > \mu_b$.

$D = \left| \dfrac{3.63 - 3.33}{.38} \right| = .79; N(.79) = .1223$

EVPI $= (60{,}000)(.38).1223 = \$2{,}800$

8-4. EVPI $= (100)(10)(.1978) = \$197.8$

where $C = 100; \sigma_0 = 10; D = \dfrac{|20 - 15|}{10} = .5;$

and $N(.5) = .1978$

b and *c*.

Sample Size n	$\sigma_{\bar{x}} = \dfrac{\sigma_p}{\sqrt{n}} = \dfrac{20}{\sqrt{n}}$	σ^*	D^*	$N(D^*)$	EVSI	Cost of Sample	ENG
10	6.32	8.46	.590	.1714	109	30	79
25	4.0	9.30	.537	.1866	173	60	113
50	2.83	9.65	.518	.1923	186	110	76

The best of the three choices is $n = 25$.

8–5. *a.* $\bar{\mu}_0 = 4.0$; $\sigma_0 = 1.5$; $\sigma_s = 2.5$; $n = 36$; $\sigma_{\bar{x}} = \dfrac{2.5}{6} = .4167$

$$\sigma^* = \sqrt{\sigma_0^2 \frac{\sigma_0^2}{\sigma_0^2 + \sigma_{\bar{x}}^2}} = \sqrt{\left(1.5^2 \frac{1.5^2}{1.5^2 + (.4167)^2}\right)} = \sqrt{2.25 \frac{2.25}{2.42}} = \sqrt{2.07} = 1.44$$

$$D^* = \left|\frac{\bar{\mu}_0 - \mu_b}{\sigma^*}\right| = \left|\frac{4.0 - 3.33}{1.44}\right| = .465$$

$N(D^*) = N(.465) = .209$; EVSI $= (60,000)(1.44)(.209) = \$18,000$

b. Sample cost $= \$3,500 + 100n = 3,500 + 100(36) = \$7,100$
ENG $= \$18,000 - 7,100 = \$10,900$
Yes, sample should be taken.

c and *d.*

n	$\sigma_{\bar{x}}$	σ^*	EVSI	COST	ENG
36	.4167	1.44	$18,000	$7,100	$10,900
50	.354	1.46	18,500	8,500	10,000
75	.288	1.465	18,700	11,000	7,700

e. Based upon these three cases, the smallest ($n = 36$) is the best.

Chapter 9

9–1.

		Player 2	
		H	T
Player 1	H	1	−1
	T	−1	1

The implication is that the players have linear utility functions for money, at least for the relevant range.

9–2. No. The minimax strategy would be to select heads at random one half of the time and tails at random one half of the time.

9–3. n cents.

9–4. *a.* A will follow strategy A_1, for it offers more to A than strategy A_2, regardless of B's strategy.

b. B will follow strategy B_2, for B will lose the least with this strategy.

c. The value of the game to A is 6. The value to B is -6.

d.

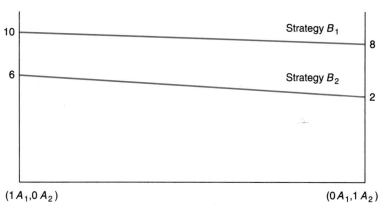

9–5. *a.* Player A will elect A_2, for it dominates A_1.

b. Player B will elect B_2, for it dominates B_1.

c. A solution of three for B and five for A.

Chapter 10

10–1. Let:

X_1 = Number of units of product A produced
X_2 = Number of units of product B produced
X_3 = Number of units of product C produced
X_4 = Number of units of product D produced

Maximize $P = 40X_1 + 24X_2 + 36X_3 + 23X_4$

Subject to: $2X_1 + 1X_2 + 2.5X_3 + 5X_4 \leq 120$ (milling constraint)

$1X_1 + 3X_2 + 2.5X_3 + 0X_4 \leq 160$ (assembly constraint)

$10X_1 + 5X_2 + 2X_3 + 12X_4 \leq 1,000$ (in-process inventory constraint)

$X_1 \leq 20$ (demand on product A)

$X_3 \leq 16$ (demand on product C)

$X_4 \geq 10$ (contract requirement on product D)

All $X_i \geq 0$

Solution: $X_1 = 10$; $X_2 = 50$; $X_3 = 0$; $X_4 = 10$; $P = 1,830$

10–2. Let:

X_1 = Funds in signature loans
X_2 = Funds in furniture loans
X_3 = Funds in automobile loans
X_4 = Funds in second home mortgages
X_5 = Funds in first home mortgages

Maximize: $P = 0.15X_1 + 0.12X_2 + 0.09X_3 + 0.10X_4 + 0.07X_5$
Subject to: $X_1 + X_2 + X_3 + X_4 + X_5 \leq 1.5$ (total funds available)
$X_1 \leq 0.10(X_1 + X_2 + X_3 + X_4 + X_5)$ or
$0.9X_1 - 0.1X_2 - 0.1X_3 - 0.1X_4 - 0.1X_5 \leq 0$
$X_1 + X_2 \leq 0.20(X_1 + X_2 + X_3 + X_4 + X_5)$ or
$0.8X_1 + 0.8X_2 - 0.2X_3 - 0.2X_4 - 0.2X_5 \leq 0$
$X_5 \geq 0.40(X_4 + X_5)$ or $- 0.4X_4 + 0.6X_5 \geq 0$
$X_5 \geq 0.20(X_1 + X_2 + X_3 + X_4 + X_5)$ or
$-0.2X_1 - 0.2X_2 - 0.2X_3 - 0.2X_4 + 0.8X_5 \geq 0$
$X_4 \leq 0.25(X_1 + X_2 + X_3 + X_4 + X_5)$ or
$-0.25X_1 - 0.25X_2 - 0.25X_3 + 0.75X_4 - 0.25X_5 \leq 0$
All $X_i \geq 0$

Solution: $X_1 = 0.15; X_2 = 0.15; X_3 = 0.525; X_4 = 0.375; X_5 = 0.30; P = 0.146$

10–3. Maximize: $P = 30A + 30B$
Subject to:
$3A + 1B \leq 30,000$
$A \leq 8,000$
$B \leq 12,000$

10–4. Let:

$X_1, X_2, \ldots, X_6$ = Number of transformers produced in regular time each month
$Y_1, Y_2, \ldots, Y_6$ = Number produced on overtime each month
$I_1, I_2, \ldots, I_6$ = Number of transformers in stock at the *end* of each month

Constraints:
Capacity:

$X_i \leq 50$ for $i = 1, 2, \ldots 6$
$Y_i \leq 20$ for $i = 1, 2, \ldots 6$

Inventory definition:

$I_1 = 15 + X_1 + Y_1 - 58$ 　　　for January
$I_i = I_{i-1} + X_i + Y_i -$ Orders$_i$ 　　for $i = 2, 3, \ldots 6$

Final inventory:

$I_6 \geq 5$

Objective function:

Minimize: $18X_1 + 17X_2 + 17X_3 + 18.5X_4 + 19X_5 + 19X_6$
$+ 20Y_1 + 19Y_2 + 19Y_3 + 21Y_4 + 22Y_5 + 22Y_6$
$+ 0.5I_1 + 0.5I_2 + 0.5I_3 + 0.5I_4 + 0.5I_5 + 0.5I_6$

Solution:

Month	Regular Production	Overtime Production	Inventory
January	43	0	0
February	50	0	14
March	50	11	41
April	50	0	22
May	50	0	0
June	48	0	5

Total cost is $5,511 (thousand).

An alternative basic solution exists that involves regular production of 50 in January, and only 4 produced on overtime in March, with appropriate modifications in ending inventories in January (7) and February (21).

10-5. Let:

$X_1 = M^3$ of earth processed at plant 1
$X_2 = M^3$ at plant 2
$X_3 = M^3$ at plant 3

Minimize $C = 0.60X_1 + 0.36X_2 + 0.50X_3$
Subject to:
$0.58X_1 + 0.26X_2 + 0.21X_3 = 148,000$ (stone count requirement)
$0.36X_1 + 0.22X_2 + 0.263X_3 \geq 130,000$ (carat requirement)

$\left. \begin{array}{l} X_1 \leq 83,000 \\ X_2 \leq 310,000 \\ X_3 \leq 190,000 \end{array} \right\}$ (capacity requirement)

Solution: $X_1 = 61,700; X_2 = 310,000; X_3 = 150,500$
Minimum cost $= C = 223,880$ rand

Chapter 11

11–1. See graph below. The solution is $X_1 = 4$, $X_2 = 4$, and $P = 28$.

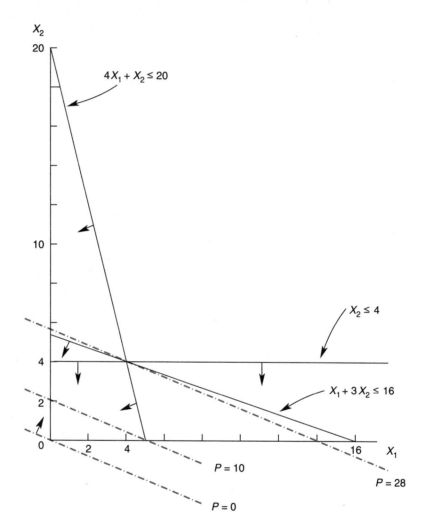

11–2. *a.* See graph below. The optimal solution is 6 thousand units of product A and 12 thousand units of B, with profit of $540 thousand.

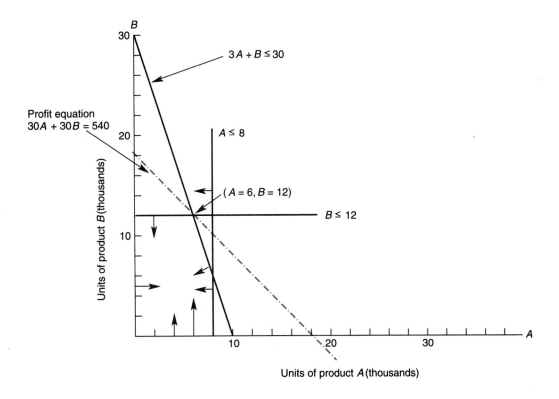

b. See graph below. Note that the constraint $A \le 8$ is not binding since $A = 6$ in the optimal solution. Hence, increasing the limit on A will have no effect on the solution or on the profit. The *dual price* is zero.

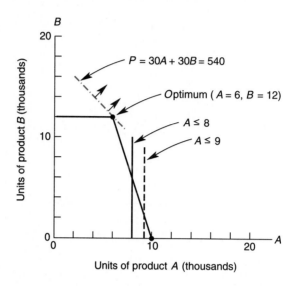

c. See graph below. Note that the optimum solution shifts to $A = 5.67$, $B = 13$, with profit of $560 thousand. This represents an increase in profit of $20 thousand from the base case ($560 − 540 = $20). Hence, the dual price is $20. That is, each unit increase in the limit on production of product B will increase profit by $20.

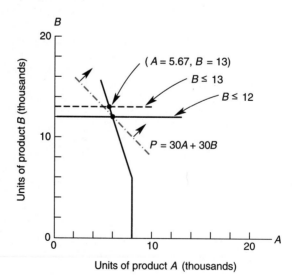

d. See graph below. Note that the optimum solution shifts to $A = 6.33$, $B = 12$, with profit $P = \$550$. This is an increase in \$10 from the base case. Hence, the dual price for labor hours is \$10.

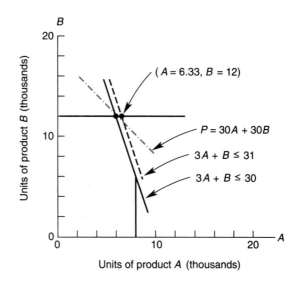

Units of product A (thousands)

e. *Sales limit on product A:* Refer to the graph associated with (b). The dual price on this constraint is zero. Note that increasing the limit on product A will have no effect at all; hence, there is no upper limit. The optimal solution includes six thousand units of product A. A reduction in the sales limit below this will affect the solution. Hence, the range is from six thousand upward (with no upper limit) and this is the range within which the dual price of zero holds.

   Sales limit on product B: Refer to the graph on the next page. Note that as additional units of B can be produced, the optimum moves up to the point ($A = 0$, $B = 30$). Beyond this point, additional sales of B cannot be made because of the labor hours. Hence, the upper limit is 30 thousand units. As the sales limit of B is reduced down to six thousand units, the corner point ($A=8$, $B=6$) is reached. Beyond this, the solution changes. Hence, six thousand units is the lower limit. In summary, the dual price of \$20 per unit of B holds over the range 6 to 30 thousand in the sales limit for product B.

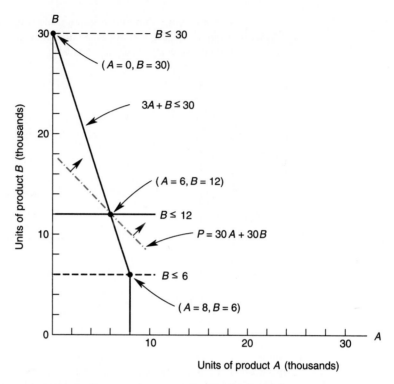

Limit on labor hours: The second graph for this problem is shown on the next page. When labor hours increase up to 36 thousand (i.e., to the constraint $3A + B \leq 36$), a new corner point ($A = 8$, $B = 12$) is reached. As hours are decreased, the corner point ($A = 0$, $B = 12$) is reached when 12 thousand hours are available. Hence, the range on labor hours is from 12 thousand hours to 36 thousand hours, and within this range, the dual price of $10 holds.

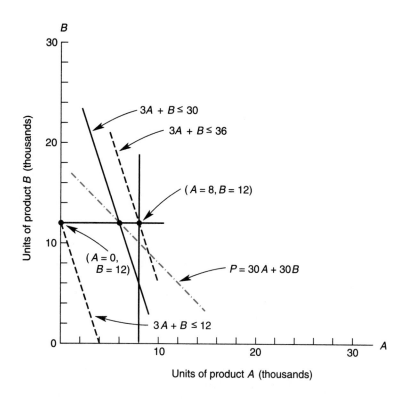

Units of product A (thousands)

11-3. The LINDO output for this problem is shown in the accompanying table. PRODA, PRODB, and so on are the variable names for units of product A, units of product B, and so on. See the formulation of the problem in the first part of the output table or refer to the answer to Problem 10–1.

a. The solution calls for 10 units of product A, 50 units of product B, no product C, and 10 units of product D, with a profit of $1,830. Also note that there is $530 of unused working capital, 10 units of unused demand for product A, and 16 units of unused demand for product B. Note that there are six constraints in the problem and exactly six nonzero solution variables. Also note that there are no alternative optimal solutions, since (1) none of the slack variables has both a zero solution value and a zero dual price, and (2) PRODC (the only decision variable with zero units) does not have a zero reduced cost.

b. Look at the dual prices for rows 2), 3), and 4). The dual price for an hour of milling time is $19.20; for an hour of assembly time the dual price is $1.60; and the dual price is zero for additional working capital.

c. Neither of these constraints is binding and hence, the dual prices are zero. The company should spend nothing to increase demand for either product.

d. Note that this constraint (row 7) is binding with a dual price of $-\$73$. A change in the constraint to require 13 units means an increase of 3 units. An examination of the right-hand side ranges indicates that this is within the range over which the dual price holds. Hence, a change in the requirement would *cost* the company $3 \cdot \$73 = \$219$.

e. Note that none of product C is produced in the optimal solution. The reduced cost is $16. Thus, the per unit profit from product C would have to increase $16 to $52 before any units would be produced. Hence, an increase of only $10 to $46 per unit would have no effect either on the solution or on the profit.

f. The opportunity cost for product E is calculated as:

Resource	*Units Required*	*Dual Price*	*Units · Dual Price*
Milling time	2	19.20	38.40
Assembly time	5	1.60	8.00
Working capital	20	0	0
Opportunity cost			46.40

Since the profit per unit of $50 is greater than the opportunity cost of $46.40, at least some units of product E should be produced.

LINDO Output for Problem 11–3

```
MAX      40 PRODA + 24 PRODB + 36 PRODC + 23 PRODD
SUBJECT TO
      2) 2 PRODA +  PRODB + 2.5 PRODC + 5 PRODD <=    120
      3)  PRODA + 3 PRODB + 2.5 PRODC <= 160
      4) 10 PRODA + 5 PRODB + 2 PRODC + 12 PRODD <=    1000
      5)  PRODA <=    20
      6)  PRODC <=    16
      7)  PRODD >=    10
END

LP OPTIMUM FOUND AT STEP 4

      OBJECTIVE FUNCTION VALUE

      1) 1830.00000

VARIABLE          VALUE        REDUCED COST
   PRODA       10.000000          .000000
   PRODB       50.000000          .000000
   PRODC         .000000        16.000000
   PRODD       10.000000          .000000

      ROW  SLACK OR SURPLUS     DUAL PRICES
      2)          .000000        19.200000
      3)          .000000         1.600000
      4)       530.000000          .000000
      5)        10.000000          .000000
      6)        16.000000          .000000
      7)          .000000       -73.000000
```

```
NO. ITERATIONS =    4

RANGES IN WHICH THE BASIS IS UNCHANGED:

                       OBJ COEFFICIENT RANGES
  VARIABLE      CURRENT      ALLOWABLE      ALLOWABLE
                 COEF        INCREASE       DECREASE
    PRODA      40.000000     8.000000      16.000000
    PRODB      24.000000    73.000000       4.000000
    PRODC      36.000000    16.000000      INFINITY
    PRODD      23.000000    73.000000      INFINITY

                      RIGHTHAND SIDE RANGES
    ROW         CURRENT      ALLOWABLE      ALLOWABLE
                 RHS         INCREASE       DECREASE
     2         120.000000   16.666670      16.666670
     3         160.000000   50.000000      50.000000
     4        1000.000000   INFINITY      530.000000
     5          20.000000   INFINITY       10.000000
     6          16.000000   INFINITY       16.000000
     7          10.000000    3.333333       3.333333
```

11–4. The LINDO output is given in the accompanying table. The variables are named SIGLOAN, FURLOAN, AUTOLOAN, SCNDMORG, and FRSTMORG for funds (millions of dollars) in signature loans, furniture loans, and so on. The formulation is contained in the LINDO output.

   a. The solution calls for $.15 million in signature loans, $.15 million in furniture loans, $.525 million in auto loans, $.375 million in second mortgages, and $.300 million in first mortgages. The total return is $.146 million.

   b. Look at the dual price on the constraint on total funds available (row 2). It is .0975 and this is the return for each additional dollar. There is no limit on the increase and 1.5 million limit on the decrease (see right-hand side ranges). This means that the incremental return is .0975 per dollar from zero on up without limit. At first this may seem strange, but note that all the constraints, except that on total funds available, are relative and limit percentages of the portfolio. Hence, once the optimal mix is obtained, the return it generates is limited only by the total funds available.

   c. Note that there is no limit on the increase in return on SCNDMORG (see objective coefficient ranges). Hence, an increase from 10 percent to 12 percent would not affect the solution at all. However, the total return would increase by .02 · .375 = .0075 million. That is, the .375 million in second mortgages would earn 2 percent more. Since there is no limit on the increase, an increase to 14 percent (or any other increase) would have no effect on the solution—other than to increase the total return.

LINDO Output for Problem 11–4

```
MAX     0.15 SIGLOAN + 0.12 FURLOAN + 0.09 AUTOLOAN + 0.1 SCNDMORG
        + 0.07 FRSTMORG
SUBJECT TO
        2) SIGLOAN + FURLOAN + AUTOLOAN + SCNDMORG + FRSTMORG <=
        1.5
        3) 0.9 SIGLOAN - 0.1 FURLOAN - 0.1 AUTOLOAN - 0.1 SCNDMORG
        - 0.1 FRSTMORG <= 0
        4) 0.8 SIGLOAN + 0.8 FURLOAN - 0.2 AUTOLOAN - 0.2 SCNDMORG
        - 0.2 FRSTMORG <= 0
        5) - 0.4 SCNDMORG + 0.6 FRSTMORG >= 0
        6) - 0.2 SIGLOAN - 0.2 FURLOAN - 0.2 AUTOLOAN -
        0.2 SCNDMORG + 0.8 FRSTMORG >= 0
        7) - 0.25 SIGLOAN - 0.25 FURLOAN - 0.25 AUTOLOAN +
        0.75 SCNDMORG - 0.25 FRSTMORG <= 0
END

LP OPTIMUM FOUND AT STEP      5

        OBJECTIVE FUNCTION VALUE

        1) .146250000

        VARIABLE          VALUE          REDUCED COST
        SIGLOAN          .150000            .000000
        FURLOAN          .150000            .000000
        AUTOLOAN         .525000            .000000
        SCNDMORG         .375000            .000000
        FRSTMORG         .300000            .000000

        ROW      SLACK OR SURPLUS       DUAL PRICES
        2)              .000000            .097500
        3)              .000000            .030000
        4)              .000000            .030000
        5)              .030000            .000000
        6)              .000000           -.020000
        7)              .000000            .010000

NO. ITERATIONS =      5

RANGES IN WHICH THE BASIS IS UNCHANGED:

                    OBJ COEFFICIENT RANGES
        VARIABLE     CURRENT    ALLOWABLE    ALLOWABLE
                     COEF       INCREASE     DECREASE
        SIGLOAN      .150000    INFINITY     .030000
        FURLOAN      .120000    .030000      .030000
        AUTOLOAN     .090000    .010000      .020000
        SCNDMORG     .100000    INFINITY     .010000
        FRSTMORG     .070000    .020000      .487500
```

```
             RIGHTHAND SIDE RANGES
ROW    CURRENT    ALLOWABLE    ALLOWABLE
        RHS       INCREASE     DECREASE
 2    1.500000    INFINITY    1.500000
 3     .000000    .150000      .150000
 4     .000000    .525000      .150000
 5     .000000    .030000     INFINITY
 6     .000000    .525000      .050000
 7     .000000    .075000      .375000
```

Chapter 12

12–1. *a.* **Add slack variables** X_3, X_4, X_5.

C_j			0	0	0	4	3
	Solution Variables	*Solution Values*	X_3	X_4	X_5	X_1	X_2
0	X_3	10	1			4	2
0	X_4	8		1		2	8/3
0	X_5	6			1	1	
	Z_j	0	0	0	0	0	0
	$C_j - Z_j$		0	0	0	4	3

b. X_1 enters; X_3 leaves.

c.

C_j			0	0	0	4	3
	Solution Variables	*Solution Values*	X_3	X_4	X_5	X_1	X_2
4	X_1	2.5	1/4	0	0	1	1/2
0	X_4	3	$-1/2$	1	0	0	5/3
0	X_5	1/2	$-1/4$	0	1	0	$-1/2$
	Z_j	10	1	0	0	4	2
	$C_j - Z_j$		-1	0	0	0	1

d. Not optimal.

e. X_2 enters; X_4 leaves.

f.

C_j			0	0	0	4	3
	Solution Variables	*Solution Values*	X_3	X_4	X_5	X_1	X_2
4	X_1	$16/10$	$4/10$	$-3/10$	0	1	0
3	X_2	$9/5$	$-3/10$	$3/5$	0	0	1
0	X_5	$44/10$	$-4/10$	$3/10$	1	0	0
	Z_j	$59/5$	0.7	$3/5$	0	4	3
	$C_j - Z_j$		-0.7	$-3/5$	0	0	0

g. Optimal: $X_1 = 16/10$; $X_2 = 9/5$; $X_5 = 44/10$; $P = 59/5 = 11.8$

12-2. *a.* The slack variable for the constraint on machine 1 is X_3. The dual price is $C_3 - Z_3 = \$.70$. The range can be calculated as:

Solution Values	X_3 *Column*	*Ratio*
$16/10$	$4/10$	4
$9/5$	$-3/10$	-6
$44/10$	$-4/10$	-11

The smallest positive value (4) determines the limit on the decrease and the smallest nonpositive value (-6) on the increase. Hence, the range is from 6 to 16 hours.

b. The slack variable for machine 2 is X_4. The dual price is $\$.60$. The range can be determined as:

Solution Values	X_4 *Column*	*Ratio*
$16/10$	$-3/10$	-5.333
$9/5$	$3/5$	3
$44/10$	$3/10$	14.667

The smallest positive value (3) determines the limit on the decrease and the smallest nonpositive value (-5.333) on the increase. Hence, the range is from 5 to 13.333 hours.

c. Slack variable X_5 is associated with the sales limit on product A. It is a solution variable with value 4.4 units, indicating that the constraint is not binding, and hence, the dual price is zero. There is no limit on the increase, and the decrease is limited by the amount of the slack. Hence, the range is from 1.6 units up without limit.

12–3. *a.*

$C_j - Z_j$	−0.7	−0.6	0	0
X_1 row	0.4	−0.3	0	1
Ratio	−1.75	2.00	—	0

The smallest positive value (2) determines the increase, and the smallest nonpositive value (−1.75) the decrease. Hence, the range is from $2.25 to $6.

b.

$C_j - Z_j$	−0.7	−0.6	0	0
X_2 row	−0.3	0.6	0	1
Ratio	2.33	−1.00	—	0

The smallest positive value (2.33) determines the increase, and the smallest nonpositive value (−1.00) the decrease. Hence, the range is from $2 to $5.33.

12–4.

Resource	Requirement	Dual Price	Requirement · Dual Price
Machine 1	2	0.70	1.40
Machine 2	2	0.60	1.20
Opportunity cost			$2.60

Since the unit profit of $3 is greater than the opportunity cost, at least some units of the new product should be produced.

12–5. *a.* Add surplus variables X_3 and X_4 and artificial variables X_5 and X_6.

C_j	Solution Variables	Solution Values	M X_5	M X_6	6 X_1	4 X_2	0 X_3	0 X_4
M	X_5	12	1	0	3	2	−1	0
M	X_6	4	0	1	½	1	0	−1
	Z_j	16M	M	M	3½M	3M	−M	−M
	$C_j - Z_j$		0	0	6 − ½M	4 − 3M	M	M

b. X_1 enters; X_5 leaves.

c.

C_j			M	M	6	4	0	0
	Solution Variables	Solution Values	X_5	X_6	X_1	X_2	X_3	X_4
6	X_1	4	$1/3$	0	1	$2/3$	$-1/3$	0
M	X_6	2	$-1/6$	1	0	$2/3$	$+1/6$	-1
	Z_j	$2M + 24$	$2 - M/6$	M	6	$4 + 2M/3$	$-2 + M/6$	$-M$
	$C_j - Z_j$		$7/6M - 2$	0	0	$-2M/3$	$2 - M/6$	M

d. Not optimal. (Also not feasible.)
b. (repeat) X_2 enters; X_6 leaves.

c.

(repeat)

C_j			M	M	6	4	0	0
	Solution Variables	Solution Values	X_5	X_6	X_1	X_2	X_3	X_4
6	X_1	2	$1/2$	-1	1	0	$-1/2$	1
4	X_2	3	$-1/4$	$3/2$	0	1	$+1/4$	$-3/2$
	Z_j	24	2	0	6	4	-2	0
	$C_j - Z_j$		$M - 2$	M	0	0	2	0

All $C_j - Z_j$'s are nonnegative; thus an optimum (minimum) solution is: $X_1 = 2$, $X_2 = 3$, and minimum cost is 24.

d. The solution is optimal, since all the $C_j - Z_j$ values are zero or positive. There are no alternative optimal solutions, since all outside variables have $C_j - Z_j$ values that are strictly positive.

12–6. a. X_1 is the entering variable (largest $C_j - Z_j$). Variable X_4 leaves.
b. The next simplex table is:

C_j			0	0	0	0	0	0.15	0.12	0.12
	Solution Variables	Solution Values	X_4	X_5	X_6	X_7	X_8	X_1	X_2	X_3
0.15	X_1	180	1					1		
0	X_5	125		1					1	1
0	X_6	45	-1		1				1	
0	X_7	75				1				1
0	X_8	0					1		-4	1
	Z_j	27	0.15	0	0	0	0	0.15	0	0
	$C_j - Z_j$		-0.15	0	0	0	0	0	0.12	0.12

c.

j	Z_j	$C_j - Z_j$
4	0.03	-0.03
5	0	0
6	0.12	-0.12
7	0	0
8	0	0
1	0.15	0
2	0.12	0
3	0	0.12
Solution value:	32.4	

X_3 is the entering variable.
X_7 is the leaving variable.

d. The solution is optimal since all the $C_j - Z_j$ values are 0 or negative. There are no alternative solutions, since all outside variables have $C_j - Z_j$ values that are strictly negative.

12–7. *a.* $0.12 per pound; a maximum of 5,000 pounds (use variable X_6).
b. $0.12 per pound; from 0 to 80,000 (use variable X_7).
c. Yes. Each pound is worth $0.03 (see $C_4 - Z_4$). This is valid in the range + 26.25 thousand pounds above 180. Total increase in profit is $(0.03)(20) =$ $0.6 thousand.
d. No effect. Current demand is not being met.
e. No limit on the increase; a drop of $0.03 on the decrease.
f. Yes. The opportunity cost is $0.50(0.12) + 0.5(0.12) = 0.12$. This is less than the profit of $0.14.

Chapter 13

13–1. The following is one possible method of arriving at a solution:

First Solution

	W_1	W_2	W_3	*Total*
F_1	10			10
F_2	5		15	20
F_3		28	2	30
	15	28	17	60

Let us test direct route F_3W_1. *Indirect route:* $+ F_3W_3 - F_2W_3 + F_2W_1$

Cost of Direct Route	*Cost of Indirect Route*
F_3W_1: 1.05	$+1.10 - .95 + 1.00 = 1.15$

The cost of the direct route ($1.05) is less than the cost of the indirect route ($1.15). Thus, the direct route F_3W_1 should be used.

The maximum number of units that can be shifted from F_3W_3 to F_3W_1 and from F_2W_1 to F_2W_3 is two units. The new table of units shipped is:

	W_1	W_2	W_3
F_1	10		
F_2	3		17
F_3	2	28	—
	15	28	17

We must now test each zero box.

Direct Route	Cost of Direct Route	Cost of Indirect Route
F_1W_2	.95	$+ F_1W_1 - F_3W_1 + F_3W_2$: $.90 - 1.05 + .85 = .70$
F_2W_2	1.40	$F_2W_1 - F_3W_1 + F_3W_2$: $1.00 - 1.05 + .85 = .80$
F_1W_3	1.30	$F_1W_1 - F_2W_1 + F_2W_3$: $.90 - 1.00 + .95 = .85$
F_3W_3	1.10	$F_3W_1 - F_2W_1 + F_2W_3$: $1.05 - 1.00 + .95 = 1.00$

The direct routes are all inferior to the indirect routes, thus an optimum solution has been found.

13–2. The following is one possible method of arriving at a solution:

First Solution–Units

	W_1	W_2	W_3	Total
F_1	10		10	20
F_2			15	15
F_3	—	26	4	30
	10	26	29	65

Testing of direct routes:

Direct Route	Cost of Direct Route	Cost of Indirect Route
F_2W_1	1.20	$1.05 - 1.20 + 1.10 = .95$
F_3W_1	1.10	$.95 - 1.20 + 1.10 = .85$
F_1W_2	1.12	$1.20 - .95 + .90 = 1.15$
F_2W_2	1.00	$1.05 - .95 + .90 = 1.00$

The cost of the direct route F_1W_2 is less than the cost of the indirect route. Thus, the direct route should be used. The maximum number of units that can be transferred is 10 units.

The second solution is as follows:

	W_1	W_2	W_3	Total
F_1	10	10		20
F_2			15	15
F_3	—	16	14	30
	10	26	29	65

Testing the unused routes:

Direct Route	Cost of Direct Route	Cost of Indirect Route
F_2W_1	1.20	$1.05 - .95 + .90 - 1.12 + 1.10 = .98$
F_3W_1	1.10	$.90 - 1.12 + 1.10 = .88$
F_2W_2	1.00	$1.05 - .95 + .90 = 1.00$
F_1W_3	1.20	$1.12 - .90 + .95 = 1.17$

The costs of the direct routes are equal to or greater than the costs of the indirect routes; thus, an optimum solution has been reached. Thus, it would not be desirable to make use of any of the direct routes currently not used. Note however that there is an alternative optimum using F_2W_2.

13–3. The first solution is degenerate (10 is the only amount in a row and column). Assume a small amount, d, in box F_1W_2, and proceed by testing the zero boxes.

First Solution—Modified

	W_1	W_2	W_3	Total
F_1	10	d		$10 + d$
F_2		20		20
F_3	$-$	8	22	30
	10	$28 + d$	22	$60 + d$

Direct Route	Cost of Direct Route	Cost of Indirect Route
F_2W_1	.90	$.70 - .85 + .80 = .65$
F_3W_1	1.00	$.60 - .85 + .80 = .55$
F_1W_3	1.45	$.85 - .60 + 1.15 = 1.40$
F_2W_3	1.05	$.70 - .60 + 1.15 = 1.25$

The cost of the direct route F_2W_3 is less than the cost of the indirect route; thus, the route F_2W_3 should be used. We can transfer 20 units.

Second Solution

	W_1	W_2	W_3	Total
F_1	10	d		$10 + d$
F_2			20	20
F_3	$-$	28	2	30
	10	$28 + d$	22	$60 + d$

Testing the Zero Boxes

Direct Route	Cost of Direct Route	Cost of Indirect Route
F_2W_1	.90	$1.05 - 1.15 + .60 - .85 + .80 = .45$
F_3W_1	1.00	$.60 - .85 + .80 = .55$
F_2W_2	.70	$1.05 - 1.15 + .60 = .50$
F_1W_3	1.45	$.85 - .60 + 1.15 = 1.40$

The direct costs are all larger than the indirect costs; thus, the second solution is an optimum solution.

13–4. *a.* $X_1 = $ Units of product A; $X_2 = $ Units of product B;
$2X_1 \leq 30$ (unskilled labor); $4X_1 + 5X_2 \leq 100$ (machine time)

b. Skilled labor: $X_1 + 5X_2 + U_1 - E_1 = 75$
   Raw material: $5X_1 + 4X_2 + U_2 - E_2 = 100$
   Profit: $15X_1 + 10X_2 + U_3 - E_3 = 300$
c. Minimize $5U_1 + 10E_1 - 5U_2 + 15E_2 + U_3 - E_3$
d. See graph below.

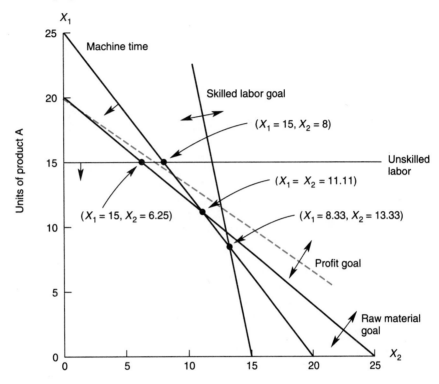

Units of product B

e. (1) $U_1 = E_1 = E_2 = E_3 = 0$; $U_2 = 5$; $U_3 = 41.7$;
       Objective function $= 16.7$
   (2) $E_1 = U_2 = E_2 = E_3 = 0$; $U_1 = 8.3$; $U_3 = 22.3$;
       Objective function $= 63.6$
   (3) $E_1 = U_2 = U_3 = 0$; $U_1 = 20$; $E_2 = 7$; $E_3 = 5$;
       Objective function $= 200$
   (4) $E_1 = U_2 = E_2 = E_3 = 0$; $U_1 = 28.75$; $U_3 = 12.5$;
       Objective function $= 156.3$
   Alternative 1 is the lowest. Note that this plan actually is under the profit
   goal by $41.7, but it has a value of $25 for returning five units of raw material.

Chapter 14

14-1. $a.$ $Y_{11} + Y_{21} + Y_{31} + Y_{41} + Y_{51} \leq 1$

$b.$ $Y_{21} \leq Y_{31}; Y_{22} \leq Y_{31} + Y_{32}$

 $Y_{23} \leq Y_{31} + Y_{32} + Y_{33}$

$c.$ $Y_{11} + Y_{21} + Y_{31} + Y_{41} + Y_{51} \geq 1$

 $Y_{12} + Y_{22} + Y_{32} + Y_{42} + Y_{52} \geq 1$

 $Y_{13} + Y_{23} + Y_{33} + Y_{43} + Y_{53} \geq 1$

$d.$ $Y_{41} + Y_{42} = 1$

$e.$ $Y_{11} + Y_{51} \leq 1; Y_{12} + Y_{52} \leq 1; Y_{13} + Y_{53} \leq 1$

14-2. $a.$ Possible branches: $X_2 = 0$ versus $X_2 = 1$; or $X_3 = 0$ versus $X_3 = 1$
Use $X_3 = 1$ branch

$b.$ Maximize $2X_1 + X_2 + 3X_4 + 4$. Subject to: $3X_1 + 2X_2 + 4X_4 \leq 5$ and $- X_2 \leq - 1$ (or $X_2 \geq 1$). Solution is: $X_1 = 0, X_2 = X_3 = 1, X_4 = .75, Z = 7.256$. Not integer.

$c.$ Not optimal. Branch again.

$a.$ Possible branches: $X_4 = 0$ versus $X_4 = 1$. Use $X_4 = 1$

$b.$ Maximize $2X_1 + X_2 + 7$. Subject to: $3X_1 + 2X_2 \leq 1$, and $-X_2 \leq - 1$. No feasible solution.

$c.$ Still not optimal. Cannot continue down this branch, since there is no feasible, and hence no integer, solution.

$a.$ Go to branch $X_4 = 0$

$b.$ Maximize $2X_1 + X_2 + 4$. Subject to: $3X_1 + 2X_2 \leq 5$ and $- X_2 \leq -1$. Solution is $X_1 = X_2 = X_3 = 1, X_4 = 0, Z = 7$

$c.$ Integer, and best so far.

$a.$ Go back to branch $X_3 = 0$

$b.$ Maximize $2X_1 + X_2 + 3X_4$. Subject to: $3X_1 + 2X_2 + 4X_4 \leq 10$ and $- X_2 \leq 0$ (or $X_2 \geq 0$). Solution is $X_1 = X_2 = X_4 = 1, X_3 = 0, Z = 6$. Integer, but not as good as previous best so far.

$c.$ Finished, since all branches have been investigated. Optimal solution is
$X_1 = X_2 = X_3 = 1, X_4 = 0, Z = 7$

The tree for the problem is given below.

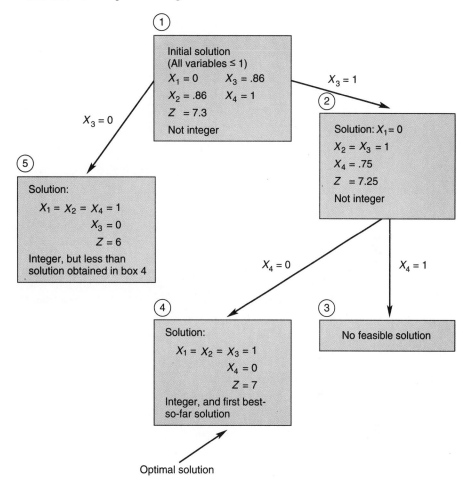

Optimal solution

14–3. Let X_1 through X_8 be zero/one variables that have a value 1 if a project is funded, and value 0 if not. Then:

Maximize: $40X_1 + 10X_2 + 80X_3 + 50X_4 + 20X_5 + 5X_6 + 80X_7 + 100X_8$
Subject to: $80X_1 + 15X_2 + 120X_3 + 65X_4 + 20X_5 + 10X_6 + 60X_7 + 100X_8 \leq$ 320 (funds constraint); $X_7 + X_8 \leq 1$ (not both projects G and H); $X_4 \leq X_1$ (no project D unless also A).

The solution calls for funding A, C, E, and H.
Total value is 240 units, and the total funds of $320,000 are all utilized.

14–4. *a.* Let Y_1 be binary variable, with $Y_1 = 1$ if stamping machine is used and 0 otherwise. An additional constraint $K \leq 200\ Y_1$ is added; and $-800\ Y_1$ is added to the objective function.

b. Let Y_2 be a binary variable, with $Y_2 = 1$ if 1,000 or more units are purchased, and 0 otherwise. Let R_1 be raw material purchased at the $.25 price, and R_2 be units of raw material purchased at the $.20 price. The following constraints are added: RMUSED $\leq R_1 + R_2$; $R_2 \geq 1,000\ Y_2$; and $R_2 \leq MY_2$, where M is a very large number. Add to the objective function: $-0.25\ R_1 - 0.20R_2$. The constraint $R_1 \leq 1,000\ (1 - Y_2)$ could also be added, but it is not necessary.

c. Let K_1 be the number of KARMAs sold at the $100 price, K_2 be the number sold at the $150 price, and K_3 be the number sold at the $120 price. Let Z_1 be a binary variable with value of 1 if 20 or less units are produced; Z_2 is also a binary variable with value of 1 if production is between 20 and 70 units; and Z_3 is a binary variable with value of 1 if production exceeds 70 units.

New constraints: $K = K_1 + K_2 + K_3$; $K_1 \leq 20Z_1$; $K_2 \leq 50Z_2$; $K_3 \leq 130Z_3$; $K_1 \geq 20Z_2$; $K_2 \geq 50Z_3$; and $Z_1 \geq Z_2$ and $Z_2 \geq Z_3$. (Actually, the last constraint isn't necessary.) Add to the objective function: $100K_1 + 150K_2 + 120K_3$.

d. Let W_1 be a binary variable that takes on a value of 1 if the campaign is to be undertaken for ANZAs and 0 otherwise; similarly, $W_2 = 1$ if the campaign is done for BOZOs. Then, the following constraints are added: $A \leq 100 + 50W_1$; $B \leq 120 + 50W_2$; $W_1 + W_2 \leq 1$. Add to the objective function: $-5,000W_1 - 5,000W_2$.

14-5. Branch as indicated in the accompanying figure (Full Solution). Compute bounds in two ways: First, consider unassigned plants, and compute the sum of the row minimums. With A assigned to 1, for example, the row minimums are as follows:

Row	Minimum in Row
B	17
C	29
D	27
	Sum = 73 (infeasible)

Full Solution*

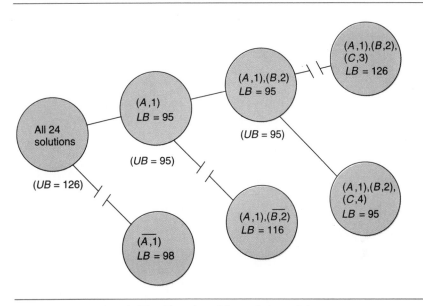

*Note: LB = Lower bound; UB = Upper bound (best solution so far).

Then, compute column minimums, considering unassigned warehouses. Given assignment A–1, the column minimums are:

Column	Minimum in Column
2	17
3	39
4	29
	Sum = 85 (feasible)

Continuing, the method produces assignment (A,1), (B,2), (C,4), (D,3) as the optimal assignment, with cost of 95.

Chapter 15

15–1. *a*. Approximately 7.5 percent.
   b. Approximately 3 percent.
   c. Approximately 95.5 percent.
   d. Approximately 53 percent.

15–2. *a.* The ranked data are: 530, 320, 225, 170, 125, 94, 70, 49, 30, 2. Cumulative data are: 530, 850, 1,075, 1,245, 1,370, 1,464, 1,534, 1,583, 1,613, 1,615. See the plot of cumulative data in the accompanying figure.

Note: After the total cumulative sales data of $1,615 are plotted, the vertical scale can be labeled 100 percent and then divided into percentages as shown.

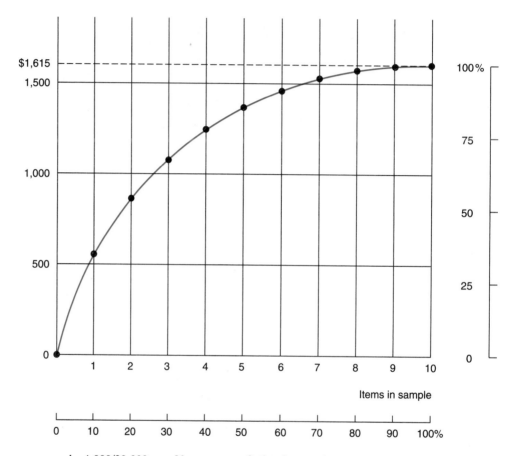

Items in sample

b. 4,000/20,000 = 20 percent of the items; in the sample, this represents 850/1,615 = 52.6 percent of sales.

c. About 85 percent of dollar sales.

d. In the sample ABC curve, the point representing 50 percent of sales falls between items with sales of 530 and 320, but is very close to the latter. Hence, we might say any item with sales above 350 would be classified as an A item. We could similarly note that at the 50 percent point on the item scale, the sales rate is 125, and use 125 as the upper limit on the C items, although a slightly more accurate method would be to average the data points (125, 94) as an estimate of the median sales rate of the sample; this averaging would produce 109.5 as the upper limit on C items. B items would be between these values.

15-3. $Q = \sqrt{\dfrac{2DK}{k_c}} = \sqrt{\dfrac{2 \cdot 1,000 \cdot 6}{30}} = \sqrt{400} = 20$ units

15-4. $a.$ $Q = \sqrt{\dfrac{2 \cdot 100,000 \cdot 60}{3}} = \sqrt{4 \cdot 10^6} = 2,000$ units

$b.$ $Q = \sqrt{\dfrac{2 \cdot 100,000 \cdot 60}{3}} = \sqrt{40,000} = \sqrt{4 \cdot 10^4} = 200$ units

Note: Daily use is $100,000/360 = 277$ units per day. Would we order 200 or 277, or more?

15-5. $a.$ $Q = \sqrt{\dfrac{2 \cdot 100,000 \cdot 15}{3}} = \sqrt{1,000,000} = 1,000$ units.

$b.$ The total cost using the original ordering cost is, using Equation 15–1:

$$TC(Q = 2,000) = \frac{2,000}{2}(3) + \frac{100,000}{2,000}(60) = 3,000 + 3,000 = \$6,000$$

The total cost using the new reduced ordering cost is:

$$TC(Q = 1,000) = \frac{1,000}{2}(3) + \frac{100,000}{1,000}(15) = 1,500 + 1,500 = \$3,000$$

The reduction in costs is $\$6,000 - \$3,000 = \$3,000$; since this $3,000 reduction exceeds the membership fee of $2,000, the company should join the co-op and order in batches of $Q = 1,000$ units.

15-6. $Q = \left(\dfrac{2DK}{k_c} \cdot \dfrac{p}{p - D}\right)^{1/2} = \left(\dfrac{2 \cdot 1,000 \cdot 4,000}{28/360} \cdot \dfrac{14,000}{14,000 - 4,000}\right)^{1/2}$

$= \left(\dfrac{8 \cdot 10^6 \cdot 360}{28} \cdot 1.4\right)^{1/2} = (4 \cdot 36 \cdot 10^6)^{1/2} = 12,000$ units

15-7. Recall from Problem 15–3 the optimal $Q = 20$ units. Total annual costs for $Q = 20$ are: $TC(Q = 20) = (20/2)(\$30) + (1,000/20)(\$6)$
$= \$300 + \$300 = \$600$

If the items were purchased in lots of 100, a price break saving of $150 − $148, or $2, would result; times 1,000 units per year $= \$2,000$. Also, the holding cost would be reduced (slightly) from $.20(150) = \$30$ to $.20(148) = \$29.60$. The net cost of $Q = 100$ is therefore:

$$TC(Q = 100) = -\$2,000 + (100/2)(\$29.60) + (\$1,000/100)(\$6)$$
$$= -\$2,000 + \$1,480 + \$60 = -\$460$$

This is compared with $+ \$600$ for $TC(Q = 20)$, for a net change of $1,060 (an improvement). Thus, the price break should be taken.

Chapter 16

16–1. *a, b.*

$$Q = \sqrt{\frac{2KD}{k_c}} = \sqrt{\frac{2 \cdot 6 \cdot 1,000}{30}} = 20 \text{ units}$$

$$F(R) = 1 - \frac{k_c Q}{k_u D} = 1 - \frac{30(20)}{2(1,000)}$$

$$= 1 - \frac{600}{2,000} = .70$$

$Z = 0.52$; $R = \bar{M} + Z\sigma_M = 50 + .52 \cdot 10 = 55$ units. Order 20 units when we have 55 units on hand.

16–2. *a, b.*

$$Q = \sqrt{\frac{2 \cdot 64 \cdot 40,000}{2}} = \sqrt{64 \cdot 40,000} = 1,600$$

$$F(R) = 1 - \frac{k_c Q}{k_u D} = 1 - \frac{2(1,600)}{10(40,000)} = 1 - \frac{3,200}{400,000} = 1 - .008 = .992$$

$Z = 2.41$; $R = 4,000 + 2.41 \cdot 500 = 5,205$. Order 1,600 when there are 5,205 units on hand.

c. Total cost $(R, Q) = [K + k_u\sigma_M N(Z)]\frac{D}{Q} + [\frac{Q}{2} + (R - \bar{M})]k_c$

$$= [64 + 10 \cdot 500 \cdot .0026] \cdot \frac{40,000}{1,600} + [\frac{1,600}{2} + (5,205 - 4,000)] \cdot 2$$

$$= 77 \cdot 25 + [800 + 1,205] \cdot 2 = 1,925 + 4,010 = \$5,935$$

For comparison, we can compute the actual optimal values for *Q, R,* and *TC.* Start from the approximate values $Q = 1,600$, $R = 5,205$ from (*a*). Using formula 16–12 from the appendix to the chapter, and noting that $N(Z) = N(2.41) = .0026$:

$$Q = \sqrt{\frac{2 \cdot 40,000}{2}(64 + 10 \cdot 500 \cdot .0026)} = (40,000(64 + 13))^{1/2}$$

$$= (40,000 \cdot 77)^{1/2} = (3,080,000)^{1/2} = 1,750$$

$$F(R) = 1 - \frac{2(1,750)}{10(40,000)} = 1 - .00875 = .99125$$

$$Z = 2.38; N(Z) = .0029$$

$$Q = [40,000(64 + 5,000 \cdot .0029)]^{1/2} = (40,000 \cdot 78.5)^{1/2} = 200(78.5)^{1/2}$$

$$= 200 \cdot 8.8 = 1,760$$

$$F(R) = 1 - \frac{2(1,760)}{10(40,000)} = .9913; Z = 2.38 \text{ (same as above)}$$

So after iterating, the true $Q = 1,760$; and $R = 4,000 + (2.38)(500) = 5,190$.
Then, using the total cost Equation 16–5,

$$TC = (78.5) \cdot \frac{40,000}{1,760} + \left(\frac{1,760}{2} + 5,190 - 4,000\right) \cdot 2$$
$$= 1,784 + 4,140 = \$5,924. \text{ The saving is only } \$11.$$

16–3. $Q = \sqrt{\dfrac{2KD}{k_c}} = \sqrt{\dfrac{2(1000)(1200)}{20}} = 346$

$F(R) = 1 - \dfrac{k_c Q}{k_u D} = 1 - \dfrac{20(346)}{200(1200)} = .9712$

From Table A, this corresponds to a $Z = 1.90$
$R = \text{mean} + Z\sigma = 100 + 1.90(40) = 176$

16–4. *a.* From formula 16–8, $\dfrac{Q(1 - P)}{\sigma_M} = \dfrac{200(.01)}{30} = 0.0667$

from Table B, $Z = 1.11$, so $R = 100 + 1.11(30) = 133.3$ or 134

b. Similarly, $\dfrac{200(.02)}{30} = 0.1333$; from Table B, $Z = 0.74$, so:

$R = 100 + .74(30) = 122.2$ or 123

c. Similarly, $\dfrac{200(.10)}{30} = 0.667$

Since this exceeds the upper limit of Table B (.3989), this means that $Z = 0$ and R is set equal to $\overline{M}$ of 100. The stated service level will actually be exceeded, due to the size of the order quantity.

Chapter 17

17–1.

Sales	$P(X = x)$	$P(X \geq x)$
0	0.05	1.00
1	0.15	.95
2	0.30	.80
3	0.35	.50
4	0.10	.15
5	0.05	.05
6	0.00	.00

a. $c_o = \$10$; $c_u = \$40$

$$p_c = \frac{c_o}{c_u + c_o} = \frac{10}{40 + 10} = .20$$

Three units should be ordered: $p_c = .20 > .15$; $p_c = .20 < .50$, where .15 is the probability that demand is four units or more, and .50 is the probability that demand is three units or more.

b. $c_u = \$40 + 20 = \$60; c_o = \$10$

$$p_c = \frac{c_o}{c_o + c_u} = \frac{10}{70} = .143$$

Four units should be ordered: $p_c = .14 < .15.; p_c = .14 > .05$

17–2. The p_c's are cumulative probabilities. We must first determine Z, the number of standard deviations necessary to move away from the mean for the probability of selling the next unit $\leq p_c$. Second, it is necessary to convert the number of standard deviations to number of units. The third step is to add or subtract the number of units from the mean. This is the optimum order size for each p_c.

	p_c	Z	σ	$Z\sigma$	$50 \pm Z\sigma$	(Subtract if $p_c > .5$)
a.	.60	0.25	10	2.5	47.5	
b.	.50	0.00	10	0.0	50.0	
c.	.45	0.12	10	1.2	51.2	
d.	.40	0.25	10	2.5	52.5	
e.	.22	0.77	10	7.7	57.7	
f.	.10	1.28	10	12.8	62.8	
g.	.02	2.05	10	20.5	70.5	

The values p_c are the probability of sales being equal to or greater than a critical amount. The higher the p_c, the smaller the optimum order size.

17–3. $p_c = \dfrac{c_o}{c_o + c_u}; c_o = \$50 - 10 = \$40; c_u = (\$100 - 70) + 50 = \$80;$

$$p_c = \frac{40}{40 + 80} = \frac{40}{120} = .33; Z = .44 \text{ standard deviations}$$

$140 + .44(20) = 140 + 8.8 = 148.8$ optimum order size

17–4. $140 + .44(50) = 140 + 22 = 162$ optimum order size. Note the increase in optimum order size caused by the increase in the standard deviation of the sales distribution. See Problem 17–5 for another comparison.

17–5. $p_c = \dfrac{c_o}{c_o + c_u} = \dfrac{40}{40 + 30} = .571$

a. $Z = .18; 140 - .18(20) = 140 - 3.6 = 136.4$
b. $140 - .18(50) = 140 - 9 = 131.0$
Note that in this problem, the larger standard deviation decreased the order size; in Problems 17–3 and 17–4, the larger deviation increased the optimum order size. The effect depends on whether $p_c > .50$ or $p_c < .50$.

Chapter 18

18–1. a. $L_q = \dfrac{\lambda^2}{\mu(\mu - \lambda)} = \dfrac{10^2}{15 \cdot 5} = 1.33$

b. $W_q = \dfrac{L_q}{\lambda} = \dfrac{1.33}{10} = .133$ hours or 8 minutes

c. Expected total time $= W_q +$ Expected service time $= 8 + 4 = 12$ minutes

18–2. *a.* $\mu = 20; L_q = \dfrac{\lambda^2}{\mu(\mu - \lambda)} = \dfrac{100}{20 \cdot 10} = .5$

b. $W_q = \dfrac{L_q}{\lambda} = \dfrac{.5}{10} = \dfrac{1}{20}$ hour or 3 minutes

18–3. Note that $\lambda = 10$ and $\mu = 15$. The standard deviation of service time is 2 minutes or $\frac{2}{60}$ hours

From Equation 18–9:

$$W_q = \frac{\dfrac{\lambda}{\mu^2} + \lambda\sigma^2}{2\left(1 - \dfrac{\lambda}{\mu}\right)} = \frac{\dfrac{10}{15^2} + 10\left(\dfrac{2}{60}\right)^2}{2(1 - {}^{10}/_{15})}$$

$W_q = 0.0833$ hours

a. $L_q = \lambda W_q = 10(0.0833) = .833$ calls

b. $W_q = 0.0833$ hours or 5 minutes

c. Use formula for W_q, but with $\sigma = 0$

$\quad W_q = 0.0667$ hour or 4 minutes (average waiting time)

$\quad L_q = 10(0.0667) = 0.667$ calls (average line length)

18–4. $\mu = 15, \lambda = 10, c = 2$

a. $L_q = \dfrac{(\lambda/\mu)^{c+1}}{c \cdot c!\left(1 - \dfrac{\lambda/\mu}{c}\right)^2} p_0$

where $p_0 = \left[\dfrac{(\lambda/\mu)^c}{c!\left(1 - \dfrac{\lambda/\mu}{c}\right)} + 1 + \dfrac{\lambda/\mu}{1!} + \dfrac{(\lambda/\mu)^2}{2!} + \ldots + \dfrac{(\lambda/\mu)^{c-1}}{(c-1)!}\right]^{-1}$

Here $p_0 = \left[\dfrac{{}^{10}/_{15}^2}{2\left(1 - \dfrac{{}^{10}/_{15}}{2}\right)} + 1 + \dfrac{{}^{10}/_{15}}{1}\right]^{-1} = [{}^1/_3 + 1 + {}^2/_3]^{-1} = {}^1/_2$

and $L_q = \dfrac{({}^{10}/_{15})^3}{2 \cdot 2\left(1 - \dfrac{{}^{10}/_{15}}{2}\right)^2} \cdot {}^1/_2 = {}^1/_{12}$

b. $W_q = \dfrac{L_q}{\lambda} = \dfrac{{}^1/_{12}}{10} = {}^1/_{120}$ hour or ½ minute. This result can also be obtained by interpolating in Table 18–2. $(\lambda/c\mu) = .33$; so from the table, $W_q\mu = 0.129$ (by interpolation) so $W_q = .129/15 = .0086$ hour $= {}^1/_2$ minute.

18–5. *a.* With $c = 1$: $W_q = 8$ minutes. There are 24 hours and 10 calls per hour (on the average) $= 240$ calls per day. Total time waiting $= 240 \cdot W_q = 1,920$ minutes. With $c = 2$: $W_q = {}^1/_2$ and total time waiting $= 240 \cdot {}^1/_2 = 120$

minutes. Hence, 1,920 − 120 or 1,800 minutes of customer time is saved. At 10 cents per minute, this is $180 per day. Hence, the second clerk (cost: $50 per day) should be utilized.

b. Break-even goodwill cost = x in dollars per minute; $1,800x = \$50$; $x = 50/1,800 = .028$ or 3 cents per minute waiting time.

c. The expected number of calls is assumed to be the same for each hour.

Chapter 19

19–1. *a.* The total number delayed to the following day is 6 (an average of .12 per day).

b. Cost of waiting with service rate of 2 is $20(.90)(250) = \$4,500$
Cost of waiting with service rate of 3 is $20(.12)(250) = \$600$
Savings = $\$4,500 − 600 = \$3,900$ per year. (Assumption of 250 working days per year.)

19–2. Results will depend on random numbers drawn. As stated in the chapter, Expected profit = $2,140. Also, a negative profit results when Price = $4 and Cost = $4 (regardless of Volume), and the probability of a loss is $0.3 \cdot 0.3 = 0.09$. Also, a loss occurs when Cost is $4 and Price is $5 and Volume = 3,000 or 4,000. Probability = $.3 \cdot .5 \cdot .6 = .09$. Also, when Price is $4 and Cost is $3 and Volume = 3,000 or 4,000. Probability = $.3 \cdot .6 \cdot .6 = .108$. Total probability = $.09 + .09 + .108 = .288$.

19–3. *a.* Since the higher price is associated with the lower volume and vice versa, this indicates that when the higher price occurs, profits will be lower than before; and when the lower price occurs, low profit margins (or negative margins) will be multiplied by larger volumes. The general effect should be to *lower* expected profit.

b. Use the following table:

	Volume			
Price	3,000	4,000	5,000	
$4	—	—	0, 1, 2	(random numbers)
$5	—	3–6	7	
$6	8, 9	—	—	

c, d, e are straightforward, using (*b*). Results depend on random numbers drawn.

Chapter 20

20–1. *a.*

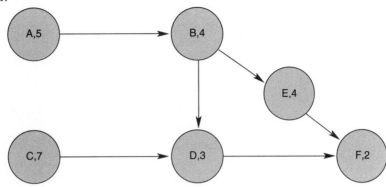

b.

Activity	ES	LS	EF	LF
A	0	0	5	5
B	5	5	9	9
C	0	3	7	10
D	9	10	12	13
E	9	9	13	13
F	13	13	15	15

Project completion time is 15 days.

c. A, B, E, F.

20–2. *a.* No; there is a three-day slack in activity C.

b. Yes; the critical path is now *CDF*, with a project completion time of 16 days.

20–3. *a.*

Activity	t_i	σ_i^2
A	4	0.44
B	8	0.44
C	6	5.44
D	5	1.78
E	8	0.44

b.

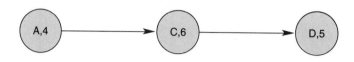

Critical path is *BE*, with a length of 16 days.

c. For path *ACD*, the expected length is 15 days and the variance is $.44 + 5.44 + 1.78 = 7.67$. Standard deviation is 2.77.
$P(\text{Time} < 16) = 1 - P(Z < 1/2.77) = .64$
For path *BE*, the variance is $.44 + .44 = .89$. Standard deviation is .94.
$P(\text{Time} < 16) = .50$.

d. $P(\text{Total project} < 16) = .64 \cdot .50 = .32$.

Chapter 21

21–1. For Machine A: $P\left(\begin{array}{c|c}\text{State 1} & \text{State 1} \\ \text{on day } n & \text{on day 1}\end{array}\right) = \dfrac{.6}{.1 + .6} = \dfrac{.6}{.7} = \dfrac{6}{7}$ as $n \to \infty$

For Machine B: $P\left(\begin{array}{c|c}\text{State 1} & \text{State 1} \\ \text{on day } n & \text{on day 1}\end{array}\right) = \dfrac{.7}{.2 + .7} = \dfrac{.7}{.9} = \dfrac{7}{9}$ as $n \to \infty$

Machine A has the higher probability of being in adjustment.

21–2. *a.* $p_1 = .95$, $p_2 = .05$ by inspection.

b. No, since according to the probability matrix, the conditional probability of paying next month's bill is the same (.95) whether or not this month's bill is paid.

21–3. *a.* $P\left(\begin{array}{c|c}\text{State 1} & \text{State 1} \\ \text{in per.}n & \text{in per.1}\end{array}\right) = (.8)P\left(\begin{array}{c|c}\text{State 1} & \text{State 1} \\ \text{in per.}n & \text{in per.1}\end{array}\right) + (.2)P\left(\begin{array}{c|c}\text{State 2} & \text{State 1} \\ \text{in per.}n & \text{in per.1}\end{array}\right)$

$+ (.2)\left\{1 - P\left(\begin{array}{c|c}\text{State 1} & \text{State 1} \\ \text{in per.}n & \text{in per.1}\end{array}\right) - P\left(\begin{array}{c|c}\text{State 2} & \text{State 1} \\ \text{in per.}n & \text{in per.1}\end{array}\right)\right\}$

or:

$(1 - .8 + .2)P\left(\begin{array}{c|c}\text{State 1} & \text{State 1} \\ \text{in per.}n & \text{in per.1}\end{array}\right) + (-.2 + .2)P\left(\begin{array}{c|c}\text{State 2} & \text{State 1} \\ \text{in per.}n & \text{in per.1}\end{array}\right) = .2$

so:

$P\left(\begin{array}{c|c}\text{State 1} & \text{State 1} \\ \text{in per.}n & \text{in per.1}\end{array}\right) = \dfrac{.2}{1 - .8 + .2} = \dfrac{.2}{.4} = \dfrac{1}{2}$ as $n \to \infty$

Also:

$$P\left(\begin{array}{c}\text{State 2}\\\text{in per.}n\end{array}\middle|\begin{array}{c}\text{State 1}\\\text{in per.1}\end{array}\right) = (.2)P\left(\begin{array}{c}\text{State 1}\\\text{in per.}n\end{array}\middle|\begin{array}{c}\text{State 1}\\\text{in per.1}\end{array}\right)$$

$$+ (.2)\left\{1 - P\left(\begin{array}{c}\text{State 1}\\\text{in per.}n\end{array}\middle|\begin{array}{c}\text{State 1}\\\text{in per.1}\end{array}\right) - P\left(\begin{array}{c}\text{State 2}\\\text{in per.}n\end{array}\middle|\begin{array}{c}\text{State 1}\\\text{in per.1}\end{array}\right)\right\}$$

or:

$$(1 + .2)P\left(\begin{array}{c}\text{State 2}\\\text{in per.}n\end{array}\middle|\begin{array}{c}\text{State 1}\\\text{in per.1}\end{array}\right) = (.2)(^1/_2) + (.2)\left\{1 - {}^1/_2\right\} = .1 + .1 = .2$$

so:

$$P\left(\begin{array}{c}\text{State 2}\\\text{in per.}n\end{array}\middle|\begin{array}{c}\text{State 1}\\\text{in per.1}\end{array}\right) = \frac{.2}{1.2} = \frac{1}{6} \text{ as } n \to \infty$$

Then:

$$P\left(\begin{array}{c}\text{State 3}\\\text{in per.}n\end{array}\middle|\begin{array}{c}\text{State 1}\\\text{in per.1}\end{array}\right) = 1 - \frac{1}{2} - \frac{1}{6} = \frac{1}{3} \text{ as } n \to \infty$$

b. Airport A would be the logical choice for a maintenance facility, since it has the highest steady-state probability. Choice of airport A would minimize the number of special trips needed to move cars to the maintenance facility at the required time.

21–4. a. A: $.8(100) + .2(100) + .2(100) = 120$
B: $.2(100) + 0 + .2(100) = 40$
C: $0 + .8(100) + .6(100) = 140$

b. A: $.8(120) + .2(40) + .2(140) = 132$
B: $.2(120) + 0 + .2(140) = 52$
C: $0 + .8(40) + .6(140) = 116$

Chapter 22

22–1. a. Optimal pricing strategy: $P_1 = 18$, $P_2 = 12$, $P_3 = 16$, $P_4 = 12$
Maximum expected profit $= 9 + 9 + 8 + 7 = 33$

b.

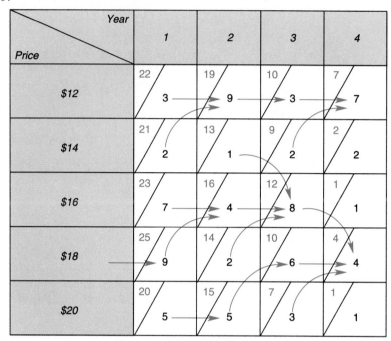

Optimal pricing strategy: $P_1 = 18; P_2 = 16; P_3 = 16; P_4 = 18$
Maximum expected profit $= 9 + 4 + 8 + 4 = 25$

22–2. *a.* $P = [200 - .2(400)] \cdot (400) = [200 - 80] \cdot (400) = (120)(400) = \$48,000$
b. $P = 150(1.4)(400) - 30(400) = 84,000 - 12,000 = \$72,000$
c. $P = [200 - .2(Y)](Y) + 150(1.4)(400 - Y) - 30(400 - Y)$
   $= 200Y - .2(Y)^2 + \$84,000 - 210Y - 12,000 + 30Y$
   $= -.2(Y)^2 + 20Y + 72,000$
d. $P_{Y=50} = -.2(50)^2 + 20(50) + 72,000 = -.2(2,500) + 1,000 + 72,000$
   $= -500 + 1,000 + 72,000 = \$72,500$
e. $\dfrac{d\{\ \}}{dy} = -.2(2)Y + 20 = 0; Y^* = \dfrac{20}{.4} = 50$
f. $f_9(400) = 180(400) + 500 = 72,000 + 500 = \$72,500$
g. $f_9(200) = 180(200) + 500 = 36,000 + 500 = \$36,500$

22–3. Formulation: Let:

   X_n = Production in period n
   I_n = Beginning inventory in period n
   D_n = Demand in period n (from table in problem)

The general recursion is:

$$f_n(I_n) = \underset{D_n - I_n \le X_n}{\text{minimum}} \left[\left\{ \begin{array}{l} 5 + X_n \text{ if } X_n > 0 \\ 0 \quad \text{ if } X_n = 0 \end{array} \right\} + I_n + f_{n+1}(I_n + X_n - D_n) \right]$$

The calculations can be performed as in Example 2 in the text. There are three alternative optimal schedules, all with cost $31:

	Schedule 1	Schedule 2	Schedule 3
January	3	3	8
February	5	10	0
March	5	0	5
April	0	0	0

22-4. *a.* $10(.2) + 9(.4) + 8(.4) = 2 + 3.6 + 3.2 = 8.8$
b. Act if best rating on day 4 is either 9 or 10. *Wait* if best rating on day 4 is 8
c. $10(.2) + 9(.4) + 8.8(.4) = 2 + 3.6 + 3.52 = 9.12$
d. Act if best rating on day 3 is 10. *Wait* if best rating on day 3 is either 8 or 9
22-5. *a.* $f_5(X_5) = X_5$

b.

$$f_4(X_4) = \text{Max.} \left\{ \underset{Act}{X_4,} \quad \underset{Wait}{10(.2) + 9(.4) + 8.8(.4)} \right\}$$

c. $X_{4b} = 10(.2) + 9(.4) + 8(.4) = 8.8$. *Act* if best rating on day 4 is greater than 8.8. *Wait* if best rating on day 4 is less than 8.8.

d.

$$f_3(X_3) = \text{Max.} \left\{ \underset{Act}{X_3,} \quad \underset{Wait}{10(.2) + 9(.4) + 8.8(.4)} \right\}$$

e. $X_{3b} = 10(.2) + 9(.4) + 8.8(.4) = 9.12$

$$f_2(X_2) = \text{Max.} \left\{ \underset{Act}{X_2,} \quad \underset{Wait}{10(.2) + 9.12(.4) + 9.12(.4)} \right\}$$

$$X_{2b} = 10(.2) + 9.12(.4) + 9.12(.4) = 9.296$$

$$f_1(X_1) = \text{Max.} \left\{ \underset{Act}{X_1,} \quad \underset{Wait}{10(.2) + 9.296(.4) + 9.296(.4)} \right\}$$
$$= \text{Max.} \{ X_1, \quad 9.4368 \}$$

$X_{1b} = 9.4368$. Optimal decision rule on day 1: *Act* if $X_1 > 9.4368$; *Wait* if $X_1 \leq 9.4368$. $f_1(9) = 9.4368$. If best rating on day 1 is 9, the manager should wait.

f.

$$f_2(X_2) = \text{Max.} \left\{ \underset{Act}{X_2,} \quad \underset{Wait}{10(.2) + 9.12(.4) + 9.12(.4)} \right\}$$

$$= \text{Max.} \left\{ \underset{Act}{X_2,} \quad \underset{Wait}{9.296} \right\}$$

The manager can obtain an expected rating of 9.296 given three days' opportunity for testing, and therefore the offer is of no help.

Index